Index to the 1800 Massachusetts Federal Census
for the County of
Bristol

Rebecca M. Sullivan
Deborah Lee Larsson

Index to the 1800 Massachusetts Federal Census
for the County of
Bristol

October 2014

ISBN: 978-1502792556

FOREWARD:

This is the fifth volume of several containing the heads of household that were enumerated in the 1800 United States Federal Census in Massachusetts. Our sixth volume is comprised of those towns in Bristol County. In order to make it easy for the researcher, towns are alphabetized, followed by an alphabetical index of Bristol county.

We have made every attempt at correctly transcribing each town. However, many of these documents are torn, covered with ink, tape marks, rips and poor handwriting. Spelling errors have been left as they were originally written. Any names & enumerations illegible are denoted with an asterisk.

This book should be used as a guide and research aid. When possible the actual image should be obtained for proper verification and citation. Visit the National Archives website to find out more on how to obtain census images. www.archives.gov/research/census.

In order to get all of the information on one page to make for easy reading we had to reduce the size of the font.

Drop us a line, we'd love to hear what you're researching: rsulli1219@aol.com

Becky & Deb
October 2014

Check out our other books:

Index to the 1800 Massachusetts Federal Census for the Counties of Barnstable, Dukes & Nantucket, Volume 1

Index to the 1800 Massachusetts Federal Census for the County of Worcester, Volume 2

Index to the 1800 Massachusetts Federal Census for the County of Essex, Volume 3

Index to the 1800 Massachusetts Federal Census for the Counties of Norfolk & Suffolk, Volume 4

Index to the 1800 Massachusetts Federal Census for the County of Plymouth, Volume 5

INDEX

Bristol County

Bristol County Stats

Microfilm Reel Number: M32-19

Town:	Page Numbers:	Enumerated By:
Attleboro	317-323	Unknown
Berkley	274-281	Apollos Tobey
Dartmouth	340-353	Benjamin Williams
Dighton	409-415	Unknown
Easton	388-394	Unknown
Freetown	281-294	Unknown
Mansfield	384-388	Unknown
New Bedford	418-432	Benjamin Church, Jr.
Norton	379-384	Unknown
Raynham	372-378	Laban Whestore
Rehoboth	296-316	Elisha May Esq'r
Somerset	404-408	Unknown
Swansea	396-404	Unknown
Taunton	356-371	Unknown
Wesport	327-339	Unknown

TOWN	PG#	LN#	LAST NAME	FIRST NAME	FREE WHITE MALES under 10	10 to 16	16 to 26	26 to 45	45 and over	FREE WHITE FEMALES under 10	10 to 16	16 to 26	26 to 45	45 and over	TOTAL ALL OTHER	TOTAL SLAVES	TOTALS	DISTRICT/ TOWNSHIP	NOTES
Attleboro	317	1	Titus	Samuel	1	1		1	1	2	1		1				8		
Attleboro	317	2	Robbins	Ezekiel				1						1			2		
Attleboro	317	3	Read	William	1			1		1	1		1				5		
Attleboro	317	4	Cushman	Joseph	2	1			1	2			1	1			8		
Attleboro	317	5	Tate	Sally		1	1							1			3		
Attleboro	317	6	Robinson	George	2		2		1		2			1			8		
Attleboro	317	7	Jillson	William			1					1					2		
Attleboro	317	8	Titus	Simeon		1	1		1				1	1			5		
Attleboro	317	9	Titus	John	1		1					1					3		
Attleboro	317	10	George	William		1	1			3	1		1				7		
Attleboro	317	11	Jillson	Levi		1			1		1	2		2			7		
Attleboro	317	12	Ide	Ichabod	1		1	1		3		1		2			9		
Attleboro	317	13	Freeman	Daniel	2		1			1			1				5		
Attleboro	317	14	Ide	Jacob	1	1	1		1	3	1			1			9		
Attleboro	317	15	Ide	Nathaniel	1			1		2			2	1			7		
Attleboro	317	16	Freeman	William	2			1		2			1				6		
Attleboro	317	17	Bullock	Richd	1		1		1	1	1	1					5		
Attleboro	317	18	Read	Levi			1					1					2		
Attleboro	317	19	Read	Azael		1	1							3			5		
Attleboro	317	20	Read	Thoma		1		1			1			1			4		
Attleboro	317	21	Read	Saml				1						1			2		
Attleboro	317	22	Read	Arnon	1		1							1			3		
Attleboro	317	23	Draper	Ebenezer				1		1	1		1				4		
Attleboro	317	24	Day	Jeremiah		3		1			1	1	1				7		
Attleboro	317	25	Draper	Stephen			2	1	1	1		1		1			7		
Attleboro	317	26	Titus	Peter	2		1	1				1					5		
Attleboro	317	27	Throop	Amos		1		2				1		2			6		
Attleboro	317	28	Wilder	John	3		1	1	1	3	1		1				11		
Attleboro	317	29	Mann	Newton	1	1		2		1	1		1				7		
Attleboro	317	30	Devens	John	3			1				2					6		
Attleboro	318	1	Tyler	Ebenezer	1	1	2		1	2	1			1			9		
Attleboro	318	2	Tyler	Zelotes	1		1		1	4		1	1	1			10		
Attleboro	318	3	Freeman	Thoms			1					1		1			3		
Attleboro	318	4	Dean	Ephraim & Asa	4	2		2		4		2	1	4			19		
Attleboro	318	5	Fuller	Caleb		1	2	2				1	3	1			10		
Attleboro	318	6	Sweet	Zebadiah		1	2		1				1				5		
Attleboro	318	7	Carpenter	Samuel		1	1	1		1			1	1			6		
Attleboro	318	8	Tyler	Walter		1		1			1	1					4		
Attleboro	318	9	Fuller	Jos		1		1		2		1		2			7		
Attleboro	318	10	Titus	Rbecca									2				2		
Attleboro	318	11	Robinson	Joel		1	1			1			1				4		
Attleboro	318	12	Robinson	Saml	2		1			1			1	2			7		
Attleboro	318	13	Hall	Josiah		1	1		1			1		1			5		
Attleboro	318	14	Fuller	Darius	3			1		1	1		1				7		
Attleboro	318	15	Fuller	Stephen		1		1		1				1			4		
Attleboro	318	16	Fuller	Frederick	2		1	1		1	1	1					7		
Attleboro	318	17	Ide	Amos		1		1	1	2		2		1			8		
Attleboro	318	18	Read	Daniel				1		1				2			4		
Attleboro	318	19	Read	Nathan	1			1		1			1				4		
Attleboro	318	20	Carpenter	Elisha		1	1		1			3		1			7		
Attleboro	318	21	Garfield	Jonathan		1			1	1		2		1			6		
Attleboro	318	22	Tiffany	Betsey	1						1	1					3		
Attleboro	318	23	Claflin	Phineas Junr	1			1				1					3		
Attleboro	318	24	Tiffany	Ebenezer	2	1		1	1	1		1	1	1			9		
Attleboro	318	25	Claflin	Phineas	1	1	1		1			2	1	1			8		
Attleboro	318	26	Claflin	Rufus		1				2			1				4		
Attleboro	318	27	Claflin	Comfort		1				1			1		1		4		
Attleboro	318	28	Claflin	Nehemiah		1		1		3				1			6		
Attleboro	318	29	Moore	Joanna		1							2	1			4		
Attleboro	318	30	Moore	Alice									2				2		
Attleboro	318	31	Daggett	Joseph				1		2		1					4		
Attleboro	318	32	Starkey	Sarah								1		1			2		
Attleboro	318	33	Bliss	Newman	2		1			1		1					5		
Attleboro	318	34	Fuller	Abial	1	1	1		1	1	1	1	1				8		
Attleboro	318	35	Robinson	Josie	1		1			2		2					6		
Attleboro	318	36	Fuller	Ebenezer	4	2	2					2		1			11		
Attleboro	318	37	Atwell	William L		1		1	1								3		
Attleboro	318	38	Liscomb	Samuel			2	1		1	2			2			8		
Attleboro	318	39	Bowen	Uriah	1	1		1					1				4		
Attleboro	318	40	Sabin	Vessel	1			1						1			3		
Attleboro	318	41	Hill	Leonard	1			1	1	2	1		1	1			8		
Attleboro	318	42	Atherton	Rufus	1			1					1	1			4		
Attleboro	318	43	Read	Ephraim		1	1	1	1	1	1		1				7		
Attleboro	318	44	Read	Moses	1				1				1	2			5		
Attleboro	318	45	Read	Joel	2	2		1	2	1	1	3	1	1			14		
Attleboro	318	46	Holmes	Samuel			2	1		1		1		1			6		
Attleboro	318	47	Field	Jos	1	1	1						1	2			6		
Attleboro	318	48	Pidge	David	1	1		1		2	3			1			10		
Attleboro	318	49	Withington	Thomas				1	1	2			1				5		

TOWN	PG#	LN#	LAST NAME	FIRST NAME	FREE WHITE MALES					FREE WHITE FEMALES					TOTAL ALL OTHER	TOTAL SLAVES	TOTALS	DISTRICT/ TOWNSHIP	NOTES
					under 10	10 to 16	16 to 26	26 to 45	45 and over	under 10	10 to 16	16 to 26	26 to 45	45 and over					
Attleboro	318	50	Pearce	Ezekiel			1		1				2	1			5		
Attleboro	318	51	Richardson	Wm	1		1	1		1			2				6		
Attleboro	318	52	Bourn	Andrew	1		3	2	1		1	3		1			12		
Attleboro	318	53	Sweet	Henry	2			1	1	1	2	2	1	1			11		
Attleboro	318	54	Robinson	Nathaniel		1	5		1		1	2	1				11		
Attleboro	318	55	Miller	Elkenah	1			1				1					3		
Attleboro	318	56	Gilmore	William	1		1					1					3		
Attleboro	318	57	Capron	Otis		1		1		2		1		1			6		
Attleboro	318	58	Capron	Elijah			2	1	1			2		1			7		
Attleboro	318	59	Richardson	Abiathar Junr			3	1				1	1				6		
Attleboro	318	60	Ingraham	Elijah	1		2	1		2			1				7		
Attleboro	318	61	Bates	Saml		1		1	1	1		3		1			8		
Attleboro	318	62	Balkom	Enoch			2	1				1		1			5		
Attleboro	318	63	Richardson	Abiathar		1	1		2	1		2		1			8		
Attleboro	318	64	Martin	John			2		1			1		1			5		
Attleboro	318	65	Wilmarth	Eliphalet					1				1	1			3		
Attleboro	318	66	Wilmarth	Eliphalet Junr	1		1			1	2		1				7		
Attleboro	318	67	Clafflin	Noah			3	2				2					7		
Attleboro	318	68	Daggett	Jesse			1			1		1					3		
Attleboro	319	1	Richardson	Daniel				1		2				1			4		
Attleboro	319	2	Richardson	Daniel Jr	3	1		1			1						6		
Attleboro	319	3	Robinson	Ebenezer	1		1					2	1				5		
Attleboro	319	4	Richardson	Vinton			1		1	1				1			4		
Attleboro	319	5	Price	Edward		1	1	1		1		2					6		
Attleboro	319	6	Woodcock	Jonathan	1			1		1	1	1	1				6		
Attleboro	319	7	Ingraham	Comfort			2	1	2			1	1	1			8		
Attleboro	319	8	Daggett	Joab	4	3		1		2		2		2			14		
Attleboro	319	9	Daggett	John			2	1	1	1	1	1		1			8		
Attleboro	319	10	Hall	John			1			1			1				3		
Attleboro	319	11	Starkey	Thoms	1				1				1	1			4		
Attleboro	319	12	Balckom	Elijah	1	1						1	1	1			6		
Attleboro	319	13	Wilkinson	John			1		1				1	1			4		
Attleboro	319	14	Richardson	Francis	1		1			1		1					4		
Attleboro	319	15	Alger	Isaac		1		1		1		1	2				6		
Attleboro	319	16	Fisher	David		1	1		1		1			1			5		
Attleboro	319	17	Starkey	Amos	1	1	1			1		1					6		
Attleboro	319	18	Balckom	Nathan		1		2	2	1	2	2	1				11		
Attleboro	319	19	Balckom	Mary	2	1		1				2		1			7		
Attleboro	319	20	Hawes	Eli	1			1		1	1		1				5		
Attleboro	319	21	Cutting	Aaron	1	2							1				4		
Attleboro	319	22	Cutting	James		2	1	1		2	1		1				8		
Attleboro	319	23	Cutting	Oliver			1			1	2		1	1			6		
Attleboro	319	24	Hall	Ephraim	2			1		1	2		1	1			8		
Attleboro	319	25	Starkey	Sibil	2		1				1		2	1			7		
Attleboro	319	26	Norton	Thoms	2	2	2		1			1		1			9		
Attleboro	319	27	Foster	Elexander		1			1			1		1			4		
Attleboro	319	28	Foster	Elexander Junr	3	1	3			1	1	2					11		
Attleboro	319	29	Briggs	Davis	2	1		1		2							6		
Attleboro	319	30	Fisher	Joel	2	1			2	4	3	2		2			16		
Attleboro	319	31	Fisher	David		1		1				1					3		
Attleboro	319	32	Mason	John	1			2		2	2		1				8		
Attleboro	319	33	Fisher	Peter		2			1	1	2		1	1			8		
Attleboro	319	34	Morse	Elijah	1		2	1		1			1				6		
Attleboro	319	35	Balckom	William				1		1		1					3		
Attleboro	319	36	Tiffany	Daniel		1		1		1		1	1				5		
Attleboro	319	37	Richardson	Benja	1		1			1		2		1			6		
Attleboro	319	38	Richardson	Seth	2		2	1		2	3	1	1	1			13		
Attleboro	319	39	Round	Hezekiah	2	1			1	1	2	3	1				11		
Attleboro	319	40	Dunham	John		1	1			2	1		1				6		
Attleboro	319	41	Smith	Cyrel		1		1				1		1			4		
Attleboro	319	42	Sweet	Michael	1		1	1				1	1	1			6		
Attleboro	319	43	Wilmarth	Martha	1		2			2	1		1				7		
Attleboro	319	44	Bassett	Joshua	3			1		2			1				7		
Attleboro	319	45	Richardson	Caleb	2	1		1	1				1	1			7		
Attleboro	319	46	Wetherell	Tisdale	1		1					1		1			4		
Attleboro	319	47	Tiffany	Noah	3	2			1	2	1	2	1				12		
Attleboro	319	48	Bourn	Seth	2	1			1	1		1	1	1			8		
Attleboro	319	49	Read	Abel		1		1		4			1	1			8		
Attleboro	319	50	Wilmarth	Stephen	2			1		2			1	2			8		
Attleboro	319	51	Parmenter	Caleb	1	1	2			1			1				6		
Attleboro	319	52	Balckom	Jacob	1	1		1			2		1				6		
Attleboro	319	53	Foster	Joseph		1	1			2			1				6		
Attleboro	319	54	Brown	Ezera	1	1	2	1		2	1		1	1			10		
Attleboro	319	55	Pike	Moses		1		1		2		1		1			6		
Attleboro	319	56	Jones	Wm				1						2			3		
Attleboro	319	57	Bates	Solomon	2	1		1	1			1		1			7		
Attleboro	319	58	Comings	David	2			2				3		1			8		
Attleboro	319	59	Cooper	Noah		2	1	1	1			2	1				9		
Attleboro	319	60	Carpenter	Cyrel		1	1		1	1	1			1			6		

TOWN	PG#	LN#	HEADS OF HOUSEHOLD		FREE WHITE MALES					FREE WHITE FEMALES					TOTAL ALL OTHER	TOTAL SLAVES	TOTALS	DISTRICT/ TOWNSHIP	NOTES
			LAST NAME	FIRST NAME	under 10	10 to 16	16 to 26	26 to 45	45 and over	under 10	10 to 16	16 to 26	26 to 45	45 and over					
Attleboro	319	61	Dunham	Abial	1	1			1	1	1	2		2			9		
Attleboro	319	62	Starkey	Thoms Junr	3	1	1			2		1					8		
Attleboro	319	63	Peck	Elizabeth										3			3		
Attleboro	319	64	Peck	Jonathan	1		1	1				1		1			5		
Attleboro	319	65	Everet	Abijah		2	1	1		1		2		1			8		
Attleboro	319	66	Sweet	Nathaniel				1						2			3		
Attleboro	319	67	Balckom	Benjamin	2		1			1	1						5		
Attleboro	320	1	Wilmarth	Amos	1			1					1				3		
Attleboro	320	2	Sweet	Gideon Junr			1			1		1					3		
Attleboro	320	3	Clafflin	Charles			1			1		1	1	1			5		
Attleboro	320	4	Carpenter	Daniel Junr	2			2					1				5		
Attleboro	320	5	Sweet	Gideon	2	2	1	1	1	1	1	3	1	1			14		
Attleboro	320	6	Snell	Lorana						1			1				2		
Attleboro	320	7	Carpenter	Daniel		1	1	2		1	1			1			7		
Attleboro	320	8	Derry	John	1		2	1		1	2		1				8		
Attleboro	320	9	Blanding	Daniel	1	1	2	1	1	1	1			1			9		
Attleboro	320	10	Wilmarth	Dan	1	1		1		2	1						6		
Attleboro	320	11	Wilmarth	Nathan Junr			1			1		1					3		
Attleboro	320	12	Wilmarth	Nathan				1		1		1		1			4		
Attleboro	320	13	Wilmarth	Larned	1	1	2			2	2			1			9		
Attleboro	320	14	French	Thoms	1		3	1		2	2			1			10		
Attleboro	320	15	Sweet	Thoms	1		1	1	1	2	1			1			8		
Attleboro	320	16	Follet	Jona		1	2	1		1	1			1			8		
Attleboro	320	17	Bishop	Zephaniah	1	1	3	1	1			2		1			10		
Attleboro	320	18	Blanding	Noah	1		1	1		1	1		1	1			7		
Attleboro	320	19	Barrows	Joseph		2	1		1	1	2		2				9		
Attleboro	320	20	Barrows	Elijah			1			3		1	1	1			7		
Attleboro	320	21	Woodcock	James			1			1				1			3		
Attleboro	320	22	Daggett	Reuben	2		1	1		1				1			6		
Attleboro	320	23	Viccory	Ruth		1		1						1			3		
Attleboro	320	24	Balckom	Saml	1			1		1	1	1		1			6		
Attleboro	320	25	Fuller	Jedithan	1							1		1			3		
Attleboro	320	26	Sanford	Saml	2		1					1		1			5		
Attleboro	320	27	Briggs	Margaret	1	1					1	2	1	1			7		
Attleboro	320	28	Titus	Timothy	3		1			1	1	1		1			8		
Attleboro	320	29	Balckom	Daniel	2		1			1		1	1	1			7		
Attleboro	320	30	Sanford	Paul	1	1	3		1	3				1			10		
Attleboro	320	31	Dunham	Sarah								1		1			2		
Attleboro	320	32	Perry	Isaac		1		1				1		2			5		
Attleboro	320	33	Perry	Ephraim	1		*	*		*	*	1					2		
Attleboro	320	34	*	Ephraim	2		1					1		1			5		
Attleboro	320	35	Briggs	Stephen	1	2		1		2			1				7		
Attleboro	320	36	Wilmarth	Elkanah				1						1			2		
Attleboro	320	37	Mason	Isaac	1		1	1		1		1		1			6		
Attleboro	320	38	Fullers	Daniel	2		1			1							4		
Attleboro	320	39	Wilmarth	Preston		1		1	2								4		
Attleboro	320	40	Freeman	Ezra			1			3			1	1			6		
Attleboro	320	41	How	William			1				1		2				4		
Attleboro	320	42	Willmarth	Jona	3		1				1		2				7		
Attleboro	320	43	Wilmarth	Stephen 2d	2		1			1			1				5		
Attleboro	320	44	Carpenter	Josiah	1		1		1			2	1	1			7		
Attleboro	320	45	French	Ezra	2	1		1		2	1	1	2				10		
Attleboro	320	46	Fuller	Zelotes			1	1		1		1					4		
Attleboro	320	47	Martin	Job				1				2		1			4		
Attleboro	320	48	Thatcher	Peter	1		1	1	1	1	3			2			10		
Attleboro	320	49	Whitaker	Richd	3	2	1	1		2		1	1				11		
Attleboro	320	50	Tyler	Ebenezer the 2nd	1	2	2			1	2	3					11		
Attleboro	320	51	Allen	Bicknall			1				1	1					3		
Attleboro	320	52	Saddler	John	2		1	1		3		1		1			9		
Attleboro	320	53	Davison	Andrew			1			2			1				4		
Attleboro	320	54	Clafflin	Calvin		1				1		1					3		
Attleboro	320	55	Wilmarth	John	2		1			1		1	1				6		
Attleboro	320	56	Clafflin	Daniel	1		1				1	1	1				5		
Attleboro	320	57	Chace	John	2	3	1	1		1	1		2				11		
Attleboro	320	58	Lune	Daniel		1		1					1				3		
Attleboro	320	59	Potter	Holliman	3	1	1	1			1		1				8		
Attleboro	320	60	Hunt	Joseph	2	1		2	1		2		1				9		
Attleboro	320	61	Carpenter	Noah				1			1		3				5		
Attleboro	320	62	Bowen	Betty										2			2		
Attleboro	320	63	Briggs	Nathl		1			1			2		1			5		
Attleboro	320	64	Carlile	Betty	1					1		1					3		
Attleboro	320	65	Cole	Richard			1			2	2	2	1				8		
Attleboro	320	66	Walcott	Benjm	3	1	1		1	1	2	1					10		
Attleboro	320	67	Lyon	John		1		1	1	1				1			4		
Attleboro	321	1	Richards	Luther	2	1		1		2	1		1				8		
Attleboro	321	2	Richards	Edwd	1			1					2				4		
Attleboro	321	3	Richards	David		1	1						2				5		
Attleboro	321	4	Richards	Nathan	1			1		1			1				4		
Attleboro	321	5	Richards	Avery	1			1		3	1		1				7		

TOWN	PG#	LN#	LAST NAME	FIRST NAME	FREE WHITE MALES under 10	10 to 16	16 to 26	26 to 45	45 and over	FREE WHITE FEMALES under 10	10 to 16	16 to 26	26 to 45	45 and over	TOTAL ALL OTHER	TOTAL SLAVES	TOTALS	DISTRICT/ TOWNSHIP	NOTES
Attleboro	321	6	Blackington	Saml					1	1				1			3		
Attleboro	321	7	Blackington	Joel	1	1	1			2		1					6		
Attleboro	321	8	Blackington	Mary								1		1			2		
Attleboro	321	9	Cheever	George		1	1					1					3		
Attleboro	321	10	Blackington	Oliver			1	1		1			1				4		
Attleboro	321	11	Blackington	Oliver Junr	1	1	1			4	2	1					10		
Attleboro	321	12	Blackington	Othnial		2		1		1			1				5		
Attleboro	321	13	Gardner	Saml	1		1					1					3		
Attleboro	321	14	Walcott	Moses				1		1				1			3		
Attleboro	321	15	Walcott	Moses Junr		1		1		2	1			1			6		
Attleboro	321	16	Walcott	Pentecost		1	1	1		1	1			1			6		
Attleboro	321	17	Blackington	Peter				1						1			2		
Attleboro	321	18	Blackington	Otis	2		1	1		1		1					6		
Attleboro	321	19	Blackington	Peter Junr	2		1			1	1	1					6		
Attleboro	321	20	Whiting	John	3		1					2		1			7		
Attleboro	321	21	Fuller	Stephen the 2nd		2		1				2	1				6		
Attleboro	321	22	Blackington	Wm	2							1	1				4		
Attleboro	321	23	Grant	Elias			1	1				1					3		
Attleboro	321	24	Holmes	Joseph	1	1		1		2	1	1		1			8		
Attleboro	321	25	Everet	Saml	1		1	1		2	2	2					9		
Attleboro	321	26	Richard	John	2		2	1				1	1	1			8		
Attleboro	321	27	Guild	Jos	1	2			1	1	1						6		
Attleboro	321	28	Cheever	Daniel	1		1			2				2			6		
Attleboro	321	29	Sprague	John		1	1		1	2		2		1			8		
Attleboro	321	30	Cutting	David	2		1			1			1				5		
Attleboro	321	31	Daggett	Elijah	1	2	1	1		3	1	1					10		
Attleboro	321	32	Daggett	E*	2	1	1			1	1						6		
Attleboro	321	33	Daggett	*		1				2		1					4		
Attleboro	321	34	Backman	Howland	1	1	1	1		2	1	1					8		
Attleboro	321	35	Daggett	Elihu		1	1				1	1	2	1			7		
Attleboro	321	36	Robinson	George W	1	1	1	1		2		1					7		
Attleboro	321	37	Orne	James Junr			1			2			1				4		
Attleboro	321	38	Maxcy	Benja	3		1						1				5		
Attleboro	321	39	Richards	Jesse	2	1	1						1				6		
Attleboro	321	40	Richards	Edwd Junr	4			1		1			1				7		
Attleboro	321	41	Gibson	Lamont				1		1			1				3		
Attleboro	321	42	Swettland	Bowen	5		2	1		5							14		
Attleboro	321	43	Draper	John	2	1	1	1				2	1	1			9		
Attleboro	321	44	Smith	David		1			2	1		3		2			9		
Attleboro	321	45	Cole	Timothy	2				1	2		1		1			7		
Attleboro	321	46	Day	Loammi	1	2	1		1			1		1			7		
Attleboro	321	47	Swetland	William		2			1	2		2		1			8		
Attleboro	321	48	Swetland	William the 2nd	1	1		1		2		2	1				8		
Attleboro	321	49	Swetland	Clark		2		1		3	1		1				8		
Attleboro	321	50	Fales	Peter	1	3			1					1			6		
Attleboro	321	51	Foster	John	2		1			1	1	1					6		
Attleboro	321	52	Mowey	James	1		1			1							3		
Attleboro	321	53	Holmes	Elizabeth	2	2		1		2		1	1	1			11		
Attleboro	321	54	Atherton	Daniel			1			2			1				4		
Attleboro	321	55	Tyron	Wm	1		1	1		1	1	1					6		
Attleboro	321	56	Cranston	Jason			1	1		1			1				4		
Attleboro	321	57	Bacon	Ebenezer		1	2	1	1	2	3	3		1			14		
Attleboro	321	58	Stanley	Catherine	2	1				1	2	1					7		
Attleboro	321	59	Lombard	James			1			1			1				3		
Attleboro	321	60	Davis	Aaron			1	1				1		1			4		
Attleboro	321	61	Field	Ebenezer	1		2	1		2	1	1					8		
Attleboro	322	1	Barrows	Ezra		1	1	1		2		2					7		
Attleboro	322	2	Slack	Samuel		1		1	1	1		3		1			8		
Attleboro	322	3	Carpenter	Ezekiel	1	1	2	1	1			1	1	1			9		
Attleboro	322	4	Robinson	Ezekiel		1	1	2	1	1				1			7		
Attleboro	322	5	Barrows	Benjm	2	1			2	1		1	1				8		
Attleboro	322	6	Sweeting	John					2					2			4		
Attleboro	322	7	Barrows	Phillbrook	3	2			1	1		2	2	1			12		
Attleboro	322	8	Barrows	Aaron		1			1	1				1			4		
Attleboro	322	9	Barrows	Milton	1			1		2				1			5		
Attleboro	322	10	Barrows	Priscilla									1	1			2		
Attleboro	322	11	Wellman	Lot	1			1		1				1			4		
Attleboro	322	12	Wellman	Rhoda			1						2	1			4		
Attleboro	322	13	Day	Eliphaz		1	1		1				1	1			5		
Attleboro	322	14	Day	Charles			1			2			1	1			5		
Attleboro	322	15	Jillson	Daniel	2	1			1			1	1	1			7		
Attleboro	322	16	Morse	William			1			1			1	1			4		
Attleboro	322	17	Morse	Wm Junr	1			1		1			1				4		
Attleboro	322	18	Morse	Charles	1			1		1	1	1					5		
Attleboro	322	19	Morse	Stephen P	2		1						1				4		
Attleboro	322	20	Read	Ebenezer	1			1		2			1				5		
Attleboro	322	21	Tingley	Lucy	1	1							1	1			4		
Attleboro	322	22	Tingley	Timothy	3			1				1		1			6		
Attleboro	322	23	Pitcher	Keziah										2			2		
Attleboro	322	24	Ingraham	Jeremiah	1	1	1		1	1		1	2	1			9		

TOWN	PG#	LN#	LAST NAME	FIRST NAME	FREE WHITE MALES					FREE WHITE FEMALES					TOTAL ALL OTHER	TOTAL SLAVES	TOTALS	DISTRICT/ TOWNSHIP	NOTES
					under 10	10 to 16	16 to 26	26 to 45	45 and over	under 10	10 to 16	16 to 26	26 to 45	45 and over					
Attleboro	322	25	Carpenter	Nathan	2			1		1			1				5		
Attleboro	322	26	Harding	Jona	2		1			1		1					5		
Attleboro	322	27	Fitton	John			1		1			1		2			5		
Attleboro	322	28	Draper	Ebenezer the 2nd	1			1		1			1				4		
Attleboro	322	29	Pearce	Jeremiah			1			1			1				3		
Attleboro	322	30	Guild	Ebenz	1		2				1	1					5		
Attleboro	322	31	Richards	Joseph A				1		1							2		
Attleboro	322	32	Tingley	Thoms				1		1	1		1				4		
Attleboro	322	33	Tingley	Thomas Junr			1			1			1				3		
Attleboro	322	34	*	Ebenezer		1		1		1							3		
Attleboro	322	35	Daggett	Isaac		1	2		1	1	1	2	1				9		
Attleboro	322	36	*	*	1	1	1		1	1	1	1	1	2			10		
Attleboro	322	37	Newel	Samuel Junr	2			1		1	1						5		
Attleboro	322	38	Newel	Samuel		3	1	2		1		1	2	1			11		
Attleboro	322	39	Holmes	Samuel		1		1		1		1		1			5		
Attleboro	322	40	Stanley	Wm	1		2	2				2		1			8		
Attleboro	322	41	Hatting	George	2		1					1					4		
Attleboro	322	42	Jackson	Samuel	2	1	2		1	1	2			1			10		
Attleboro	322	43	Sally	Nelly		1					1	1					3		
Attleboro	322	44	White	Edward	1		1			2		1					5		
Attleboro	322	45	Brown	David	4	1		1			1	1					8		
Attleboro	322	46	Farebrother	Thoms		1	1	1		3	2		1				9		
Attleboro	322	47	Peck	Jeremiah	3	3	1			1	2	1	1				12		
Attleboro	322	48	Young	Mary		1		1					1				3		
Attleboro	322	49	Blackington	Jona				1				1		1			3		
Attleboro	322	50	Swetland	George			1			1		1		1			4		
Attleboro	322	51	Swetland	John				1		1		1		1			4		
Attleboro	322	52	Swetland	Oliver	1	1	1			2	1	1					7		
Attleboro	322	53	Brown	David the 2nd	1		1					1					3		
Attleboro	322	54	Wood	Mary								2	1				3		
Attleboro	322	55	May	Elisha		2	2	1				2		1			8		
Attleboro	322	56	Bicknell	Thoms	1	2	1		1	1	1	1		1			9		
Attleboro	322	57	Swan	Robert	1	1			1				1				4		
Attleboro	322	58	Swan	Dutey	1		1					1					3		
Attleboro	322	59	Draper	James		1	1			2	1	1		1			7		
Attleboro	322	60	Draper	Lewis	2		1			1	1						5		
Attleboro	322	61	Ellis	Jabez	1	1	1	1						1			5		
Attleboro	322	62	Ellis	Richd	1	1	2		1			1		1			7		
Attleboro	322	63	Whipple	Ephraim				1		1				1			3		
Attleboro	322	64	Whipple	Jenkes	2		1			2		1					6		
Attleboro	322	65	Carpenter	John		2	1					1					4		
Attleboro	322	66	Richards	Lydia	3	1						2					6		
Attleboro	322	67	Blackington	David	2		1				1	1		2			7		
Attleboro	322	68	Jackson	James	1	1		1		2	2		1				8		
Attleboro	322	69	Lane	Levi	1		1					1					3		
Attleboro	322	70	Lane	Jona		1		1		2				1			5		
Attleboro	322	71	Ellis	Joel	1		1			1	1						4		
Attleboro	323	1	Casse	Bowdoin	1	1	1			1	1	1					6		
Attleboro	323	2	Fisher	Samuel	2	1				1		1					5		
Attleboro	323	3	Robinson	Zephariah	1			1		1	1		2				6		
Attleboro	323	4	Stanley	Jesse	1	1		1	1	2	3	2		1			12		
Attleboro	323	5	Stanley	Stephen	1	1		1		2		1					6		
Attleboro	323	6	Stanley	Jona	1	2	1		1	2	1	1		1			10		
Attleboro	323	7	Read	Jona	1		1	1				1					4		
Attleboro	323	8	Perry	Jacob	1		1		1	1	1			2			7		
Attleboro	323	9	Stanley	Amos			1		1			1		1			4		
Attleboro	323	10	Carpenter	John		1		1			2	2					6		
Attleboro	323	11	Town	Gideon	3		1		1	1		3					9		
Attleboro	323	12	Stanley	George	1	1		1		1	1		1				6		
Attleboro	323	13	Perry	Joseph	1		1			1	1	1					5		
Attleboro	323	14	Roginson	Robert	2	1	2	1		3			1				10		
Attleboro	323	15	Robinson	Obed	5		3	2		3	1	1	1				16		
Attleboro	323	16	Stratton	Lemuel	1			1		1	1	2		1			7		

TOWN	PG#	LN#	LAST NAME	FIRST NAME	FREE WHITE MALES					FREE WHITE FEMALES					TOTAL ALL OTHER	TOTAL SLAVES	TOTALS	DISTRICT/ TOWNSHIP	NOTES
					under 10	10 to 16	16 to 26	26 to 45	45 and over	under 10	10 to 16	16 to 26	26 to 45	45 and over					
Berkley	274	1	Tobey	Samuel		1	3	1	1	1	1	2	1	1			12		
Berkley	274	2	Tobey	Nathaniel	1	1	1		1			2		1			7		
Berkley	274	3	Tobey	Appolos	2			1			1		1				5		
Berkley	274	4	Atwood	Joseph			2		1			3	1	1			8		
Berkley	275	1	Porter	Tisdale			1			1		1					3		
Berkley	275	2	Andros	Thomas	3	1		1		3	2	1					11		
Berkley	275	3	Briggs	Ezra			1		1	2			1				5		
Berkley	275	4	Babbit	Elkanah		1	1		1					1			4		
Berkley	275	5	Babbit	Isaac 2nd	1		1	1		1		1					5		
Berkley	275	6	Babbit	Warren			2				1		1				4		
Berkley	275	7	Hathaway	Nathaniel	2			1		4			1				8		
Berkley	275	8	French	Ephraim	2		1			1		1					5		
Berkley	275	9	Crane	Bernice			1		1			1		1			4		
Berkley	275	10	Dean	Weltha Wid	2	2						2	1				7		
Berkley	275	11	Phillips	Phebe									1				1		
Berkley	275	12	Sanford	Robert			1			2	1	1					5		
Berkley	275	13	Upton	Adonijah			1	1									2		
Berkley	275	14	Hathaway	Elkanah			1					1					2		
Berkley	275	15	Hathaway	Stephen				1									1		
Berkley	276	1	Hathaway	Ezra		1			1	1	1	1	1	1			7		
Berkley	276	2	Babbit	John		1	2		1			1		1			6		
Berkley	276	3	Hathaway	Peter	1			1		1		1					4		
Berkley	276	4	Bragg	Samuel	1			1		1		1					4		
Berkley	276	5	Hathaway	Abijah				1						3			4		
Berkley	276	6	Hathaway	Abijah Jnr	2	2	1	1		1		1	1				9		
Berkley	276	7	Hathaway	Benanuel			1			1			1				3		
Berkley	276	8	Hathaway	Alice Wid								3		1			4		
Berkley	276	9	Hathaway	Barzilla	2	1		1		1			1				6		
Berkley	276	10	Babbit	Abijah		1			1	1		1	1				5		
Berkley	276	11	Babbit	Isaac	1			1		2			1				5		
Berkley	276	12	Newhall	Nehemiah			1		1				1	1			4		
Berkley	276	13	Newhall	Darius	1	1	1		1	2	2		1				9		
Berkley	276	14	Newhall	Nehemiah Jr	3		1	1					1				6		
Berkley	276	15	Booth	Samuel			1			1			1				3		
Berkley	276	16	Crane	Benjamin	1				1	2	2		1				7		
Berkley	276	17	Crane	Abiather	1			1	1	3			1				7		
Berkley	276	18	Crane	Abel				1	1	1		1		1			4		
Berkley	276	19	Crane	Luther	4		1	1		2	2		1				11		
Berkley	276	20	Crane	Anna Wd			2					1	1				4		
Berkley	276	21	Briggs	Jedidiah		2	2	1	1	2	1	3	1	1			14		
Berkley	276	22	Briggs	Gershom	2			1		1			1				5		
Berkley	276	23	Briggs	Seth			1		1					1			3		
Berkley	276	24	Hoard	David				1					1	1			3		
Berkley	276	25	French	James	1			1		1	2	2		1			9		
Berkley	276	26	Briggs	Thomas			1	1				1	1	1			5		
Berkley	276	27	Briggs	Keturah Wid															
Berkley	276	28	Phillips	Ralph	1				1	1	1		1				5		
Berkley	276	29	Phillips	Samuel			2		1	2	2		1				8		
Berkley	276	30	Phillips	Mary Wid									1				1		
Berkley	277	1	Burt	Stephen	3		3		1	2	2	1	2				14		
Berkley	277	2	Burt	Simeon	1	2	3		1	1	1	2		1	1		13		
Berkley	277	3	Burt	Edmond		1		1		1			1				4		
Berkley	277	4	Burt	Abner		1	2	3	1			1	3	1			12		
Berkley	277	5	Tisdale	Thomas		1	2						1				4		
Berkley	277	6	French	Nathan	1			1	2		1	1	2	2			10		
Berkley	277	7	Phillips	Nathaniel		1			1			1					3		
Berkley	277	8	Paull	Jacob	1			1		1		1					4		
Berkley	277	9	Briggs	Fobes	1			1		2			1				5		
Berkley	277	10	Colby	Jeremiah			1					1					2		
Berkley	277	11	French	Levi		1	1		1			2	2	1			8		
Berkley	277	12	French	Content Wid										1			1		
Berkley	277	13	French	Samuel	1	1	1		1			1		2			7		
Berkley	277	14	French	Israel	1				1					1			3		
Berkley	277	15	French	Elijah				1						1			2		
Berkley	277	16	French	Phillip	1		1	1		3			1				7		
Berkley	277	17	Paull	John 2d				1		2	1			2			6		
Berkley	277	18	French	Israel Junr		1	1		1	1	1	1		1			7		
Berkley	277	19	Burt	Abner Junr	1		1	1		2			1				6		
Berkley	277	20	French	Ebenezer				1					1				2		
Berkley	277	21	French	Keziah										1			1		
Berkley	277	22	Cranson	Bathsheba						1			1	1			3		
Berkley	277	23	Jones	Zephiniah		1			1			2		2			6		
Berkley	277	24	Hervery	William				1					1				2		
Berkley	277	25	Paull	John 1st				1		1				1			3		
Berkley	277	26	Paull	Roger	1			1		4			1				7		
Berkley	277	27	Macomber	Elijah	2		1		1	1		2	1				8		
Berkley	277	28	Gavin	Paul	2			1		1			1	1			6		
Berkley	277	29	Briggs	Israel	2			1		1			1		1		6		
Berkley	277	30	Macomber	James					1				1				2		

TOWN	PG#	LN#	HEADS OF HOUSEHOLD		FREE WHITE MALES					FREE WHITE FEMALES					TOTAL ALL OTHER	TOTAL SLAVES	TOTALS	DISTRICT/ TOWNSHIP	NOTES
			LAST NAME	FIRST NAME	under 10	10 to 16	16 to 26	26 to 45	45 and over	under 10	10 to 16	16 to 26	26 to 45	45 and over					
Berkley	278	1	Macomber	Venns	1		1			1							3		
Berkley	278	2	Burt	Joseph				1						1			2		
Berkley	278	3	Burt	John	1	1		1					1				4		
Berkley	278	4	Caswell	Abner				1		1				1			3		
Berkley	278	5	Mirich	Simeon	2			1		2			1				6		
Berkley	278	6	Caswell	Ephraim	1		1	1					1	1			5		
Berkley	278	7	Caswell	Abraham	2	1			1	2			1				7		
Berkley	278	8	Mirich	Nathan				1						1			3		
Berkley	278	9	Paull	Joseph		1		1				2	1				5		
Berkley	278	10	Staples	Joseph		1		1				1		1			4		
Berkley	278	11	Paull	Ebenezer 2d			2		1		2	2		1			8		
Berkley	278	12	Townsand	Gilbert	2	1		1					1	1			6		
Berkley	278	13	Seekels	John			1					1					2		
Berkley	278	14	Briggs	John		1	2		1	2	1	1	1	1			10		
Berkley	278	15	Briggs	Hathaway	1			1		3	1		1				7		
Berkley	278	16	Skiff	Isaac			1					1					2		
Berkley	278	17	Paull	Ebenezer	1			1	1		4	1	1				9		
Berkley	278	18	Richard	Verdy									1				1		
Berkley	278	19	Sanford	George				1				2					3		
Berkley	278	20	Sanford	Joseph	3	2		1		1			1				8		
Berkley	278	21	Sanford	George Junr	4			1		2		1	1				9		
Berkley	278	22	Hervery	James	2			1				1	1				5		
Berkley	278	23	Macomber	Wd Susan	1							1					2		
Berkley	278	24	Chace	Ezra	2		2	1		2	3	1	1	1			13		
Berkley	278	25	Haskens	Phillip	1		2		1		2	3		1			10		
Berkley	278	26	Read	Barney	1			1		1			1				4		
Berkley	278	27	Parris	Olive	1							1					2		
Berkley	278	28	Mirich	Ebenezer	1			1		2	1	1	1				7		
Berkley	278	29	Briggs	Abraham				1		2	2			1			6		
Berkley	278	30	Clemmons	Lydia										1			1		
Berkley	279	1	Winslow	Avery			2		1			1		1			5		
Berkley	279	2	Winslow	Avery Jun			1			1		1					3		
Berkley	279	3	Winslow	Ebenezer	1		1		1				1	1			5		
Berkley	279	4	Paull	Benjamin	3	1			1		1	1	1				8		
Berkley	279	5	Paull	Samuel	2		1		1	2	2		2				10		
Berkley	279	6	Farrington	Abial		1		1		1			1				4		
Berkley	279	7	Paull	James	2		1	1		2	3	1	1				11		
Berkley	279	8	Paull	Isaac	2			1		3	2		1	1			10		
Berkley	279	9	Briggs	Sarah	1						1		1				3		
Berkley	279	10	Paull	Israel		1	1	1		3	1	1	1				9		
Berkley	279	11	Hathaway	Phillip			1			1			1				3		
Berkley	279	12	Cudworth	David	1	1	2	1					1				6		
Berkley	279	13	Tubbs	Samuel	3	2		1		3			1				10		
Berkley	279	14	Chace	Simeon	1	1	2	1		3	1		1				10		
Berkley	279	15	Briggs	Amos 2d	1	1	1		2	3	1		1				10		
Berkley	279	16	Haskens	Ruth Wid	3		2					3		1			9		
Berkley	279	17	Briggs	Job			1					1					2		
Berkley	279	18	Briggs	Amata Wid						1	1			1			3		
Berkley	279	19	Strange	Joseph			1					1					2		
Berkley	279	20	Evens	William	2	1			1	2	1	1	1	1			10		
Berkley	279	21	Goff	John	2	2	2	1	1	1			1	1			11		
Berkley	279	22	Briggs	George	2	2	1						1				6		
Berkley	279	23	Hathaway	Henry	2	2	2	1		1				1			9		
Berkley	279	24	Nicholas	Joseph	1			1		1			1				4		
Berkley	279	25	Crane	Ebenezer		1			1		2			2			6		
Berkley	279	26	Briggs	Abial		1	1	1		1	1		1				6		
Berkley	279	27	Hathaway	Benjamin		1	1	1					1	1			5		
Berkley	279	28	Hathaway	Enoch	1			1		1	1		1				5		
Berkley	279	29	Crane	Henry	1		1						1				3		
Berkley	279	30	Briggs	Nathan		2		1		1			1	1			6		
Berkley	279	31	Phillips	Ralph Jun	2		1						1				4		
Berkley	279	32	Briggs	Mary Wid				1					1	1			3		
Berkley	280	1	Shove	Edward		1	2		1	1			2	1			8		
Berkley	280	2	Shove	Theophelus		1							1				2		
Berkley	280	3	Macomber	Joel	2			1			1		1				5		
Berkley	280	4	Jones	Sargent	2		1						1				4		
Berkley	280	5	Crane	Elisha			2		1				3	1			7		
Berkley	280	6	Nicholas	James			1	2	1			2		1			7		
Berkley	280	7	Dillingham	John	2			2		2			1				7		
Berkley	280	8	Babbit	Dean	2			1		1			1				5		
Berkley	280	9	Nicholas	Edward				1						1			2		
Berkley	280	10	Gregory	Elisha	1	1	1		1				1	1			6		
Berkley	280	11	Shove	Asa		1	1		1	1		2		1			7		
Berkley	280	12	Shove	Samuel		1		1		3			1				6		
Berkley	280	13	Crane	Benjamin 2d	1			1					1				3		
Berkley	280	14	Shove	George		1	2		1	1			3	1			9		
Berkley	280	15	Crane	Nathaniel			1			2			1				4		
Berkley	280	16	Hathaway	Benjamin Jr			1			2			1				4		
Berkley	280	17	Chace	Hannah									1				1		

TOWN	PG#	LN#	HEADS OF HOUSEHOLD		FREE WHITE MALES					FREE WHITE FEMALES					TOTAL ALL OTHER	TOTAL SLAVES	TOTALS	DISTRICT/ TOWNSHIP	NOTES
			LAST NAME	FIRST NAME	under 10	10 to 16	16 to 26	26 to 45	45 and over	under 10	10 to 16	16 to 26	26 to 45	45 and over					
Berkley	280	18	Shove	William			1	1		1	2	1					6		
Berkley	280	19	Boyce	John	1			1			1		1	1			5		
Berkley	280	20	Shove	Hannah Wid								1	1	1			3		
Berkley	280	21	Nicholas	Hannah Wid									1	1			2		
Berkley	280	22	Nicholas	Aaron				1		2	1	2	1				7		
Berkley	280	23	Briant	Jonathan			1	1			1	1	1				5		
Berkley	280	24	Drinkwater	Desire									2				2		
Berkley	280	25	Peirce	Ebenezer				1					1				2		
Berkley	280	26	Peirce	Ebenezer Junr	2	1		1		2			1				7		
Berkley	280	27	Dean	David		1			1	1		1	1	1			6		
Berkley	280	28	Dean	David Jur	1			1		1			1				4		
Berkley	280	29	Dean	Joseph		1			1					1			3		
Berkley	280	30	Dean	Walter	1			1					2	1			5		
Berkley	280	31	Dean	James			2		1			2			1		6		
Berkley	280	32	Dean	James Junr				1		1	1		1				4		
Berkley	281	1	Dean	Aaron	2			1		3			1				7		
Berkley	281	2	Dean	Mary Wid			2					1	1	1			5		
Berkley	281	3	Tew	Dan			1	2	1	1		2	2	1			10		
Berkley	281	4	Tew	Abigal Wid	1	1				1	2		1				6		
Berkley	281	5	Tew	Henry				1				2		2			5		
Berkley	281	6	Tew	Henry Junr	2	1	2		1	2	1		1				10		
Berkley	281	7	Phillips	Ebenezer		1		1									2		
Berkley	281	8	Phillips	John	1			1					2				4		
Berkley	281	9	Phillips	Abigal Wid				1					1				2		
Berkley	281	10	Peirce	Elisha			1	1					1				3		
Berkley	281	11	Cotton	William		1		1					1				3		
Berkley	281	12	Tew	Margaret Wid								2	1				3		
Berkley	281	13	Briggs	Amos 3d	1		1			1		1					4		

| TOWN | PG# | LN# | HEADS OF HOUSEHOLD | | FREE WHITE MALES | | | | | FREE WHITE FEMALES | | | | | TOTAL ALL OTHER | TOTAL SLAVES | TOTALS | DISTRICT/ TOWNSHIP | NOTES |
			LAST NAME	FIRST NAME	under 10	10 to 16	16 to 26	26 to 45	45 and over	under 10	10 to 16	16 to 26	26 to 45	45 and over					
Dartmouth	340	1	Allen	Obediah	2	1		1					1				5		
Dartmouth	340	2	Almy	Jiles			1		1	2			1				8		
Dartmouth	340	3	Akins	John			1	1	1	1	1	1	1	2			9		
Dartmouth	340	4	Almy	Peleg	1		1			1		1					7		
Dartmouth	340	5	Anthony	Abraham										5			5		
Dartmouth	340	6	Anthony	Quanh										5			5		
Dartmouth	340	7	Anthony	Joseph										4			4		
Dartmouth	340	8	Akins	Mary		1						1	1				3		
Dartmouth	340	9	Akins	Timothy	1	1	1		1				1				7		
Dartmouth	340	10	Akins	Ruth	1							1	1				3		
Dartmouth	340	11	Akins	James		1		2			1		2				6		
Dartmouth	340	12	Akins	Jacob	1		2				1	1					5		
Dartmouth	340	13	Anthony	Jacob			1	2					1				4		
Dartmouth	340	14	Almy	George		1		1		1			1				4		
Dartmouth	340	15	Allen	Judah		1		1		2			1				5		
Dartmouth	340	16	Allen	Thomas		2		1				1	1				5		
Dartmouth	340	17	Allen	Daniel			1		1	1							3		
Dartmouth	340	18	Allen	Benjamin			2						1				3		
Dartmouth	340	19	Andrew	Stephen			1			1			1				3		
Dartmouth	340	20	Andrew	Mary		2		1					1				4		
Dartmouth	340	21	Andrew	John		1						1					4		
Dartmouth	340	22	Allen	Jethrow			1						1				2		
Dartmouth	341	1	Allen	Joseph			1	1	4			1	1				11		
Dartmouth	341	2	Allen	Sylvanus		1		1			1		1				4		
Dartmouth	341	3	Allen	Philip		1		2				1					6		
Dartmouth	341	4	Allen	Russel	2	1		1	1	2	1		2				10		
Dartmouth	341	5	Allen	Jedediah	1	1	1			2	1		1				8		
Dartmouth	341	6	Allen	Thomas			1			2		1					6		
Dartmouth	341	7	Auker	Joseph										1					
Dartmouth	341	8	Almy	Christopher			1						1				2		
Dartmouth	341	9	Almy	Thomas		1				1							3		
Dartmouth	341	10	Almy	Richard		1				1							2		
Dartmouth	341	11	Allen	Ruben	1		1	2			1						6		
Dartmouth	341	12	Allen	Margaret	1					1	1		1				4		
Dartmouth	341	13	Allen	Thomas	1		2						1				4		
Dartmouth	341	14	Allen	Ebenezar 2nd	1	1						1					4		
Dartmouth	341	15	Anthony	Simon									2				2		
Dartmouth	341	16	Anthony	Caleb	1		1	2				1	1				10		
Dartmouth	341	17	Akins	Thomas	1		1			1		1					4		
Dartmouth	341	18	Allen	Ebenezar			1			1		1					3		
Dartmouth	341	19	Akins	William	1			1	1				1				5		
Dartmouth	341	20	Anthony	William		1							1	1			4		
Dartmouth	341	21	Anthony	Daniel		1		1			1						4		
Dartmouth	341	22	Anthony	Gidion		1		1			1						6		
Dartmouth	341	23	Almy	Joseph									3				3		
Dartmouth	341	24	Brightman	Wanton	2	1		1		1	1						8		
Dartmouth	341	25	Butts	Abraham	1			1		2	1						7		
Dartmouth	341	26	Briggs	John		1		4			1						7		
Dartmouth	341	27	Butts	Stephen	2		1	1			1		1				7		
Dartmouth	341	28	Butts	Stephen 2nd		1		1		1							3		
Dartmouth	341	29	Butts	Peleg		1		2		1							4		
Dartmouth	341	30	Bedon	Henry			1			1		1					3		
Dartmouth	341	31	Bedon	Sampson			1	2		1		1					8		
Dartmouth	341	32	Bedon	Richard			1			1	1						6		
Dartmouth	341	33	Briggs	Daniel			1						1				2		
Dartmouth	341	34	Briggs	Wesson		1	1		1	1		1					6		
Dartmouth	341	35	Briggs	Hannah								1	1				2		
Dartmouth	341	36	Bard	Molly	2	1					1	1					5		
Dartmouth	342	1	Baker	John		1		1				1					6		
Dartmouth	342	2	Briggs	Caleb		1	1			1							3		
Dartmouth	342	3	Baker	Jabez			1					1	1				3		
Dartmouth	342	4	Baker	Lemuel		1						1					4		
Dartmouth	342	5	Baker	Stephen	3	1	1	1				1	2	1			10		
Dartmouth	342	6	Bard	Mary	3								1				4		
Dartmouth	342	7	Buffington	Stephen		1	1	1				1	1				5		
Dartmouth	342	8	Biss	Arnold		1		4		2	1	1					10		
Dartmouth	342	9	Baley	Zuacke									3				3		
Dartmouth	342	10	Babcock	Benjamin			1	2				1					5		
Dartmouth	342	11	Baker	Benjamin	1		1	1				1	1				5		
Dartmouth	342	12	Babcock	Peleg	2	1		1					1				6		
Dartmouth	342	13	Briggs	Joseph		3						1					4		
Dartmouth	342	14	Briggs	William			1						1				2		
Dartmouth	342	15	Brown	Benjamin Jr			1						1				4		
Dartmouth	342	16	Blackman	Ebenezer	1	1		1	1	2	1		1				10		
Dartmouth	342	17	Booth	Moten		1	1		3	1		1					9		
Dartmouth	342	18	Brown	Benjamin	1	1		1	2	1		1	1				8		
Dartmouth	342	19	Bowles	Ezra		1		1		1							4		
Dartmouth	342	20	Booth	Anthony			1						1				2		
Dartmouth	342	21	Borden	Alexander		1		3		1							6		

TOWN	PG#	LN#	LAST NAME	FIRST NAME	FREE WHITE MALES					FREE WHITE FEMALES					TOTAL ALL OTHER	TOTAL SLAVES	TOTALS	DISTRICT/ TOWNSHIP	NOTES
					under 10	10 to 16	16 to 26	26 to 45	45 and over	under 10	10 to 16	16 to 26	26 to 45	45 and over					
Dartmouth	342	22	Bowdsh	William	1	1		2		1	1		1				7		
Dartmouth	342	23	Bennet	John			1						1				2		
Dartmouth	342	24	Bedon	Ruth				2				1					3		
Dartmouth	342	25	Bedon	Benjamin			1	1			2		1				6		
Dartmouth	342	26	Bedon	Richard			1			1		1					3		
Dartmouth	342	27	Cornell	Eunice	1					1			1				3		
Dartmouth	342	28	Cornell	Gidion		1	1	1	2			1	1				7		
Dartmouth	342	29	Cornell	Timothy			1						2				3		
Dartmouth	342	30	Cornell	Sarah					3			1	1				6		
Dartmouth	342	31	Case	Rachel		1							1				2		
Dartmouth	342	32	Cornell	Stephen		1	1					1					3		
Dartmouth	342	33	Crapo	Ruben		1						1					3		
Dartmouth	342	34	Crossman	Zelotes		1						1					2		
Dartmouth	342	35	Cory	William		2	1		3			1					9		
Dartmouth	342	36	Craw	David			1	1				1					5		
Dartmouth	342	37	Chase	Abner		2		2				1	1				6		
Dartmouth	342	38	Chase	Nathaniel	1	1		1			2		1				6		
Dartmouth	343	1	Chase	John		1		1				2					4		
Dartmouth	343	2	Chase	Benjamin		1		1				1					3		
Dartmouth	343	3	Cushman	Obed	1			1	1	2	1	1					9		
Dartmouth	343	4	Collins	William			1	1				1					3		
Dartmouth	343	5	Cummings	Benjamin	1			1	2	3	1	1					11		
Dartmouth	343	6	Chase	David			1	2					1				4		
Dartmouth	343	7	Chandeler	Jeremiah	1		1		2		1	1					8		
Dartmouth	343	8	Crank	George											6		6		
Dartmouth	343	9	Collins	Benjamin		2		1		1							6		
Dartmouth	343	10	Collins	Richard			1						1				2		
Dartmouth	343	11	Cowing	Zebah		1	1			1		1					4		
Dartmouth	343	12	Cowing	Joshua	1		1		2	1		1					9		
Dartmouth	343	13	Cowing	Mary		1					1	1					3		
Dartmouth	343	14	Cornell	Amos		1		1					2				5		
Dartmouth	343	15	Cornell	John	1		1		2			1					8		
Dartmouth	343	16	Cornell	William		1		1		1							4		
Dartmouth	343	17	Chase	Simeon Junr		1						1					4		
Dartmouth	343	18	Chase	Simeon	1		1			1		1					5		
Dartmouth	343	19	Chase	Allen		1		1		1							4		
Dartmouth	343	20	Chase	Jeremiah		1				1	1						4		
Dartmouth	343	21	Chase	David			1			1		1					3		
Dartmouth	343	22	Chase	John		1				1							3		
Dartmouth	343	23	Chase	Preserved		1		1		1							3		
Dartmouth	343	24	Collins	Richard			1			1		1	1				6		
Dartmouth	343	25	Chase	Ebenezer	1			1		1	1		1				5		
Dartmouth	343	26	Crapo	Peter Junr			1	1				2					5		
Dartmouth	343	27	Crapo	Richard			1	2				1					4		
Dartmouth	343	28	Cook	Audra		1	1			2			1				5		
Dartmouth	343	29	Cook	Benjamin											6		6		
Dartmouth	343	30	Cowing	Ebenezer		2		1		1		1					5		
Dartmouth	343	31	Chase	Ezekiel	1			1		2	2		1				9		
Dartmouth	343	32	Cornell	Richard		1						1					3		
Dartmouth	343	33	Cornell	Isaac			1					1	1				3		
Dartmouth	343	34	Craw	Nathan			1	3				1					7		
Dartmouth	343	35	Devol	David	2	2	1		1	?	1						11		
Dartmouth	343	36	Dick	Silas										10			10		
Dartmouth	343	37	Davis	Richard			1				1	1	1				5		
Dartmouth	343	38	Derry	Lucina										7			7		
Dartmouth	343	39	Devil	Job	2		1					1					5		
Dartmouth	343	40	Davis	William			1			1		1					6		
Dartmouth	343	41	Davis	James			1					1					2		
Dartmouth	343	42	Demoranvel	Shoman		1		4				1					6		
Dartmouth	344	1	Demoranvel	Nehemiah		1		1		1							4		
Dartmouth	344	2	Doty	John	1		1	1	2	1		1					9		
Dartmouth	344	3	Eastons	Joseph	1	1	1		2	1		1					7		
Dartmouth	344	4	Easton	Walter	1	1	1		1	1	1	1					7		
Dartmouth	344	5	Eddy	Zephaniah			1			1		1					3		
Dartmouth	344	6	Freborn	Cuffe										6			6		
Dartmouth	344	7	Fisher	Seth	1	1				1		1	1				5		
Dartmouth	344	8	Fowler	Thomas									2		2		2		
Dartmouth	344	9	Francis	Nathan	1		1			2	3	1					9		
Dartmouth	344	10	Fisher	Nathan															Enumeration left blank
Dartmouth	344	11	Fisher	William	1		1	1					1	1			5		
Dartmouth	344	12	Frelove	John			1					1					2		
Dartmouth	344	13	Faunce	Thomas	1	1	1	1		1	3		2				10		
Dartmouth	344	14	Gidley	Thomas			1	2				1					5		
Dartmouth	344	15	Gidley	Samuel	2		1			2		1					9		
Dartmouth	344	16	Gidley	Henry			2			1		3	2				8		
Dartmouth	344	17	Gifford	Timothy		1	1	1		1		1	3	2			10		
Dartmouth	344	18	Gifford	Nathaniel			1	2				1					6		
Dartmouth	344	19	Gifford	Joseph		1		1				1					4		
Dartmouth	344	20	Gifford	Samuel		2	1			1			1	1			7		
Dartmouth	344	21	Gillis	John			1						1				6		

TOWN	PG#	LN#	LAST NAME	FIRST NAME	FREE WHITE MALES					FREE WHITE FEMALES					TOTAL ALL OTHER	TOTAL SLAVES	TOTALS	DISTRICT/ TOWNSHIP	NOTES
					under 10	10 to 16	16 to 26	26 to 45	45 and over	under 10	10 to 16	16 to 26	26 to 45	45 and over					
Dartmouth	344	22	Gifford	Thomas			1			1		1					3		
Dartmouth	344	23	Gifford	Abraham	1		1		2	1	1	1					8		
Dartmouth	344	24	Gifford	Stephen	1	2		1				2	1				8		
Dartmouth	344	25	Gifford	Josiah		1						1	1				4		
Dartmouth	344	26	Gifford	David	1	2		1	1			1	2				8		
Dartmouth	344	27	Gifford	Elihew		3		1		1		1	1				8		
Dartmouth	344	28	Gifford	Isaac			1		2				1				5		
Dartmouth	344	29	Gifford	William	1	1			1				1				6		
Dartmouth	344	30	Gifford	Silas			1		1	1							4		
Dartmouth	344	31	Gifford	James			1			1			1				4		
Dartmouth	344	32	Gifford	Joseph	1			2				1	1				5		
Dartmouth	344	33	Gifford	Gidion		1	1					2	1				5		
Dartmouth	344	34	Gifford	David 2d	1			2	1				1				6		
Dartmouth	344	35	Gifford	Anne	2	1							1				4		
Dartmouth	344	36	Gifford	Luis	1			1	2	1			1				8		
Dartmouth	345	1	Gifford	Jonathan		2		1	1	2			1				7		
Dartmouth	345	2	Gifford	Silus Wdo									4				4		
Dartmouth	345	3	Gifford	Jeremiah	1		2		2	1	1		2				9		
Dartmouth	345	4	Gidly	Benjamin			2		2				2				6		
Dartmouth	345	5	Giford	Benjamin			1		2				1				6		
Dartmouth	345	6	Howland	Thomas	1		1	1				1	1				6		
Dartmouth	345	7	Head	Henry			1	1		2	2		1				8		
Dartmouth	345	8	Hicks	Thomas			1						2				3		
Dartmouth	345	9	Handy	John	3	1		1	2				1	1			9		
Dartmouth	345	10	Howland	Henry	1		1		2				1	1			8		
Dartmouth	345	11	Howland	Nathaniel	1	1	1		4	1	1	1	1				12		
Dartmouth	345	12	Hicks	Deborah									2				2		
Dartmouth	345	13	Howland	Isaac	1	1		1	1	1	1	1	1				11		
Dartmouth	345	14	Howland	Benjamin			1						1				2		
Dartmouth	345	15	Howland	Stephen		1		2				1					6		
Dartmouth	345	16	Howland	Gideon	1		1	1					2	2			7		
Dartmouth	345	17	Howland	Thomas			1		1		1						4		
Dartmouth	345	18	Howland	John	1		1		1	1		1	1				9		
Dartmouth	345	19	Howland	Joseph			1				1		1				4		
Dartmouth	345	20	Head	John	1	1	1	1	2		2		1				11		
Dartmouth	345	21	Hicks	Daniel		1	1		1				1				5		
Dartmouth	345	22	Hull	John	2		1	1					2				8		
Dartmouth	345	23	Howland	William	1		1		2	1			1				6		
Dartmouth	345	24	Howland	Jonathan		1		1	1	1	1	1					7		
Dartmouth	345	25	Howland	Lucy		1	1			1	2		2				7		
Dartmouth	345	26	Hathaway	Elizabeth		1						1	2				4		
Dartmouth	345	27	Howland	Asa		1						2	2				5		
Dartmouth	345	28	Howland	Luthern		1		1					2				4		
Dartmouth	345	29	Howland	Daniel	1		1	1	2	1			1				9		
Dartmouth	345	30	Howland	Cady									2				2		
Dartmouth	345	31	Howland	Joshua			1			2			1				5		
Dartmouth	345	32	Howland	Caleb	1	1		1	1	2	1	1					8		
Dartmouth	345	33	Handy	George		1							1				3		
Dartmouth	345	34	Howland	Joseph			2		3				1				6		
Dartmouth	345	35	Howland	Warren		1		1	4	1			1				8		
Dartmouth	345	36	Howland	Reserved	1		1				1	1					6		
Dartmouth	345	37	Howland	David			1		4	1							6		
Dartmouth	345	38	Howland	Pero										4			4		
Dartmouth	345	39	Howland	Gideon 2d		3		1	1	1	1	1					8		
Dartmouth	345	40	Hoskins	George	2	1		1		2		1					8		
Dartmouth	345	41	Hathaway	Paul	2		1		2	3	1						11		
Dartmouth	345	42	Hathaway	Maltiah			1						1				2		
Dartmouth	345	43	Hathaway	Henry	1		1		1	1			1				5		
Dartmouth	345	44	Hart	Joseph			1		1	2	1	1					7		
Dartmouth	345	45	Hart	Hannah									3				3		
Dartmouth	345	46	Howland	John	1	2		1	1	2			1				12		
Dartmouth	345	47	Hart	William	1	1		1		3		1	1				8		
Dartmouth	346	1	Joy	Samuel		1		1				1	1				4		
Dartmouth	346	2	Jones	Zebedee			1		3				1				5		
Dartmouth	346	3	Jones	Zepheniah			1		2				1				4		
Dartmouth	346	4	Jones	Abial			1		1				1				5		
Dartmouth	346	5	Jonson	Laurance										4			4		
Dartmouth	346	6	Kerby	Silas			1		2				1				6		
Dartmouth	346	7	Kerby	Rescom			1				1						6		
Dartmouth	346	8	Kerby	Benjamin			1		1	1			1				6		
Dartmouth	346	9	Kerby	Wesson			1				1						2		
Dartmouth	346	10	Kerby	Luthern			1		1				1				4		
Dartmouth	346	11	Knapp	Asael			1		1	2			1				7		
Dartmouth	346	12	Knap	Eben				1					1				2		
Dartmouth	346	13	Lawton	Abraham										4			4		
Dartmouth	346	14	Lewis	John										4			4		
Dartmouth	346	15	Lapham	Humphrey	2		1		2	1		1					8		
Dartmouth	346	16	Lapham	Nicholas			1		1		1						3		
Dartmouth	346	17	Lapham	Mary		1							1				2		

			HEADS OF HOUSEHOLD		FREE WHITE MALES					FREE WHITE FEMALES					TOTAL ALL OTHER	TOTAL SLAVES	TOTALS	DISTRICT/ TOWNSHIP	NOTES
TOWN	PG#	LN#	LAST NAME	FIRST NAME	under 10	10 to 16	16 to 26	26 to 45	45 and over	under 10	10 to 16	16 to 26	26 to 45	45 and over					
Dartmouth	346	18	Lawton	Jonathan				1	1	1			1				5		
Dartmouth	346	19	Lincoln	Isaac					1				1	2			5		
Dartmouth	346	20	Luther	Jonathan				1					1				3		
Dartmouth	346	21	Liscom	Richard			1		2			1					6		
Dartmouth	346	22	Little	Barker	3			1		3		1					8		
Dartmouth	346	23	Little	Nathaniel			1					1					3		
Dartmouth	346	24	Macomber	Elijah	1			1	2				1	1			8		
Dartmouth	346	25	Macomber	Perry	1		1		2	2		1					9		
Dartmouth	346	26	Mosher	Ruben		1						1					2		
Dartmouth	346	27	Macomber	Anson	3	1	1		2	1		1					12		
Dartmouth	346	28	Mosher	Ebenezer		1		1		1			1				5		
Dartmouth	346	29	Mosher	Maxon	1	1		1		1		1	1				7		
Dartmouth	346	30	Mosher	Jethrow			1					1					3		
Dartmouth	346	31	Mosher	Stephen			1			2		1					4		
Dartmouth	346	32	Mosher	Elizabeth								1	2				4		
Dartmouth	346	33	Maxfield	Edmond		1	1	2			1		1				6		
Dartmouth	346	34	Maxfield	Zadock		1		3	1		1	1				7		
Dartmouth	346	35	Michal	Elkanah			1		1			1					3		
Dartmouth	346	36	Michel	Nathan		1						1					3		
Dartmouth	347	1	Maxfield	Timothy			1	1	1	3	1						8		
Dartmouth	347	2	Maxfield	David		1	1		4			1					7		
Dartmouth	347	3	Maxfield	John			1					1					2		
Dartmouth	347	4	Maxfield	Abraham		1	1		1	1	1						7		
Dartmouth	347	5	Mosher	Barney			1					1					2		
Dartmouth	347	6	Mosher	Barney Junr	4	1	1		1			1					9		
Dartmouth	347	7	Mosher	Hannah								1	1				2		
Dartmouth	347	8	Mosher	Lemuel		2		1		1		1					5		
Dartmouth	347	9	Mott	Thomas			1	1		1	1	1					6		
Dartmouth	347	10	Miller	John		1		2			1	1					7		
Dartmouth	347	11	Mosher	Jesse	1			1		1		1					4		
Dartmouth	347	12	Mosher	George	1			1		1		1					4		
Dartmouth	347	13	Mosher	John	2	1		1	1	2		1					10		
Dartmouth	347	14	Mosher	John Junr		1			1			1					4		
Dartmouth	347	15	Mosher	Elijah			1				1						4		
Dartmouth	347	16	Mosher	Isaac		1		1		1							4		
Dartmouth	347	17	Macomber	Constant	1			1	1			1					7		
Dartmouth	347	18	Petty	David			1	1	1		1						7		
Dartmouth	347	19	Potter	Gardner		1				1	1						6		
Dartmouth	347	20	Prince	Elizabeth										4			4		
Dartmouth	347	21	Pratt	Thomas		1		2	1	1	1						8		
Dartmouth	347	22	Packard	Joel	1		1		1		1						4		
Dartmouth	347	23	Perkins	Benjamin		1		5			1						7		
Dartmouth	347	24	Prince	Job									3				3		
Dartmouth	347	25	Peabody	Peleg	1						1						2		
Dartmouth	347	26	Peabody	Daniel	1		1			1	1	1					5		
Dartmouth	347	27	Page	Ebenezar									1				1		
Dartmouth	347	28	Peckham	Caleb				1		2	3	1	1				11		
Dartmouth	347	29	Peckham	Isaiah			1				1						2		
Dartmouth	347	30	Peckham	James			1		3		1						6		
Dartmouth	347	31	Palmer	Abigail						2		1					4		
Dartmouth	347	32	Potter	Wm Holiday	2		1		2	2		1					8		
Dartmouth	347	33	Potter	Abner	1	1			1	1							5		
Dartmouth	347	34	Potter	Joshua	1			1		2		1	1				6		
Dartmouth	347	35	Potter	Prince		2		1		3	1		1				8		
Dartmouth	347	36	Potter	Humphrey	2	2		1					1				7		
Dartmouth	347	37	Parce	Clothier		1		1					1				3		
Dartmouth	347	38	Peckham	Bristol									3				3		
Dartmouth	347	39	Philips	Ira	2		1		2	1	1						9		
Dartmouth	347	40	Pool	Safinas	2		1			2		1					9		
Dartmouth	347	41	Potter	Weaver			1					1					3		
Dartmouth	347	42	Petty	Simpson	1			1		1	1	1					5		
Dartmouth	348	1	Quan	James											6		6		
Dartmouth	348	2	Quan	Deborah											3		3		
Dartmouth	348	3	Quan	Joseph											10		10		
Dartmouth	348	4	Quan	Martha											3		3		
Dartmouth	348	5	Russel	Elihu			1		1		1						4		
Dartmouth	348	6	Russel	Joseph	1		1		3	1		1					9		
Dartmouth	348	7	Rickdson	Sarah		2					3		1				6		
Dartmouth	348	8	Russel	Otes			1		2			1	1				6		
Dartmouth	348	9	Russel	Humphrey	1			1		2	1	1	1				7		
Dartmouth	348	10	Russel	Philip			1				2	1					6		
Dartmouth	348	11	Russel	Elijah			1	1		3		1					6		
Dartmouth	348	12	Russel	Jonathan				2	2	1		1					8		
Dartmouth	348	13	Ricketson	Henry	1		1		2			1					6		
Dartmouth	348	14	Ricketson	John				1				2	2				6		
Dartmouth	348	15	Ricketson	Clark	1		1		1			1					4		
Dartmouth	348	16	Russel	Perry		2	1				1						4		
Dartmouth	348	17	Russel	Elizabeth									2	1			3		
Dartmouth	348	18	Russel	Michael			1			1			4	2			8		
Dartmouth	348	19	Rider	Benjamin		1		1			1	1					4		

TOWN	PG#	LN#	LAST NAME	FIRST NAME	FREE WHITE MALES under 10	10 to 16	16 to 26	26 to 45	45 and over	FREE WHITE FEMALES under 10	10 to 16	16 to 26	26 to 45	45 and over	TOTAL ALL OTHER	TOTAL SLAVES	TOTALS	DISTRICT/ TOWNSHIP	NOTES
Dartmouth	348	20	Rider	Rowland		1				1							3		
Dartmouth	348	21	Rider	William	2		1			1	1	1					6		
Dartmouth	348	22	Rider	John		1		1		1							4		
Dartmouth	348	23	Rider	Abigale									2				2		
Dartmouth	348	24	Rider	Samuel	1		1			1			1				5		
Dartmouth	348	25	Rider	Henry		1				1	1						4		
Dartmouth	348	26	Reed	William	1	1		3				1					8		
Dartmouth	348	27	Rogers	Gidion	1		1	3		2	1	1					9		
Dartmouth	348	28	Reed	Benjamin	2	2	1		2	2		1	1				11		
Dartmouth	348	29	Reed	John	1		1			2			1				8		
Dartmouth	348	30	Reed	Thomas Junr		2	1		1	3	1		1				12		
Dartmouth	348	31	Reed	Elijah Warren		1		3				1					6		
Dartmouth	348	32	Reed	Thomas			1						1				2		
Dartmouth	348	33	Reed	Lemuel	1		1	2	1			1					8		
Dartmouth	349	1	Ricketson	Cook		1		1		1							6		
Dartmouth	349	2	Russel	Isaac			1				1						2		
Dartmouth	349	3	Russel	Luthern		2	1			1	1						5		
Dartmouth	349	4	Russel	Joseph			1	2	1		1						6		
Dartmouth	349	5	Russel	David			1				1						2		
Dartmouth	349	6	Russel	Barney		1	1					1					3		
Dartmouth	349	7	Russel	Stephen	1		1					1					5		
Dartmouth	349	8	Ricketson	Peleg		1				1		1					3		
Dartmouth	349	9	Russel	Clark	1		1		1	1		1					5		
Dartmouth	349	10	Russel	Stephen			1		1			1					5		
Dartmouth	349	11	Russel	William	1	1	1		3			1					7		
Dartmouth	349	12	Russel	Paul		1			1	1	2						6		
Dartmouth	349	13	Reynolds	Benjamin	2		1						1				4		
Dartmouth	349	14	Rogers	John			1			1		1					3		
Dartmouth	349	15	Slocum	Jonathan Junr			1					1					5		
Dartmouth	349	16	Slocum	Jonathan			1		1	1	1						4		
Dartmouth	349	17	Slocum	Jonas	1	1		1	3	2		1					10		
Dartmouth	349	18	Slocum	Elihu	2	1		1	1	1	1		1				11		
Dartmouth	349	19	Smith	Deliverance		1			2	1							5		
Dartmouth	349	20	Smith	Caleb		1			1	1							3		
Dartmouth	349	21	Slocum	Peleg 1st	1		1	1				3	1				7		
Dartmouth	349	22	Slocum	Giles		1		1				1	1				6		
Dartmouth	349	23	Smith	George 2nd	1	1	1		2	1		1	1				10		
Dartmouth	349	24	Smith	H. Benjamin		1	1			1							6		
Dartmouth	349	25	Slocum	Ceasar										3			3		
Dartmouth	349	26	Shearman	Benjm Junr	1		1		2	1		1					8		
Dartmouth	349	27	Shearman	Benjm				1				1	1				3		
Dartmouth	349	28	Shearman	Abraham			1		2	1		1					6		
Dartmouth	349	29	Shearman	Barney	1	1		1			1		2				7		
Dartmouth	349	30	Smith	Meribah									2				2		
Dartmouth	349	31	Smith	Benjamin	1		1		2	1		1					7		
Dartmouth	349	32	Smith	George	1	1	1	1				1	1				6		
Dartmouth	349	33	Smith	Mary	1	1					1	1	1				5		
Dartmouth	349	34	Smith	Increas				1					1				2		
Dartmouth	349	35	Smith	Perry			1		1			1					6		
Dartmouth	349	36	Smith	Samuel			1		1	1							4		
Dartmouth	349	37	Smith	Benjamin			1					1					2		
Dartmouth	349	38	Smith	Jiles	1		1		3	1							7		
Dartmouth	349	39	Smith	Collins	1		1		3		1						8		
Dartmouth	349	40	Smith	Peleg		1	1	1		1		1					5		
Dartmouth	350	1	Smith	Elihu		1		2			1						5		
Dartmouth	350	2	Shearman	William		1	1					2					4		
Dartmouth	350	3	Shearman	Peleg	2	2	1					1					6		
Dartmouth	350	4	Shearman	Elihu		1		1				1					3		
Dartmouth	350	5	Smith	Ruben			1	2		1		1					7		
Dartmouth	350	6	Shearman	Peleg 2d	1					1							3		
Dartmouth	350	7	Slocum	Santo										3			3		
Dartmouth	350	8	Shearman	Ruben		1	1		2			1	1				8		
Dartmouth	350	9	Shearman	George		2		1	2	1		1					7		
Dartmouth	350	10	Shearman	Shadrach	1		1	1	4	2		2	3				16		
Dartmouth	350	11	Shearman	Russel		2	1		1			1					7		
Dartmouth	350	12	Smith	Henry	1	1		1			1		1				5		
Dartmouth	350	13	Stafford	Lilly		1		2		1	1	1					7		
Dartmouth	350	14	Shearman	Josiah		1					2		2				5		
Dartmouth	350	15	Sisson	Stephen			1		2			1	1				7		
Dartmouth	350	16	Stratton	Udel			2					1					3		
Dartmouth	350	17	Sandford	George			1					1					2		
Dartmouth	350	18	Sandford	Peleg		1		2		1	1						6		
Dartmouth	350	19	Sandford	Isaac		1				1		1					5		
Dartmouth	350	20	Sandford	Elisha		1	1				1	1					4		
Dartmouth	350	21	Sandford	John		1		3			1						6		
Dartmouth	350	22	Sowle	William	1	1	1			1							4		
Dartmouth	350	23	Sandford	Paul		1					1						2		
Dartmouth	350	24	Sandford	William	1	1		2			1						5		
Dartmouth	350	25	Slocum	Holder		1		1				1	2				5		
Dartmouth	350	26	Shearman	David	1	1	1		1			1					5		
Dartmouth	350	27	Shearman	Philip		1	1	1			1	2					6		
Dartmouth	350	28	Shearman	Paul			1			2	1	1					6		
Dartmouth	350	29	Sandford	David	1		1		1		1						6		
Dartmouth	350	30	Shearman	Mary		1		1		1	1						4		
Dartmouth	350	31	Shearman	Caleb		1	1		2	1	1						8		
Dartmouth	350	32	Shearman	Prince			1			1		1					3		
Dartmouth	350	33	Shearman	Jerih	1	1		1		1							5		
Dartmouth	350	34	Shearman	Butler		1	1	1				1					4		
Dartmouth	350	35	Shearman	Ira		1		3		1		1					6		

TOWN	PG#	LN#	LAST NAME	FIRST NAME	FREE WHITE MALES under 10	10 to 16	16 to 26	26 to 45	45 and over	FREE WHITE FEMALES under 10	10 to 16	16 to 26	26 to 45	45 and over	TOTAL ALL OTHER	TOTAL SLAVES	TOTALS	DISTRICT/ TOWNSHIP	NOTES
Dartmouth	350	36	Shearman	Daniel				1					2			4			
Dartmouth	350	37	Slocum	Elihu 2nd			1					1	1			5			
Dartmouth	350	38	Shearman	James			1		2	1		1		3		11			
Dartmouth	350	39	Shearman	Jonathan	1			1		1	1		1			5			
Dartmouth	350	40	Smith	Benjamin Jr				1				1	1			4			
Dartmouth	350	41	Smith	Benjamin Junr		1						1				5			
Dartmouth	350	42	Slaid	Edward	1	1		1	1	1	1		1			8			
Dartmouth	350	43	Shepherd	Abner	1		1		1			1				6			
Dartmouth	350	44	Smith	Lowrey			1		1	1		1				5			
Dartmouth	350	45	Sekel	Caleb			1		2			1				4			
Dartmouth	350	46	Smith	John	1			1		1		1	1			5			
Dartmouth	351	1	Shearman	Timothy				1		1	1		1			4			
Dartmouth	351	2	Shearman	Deavenport		1		3		1						7			
Dartmouth	351	3	Shearman	Zoath	2	1		3				1				8			
Dartmouth	351	4	Sheldon	John	1		1	3		2		1				10			
Dartmouth	351	5	Shearman	Butler 2nd		1		1				1				5			
Dartmouth	351	6	Shearman	Charles		1		2		2		1				8			
Dartmouth	351	7	Slocum	Peleg 2nd		1	1					1				3			
Dartmouth	351	8	Shearman	Josiah		1				1						2			
Dartmouth	351	9	Shepherd	John			1				1	1				3			
Dartmouth	351	10	Shepherd	Barney		1	1	2				1				6			
Dartmouth	351	11	Slocum	Christopher		1	1					1				3			
Dartmouth	351	12	Sandford	Richard	1		1		1			1				6			
Dartmouth	351	13	Toby	Cornelius		1		1				1		1		6			
Dartmouth	351	14	Tucker	Sambo											5	5			
Dartmouth	351	15	Tripp	Abner		1		2				1				5			
Dartmouth	351	16	Tripp	Ephraim			1		1	1		1				4			
Dartmouth	351	17	Tucker	Joseph		1		1			1		1			4			
Dartmouth	351	18	Tucker	Edward			1		3			1				5			
Dartmouth	351	19	Tucker	Abraham		1	1					1				3			
Dartmouth	351	20	Tucker	John		2		1		2	2	1				9			
Dartmouth	351	21	Tucker	Berzilla		1	1						1			3			
Dartmouth	351	22	Tucker	Benjamin	1	1		1	1		1		1			7			
Dartmouth	351	23	Tripp	John			1		1		1		1			5			
Dartmouth	351	24	Taber	Amos	1		1		1			1				6			
Dartmouth	351	25	Tucker	Rebeccah									2			2			
Dartmouth	351	26	Tucker	Jonathan	1			1	1	1	1			1		7			
Dartmouth	351	27	Tripp	William			1				1		1			3			
Dartmouth	351	28	Tripp	Othnial		1						2	1			4			
Dartmouth	351	29	Tucker	Holder			1			1	2					5			
Dartmouth	351	30	Trafford	Joseph	1			1	1		2	1				7			
Dartmouth	351	31	Taber	Benjamin	1	1	1			1		1				8			
Dartmouth	351	32	Tucker	Henry	2	1	1		1			1		1		8			
Dartmouth	351	33	Valentine	Lydia										4		4			
Dartmouth	351	34	Upham	James			1					1				3			
Dartmouth	351	35	Wilkey	Peter				1		1	1		1			5			
Dartmouth	351	36	Wilkey	George		1			1	1						3			
Dartmouth	351	37	Wilcox	William	1	1		1			2		1			6			
Dartmouth	352	1	Wing	John	1	1	1		2	2		1				9			
Dartmouth	352	2	Wilbur	David				1		2		1				4			
Dartmouth	352	3	Wilbur	Stephen			1		2	1		1				5			
Dartmouth	352	4	Wilbur	Jonathan		2		1			1	2	1	1		8			
Dartmouth	352	5	Weeks	Joshua	1		1		2			1				7			
Dartmouth	352	6	Woodmancy	Gideon	2		1		1			1				6			
Dartmouth	352	7	Waste	Nathan		1	1				1	1				4			
Dartmouth	352	8	Washborn	Peter	1			1			2					4			
Dartmouth	352	9	Wheeler	Calven		1					1		1			4			
Dartmouth	352	10	Wood	Marlborough		1		1				1	1			7			
Dartmouth	352	11	Wilcox	Benjamin		1			3	1						5			
Dartmouth	352	12	Wood	Luthern			1	1				2				4			
Dartmouth	352	13	Wood	Josiah				1				1	1			3			
Dartmouth	352	14	Wood	Jonathan			1					1				3			
Dartmouth	352	15	Wilcox	Thomas	1	1	1	1		1	2		1			8			
Dartmouth	352	16	Wood	John	1	2		1	2	1	1	1				10			
Dartmouth	352	17	Wade	John	1			1			1	1	2			7			
Dartmouth	352	18	Wilcox	Henry		1	1					1				3			
Dartmouth	352	19	Wady	Humphrey		1	1						1			3			
Dartmouth	352	20	Wait	Henry	2			1			2		1			6			
Dartmouth	352	21	Winslow	Richard				1					1			4			
Dartmouth	352	22	Winslow	Nelson			1		1		1	1				5			
Dartmouth	352	23	Wing	Primus										3		3			
Dartmouth	352	24	Whalon	Daniel		1		1		2	2					7			
Dartmouth	352	25	Winslow	Benjam Junr			1		1	1						4			
Dartmouth	352	26	Webster	Abigail					1			1	1			3			
Dartmouth	352	27	Winslow	Benjamin	1	1		1	1	1		1				8			
Dartmouth	352	28	Winslow	John			1		2	1		1				5			
Dartmouth	352	29	Winslow	Abigale							1	1				2			
Dartmouth	352	30	Winslow	Thomas			1		1	1						3			
Dartmouth	352	31	Washborn	Ira	1		1		1	1		1				7			
Dartmouth	352	32	Wilbur	Henry			1	1				1				4			
Dartmouth	352	33	Wilbur	Isaac			1		1		1	1				7			
Dartmouth	352	34	Washborn	Bazaleal	2			1	2	1	1	1				10			
Dartmouth	352	35	Whalon	Joseph			1		2			2				6			
Dartmouth	353	1	Williams	James	1	3		1			1		1			7			
Dartmouth	353	2	Williams	Joshua		1	1		2		1	1				9			
Dartmouth	353	3	Williams	Benjamin		1	1		1			1		1		7			
Dartmouth	353	4	Williams	Mary Wid	1		1		1		1	1				6			

TOWN	PG#	LN#	HEADS OF HOUSEHOLD LAST NAME	FIRST NAME	FREE WHITE MALES under 10	10 to 16	16 to 26	26 to 45	45 and over	FREE WHITE FEMALES under 10	10 to 16	16 to 26	26 to 45	45 and over	TOTAL ALL OTHER	TOTAL SLAVES	TOTALS	DISTRICT/ TOWNSHIP	NOTES
Dighton	409	1	Baylee	William			2		1			2		1			6		
Dighton	409	2	Richmond	Ezra					1					2			3		
Dighton	409	3	Barrows	John			1		1				1	1			4		
Dighton	409	4	Baylee	Thomas		1	1	1		1		1					5		
Dighton	409	5	Smith	John	3	2	2		1	1	1	2		1			13		
Dighton	409	6	Baylee	Hodijah		2	1	1			1		1	1			7		
Dighton	409	7	Andrews	William	1	1			1	1			1				5		
Dighton	409	8	Kimble	Asa	1		1			1	1	1					5		
Dighton	409	9	Dean	Saml	3		1				1	1	1				7		
Dighton	409	10	Peirce	Caleb	1	2	1	1			1	1					7		
Dighton	409	11	Stetson	Ebenz			1		1	2	2		1				7		
Dighton	409	12	Wright	Benja	1	2	1		1	1	1		1				8		
Dighton	409	13	Richmond	Jonah	3	3	3		1		2			1			13		
Dighton	409	14	Babbit	Gideon		2	1		1					1			5		
Dighton	409	15	Hathaway	Isaac		1			1	4	2			1			9		
Dighton	409	16	Trafton	Snow			1			3			1				5		
Dighton	409	17	Reed	Seth	1	1		1		1			1				5		
Dighton	409	18	Trafton	Benja		1	1					1		1			5		
Dighton	409	19	Butlar	Kate			1							1			2		
Dighton	409	20	Reed	Jemima									2	1			3		
Dighton	409	21	Reed	Samuel	4	1			1	1				1			8		
Dighton	409	22	Briggs	Ebz					1				4	1			6		
Dighton	409	23	Briggs	Saml 3d	1	3		1		4			1				10		
Dighton	409	24	Smith	Saml	1	2		1	1	2	3			1			11		
Dighton	409	25	Simons	Hannah Wido		1					1	1		1			4		
Dighton	409	26	Simmons	Constant 2d	1		1						1				3		
Dighton	409	27	Phillips	Elizt Wido	2	1		1		1	2	1		1			9		
Dighton	409	28	Briggs	George	1	1		1	1	2	2	2		1			11		
Dighton	409	29	Briggs	Nathan			1	1						1			3		
Dighton	409	30	Simmons	Joshua		1			1	4	2			1			9		
Dighton	409	31	Simmons	Jereh					1					1			2		
Dighton	409	32	Mason	Amos	1	1	1		1	1	2			1			8		
Dighton	409	33	Cummings	David			1						1				2		
Dighton	409	34	Fish	Daniel	2	1			1	1	3	1		1			10		
Dighton	409	35	Smith	Stephen	1				1					1			3		
Dighton	409	36	Smith	Asa	2		1			1		1					5		
Dighton	409	37	Smith	Daniel			1			1		1					3		
Dighton	409	38	Briggs	Abner	4	1			1	1	1		1				9		
Dighton	409	39	Teaston	Seth			2		2			4		1			9		
Dighton	409	40	Briggs	Saml			1	1						1			3		
Dighton	409	41	Briggs	Eliakim 2d			1	1		4	1		1				8		
Dighton	410	1	Briggs	Abiezer	3	1			1	1	3			1			10		
Dighton	410	2	Briggs	Saml 2d					1					1			2		
Dighton	410	3	Briggs	Zebedec	2			1		3			1	1			8		
Dighton	410	4	Horton	Seth	1			1		1		1					4		
Dighton	410	5	Simmons	Constant		1	1	1	1			3		1			8		
Dighton	410	6	Paul	William	3	1			1	3	1	3		1			13		
Dighton	410	7	West	Nathan			1			2		1					4		
Dighton	410	8	Shaw	Lavina								1		3			4		
Dighton	410	9	Cornell	Stephen Jr	1			1		1		1					4		
Dighton	410	10	Lewis	Benja	2	2		1			2	1					8		
Dighton	410	11	Phillips	Saml	1		2	1	1		1			1			7		
Dighton	410	12	Phillips	Baylies			1						1				2		
Dighton	410	13	Pitts	Philip	1		1			2			1				5		
Dighton	410	14	Shaw	Abraham	1		1			2			1				5		
Dighton	410	15	Phillips	Abiezer			2		1		1	2		1			7		
Dighton	410	16	Phillips	Ephraim	2	1		1		1			1	1			7		
Dighton	410	17	Paul	Richard	2	1		1					1				5		
Dighton	410	18	Jones	Henry				1			2			1			4		
Dighton	410	19	Paul	Zebedee			1						1	1			3		
Dighton	410	20	Smith	Stephen Jr	1			1		4	1			1			8		
Dighton	410	21	Paul	Lemuel	1	2		1		3	1			1			9		
Dighton	410	22	Church	Gamaliel	1		1	1		1		2	1	1			8		
Dighton	410	23	Atwood	George	2			2		2		1					7		
Dighton	410	24	Atwood	John		1	1					1					3		
Dighton	410	25	Gooding	Matthew	2				1	1	1	1	1				7		
Dighton	410	26	Gooding	George			1	1				1					3		
Dighton	410	27	Gooding	Joseph		2		1			1			1			5		
Dighton	410	28	Gooding	Joseph Jr		2	1	1		1		1					6		
Dighton	410	29	Standish	David			1			3	1	1	1				7		
Dighton	410	30	Perry	Luther			1					1					2		
Dighton	410	31	Atwood	Joseph		1			2	1			1	1			6		
Dighton	410	32	Austin	Seth		3			1		1			1			6		
Dighton	410	33	Clouston	Hannah		1							1	2			4		
Dighton	410	34	Hathaway	Leonard	2			1		1	1		1				6		
Dighton	410	35	Rose	Thomas Jr	3			1		2			1	1			8		
Dighton	410	36	Walker	William	1	3	2		1	1	1			1			10		
Dighton	410	37	Walker	William Jr			1			2			1				4		
Dighton	410	38	Briggs	James	1	4			1	1	1			3			11		

TOWN	PG#	LN#	LAST NAME	FIRST NAME	FREE WHITE MALES under 10	10 to 16	16 to 26	26 to 45	45 and over	FREE WHITE FEMALES under 10	10 to 16	16 to 26	26 to 45	45 and over	TOTAL ALL OTHER	TOTAL SLAVES	TOTALS	DISTRICT/TOWNSHIP	NOTES
Dighton	410	39	Walker	Sylvester	1			1		2			1				5		
Dighton	410	40	Church	Frances	2			1					1				4		
Dighton	410	41	Atwood	Sylvest						1		2	2				5		
Dighton	410	42	Atwood	Sylv Jr	2	1		1		2	1		1				8		
Dighton	410	43	Pool	Isaac	4		2		1	2	2	3		2			16		
Dighton	410	44	Pool	Jonah				1		2			1	1			5		
Dighton	410	45	Kneeder	Thomas		1		1					1				3		
Dighton	411	1	Knowles	Jonathan	2			1		1			1				5		
Dighton	411	2	Marble	James				1					1				2		
Dighton	411	3	Walker	John	2			1		2			1				6		
Dighton	411	4	Wilbour	Josiah	1			1					1				3		
Dighton	411	5	Stephens	Benja				1				2		1			4		
Dighton	411	6	Stephens	John		3		1					1	1			6		
Dighton	411	7	Carwell	Elijah		4	1	1				2		2			10		
Dighton	411	8	Stephen	Saml		2		1		1	3			1			8		
Dighton	411	9	Carey	Daniel	2			1		2			1				6		
Dighton	411	10	Carey	Wido		1						3		1			5		
Dighton	411	11	Elmes	Elkanah				1					1				2		
Dighton	411	12	Waldron	George Jr	1			1		2			1				5		
Dighton	411	13	Waldron	Benja 2d	2			1		1			1				5		
Dighton	411	14	Jones	John	1			1		1			1				4		
Dighton	411	15	Waldron	George	1		4	1				2	1				9		
Dighton	411	16	Baylies	Thomas S	2	2	2			2			1				9		
Dighton	411	17	Lincoln	Lott	4	2		1		2							9		
Dighton	411	18	Walker	Nathll	2	3	1	1		1		3		1			12		
Dighton	411	19	Walker	Jonathan		2		1					1	2			6		
Dighton	411	20	Walker	Jonathan Jr	1		1			2			1				5		
Dighton	411	21	Wetherell	Daniel	1	3		1		2	2						9		
Dighton	411	22	Wheeler	John		2		1		2				1			6		
Dighton	411	23	Briggs	Matthew	1	1	1	1			2	1		1			8		
Dighton	411	24	Davis	John	2	3		1		2	1	1		1			11		
Dighton	411	25	Briggs	Eliakim		1		1									2		
Dighton	411	26	Briggs	Edward			1			1		1					3		
Dighton	411	27	Hathaway	Job											4		4		
Dighton	411	28	Winslow	Job	1		1	1		2	1		1				7		
Dighton	411	29	Williams	Simeon	1			1		1			2				5		
Dighton	411	30	Williams	Jonathan	1			1		2	3		1				8		
Dighton	411	31	Williams	Joshua				1		2			1				4		
Dighton	411	32	Williams	Jared	1		1						1	2			5		
Dighton	411	33	Williams	George Jr	1		1	1		1			1				5		
Dighton	411	34	Williams	William		1				1			1				3		
Dighton	411	35	Talbot	Josiah	2	1	2	1		2	1	1		2			12		
Dighton	411	36	Williams	David		2		1		1		3					7		
Dighton	411	37	Williams	George		2	1	1		2		2		1			9		
Dighton	411	38	Walker	Nehemiah	2		1	1					1	1			6		
Dighton	411	39	Waldren	Elijah				3						2			5		
Dighton	411	40	Walker	Perez		1		1						1			3		
Dighton	411	41	Walker	Eliakim		1							1				2		
Dighton	411	42	Curtin	Jonathan		1		1					1				3		
Dighton	411	43	Curtin	Jonathan Jr	1			1					1				3		
Dighton	412	1	Waldron	Abraham			5	1					2	1			9		
Dighton	412	2	Waldron	Abraham Jr	1			1					1				3		
Dighton	412	3	Waldron	Benja				1					1				2		
Dighton	412	4	Waldron	Robert				1					1				2		
Dighton	412	5	Reed	Simeon			4	1						1			6		
Dighton	412	6	Reed	Simeon Junr		1		1		1	1		1				5		
Dighton	412	7	Walker	Ebenezer				1			1	2		1			5		
Dighton	412	8	Wheeler	Benjamin	4	3	1	1		2	2		1				15		
Dighton	412	9	Goff	Enoch		1		1						1			3		
Dighton	412	10	Goff	Enoch Junr		1							1				2		
Dighton	412	11	Gardner	Stephen	2		1	1		3	1		1				9		
Dighton	412	12	Mason	John	2			1		1			1				5		
Dighton	412	13	Gooding	Ephraim	4		1	1		1	1		1	1			10		
Dighton	412	14	Peirce	Jabez		1		1						1			3		
Dighton	412	15	Peirce	Thomas	1			1		1		1					4		
Dighton	412	16	Ide	Nathan		1		1		1	1		1	1			6		
Dighton	412	17	Whitmarsh	Rufus		1		1				3		1			6		
Dighton	412	18	Peirce	Holmes		1	1			1		1					4		
Dighton	412	19	Whitmarsh	Walter		1							1				2		
Dighton	412	20	Whitmarsh	John	1	2	1	1		1	1	1		1			9		
Dighton	412	21	Brown	William		1	1	1		1	1	1		1			7		
Dighton	412	22	Lockwood	James	1	1		1		1			1				5		
Dighton	412	23	Perry	Saml Junr	2		1	1		2			1				7		
Dighton	412	24	Godbey	Seth			2							2			4		
Dighton	412	25	Hathaway	Stephen	1		1	1		2			1				6		
Dighton	412	26	Crandle	John			1					1	1	1			4		
Dighton	412	27	Bozworth	Isiah		1								1			2		
Dighton	412	28	Norton	Benja			1			1		1					3		
Dighton	412	29	Whitmarsh	Jonathan	1	2			1	2			1				7		

TOWN	PG#	LN#	LAST NAME	FIRST NAME	FREE WHITE MALES					FREE WHITE FEMALES					TOTAL ALL OTHER	TOTAL SLAVES	TOTALS	DISTRICT/ TOWNSHIP	NOTES
					under 10	10 to 16	16 to 26	26 to 45	45 and over	under 10	10 to 16	16 to 26	26 to 45	45 and over					
Dighton	412	30	Whitmarsh	Abial		1			1					1			3		
Dighton	412	31	Whitmarsh	Robert	2			1		2	1		1				7		
Dighton	412	32	Talbot	Jedediah		1			1					1			3		
Dighton	412	33	Hide	James											8		8		
Dighton	412	34	Talbot	Zepha	3			1		1	1			1			7		
Dighton	412	35	Ware	George	1	1		1		2	2	1	1	2			11		
Dighton	412	36	Wright	Wido		1	1	1				3	1	1			8		
Dighton	412	37	Simmons	Seth	1	1		1		1	1	1					7		
Dighton	412	38	Richmond	William	1		2	1	1	2			1	1			9		
Dighton	412	39	Whitmarsh	Holmes Wido of	1	1				1			1				4		
Dighton	412	40	Whitmarsh	Sarah		1	1							1			3		
Dighton	412	41	Palmer	Mary		1							1				2		
Dighton	412	42	Masden	Hannah	1								1				2		
Dighton	412	43	Henry	Alexnader	1		1			1		1		1			5		
Dighton	412	44	Richmond	Abigail			2			1		4		1			8		
Dighton	412	45	Andrews	Stephen	2	1	1			1	2		1				8		
Dighton	412	46	Smith	William				1					1				2		
Dighton	412	47	Richmond	Jim											6		6		
Dighton	412	48	Wheelor	Phebe											5		5		
Dighton	413	1	Reed	William	3	1			1	1	1		1				8		
Dighton	413	2	Chase	Caleb Jr	4				1	1	2		1				9		
Dighton	413	3	Fish	Robert		1			1			1	1				4		
Dighton	413	4	Eddy	Joshua	3		1			1		1					6		
Dighton	413	5	Chase	Aaron	2	1		1		2	2	1					9		
Dighton	413	6	Reed	Loved		2			1	1	1		1				6		
Dighton	413	7	Reed	Joshua	2		1					1					4		
Dighton	413	8	Cummings	John		2			1	1	2		1				7		
Dighton	413	9	Jones	Salathiel	3		1	1	1	1		1	1				9		
Dighton	413	10	Cummings	Jona	1	1	1					1					4		
Dighton	413	11	Jones	Asa	1	1		1		3	1		1				8		
Dighton	413	12	Jones	Wido									2				2		
Dighton	413	13	Phillips	Abiezer Jr		2		1		3	3		1				10		
Dighton	413	14	Jones	Isaac	2			1			1	2	2				8		
Dighton	413	15	Talbot	Saml	2	1	1		1			2		1		1	9		
Dighton	413	16	Talbot	Silas	1			1		3		1					6		
Dighton	413	17	Brayton	Ned											5		5		
Dighton	413	18	Burt	Clothier			2	1					1				4		
Dighton	413	19	Pells	George	1	1	2		1	1	2		1				9		
Dighton	413	20	Shaw	Jabez	1			2					1				4		
Dighton	413	21	Atwood	James	2	1			1	1			1				6		
Dighton	413	22	Richmond	Thomas B.	3		2		1		2	1		1			10		
Dighton	413	23	Whitmarsh	Matthew	1	1			1	1	1	1		1			7		
Dighton	413	24	Richmond	John	1			1		2	1	1		1			7		
Dighton	413	25	Wright	Joshua		1		1				1					3		
Dighton	413	26	Andrews	David	2			1		3		1	1	1			9		
Dighton	413	27	Raymond	Saria						1	1		1				3		
Dighton	413	28	Perry	Edward				1				1	1				3		
Dighton	413	29	Perry	Sylvester	2	1		1		2	1	1					8		
Dighton	413	30	Andrews	Joseph	2			1		1			1	1			6		
Dighton	413	31	Bowen	Benamiel	1				1	3	2		1				8		
Dighton	413	32	Luther	Benja	2	2	1		1	1	1		1	1			10		
Dighton	413	33	Talbot	Hannah		1	2							1			4		
Dighton	413	34	Jones	Jeremiah				1		1		1					3		
Dighton	413	35	Andrews	Elkanah	3	2			1	1			1		1		9		
Dighton	413	36	Andrews	Thomas		2		1				1	1				5		
Dighton	413	37	Talbot	Joseph 2d	1			1		1			1				4		
Dighton	413	38	Bragg	John		1	1		1			2		2			7		
Dighton	413	39	Richmond	Gamiel		1			1	3	1		1				7		
Dighton	413	40	Smith	James	1	2			1	1	1	4		1			11		
Dighton	413	41	Briggs	James 2d	1			1		1	1		1				5		
Dighton	413	42	Shaw	Jahaziah				1		3	2		1				7		
Dighton	413	43	Cartwright	Daniel Jr	2	2		1	1	1			1				8		
Dighton	413	44	Cartwright	Jona	1							1					2		
Dighton	414	1	Cartwright	Daniel		1	1		1		1		1				5		
Dighton	414	2	Hathaway	John	4	1			1	1		1	3		3		14		
Dighton	414	3	Spooner	James	1		1		1				1				4		
Dighton	414	4	Wardwell	Josiah	2			1		2	1		1				8		
Dighton	414	5	Simmons	Eliphalet	2			1		1	1		1				6		
Dighton	414	6	Peirce	John	2	1		1		2	2		1	1			10		
Dighton	414	7	Simmons	Edward	2	1			1	3			1				8		
Dighton	414	8	Talbot	Elka		2		1		1			1				5		
Dighton	414	9	Snell	Anthony				1				1					2		
Dighton	414	10	Talbot	Joseph	1	3			1	1	3			1			11		
Dighton	414	11	Hathaway	Ephraim Jr	1	2		1	1	1	2		1				9		
Dighton	414	12	Cummings	William	1	1	1	1					1				5		
Dighton	414	13	Andrews	John	3	1		1					1	1			7		
Dighton	414	14	Snell	John		1		1				1		1			4		
Dighton	414	15	Pratt	Jona			1		1					3			5		
Dighton	414	16	Pratt	Jabez		2			1			5		1			9		

TOWN	PG#	LN#	LAST NAME	FIRST NAME	FREE WHITE MALES					FREE WHITE FEMALES					TOTAL ALL OTHER	TOTAL SLAVES	TOTALS	DISTRICT/ TOWNSHIP	NOTES
					under 10	10 to 16	16 to 26	26 to 45	45 and over	under 10	10 to 16	16 to 26	26 to 45	45 and over					
Dighton	414	17	Hathaway	Joshua Jr	1				1		1		1				4		
Dighton	414	18	Hathaway	Joshua			1	1						3			5		
Dighton	414	19	Hathaway	Ephraim				1				1		2			4		
Dighton	414	20	Upham	Barnet				1						1			2		
Dighton	414	21	Upham	Abijah	1		1			1	1	1					5		
Dighton	414	22	Simmons	Mercy		1	1			2	2		1				7		
Dighton	414	23	Hathaway	William	1	1	3	1			3	1		1			11		
Dighton	414	24	Case	Jonathan J	3	1			1	1			1				7		
Dighton	414	25	Baker	Seth	2	1			1	1			1	1			7		
Dighton	414	26	Jones	Jonathan			2		1			1	2		1		7		
Dighton	414	27	Perry	Simeon			2		1			1	2		1		7		
Dighton	414	28	Bun	Nathll	1	1		1		1	1		1				6		
Dighton	414	29	Codding	William			1		1			1		1			4		
Dighton	414	30	Walker	Perez Junr	1			1		2			1				5		
Dighton	414	31	Walker	George	1			1		2			1				5		
Dighton	414	32	Waldron	Joseph		1	1	1	1	1		1	1		1		8		
Dighton	414	33	Austin	Zachariah				1			1	3		1			6		
Dighton	414	34	Austin	Abijah			1			1		1					3		
Dighton	414	35	Goff	Shubal	1	1			1	5	1		1				10		
Dighton	414	36	Bowen	Zenas	2		1					1					4		
Dighton	414	37	Hale	Job			1			1		1					3		
Dighton	414	38	Peirce	Nathll	3	1			1	2			1				8		
Dighton	414	39	Bowen	Jeremiah	1	1	1		1		3			1			8		
Dighton	414	40	Francis	Peleg			2		1			1		1			5		
Dighton	415	1	Francis	Peleg Jr			1			2			1				4		
Dighton	415	2	Horton	Solomon	1	2	3	1	1			1	1	1			11		
Dighton	415	3	Wescoat	Cornelius				1						1			2		
Dighton	415	4	Wescoat	Richard			1			1			1				3		
Dighton	415	5	Wescoat	John	2	1			1	1	1			2			8		
Dighton	415	6	Miller	Henry			1					1					2		
Dighton	415	7	Lewis	Timothy	1			1		3	1		1				7		
Dighton	415	8	Lewis	Aaron	1	1	1	1		1	1			1			7		
Dighton	415	9	Tosolong	Leander											3		3		
Dighton	415	10	Paul	Peter	3	2		1		1	1		1				9		
Dighton	415	11	Read	Ebenezer		3		1		2	1	1	1				9		
Dighton	415	12	Lee	Abiather	1		1					1					3		
Dighton	415	13	Stephens	Benja Jr				1		1		1					3		
Dighton	415	14	Rose	Thomas			2		1			2	2	1			8		
Dighton	415	15	Pendleton	Gidion	1	1	1		1	2			1				7		
Dighton	415	16	Rose	Nath	1				1					1			3		
Dighton	415	17	Perry	Joseph	1		1		1	1		3		1			8		

TOWN	PG#	LN#	LAST NAME	FIRST NAME	FREE WHITE MALES					FREE WHITE FEMALES					TOTAL ALL OTHER	TOTAL SLAVES	TOTALS	DISTRICT/ TOWNSHIP	NOTES
					under 10	10 to 16	16 to 26	26 to 45	45 and over	under 10	10 to 16	16 to 26	26 to 45	45 and over					
Easton	388	1	Ames	Permenas		1			1	2				1			5		
Easton	388	2	Alger	Isaac	1	2			1	2			1				7		
Easton	388	3	Alger	Benjamin			1			1	1		1				4		
Easton	388	4	Austin	William			1			2			1				4		
Easton	388	5	Allen	Experience															Enumeration left blank
Easton	388	6	Ames	Jotham		1			1	1		1		1			5		
Easton	388	7	Bailey	Seth	1		2		1	2				1			7		
Easton	388	8	Bryant	Dependence F	1		1			1			1				4		
Easton	388	9	Buler	Atherton															Enumeration left blank
Easton	388	10	Bartlett	Isaac	3		2	1				1	1				8		
Easton	388	11	Bates	Benjamin		1	1	1		1			1				5		
Easton	388	12	Buck	Thomas				1					2	1			4		
Easton	388	13	Bartlett	Peter	1		1					1		1			4		
Easton	388	14	Buck	Barnabas	1			1		1			1				4		
Easton	388	15	Buck	Benjamin	2			1		3			1				7		
Easton	388	16	Britton	William	1	1	2		1	1	1		1				8		
Easton	388	17	Britton	John	2	1	2		1	3			1				10		
Easton	388	18	Brett	Calvin	2	1		1		2	1	1	1	1			10		
Easton	388	19	Britton	Zachariah				1						1			2		
Easton	388	20	Bonney	William	2	1		1					1				5		
Easton	389	1	Britton	Joshua	2		1			3			1				7		
Easton	389	2	Britton	Pendleton		1		1						1			3		
Easton	389	3	Bisby	Sauel		1		1		2	1	1		1			7		
Easton	389	4	Buck	Tertius		1				1			1				3		
Easton	389	5	Buck	Nathan	2		1						2				1		
Easton	389	6	Bartlett	Susannah	2	1									1		4		
Easton	389	7	Chipman	Jacob	1			1		2			1				5		
Easton	389	8	Copeland	Elijah		1		1		1	2		1				6		
Easton	389	9	Copeland	Elijah Jr	2			1			1		1				5		
Easton	389	10	Copeland	Josiah	2	2		1		1		1	1				8		
Easton	389	11	Carr	Caleb	1			1		1			2	1			6		
Easton	389	12	Drake	Jonah				1						1			2		
Easton	389	13	Drake	Timothy	2			1		2			1				6		
Easton	389	14	Drake	Elijah	2			1		1			1				5		
Easton	389	15	Drake	Elijah Jr				1		1			1				3		
Easton	389	16	Drake	Bethuel		2		1		1	1		1	1			7		
Easton	389	17	Drake	Bethuel Jr			1			2			1				4		
Easton	389	18	Drew	Nicholas	1			1		2			1				5		
Easton	389	19	Deane	James		1	1	1						1	1		5		
Easton	389	20	Deane	Elisha				1					1	1			3		
Easton	389	21	Deane	Elisha Junr	2			1		1	1		1				6		
Easton	389	22	Drake	Lot	3	2		1				1	1				8		
Easton	389	23	Drake	Adam		2		1				1	1	1			6		
Easton	389	24	Drake	Titus	4			1					1				6		
Easton	389	25	Drake	Robert	1		1		1	1	2		1				7		
Easton	389	26	Drake	Elizabeth	3		1			1	1	1	1				8		
Easton	389	27	Drake	Joseph				1						2			3		
Easton	389	28	Dickerman	Ebenezer		1		1						1			3		
Easton	389	29	Dickerman	James	2			1		2				1			6		
Easton	389	30	Drake	Thomas	1	3	2		1	3			1				11		
Easton	389	31	Deane	Edward	1			1						1			3		
Easton	389	32	Deane	James 2d			1			3		1					5		
Easton	389	33	Drake	Zachariah	2			1			1	3		1			8		
Easton	389	34	Drew	John	2	1		2		1	1		1	2			10		
Easton	389	35	Downing	Moses		1		1		2	1		1				6		
Easton	389	36	Drake	Cyrus			1						1				2		
Easton	389	37	Dickerman	Nehemiah		1							1				2		
Easton	389	38	Drake	Patty	2					1			1				4		
Easton	389	39	Drake	Isaac			1			1			1				3		
Easton	389	40	Drake	Edward	2	1	1			2			1				7		
Easton	390	1	Fobes	Libeus				1					1	2			4		
Easton	390	2	Fuller	Isaac		2		1		1			1	1			6		
Easton	390	3	Ferguson	George		2				1			1				5		
Easton	390	4	Ford	Joseph	1			1		1				1			4		
Easton	390	5	Fuller	Barzillia	2			1		2			1				6		
Easton	390	6	Fillebrown	Bethuel	3			1		3			1				8		
Easton	390	7	Godfrey	Abigail									1	1			2		
Easton	390	8	Godfrey	Joseph		1		1						1			3		
Easton	390	9	Godfrey	Joseph Jr	1	2	1	1		1			1				7		
Easton	390	10	Guild	Samuel	1	1	1			2	1		1				8		
Easton	390	11	Guild	Samuel Jur			1					1					2		
Easton	390	12	Gilmore	Joshua	3	1	2	1				1	1				9		
Easton	390	13	Gay	Solomon		1		1		4			1				7		
Easton	390	14	Gwinell	Hannah	1							3		1			5		
Easton	390	15	Goodwin	Daniel	1			1		1		2	1				6		
Easton	390	16	Goward	Francis	1		1	1					1				4		
Easton	390	17	Gilbert	Apollos			1						1				2		
Easton	390	18	Gilbert	Nathaniel			1	1		2				1			5		
Easton	390	19	Goward	Mary			1						1	1			3		
Easton	390	20	Hayward	Joshua	1			1		5	2		1				10		
Easton	390	21	Hayward	Edward	4	1			1		1	1	1				9		
Easton	390	22	Harlow	Ruben	2	1		1		1			1				6		
Easton	390	23	Hayward	Jonathan	1		1			1			1				4		
Easton	390	24	Hayward	Oliver	1	3	2	1		3		1	1				12		
Easton	390	25	Haney	Elisha		1		1	1				1	1			5		
Easton	390	26	Howard	Nehemiah		1		1					1	1			4		
Easton	390	27	Howard	Roland	3			1		1		1	2	1			9		
Easton	390	28	Howard	Calvin	1		1			4			1				7		
Easton	390	29	Howard	Elijah	1	2			1	2				1			7		
Easton	390	30	Howard	Joseph	2	2	1		1	2		1	1	1			11		

TOWN	PG#	LN#	LAST NAME	FIRST NAME	FREE WHITE MALES under 10	10 to 16	16 to 26	26 to 45	45 and over	FREE WHITE FEMALES under 10	10 to 16	16 to 26	26 to 45	45 and over	TOTAL ALL OTHER	TOTAL SLAVES	TOTALS	DISTRICT/ TOWNSHIP	NOTES
Easton	390	31	Hayward	Abner				1				2		1			4		
Easton	390	32	Hayward	Ebenezer	1		1	1		1	1			1			6		
Easton	390	33	Hayden	Charles			1	1			1		1				4		
Easton	390	34	Howard	Barnabas	3	1		1			1		1				7		
Easton	390	35	Howward	Deane		1		1				1					3		
Easton	390	36	Jones	Abigail									3	1			4		
Easton	390	37	Johnson	David	2			1		2			1				6		
Easton	390	38	Johnson	Edward											4		4		
Easton	390	39	Keith	Josiah	2	1			1		2			1			7		
Easton	390	40	Keith	Lemuel		1	2		1	1	1			1			7		
Easton	390	41	Keith	Benjamin			1	1					1				3		
Easton	391	1	Kimball	Samuel	2		1	1		3			1	1			9		
Easton	391	2	Kimball	Isaac			1			1		1					3		
Easton	391	3	Keith	Scot	2	1	1		1	1	1	1		1			9		
Easton	391	4	Keith	Mary		1								1			2		
Easton	391	5	Keith	David		1	2		1		1	2		1			8		
Easton	391	6	Kinsley	Zebudiah	1	1			1	1			4	1			9		
Easton	391	7	Kinsley	Benjamin			1		1	1	1			1			5		
Easton	391	8	Kingsman	Edward	2	1		1		2				1			7		
Easton	391	9	Keith	Alexander			1			2	1	1					5		
Easton	391	10	Keith	Nehemiah		1				1			1		1		4		
Easton	391	11	Keith	Bethiah		1							1	3			5		
Easton	391	12	Keith	David				1		1		1		1			4		
Easton	391	13	Littlefield	Abiah															Enumeration left blank
Easton	391	14	Littlefield	Daniel															Enumeration left blank
Easton	391	15	Lathrop	Edmund		1	1		1					1			3		
Easton	391	16	Leach	Abisha	2	1	3	1	1		1			1			10		
Easton	391	17	Lathrop	Ambrose															Enumeration left blank
Easton	391	18	Leonard	Eliphalet			1	1		1			2				5		
Easton	391	19	Leonard	Eliphalet Jr	1		1	1		3		1	1				8		
Easton	391	20	Leonard	Jacob	2		1			1			1				5		
Easton	391	21	Lathrop	Isaac	1	1	2	1		2	2	1		1			11		
Easton	391	22	Lathrop	John		2		1		1	2		1				7		
Easton	391	23	Lathrop	John 2d	1		1			1		1					4		
Easton	391	24	Lincoln	Paul		1	2	1		2			1				7		
Easton	391	25	Leonard	Isaac	1	1		1		1			1				5		
Easton	391	26	Littlefield	Seth	1		1	1		1	2		1				7		
Easton	391	27	Littlefield	Ebenezer	2			1		1			1				5		
Easton	391	28	Lathrop	Solomon	2	1		1		2		1	1				8		
Easton	391	29	Leonard	Samuel		1		1		4	2	1	1				10		
Easton	391	30	Lathrop	Isaac 2d			1						1				2		
Easton	391	31	Leonard	David	1		1						1				3		
Easton	391	32	Leach	Rufus			2						1				3		
Easton	391	33	Lathrop	Joseph		1		1		2	1		1				6		
Easton	391	34	Lathrop	Joseph 2d				1						2			3		
Easton	391	35	Manley	David		1	1	1		1				1			5		
Easton	391	36	Manley	David Jr	1			1		1			1				4		
Easton	391	37	Manley	William		2							1				3		
Easton	391	38	Mitchel	Thomas		3	1	1		4	1		1				11		
Easton	391	39	Manley	Seth				1				1		1			3		
Easton	391	40	Manley	Seth Jr	4			1		1			1				7		
Easton	391	41	Manley	Abiah				1				1					2		
Easton	391	42	Manley	Daniel	1			1		1		2					5		
Easton	391	43	Monk	George	1		1	1						2			5		
Easton	391	44	Macomber	Daniel		1		1					1	1			4		
Easton	391	45	Morse	Ephraim	1		1			3		1					6		
Easton	391	46	Mitchel	Abiel			1			1	3	1					6		
Easton	392	1	Mitchel	Timothy	1		1			1		1					4		
Easton	392	2	Mitchel	Eliphalet	1		1					1					3		
Easton	392	3	March	Anthony											4		4		
Easton	392	4	Niles	Elijah	2			1		1	1		2				7		
Easton	392	5	Packard	Joseph				1						1			2		
Easton	392	6	Pool	Samuel	1	1	1	1					1	1			6		
Easton	392	7	Pratt	Josiah			1			1		1					3		
Easton	392	8	Pratt	Caleb	3			1					1				5		
Easton	392	9	Packard	Barnabas	2	2		1		3			1				9		
Easton	392	10	Perry	Samuel	2			1				1	1				5		
Easton	392	11	Packard	Calvin	1	1		1		1	1		1				6		
Easton	392	12	Perry	James			2	1			1			1			5		
Easton	392	13	Perry	James Jur				1			1		2	2	1		7		
Easton	392	14	Pratt	Seth			2	1						1			4		
Easton	392	15	Pratt	William		1		1	1			1		1			5		
Easton	392	16	Pratt	William 2d		1			1					2	1		5		
Easton	392	17	Pratt	William 3d	1	1		1					1				4		
Easton	392	18	Pratt	Jonathan			1	1	1		1			1			5		
Easton	392	19	Pool	John	2			1		1		2					6		
Easton	392	20	Packard	Jedidiah	1	1		1		3			1				7		
Easton	392	21	Packard	Jedidiah 2d		1											1		
Easton	392	22	Phillips	Silas		2		1			1	1	1				6		
Easton	392	23	Phillips	Asa		1	1		1	1			1	2			7		
Easton	392	24	Phillips	Jacob				1				2	2				6		
Easton	392	25	Packard	James	2			1		1	1			2			7		
Easton	392	26	Quinley	James			1			1			1				3		
Easton	392	27	Riply	Abiel	1			1		3			1				6		
Easton	392	28	Randell	Absolon			1						1				2		
Easton	392	29	Read	William	3	2		1				1	1				8		
Easton	392	30	Read	Abijah		2		1		1	1		1				6		
Easton	392	31	Randell	Abiah				1				1	2		1		4		
Easton	392	32	Randell	John		2	2	1				2					7		
Easton	392	33	Randell	Jonathan	1		1		1	4			1				8		

26

TOWN	PG#	LN#	LAST NAME	FIRST NAME	M under 10	M 10 to 16	M 16 to 26	M 26 to 45	M 45 and over	F under 10	F 10 to 16	F 16 to 26	F 26 to 45	F 45 and over	TOTAL ALL OTHER	TOTAL SLAVES	TOTALS	DISTRICT/ TOWNSHIP	NOTES
Easton	392	34	Randell	Daniel	2			1		2			1				6		
Easton	392	35	Randell	Timothy	1	1		1		3	1		1				8		
Easton	392	36	Record	Amasa			1		1		1			1	1		5		
Easton	392	37	Ripley	Samu		2		1				1		1			5		
Easton	392	38	Randell	Robert					1					1			2		
Easton	392	39	Randell	Job	3	2	1		1	2	1	1	1				12		
Easton	392	40	Randell	Caleb	1		1	1		1			1				5		
Easton	392	41	Randell	Abner		2			1				2	1			6		
Easton	392	42	Randell	Solomon			1	1					2	1			5		
Easton	392	43	Randell	Barnabas			1										1		
Easton	392	44	Randell	Ephraim	1		3		1		2			1			8		
Easton	393	1	Randell	Ziba		2		1		1	1			1			6		
Easton	393	2	Randell	Nehemiah	1			1				1	1	1			5		
Easton	393	3	Randell	Apollos	1			1		2			1				5		
Easton	393	4	Randell	Hopestill	1	1	1		1	1		1	1	1			8		
Easton	393	5	Randell	Phinehas	4		1						1				6		
Easton	393	6	Randell	Thomas	2	4		1				1	1				9		
Easton	393	7	Randell	Luther	2			1		1	1		1				6		
Easton	393	8	Randell	John 2d	4			1		2				1			9		
Easton	393	9	Randell	Ebinezer			1	1		1			1				4		
Easton	393	10	Randell	Timothy	1	1		1		3	1		1				8		
Easton	393	11	Randell	Thomas	4	2		1				1	1				9		
Easton	393	12	Randell	Daniel	2			1		2	1		1				7		
Easton	393	13	Selee	Nathan	2			1		1	3	1		1			9		
Easton	393	14	Shaw	Joshua	1			1						1			3		
Easton	393	15	Stone	Ephraim	2		1						1				4		
Easton	393	16	Shepard	Samuel	1		1			2			1				5		
Easton	393	17	Snow	Calvin	2	1		1		4	1		1				10		
Easton	393	18	Storey	Thomas		2	1	1			1		1				6		
Easton	393	19	Shaw	Nicholas			1		1				1				3		
Easton	393	20	Shaw	Eliphalet	3			1					1				5		
Easton	393	21	Stone	Solomon	2			1		3			1	1			8		
Easton	393	22	Snow	William	3			1		1			1	1			7		
Easton	393	23	Stokes	Ira	1			1		2				1			5		
Easton	393	24	Stearns	Simeon				1				1		1			3		
Easton	393	25	Turner	Bethael	1	2		1		3	1		1				9		
Easton	393	26	Thayer	Nathaniel	2	1	1	1	1	2	1	1	1				11		
Easton	393	27	Tisdale	John	2	1	1	1		2	1		1				9		
Easton	393	28	Thompson	David		1		1					1				3		
Easton	393	29	Thompson	David Jr	1			1		4			1				7		
Easton	393	30	Turner	Elijah	2			1		2	2	1	1				9		
Easton	393	31	Thayer	Stephen	3	1			1	1	1		1	1			9		
Easton	393	32	Thayer	Jacob		2	1		1	2	1			1			8		
Easton	393	33	Tilden	David		1		1		2			1				5		
Easton	393	34	Thayer	Samuel	2	1		1		2	1		1				8		
Easton	393	35	Taylor	David	3			1		2	1		1				8		
Easton	393	36	Vose	Reuben	1			1		3	1	1					7		
Easton	394	1	Willis	Thomas		3			1	1	1	1		1			8		
Easton	394	2	Willis	Thomas Jr	2	2		1		4	1		1				11		
Easton	394	3	Williams	Edward		1	3		1	3	1			1			10		
Easton	394	4	Williams	Marlboro	1	2			1	1	2		1				8		
Easton	394	5	Williams	Josiah			1		1		1	2					5		
Easton	394	6	Williams	Anna			1			1				1			3		
Easton	394	7	Wetherell	Abijah		2		1						1			4		
Easton	394	8	Wetherell	Abijah Jr	2			1		4	1		1				9		
Easton	394	9	Willis	Phillip	1				1	4				1			7		
Easton	394	10	Williams	John	1		3		1	3	1	3	1				13		
Easton	394	11	Wheaton	Daniel	2			1		1				1			5		
Easton	394	12	Wade	David	5		2	1		1	2	1	1	1			14		
Easton	394	13	Whalock	Lymon		2		1		1	1		1	2			8		
Easton	394	14	Wilbore	Ebinezer	2	2		1		3	1			1			10		
Easton	394	15	Wilbore	George	3	2	1	1		2			1				10		
Easton	394	16	Williams	Sarah		1	1	1		2	1		1	2			9		
Easton	394	17	Willis	Lemuel			1		1			1	2	1			6		
Easton	394	18	Williams	Ezra	2			1		2	1		1				7		
Easton	394	19	White	David	2			1		3				1			7		
Easton	394	20	White	John	2			1		1				1			5		
Easton	394	21	Williams	Benjamin			1			3				1			5		
Easton	394	22	Wetherell	Darius	2				1	1				1			5		
Easton	394	23	Williams	Joshua	2			1		2				1			6		
Easton	394	24	Woode	Mary								1		1			2		
Easton	394	25	White	Adonijah	3			1		1				1			6		
Easton	394	26	White	Josiah			1		1				1				3		
Easton	394	27	Williams	Thomas	3	1		1		2		1		1			10		
Easton	394	28	White	Royal					1		1	1		1			4		
Easton	394	29	Ward	Joseph		2	1		1	3		1	1				9		
Easton	394	30	Woode	Mary								2	1	1			4		
Easton	394	31	Wild	John	2			1		1				1			5		
Easton	394	32	West	Peleg	1			1		1				1			4		
Easton	394	33	Woodcock	Martha	1								1	1			3		
Easton	394	34	Weatherby	Nathaniel	2	1		1		1		1	1	1			8		
Easton	394	35	Williams	Oliver	2			1		1				1			5		
Easton	394	36	White	Edward			2		1			1	1	1			6		
Easton	394	37	White	Howard				1						1			2		
Easton	394	38	Washburn	Hugh				1		1	1		1				4		
Easton	394	39	Wade	Thomas	2	1		1		3				1			8		

TOWN	PG#	LN#	LAST NAME	FIRST NAME	FREE WHITE MALES under 10	10 to 16	16 to 26	26 to 45	45 and over	FREE WHITE FEMALES under 10	10 to 16	16 to 26	26 to 45	45 and over	TOTAL ALL OTHER	TOTAL SLAVES	TOTALS	DISTRICT/ TOWNSHIP	NOTES
Freetown	281	1	Dean	Levi	1	1	1	2		1			2				8		
Freetown	281	2	Cudworth	Phebe Wid									2	1			3		
Freetown	281	3	Cudworth	William	2			1		2			1				6		
Freetown	281	4	Boyce	William	2			1		2	1		1				7		
Freetown	281	5	Shove	Azrah	1	1	1		1	3			1				8		
Freetown	281	6	Cudworth	Jessee					1			1	1	1			4		
Freetown	281	7	Cudworth	David	1			1					1				3		
Freetown	281	8	Strange	Charles	2	1	1	1		3	2	1	1	1			13		
Freetown	281	9	Strange	John	1	2		1			1	2	1				8		
Freetown	281	10	Briggs	Abner	2		1		1	1			1				6		
Freetown	281	11	Babbit	Ebenezer	1			1		2			1				5		
Freetown	281	12	Marvill	Charles	1		1	1		2			1				6		
Freetown	281	13	Read	William			3		1			3	1				8		
Freetown	281	14	Wilkenson	John	3			1		1	3		1				9		
Freetown	281	15	S*intine	Thomas	1			1		1		1	1				5		
Freetown	282	1	Shore	Joseph		1		1					1				3		
Freetown	282	2	Pratt	William	4		2	1			1		1				9		
Freetown	282	3	Paddock	Josiah			2			1			1				4		
Freetown	282	4	Richmond	Paddoch			1						1				2		
Freetown	282	5	Burbank	Isaac		1	1	1		1	2		1				7		
Freetown	282	6	Burbank	Isaac Jnr	1		1			1	1		1				5		
Freetown	282	7	Winslow	Oliver			3				2		1	1			7		
Freetown	282	8	Grinnel	Oliver	1		1			1			1				4		
Freetown	282	9	Tisdale	Abigail Wid.						1			1				2		
Freetown	282	10	Hinds	Ebenezer	1	2			1	1	2	2	1				10		
Freetown	282	11	Paine	Ebenezer	1	2	1		1	1	2		1				10		
Freetown	282	12	Briggs	John			3	1	1		1		1	1			8		
Freetown	282	13	Nicholas	Eleazer	1	2		2		2			3				10		
Freetown	282	14	Pickens	Samuel	2	1		1		2	1	1	1				9		
Freetown	282	15	Hathaway	Calven				1					2				3		
Freetown	282	16	Porter	Benjamin 2d	1			1					1				3		
Freetown	282	17	Weaver	Benjamin		2	1		1	1		1	1		1		8		
Freetown	282	18	Winslow	Ephraim	1	1		1	1	1	2	1	1	1			10		
Freetown	282	19	Davis	Paul	1			1		1			1	1			5		
Freetown	282	20	Duglap	Daniel	1	2		2		1			1	1			8		
Freetown	282	21	Read	Benjamin	3	1	1		1		1	2	1				10		
Freetown	282	22	Porter	Benjamin	1	1	2		2			2	2				10		
Freetown	282	23	Porter	Robert	1	1	1	1		1			1				6		
Freetown	282	24	Goff	Thomas	2	1			1		1		1				6		
Freetown	282	25	Ennis	William			1				1	1	1				4		
Freetown	282	26	Chace	Jessee			1						1				2		
Freetown	282	27	Bliffens	Anson	2			1			1		1				5		
Freetown	282	28	Bullock	Jessee				1					1				2		
Freetown	282	29	Winslow	Joseph	2	1			1	1	2	1	1				9		
Freetown	282	30	Briggs	Ephraim	4			1		1		1	1				8		
Freetown	282	31	Briggs	Elijah			1	1					1				3		
Freetown	282	32	Babbit	Ebenezer 2d	2			1		2			1				6		
Freetown	283	1	Chace	Gilbert	3		1	1		2		1	1				9		
Freetown	283	2	Chace	Augustine	1				1	4	1		1				8		
Freetown	283	3	Hathaway	Nicholas	1			1		1			1				4		
Freetown	283	4	Peirce	Ebenezer		1		1					1				3		
Freetown	283	5	Clark	Richard	3		1	1			1		1				7		
Freetown	283	6	Chace	Darius	2	2	2	1		1	1		1				10		
Freetown	283	7	Hathaway	Phillip 2d	2		1	1			1	1	1				7		
Freetown	283	8	Bliss	Phebe									2				2		
Freetown	283	9	Chace	Noah		2		1		3			1				7		
Freetown	283	10	Winslow	James		1	3	1		1			2				8		
Freetown	283	11	Carpenter	William			1			1			1		1		4		
Freetown	283	12	Cudworth	Dolly Wid.		1							2	1			4		
Freetown	283	13	Cudworth	Drinkwater			1					1					2		
Freetown	283	14	Peirce	Bethnel	3	2	1	1					1				9		
Freetown	283	15	Briggs	Joseph		1		1		4	1		1				8		
Freetown	283	16	Webester	Simeon P	1			1		2			1	1			6		
Freetown	283	17	Hathaway	Joseph	4		1		1		2	1	1				10		
Freetown	283	18	Hathaway	Weltha Wid.	1							1	2				4		
Freetown	283	19	Hathaway	Gilbert	2	2	1		1	1		1	1	2			11		
Freetown	283	20	Hathaway	Nathaniel				1		3	1		1	1			8		
Freetown	283	21	Winslow	Benjamin	2			1	1	2			1	1			8		
Freetown	283	22	Hathaway	Deborough Wid.									1				1		
Freetown	283	23	Howland	George		1			1	3	1	1	1				8		
Freetown	283	24	Howland	Joshua		1			1			2	1				5		
Freetown	283	25	Briggs	John 2d	1	1	1			1			1				9		
Freetown	283	26	Brown	Benjamin W.	1	1	1						1				4		
Freetown	283	27	Evens	John	3		1		1	1	2	1	1				10		
Freetown	283	28	Hathaway	Joseph	1				1	1		1	1	1	3		8		
Freetown	283	29	Hathaway	John	1			1		1			1			1	5		
Freetown	283	30	Hathaway	Phillip				1		1		1				1	5		
Freetown	283	31	Hathaway	Cloather	2			1		1			1				5		
Freetown	283	32	Hathaway	Dorcas Wid.										3			3		

TOWN	PG#	LN#	LAST NAME	FIRST NAME	FREE WHITE MALES					FREE WHITE FEMALES					TOTAL ALL OTHER	TOTAL SLAVES	TOTALS	DISTRICT/ TOWNSHIP	NOTES
					under 10	10 to 16	16 to 26	26 to 45	45 and over	under 10	10 to 16	16 to 26	26 to 45	45 and over					
Freetown	284	1	Merrick	Isaac		1	2		1		2			1			7		
Freetown	284	2	Hathaway	Thomas	1			1			1	1					4		
Freetown	284	3	Hathaway	Samuel	2	1	2	1		2	2		1				11		
Freetown	284	4	Read	George	2	1		1					1				5		
Freetown	284	5	Southwick	Joshua				1					1				2		
Freetown	284	6	Hathaway	Abial				1		1			1				3		
Freetown	284	7	Chace	Beloney	1		1	1		2	2		1				8		
Freetown	284	8	Mackson	Jonathan	2	1			1	2			1	1			8		
Freetown	284	9	Terry	Job		2			1	1		1	1				6		
Freetown	284	10	Hathaway	Silas	3	2	1		1	2	1	1	1				12		
Freetown	284	11	Winslow	Abner		1	2		1	1	1	1		1			8		
Freetown	284	12	Cleveland	Ambros	1	2		1		7	1	1	1				14		
Freetown	284	13	Barnaby	Ambrose		4	1	1					4	1			12		
Freetown	284	14	Sallintine	Wid. Mary			2			1	1	1	1				6		
Freetown	284	15	Sallintine	William	1		1	2	2	1		4	1	2	1		15		
Freetown	284	16	Sallintine	David	1	1		1	1	1		2		1	1		9		
Freetown	284	17	Winslow	Luther	2	1	3		1	1	1		1				10		
Freetown	284	18	Simmons	Abraham	1		1		1				1	1			5		
Freetown	284	19	Hathaway	Jail	1	1		1	1	1	1			2			8		
Freetown	284	20	Davis	Thomas			1	1					1				3		
Freetown	284	21	Weaver	Sheffield		1		1		3	1	1	1	1			9		
Freetown	284	22	Simmons	Harvey	2			2		2			1		1		8		
Freetown	284	23	Read	Jonathan	2		3		1	1		1	2	1			11		
Freetown	284	24	Borden	Joseph	1	1		1		2	1		1				7		
Freetown	284	25	Read	Daniel	4			2	1				2	1			10		
Freetown	284	26	Watson	Elkanah	1	1		1	1	1	1		1				6		
Freetown	284	27	Brightman	Joseph Jr	1	3	2		1				1				8		
Freetown	284	28	Tompkins	Benjamin			1			5			1				7		
Freetown	284	29	Phillips	Peirce	2	2		1		2		1	1				9		
Freetown	284	30	Read	Dolly		1							3	3			7		
Freetown	284	31	Browmall	Jonathan	3	2			1	1	1		1	3			12		
Freetown	285	1	Durffee	Benjamin	2	1		1	1		1	2	1				9		
Freetown	285	2	Turner	John	2				1				1	1			5		
Freetown	285	3	Durffee	Charles	1			1	1	3	2		3	1			12		
Freetown	285	4	Borden	Mary Wid.	1	1		1		1	1			1			6		
Freetown	285	5	Cook	John	2			1					1				4		
Freetown	285	6	Borden	Nathan	2	1	2	1		1	2		1				10		
Freetown	285	7	Borden	Richard	3	1		1		1			1				7		
Freetown	285	8	Borden	Thomas	3	2	2	1	1	3	1	1	1				15		
Freetown	285	9	Bowen	Nathan	2		3		1		1	1	2	1			11		
Freetown	285	10	Bowen	Abraham	2			1		2			1				6		
Freetown	285	11	Borden	Perry		2		1			2		1		2		8		
Freetown	285	12	Borden	Simeon P	1	1	1		1	2	1		1	1			9		
Freetown	285	13	Strange	Lot			1		1	1	2	2		1			8		
Freetown	285	14	Smith	Abner	1		1	1	1		1	1	1	1			8		
Freetown	285	15	Hathaway	Dudlee		2	3	1	1	1		2		1			11		
Freetown	285	16	Chace	Ebenezer				1	1	2				1			4		
Freetown	285	17	Cummons	Alanson	2			1						1			4		
Freetown	285	18	Cummons	Phillip	2	1		1		3			1				8		
Freetown	285	19	Clark	Asa	2	2			1	1			1				7		
Freetown	285	20	Rounsevill	Levi			2		1			2		1			6		
Freetown	285	21	Rounsevill	Thomas	1	3	1		1			4		1			11		
Freetown	285	22	Rounsevill	Phillip	3	1	2		1	1	1	1	1				11		
Freetown	285	23	Rounsevill	William	1			1		2		1					5		
Freetown	285	24	Morton	Nathaniel Jr		1		1		2		1					5		
Freetown	285	25	Morton	Nathaniel		2		2		1				2			7		
Freetown	285	26	Morton	Job			1						1				2		
Freetown	285	27	Tinkam	Arther	2			1		1			1				5		
Freetown	285	28	Jucket	Thankfull			1				1	1		1			4		
Freetown	285	29	Parris	Desire		1	1						1	1			4		
Freetown	285	30	Hinds	Ebenezer Junr	1		1						1				3		
Freetown	285	31	Chace	Job	2	1		1		1	2		1				8		
Freetown	285	32	Richmond	Samuel	2	1		1	1	2		1		1			9		
Freetown	286	1	Richord	Isaac			1		1	1							3		
Freetown	286	2	Haskens	Elijah	1			1		2			1				5		
Freetown	286	3	Clark	Theophelus				1						1			2		
Freetown	286	4	Clark	Theophelus Jr	1		2	1		3	1		1				9		
Freetown	286	5	Edmister	Noah			1	1				1		1			4		
Freetown	286	6	Torry	Benjamin		1		1		1			1				4		
Freetown	286	7	Torry	Susannah Wd									1	1			2		
Freetown	286	8	Winslow	David		1			1	2				1			5		
Freetown	286	9	Daggett	Benjamin			1		1	2		1	1				5		
Freetown	286	10	Winslow	William	3		2		1				1	1			8		
Freetown	286	11	Davis	Jonathan Jr	1			1		2			1				5		
Freetown	286	12	Bennet	Peter			1						1				2		
Freetown	286	13	Winslow	Nathan	1		2	1				2		1			7		
Freetown	286	14	Davis	Wd Dinah			1						1				2		
Freetown	286	15	Winslow	George				1						1			2		
Freetown	286	16	Bliffins	Vallintine	3			1		1	1		1				7		

TOWN	PG#	LN#	LAST NAME	FIRST NAME	FREE WHITE MALES under 10	10 to 16	16 to 26	26 to 45	45 and over	FREE WHITE FEMALES under 10	10 to 16	16 to 26	26 to 45	45 and over	TOTAL ALL OTHER	TOTAL SLAVES	TOTALS	DISTRICT/ TOWNSHIP	NOTES
Freetown	286	17	Miles	Abigail Wid						2		1		1			4		
Freetown	286	18	Winslow	John	3	2			1	2	1		1				10		
Freetown	286	19	Chace	Benjamin	2			1					1				4		
Freetown	286	20	Simmons	Abraham Jun	1			1		1		1					4		
Freetown	286	21	Peirce	Lydia Wid						1			1				2		
Freetown	286	22	Runnolds	John	2			1					1	1			5		
Freetown	286	23	Simmons	Silvester	1	1			1			2		1			6		
Freetown	286	24	Thurston	Thomas			2	1					1	1			5		
Freetown	286	25	Thurston	Peleg	1		2	1					1				5		
Freetown	286	26	Winslow	Luther Jr	2			1		2			1				6		
Freetown	286	27	Thurston	Samuel				1					2		1		4		
Freetown	286	28	Simmons	Job			1			1		1					3		
Freetown	286	29	Cleveland	Benjamin			1	1				2		1			5		
Freetown	286	30	Chace	Dudlee	3		1					1	1				6		
Freetown	286	31	Cleveland	David	1	1	1			1	1	1					6		
Freetown	286	32	Miller	Robert	1	1	1	1		1	1		1				7		
Freetown	287	1	Hathaway	Robert	1	2		1		2	1		1				8		
Freetown	287	2	Davis	Cornelius Jr	1			1		1		1					4		
Freetown	287	3	Butts	Gideon			1	1				1		1			4		
Freetown	287	4	Winslow	Isaac	1			1		2	3		1				8		
Freetown	287	5	Cleveland	Elphas	2			1		2			1				6		
Freetown	287	6	Read	Jonathan Jr	2			1		2			1				6		
Freetown	287	7	Read	Elizabeth Wid										1			1		
Freetown	287	8	Dodson	Jonathan 2d	1	1		1		1			2				6		
Freetown	287	9	Brightman	Benjamin	2			1		1	1		1				6		
Freetown	287	10	Brightman	George		1		1	2	2		2		1			9		
Freetown	287	11	Brightman	Pardon				1		2		1					4		
Freetown	287	12	Brightman	Henry			1	1				1		1			4		
Freetown	287	13	Brightman	Jonathan	2			1		1			1				5		
Freetown	287	14	Brightman	Joseph				2				1		1			4		
Freetown	287	15	Lawton	Daniel	4	2			1	4	1		1				13		
Freetown	287	16	Eldridge	Gideon	1				1				1	1	2		6		
Freetown	287	17	Dennison	James		1		1		1	1		1	1			6		
Freetown	287	18	Harrison	John		1		1			2	1		2			7		
Freetown	287	19	Davol	Pardon		1	2	1		1		1		2			8		
Freetown	287	20	Borden	Louisa Wid		1							1				2		
Freetown	287	21	Wilbour	Isaac	2	1		1		2	2		1				9		
Freetown	287	22	Wrightington	James			1			3		1					5		
Freetown	287	23	Borden	Aaron	1	1		1		1			1				5		
Freetown	287	24	Brown	Hannah Wid		1							1	1			3		
Freetown	287	25	Church	Betsey Wid	3	3	1			2		3		1			13		
Freetown	287	26	Borden	Stephen				1				1	2	1			5		
Freetown	287	27	Church	Joseph	1		1	1		1	2	2		1			9		
Freetown	287	28	Read	Mary Wid		1		1					2	1			5		
Freetown	287	29	Borden	Abel	2			1		2	1		1				7		
Freetown	287	30	Borden	Seth	1			1		2			1				5		
Freetown	287	31	Borden	William	2			1		1			1				5		
Freetown	287	32	Saben	Samuel	3			1			1		1				6		
Freetown	288	1	Luther	Benjamin		1	1	1		1		1					5		
Freetown	288	2	Davol	Abner			1				1						2		
Freetown	288	3	Thomas	Elihu	2			1		1			1				5		
Freetown	288	4	Borden	Arnold	2			1				1					4		
Freetown	288	5	Peckum	Barbor	1				1	2	2		1				7		
Freetown	288	6	Borden	Daniel					1		1	1		1			4		
Freetown	288	7	Borden	George 2d	3		2	2	1		1	2		1			12		
Freetown	288	8	Rogers	Jeremiah	2			1		1	2		1				7		
Freetown	288	9	Borden	Thomas 2d	1			1				1					3		
Freetown	288	10	Sherman	Silas	2			1				1					4		
Freetown	288	11	Braton	Benjamin		1	1	1					1				4		
Freetown	288	12	Chandler	Walter	1				1		1		1	1			5		
Freetown	288	13	Winslow	Ezra	1			1					1	1			4		
Freetown	288	14	Borden	Abner	3			1					1				5		
Freetown	288	15	Braton	Frances					1				1	1			3		
Freetown	288	16	Cook	Elihu	2		1	1		1			1				6		
Freetown	288	17	Durffee	Ruth Wid						1			1				2		
Freetown	288	18	Wodwell	Pardon			1			2		1					4		
Freetown	288	19	Sanford	Stephen	1			1				1	1				4		
Freetown	288	20	Elsbree	Boomer	3	1	3		1		1			1			10		
Freetown	288	21	Brightman	Joseph 3d				1		2			1				4		
Freetown	288	22	Freelove	Thomas		2	1	1		3			1				8		
Freetown	288	23	Brightman	Peleg	4			1			1		1				7		
Freetown	288	24	Lawton	Hannah Wid		1							2	1			4		
Freetown	288	25	Boomer	Martin	2	2	2		1			2		1			10		
Freetown	288	26	Boomer	James	3			2		1			1	2			9		
Freetown	288	27	Terry	Robert	3			2		1			1	2			9		
Freetown	288	28	Terry	Robert Jr		1			1		1	1		1			5		
Freetown	288	29	Bennet	Isaac	1			1		1	1		1	1			6		
Freetown	288	30	Bennet	Benjamin Jr	1			1		1			1				4		
Freetown	288	31	Cleveland	Jonathan	1		1	1	1	2			1	1			8		

TOWN	PG#	LN#	LAST NAME	FIRST NAME	FWM under 10	FWM 10 to 16	FWM 16 to 26	FWM 26 to 45	FWM 45 and over	FWF under 10	FWF 10 to 16	FWF 16 to 26	FWF 26 to 45	FWF 45 and over	TOTAL ALL OTHER	TOTAL SLAVES	TOTALS	DISTRICT/ TOWNSHIP	NOTES
Freetown	288	32	Lawton	George	3	1			1		2		1				8		
Freetown	289	1	Law	James			1			2			1				4		
Freetown	289	2	Boomer	Nathaniel	1	1		1		2			1				6		
Freetown	289	3	Butts	David	1			1		3			1				6		
Freetown	289	4	Davis	Edmond	1		1			2		1					5		
Freetown	289	5	Read	Nathan	2			1		2			1		4		10		
Freetown	289	6	Read	George 2d	3			2				1	1				7		
Freetown	289	7	Read	Joseph	1	1	1		1		1	3		2			10		
Freetown	289	8	Read	Gideon	1			1		3		1	1				7		
Freetown	289	9	Bron	Frances					1	1	1		2	1			6		
Freetown	289	10	Boomer	Ephraim	2			1		1	1		1				6		
Freetown	289	11	Elsbree	Ephraim				1		1	1	1					4		
Freetown	289	12	Durffee	Thomas				1		1			1				3		
Freetown	289	13	Davis	Benjamin				1			1		1				3		
Freetown	289	14	Cotton	Thomas	4			1			1		1				7		
Freetown	289	15	Read	Braton			1			2		1	1				5		
Freetown	289	16	Hathaway	Elisha	1			1		2	2		1				7		
Freetown	289	17	Read	Oliver	2			1		1	2		1				7		
Freetown	289	18	Davis	Aaron	1	1		1	1	2		2	1				9		
Freetown	289	19	Davis	Joseph		1	3	1	1	3			1	1			11		
Freetown	289	20	Blossom	Elijah	1		1		1	2	1		1				7		
Freetown	289	21	Brightman	George	3	1		1		1	3		1	1			11		
Freetown	289	22	Snell	George	2			1		2	2		1		2		10		
Freetown	289	23	Snell	Amos				1					1		3		5		
Freetown	289	24	Snell	Amos Jr	2			1		2			1		4		10		
Freetown	289	25	Boomer	Daniel		1	1	1		1		2	1				7		
Freetown	289	26	Blossom	Charity								1	1				2		
Freetown	289	27	Haskell	William	1		1					1					3		
Freetown	289	28	Booth	Jesse	2		1					1	1				5		
Freetown	289	29	Blossom	Rufus	1			1		1		1					4		
Freetown	289	30	Hathaway	Mary Wid	1						1	1	1				4		
Freetown	289	31	Hathaway	Jail	1		1			1		1					4		
Freetown	290	1	Borden	George		1	1		1	1	2		1		1		8		
Freetown	290	2	Combs	Elnathan	1			1		1			1				4		
Freetown	290	3	Wilson	David			3	1				1		1			6		
Freetown	290	4	Rider	Benjamin	1		1			1		1					4		
Freetown	290	5	Miller	David		1	2		1	1	1	1					8		
Freetown	290	6	Samson	Ebenezer	2			1				1	1				6		
Freetown	290	7	Wilbour	Elizabeth Wid		1	1					1					4		
Freetown	290	8	Terry	Ebenezer	2	2	1		1			1	1	1			9		
Freetown	290	9	Miller	Jeb	2		1			2		1					6		
Freetown	290	10	Samson	John	1	2		1		2			1				7		
Freetown	290	11	Davis	Cornelius		2	1		1	1			1				7		
Freetown	290	12	Chase	Chloe Wid	1					1		1					3		
Freetown	290	13	Thurston	Edward			2	1		2		2	2				10		
Freetown	290	14	Davis	Kiah	2	1		1		1		1		1			7		
Freetown	290	15	Burt	Thomas		1		1						1			3		
Freetown	290	16	Hunter	Elexander	1	1		1		2			1				6		
Freetown	290	17	Davis	James	1		1					1					4		
Freetown	290	18	Davis	Eleazer	1			1	1	1		1	1				6		
Freetown	290	19	Horton	Jonathan				1		1		1	1				4		
Freetown	290	20	Pain	John				1			1	1	1				4		
Freetown	290	21	Davis	Nichademos				2			1	1	2				6		
Freetown	290	22	Winslow	George 2d			1	1		1	1	1					5		
Freetown	290	23	Hathaway	Zepheniah Jr	2			1		2		1					6		
Freetown	290	24	Hathaway	Micah				1		2		1					4		
Freetown	290	25	Hathaway	Zepheniah			1	1				1		1			4		
Freetown	290	26	Hathaway	William				1						1			2		
Freetown	290	27	Pain	John 2d			1	1				1					4		
Freetown	290	28	Hathaway	Israel	1	1	1		1	1			1				6		
Freetown	290	29	Winslow	James 2d	1			1		2	1		1				6		
Freetown	290	30	Barrows	Isaac	4			1		1	1		1				8		
Freetown	291	1	Terry	Zepheniah			2	1	1	1	2		1				8		
Freetown	291	2	Lawton	Job	2		1						1				4		
Freetown	291	3	Pain	Mary Wid	1	1	1						1	1			5		
Freetown	291	4	Evens	Gilford	1	1			1	1	1						5		
Freetown	291	5	Chace	Greenfield	1				1	3	1	2	1				9		
Freetown	291	6	Conley	John	1			1		2		1					5		
Freetown	291	7	Strange	William	2		1			1		1					5		
Freetown	291	8	Chace	Otis	2		1			2		1					6		
Freetown	291	9	Clark	Seth	1		1					1					3		
Freetown	291	10	Bisemore	John	2			1		1		1	1				6		
Freetown	291	11	Pain	Joseph	1	1		1		2		1					7		
Freetown	291	12	Pain	Gilford			1			1		1					3		
Freetown	291	13	Brosman	Olive	2					1		1		1			5		
Freetown	291	14	Pain	Ichabod	1		1					1					3		
Freetown	291	15	Cummons	Jail		1				3		1					5		
Freetown	291	16	Davis	Jonathan	1				1					1			3		
Freetown	291	17	Haskell	Benjamin	3	1		1		1	1		1				8		
Freetown	291	18	Simmons	John				1					1				2		

TOWN	PG#	LN#	LAST NAME	FIRST NAME	FREE WHITE MALES					FREE WHITE FEMALES					TOTAL ALL OTHER	TOTAL SLAVES	TOTALS	DISTRICT/ TOWNSHIP	NOTES
					under 10	10 to 16	16 to 26	26 to 45	45 and over	under 10	10 to 16	16 to 26	26 to 45	45 and over					
Freetown	291	19	Haskell	Josiah	1	1		1		3			1	1			8		
Freetown	291	20	Westcoat	William			1			2		2	1				6		
Freetown	291	21	Haskell	John	1	1		1					1	1			5		
Freetown	291	22	Haskell	Isaac	1	1		1		2			1				6		
Freetown	291	23	Braley	Nathaniel	1	1	2		1				1				6		
Freetown	291	24	Haskell	Josiah 2d	2			1		1			1				5		
Freetown	291	25	Braley	William			1			1			1				3		
Freetown	291	26	Braley	Benjamin	4		1			1			1				7		
Freetown	291	27	Pigesley	Robert	2			1		1	2		1				7		
Freetown	291	28	Braley	Ephraim	1	1				2	1		1				7		
Freetown	291	29	Bolton	John		3		1		4			1				9		
Freetown	291	30	White	Perregrin		1	1	1	1			1		1			6		
Freetown	291	31	Crapo	Benjamin	1			1					1				3		
Freetown	292	1	Borden	John		1			1				1				3		
Freetown	292	2	Bolton	Jonathan		1			1					1			3		
Freetown	292	3	Crapo	Joshua					1	2	2		1				6		
Freetown	292	4	Jucket	Micah	3	1			1	1			1				7		
Freetown	292	5	Ashley	Abraham	4	1	2		1	2	1	1					12		
Freetown	292	6	Crapo	Peter	1	1	2		1	3				1			9		
Freetown	292	7	Cottle	Thomas		1	1		1	1	2		1				7		
Freetown	292	8	Cottle	Samuel	1				1			1		1			4		
Freetown	292	9	Laramee	Benjamin Jun	2	2		1		1	1		1				8		
Freetown	292	10	Ashley	Taber	2		1					1					4		
Freetown	292	11	Ronnalds	Micah				1	1	1		1		1			4		
Freetown	292	12	Lucus	Elijah		2	2	1		3		1	1				10		
Freetown	292	13	Saller	Silas	1	1			1				1	1			5		
Freetown	292	14	Westcoat	Benjamin					1			1					2		
Freetown	292	15	Jabez	George		2	1		2	1	1	2	1				10		
Freetown	292	16	Ashley	Micah	1		1		1	3	3		1				10		
Freetown	292	17	Rounswill	Abner	1			1		2			1				5		
Freetown	292	18	Haskens	Anthony	1		1						1				3		
Freetown	292	19	Mason	Hezekiah	1		1		1					1			4		
Freetown	292	20	White	Merchant	2			1					1	1			5		
Freetown	292	21	Pigesley	Joseph	2	3			1	2	2		1				12		
Freetown	292	22	Westcoat	Thomas	2	2		1		3			1				9		
Freetown	292	23	Foster	John	1	1	1		1	1	1	2	1		1		10		
Freetown	292	24	Allen	John			1			3		1			1		6		
Freetown	292	25	Pratt	David		1		1			1		1				4		
Freetown	292	26	Johnson	Ichabod				1		3			2	1			7		
Freetown	292	27	Howland	Job Jr	1		1	1		1			1				5		
Freetown	292	28	Ashley	Percival		1							1	1	1		4		
Freetown	292	29	Ashley	Abraham Jr			1			4			1				6		
Freetown	292	30	Ashley	Enoch	1			1			1						3		
Freetown	292	31	Braley	Ezekel	1	2		1		2			1				7		
Freetown	292	32	Braley	Amos	2		1			2			1				6		
Freetown	293	1	Braley	Asa	1		1			2			1				5		
Freetown	293	2	White	Samuel	1	2	1			1	4		1				9		
Freetown	293	3	White	Thomas		1		1		1		2	1				6		
Freetown	293	4	Laramee	John		1		1	1	3		2	1				9		
Freetown	293	5	Ashley	Percival Junr	3		1			1		1					6		
Freetown	293	6	Ashley	Barnabas		1		1		1			1				4		
Freetown	293	7	White	Ebenezer				1		1			1				3		
Freetown	293	8	Denno	Nathaniel			2	1	1	3	1	1	1				10		
Freetown	293	9	Haskens	Abner	1	1			1	1	1	1					6		
Freetown	293	10	Parker	Elijah	2	2	2	1		2	1		1		1		12		
Freetown	293	11	Durffee	David		1			1				1				3		
Freetown	293	12	Foster	Gload		1		1				1					3		
Freetown	293	13	Macomber	Samuel	1			1		1		1					4		
Freetown	293	14	Thomas	Jedidiah	1			1					1				3		
Freetown	293	15	Morton	Abraham	1		1	1		2			1				6		
Freetown	293	16	Rounswill	Gabriel Wid	1	2	1					3		1			8		
Freetown	293	17	Smith	Gilbert	2			1		1			1				5		
Freetown	293	18	Whitmarsh	Asa	2			1					1				4		
Freetown	293	19	Gurney	Silas			1		1	1	2		1				6		
Freetown	293	20	Chace	Edward	2	1	1	1		1		1	1				8		
Freetown	293	21	Jucket	Stephen	1		1			1	1						4		
Freetown	293	22	Read	James	1			1					1		1		4		
Freetown	293	23	Smith	Edward				1		2		1	1				5		
Freetown	293	24	Pain	Ebenezer 2d	1			1		1			1				4		
Freetown	293	25	Goff	Paul		1					1		1				3		
Freetown	293	26	Hathaway	John	4	1		1		1	1		1		1		10		
Freetown	293	27	Shore	Mary Wid	1		1			2		1	1				6		
Freetown	293	28	Read	Benjamin Jun			1					1					2		
Freetown	293	29	Burr	Elizabeth Wid						2			1				3		
Freetown	293	30	Borden	Stephen				1					1	1			3		
Freetown	294	1	Chace	Isaac	1					2			1				4		
Freetown	294	2	Dodson	Jonathan				1									1		
Freetown	294	3	Brown	Josiah			1			3			1				5		
Freetown	294	4	Demoranoil	Josiah	1			1		1			1				4		
Freetown	294	5	Evens	Mary Wid								1		1			2		
Freetown	294	6	Hathaway	Malbone	3			1		1			1				6		
Freetown	294	7	Hathaway	James				1				1	1				3		
Freetown	294	8	Haskens	Nathaniel		1		1		2	1		1				6		
Freetown	294	9	Phillips	Ebenezer Junr		2				1			1				4		
Freetown	294	10	Pain	Job			2	1			1	1	1				6		
Freetown	294	11	Hathaway	Gilford	1			1					1				4		
Freetown	294	12	Hathaway	Sally Wid		1				1			1				3		
Freetown	294	13	Pain	Warden	1	1			1	2		2		2			9		
Freetown	294	14	Hathaway	Gilford 2d	1	1		1		1			1				5		

TOWN	PG#	LN#	HEADS OF HOUSEHOLD		FREE WHITE MALES					FREE WHITE FEMALES					TOTAL ALL OTHER	TOTAL SLAVES	TOTALS	DISTRICT/ TOWNSHIP	NOTES
			LAST NAME	FIRST NAME	under 10	10 to 16	16 to 26	26 to 45	45 and over	under 10	10 to 16	16 to 26	26 to 45	45 and over					
Freetown	294	15	Perkens	David	1			1		4			1				7		
Freetown	294	16	Chace	Phebe Wid						1			2				3		
Freetown	294	17	Chace	Phillip				1		3	2		1				7		
Freetown	294	18	Chace	Benjamin 2d			1	1					1				3		
Freetown	294	19	Chace	Michal					1		1	2		1			5		
Freetown	294	20	Chace	Seth			2		1	1				1			5		
Freetown	294	21	Richmond	Jonathan	1			1		2	1		1				6		
Freetown	294	22	Cudworth	David 2d	1			1		1			1				4		
Freetown	294	23	Hathaway	Ephraim					1				1	1			3		
Freetown	294	24	Winslow	John 2d				1				1					2		
Freetown	294	25	Dean	Benjamin	3	1		1		1			1				7		
Freetown	294	26	Briggs	George			1	1		3			1				6		
Freetown	294	27	Cudworth	Jessee	2			1		1		1					5		

TOWN	PG#	LN#	LAST NAME	FIRST NAME	FREE WHITE MALES under 10	10 to 16	16 to 26	26 to 45	45 and over	FREE WHITE FEMALES under 10	10 to 16	16 to 26	26 to 45	45 and over	TOTAL ALL OTHER	TOTAL SLAVES	TOTALS	DISTRICT/ TOWNSHIP	NOTES
Mansfield	384	1	Allen	Micah	1		1		1		1			4			8		
Mansfield	384	2	Allen	Joseph	1		1		1		2	1		1			7		
Mansfield	384	3	Allen	Elijah	2		1					1					4		
Mansfield	384	4	Atherton	Phillip	1	2		1					1	1			6		
Mansfield	384	5	Blanchard	Judith	1			2				1		1			5		
Mansfield	384	6	Bates	Benjamin	1		3		1		2	1		1			9		
Mansfield	384	7	Billings	Benjamin		1						1	1				4		
Mansfield	384	8	Bates	Leavit		1	1		1	1	2			1			7		
Mansfield	384	9	Bates	Spencer	1			1					1				3		
Mansfield	384	10	Briggs	Jacob		1		1	1		1	1	1				6		
Mansfield	384	11	Bates	John			1			2		1					4		
Mansfield	384	12	Brintnell	Nathaniel	1			1				1		2			5		
Mansfield	384	13	Brintnell	Job		1		1		1	1	2		1			7		
Mansfield	384	14	Bird	Elijah	2	1		1		2	1	1		1			9		
Mansfield	384	15	Bailey	Samuel			1	1					1	1			4		
Mansfield	384	16	Brintnell	Ebenezer			1	1					1				3		
Mansfield	384	17	Brintnell	Ebenezer Jr	3		1			2			1				7		
Mansfield	384	18	Bailey	Abner			2			1	3	1	1				8		
Mansfield	384	19	Briggs	Solomon				1		1		1		1			4		
Mansfield	385	1	Clap	Elkanah		1		1	1	2	1		1	1			8		
Mansfield	385	2	Copeland	Moses		1		1	1	1	2			1			7		
Mansfield	385	3	Cobb	Benjamin				1						1			2		
Mansfield	385	4	Cobb	David	2			1					1				4		
Mansfield	385	5	Cobb	Benjamin Junr	3	1	1		1	1			1				8		
Mansfield	385	6	Cobb	John	1	1		1		1			1				5		
Mansfield	385	7	Cobb	mason	3	2			1				1				7		
Mansfield	385	8	Cobb	Salmon	2			1		2	2			1			8		
Mansfield	385	9	Cobb	Daniel				1					1	1			3		
Mansfield	385	10	Copeland	William	1	1	1		1	2	1	1		1			9		
Mansfield	385	11	Crosman	Thephilus			3		1					1			5		
Mansfield	385	12	Crawley	Abraham	1	2			1	2		1	1	1			9		
Mansfield	385	13	Cobb	Jonathan	2			1		2			1				6		
Mansfield	385	14	Codding	Samuel	4	1	1	1		2			1	1			11		
Mansfield	385	15	Chapman	John	2			1		1			1				5		
Mansfield	385	16	Copeland	Amasa	1		1						1				3		
Mansfield	385	17	Doane	Isaac		1		1				1	1	1			5		
Mansfield	385	18	Doane	William			1	1		1			1				4		
Mansfield	385	19	Doane	John			3		1			2	1	1			8		
Mansfield	385	20	Doane	Elijah		1		1		1			1				4		
Mansfield	385	21	Doane	Dwight	3			2		1	1		1				8		
Mansfield	385	22	Dunham	William	4	3			1	2							11		
Mansfield	385	23	Dunham	Elizabeth									1	2			3		
Mansfield	385	24	Doane	William 2d	2			1		2			1				6		
Mansfield	385	25	Drake	Oliver	2	3			1	2			1				9		
Mansfield	385	26	Drake	Benjamin	1			1				1					3		
Mansfield	385	27	Eliot	Nehemiah				1									1		
Mansfield	385	28	Francis	Apollos	2		1	1		1			1	1			7		
Mansfield	385	29	Fisher	Samuel		2			1			1		1			5		
Mansfield	385	30	Fisher	Samuel Jr	1		1						1				3		
Mansfield	385	31	Fisher	Lemuel		1		1				2		2			6		
Mansfield	385	32	Fisher	Nathan	1	2		1		3	2		1				10		
Mansfield	385	33	Field	Joseph	2			1			1	2					7		
Mansfield	385	34	Fillebrown	Catharine	1			1		1		2	1				6		
Mansfield	385	35	Field	Richard				1					1				2		
Mansfield	385	36	Field	William	1			1		2			1				5		
Mansfield	385	37	Fuller	Isaac	1			1		1	1						4		
Mansfield	385	38	Francis	Levi Jur	1			1		2			1				5		
Mansfield	385	39	Fisher	Jacob	1		1						1				3		
Mansfield	385	40	Gilbert	David	1			1					2				4		
Mansfield	385	41	Gilbert	James			1						1	1			3		
Mansfield	385	42	Gilbert	Daniel			4	2						1	1		8		
Mansfield	385	43	Grover	David			2		1					1			4		
Mansfield	385	44	Grover	David Jur	1			1		2	2		1				7		
Mansfield	385	45	Grover	Jesse				1					1				2		
Mansfield	385	46	Grover	Samuel	2			1					1				4		
Mansfield	385	47	Grover	Joseph				1					1				2		
Mansfield	385	48	Grover	Thomas					1					1			2		
Mansfield	385	49	Grover	Levi		1			1			2		1			5		
Mansfield	385	50	Grover	Seth		2		1		2			1				6		
Mansfield	385	51	Grover	Samuel				1		1			1				3		
Mansfield	385	52	Grover	Abiel		1		1		2				1			5		
Mansfield	386	1	Green	Roland		1		1				1	1	1	1		6		
Mansfield	386	2	Green	Roland Jur			1						1				2		
Mansfield	386	3	Grover	Simeon			1			1	1	1					4		
Mansfield	386	4	Grover	Benjamin		1			1		1	3		1			7		
Mansfield	386	5	Grover	William	1	1	1	1				1	1	1			7		
Mansfield	386	6	Hall	Elkanah	2		1	1					1				7		
Mansfield	386	7	Harden	John	2		1		1	1		2	1	1			9		
Mansfield	386	8	Hodges	Job				1					1	1			3		

TOWN	PG#	LN#	LAST NAME	FIRST NAME	FREE WHITE MALES					FREE WHITE FEMALES					TOTAL ALL OTHER	TOTAL SLAVES	TOTALS	DISTRICT/ TOWNSHIP	NOTES
					under 10	10 to 16	16 to 26	26 to 45	45 and over	under 10	10 to 16	16 to 26	26 to 45	45 and over					
Mansfield	386	9	Hodges	Elisha	2			1		2	1		1				7		
Mansfield	386	10	Hodges	John	3	1		1		1			1				7		
Mansfield	386	11	Hodges	Jesse		1		1		1	1		1				5		
Mansfield	386	12	Hardon	Susannah									1	1			2		
Mansfield	386	13	Hardon	Isaac		1				4			1	1			7		
Mansfield	386	14	Hardon	David		3	2		1	1	1		1	1			10		
Mansfield	386	15	Hardon	Jacob	1	1		1		2		2	1				8		
Mansfield	386	16	Hodges	Nathaniel		2	2		1	2		1	1				9		
Mansfield	386	17	Hunt	James				1					3				4		
Mansfield	386	18	Haskel	zuriel				1					1				2		
Mansfield	386	19	Hodges	Elijah				1					1				2		
Mansfield	386	20	Harris	Thomas		1	2		1	1			1				6		
Mansfield	386	21	Hunt	Quincy	1			2		1		1	1				6		
Mansfield	386	22	Hitchcock	Thomas			1			2		2					5		
Mansfield	386	23	Knapp	John			1		2				1	1			5		
Mansfield	386	24	Knapp	John Jur			1					1					2		
Mansfield	386	25	Lane	Joseph	1	1			1	1	1		1				6		
Mansfield	386	26	Lane	Ebenezer			1		1	1		1					4		
Mansfield	386	27	Lane	Seth				1					1				2		
Mansfield	386	28	Lane	Seth Junr	1		1	1		1	1	1					6		
Mansfield	386	29	Lane	Abiel		1		1		1			1				4		
Mansfield	386	30	Leonard	Abiel				1					1				2		
Mansfield	386	31	Leonard	Abijah	1		2		1	1	1	1					8		
Mansfield	386	32	Leonard	Nehemiah	2	2			2	1	1	1		2			11		
Mansfield	386	33	Lovel	Isaac		2			1			1		2			6		
Mansfield	386	34	Lovel	David		2			1			1		3			7		
Mansfield	386	35	Makepeace	Isaac		2	1			5		1					9		
Mansfield	386	36	Newland	Jacob			2		2	1	1		1	1			8		
Mansfield	386	37	Newcomb	Jonathan			3		2	1		1		3			10		
Mansfield	386	38	Osgood	John				1					1				2		
Mansfield	386	39	Pain	John		1		1	1	2		1		1			7		
Mansfield	386	40	Pratt	John	1		2		1			1		1			6		
Mansfield	386	41	Pratt	John Jur	3	2		1		2		1	2				11		
Mansfield	386	42	Pratt	David			1		1	1	2		1				6		
Mansfield	386	43	Pratt	Amasa		1						1					2		
Mansfield	387	1	Pratt	Josiah Jr		1	1			2	2						6		
Mansfield	387	2	Pratt	Josiah	2			1		1			1				5		
Mansfield	387	3	Penny	John					1					1			2		
Mansfield	387	4	Phillips	John		2			1	1			1				5		
Mansfield	387	5	Pratt	Spencer		2			1		1		1				5		
Mansfield	387	6	Pain	Joel	2	1		1		1	2	1					8		
Mansfield	387	7	Pratt	Lucy						1		1	1				3		
Mansfield	387	8	Rogers	Benjamin				1				1	1				3		
Mansfield	387	9	Richardson	Stephen				1					1				2		
Mansfield	387	10	Richardson	Ebenezer				1		2		1					4		
Mansfield	387	11	Richardson	Thomas			1			1		1					3		
Mansfield	387	12	Rogers	Daniel			1					1					2		
Mansfield	387	13	Snow	Reuben		1	1	1	1			1	1				6		
Mansfield	387	14	Skinner	David		1			1			2	1				5		
Mansfield	387	15	Skinner	James	1			1		4	1	1	1				9		
Mansfield	387	16	Skinner	Jacob	1	1	2		1	1			1				7		
Mansfield	387	17	Skinner	Robert	1	1		1		2			1				6		
Mansfield	387	18	Skinner	Isaac	1			1				1					3		
Mansfield	387	19	Skinner	Thomas				1					1				2		
Mansfield	387	20	Skinner	Thomas Jur	1		1		1	2	2	1		1			9		
Mansfield	387	21	Smith	Nicholas				1					2				3		
Mansfield	387	22	Shepard	Seth	1		1		1	1				2			6		
Mansfield	387	23	Sweet	Benjamin		1	2		1				1	1			6		
Mansfield	387	24	Skinner	Rufus			1					1		1			3		
Mansfield	387	25	Smith	Stephen	2	1			1	1	2		1				8		
Mansfield	387	26	Skinner	David Jr			1			2	1	1					5		
Mansfield	387	27	Stearns	Isaac	1	1		1		2		1					6		
Mansfield	387	28	Skinner	William			1			3		1					5		
Mansfield	387	29	Skinner	Hewit	1		1			3		1		1			7		
Mansfield	387	30	Smith	Spencer	1			1		2		1					5		
Mansfield	387	31	Slack	Lewis	3			1	1			1					6		
Mansfield	387	32	Skinner	Ezra	1	2		1		3	1		1				9		
Mansfield	387	33	Skinner	Otis				1		1		1					3		
Mansfield	387	34	Todd	Archibald	1	1		1		1	1	1					6		
Mansfield	387	35	Titus	Joseph	1			1			1	1	1				5		
Mansfield	387	36	Tiffany	William				1					1				2		
Mansfield	387	37	Thayer	Christopher				1					1				2		
Mansfield	387	38	Thayer	Remember	1						1		1				3		
Mansfield	387	39	Tripp	Ephraim	1	2	1		2	1		1		2			10		
Mansfield	387	40	Tucker	John											4		4		
Mansfield	387	41	Williams	Ebenezer		1				1	1						3		
Mansfield	387	42	Williams	Bates		1				1	1						3		
Mansfield	387	43	Wellman	Ebenezer	1		1			2			1				5		
Mansfield	387	44	Waterman	Mary									1	1			2		

TOWN	PG#	LN#	LAST NAME	FIRST NAME	FREE WHITE MALES					FREE WHITE FEMALES					TOTAL ALL OTHER	TOTAL SLAVES	TOTALS	DISTRICT/ TOWNSHIP	NOTES
					under 10	10 to 16	16 to 26	26 to 45	45 and over	under 10	10 to 16	16 to 26	26 to 45	45 and over					
Mansfield	387	45	White	Mehetable	1	1						2		1			5		
Mansfield	387	46	White	Lemuel	1		1		1		1		1	1			6		
Mansfield	387	47	White	John		3		1					1				5		
Mansfield	387	48	White	Amos	1				1		1		1	1			5		
Mansfield	387	49	Wheaton	Calvin	2			2		1			2				7		
Mansfield	387	50	Williams	John	1	1	2		1	1		1	1				8		
Mansfield	388	1	Wetherell	Solomon	1	2	1	1	1	1			2				9		
Mansfield	388	2	White	Matthew	1			1					1				3		
Mansfield	388	3	Williams	Jacob	2			1		1	1	1	1				7		
Mansfield	388	4	Williams	Benjamin			1		1			2		1			5		
Mansfield	388	5	Williams	Daniel	2			1		2			1				6		
Mansfield	388	6	Williams	Elijah					1					1			2		
Mansfield	388	7	Wellman	Isaac			1		1			1		2			5		
Mansfield	388	8	White	Simeon	3		1		2	2	1		1	1			11		
Mansfield	388	9	White	Eliab			1		1				1	1			4		
Mansfield	388	10	White	David				1	1				1				3		
Mansfield	388	11	White	Sarah		1				1	1	1					4		
Mansfield	388	12	Wetherell	Benjamin		1		1			1		1				4		
Mansfield	388	13	Weatherby	Ebenezer			1			2		1					4		
Mansfield	388	14	Wellman	John	1				1				2				4		
Mansfield	388	15	White	Jonathan					1					1			2		
Mansfield	388	16	Whilbore	Benjamin				1		2			1				4		
Mansfield	388	17	Williams	Benjamin Jr			1			1		1					3		
Mansfield	388	18	White	Daniel		1		1				1		1			4		
Mansfield	388	19	White	Samuel				1		2			1				4		
Mansfield	388	20	Walker	Eleazer		1		1	1	2	1	1		1			8		
Mansfield	388	21	White	Jonathan Jr			1		1	2	1	1		1			7		
Mansfield	388	22	Williams	Amasa	3			1		1			1				6		
Mansfield	388	23	White	Ebenezer	1		1	1	1	1		1		1			7		
Mansfield	388	24	White	Nathan	2			1		2			1				6		
Mansfield	388	25	White	Leonard	1			1				1					3		
Mansfield	388	26	White	Oliver				1				1					2		

TOWN	PG#	LN#	HEADS OF HOUSEHOLD LAST NAME	FIRST NAME	FREE WHITE MALES under 10	10 to 16	16 to 26	26 to 45	45 and over	FREE WHITE FEMALES under 10	10 to 16	16 to 26	26 to 45	45 and over	TOTAL ALL OTHER	TOTAL SLAVES	TOTALS	DISTRICT/ TOWNSHIP	NOTES
New Bedford	418	1	Allen	Jethro	1		4		1		1	1	1	1			10		
New Bedford	418	2	Allen	Ebenezer	2	3		1		1	1		1				9		
New Bedford	418	3	Allen	Silvanus		1		1			1			1			4		
New Bedford	418	4	Allen	Eunice		1						2	1				4		
New Bedford	418	5	Allen	Anthony			1										1		
New Bedford	418	6	Allen	Rufus		2	3	1					1				7		
New Bedford	418	7	Allen	Paul	1	2		1		3	1		1				9		
New Bedford	418	8	Adams	Elizabeth		2	2			1			1				6		
New Bedford	418	9	Alden	John		1	2	1				2	2				8		
New Bedford	418	10	Alden	Otis	1			1					1				3		
New Bedford	418	11	Alden	John Jun	2			1		1	1	1					6		
New Bedford	418	12	Akin	Bartholomew	1	2		2		1	1	1					8		
New Bedford	418	13	Akin	Deborah		1				1			1				3		
New Bedford	418	14	Anible	Isaac			1										1		
New Bedford	418	15	Allen	Elizabeth	1					2	1	1	1				6		
New Bedford	418	16	Allen	William			1		3			2					6		
New Bedford	418	17	Ayers	Edward			1		1	2		1					5		
New Bedford	418	18	Adams	Knowles		1	1		1			1					4		
New Bedford	418	19	Allen	Job			1				1						2		
New Bedford	418	20	Austin	Joseph		1	1		1	1	1	1		1	1		8		
New Bedford	418	21	Ayers	Joseph	1	1		1		2	2	2	1	1			11		
New Bedford	418	22	Ashley	William			1						1		1		3		
New Bedford	418	23	Anthony	William											4		4		
New Bedford	418	24	Allen	James		1	2	1		2	1		1				8		
New Bedford	418	25	Allen	James 2nd	3	1	1	1		2	1	1	1				11		
New Bedford	418	26	Allen	Humphrey	1		1					1					3		
New Bedford	420	1	Allen	Jonathan 2d	1	1		1		1		1					5		
New Bedford	420	2	Allen	Abraham	2	1		1		1			1				6		
New Bedford	420	3	Allen	David	5			1	1			3	1				11		
New Bedford	420	4	Allen	Peleg	1	1		1		2			1				6		
New Bedford	420	5	Allen	Francis			1										1		
New Bedford	420	6	Allen	Jonathan				1									1		
New Bedford	420	7	Allen	Eleazer	1			1					1				3		
New Bedford	420	8	Armstrong	Susanna	1								1				2		
New Bedford	420	9	Allen	Robert	2	2		1		2	1	1	1				10		
New Bedford	420	10	Andrews	Abial	2			1					1				4		
New Bedford	420	11	Adams	Wally			1		1			1		1			4		
New Bedford	420	12	Anthony	Daniel	2	1		1			1	1					6		
New Bedford	420	13	Anthony	John											6		6		
New Bedford	420	14	Burges	Isaiah	1	2		1		1			2				7		
New Bedford	420	15	Baylis	Frederic	2			1		1		1					5		
New Bedford	420	16	Blossom	Benjamin	1		2	1		4	1	1	1				11		
New Bedford	420	17	Blossom	Samuel		1	1			1			1				4		
New Bedford	420	18	Bates	Nathan			1						1				2		
New Bedford	420	19	Brownell	John	1			1						2			4		
New Bedford	420	20	Brownell	Robert		1							1				2		
New Bedford	420	21	Blossom	Joseph	3			1		3			1				8		
New Bedford	420	22	Babcock	Phebe	1	1	2			2	1	1		1			9		
New Bedford	420	23	Babcock	Joseph			1			1	1	1					4		
New Bedford	420	24	Bosworth	Joseph			1							1			2		
New Bedford	420	25	Bolles	Prudence		1							1				2		
New Bedford	420	26	Bennett	Robert	2	1	2		1	1		2		1			10		
New Bedford	420	27	Bennett	Elisha	2	1		1			1		1				6		
New Bedford	420	28	Bennett	Joseph	3			1		2			1				7		
New Bedford	420	29	Bartlett	Silvanus	1		1	1					1				4		
New Bedford	420	30	Bates	Joseph	3	1		1		2	1		1				9		
New Bedford	420	31	Braley	Seth	1			1					1				3		
New Bedford	420	32	Blackmore	John	1			1		2			1	1			6		
New Bedford	420	33	Bennett	Gilbert	1			1			1	1	1				5		
New Bedford	420	34	Bennett	Meribah								2	1				3		
New Bedford	420	35	Brown	Dedford											2		2		
New Bedford	420	36	Bennett	William		1			1					1			3		
New Bedford	420	37	Bennett	Edward			1	1	1		1	2	1		2		9		
New Bedford	420	38	Bennett	Joseph 2d	3			1		2			1				7		
New Bedford	420	39	Bumpus	Silvester	1		2		1	1	2	1		1			9		
New Bedford	420	40	Bliss	William	2	2		1		1	1		1				8		
New Bedford	420	41	Bates	Worth		1	2		2	1	1		1				8		
New Bedford	420	42	Butler	Peter	1			1		2		1	1	1			7		
New Bedford	420	43	Barrow	Thomas	3			1		2	1		1				8		
New Bedford	420	44	Bryant	Gamaliel				1		1				1			3		
New Bedford	420	45	Bryant	Gamaliel Jr				1		3		1			1		6		
New Bedford	421	1	Beetle	Henry	2	1		1		2	1	1	1				9		
New Bedford	421	2	Brownell	Uriah		1		1		2			1				5		
New Bedford	421	3	Brightman	John		1	1						1				3		
New Bedford	421	4	Brown	Scipio											6		6		
New Bedford	421	5	Barker	Abraham		1											1		
New Bedford	421	6	Barker	Thomas											3		3		
New Bedford	421	7	Bunker	Sheubael		1		1		1	1	1					5		
New Bedford	421	8	Bonney	Samuel			2			1		1					4		

TOWN	PG#	LN#	LAST NAME	FIRST NAME	FREE WHITE MALES under 10	10 to 16	16 to 26	26 to 45	45 and over	FREE WHITE FEMALES under 10	10 to 16	16 to 26	26 to 45	45 and over	TOTAL ALL OTHER	TOTAL SLAVES	TOTALS	DISTRICT/ TOWNSHIP	NOTES
New Bedford	421	9	Butterfield	Easther											1		1		
New Bedford	421	10	Bennett	Daniel			1			2	2		1				6		
New Bedford	421	11	Burrill	Joshua	1	1		1		2	1		1				7		
New Bedford	421	12	Butler	Benjamin			1		1			2		1			5		
New Bedford	421	13	Bowen	Charles											4		4		
New Bedford	421	14	Butler	Benjamin Jr			1			2	1		1				5		
New Bedford	421	15	Butler	Obadiah	2		1			1			1				5		
New Bedford	421	16	Bowdish	James				1			1		1				3		
New Bedford	421	17	Barker	Joshua	1		2					2					5		
New Bedford	421	18	Bennett	Thomas	1		1		1	1	2	1	1				8		
New Bedford	421	19	Bennett	Benjamin			1				1		1				3		
New Bedford	421	20	Butler	Daniel			1			3			1	1			6		
New Bedford	421	21	Booth	Isaiah				1				1		1			3		
New Bedford	421	22	Booth	Benjamin	1			1		3			1				6		
New Bedford	421	23	Bennett	Jeremiah			1	1						1			3		
New Bedford	421	24	Clark	David		2	1	1			1		1				6		
New Bedford	421	25	Crandon	Thomas				1									1		
New Bedford	421	26	Crandon	Consider			1						1				2		
New Bedford	421	27	Cornish	Hananiah				1						2			3		
New Bedford	421	28	Church	Benjamin		1		1		1	1		1				5		
New Bedford	421	29	Church	Benjamin Jr		1				1	1	1					4		
New Bedford	421	30	Church	Charles	1	2		1		2		2	2				10		
New Bedford	421	31	Clark	John			2							2			4		
New Bedford	421	32	Crandon	John			1										1		
New Bedford	421	33	Copeland	Elisha		1		1		2	2		1				7		
New Bedford	421	34	Cornish	Patience								2	2	1			5		
New Bedford	421	35	Church	Gamaliel	2			1		1			1				5		
New Bedford	421	36	Church	Joseph	2	1	1		1	1	1	1	1				9		
New Bedford	421	37	Cunningham	Stephen		2	2	1					1	1			7		
New Bedford	421	38	Crowel	John			1			1			1				3		
New Bedford	421	39	Crandon	Joseph	1		1			1			1				4		
New Bedford	421	40	Clasby	Lot	1		1	1		1			1				5		
New Bedford	421	41	Cook	Robert			1			1			1				3		
New Bedford	422	1	Cook	Pardon		1		1		2	1	1	1				7		
New Bedford	422	2	Cook	Paul				1					1				2		
New Bedford	422	3	Cushman	Elisha				1									1		
New Bedford	422	4	Cushman	Mary	1	1					1		1				4		
New Bedford	422	5	Crandon	Phillip	2		1						1				4		
New Bedford	422	6	Churchill	Jedidah									1				1		
New Bedford	422	7	Churchill	David		1		1		1			1				4		
New Bedford	422	8	Church	Stephen	1		1			1			1				4		
New Bedford	422	9	Claghorn	George	1	2		1		2	1	3		1			11		
New Bedford	422	10	Church	Gilbert			1						1				2		
New Bedford	422	11	Church	Elizabeth			1						1	1			3		
New Bedford	422	12	Church	Charles 2d	1	1	1	1					1				5		
New Bedford	422	13	Cannon	Phillip	1	1	2	1		1			1				7		
New Bedford	422	14	Carriwill	Phillip											5		5		
New Bedford	422	15	Chadwick	John	1			1					2				4		
New Bedford	422	16	Cathaway	Lot											3		3		
New Bedford	422	17	Cushman	Ezra	2	1	3	2			1	1	1		1		12		
New Bedford	422	18	Chace	Joseph		1	4			1			1				7		
New Bedford	422	19	Cross	Latham				1					1				2		
New Bedford	422	20	Congdon	Caleb	2			1		3			1	1			8		
New Bedford	422	21	Congdon	Joseph				1						1			2		
New Bedford	422	22	Coval	William	4	1	2		1	1	1		1				11		
New Bedford	422	23	Coggenhall	John Jr	1		4				1	1					7		
New Bedford	422	24	Crocker	Joshua		1	1			4	1	3	1				11		
New Bedford	422	25	Case	Job	1					3	1		1				7		
New Bedford	422	26	Card	Jonathan	1		1	1					1				4		
New Bedford	422	27	Cairsley	Thomas	1			1		3			1				6		
New Bedford	422	28	Cairsley	Elijah	2		1						1				4		
New Bedford	422	29	Crocker	Rowland	2	1		1					1	1			6		
New Bedford	422	30	Coleman	Benjamin			1						1				2		
New Bedford	422	31	Chase	Ariel	1			1		1			1				4		
New Bedford	422	32	Cannon	John	2	2		1		2			2	1			10		
New Bedford	422	33	Congdon	John		1		1		1			1	1	1		6		
New Bedford	422	34	Coggeshall	John		2	1	2					1	1	1		8		
New Bedford	422	35	Coggeshall	Gideon	1		1	1		4	2		1				10		
New Bedford	422	36	Churchill	Thomas	1			1			1		2				5		
New Bedford	422	37	Chandler	Joshua				1		2			1				4		
New Bedford	422	38	Cushman	Mial	1	1		1					1				4		
New Bedford	422	39	Cornal	Levi				1		2			1				4		
New Bedford	422	40	Cole	Archipus			1	1		3			1				6		
New Bedford	422	41	Crane	Cesar											2		2		
New Bedford	422	42	Chace	Benjamin	1			1		2		2		1			7		
New Bedford	422	43	Chaffee	John	3	1		1	1				1	1			8		
New Bedford	422	44	Chace	Michael	2			1		1			1				5		
New Bedford	422	45	Coombs	Ithamar	3			1					1				5		
New Bedford	422	46	Cowen	Luella		1					1	1	1				4		

TOWN	PG#	LN#	LAST NAME	FIRST NAME	FREE WHITE MALES					FREE WHITE FEMALES					TOTAL ALL OTHER	TOTAL SLAVES	TOTALS	DISTRICT/ TOWNSHIP	NOTES
					under 10	10 to 16	16 to 26	26 to 45	45 and over	under 10	10 to 16	16 to 26	26 to 45	45 and over					
New Bedford	422	47	Chace	Jared	2	1		1		1	2		1				8		
New Bedford	422	48	Delano	Joshua	1	4	3		1	2		2		1			14		
New Bedford	422	49	Delano	Dinah		1								1			2		
New Bedford	423	1	Delano	Jabez	2			1					1		1		5		
New Bedford	423	2	Delano	Thomas		2	1		1		1	1		1			7		
New Bedford	423	3	Delano	Richard	2			1		2			1		1		7		
New Bedford	423	4	Drew	Joshua		3	1	1		4		1	2				12		
New Bedford	423	5	Delano	John	2	1	1	1				1	1	1			8		
New Bedford	423	6	Delano	Paul	1	1	1						1				4		
New Bedford	423	7	Delano	Ephraim			1	1	1			4		1			8		
New Bedford	423	8	Delano	Reuben			1		1			2	1	1			6		
New Bedford	423	9	Dexter	William				1									1		
New Bedford	423	10	Drew	Isaac			1		1			1		1			4		
New Bedford	423	11	Delano	Calvin			1		1			2		1			5		
New Bedford	423	12	Delano	Nathan	1			1		4	1		1				8		
New Bedford	423	13	Delano	John	2	2		1		2	1		1				9		
New Bedford	423	14	Delano	Seth	1			1					1				3		
New Bedford	423	15	Delano	Amaziah	1			1					1				3		
New Bedford	423	16	Delano	Marcy	1									1			2		
New Bedford	423	17	Darnon	Joseph	1				1		1	1		1	1		6		
New Bedford	423	18	Darnon	Joseph Jun			1					2					3		
New Bedford	423	19	Doane	Elizabeth									2				2		
New Bedford	423	20	Delano	Joseph		1	2		1	1	1	1	1				8		
New Bedford	423	21	Dillingham	Cornelius				1					1				2		
New Bedford	423	22	Dillingham	Benjamin		1	3	1	1			2		1			9		
New Bedford	423	23	Davis	Nicholas		2		1		2			1				6		
New Bedford	423	24	Davis	Humphrey	1			1		1			1				4		
New Bedford	423	25	Davis	Jethro	2			1				1		1			5		
New Bedford	423	26	Davis	Nicholas 2nd			1	1		1			1				4		
New Bedford	423	27	Davis	Nathan	1	2			1	1		2		1			8		
New Bedford	423	28	Davis	Ruth									1				1		
New Bedford	423	29	Davis	James 2nd	4			1					1				6		
New Bedford	423	30	Davis	Aaron	1		1		1	3	1	1	1				9		
New Bedford	423	31	Drew	Sarah									1				1		
New Bedford	423	32	Davis	Abraham	1	1		1		1	1		1				6		
New Bedford	423	33	Dudley	George	2			1		1			1				5		
New Bedford	423	34	Drew	Benjamin	1			1		2			1				5		
New Bedford	423	35	Delano	Hannah	2								1				3		
New Bedford	423	36	Doty	Elihu			1					1		1			3		
New Bedford	423	37	Doty	Theodore			1										1		
New Bedford	423	38	Davis	Russell		1	1						1				3		
New Bedford	423	39	Delano	Gideon				1									1		
New Bedford	423	40	Deane	William		1						1					2		
New Bedford	423	41	Delano	Abisha	1			1		1		1			3		7		
New Bedford	423	42	Dunbar	Fanny	2	2				2	1		1				8		
New Bedford	423	43	Delano	Allerton	1			1		1			1				4		
New Bedford	423	44	Delano	Thomas 2nd	1			1		2	1		1				6		
New Bedford	423	45	Dunham	George L.			1			1		1					3		
New Bedford	423	46	Davis	James		2	1		1			3		1			8		
New Bedford	423	47	Durfee	James	2		1	1		4			1				9		
New Bedford	423	48	Drew	Josiah	1		1	1			1		2				6		
New Bedford	424	1	Davis	James 2nd	1	1	1		1	4	1	2	1	1			13		
New Bedford	424	2	Dillingham	Bejamin Jr		2	1			2		1					6		
New Bedford	424	3	Davis	David	1	1		1		5	1		1				10		
New Bedford	424	4	Eldredge	John				1					1				2		
New Bedford	424	5	Eldredge	Killey			1			3	1		1				6		
New Bedford	424	6	Eldredge	Isaiah				1					1				2		
New Bedford	424	7	Eldredge	Elnathan	2		2		1			1		1			7		
New Bedford	424	8	Eldredge	Rebecca	1							1					2		
New Bedford	424	9	Eldredge	Salathiel	1			1				1	1				4		
New Bedford	424	10	Eldredge	Amos	1	1		1		1	1		1				6		
New Bedford	424	11	Ellis	Seth				1				1	1				3		
New Bedford	424	12	Ellis	John				1									1		
New Bedford	424	13	Ellis	Elijah		1				1			1				3		
New Bedford	424	14	Ellis	Luke			1	1		4	2	1	1				10		
New Bedford	424	15	East	George				1					1				2		
New Bedford	424	16	Eddy	Job			1										1		
New Bedford	424	17	Eddy	John	1			1		1			1				4		
New Bedford	424	18	Earl	Job	1	1			1			2	1				6		
New Bedford	424	19	Freeman	Obed		2			1			4	1				8		
New Bedford	424	20	Fuller	Peter		1	1		1	2	1	1		1			8		
New Bedford	424	21	Freeman	Charles B.		1	1			1		1					4		
New Bedford	424	22	Fisk	Brownell	1			1		3			1				6		
New Bedford	424	23	Fisk	David	1			1		1	1		1				5		
New Bedford	424	24	Fisk	Turner		1		1		1		1	1				5		
New Bedford	424	25	Folger	Obed	1	1		1		2			1				6		
New Bedford	424	26	Fuller	Francis	2			1		1	2	1	1				8		
New Bedford	424	27	Fuller	John			1			1		1					3		
New Bedford	424	28	Fisk	Preserved			1					1		1			3		

TOWN	PG#	LN#	LAST NAME	FIRST NAME	FREE WHITE MALES					FREE WHITE FEMALES					TOTAL ALL OTHER	TOTAL SLAVES	TOTALS	DISTRICT/ TOWNSHIP	NOTES
					under 10	10 to 16	16 to 26	26 to 45	45 and over	under 10	10 to 16	16 to 26	26 to 45	45 and over					
New Bedford	424	29	Foster	Peter		2				2			1				5		
New Bedford	424	30	Fuller	Mary				1			1	1	1	1			5		
New Bedford	424	31	Gelat	John	3		1	1		2	1		1				9		
New Bedford	424	32	Grinnel	Benjamin	3	1	1	1		2			1				9		
New Bedford	424	33	Gibbs	Alfred			1			1		1					3		
New Bedford	424	34	Gibbs	Ancel		1		1									2		
New Bedford	424	35	Gibbs	Rowland				1									1		
New Bedford	424	36	Gordon	William	2	1	1		1	2		2	1	1			11		
New Bedford	424	37	Gifford	Abner				1									1		
New Bedford	424	38	Green	Christopher	1			1					1	1			4		
New Bedford	424	39	Gifford	James	2	1	3		1	3	1	1		1			13		
New Bedford	424	40	Gifford	William	1			1		2			1				5		
New Bedford	424	41	Gifford	Thomas	2		1		1	2	1		1	1			9		
New Bedford	424	42	Gerish	John	1			1					1				3		
New Bedford	425	1	Grinnel	Cornelius	2	2		1		1			1				7		
New Bedford	425	2	Graham	Michael				1									1		
New Bedford	425	3	Gilbert	John		1		2		1			1				5		
New Bedford	425	4	Gelat	David			1										1		
New Bedford	425	5	Greene	Caleb		2			1	2			1				6		
New Bedford	425	6	Grinnel	Susanna	1		1			1	4		2	1			10		
New Bedford	425	7	Gerish	John		1			1			2		1			5		
New Bedford	425	8	Gardner	Andrew	4	1		1				1	1				8		
New Bedford	425	9	Gifford	Stephen				1		1		2					4		
New Bedford	425	10	Green	Thomas				1		1			1				3		
New Bedford	425	11	Gifford	Thomas					1					1			2		
New Bedford	425	12	Gifford	Noah	2			1		1			1				5		
New Bedford	425	13	Gifford	Ruamy	1		2			1		2	1				7		
New Bedford	425	14	Greive	David	1			1		3	1	1	1				8		
New Bedford	425	15	Hicks	Galen				1				1	1				3		
New Bedford	425	16	Huttleston	Peleg			1	1		1		2					5		
New Bedford	425	17	Hathaway	Elizabeth	1	2						3					6		
New Bedford	425	18	Hills	Jabez	1			1		1			1				4		
New Bedford	425	19	Hathaway	Robert			2		1			3		1			7		
New Bedford	425	20	Hammond	Richard	1	1		1		2	1		1				7		
New Bedford	425	21	Huttleston	Henry	1	1		1		1			1				5		
New Bedford	425	22	Hathaway	Bridget										2			2		
New Bedford	425	23	Hathaway	Clark	1			1	1		1			1			5		
New Bedford	425	24	Hathaway	Reuben				1					3	1			5		
New Bedford	425	25	Hitch	Hardy	1		1						2				4		
New Bedford	425	26	Hammond	Seth	2			1	1	1			1	1			7		
New Bedford	425	27	Hammond	Barnabas	4	1	1	1		1	1	2	1				12		
New Bedford	425	28	Handy	Thomas					1					1			2		
New Bedford	425	29	Handy	Rose			1							1			2		
New Bedford	425	30	Hammond	Sarah	1					2	1		1				5		
New Bedford	425	31	Hammond	Prince				1		3		1					5		
New Bedford	425	32	Hamblin	Wealthy	1					1			1				3		
New Bedford	425	33	Handy	Isaac	3			1					1				5		
New Bedford	425	34	Hathaway	George	1			1					1				3		
New Bedford	425	35	Hathaway	Eleazer	1	1			1	2			1	1			7		
New Bedford	425	36	Holmes	John	2		1	1		2			1				7		
New Bedford	425	37	Handy	Gamaliel		1		1					1				3		
New Bedford	425	38	Howard	Abner		2		1		6	1			1			11		
New Bedford	425	39	Hitch	George				1			1	2		1			5		
New Bedford	425	40	Hathaway	Arthur	2	2		1		2	1		1				9		
New Bedford	425	41	Howland	Wing		2	2	1		3	1	2	1				12		
New Bedford	425	42	Hathaway	Samuel		1		1		2		3		1			8		
New Bedford	425	43	Hitch	Samuel			3	1				1	1	1			7		
New Bedford	425	44	Hathaway	Stephen		1	2	1		1	1	3		1			10		
New Bedford	425	45	Hathaway	Micah		1	2	1		1	3	3					11		
New Bedford	426	1	Hathaway	Lois										1			1		
New Bedford	426	2	Hitch	Elget		1		1						1			3		
New Bedford	426	3	Hathaway	Thomas				1		2			1				4		
New Bedford	426	4	Huttleston	Thomas	1			1					1				3		
New Bedford	426	5	Holmes	Joseph	2			1		3			1				7		
New Bedford	426	6	Hathaway	Obed		1		1					1	1			4		
New Bedford	426	7	Hathaway	Samuel		1		1		1	1			1			5		
New Bedford	426	8	Hathaway	Elnathan				1						1			2		
New Bedford	426	9	Hammond	Alden	1			1						1			3		
New Bedford	426	10	House	John	1	2		1		1			1	1			7		
New Bedford	426	11	House	Benjamin				1									1		
New Bedford	426	12	Hathaway	Jabez				1				1	1				3		
New Bedford	426	13	Hicks	Abraham	3	1		1		2			1				8		
New Bedford	426	14	Hathaway	John				1				1	1	1			4		
New Bedford	426	15	Hillman	Zachariah	1	2		1		2	1		1				8		
New Bedford	426	16	Hatch	James		1	1	1		1	1		1				6		
New Bedford	426	17	Haskins	William	2		2	1		1	1		1				8		
New Bedford	426	18	Hammond	Barzilla	1	1	1	1					1				5		
New Bedford	426	19	Hammond	Jabez	1				1					1			3		
New Bedford	426	20	Hitch	George Jr			1			1			1				3		
New Bedford	426	21	Hammond	Heart	1					1			1				3		

TOWN	PG#	LN#	LAST NAME	FIRST NAME	FWM under 10	FWM 10 to 16	FWM 16 to 26	FWM 26 to 45	FWM 45 and over	FWF under 10	FWF 10 to 16	FWF 16 to 26	FWF 26 to 45	FWF 45 and over	TOTAL ALL OTHER	TOTAL SLAVES	TOTALS	DISTRICT/ TOWNSHIP	NOTES
New Bedford	426	22	Henshaw	William	2	1	3	1			1		1				9		
New Bedford	426	23	Howland	Mathew	2	1	3		1	1	1		1				10		
New Bedford	426	24	Hammond	Jabez Jr	1					2			1				5		
New Bedford	426	25	Hazard	Thomas	2	1	1	1		1	1	2	1		2		12		
New Bedford	426	26	Howland	Weston	2		1	1		1			1		1		7		
New Bedford	426	27	Howland	Cornelius			1	1		3	1		1				7		
New Bedford	426	28	Howland	Gideon		1		1				2					4		
New Bedford	426	29	Howland	Isaac Jun				1			1			1			3		
New Bedford	426	30	Howland	James		1	1	1	1	1			1				6		
New Bedford	426	31	Howland	Isaac				1			2		1		1		5		
New Bedford	426	32	Howland	Humphrey	1	3	1	1		1		1	1				9		
New Bedford	426	33	Haskell	Roger	1		1	1		1			1		1		6		
New Bedford	426	34	Howland	Gilbert	3		1	1		1	1	1					8		
New Bedford	426	35	Heffords	Jonathan	3	1		1		1	1		1				8		
New Bedford	426	36	Hart	Lemison	1			1		2	1		1				6		
New Bedford	426	37	Helm	John	2			1		1			1				5		
New Bedford	426	38	Hussey	Isaiah				1		2			1	1			5		
New Bedford	426	39	Howland	Peleg	3		1	1		1	1	1					8		
New Bedford	426	40	Hill	Benjamin	2		1		1	4	2			1			11		
New Bedford	426	41	Howland	Benjamin	2			1				1	1				5		
New Bedford	426	42	Howland	John	1	1	3		1	2	1	1	2		1		13		
New Bedford	426	43	Howland	Joseph		1		2				1	1		1		6		
New Bedford	426	44	Howland	Timothy	1	2	1		1				1				6		
New Bedford	426	45	Haskins	Jonathan			1			1			1				3		
New Bedford	427	1	Hatch	Seth			1			1			1				3		
New Bedford	427	2	Howland	Jonathan	2	1			1	1	1		1				7		
New Bedford	427	3	Hathaway	Hannah		1						1	1				3		
New Bedford	427	4	Hammond	Thomas	1			1		1		2	1		1		7		
New Bedford	427	5	Hathaway	Nathaniel			1			2			1				4		
New Bedford	427	6	Hathaway	Humphrey	3	1		1		1			1				7		
New Bedford	427	7	Hathaway	Richard		1	4		1	2	1		1	1	1		12		
New Bedford	427	8	Holmes	William	1	1		1		3			1				7		
New Bedford	427	9	Hathaway	William	1			1		1			1				4		
New Bedford	427	10	Howard	Solomon		1	1		1	1	2						6		
New Bedford	427	11	Hammond	Mary		1							3				4		
New Bedford	427	12	Holmes	James				1					1	1			3		
New Bedford	427	13	Hopkins	John	2			1		2			1				6		
New Bedford	427	14	Hathaway	Elihu				2	1				1	1			5		
New Bedford	427	15	Hathaway	Noah	2			1		1			1				5		
New Bedford	427	16	Hathaway	Seth		1		1					1				3		
New Bedford	427	17	Howland	Reuben	1		1	1		1		1	1				6		
New Bedford	427	18	Hathaway	Silvanus	1		1					1					3		
New Bedford	427	19	Hathaway	Hannah			1							1			2		
New Bedford	427	20	Hathaway	James			1							1			2		
New Bedford	427	21	Hathaway	Prince	1		1						1				3		
New Bedford	427	22	Hathaway	Isaac		1	1					1					3		
New Bedford	427	23	Hathaway	Deborah	1									1			2		
New Bedford	427	24	House	Sheubal		1				1		1					3		
New Bedford	427	25	Hathaway	William Jr		1						1					2		
New Bedford	427	26	Jones	Isaiah	1	1	2	1					1				6		
New Bedford	427	27	Jenne	Israel	2	1		1		2	1	1	1				9		
New Bedford	427	28	Jenne	Nathaniel				1					2				3		
New Bedford	427	29	Jenne	Jabez	1			1					1	1			4		
New Bedford	427	30	Jenne	David	1		1			2			1				5		
New Bedford	427	31	Jenne	Abner	1	1		1		1		1	1	1			7		
New Bedford	427	32	Jacobs	David			1			1			1				3		
New Bedford	427	33	Jenne	Levi	3	1	2		1	2	1		2				12		
New Bedford	427	34	Johnson	Ebenezer		1											1		
New Bedford	427	35	Jenne	Weston	2		1						1				4		
New Bedford	427	36	Jenne	Caleb		1	1		1	3			1				7		
New Bedford	427	37	Jenne	Jethro				1		1			1				3		
New Bedford	427	38	Jenne	Jonathan	1	1	1		1				1				5		
New Bedford	427	39	Jenne	Patience									1	2			3		
New Bedford	427	40	Jenne	Marcy						1		1					2		
New Bedford	427	41	Jenne	Sarah									1				1		
New Bedford	427	42	Jenne	Elizabeth			2						1				3		
New Bedford	427	43	Jenne	Jeptha	1		1			1			1				4		
New Bedford	427	44	Jenne	Reuben	2		1	1		1			1				6		
New Bedford	427	45	Jenne	Josiah		1											1		
New Bedford	428	1	Jenne	Sarah		1				1	1	1		1			5		
New Bedford	428	2	Joseph	Christopher	2	1		1		1	1	1					7		
New Bedford	428	3	Jenne	Job		1	1	2	1	1	2		1				9		
New Bedford	428	4	Jenne	Seth		1			1				1				3		
New Bedford	428	5	Jenne	William			1			1							2		
New Bedford	428	6	Jenne	John	2		1			2			1		1		7		
New Bedford	428	7	Jenne	Weston2nd		1							1				2		
New Bedford	428	8	Jenne	Peleg	2	3							1				6		
New Bedford	428	9	Ingraham	Timothy		1	2	1	1	1			1	1			8		
New Bedford	428	10	Jenne	Jahariel		1	1			2			1	1			6		
New Bedford	428	11	Jenne	Caleb Jr	2		2	1				2					7		
New Bedford	428	12	Johnson	Samuel											7		7		
New Bedford	428	13	Ingraham	Thomas		1	2		1	1	2	1	1				9		
New Bedford	428	14	Ingraham	Paul				1			1	1					3		
New Bedford	428	15	James	William			2					2					4		
New Bedford	428	16	Jenne	Patience									1				1		
New Bedford	428	17	Kinney	Samuel		1		1					1				3		
New Bedford	428	18	Kempton	Paul		1							1				2		
New Bedford	428	19	Kinney	Jacob	1	1	2		1				1				6		
New Bedford	428	20	Kempton	William		2			1	2	1		1	1			8		

TOWN	PG#	LN#	HEADS OF HOUSEHOLD LAST NAME	FIRST NAME	FREE WHITE MALES under 10	10 to 16	16 to 26	26 to 45	45 and over	FREE WHITE FEMALES under 10	10 to 16	16 to 26	26 to 45	45 and over	TOTAL ALL OTHER	TOTAL SLAVES	TOTALS	DISTRICT/ TOWNSHIP	NOTES
New Bedford	428	21	Kempton	Asa	1			1		3			1				6		
New Bedford	428	22	Kempton	Stephen			1		1			1	1	1			5		
New Bedford	428	23	Kempton	James	2	3		1		1		2	1	1			11		
New Bedford	428	24	Kempton	Jonathan	1	1		1		4	1		1				9		
New Bedford	428	25	Killey	amos	2	1		1		2			1				7		
New Bedford	428	26	Kempton	William Jr	1		1					1					3		
New Bedford	428	27	Keen	Jesse	2	1		1			1	1	1				7		
New Bedford	428	28	Keen	Ebenezer		1		1				1		1			4		
New Bedford	428	29	Keen	Ebenezer Jr				1		1			1		1		4		
New Bedford	428	30	Kempton	Sarah										1			1		
New Bedford	428	31	McKenzie	Martin	2			1					1				4		
New Bedford	428	32	Kempton	Elijah	2			1		2	3		1				9		
New Bedford	428	33	Kempton	Obed	1	1		1			2		1				6		
New Bedford	428	34	Kempton	Manasseh		2	2	1				1		1	1		8		
New Bedford	428	35	Kempton	Manasseh Jr	2	1	5	1		2			1	1			13		
New Bedford	428	36	Kempton	Thomas		2			1	1				2			6		
New Bedford	428	37	Kempton	Ephraim				1		1		1	2	1	1		7		
New Bedford	428	38	Kempton	Ephraim Jr		1	2	1		1		1		1	1		8		
New Bedford	428	39	Kempton	David	2			1		3	2		1				9		
New Bedford	428	40	Kempton	Joseph				1					2				3		
New Bedford	428	41	Landers	Jane	2					1			1				4		
New Bedford	428	42	Levett	Joseph			1			1			1				3		
New Bedford	428	43	Lewis	Robinson	1		1					1					3		
New Bedford	428	44	Langworthy	John	1		2	1					1		1		6		
New Bedford	429	1	Lincoln	Benjam	1	1	2	1				2					7		
New Bedford	429	2	Lowden	John			1			1		1					3		
New Bedford	429	3	Littlefield	Sarah											7		7		
New Bedford	429	4	Lewis	Abner				1					1				2		
New Bedford	429	5	Morton	Seth				1					3				4		
New Bedford	429	6	Morton	Jethro	1	1		1		3	1		1				8		
New Bedford	429	7	Mendal	Thomas	1	1	1	1			1		1				6		
New Bedford	429	8	Mitchel	Seth	1		1	1		1		1					5		
New Bedford	429	9	Mitchel	David				1			1		1				3		
New Bedford	429	10	Martin	Hannah											3		3		
New Bedford	429	11	Mosher	Abner	2		1					1					4		
New Bedford	429	12	Mendal	Ellis	2		1	1		2		1	1	1	1		10		
New Bedford	429	13	Miller	Robert		1		1					1				3		
New Bedford	429	14	Mendal	Lemuel				1				1	1				3		
New Bedford	429	15	Maxfeld	Zadock		1	1	1		1	3			1			8		
New Bedford	429	16	Maxfeld	Isaac			1			1			1				3		
New Bedford	429	17	Maxfeld	Joseph	3		1			1			1				6		
New Bedford	429	18	Mosher	Elihu		2		1		1		1	1				6		
New Bedford	429	19	Mosher	Phillip	2		1			1			1		1		6		
New Bedford	429	20	Mosher	Samuel	1		1			3		1	1				7		
New Bedford	429	21	Mosher	Benjamin				1			1		1				3		
New Bedford	429	22	Myrick	Mathew	1		1						1				3		
New Bedford	429	23	Mayhew	Jeremiah		1	1	1		1			1	1	1		6		
New Bedford	429	24	Mosher	Ruth									1				1		
New Bedford	429	25	Mason	Benajah				1		1			1				3		
New Bedford	429	26	Medar	William	1			1		2	1		1				6		
New Bedford	429	27	Manchester	Job				1				1		1			3		
New Bedford	429	28	Maxfeld	Warren	1			1					1				3		
New Bedford	429	29	Merrihew	Peter	2			1		3			1	1			8		
New Bedford	429	30	Mason	Reuben	1	1	1	1		1	2	1	1				9		
New Bedford	429	31	Meranville	Simeon	2			1		4	2		1				10		
New Bedford	429	32	Norton	Hannah		1				1	1		1				4		
New Bedford	429	33	Nye	Mary						1	1		1				3		
New Bedford	429	34	Nye	Daniel		1		1					1				3		
New Bedford	429	35	Nye	Thomas	2			1					2	1			6		
New Bedford	429	36	Nye	Stephen	1			1		1			1				4		
New Bedford	429	37	Norton	Constant		1		1		2			1				5		
New Bedford	429	38	Nye	Thomas Junr	2	1		1		3	1		1				9		
New Bedford	429	39	Nye	Jonathan	1	1		1		4	2		1				10		
New Bedford	429	40	Nye	Obed			1		1			2		1	1		6		
New Bedford	429	41	Nye	Barnabas		1			1			3		1			6		
New Bedford	429	42	Nash	Simeon	1	2			1			2		1			7		
New Bedford	429	43	Nye	Nathan	1		1		1			1		1			5		
New Bedford	429	44	Newport	Prince										1	1		2		
New Bedford	429	45	Onan	John			2		1		1		1				5		
New Bedford	430	1	Onan	Simeon		1			1			1		2			5		
New Bedford	430	2	Onan	Joshua				1					1				2		
New Bedford	430	3	Ornsby	Brownell	2			1	1				1				5		
New Bedford	430	4	Perry	Freeman	2			1		1		1	1				6		
New Bedford	430	5	Procter	Samuel		1	2	1					1		1	2	8		
New Bedford	430	6	Pope	Thomas	1		1			2			1				5		
New Bedford	430	7	Pope	Freeman	2		1						2	1			6		
New Bedford	430	8	Pope	Edmund		1		1				1	2	1			6		
New Bedford	430	9	Pope	Nathaniel	4			1					2				7		
New Bedford	430	10	Pope	William		1		1					1	1			4		
New Bedford	430	11	Pease	Abner			1						1	1			3		
New Bedford	430	12	Parker	Zalmena			1										1		
New Bedford	430	13	Procter	Susanna	1	1	1			1			2	1			7		
New Bedford	430	14	Price	John	1			1		2			2	1			7		
New Bedford	430	15	Pope	Samuel		1	1	1		1		1	1	1			7		
New Bedford	430	16	Pope	Ephraim				1						1			2		
New Bedford	430	17	Pinkham	Andrew	1		1						1				3		
New Bedford	430	18	Peckham	Isaiah	2			1		3			1				7		
New Bedford	430	19	Peckham	Lucy										2			2		
New Bedford	430	20	Peckham	Peleg		1		1					1				3		
New Bedford	430	21	Pope	Seth					1					1			2		

TOWN	PG#	LN#	LAST NAME	FIRST NAME	M under 10	M 10 to 16	M 16 to 26	M 26 to 45	M 45 and over	F under 10	F 10 to 16	F 16 to 26	F 26 to 45	F 45 and over	TOTAL ALL OTHER	TOTAL SLAVES	TOTALS	DISTRICT/ TOWNSHIP	NOTES
New Bedford	430	22	Procter	Josiah				1					1	1			3		
New Bedford	430	23	Pickhens	John										1			1		
New Bedford	430	24	Pickhens	Thaddeus	1		1					1					3		
New Bedford	430	25	Pope	Yet Seth	1			1		3	1		1				7		
New Bedford	430	26	Pope	Jonathan	1		1	1		2			1				6		
New Bedford	430	27	Phillips	Peter				1					1				2		
New Bedford	430	28	Perry	Lemuel		1		1				3	2				7		
New Bedford	430	29	Parker	Elventon			1										1		
New Bedford	430	30	Pope	Marcy									1				1		
New Bedford	430	31	Pope	Ebenezer			1					1					2		
New Bedford	430	32	Pope	Lemuel			1										1		
New Bedford	430	33	Price	Simeon		1		1		1			1	1			5		
New Bedford	430	34	Potter	Pardon		2	1			2		2					7		
New Bedford	430	35	Peckham	John Jur	1	2				1		1					5		
New Bedford	430	36	Potter	Southworth	1		1						1				3		
New Bedford	430	37	Price	Oliver	3	1		1		3			1				9		
New Bedford	430	38	Potter	Thurston		1		1				1	1				4		
New Bedford	430	39	Parker	Jonathan	3		1			1			1				6		
New Bedford	430	40	Potter	Stephen	1		1			1		1					4		
New Bedford	430	41	Pratt	Lewis	1		1						1				3		
New Bedford	430	42	Pearce	Cesar											6		6		
New Bedford	430	43	Prior	Susanna										1			1		
New Bedford	430	44	Perry	Ebenezer	1		1	1		1			1				5		
New Bedford	430	45	Proud	John	1	1		1		1	2	3	1				10		
New Bedford	430	46	Plumb	Joshua	1		1			1		2					5		
New Bedford	430	47	Packard	Abijah		1		1		1		1					4		
New Bedford	431	1	McPherson	John		1	1	1		1			1				5		
New Bedford	431	2	Pope	Edward	2	1		2				3	2	2			12		
New Bedford	431	3	Peckham	John			1				1		1	1	1		5		
New Bedford	431	4	Peckham	Mary										1			1		
New Bedford	431	5	Peckham	William	1		1			2			1	1			6		
New Bedford	431	6	Perry	Samuel			1						1	1	1		4		
New Bedford	431	7	Perry	Samuel Jun	2		1	1				1	1	1			7		
New Bedford	431	8	Pope	Worth	1		2	1		2			1	1			8		
New Bedford	431	9	Parker	William	2	1	2		1	2			1				9		
New Bedford	431	10	Pratt	Amos	1	1		1		1			1				6		
New Bedford	431	11	Pearce	Joseph		1	2	1		3	1	1	1				10		
New Bedford	431	12	Perkins	Henry	2			1		3	2	4		1			13		
New Bedford	431	13	Potter	Jonathan	3		1			2	2		1				9		
New Bedford	431	14	Parker	Nathan		1				1		1					3		
New Bedford	431	15	Russell	Phillip	3		1			2			1				7		
New Bedford	431	16	Russell	Wing	1		1			1			1				4		
New Bedford	431	17	Randall	Putnam	1	1				1			1				4		
New Bedford	431	18	Rouse	John			1				2		1				4		
New Bedford	431	19	Russell	John		1	1	1						1			4		
New Bedford	431	20	Russell	William 2nd	1		1		1	1	3	1		1			9		
New Bedford	431	21	Robinson	William				1				1		1			3		
New Bedford	431	22	Russell	Jonathan	2			1				1	1	1			6		
New Bedford	431	23	Russell	Seth Jun		1		1		1	1	1			2		7		
New Bedford	431	24	Russell	Gilbert		1		1		4	2	1	1		1		11		
New Bedford	431	25	Rotch	William		1		1		2	2	1	2		1		10		
New Bedford	431	26	Rotch	Thomas			1	1				1	1	1			5		
New Bedford	431	27	Rotch	William Jun	2	1	3	2		2		2		3	2		16		
New Bedford	431	28	Russell	Charles	1	1				1	1	1					7		
New Bedford	431	29	Russell	Barnabas	1	1	1		1	5	2	2	1	1	1		16		
New Bedford	431	30	Russell	William Jr	2	1	3	1		1			1	1			10		
New Bedford	431	31	Rickelson	Daniel		1	1	1					1	1	1		6		
New Bedford	431	32	Rickelson	Joseph		1	1						1				3		
New Bedford	431	33	Ross	William	1			1		2	1		1				6		
New Bedford	431	34	Russell	William	1	1	1			1	1		1				7		
New Bedford	431	35	Rotch	Joseph				1				1	1	1			4		
New Bedford	431	36	Rickelson	Charles		1											1		
New Bedford	431	37	Right	Thomas				1					2				3		
New Bedford	431	38	Russell	Caleb				1				1	1				3		
New Bedford	431	39	Russell	Caleb Jur		2	1	1		2			1				7		
New Bedford	431	40	Russell	Pero											3		3		
New Bedford	431	41	Russell	Joseph				1					1	1			3		
New Bedford	431	42	Russell	Abraham	4			4				3	1		7		19		
New Bedford	431	43	Russell	John J	1		1			1			1				4		
New Bedford	431	44	Russell	Seth	1			1					1	1			4		
New Bedford	431	45	Rickelson	Abraham	2			1		2			1		1		7		
New Bedford	431	46	Rodman	Samuel	2		1	1		1	2	3	1		1		12		
New Bedford	431	47	Raynolds	Michael	1		1						1				3		
New Bedford	432	1	Raynolds	William	3	1		1		2	1		1				9		
New Bedford	432	2	Shearman	Jabez		1				2			1				4		
New Bedford	432	3	Spooner	Benjamin			1	1		1	1	1		1			6		
New Bedford	432	4	Stetson	Joseph				1			1		1				3		
New Bedford	432	5	Stevens	Seth	1		1	1		4	1	1	1				10		
New Bedford	432	6	Sisson	Jonathan		1	1			1			1				4		
New Bedford	432	7	Stoddard	Nichols	2			1		1		1	1				6		
New Bedford	432	8	Stoddard	Noah	1	1		1	1	1		1	1				7		
New Bedford	432	9	Shearman	John 2nd		1		1		1			1				4		
New Bedford	432	10	Shaw	William	4	1		1		2	1		1	1			11		
New Bedford	432	11	Swift	Asa	2		1						1	1			5		
New Bedford	432	12	Stetson	Nathaniel	1	3	1		1			1	1	1			9		
New Bedford	432	13	Shearman	Isaac	1		1		1	2	3		1				9		
New Bedford	432	14	Stetson	William			1			1			1				3		
New Bedford	432	15	Sampson	Isacher	5		1					1	1				9		
New Bedford	432	16	Sisson	Mary										1			1		
New Bedford	432	17	Sisson	Benjamin	2	2		1		2	2		1				10		

TOWN	PG#	LN#	LAST NAME	FIRST NAME	FREE WHITE MALES					FREE WHITE FEMALES					TOTAL ALL OTHER	TOTAL SLAVES	TOTALS	DISTRICT/ TOWNSHIP	NOTES
					under 10	10 to 16	16 to 26	26 to 45	45 and over	under 10	10 to 16	16 to 26	26 to 45	45 and over					
New Bedford	432	18	Stevens	Eunice			2						1	1			4		
New Bedford	432	19	Stoddard	Samuel		1	1						1				3		
New Bedford	432	20	Stevens	William				1						1			2		
New Bedford	432	21	Stevens	Job	1		1			1	1						4		
New Bedford	432	22	Spooner	John	1		1			3			1				6		
New Bedford	432	23	Sharpes	Hezekiah											2		2		
New Bedford	432	24	Spooner	Elnathan		2		1	1	1			2	1			8		

TOWN	PG#	LN#	HEADS OF HOUSEHOLD		FREE WHITE MALES					FREE WHITE FEMALES					TOTAL ALL OTHER	TOTAL SLAVES	TOTALS	DISTRICT/ TOWNSHIP	NOTES
			LAST NAME	FIRST NAME	under 10	10 to 16	16 to 26	26 to 45	45 and over	under 10	10 to 16	16 to 26	26 to 45	45 and over					
Norton	379	1	Austin	David	1	1	1		1		1	3	1				9		
Norton	379	2	Austin	Stephen					1					1			2		
Norton	379	3	Arnold	Asa	1			1		1			1				4		
Norton	379	4	Briggs	Timothy Jr	1		1		1	1				1			5		
Norton	379	5	Briggs	Jonathan	3				2	1	3		1				10		
Norton	379	6	Briggs	Daniel	3		1			2			2				8		
Norton	379	7	Babbet	Edward	2		1	1		2			2				8		
Norton	379	8	Burt	Dinah		1						1		1			3		
Norton	379	9	Babbit	Betty			2			1	1						4		
Norton	379	10	Burt	Joseph					1	1		1	2				5		
Norton	379	11	Burt	Joseph Jr	2			1		1	1		1				6		
Norton	379	12	Burt	William	2	1	1		1	1	1	1	1	1			10		
Norton	379	13	Braman	Silvanus	2		1		1			1	1				6		
Norton	379	14	Briggs	Hezekiah	3		1	1					1				6		
Norton	379	15	Briggs	John		1	1		1			1		1			5		
Norton	379	16	Benson	John	4			1		1	1		1				8		
Norton	379	17	Braman	Thomas	1		1		1			1		1			5		
Norton	379	18	Balkcom	Samuel	1	1		2		1		1					6		
Norton	379	19	Balkcom	Alexander				1				1	1				3		
Norton	379	20	Balkcom	David			2		1	1	1	1	1				7		
Norton	379	21	Balkcom	James	3		1			1		1					6		
Norton	379	22	Balkcom	Jacob			1			1		1					3		
Norton	379	23	B*n	Seth	4	2		1			2		1				10		
Norton	380	1	Burt	David	2	2	2	1		1							8		
Norton	380	2	Burt	David Jr	1			1		2		1					5		
Norton	380	3	Bruton	William				1		3		1					5		
Norton	380	4	Bates	Leavit				1		1		1					3		
Norton	380	5	Basset	Daniel				1		2			2				5		
Norton	380	6	Blandin	Benja	1	1	1		1	2	1			3			10		
Norton	380	7	Basset	Isaac	1		3	1		2	1		1				9		
Norton	380	8	Briggs	Nehemiah	3			1		2			1				7		
Norton	380	9	Briggs	Simeon					1				1	2			4		
Norton	380	10	Cobb	Silas			2	2	2		2	1	1	1	1		12		
Norton	380	11	Cobb	Lyman	1			1		3			1	1			7		
Norton	380	12	Cobb	Pliny	1		1			1		1					4		
Norton	380	13	Crane	Terry	2		1	1			1			1			6		
Norton	380	14	Clap	David	1	1	1		2	1	2			2			10		
Norton	380	15	Cobb	William				1				1		1			3		
Norton	380	16	Cobb	Elisha	1	1	1	1		4	2	1	1				12		
Norton	380	17	Copeland	Asa		3	1		1	3	1			1			10		
Norton	380	18	Copeland	Samuel	1	2			1	1			1	1			7		
Norton	380	19	Carpenter	William	3		2			1	3	1	1				12		
Norton	380	20	Carpenter	Peter		1	1	1					1				5		
Norton	380	21	Clark	Pitt	1			1		1			1	1			5		
Norton	380	22	Clark	William		1		1		2			1				5		
Norton	380	23	Clafflin	Nathaniel			2		1	1	1		1				6		
Norton	380	24	Capron	Elisha	1			1		3			1				6		
Norton	380	25	Clark	Asa	1			1		2			1				5		
Norton	380	26	Crosman	Elisha	1			1		2			1				5		
Norton	380	27	Deane	Daniel			1		1					1			3		
Norton	380	28	Deane	Asahel	2		1		1	1	1	1	1				8		
Norton	380	29	Deane	Noah	1	1		1		1	1		1				6		
Norton	380	30	Deane	Pliny	2		1	1				1	1				7		
Norton	380	31	Deane	Nathan				1				1		1			3		
Norton	380	32	Deane	Nathan Jr	3	2		2		1			2	1			11		
Norton	380	33	Deane	Richard	2	1	6		1	1	2			1			11		
Norton	380	34	Danforth	Elijah		3	1	1			1	1		1			8		
Norton	380	35	Danforth	Thomas	2	1		1		3	1	1		1			10		
Norton	380	36	Deane	Asahel Jun	1		1	1		1	1	1	1				7		
Norton	380	37	Daggett	Josiah	1			1		1			1				4		
Norton	380	38	Derry	Wilks				1		1		1					3		
Norton	380	39	Drake	Otis	3			1		1			2				7		
Norton	380	40	Eddy	Rachel				1			1			1			3		
Norton	380	41	Eddy	Abiel				1						1			2		
Norton	380	42	Eddy	Ezra			1	1						1			3		
Norton	380	43	Eddy	Elijah	1	1	1		1	1	1			1			7		
Norton	380	44	Eddy	John	1			1					1				3		
Norton	380	45	Eddy	Samuel			1		1	1	1	2		1			7		
Norton	381	1	Francis	Levi		1			1		1			1			4		
Norton	381	2	Freeman	Bethiah			2			2	1	1	1				7		
Norton	381	3	Freeman	John	2			2		3			1				8		
Norton	381	4	Francis	Tisdale	1			1		2			1	1			6		
Norton	381	5	Franklin	Record				1					1	1			3		
Norton	381	6	French	James	2			1		1			1	1			6		
Norton	381	7	Field	Solomon	2			1		3			2				8		
Norton	381	8	Foster	Joseph	1			1		1				1			4		
Norton	381	9	Frazier	Hugh		1		1					1				3		
Norton	381	10	Foster	Josiah	1			1					1				3		
Norton	381	11	Field	Darius	1			1		1			1				4		

TOWN	PG#	LN#	LAST NAME	FIRST NAME	FWM under 10	FWM 10 to 16	FWM 16 to 26	FWM 26 to 45	FWM 45 and over	FWF under 10	FWF 10 to 16	FWF 16 to 26	FWF 26 to 45	FWF 45 and over	TOTAL ALL OTHER	TOTAL SLAVES	TOTALS	DISTRICT/ TOWNSHIP	NOTES
Norton	381	12	Field	David			1						1				2		
Norton	381	13	Grey	John		1	1	1					2				5		
Norton	381	14	Gilbert	John	1	1		1				2	1				6		
Norton	381	15	Gilbert	George		1	2	1		1		1	1				7		
Norton	381	16	Godfrey	Gersham	1			1		1			1				4		
Norton	381	17	Godfrey	James	1	3		1		1			1	1			8		
Norton	381	18	Godfrey	Samuel					2			2		1	1		6		
Norton	381	19	Godfrey	Mary									1	1			2		
Norton	381	20	Guillo	Francis	1	2		1			2		1				7		
Norton	381	21	Hodges	Leonard	1			1		1	1						4		
Norton	381	22	Horton	Benjamin		1				3		1		1			6		
Norton	381	23	Hodges	James	1		4	1	1	1	2	1	1				12		
Norton	381	24	Hodges	George		1		1					1				3		
Norton	381	25	Hodges	Elijah	1				1			2	1				5		
Norton	381	26	Hodges	Tisdale	1	1	3		1			2		1			9		
Norton	381	27	Hodges	John				1		2	2	1	1				7		
Norton	381	28	Hodges	Jonathan	1	1	1	1		2			1				7		
Norton	381	29	Hodges	Joseph		1	1		1	1	1		1				7		
Norton	381	30	Hodges	Isaac		1			1		1		1				4		
Norton	381	31	Hodges	Seth	1		1	1		2	1		1				7		
Norton	381	32	Hodges	Rufus		1		1									2		
Norton	381	33	Hodges	Josiah			1	1	1				1				4		
Norton	381	34	Hodges	Isaac Junr	2	2	1	1		2		1	1				10		
Norton	381	35	Hodges	Joseph 2d	1			1		3			1				6		
Norton	381	36	Hodges	David		2			1	2		1	1				7		
Norton	381	37	Hall	Brian	2	1		1		2	1		2				9		
Norton	381	38	Hall	Silas	2			1		1			1				5		
Norton	381	39	Hall	John	1			1	1					1			4		
Norton	381	40	Hall	John 3d	1			1		2	1		1				6		
Norton	381	41	Hervey	Josiah				1			1		1				3		
Norton	381	42	Hunt	Joseph		1	2	1		1	1		1				7		
Norton	381	43	Hunt	Samuel	5	1		1		1		1	1				10		
Norton	381	44	Hunt	Josiah		1	1					1	2	2			7		
Norton	381	45	Hill	Joseph				1					1				2		
Norton	381	46	Haradon	Isaac	1			1		3			1				6		
Norton	382	1	Heard	Enos				1		1		1					3		
Norton	382	2	Holmes	John		1		1		1			1				4		
Norton	382	3	Jackson	Nathaniel		1		1				1		1			4		
Norton	382	4	Jackson	Hezekiah		1		1		1			1				4		
Norton	382	5	Jewitt	Jedediah	1			1		1			1				4		
Norton	382	6	Knowles	Asa	1		1			1			1				4		
Norton	382	7	King	John	1			1	1			1	1	2			7		
Norton	382	8	Keith	Seth	1	1	1	1			1	2	1				8		
Norton	382	9	Knapp	Daniel		1	1	1				1	1	1			6		
Norton	382	10	King	Calvin	1	1		1		1			1				5		
Norton	382	11	King	Josiah	1				1		1			1	1		5		
Norton	382	12	Lincoln	David					1					2			3		
Norton	382	13	Lincoln	David Jun		3	1		1					1			6		
Norton	382	14	Lincoln	Levi		1			1	3	1		1				7		
Norton	382	15	Lincoln	Luther	2		2	1		3			1	1			10		
Norton	382	16	Leonard	George		1		1	2		1	1	1	2			9		
Norton	382	17	Lane	William	2			1		3			2				8		
Norton	382	18	Lane	Ephraim		1	3				1	1		1			8		
Norton	382	19	Leonard	Jonathan		1	1	1		1		2		1			7		
Norton	382	20	Lincoln	Simeon	3			1		1	1		1				7		
Norton	382	21	Lane	Isaac		1		1		1			1				4		
Norton	382	22	Lane	Daniel	3			1		1			1				6		
Norton	382	23	Leonard	Thomas	1		1	1		1			1				5		
Norton	382	24	Lincoln	Rufus				1		1	2		1				5		
Norton	382	25	Lincoln	Abiel				1						4			5		
Norton	382	26	Lincoln	Abiel Jr	2	1	2		1	2		2	1				11		
Norton	382	27	Lincoln	Asa	2	1			1	1		1	1				7		
Norton	382	28	Lincoln	Hannah										2			2		
Norton	382	29	Lincoln	Marcy			1	1						2			4		
Norton	382	30	Lincoln	Abner		1				1			1				3		
Norton	382	31	Lazell	Ebenezer	1			1					1				3		
Norton	382	32	Morey	Ruhanah				1					2	1	1		5		
Norton	382	33	Morey	Samuel	1		1	1		1	1		2	1			8		
Norton	382	34	Munro	Nathaniel	2			1		2			1				6		
Norton	382	35	Makepeace	Masa		1					1	1	1				4		
Norton	382	36	Makepeace	Lysander				1		3			1	1			6		
Norton	382	37	Makepeace	William					1			3		1			5		
Norton	382	38	Makepeace	David	1			1		1			1				4		
Norton	382	39	Martin	Amos		2	2	1				2		1			8		
Norton	382	40	Martin	William	2			1		2	2	1					8		
Norton	382	41	Macomber	Ezra	1			1		3			1				6		
Norton	382	42	Morey	Cesar											8		8		
Norton	382	43	Newcomb	Silvester	1			1		2			2				6		
Norton	382	44	Newcomb	Samuel					1				1				2		

TOWN	PG#	LN#	HEADS OF HOUSEHOLD		FREE WHITE MALES					FREE WHITE FEMALES					TOTAL ALL OTHER	TOTAL SLAVES	TOTALS	DISTRICT/ TOWNSHIP	NOTES
			LAST NAME	FIRST NAME	under 10	10 to 16	16 to 26	26 to 45	45 and over	under 10	10 to 16	16 to 26	26 to 45	45 and over					
Norton	382	45	Newcomb	Joseph		2			1				1	1			5		
Norton	382	46	Newcomb	Josiah	1	1		1				1	1				5		
Norton	382	47	Newcomb	Richard	1	1		1		2		1	3	1			10		
Norton	382	48	Newcomb	Asa	1		1	1		1			1				5		
Norton	382	49	Newcomb	John	2	1	1		2	2	1	2	1	1			13		
Norton	383	1	Newland	Jeremiah	1			1	1				2	1			6		
Norton	383	2	Newland	Jonathan					1				1	1			3		
Norton	383	3	Newland	Enos	1			1				1					5		
Norton	383	4	Norton	William					1				1	1			3		
Norton	383	5	Newland	David	1			1		3			1				6		
Norton	383	6	Parker	Daniel		1	1		1	1	1	2		1			8		
Norton	383	7	Pattin	John				2	1				2				5		
Norton	383	8	Presbrey	Simeon	2	2	2	1		3			1	1			12		
Norton	383	9	Perry	Nathan		2	2		1	1	2	2		1			11		
Norton	383	10	Perry	Ichabod		1	1		1	2		1		1			7		
Norton	383	11	Penno	Peter	2		3		1	2	1	1		1			11		
Norton	383	12	Puffin	Benjamin		1		1				1	1				4		
Norton	383	13	Prior	Hepzebah										1			1		
Norton	383	14	Powers	Edward					1			1	1	1			4		
Norton	383	15	Phillips	Daniel		2			1			1		1			5		
Norton	383	16	Palmer	Joseph		1		1		3			1				6		
Norton	383	17	Pratt	Joseph					1				1				2		
Norton	383	18	Raymond	Ephraim	1		2	1		3	1	1	1				10		
Norton	383	19	Richardson	George	1		1					1					3		
Norton	383	20	Richmand	George	1			1	3	1	2		1				9		
Norton	383	21	Smith	Timothy			1	1	1	1		2		1			7		
Norton	383	22	Shepard	Jacob	1	1	1	1	1		1	1		1			8		
Norton	383	23	Smith	David					1					1			2		
Norton	383	24	Smith	Seth		1			1					1			3		
Norton	383	25	Smith	Anna	1		2			1		1					5		
Norton	383	26	Stone	Nathaniel	3	1	1		1	4	2	2	1				15		
Norton	383	27	Storey	William	1		1		1	2				1			6		
Norton	383	28	Smith	Arunah	3			1		2		1		1			8		
Norton	383	29	Smith	Jonathan		1		1		3			1				6		
Norton	383	30	Storey	Thomas			1		1			2		2			6		
Norton	383	31	Sweet	Michael	2	2		1		3		1	1				10		
Norton	383	32	Shearman	Mary	1		1		1					4			7		
Norton	383	33	Sweet	John	1			1		1	1		1				5		
Norton	383	34	Smith	Abisha	1			1		3	2		1				8		
Norton	383	35	Storey	Elijah	2	2		1		2	1		1				9		
Norton	383	36	Stanley	Benjamin		1		1		1		1	2	1			7		
Norton	383	37	Smith	Jacob		1	1		1			1	1	1			6		
Norton	383	38	Shaw	Sarah	2							1		2			5		
Norton	383	39	Shaw	Benjamin	1			1		1			1				4		
Norton	383	40	Skinner	Zophir	1			1				1					3		
Norton	383	41	Shelley	Joseph		1			1	1		1	2				6		
Norton	383	42	Tisdale	Polly							1	1					2		
Norton	383	43	Titus	Ebenezer		1	1		1		2	3		2			10		
Norton	383	44	Tucker	Asahel	3			1		1		1	1				7		
Norton	383	45	Tucker	Jedediah					1	1		2	1				5		
Norton	383	46	Tucker	Hezekiah	2		1	1		1	2	1	1	1			10		
Norton	383	47	Titus	Silvester	1			1		1		1					4		
Norton	383	48	Tucker	Jereth		1						1					2		
Norton	384	1	Verry	William	1		1	1		2	2		2	1			10		
Norton	384	2	Woodward	Hannah					1		1	2		1			5		
Norton	384	3	Woodward	Elkanah Jr	1		1						1				3		
Norton	384	4	Wheaton	George		2			1				1	1			5		
Norton	384	5	Wheaton	Laban	1	1		1	1	1		1	1				7		
Norton	384	6	Wiswall	Elijah	2		1	1		1			1	1			7		
Norton	384	7	Wiswall	Amasa	1		1	1		2	1		1	1			8		
Norton	384	8	Witherell	William			2	1				2	2				7		
Norton	384	9	Witherell	William Jun	2			1		1			1				5		
Norton	384	10	Willis	Beriah	3			1		1		1					7		
Norton	384	11	Woodward	Anna										2			2		
Norton	384	12	Wiswall	Noah		2			1		1	1		1			6		
Norton	384	13	Wilbore	Ephraim	2	1	1		1	1	1			2			9		
Norton	384	14	Wild	Benjamin		2	1		1		2	1		1			8		
Norton	384	15	Witherell	Abijah		1		1				1		1			4		
Norton	384	16	Witherell	James	2	2					1		1				6		
Norton	384	17	Woodward	Josiah		1	3	2	1		1	1	1	3			13		
Norton	384	18	Woodward	Elkanah	1		1						1				3		
Norton	384	19	White	John	1	2	1			1	1		1				8		
Norton	384	20	Witherell	John		2		1				1					5		
Norton	384	21	Witherell	Samuel	1		1					1					3		
Norton	384	22	Witherell	Elisha				1				1					2		
Norton	384	23	White	Abraham			1	1					1				3		
Norton	384	24	Woodward	Isaac	2				1	3	1	2		1			10		
Norton	384	25	White	Zebulon	1	3				2		3		1			11		
Norton	384	26	Washburn	Malatiah					1					1			2		

47

TOWN	PG#	LN#	HEADS OF HOUSEHOLD		FREE WHITE MALES					FREE WHITE FEMALES					TOTAL ALL OTHER	TOTAL SLAVES	TOTALS	DISTRICT/ TOWNSHIP	NOTES
			LAST NAME	FIRST NAME	under 10	10 to 16	16 to 26	26 to 45	45 and over	under 10	10 to 16	16 to 26	26 to 45	45 and over					
Norton	384	27	Witherell	George	1			1				2					4		
Norton	384	28	Wilbore	Joel	1			1					1				3		
Norton	384	29	West	Robert				1				1					2		
Norton	384	30	Woodward	Levi	2			1		1		1					5		

TOWN	PG#	LN#	LAST NAME	FIRST NAME	FWM under 10	FWM 10 to 16	FWM 16 to 26	FWM 26 to 45	FWM 45 and over	FWF under 10	FWF 10 to 16	FWF 16 to 26	FWF 26 to 45	FWF 45 and over	TOTAL ALL OTHER	TOTAL SLAVES	TOTALS	DISTRICT/TOWNSHIP	NOTES
Raynham	372	1	Shaw	Mason		1	1		1					1			4		
Raynham	372	2	Leonard	Zephanah			1		1	1				1			4		
Raynham	372	3	Jones	Seth		1			1			1		1			4		
Raynham	372	4	Leonard	Joshua	1		1		1	1				1			5		
Raynham	372	5	Byram	William	1	2		1		2		2		1			9		
Raynham	372	6	Campbell	Oliver	1			1		4			1	1			8		
Raynham	372	7	Leonard	Elijah			2	1					1	1			5		
Raynham	372	8	Graves	Samuel	2				1					1			4		
Raynham	372	9	Hathaway	Abraham	1	1	1		1	1	1	1		1			8		
Raynham	372	10	Gilmore	Elisha	3	1		1		1	1	2	1				10		
Raynham	372	11	King	Philip		1	2		1		1	1		1			7		
Raynham	372	12	Hall	Reuben		1	2		1	1	2	2		1			10		
Raynham	372	13	Hall	Hannah Wid	1							1		2			4		
Raynham	372	14	Dean	Josiah		2	4		1	1		2		1			11		
Raynham	372	15	Hall	Amos				1						2			3		
Raynham	372	16	Hall	Lewis		2		1		1				1			5		
Raynham	372	17	Jones	Nehemiah	1			1		2			1				5		
Raynham	372	18	Alden	Lois										1			1		
Raynham	372	19	Campbell	Joshua	1			1		2			1				5		
Raynham	372	20	Hall	Caleb	1			1					1				3		
Raynham	372	21	White	Rufus	3		1					1					5		
Raynham	372	22	Snow	Solomon	1	1			1		1			1			5		
Raynham	372	23	Dean	Benaiah	1	2	2		1	2	1		1				10		
Raynham	372	24	Jones	Samuel			1	1		2				1			5		
Raynham	372	25	Wilbore	Isaiah		1	1	1			1	1	1				6		
Raynham	372	26	Carver	John		1	1		1		1			1			5		
Raynham	372	27	Knap	Philip		1	1		1				1				4		
Raynham	372	28	Welbore	Meshach	2			1		2		1	1				7		
Raynham	372	29	Knap	Sarah Wid										1			1		
Raynham	372	30	Knap	Atherton		1	2		1	1		1	1				7		
Raynham	372	31	Ellis	Sarah Wid						1		1	2				4		
Raynham	372	32	Hall	Mason	1			1		2			1				5		
Raynham	372	33	Gushee	Samuel		1		1			1	1	1				5		
Raynham	372	34	Gushee	Elijah	1		2		1	1	1		1				7		
Raynham	372	35	White	Apollos	1			1		1			1				4		
Raynham	372	36	Gushee	Seth			1					2					3		
Raynham	372	37	Andrews	Reuben	1				1	2	2	1		1			8		
Raynham	372	38	White	Perez	2		1			1			1				5		
Raynham	372	39	Washburn	Nehemiah	5		1	1		1	3		1				12		
Raynham	372	40	Washburn	Israel	4	2			1		1		1				9		
Raynham	372	41	Washburn	Oliver	1			1		4	1		1				8		
Raynham	372	42	Knap	Eliab	2	1			2	1	1	1	1				9		
Raynham	372	43	Hall	Nathan				1						2			3		
Raynham	372	44	Hall	Nathan Junior				1				1		1			3		
Raynham	373	1	Hall	Job	1	1			1	1	3		1				8		
Raynham	373	2	Hall	Luther			1						1				2		
Raynham	373	3	Crosman	Gabriel	1	2			1					1			5		
Raynham	373	4	King	John Junior	1			1		1	3	3		1			10		
Raynham	373	5	Williams	John			1		1	1		1					5		
Raynham	373	6	Crosman	Elhanan	1			1				1					3		
Raynham	373	7	Andrews	Zephaniah	4	2		1					1				8		
Raynham	373	8	Hoard	David	1	1			1	2			1				6		
Raynham	373	9	Fobes	Perez				1						1			2		
Raynham	373	10	Andrews	George			1		1	1	1	1					6		
Raynham	373	11	Bryant	Lemuel			1			1			1				3		
Raynham	373	12	Noyes	Samuel	3	1		1			1		1				7		
Raynham	373	13	Richmond	Seth	1	1	1	1	1	1			1				7		
Raynham	373	14	Hacket	Asahel	3	1		1		1			1	2			9		
Raynham	373	15	Leonard	Cuff											10		10		
Raynham	373	16	French	William				1					1				2		
Raynham	373	17	Dean	Jonathan				1					1				2		
Raynham	373	18	Dean	Jonathan Junr	2	1		1					1				5		
Raynham	373	19	Dean	Job 2d	1		1		2		1	2					8		
Raynham	373	20	King	George	1				1				1				3		
Raynham	373	21	Frazier	Charles	4	1		1			1		1				8		
Raynham	373	22	Williams	Jonathan	1	1		1		2	1		1				7		
Raynham	373	23	Boodry	Joseph		1			1	2				1			5		
Raynham	373	24	Boodry	John	1			1		2			1				5		
Raynham	373	25	Williams	Macey	1			1		2			1				5		
Raynham	373	26	Williams	Abiel	1		1		1			1	1	1			6		
Raynham	373	27	Williams	Lemuel		2		1			1						4		
Raynham	373	28	Shaw	Samuel	2			1		2			1				6		
Raynham	373	29	Williams	Nathan	1				1	2	1	1		1			8		
Raynham	373	30	Leonard	Samuel 3d	1	1		1		3			1				7		
Raynham	373	31	Shaw	Joseph Junior			1		1		1		1				4		
Raynham	373	32	Shaw	Joseph				1						1			2		
Raynham	373	33	Shaw	Silas		1	1		1	1		1	1				6		
Raynham	373	34	Williams	Stephen		2		1				1		1			5		
Raynham	373	35	Hall	William				1									1		

TOWN	PG#	LN#	HEADS OF HOUSEHOLD		FREE WHITE MALES					FREE WHITE FEMALES					TOTAL ALL OTHER	TOTAL SLAVES	TOTALS	DISTRICT/ TOWNSHIP	NOTES
			LAST NAME	FIRST NAME	under 10	10 to 16	16 to 26	26 to 45	45 and over	under 10	10 to 16	16 to 26	26 to 45	45 and over					
Raynham	373	36	Warren	Thomas			1	1						1			3		
Raynham	373	37	Hall	Joseph 2d			1	1									2		
Raynham	373	38	Hall	Asa	1		1			2			1				5		
Raynham	373	39	Leonard	Simeon 2d			1			1			1				3		
Raynham	373	40	Leonard	Gamaliel				1						1			2		
Raynham	373	41	Hall	Edmund			3	1					1	1			6		
Raynham	373	42	Cain	Benjamin	1			1		2	1	2	1				8		
Raynham	373	43	Hall	Silas		1		1		1	1		1				5		
Raynham	374	1	Leonard	Eliakim	2			1		1			1				5		
Raynham	374	2	Leonard	Thomas	2			1		2	2		1				8		
Raynham	374	3	Leonard	Mary Wid			3							1			4		
Raynham	374	4	Shaw	Nathaniel		1		1				1	1	1			5		
Raynham	374	5	Hall	Abigail Wid			1	1						1			3		
Raynham	374	6	Williams	Silas	2		1			3			1				7		
Raynham	374	7	Dean	Seth			2	1		4	2	1	1				11		
Raynham	374	8	Robinson	Hendrick	1	2		1		1	1		1				7		
Raynham	374	9	Robinson	Godfrey	3		1	1		1			1				7		
Raynham	374	10	Robinson	Nathan	3	2		1		1		1	1				9		
Raynham	374	11	Robinson	Josiah	1			1		1	1	2	1				7		
Raynham	374	12	Andrews	Nathaniel Junr	1		1			2			1	1			6		
Raynham	374	13	King	Isaac	2	1	1				1		1				6		
Raynham	374	14	King	Silas	2	1	1			1			1				6		
Raynham	374	15	Dean	Thomas		1		1				1	1	1			5		
Raynham	374	16	Dean	Jonathan 3d	3		1			1	1		1				7		
Raynham	374	17	Cole	Joseph Junr		1											1		
Raynham	374	18	King	Stephen	4		1			1		1	1				8		
Raynham	374	19	Williams	Noah			1			1				2			4		
Raynham	374	20	King	John				2			2		1				5		
Raynham	374	21	Williams	George Junr	2	1	1						1				5		
Raynham	374	22	King	Nathan	2	1	2	1		2	1	1	1	1			12		
Raynham	374	23	Richmond	Ezra	1			1		1	1	1	1				6		
Raynham	374	24	Andrews	Nathan	2	1		1		1	1	2	1				9		
Raynham	374	25	Hall	Joseph			1	1			2		1				5		
Raynham	374	26	Williams	George		1	3	1	1	1		2		1			10		
Raynham	374	27	King	Barzilla			1			1			1				3		
Raynham	374	28	King	Benjamin	1		1			2		1		1			6		
Raynham	374	29	White	Samuel				1						1			2		
Raynham	374	30	White	Isaac	2		1			2		1	2				8		
Raynham	374	31	Collins	Pomp											5		5		
Raynham	374	32	Gilmore	Toby											9		9		
Raynham	374	33	Holmes	Otis	2		1					1					4		
Raynham	374	34	Washburn	Seth	1		2	1		4	1	1	1				11		
Raynham	374	35	Presho	James				1					1				2		
Raynham	374	36	Presho	Zadoc	5		1			1			2				9		
Raynham	374	37	Briant	David	1	1	1	1					1	1			6		
Raynham	374	38	Makepeace	Seth	1	1	1			2			1				6		
Raynham	374	39	Bolton	Seth				1				1		1			3		
Raynham	374	40	Holmes	John			1			1			1				3		
Raynham	374	41	Huron	Benjamin		1						1					2		
Raynham	374	42	Chamberlain	James			1	3					1				5		
Raynham	375	1	Leonard	Seth				2					2				4		
Raynham	375	2	Carter	Stanley	4		1	1		2	1		1				10		
Raynham	375	3	Leonard	Simeon	3	2				1	1		1				8		
Raynham	375	4	Andrews	John	2	3	1			2			1				9		
Raynham	375	5	Wilbore	Libus		1	2						1				4		
Raynham	375	6	Wilbore	Josiah		1	2	1				2		1			7		
Raynham	375	7	Andrews	Rufus	1			1		1	1	1		1			6		
Raynham	375	8	White	Daniel			1	1				1	1				4		
Raynham	375	9	White	Hannah Wid								1		2			3		
Raynham	375	10	White	Israel	3	1	1	1		2		1	1				10		
Raynham	375	11	Wilbore	Jacob	2			1		1	1		1				6		
Raynham	375	12	Wilbore	Adam		1							1				2		
Raynham	375	13	Hewett	Rufus	1		1			1		1					4		
Raynham	375	14	Timberlake	James	1		1						1				3		
Raynham	375	15	Crane	Henry		1		1						1			3		
Raynham	375	16	Wilbore	Simeon Junr	3			1		1		1					6		
Raynham	375	17	Presho	Sampson	2	2		1		2		1	1				9		
Raynham	375	18	Hall	Samuel		1	1						1				3		
Raynham	375	19	White	Asa	1		2	1		3	1		1				9		
Raynham	375	20	Dean	Stephen Junr	1		1			1			1	1			5		
Raynham	375	21	Leach	Asa	1	1		1		3			1				7		
Raynham	375	22	Dean	Stephen			1	1			1	2		1			6		
Raynham	375	23	Robinson	Seth	1	2		1		2	1	1	1	2			11		
Raynham	375	24	Hall	Hannah Wid	1					2	2		1				6		
Raynham	375	25	Hall	Seth	4			1		1			1				7		
Raynham	375	26	Keith	Asa	2	1	2	1				1	1				8		
Raynham	375	27	Leach	Eliphalet			1			1		1					3		
Raynham	375	28	Snow	Ebenezer Junior	2	1				1	1		1				7		
Raynham	375	29	Snow	Ebenezer				1						1			2		

TOWN	PG#	LN#	LAST NAME	FIRST NAME	FREE WHITE MALES under 10	10 to 16	16 to 26	26 to 45	45 and over	FREE WHITE FEMALES under 10	10 to 16	16 to 26	26 to 45	45 and over	TOTAL ALL OTHER	TOTAL SLAVES	TOTALS	DISTRICT/ TOWNSHIP	NOTES
Raynham	375	30	Robinson	Abishai			1			1		1					3		
Raynham	375	31	Wilbore	Samuel	4	1			1	1	1	2	1				11		
Raynham	375	32	Robinson	John	1		1		1	1	1			1			6		
Raynham	375	33	Hall	Stephen			1		1		1		1	1			5		
Raynham	375	34	Dean	Nathaniel	2	2	1	1	1			2		1			10		
Raynham	375	35	Hall	Nathaniel	1		1	1	1			1					5		
Raynham	375	36	Hewitt	Richard	1		1			1		1					4		
Raynham	375	37	Robinson	Eliab			1	1				1	1				4		
Raynham	375	38	Gilmore	John Junior		1	1	1		2		1	2				8		
Raynham	375	39	Shaw	Jonathan	1	1		1		2			1				6		
Raynham	375	40	Dean	Joseph				1					1				2		
Raynham	375	41	Dean	Joseph Junr	1	1		1		1			1				5		
Raynham	375	42	Dean	Johith		1		1		4			1				7		
Raynham	376	1	Bolton	Gamaliel			1					1					2		
Raynham	376	2	Lincoln	Ambros	2	2		1		1	1		1				8		
Raynham	376	3	Dean	Hoitstill Wid											1		1		
Raynham	376	4	Wilbore	Joseph Junior	1	1		1		2			1				6		
Raynham	376	5	Witherell	Solomon Junr			1			1		1					3		
Raynham	376	6	Shelly	Eliab		1	1		1	2			1	1			7		
Raynham	376	7	Dean	Lazell	2		1			2	1		1				7		
Raynham	376	8	Carver	Jabez	1		1		1	2	1		1				7		
Raynham	376	9	Pollard	John Junior	1		1					1					3		
Raynham	376	10	Gilmore	John	1		2	1	1	2			1				8		
Raynham	376	11	Dean	Job 2d	3	3			1	1		3		1			12		
Raynham	376	12	Wilbore	Zephaniah	1		1	1		1		2					6		
Raynham	376	13	Wilbore	Simeon		3		1		1		2		1			8		
Raynham	376	14	Howard	Molly Wid	1								1				2		
Raynham	376	15	Wilbore	Elkanah			1	1				1		1			4		
Raynham	376	16	Wilbore	Elkanah Junr			1			1			1				3		
Raynham	376	17	Wilbore	Apollos	1		1			1		1					4		
Raynham	376	18	Britten	Robert				1				1	1	2			5		
Raynham	376	19	Britten	Henry	1		2	1		1	1	1					7		
Raynham	376	20	Britten	Nathaniel	2			1		1	2	1	1				8		
Raynham	376	21	Leonard	Samuel Junr	1	1		1		2	1		1				7		
Raynham	376	22	Howard	Rufus			1						1				2		
Raynham	376	23	Smith	Ebenezer			1						1				2		
Raynham	376	24	Smith	William Junior	1			1		2	1						5		
Raynham	376	25	Simmons	Thomas	2			1			1		1				5		
Raynham	376	26	Smith	Isaac				1					1				2		
Raynham	376	27	White	Elijah				1			1	1		1			4		
Raynham	376	28	Smith	William	1	1		1		1		1		1			6		
Raynham	376	29	Wilbore	Ebenezer	1	2		1		2	1		1				8		
Raynham	376	30	Dean	Linus	3			1		1			1				6		
Raynham	376	31	Howard	William	3	2	2	1		2	1	1	1				13		
Raynham	376	32	Presho	Joseph	2			1		2	1		1				7		
Raynham	376	33	Wilbore	Zibean			1			1		1		1			4		
Raynham	376	34	Leonard	Samuel	1	1			1					1			4		
Raynham	376	35	Makepeace	William		1			1	1	1			1			5		
Raynham	376	36	Makepeace	William Junr	2		1						1				4		
Raynham	378	1	Andrews	Joseph	2		1						1				4		
Raynham	378	2	Arnold	David		1	1	1	1	1		1		1			7		
Raynham	378	3	Arnold	John	1			1	1	1		1					5		

TOWN	PG#	LN#	LAST NAME	FIRST NAME	FREE WHITE MALES under 10	10 to 16	16 to 26	26 to 45	45 and over	FREE WHITE FEMALES under 10	10 to 16	16 to 26	26 to 45	45 and over	TOTAL ALL OTHER	TOTAL SLAVES	TOTALS	DISTRICT/ TOWNSHIP	NOTES
Rehoboth	296	1	Abel	Robert			1										1		
Rehoboth	296	2	Abel	Caleb	1		1	1	3	1		1					9		
Rehoboth	296	3	Allen	Stephen	1		1	1			1	1					5		
Rehoboth	296	4	Armington	John			1			1		1					3		
Rehoboth	297	1	Armington	Asa	1				1			1					6		
Rehoboth	297	2	Armington	Walker			1					1					3		
Rehoboth	297	3	Allen	Samuel 2d	1	1		1	1	1		1					6		
Rehoboth	297	4	Allen	Oliver		1						1					3		
Rehoboth	297	5	Allen	James	1		1	1	1	1		2		1			8		
Rehoboth	297	6	Allen	Ebenezer			1			1			1				3		
Rehoboth	297	7	Allen	John			1	1			1		1				5		
Rehoboth	297	8	Allen	Abner	1			2				1	1				5		
Rehoboth	297	9	Allen	Samuel			1	1	1			1	1	1			6		
Rehoboth	297	10	Allen	Amaziah	1		1			1		1					6		
Rehoboth	297	11	Allen	George			1			2		1					5		
Rehoboth	297	12	Anthony	Abner	1		1					1					3		
Rehoboth	297	13	Adams	John Jun		3	1	1		3		1					10		
Rehoboth	297	14	Allen	Elisha			1					1					2		
Rehoboth	297	15	Allen	Deborah															Enumeration left blank
Rehoboth	297	16	Smith	Joshua			1	1		1		1					5		
Rehoboth	297	17	Smith	Samuel	1		1			1		1	1				5		
Rehoboth	297	18	Brown	John			1			1	1		1				5		
Rehoboth	298	1	Reed	Elijah A.		1	1				1						4		
Rehoboth	298	2	Bullock	Barrak	1	1	1	1		4		2					10		
Rehoboth	298	3	Bullock	Stephen	1			1		2		1	1				6		
Rehoboth	298	4	Bullock	Stephen Jr			1			1			1				4		
Rehoboth	298	5	Davis	Daniel		1	1	1		1		1					6		
Rehoboth	298	6	Davis	Daniel Jr			1		1	1							5		
Rehoboth	298	7	Bullock	Asa	1		1		3	1	1			1			9		
Rehoboth	298	8	Peck	Gideon 2d	1		1		3	1		1					9		
Rehoboth	298	9	Bullock	William			1				1		1				3		
Rehoboth	298	10	Bullock	Calvin	1	1		1		2		1					8		
Rehoboth	298	11	Bullock	Samuel	2	1	1	1				2	1	1			9		
Rehoboth	298	12	Bullock	Kent	1			1	1			2	1	1			8		
Rehoboth	298	13	Bullock	Eleazer			1			1		1					3		
Rehoboth	298	14	Miller	Philop	2	1		1				2	1				8		
Rehoboth	298	15	Martin	James	1		1					1	1	1			5		
Rehoboth	298	16	Watson	John	2	2		1				2	2				9		
Rehoboth	298	17	Barney	Benajer	1			1				1	1				4		
Rehoboth	298	18	Barney	Cyrenius		1		2		1							5		
Rehoboth	298	19	Frankton	Elisha		1		2		1							6		
Rehoboth	298	20	Wheeler	Aaron	2	1		1		1		2	1				10		
Rehoboth	298	21	Thurber	Daniel		1		1		1		2	1				6		
Rehoboth	298	22	Hale	Job	1	1		1	2				1				7		
Rehoboth	298	23	Peck	Jonathan		2		1					1				4		
Rehoboth	298	24	Peck	Jonathan Jr	1	1	1		3	1		1					9		
Rehoboth	298	25	Pears	Peleg	2	1	1			1	1		1				10		
Rehoboth	298	26	Cole	Nehemiah	1	1		1	1				1				6		
Rehoboth	298	27	Bosworth	Peleg	1	3		1		1			1				7		
Rehoboth	298	28	Pears	Isaac	1		1		3	1	1	1	1				12		
Rehoboth	298	29	Horton	Willm			1	1					1				4		
Rehoboth	298	30	Case	Gardner		1	1		3	1		1					8		
Rehoboth	298	31	Baker	James	1		1						2				6		
Rehoboth	298	32	Baker	Nathaniel		1		1		1			1				4		
Rehoboth	298	33	Ingals	Hezekiah	1	1		1		5		1					9		
Rehoboth	298	34	Carpenter	Peter	1	1		1			1	1					5		
Rehoboth	298	35	Tucker	Joshua			1		4			1					6		
Rehoboth	298	36	Fuller	Giberd			1	1				1					4		
Rehoboth	298	37	Beers	Mary									1				1		
Rehoboth	298	38	Whitaker	Daniel			1						2				3		
Rehoboth	298	39	Whiaker	Margret									3				3		
Rehoboth	298	40	Lake	Laben	1	2		1		1	1		1				9		
Rehoboth	298	41	Lindsey	Benjamin	1			1	1	2		1					8		
Rehoboth	298	42	Peck	Phillip	1	1	1	1		1	3		1				9		
Rehoboth	298	43	Wheaton	Jonathan	1		1			2		1					8		
Rehoboth	298	44	Bliss	James	1	1	1		2	2	1		1				11		
Rehoboth	298	45	French	Elkanah	1	2	1		4	2	1						13		
Rehoboth	299	1	Bullock	Aaron	2	1		1	1			1	1				8		
Rehoboth	299	2	Bullock	Ebenezer		1		1		1	1	1	1				7		
Rehoboth	299	3	Hix	Hezekiah		1	1	1	1	1		1					7		
Rehoboth	299	4	Bliss	Nathaniel			1	2				1	1				5		
Rehoboth	299	5	Sprague	Samuel		1	1		1	1	2		3				9		
Rehoboth	299	6	Wheaton	Lewis	1	1	1		5		1	1					11		
Rehoboth	299	7	Bliss	Lydia	1	2					2		1				7		
Rehoboth	299	8	Bliss	James 2nd	2		1		2	1		1					7		
Rehoboth	299	9	Bliss	Asahel	1		1	1	1		1	1					7		
Rehoboth	299	10	Bliss	Ephraim			1						1				2		
Rehoboth	299	11	Bliss	Obediah			1		1			1					4		
Rehoboth	299	12	Bliss	Charles			1		1	1		1					5		
Rehoboth	299	13	Goff	Nathan	1		1			1	1		1				5		

TOWN	PG#	LN#	LAST NAME	FIRST NAME	FREE WHITE MALES under 10	10 to 16	16 to 26	26 to 45	45 and over	FREE WHITE FEMALES under 10	10 to 16	16 to 26	26 to 45	45 and over	TOTAL ALL OTHER	TOTAL SLAVES	TOTALS	DISTRICT/TOWNSHIP	NOTES
Rehoboth	299	14	Peck	Mary				1					1			2			
Rehoboth	299	15	Peck	Elemuel			1					1				2			
Rehoboth	299	16	Hix	Azariah		1	1					1	2			5			
Rehoboth	299	17	Brown	John 3rd			1	2		1			1			4			
Rehoboth	299	18	Hix	Jotham	1	1		1		1			1			5			
Rehoboth	299	19	Pears	Stephen		1		1		1			1			4			
Rehoboth	299	20	Bliss	Samuel		1	1			1	1					4			
Rehoboth	299	21	Smith	John		1		1		1			1			4			
Rehoboth	299	22	Rounds	Esther		1				1	1	1				4			
Rehoboth	299	23	Carpenter	Stephen	1	1	1		2	1			1			9			
Rehoboth	299	24	Carpenter	Thomas	1		1			1			1			6			
Rehoboth	299	25	Horton	Abial	1	1		1	1	1			1			6			
Rehoboth	299	26	Peck	Gideon 2d			1	1					1			4			
Rehoboth	299	27	Peck	Ambrose			1			1			1			3			
Rehoboth	299	28	Carpenter	Abel		1	1	1		1			1			7			
Rehoboth	299	29	Lawton	Sebray			1	1				1	1	1		8			
Rehoboth	299	30	Carpenter	James	1		1	4				1	1			8			
Rehoboth	299	31	Blanding	William	1	1	1	1		2	1		1			10			
Rehoboth	299	32	Carpenter	Christopher		1	1			1		2				6			
Rehoboth	299	33	Carpenter	Amy								1	1			2			
Rehoboth	299	34	Jones	John			1			1			1			3			
Rehoboth	299	35	Lawton	Thomas			1	2					1			5			
Rehoboth	299	36	Servis	Reuben			1						1			3			
Rehoboth	299	37	Field	John			1	1					1			4			
Rehoboth	299	38	Bliss	Nathan	1	1		1		1			1			5			
Rehoboth	299	39	Bliss	Abel 2nd	1		1						1			3			
Rehoboth	299	40	King	Robert	1	1		1			2		1			8			
Rehoboth	299	41	Woodmansie	Squire			1	1					1			3			
Rehoboth	299	42	Woodmansie	Eleazer		1		2				1				8			
Rehoboth	299	43	Carpenter	Thomas		1	1						1			3			
Rehoboth	299	44	Carpenter	Ebenezer		1						1				3			
Rehoboth	299	45	Wheeler	Jeremiah Jr	1	1		1			2		1			7			
Rehoboth	299	46	Salsburg	William		1		2				1				5			
Rehoboth	300	1	Goff	Lovel		1		1		1			1			5			
Rehoboth	300	2	Gooff	James	1		1		1			1	1			8			
Rehoboth	300	3	Goff	Amos	1	1		1		1	1		1			6			
Rehoboth	300	4	Goff	Charles			1			2		1				4			
Rehoboth	300	5	Goff	Squire			1						1			2			
Rehoboth	300	6	Horton	Nathan		1		1				1	1			5			
Rehoboth	300	7	Goff	Samuel	1		1	2		1			1	1		11			
Rehoboth	300	8	Horton	Shubel			1			1			1			5			
Rehoboth	300	9	Goff	Levi Junior			1	2					1			4			
Rehoboth	300	10	Boroen	Nathan	2		1	3		1			1			12			
Rehoboth	300	11	Walker	Phillip	1	1		1		1	1		2			8			
Rehoboth	300	12	Hilton	Edward	1		1			1			1			5			
Rehoboth	300	13	Nash	Jonathan		1		1					1			4			
Rehoboth	300	14	Brown	Abel		1	1		3		1	1				7			
Rehoboth	300	15	Brown	David		1	1						1	1		4			
Rehoboth	300	16	Brown	James		1		1				1		1		5			
Rehoboth	300	17	Drown	Roial		1	1		1				1			6			
Rehoboth	300	18	Drown	Nathaniel		1		1		1		1	1			6			
Rehoboth	300	19	Drown	Jesse			1				1					3			
Rehoboth	300	20	Pidge	Benjamin	2	3		1	1	1	1	1	2			12			
Rehoboth	300	21	Hunt	Simeon			2	1		1	1	1	1			7			
Rehoboth	300	22	Turner	Nathan		1						2				3			
Rehoboth	300	23	Cushon	David		1		1		1			1			4			
Rehoboth	300	24	Turner	Amos		1		1		1			1			4			
Rehoboth	300	25	Lewis	Daniel		1						1	1			4			
Rehoboth	300	26	Francis	John		1						1				4			
Rehoboth	300	27	Lindsey	John	2	1		1		1	1		1			9			
Rehoboth	300	28	Carpenter	Obediah	2	1		1	3	1	1	1	1			13			
Rehoboth	300	29	Bliss	Samuel			1	1					1			3			
Rehoboth	300	30	Medbury	Abel		1				1			1			5			
Rehoboth	300	31	Lyon	Aaron			2			1			1			4			
Rehoboth	300	32	Lyon	William		1							1			2			
Rehoboth	300	33	Medbury	Ebenezer	2		1	1	2				1			8			
Rehoboth	300	34	Perry	Noah	1	3		1				1	2			8			
Rehoboth	300	35	Allen	Deborah						1			2			3			
Rehoboth	300	36	Allen	Elizabeth		1			1	1		1				5			
Rehoboth	300	37	Lyon	Samuel		1		1		1	1		1			6			
Rehoboth	300	38	Robinson	Noah															Enumeration left blank
Rehoboth	300	39	Willmarth	Daniel	1	1		1	1		4		1			12			
Rehoboth	300	40	Wheaton	Joseph	1	1		1		1			1			7			
Rehoboth	300	41	Lane	Amos		2		1			1	1	1			6			
Rehoboth	300	42	Blanding	Christopher	1	1		1	1		1	1				11			
Rehoboth	300	43	Bliss	Oliver		2		1		1	2	1				7			
Rehoboth	300	44	Fairbrother	William	1	2		1	2	1			1			8			
Rehoboth	300	45	Carpenter	Thomas 2d	1						2	1	1			6			
Rehoboth	300	46	Carpenter	Peter 2d	2	1			1	1						6			
Rehoboth	301	1	Carpenter	Samuel	1			1	1			1				5			

TOWN	PG#	LN#	LAST NAME	FIRST NAME	FREE WHITE MALES under 10	10 to 16	16 to 26	26 to 45	45 and over	FREE WHITE FEMALES under 10	10 to 16	16 to 26	26 to 45	45 and over	TOTAL ALL OTHER	TOTAL SLAVES	TOTALS	DISTRICT/ TOWNSHIP	NOTES
Rehoboth	301	2	Gooff	Richard	1			1		1		1					7		
Rehoboth	301	3	Gooff	Joseph				1		1			1	1			4		
Rehoboth	301	4	Gooff	Joseph Jr			1					1					2		
Rehoboth	301	5	Perry	Joseph		1	1			1		1					5		
Rehoboth	301	6	Palmer	John			1	1				1					4		
Rehoboth	301	7	Carpenter	Elizabeth		1	1			2			1				5		
Rehoboth	301	8	Carpenter	Caleb	1		1	2		1	1		1				7		
Rehoboth	301	9	Wheeler	Huldah	1			1					1				5		
Rehoboth	301	10	Goff	Squire			1	3		2			1				8		
Rehoboth	301	11	Goff	Levi Junior		1	1	1	1		2	1	1				9		
Rehoboth	301	12	Pettis	Ezekiel		1		1	1				1				5		
Rehoboth	301	13	Wheeler	Samuel			1						1				4		
Rehoboth	301	14	Goff	Aaron	2			1	1				1				5		
Rehoboth	301	15	Goff	Abel	2		1		1	1	1						7		
Rehoboth	301	16	Marker	Burden			1	1		1	1	1					7		
Rehoboth	301	17	Vicory	Robert	2		1		2	1		1					8		
Rehoboth	301	18	Davis	Barney				1		1			1				3		
Rehoboth	301	19	Fisher	Ana	1								1				2		
Rehoboth	301	20	Marker	John			1			2		1					4		
Rehoboth	301	21	Marker	John Jun			1		2			1					6		
Rehoboth	301	22	Bliss	Asa	1	1	1		3	2		1					11		
Rehoboth	301	23	Rogerson	John	1		1		1			1					5		
Rehoboth	301	24	Pears	James				1			1						6		
Rehoboth	301	25	Webber	John				1		2	1		1				6		
Rehoboth	301	26	Webber	James			1			1							4		
Rehoboth	301	27	Martin	George W.		1		1		1		1					6		
Rehoboth	301	28	Peck	Samuel	1		1	1		1		1					5		
Rehoboth	301	29	Peck	George		1	1	3				1					6		
Rehoboth	301	30	Martin	Calvin		1	1	3				1					7		
Rehoboth	301	31	Martin	Valentine		1		1	2			1					5		
Rehoboth	301	32	Martin	Valentine Jr		1					1	1					4		
Rehoboth	301	33	Martin	Sylvenus		1						1					2		
Rehoboth	301	34	Peck	Allen		2	1	1	1	2		1					9		
Rehoboth	301	35	Lake	Elethean	1			1		1			1				6		
Rehoboth	301	36	Peck	Joseph			1					1					5		
Rehoboth	301	37	Ornsbee	Benjamin			1		1			1					3		
Rehoboth	301	38	Chaffe	Samuel				1			1	2	1				6		
Rehoboth	301	39	Ornsbee	Abraham		1		1			1		1				4		
Rehoboth	301	40	Goff	Constant	1		1		1			1					5		
Rehoboth	301	41	Horton	Daniel	1	1		1	2	1	1						8		
Rehoboth	301	42	Horton	Constant				1			1		1				3		
Rehoboth	301	43	Horton	Aaron			1				1						3		
Rehoboth	301	44	Goff	Asa	2	1		1		1		1					7		
Rehoboth	301	45	Pears	Nathaniel	1			1	1								3		
Rehoboth	301	46	Pears	Nathan		1				1							3		
Rehoboth	302	1	Wheaton	Joseph	1			1	2	2	2	1	1				11		
Rehoboth	302	2	Goff	Israle			1		2	1		1					7		
Rehoboth	302	3	Cambel	Rode									1				1		
Rehoboth	302	4	Millard	Josiah			1				1						2		
Rehoboth	302	5	Martin	Marther									1				1		
Rehoboth	302	6	Dagget	Timothy		1		1					1				3		
Rehoboth	302	7	Dagget	James			1						1				6		
Rehoboth	302	8	Bullock	Benjamin	1			1	2	1	1						8		
Rehoboth	302	9	Fuller	Timothy	1			1	3			1	2				9		
Rehoboth	302	10	Allen	Comfort	2						1						4		
Rehoboth	302	11	Allen	Isaiah	1			1	1	1		1					6		
Rehoboth	302	12	Kent	Ezekel		1	1	1		1	2		1				7		
Rehoboth	302	13	Bliss	Abiah				1				1	1				3		
Rehoboth	302	14	Bliss	Abiah Junr	1	1	2		4	1		1					11		
Rehoboth	302	15	Bliss	Abel	1	1	1		3	1		1					9		
Rehoboth	302	16	Bliss	Noah	1	1		1			1		1				6		
Rehoboth	302	17	Turner	Ephraim	2			1			1	1	1				6		
Rehoboth	302	18	Bliss	Jacob	2		1	1			2	1	3				10		
Rehoboth	302	19	Bowen	Uriah				1			2		1				4		
Rehoboth	302	20	Bowen	Ephraim		1		1		1							4		
Rehoboth	302	21	Bowen	Benjamin		1		2		1							3		
Rehoboth	302	22	Turner	William		1		2				1					5		
Rehoboth	302	23	Pears	Ebenezer		2		2		2		1					9		
Rehoboth	302	24	Baldwin	Nathan			1	1		1	1						6		
Rehoboth	302	25	Hix	Nathan 2	2	1	1		1	1			1				11		
Rehoboth	302	26	Wheeler	Comfort	3		1						1				6		
Rehoboth	302	27	Wheeler	Nathan				1	2				1				5		
Rehoboth	302	28	Wheeler	Mason			1			1	1		1				4		
Rehoboth	302	29	Cole	Simeon	1	1		2	2	1	1	1	1				11		
Rehoboth	302	30	Peck	Ebenzer 2nd		1	1	2		1							6		
Rehoboth	302	31	Millard	Spice		1	1	1		1	1	1	1				7		
Rehoboth	302	32	Millard	Aaron		1	1			1		1					7		
Rehoboth	302	33	Peckam	Aaron	2		1	1		1	2	1	1				14		
Rehoboth	302	34	Bowen	John		1		1			1	1					5		

| TOWN | PG# | LN# | LAST NAME | FIRST NAME | FREE WHITE MALES | | | | | FREE WHITE FEMALES | | | | | TOTAL ALL OTHER | TOTAL SLAVES | TOTALS | DISTRICT/ TOWNSHIP | NOTES |
					under 10	10 to 16	16 to 26	26 to 45	45 and over	under 10	10 to 16	16 to 26	26 to 45	45 and over					
Rehoboth	302	35	Pears	Samuel	2		1		1				1				8		
Rehoboth	302	36	Cole	Otis			1		2			1					5		
Rehoboth	302	37	Perry	Jesse		3		1	1	2	1		1				9		
Rehoboth	302	38	Fuller	Jesse			1	2	2				1				7		
Rehoboth	302	39	Fuller	Nathaniel	1			1		1	1	2	2				8		
Rehoboth	302	40	Rounds	James			1		3				1				5		
Rehoboth	302	41	Horton	Nathan	1		1		1	1		1	1				9		
Rehoboth	302	42	Horton	James		2		1		1	1	1	1				7		
Rehoboth	302	43	Whiting	William	1		1		2	1		1					7		
Rehoboth	302	44	Millard	Hezekiah		1	1						1				3		
Rehoboth	302	45	Miller	Nathaniel	2	1	1					1					7		
Rehoboth	302	46	Horton	Joseph		3	1	1	2			1	1	2			11		
Rehoboth	303	1	Kingsley	David		2		1				1	2	1			7		
Rehoboth	303	2	Pears	Israel	2		1		1	2	1						8		
Rehoboth	303	3	Martin	Ephraim	2	1	1		2	1		2					11		
Rehoboth	303	4	Marten	Hezekiah	2	2		1		1	2	1	1				11		
Rehoboth	303	5	Round	Nathaniel			1		2	2	1	1					8		
Rehoboth	303	6	Bowen	Ephraim	1		1	1	1	1	1						7		
Rehoboth	303	7	Round	Marten	1			1			2		1				5		
Rehoboth	303	8	Round	Chase	1			1		3	2		1				9		
Rehoboth	303	9	Round	John			2		1			1	1				8		
Rehoboth	303	10	Round	Amos				1					1				3		
Rehoboth	303	11	Horton	Eliphlet		1		2				1					6		
Rehoboth	303	12	Hix	Stephen	1			1	1	1	2	1					10		
Rehoboth	303	13	Pearse	Joshua		1		2	1	2	2		3				12		
Rehoboth	303	14	Pearse	Leonard		1			1			1					4		
Rehoboth	303	15	Pearse	Barnard	2		1		1			1					6		
Rehoboth	303	16	Perry	William			1			1		2		1			5		
Rehoboth	303	17	Round	Georg	2		1	2				1					6		
Rehoboth	303	18	Baker	Joseph	1			1		2	1	1	1				7		
Rehoboth	303	19	Baker	James	1		1						1				5		
Rehoboth	303	20	Baker	Nathaniel		1		1		1			1	1			5		
Rehoboth	303	21	Pears	Preserved	1		1		2	3		1					10		
Rehoboth	303	22	Bosworth	Ichabod	1			1	1				1				4		
Rehoboth	303	23	Bosworth	Ichabod Jr	1		1		1	1							4		
Rehoboth	303	24	Pears	Joseph	1	1		1	1	2	2	1					11		
Rehoboth	303	25	Goff	Amos	1			1			2		1				5		
Rehoboth	303	26	Barton	Hail	2	1		1		1	3		1				9		
Rehoboth	303	27	Pears	Nathaniel 2nd	1		1		1	1		1					7		
Rehoboth	303	28	Mason	Joseph	1			1	1	2	1		1				10		
Rehoboth	303	29	Pears	Henery	1			1	1	1	2		1				8		
Rehoboth	303	30	Marbel	Stephen				1			2	1	2				6		
Rehoboth	303	31	Case	Joseph	2	1	1		4		2	1					11		
Rehoboth	303	32	Kilton	Nathaniel				1					1				2		
Rehoboth	303	33	Kilton	John 2nd	1	1	1		1	2	1		1				8		
Rehoboth	303	34	Simmons	Thomas				1			1		1				3		
Rehoboth	303	35	Simmons	Comfort	1	1	1		3	2	1	1					11		
Rehoboth	303	36	Horton	Thomas		1	1	1		1		1					6		
Rehoboth	303	37	Baker	Joseph Jr		1			2		1						4		
Rehoboth	303	38	Mason	Avis		2						1					3		
Rehoboth	303	39	Lee	Israel			1				1						4		
Rehoboth	303	40	Horton	William 3rd			1				1						2		
Rehoboth	303	41	Baker	Phebe						1		1					5		
Rehoboth	303	42	Horton	William	1			1	1		1		2				7		
Rehoboth	303	43	Gardner	James	1	1		1	1	1	2		1				9		
Rehoboth	303	44	Cole	Constant	2	1		1		1	2		1				9		
Rehoboth	304	1	Goff	Nathaniel	1			1					1				4		
Rehoboth	304	2	Miller	William			1			1		1					3		
Rehoboth	304	3	Bowen	Jeremiah			1		1			1					3		
Rehoboth	304	4	Edson	Nathan			1	1		2		1					6		
Rehoboth	304	5	Peck	Josiah			1				1	1	1				4		
Rehoboth	304	6	Peck	Josiah Jr		1		1				1					4		
Rehoboth	304	7	Baker	Jeremiah			1				1		1				3		
Rehoboth	304	8	Baker	Lewin		2	1				1						5		
Rehoboth	304	9	Barns	John	2		1		1	1		1					8		
Rehoboth	304	10	Wood	John 2nd			1				1		1				4		
Rehoboth	304	11	Wheeler	Cyrel			1		3			1					7		
Rehoboth	304	12	Grant	Thomas	1	1		1			2		1				6		
Rehoboth	304	13	Peck	Nicholas		3		1					1				5		
Rehoboth	304	14	Barney	Christopher		1		1					1				3		
Rehoboth	304	15	Barney	Caleb		1			1	1							4		
Rehoboth	304	16	Barney	William			1		1			1					3		
Rehoboth	304	17	Thurber	Leonard			1			1			1				3		
Rehoboth	304	18	Thurber	Benjamin			1		1			1	1				6		
Rehoboth	304	19	Thurber	David			1		3			1					6		
Rehoboth	304	20	Thurber	Reuben			1		1			1					4		
Rehoboth	304	21	Thurber	James 2nd		1					1						2		
Rehoboth	304	22	Threeshear	Aaron	1		1			1		1					8		
Rehoboth	304	23	Threeshear	Barnabas			1		1	1	1		1				4		
Rehoboth	304	24	Bullock	Richard	1		1	1	1		1		1				7		

TOWN	PG#	LN#	LAST NAME	FIRST NAME	FREE WHITE MALES under 10	10 to 16	16 to 26	26 to 45	45 and over	FREE WHITE FEMALES under 10	10 to 16	16 to 26	26 to 45	45 and over	TOTAL ALL OTHER	TOTAL SLAVES	TOTALS	DISTRICT/ TOWNSHIP	NOTES
Rehoboth	304	25	Campbell	Sylvanus			1		1	1							5		
Rehoboth	304	26	Mason	Elisha	2	1	1	1	3	1		1	1				14		
Rehoboth	304	27	Simmons	Edward		1	1	1			2		1				8		
Rehoboth	304	28	Miller	Samuel				1	2	1		1					8		
Rehoboth	304	29	Miller	Samuel 2nd		1		1			1		1				4		
Rehoboth	304	30	Nichols	Israel		1		1			1		1				4		
Rehoboth	304	31	Nichols	Israel Jun		1	1				1						6		
Rehoboth	304	32	Ingals	Elkanah	1	1		1		1		1	1				6		
Rehoboth	304	33	Nichols	Joseph	1		1				1						3		
Rehoboth	304	34	Hix	Nathan	2		1	2		2			1				8		
Rehoboth	304	35	Baker	Samuel	1	2	1			1	1	1					7		
Rehoboth	304	36	Bosworth	Amos		3		1		1			1				6		
Rehoboth	304	37	Horten	Volentine				1					1				3		
Rehoboth	304	38	Hix	Jacob				1			1		1				4		
Rehoboth	304	39	Bullock	Abel		1		1			1						4		
Rehoboth	304	40	Wheeler	Rusel	1		1		1	1							4		
Rehoboth	304	41	Moulton	William	1		1	2		1		1					7		
Rehoboth	304	42	Horton	Comfort		2		1	1	2	1		1				9		
Rehoboth	304	43	Horton	Job	1	1		1					1				4		
Rehoboth	304	44	Hilton	John				1			1		1				4		
Rehoboth	304	45	Pears	Joseph 2d	1		1		1			1	1				7		
Rehoboth	305	1	Pears	John		1	2			1	1	1					7		
Rehoboth	305	2	Bowen	Amy									1				2		
Rehoboth	305	3	Pears	Comfort		1			1		1						6		
Rehoboth	305	4	Pearse	Noah			1	1	1		1						5		
Rehoboth	305	5	Pearse	Squeir	1		1		3	2	1						9		
Rehoboth	305	6	Bullock	Jabez	3	1	1				1	1					7		
Rehoboth	305	7	Bowen	Marten				1	2		1						6		
Rehoboth	305	8	Knap	Seth	1		1	1	1	1		1					6		
Rehoboth	305	9	Follet	Robert			1		1		1						5		
Rehoboth	305	10	Numan	Samuel		1		1		1		1					4		
Rehoboth	305	11	Numan	David		1		2			1						4		
Rehoboth	305	12	Numan	Daniel		1		2			1						5		
Rehoboth	305	13	Davison	William		1					1						3		
Rehoboth	305	14	Davis	William	2	1		4		1		1					10		
Rehoboth	305	15	Round	Nathaniel	1		1			1		1					4		
Rehoboth	305	16	Allen	Jonathan	2	2		1	1	2		1					10		
Rehoboth	305	17	Brayton	David	2		1		1	1	1	1					9		
Rehoboth	305	18	Thurber	Nathaniel		1		2	2		1	1					8		
Rehoboth	305	19	Franklin	Daniel		1		1			1						6		
Rehoboth	305	20	Burr	Nathaniel		1	1	1		1	2	1	1				8		
Rehoboth	305	21	Burr	Elisha		1	1				1						3		
Rehoboth	305	22	Ormsbee	Daniel		1		1		2	1	1					7		
Rehoboth	305	23	West	Amost	1	2		1	1	2		1					8		
Rehoboth	305	24	Goff	Sylvester		1		3			1						7		
Rehoboth	305	25	West	Henery	1		1				1						3		
Rehoboth	305	26	West	Benjamin		1		2	1		1						6		
Rehoboth	305	27	Millard	Jacob		1	1	1			1						4		
Rehoboth	305	28	Horton	Conten	1	1			1	1		1					5		
Rehoboth	305	29	Martin	Edward	1		1					2					4		
Rehoboth	305	30	Marten	Hail		1		2			1						7		
Rehoboth	305	31	Short	Ebenzer		1		1	1		1						5		
Rehoboth	305	32	Miller	John		1		1			2	1					5		
Rehoboth	305	33	Pears	Richard				1			1	1	1	1			5		
Rehoboth	305	34	Pears	Robert		1			1		1						3		
Rehoboth	305	35	Wheeler	Jeremiah		2		1			1		1				5		
Rehoboth	305	36	Weber	Nathaniel	1			1			1		1				7		
Rehoboth	305	37	Wheeler	Jarvis			1		3		1						5		
Rehoboth	305	38	Drown	Frederic	1			1	1		2		1				7		
Rehoboth	305	39	Drown	Jonathan				1			1		1				3		
Rehoboth	305	40	Crowell	James	1			1		1	2		1				6		
Rehoboth	305	41	Moulton	Chase		1	1		2		1	1					8		
Rehoboth	305	42	Smith	Joseph		1	1				1						4		
Rehoboth	305	43	Bliss	Joseph	1	1		1			1	2	1				7		
Rehoboth	305	44	Whitaker	Noah	1	3		1			2		1				8		
Rehoboth	305	45	Weber	Richard	1	1		1	1	1		1		1			7		
Rehoboth	305	46	Wheeler	William		1		1				1					6		
Rehoboth	306	1	Burr	Isaac	1	1		1	1	1			1				6		
Rehoboth	306	2	Burr	Cromwel		1	1	1		1							4		
Rehoboth	306	3	Fowler	Isaac		1	1	1			1	1					8		
Rehoboth	306	4	Right	Joseph	1			1		2	1	1					6		
Rehoboth	306	5	Engals	Edmun		3		1			1		1				6		
Rehoboth	306	6	Moulton	Stephen	2	2	1			1		1					8		
Rehoboth	306	7	Forbs	Daniel	1			1		2			1				6		
Rehoboth	306	8	Woodward	Samuel Jr		1		1					1				3		
Rehoboth	306	9	Mason	John	1			1	2	2	1						7		
Rehoboth	306	10	Ormsbee	Luis	2		1			1		1					8		
Rehoboth	306	11	Bliss	Abedial	1				3	2		1					11		
Rehoboth	306	12	Bullock	James		1	1	1				1	1				5		
Rehoboth	306	13	Bowen	Stephen			1		2			1	1				7		
Rehoboth	306	14	Blacington	Samuel	1	1	2		1		1		1				7		
Rehoboth	306	15	Burt	Rufus	1		1			1		1					7		
Rehoboth	306	16	Bliss	John	1	2		1			1		1				10		
Rehoboth	306	17	Cole	Simeon															Enumeration left blank
Rehoboth	306	18	Cole	Aaron	1	2		1	1		1	1					12		
Rehoboth	306	19	Cole	Amos			1						1				2		
Rehoboth	306	20	Carpenter	John			1						1				2		
Rehoboth	306	21	Carpenter	Thomas	1		1		2	1	2	1					9		
Rehoboth	306	22	Carpenter	Thoms 2nd															Crossed out

TOWN	PG#	LN#	LAST NAME	FIRST NAME	FREE WHITE MALES under 10	10 to 16	16 to 26	26 to 45	45 and over	FREE WHITE FEMALES under 10	10 to 16	16 to 26	26 to 45	45 and over	TOTAL ALL OTHER	TOTAL SLAVES	TOTALS	DISTRICT/ TOWNSHIP	NOTES
Rehoboth	306	23	Conant	Timothy		2		1		2	1	1					9		
Rehoboth	306	24	Darby	Abner			1	3			1						6		
Rehoboth	306	25	Darby	John			1										1		
Rehoboth	306	26	Davis	Joseph	1	2		1			1		1				7		
Rehoboth	306	27	Glading	James			1			1		1	1				8		
Rehoboth	306	28	Gladinig	William			1	2			1						5		
Rehoboth	306	29	Goff	Levi															Enumeration left blank
Rehoboth	306	30	Goff	Squier Jr															Enumeration left blank
Rehoboth	306	31	Haskins	John	2	3		1			1		1				9		
Rehoboth	306	32	Hix	Nathan 2nd	2	1	1	1	1		1						11		
Rehoboth	306	33	Horten	Barnard		1		1		1	2		1				6		
Rehoboth	306	34	Kent	Joseph	2			1			1		1				5		
Rehoboth	306	35	Hix	Jotham 2nd			1				1						2		
Rehoboth	306	36	Kent	Ezkiel			1			1			1				3		
Rehoboth	306	37	Munro	Benjamin		2	1	1	1				1				6		
Rehoboth	306	38	Martin	Daniel		1		1				1					4		
Rehoboth	306	39	Perry	Timothy			1		1		1	1	1				5		
Rehoboth	306	40	Perry	Josial		2		1	1	2	1		1				8		
Rehoboth	306	41	Peck	Oliver	2		1	1				1	1				9		
Rehoboth	306	42	Peck	James	1			1	1	1		1					7		
Rehoboth	306	43	Pettis	Ezekiel		1		1	1				1				5		
Rehoboth	306	44	Peck	Jethnial		1	1	1				1	1				5		
Rehoboth	306	45	Perry	Ezra		2		1	1	2	2		1				9		
Rehoboth	306	46	Perry	Ezra Jr	1		1		1	1		1					8		
Rehoboth	307	1	Turner	Judah							1		1				2		
Rehoboth	307	2	Round	Jabez		3		1			1	1	1				7		
Rehoboth	307	3	Round	Sylvester	1	1	1		3	2	1	1					11		
Rehoboth	307	4	Round	Simeon	1	2		1	1		1	1	1				9		
Rehoboth	307	5	Round	Lane		1			1		2		1				5		
Rehoboth	307	6	Round	Abner			1	1		1							4		
Rehoboth	307	7	Smith	John		2	1		1	1		1	1				8		
Rehoboth	307	8	Reed	Sarrah & Huldah									2				2		
Rehoboth	307	9	Bucklin	Joseph	1	1		1			2		1				6		
Rehoboth	307	10	Bucklin	Barrak		1					1	1					4		
Rehoboth	307	11	Bucklin	Joseph 2nd		1				1	2	1					6		
Rehoboth	307	12	Bois	George			1					1					5		
Rehoboth	307	13	Bucklin	James 2nd			1					1					2		
Rehoboth	307	14	Bowen	Noah	1			1	2	1		1					8		
Rehoboth	307	15	Carpenter	Ezeikel															Crossed out
Rehoboth	307	16	Starkweather	Ephraim			1						1				2		
Rehoboth	307	17	Starkweather	Oliver	1		1			1		1					6		
Rehoboth	307	18	Black	Eliphalet		1		1				1	1				5		
Rehoboth	307	19	Sabin	Dolly			1	1		1	1	3					7		
Rehoboth	307	20	Kenedy	David	1		1	1				1					4		
Rehoboth	307	21	Goff	Caleb			1			2	1		1				6		
Rehoboth	307	22	Bowers	Sylvester Jr		1					3						5		
Rehoboth	307	23	Bowers	Edward	1	1		3		1		1					7		
Rehoboth	307	24	Bowers	Asa		1		2				1					5		
Rehoboth	307	25	Jenks	Levi		1		3		2		1					9		
Rehoboth	307	26	Carpenter	Elihu		1				1							3		
Rehoboth	307	27	Brown	Samuel		1		1					2				6		
Rehoboth	307	28	Brown	John 2nd	1	2		1	1	1	3		1				11		
Rehoboth	307	29	Bourn	Stephen	1	2		1	3	2	1	1					11		
Rehoboth	307	30	Bliss	Jacob Jr															Enumeration left blank
Rehoboth	307	31	Peck	Henery		2	1	1		2	1		1				8		
Rehoboth	307	32	Bowen	Eleazer	3			1	2			1					7		
Rehoboth	307	33	Bowen	Numan			1		3			1					6		
Rehoboth	307	34	Carpenter	Caleb 2nd		1	1	1		1	1		1				6		
Rehoboth	307	35	Carpenter	Elihu	2			1		1	1	1					11		
Rehoboth	307	36	Carpenter	Benjamin	1	2		1			1		1				10		
Rehoboth	307	37	Carpenter	Mary		3			2	2			1				8		
Rehoboth	307	38	Cushin	Josiah	2			1		1	1		1				6		
Rehoboth	307	39	Cushin	Jacob	2	1		1		1	2		1				9		
Rehoboth	307	40	Cooper	David	1	1	1		3	3	1	1	1				13		
Rehoboth	307	41	French	Elkanah	1		1			1			1				4		
Rehoboth	307	42	Dagget	Jacob	1		2		2			1	1				10		
Rehoboth	307	43	French	Abel	1		1		3	1			1				10		
Rehoboth	307	44	French	James	1	1		1		1	1	1	1				7		
Rehoboth	307	45	French	John	2		1	1		1	1		1				8		
Rehoboth	307	46	Ide	Mary							2		1				4		
Rehoboth	308	1	Jacobs	Calvin	1		1	1		1			2				6		
Rehoboth	308	2	Medbury	Ebenezer			1										2		
Rehoboth	308	3	Medbury	Ebenezer 2nd	3		1		2			1					7		
Rehoboth	308	4	Numan	David 2nd		2	1					1					6		
Rehoboth	308	5	Ormsbee	Abraham Jr		1	1		2	2		1					9		
Rehoboth	308	6	Perren	Daniel		1		1				1					4		
Rehoboth	308	7	Perren	Zepheriah Sen		1	1	3			1	1					7		
Rehoboth	308	8	Chaffe	Shubel			1			1			1				3		
Rehoboth	308	9	Peck	Marry									1				1		
Rehoboth	308	10	Robinson	Rachel						1			1				2		
Rehoboth	308	11	Reed	Nathan			1			1	3						6		
Rehoboth	308	12	Reed	Nathaniel	2		1		3	1	1	1					9		
Rehoboth	308	13	Sabin	William		1		1			1		1				4		
Rehoboth	308	14	Shory	Abel 2nd			1		1	2		1					7		
Rehoboth	308	15	Tittas	Comfort	1		1			1			1				4		
Rehoboth	308	16	Walker	Luis	2		1		2		1	1					8		
Rehoboth	308	17	Walker	Ephraim	1	1		1		1	1	1	1				8		
Rehoboth	308	18	Walker	Moses	1						1	2					6		
Rehoboth	308	19	Walker	Moses 2nd		1	1		3		1	1					10		
Rehoboth	308	20	Walker	Richard 2nd															Enumeration left blank

TOWN	PG#	LN#	LAST NAME	FIRST NAME	M under 10	M 10 to 16	M 16 to 26	M 26 to 45	M 45 and over	F under 10	F 10 to 16	F 16 to 26	F 26 to 45	F 45 and over	TOTAL ALL OTHER	TOTAL SLAVES	TOTALS	DISTRICT/ TOWNSHIP	NOTES
Rehoboth	308	21	Whitaker	Peter	2			1	1	1			1			8			
Rehoboth	308	22	Carpenter	Caleb		1	1	1		1	1		1			6			
Rehoboth	308	23	Brown	Samuel Jr		2	1					1				5			
Rehoboth	308	24	Bowen	Uriah Jr			1						1			3			
Rehoboth	308	25	Walker	Ephraim 2nd	1	3		1	1	1			1	1		10			
Rehoboth	308	26	Lyon	Samuel Jr	3	1						1				5			
Rehoboth	308	27	Lyon	Aaron			1	1				1	1	1		5			
Rehoboth	308	28	Abel	Medbery		1				1		1		1		5			
Rehoboth	308	29	Fuller	Jesse			1	2		2		1				7			
Rehoboth	308	30	Turner	Ephram	1	1		1			1	1	1			6			
Rehoboth	308	31	Fuller	Timothy	1			1	3			1	2			9			
Rehoboth	308	32	Wheeler	Philip	1		1	2		1		1				8			
Rehoboth	308	33	Bliss	Abel	1		1		3	1	1					8			
Rehoboth	308	34	Martin	John	1		1		3	1		1				9			
Rehoboth	308	35	Fuller	Benjamin 2nd		2		1	1	1			1			8			
Rehoboth	308	36	Reed	Rachel		1				1	1		1			5			
Rehoboth	308	37	Boston	Richard			1	3				1				5			
Rehoboth	308	38	Round	Amos 2		1			1	1						3			
Rehoboth	308	39	Jones	Jenken			1	2		1		1				7			
Rehoboth	308	40	Jones	Josiah		1	1	1		1		1				6			
Rehoboth	308	41	Norton	John	1		1	2				1				6			
Rehoboth	308	42	Graham	Rebeckah							1	1	2			4			
Rehoboth	308	43	Bonna		1					1						2			First name left blank
Rehoboth	308	44	Smith	John 2nd		1		1			1		1	1		5			
Rehoboth	308	45	Smith	Oliver	2		1	2		1	1					9			
Rehoboth	308	46	Smith	Ezekiel		1		1				1	1			5			
Rehoboth	309	1	Smith	Aron			1	2				1	1			6			
Rehoboth	309	2	Smith	Narthaniel	2			1	1	1	2		1			10			
Rehoboth	309	3	Shaw	Nathaniel & Son			1	2				1	1			9			
Rehoboth	309	4	Short	Philip		1		2	1	1		1				9			
Rehoboth	309	5	Short	Daniel		1		1	1	1			1			5			
Rehoboth	309	6	Wheeler	Barnard		1	1		2	2		1				8			
Rehoboth	309	7	Wheeler	Job			1		2	1						5			
Rehoboth	309	8	Peck	Otis	1	1		1		2	3		1			9			
Rehoboth	309	9	Round	Enos	1			1				1				3			
Rehoboth	309	10	Wade	Luis	5			1		1	2		1			10			
Rehoboth	309	11	Armington	Benjamin	1			1		1			1			4			
Rehoboth	309	12	Armington	Joseph	3	2	2	1	2	1	1	1	1	1		18			
Rehoboth	309	13	Antrum	Darius			1						1			2			
Rehoboth	309	14	Bowen	Ruth						3			1			4			
Rehoboth	309	15	Bowen	Elizabeth									1			1			
Rehoboth	309	16	Bowen	Cyrrel		1	1									2			
Rehoboth	309	17	Bucklin	George	1		1	1					1			4			
Rehoboth	309	18	Bucklin	David	1	1	1			1						6			
Rehoboth	309	19	Bucklin	Ebenezer	1			1	1				2			6			
Rehoboth	309	20	Bucklin	James	1	2		1		1	2		1			8			
Rehoboth	309	21	Barney	Nathaniel			1	1					1			4			
Rehoboth	309	22	Wheeler	Job		1		2		1						5			
Rehoboth	309	23	Bowen	Mary		1						2	1			4			
Rehoboth	309	24	Barney	Jonathan	1	1	2		1				1			7			
Rehoboth	309	25	Bowen	Barzillia	1		1						1			3			
Rehoboth	309	26	Carpenter	Aseph		1		1	1	1		2				6			
Rehoboth	309	27	Bishop	John		2		1	1				1			5			
Rehoboth	309	28	Butterworth	Oliver			1				2		1			4			
Rehoboth	309	29	Bishop	Phanuel		1		1		1			1			4			
Rehoboth	309	30	Bishop	Comfort	2		1		2	2			1			9			
Rehoboth	309	31	Bishop	Ebenezer				1					2			3			
Rehoboth	309	32	Bowen	Simeon			1			1			1			3			
Rehoboth	309	33	Bullock	Jabez 2nd		1		1			1					4			
Rehoboth	309	34	Brown	Sarah						1		1				2			
Rehoboth	309	35	Brown	Anna		3				2		1				6			
Rehoboth	309	36	Brown	Gideon 2d	1	2		1		1		1				6			
Rehoboth	309	37	Brown	Oliver	1		1		1	1	1	2				8			
Rehoboth	309	38	Carpenter	Daniel Jr		1		1		1						3			
Rehoboth	309	39	Carpenter	Otis		1						1				5			
Rehoboth	309	40	Cole	Joseph	1	1		1	1	1			1			6			
Rehoboth	309	41	Cole	William	1			1	3	1	1		1			9			
Rehoboth	309	42	Coomer	John			1						1			2			
Rehoboth	309	43	Cole	Allen		2				1		1				5			
Rehoboth	309	44	Chaffe	Bradock	1		1	2		1	1					8			
Rehoboth	309	45	Chaffe	Joseph	1	1	1	2				1				8			
Rehoboth	310	1	Chandler	Jacob		2		1	2	1	1	1				9			
Rehoboth	310	2	Dagget	Willm			3	1				2	1			7			
Rehoboth	310	3	Dagget	Robert		1	1		1	2		1				10			
Rehoboth	310	4	Dagget	Levi			1		3	2		1				9			
Rehoboth	310	5	Bowen	Joel	2		1		3	3		1				13			
Rehoboth	310	6	Bicknal	Peter		2		1			2		1			6			
Rehoboth	310	7	Bowen	Simeon Jr	2		1		1	3		1				8			
Rehoboth	310	8	Brown	Nathaniel			1			1		1				4			
Rehoboth	310	9	Brown	Jonathan		1		1			1					5			
Rehoboth	310	10	Brown	Aaron		1		1			1					4			
Rehoboth	310	11	Bowen	Ichabod			1	1	1				1			5			
Rehoboth	310	12	Bowen	Samuel			1	1	1	1		1				5			
Rehoboth	310	13	Bowen	Eleazer															Enumeration left blank
Rehoboth	310	14	Carpenter	Daniel	2	1		1	1	1			1			10			
Rehoboth	310	15	Carpenter	Benjamin		1		1				1				4			
Rehoboth	310	16	Carpent	Ashel		2		1		3	3	1				10			
Rehoboth	310	17	Carpenter	Jonathan	1		1	1	1	1		1				6			
Rehoboth	310	18	Cushing	Level				1					1			3			
Rehoboth	310	19	Cushin	Charles			1		1	1	1					8			

TOWN	PG#	LN#	LAST NAME	FIRST NAME	FREE WHITE MALES					FREE WHITE FEMALES					TOTAL ALL OTHER	TOTAL SLAVES	TOTALS	DISTRICT/ TOWNSHIP	NOTES
					under 10	10 to 16	16 to 26	26 to 45	45 and over	under 10	10 to 16	16 to 26	26 to 45	45 and over					
Rehoboth	310	20	Carben	Robert	1			1					1				3		
Rehoboth	310	21	Chaffe	Jonathan	1	2		1	1				1	1			7		
Rehoboth	310	22	Chaffe	Jonathan		1	1		2				1				7		
Rehoboth	310	23	Numan	Nathan			1		1				1				5		
Rehoboth	310	24	Fuller	Benjamin	1	3		1	1	1		1	1				9		
Rehoboth	310	25	Chaffe	Nathaniel		2		1		1			1	1			6		
Rehoboth	310	26	Chaffe	Daniel			1		1				1				7		
Rehoboth	310	27	Cooper	Nathaniel		2		1	1	1	2		1				8		
Rehoboth	310	28	Cole	David			1		1				1				3		
Rehoboth	310	29	Fisher	Daniel	1			1			1	1	1				5		
Rehoboth	310	30	Fisher	Daniel Jr			1		1				1				4		
Rehoboth	310	31	French	Elkana Jr	1	2	1		4		2	1	1				13		
Rehoboth	310	32	Fuller	Asa			1			2			1				6		
Rehoboth	310	33	Fuller	Noah		1		1	1		1	1	1				6		
Rehoboth	310	34	Lyon	Obediah	1		1						1				5		
Rehoboth	310	35	Miller	Mary	1		1	1		1		1	2				8		
Rehoboth	310	36	Miller	Ellis	2		1		3				1				8		
Rehoboth	310	37	Medbury	John	3	1		1					1				9		
Rehoboth	310	38	Perry	John	1			1		1	2		1				6		
Rehoboth	310	39	Peck	Ebenezer	1			1		1			1				4		
Rehoboth	310	40	Peck	Charles	1			1		1		1					5		
Rehoboth	310	41	Peck	John	1	2							1				4		
Rehoboth	310	42	Peck	Thomas			1		3				1				8		
Rehoboth	310	43	Robinson	Noah	1		1		3				1	1			8		
Rehoboth	310	44	Reed	Thomas	2			1		1			1				9		
Rehoboth	310	45	Read	Oliver				1			2						3		
Rehoboth	310	46	Read	Oliver Jr			1						1				4		
Rehoboth	311	1	Read	Simeon	1	1		1	1	1			1				6		
Rehoboth	311	2	Read	Amos			1	1					1				3		
Rehoboth	311	3	Shory	John			1					1	1				3		
Rehoboth	311	4	Peck	Edmond		1				1							5		
Rehoboth	311	5	Peck	Stephen			1			1			1				3		
Rehoboth	311	6	Shory	Abel		2	1		5				1				10		
Rehoboth	311	7	Shory	Zepheniah							1	1	1				3		
Rehoboth	311	8	Shory	Jacob			1						1				2		
Rehoboth	311	9	Short	Ebenezer		1		1		1			1				5		
Rehoboth	311	10	Woodward	Samuel			1				3		3				7		
Rehoboth	311	11	Woodward	John		1		1			1		1				5		
Rehoboth	311	12	West	Joseph	1		1		1	1		1					7		
Rehoboth	311	13	West	Oliver	1			1	1	1			1				6		
Rehoboth	311	14	Wood	Jonathan	1	2		1	1	2	1	1	1				10		
Rehoboth	311	15	Wood	Oliver			1						1				6		
Rehoboth	311	16	Wood	Jonathan Jr		1							1				3		
Rehoboth	311	17	Humphrey	Jonathan	2	3		1	3	1			1				11		
Rehoboth	311	18	Barney	James		1		1		1							3		
Rehoboth	311	19	Wheaton	Lucas	1			1	1	1		1	2				10		
Rehoboth	311	20	Martin	Asa	1		1		3	1		1					9		
Rehoboth	311	21	Iney	Benjamin			1						1				2		
Rehoboth	311	22	Branch	Aholiab		1				2			1				4		
Rehoboth	311	23	Macliss	Thomas				1					1				2		
Rehoboth	311	24	Perry	David Jr	1	2		2		1	1		2				9		
Rehoboth	311	25	Bullock	Thomas	1		1	1				1					6		
Rehoboth	311	26	Drier	William			1						2				3		
Rehoboth	311	27	Willmarth	Joseph		2		1	1				1				6		
Rehoboth	311	28	Hor	Jacob		1		1			2		1				7		
Rehoboth	311	29	Hor	Jacob Jr		1						1					3		
Rehoboth	311	30	Perry	Ezra		1		1			1		1				5		
Rehoboth	311	31	Macomber	Elemuel		1	1			2							4		
Rehoboth	311	32	Bowen	Benjamin		1				1		1					5		
Rehoboth	311	33	Edson	Ebenezer	1	2		1	1	1			1				8		
Rehoboth	311	34	Lincoln	Sandford			1		2	1		1					6		
Rehoboth	311	35	Darby	Abner		1		1	2		1		1				8		
Rehoboth	311	36	Macomber	John	2			1		2		1					6		
Rehoboth	311	37	Smith	Huldah						1	1	1					3		
Rehoboth	311	38	Threeshear	Asa		1						2					3		
Rehoboth	311	39	Miller	John 2nd			1						1				2		
Rehoboth	311	40	Miller	James			1			1	1		1				4		
Rehoboth	311	41	Salsbury	Hezekiah	1		1				1		1				4		
Rehoboth	311	42	Mason	John	1		1	2		2	1						7		
Rehoboth	311	43	Medbury	Nathan		1		3		1		2	2				10		
Rehoboth	311	44	Medbury	Siah	1		1	2		1	1						8		
Rehoboth	311	45	Medbury	Nathaniel	1		1					1	1				4		
Rehoboth	311	46	Mur	Nathan		1	1	1					1				4		
Rehoboth	312	1	Munro	Allen	1			1		1			1				6		
Rehoboth	312	2	Medbury	Thomas	1	1	1						1				4		
Rehoboth	312	3	Pain	Jonathan	1			1		1	2		1				7		
Rehoboth	312	4	Peck	Cyrrel	3		1		2		1	1					10		
Rehoboth	312	5	Perry	Constant	1		1	1		1		1					6		
Rehoboth	312	6	Pain	Nathaniel			1					1	1	1			3		
Rehoboth	312	7	Pain	Pelig	1		1	2		2	1		1				8		
Rehoboth	312	8	Pain	Nathaniel Jr	1		1			2	2		1				9		
Rehoboth	312	9	Peck	Comfort		1		1				1	1				5		
Rehoboth	312	10	Peck	James			1		2				1				6		
Rehoboth	312	11	Peck	Comfort Jr	2		1		3				1				8		
Rehoboth	312	12	Peck	Solmomon	1		1		2				1				6		
Rehoboth	312	13	Peck	Darius		1			1		1						3		
Rehoboth	312	14	Peeks	Thomas		1					1						3		
Rehoboth	312	15	Read	Perres		1		1			1	1					5		
Rehoboth	312	16	Read	Abel			1						1				2		
Rehoboth	312	17	Rodliaf	Frederic	2	1		1	1				1				10		

TOWN	PG#	LN#	LAST NAME	FIRST NAME	FREE WHITE MALES					FREE WHITE FEMALES					TOTAL ALL OTHER	TOTAL SLAVES	TOTALS	DISTRICT/ TOWNSHIP	NOTES
					under 10	10 to 16	16 to 26	26 to 45	45 and over	under 10	10 to 16	16 to 26	26 to 45	45 and over					
Rehoboth	312	18	Rude	William			1	1		1			1				4		
Rehoboth	312	19	Renuff	Philip			1	1					1				3		
Rehoboth	312	20	Read	Bashabee										2			2		
Rehoboth	312	21	Richmond	John R	1	2	1	1			2		1	1			9		
Rehoboth	312	22	Shependson	Zebadiah				1						2			3		
Rehoboth	312	23	Stephens	Samuel		1		1	2	2	1	1					9		
Rehoboth	312	24	Titas	Comfort			1			1							3		
Rehoboth	312	25	Smith	Abial		1		1				1	1				4		
Rehoboth	312	26	Showry	Sarah										2			2		
Rehoboth	312	27	Sheperson	Benager				1				2		1			4		
Rehoboth	312	28	Shores	Zepheniah		2		1		1		1		1			6		
Rehoboth	312	29	Vial	Nathaniel	1		1		3				1				7		
Rehoboth	312	30	Vial	Benjamin				1		1			1				3		
Rehoboth	312	31	Vial	Allen			1	1					1	1			4		
Rehoboth	312	32	Vial	Rachel								2	2				4		
Rehoboth	312	33	Vial	John		2	1			2			1				6		
Rehoboth	312	34	Vial	Constant		1		1		1			1				4		
Rehoboth	312	35	Walker	Richard	1			1	1	1			1	1	1		7		
Rehoboth	312	36	Walker	Timothy	1	3		1	3			1	1				10		
Rehoboth	312	37	Windsor	Ira	1		1	1		1			1				6		
Rehoboth	312	38	Salsbury	Samuel			1		3				1				5		
Rehoboth	312	39	Whitaker	Richard		1		1	1				1	1			5		
Rehoboth	312	40	Bowers	Sylvester				1		1							2		
Rehoboth	312	41	Carpenter	Caleb				1		1		3	1				7		
Rehoboth	312	42	Carpenter	Caleb 2rd	2		1		3				1				7		
Rehoboth	312	43	Perrin	Thomas			1	1					1				7		
Rehoboth	312	44	Carpenter	Amos			1										1		
Rehoboth	312	45	Hunt	Hezekiah		2		2		1	1		2				8		
Rehoboth	312	46	Chaffe	Samuel				1		2	1		2				6		
Rehoboth	313	1	Carpenter	Oliver			1	1					1				4		
Rehoboth	313	2	Dagget	William 2nd			1		1			1					6		
Rehoboth	313	3	Debens	Charles				1									1		
Rehoboth	313	4	Dagget	James		2	1			1			1				6		
Rehoboth	313	5	Ellis	James			1			1		1					5		
Rehoboth	313	6	Ellis	Ashur			1			1		1					5		
Rehoboth	313	7	Fisher	Joshua	1	1		1	1	1	2	1					9		
Rehoboth	313	8	Fitts	David	1		1	1					1				5		
Rehoboth	313	9	French	James Jr	1		1		3	1			1				7		
Rehoboth	313	10	French	Samuel				1				1	2				4		
Rehoboth	313	11	French	Samuel Jr	1		1			1			1				7		
Rehoboth	313	12	Grand	Benjamin	2			1		1							4		
Rehoboth	313	13	Gage	Benjamin	1	1	1		1			1	1				8		
Rehoboth	313	14	Gooff	Ezra			1					1	2				8		
Rehoboth	313	15	Gooduff	Isaac		1		2		1							5		
Rehoboth	313	16	Hunt	John		1	1			1							3		
Rehoboth	313	17	Hunt	Peter	1		1	1		2		1					8		
Rehoboth	313	18	Hunt	Nathaniel	3		1	1		1	1						9		
Rehoboth	313	19	Hunt	Josiah			1	1		1	1						5		
Rehoboth	313	20	Hill	James			1		1	1		2					4		
Rehoboth	313	21	Hunt	John 2nd	1		1	1				1					5		
Rehoboth	313	22	Hare	Jonathan	1	1		1		1	1		1				9		
Rehoboth	313	23	Harris	Benjamin		1		1	2	1		1					7		
Rehoboth	313	24	Hannon	John		1	2				1		2				6		
Rehoboth	313	25	Hill	Benjamin			1		1	1		1					6		
Rehoboth	313	26	Hunt	William		2	1	1		1			1				6		
Rehoboth	313	27	Handy	William			1			1		1					4		
Rehoboth	313	28	Humphrey	David		1		1	2	1	1						6		
Rehoboth	313	29	Hudson	Reuben		1		1				1	1	1			5		
Rehoboth	313	30	Hill	David		1		1		1	1	1	1				6		
Rehoboth	313	31	Hill	David Jr			1	1					1				4		
Rehoboth	313	32	Ide	Abel	1		1	1					1				5		
Rehoboth	313	33	Ide	Ezra			1		2				1				6		
Rehoboth	313	34	Ide	John	2		1	1					1				8		
Rehoboth	313	35	Ide	Willm	1		1	1					1				5		
Rehoboth	313	36	Ide	Nathaniel	1	2	2	1		1			1				8		
Rehoboth	313	37	Jacobs	John	2			1					2	1			8		
Rehoboth	313	38	Jacobs	Allen		1		1					2				4		
Rehoboth	313	39	Jones	William	1			1	2	1		2	1				8		
Rehoboth	313	40	Jones	Ebenezer	1		1		3		1	1					9		
Rehoboth	313	41	Kent	Elijah & Son	2			2		1	1	1	2				14		
Rehoboth	313	42	Kent	Josiah	1	2		1		1	1						7		
Rehoboth	313	43	Kent	Jabez EB		1				1	1						3		
Rehoboth	313	44	Kent	Ezra			1	1		1			1				6		
Rehoboth	313	45	Kent	Elizabeth									1				1		
Rehoboth	313	46	Kent	Noah			1	1					1				3		
Rehoboth	314	1	Kent	James		1		1		1			1				4		
Rehoboth	314	2	Kent	John			1		2				1				4		
Rehoboth	314	3	Lawton	Caleb	1		1	1					1				4		
Rehoboth	314	4	Mason	James		1		1			1		2				5		
Rehoboth	314	5	Mason	David			1		2				1				5		
Rehoboth	314	6	Mason	Caleb				1				1	2				4		
Rehoboth	314	7	Mason	Nathan			1	3		1		1	2				9		
Rehoboth	314	8	Mason	Jonathan	2		1		2				1				8		
Rehoboth	314	9	Peck	Ebenezer 2nd						1							1		
Rehoboth	314	10	Bliss	Cromel 2nd		1				1							3		
Rehoboth	314	11	Numan	Jesse		1	1	1	1	1		1	1				7		
Rehoboth	314	12	Smith	Joshua Jr				1	2				1				7		
Rehoboth	314	13	Chaffe	Ephraim		1	1		3				1				6		
Rehoboth	314	14	Peck	Abiah				1					1				3		
Rehoboth	314	15	Chaffe	Jonathan															Enumeration left blank

60

			HEADS OF HOUSEHOLD		FREE WHITE MALES					FREE WHITE FEMALES									
TOWN	PG#	LN#	LAST NAME	FIRST NAME	under 10	10 to 16	16 to 26	26 to 45	45 and over	under 10	10 to 16	16 to 26	26 to 45	45 and over	TOTAL ALL OTHER	TOTAL SLAVES	TOTALS	DISTRICT/ TOWNSHIP	NOTES
Rehoboth	314	16	Miller	Clark		1				1							2		
Rehoboth	314	17	Miller	Joseph			1		2	1							4		
Rehoboth	314	18	Vial	Hezekiah	1		1		1			1					5		
Rehoboth	314	19	Windsor	Mary					1	1		1		1			6		
Rehoboth	314	20	Wade	Ichabod	1			1		1		1					4		
Rehoboth	314	21	Willmarth	Mary							2	1					3		
Rehoboth	314	22	Willmarth	Thomas			1					1					2		
Rehoboth	314	23	Hunt	Chris															Enumeration left blank
Rehoboth	314	24	Walker	John			1					1					2		
Rehoboth	314	25	Walker	George H		1				1		1	2				7		
Rehoboth	314	26	Walker	Joseph		1		2				2	1				6		
Rehoboth	314	27	Whitman	Samuel	1			1			1	1					4		
Rehoboth	314	28	Whitman	Frederic		1				1		1					3		
Rehoboth	314	29	Whitman	Samuel Jr		1						1					2		
Rehoboth	314	30	Whitman	Israel		1		3		1		1					7		
Rehoboth	314	31	Wiett	Lemuel	1		1						2				4		
Rehoboth	314	32	Wood	Luis		1	1					1					3		
Rehoboth	314	33	Wood	John		1		2		2		1					8		
Rehoboth	314	34	Wood	David	1		1				2		1				5		
Rehoboth	314	35	Weaton	Peter	1	2						1					4		
Rehoboth	314	36	Read	Peter			1					1					2		
Rehoboth	314	37	Brown	Zebedee	2	1	1		2	1	1	1					10		
Rehoboth	314	38	Carpenter	Noah		1				1							3		
Rehoboth	314	39	Jenings	Nathan			1	1		1		1					4		
Rehoboth	314	40	Jenings	Squier Jr			1		1			1					7		
Rehoboth	314	41	Anthony	Reuben	1		1		2	1		1					8		
Rehoboth	314	42	Horton	Wheeler			1		1		1						5		
Rehoboth	314	43	Gardner	Edward		1		1				1					3		
Rehoboth	314	44	Miller	James 2nd		1			1		1			1			5		
Rehoboth	314	45	Brayton	Alderman										1	1		1		
Rehoboth	314	46	Moss	Pero										5	5		5		
Rehoboth	314	47	Witeman	Richard										2	2		2		
Rehoboth	315	1	Slocum	Prime										8	8		8		
Rehoboth	315	2	Sips	Stephen										4	4		4		
Rehoboth	315	3	Brayton	Sip										8	8		8		
Rehoboth	315	4	Moore	Robert										3	3		3		
Rehoboth	315	5	Hill	Barbary										4	4		4		
Rehoboth	315	6	Bliss	Elizabeth									3		3		3		
Rehoboth	315	7	Freeman	Joseph										5	5		5		
Rehoboth	315	8	Barney	Paul										4	4		4		
Rehoboth	316	1	Allen	Benjamin			1				1	1					3		
Rehoboth	316	2	Allen	Ephraim		2		1	1	2	1	1					9		
Rehoboth	316	3	Allen	Josiah	2	1	1					1					10		

61

TOWN	PG#	LN#	LAST NAME	FIRST NAME	FREE WHITE MALES					FREE WHITE FEMALES					TOTAL ALL OTHER	TOTAL SLAVES	TOTALS	DISTRICT/ TOWNSHIP	NOTES
					under 10	10 to 16	16 to 26	26 to 45	45 and over	under 10	10 to 16	16 to 26	26 to 45	45 and over					
Somerset	404	1	Peirce	Asa	3	1		1		1	1	1	1				9		
Somerset	404	2	Peirce	Mial				1						1			2		
Somerset	404	3	Chase	James	2	1		1		1	3		1				9		
Somerset	404	4	Shove	Theophelus		3		1		2	1		1				8		
Somerset	404	5	Simmons	Brown	1	1		1		1	2	4	1				11		
Somerset	404	6	Blithens	Royal				1					1				2		
Somerset	404	7	Hood	John	3	2	1						1				7		
Somerset	404	8	Hood	William			1			1		1					3		
Somerset	404	9	Marble	Joseph	3	1		1					1	1			7		
Somerset	404	10	Chase	Collins				1		1			1				3		
Somerset	404	11	Davis	Benj		2		1				1		2			6		
Somerset	404	12	Robinson	Gideon		1						1					2		
Somerset	404	13	Walker	Gilbert		1		1		3		1	1				7		
Somerset	404	14	Candage	John		1						1					2		
Somerset	404	15	Shea	John		1				1		1	1				4		
Somerset	404	16	Gillet	Peter	1	1		1		2			1				6		
Somerset	404	17	Brown	E. Wid		1						1	1	1			4		
Somerset	404	18	Brown	John	1			1		2			1				5		
Somerset	404	19	Earl	Oliver	1			1		1			1				4		
Somerset	404	20	Rounds	Chase		1				1		1					3		
Somerset	404	21	Place	James	1			1		1	1		1				5		
Somerset	404	22	Luther	Dyer			1					1					2		
Somerset	404	23	Swasey	Jerathmeel	1	3		1		1	2		1				9		
Somerset	404	24	Swasey	Polly Wido		1						1	1				3		
Somerset	404	25	Marble	Thomas	1			1		1		1					4		
Somerset	404	26	Shaw	Eliphalet	1			1		4	1	1					8		
Somerset	404	27	Evans	Jacob	4	1		1		1	1		2				10		
Somerset	404	28	Chase	Shadrach				1		2		1					4		
Somerset	404	29	Evans	Caleb	4		1						1				6		
Somerset	404	30	Marble	Lloyd	1		1			1		1					3		
Somerset	404	31	Davis	Silas			1	1					1				3		
Somerset	404	32	Neel	James	1	2		1			1		1				6		
Somerset	404	33	Davis	Arthur	2	2		1		1			1				7		
Somerset	404	34	Bragg	Henry				1		1			2				4		
Somerset	404	35	Clark	Henry	2			1		1	1		1				6		
Somerset	404	36	Fish	Widow	1					1			1				3		
Somerset	404	37	Sherdon	William	3			1		2			2				8		
Somerset	404	38	Chase	James 3d	4	1		1			1		1				8		
Somerset	404	39	Palmer	Wido		1				1	2		1				5		
Somerset	404	40	Robinson	Joseph	2	1		1		2	2				1		9		
Somerset	404	41	Luther	David Junr		1				1	1						3		
Somerset	404	42	Sherdon	John			1	1	1								3		
Somerset	404	43	Borland	Frances	2	3		1		2		1					9		
Somerset	404	44	Buffinton	Moses		2		1		2			2				7		
Somerset	404	45	Anthony	Caleb			1		2			1					4		
Somerset	404	46	Buffinton	Benja	4	1	1			2			1				9		
Somerset	405	1	Chase	Ezra				1				1		1			3		
Somerset	405	2	Chase	Ezra Jun	1		1					1					3		
Somerset	405	3	Kellog	Joseph			1			2	1		1				5		
Somerset	405	4	Marble	George	3	1	1	1			1		1				8		
Somerset	405	5	Hill	Ruth							1		1				2		
Somerset	405	6	Bowers	Cash V Flora											3		3		
Somerset	405	7	Bowers	Rose											1		1		
Somerset	405	8	Bowers	Mary Widow				1						2			3		
Somerset	405	9	Benson	William	2			1		2	1		1				7		
Somerset	405	10	Hellon	John	2			1		1	2		1				7		
Somerset	405	11	Pettis	Henry	1			1		1	2	1	1				7		
Somerset	405	12	Cummings	Noble	1	2	1			2	2	1					9		
Somerset	405	13	Read	Wid						1		1	1				3		
Somerset	405	14	Davis	Benja Jun		1		1		4	2	1	1				10		
Somerset	405	15	Chase	Stephen	2	1		1			1		1				6		
Somerset	405	16	Bowers	David Widow of									1	1			2		
Somerset	405	17	Forrester	Wido	1						1		1				3		
Somerset	405	18	Chase	Isaac				1		2	1		1				5		
Somerset	405	19	Bowen	John	1		1	1	1	1	4		1				10		
Somerset	405	20	Head	Baker	3	2		1		2	1		1				10		
Somerset	405	21	Swasey	Joseph	2		1			3	2						9		
Somerset	405	22	Kain	Robert				1					1				2		
Somerset	405	23	Marble	Thomas 2d	1	1		1		1	2		1				7		
Somerset	405	24	Harris	John			1			2			1				4		
Somerset	405	25	Hoar	Gideon	1	5	1	1		2	1		1				12		
Somerset	405	26	Tubb	Samuel		2	2	1			2						8		
Somerset	405	27	Potts	Widow			1				2		1				4		
Somerset	405	28	Simmons	Zephaniah	2	2	1	1	1	1	1		1				10		
Somerset	405	29	Kain	Robert Jr		2		1		2	1		1				7		
Somerset	405	30	Burke	Benjamin				1				1		1			3		
Somerset	405	31	Dennis	Arther	2	2		1		2	4		1				12		
Somerset	405	32	Dennis	John				1									1		
Somerset	405	33	Buffington	Benka	1	2		1			5		1				10		

TOWN	PG#	LN#	LAST NAME	FIRST NAME	FREE WHITE MALES					FREE WHITE FEMALES					TOTAL ALL OTHER	TOTAL SLAVES	TOTALS	DISTRICT/ TOWNSHIP	NOTES
					under 10	10 to 16	16 to 26	26 to 45	45 and over	under 10	10 to 16	16 to 26	26 to 45	45 and over					
Somerset	405	34	Bardine	John				1						1			2		
Somerset	405	35	Shaw	Oliver		1		1		2		1					5		
Somerset	405	36	Buffinton	Jona		1		1			4		1				7		
Somerset	405	37	Head	Job		1			1		4			1			7		
Somerset	405	38	Head	Job Junr			1				1		1				3		
Somerset	405	39	Luther	Theophelus	1			1		3			1				6		
Somerset	405	40	Wilbour	James	2	1		1			2			1			7		
Somerset	405	41	Wilbour	Mary Wido	1	2	1				2	1					8		
Somerset	405	42	Eddy	Lydia Wido		1							1				2		
Somerset	405	43	Head	Caleb		2		1		1	1		1				6		
Somerset	405	44	Read	David	2		1			1	3		1	1			9		
Somerset	405	45	Bowers	Jonathan		2			1	4	1			1			9		
Somerset	405	46	Bowers	Philip	3	1		1		1	4			1			11		
Somerset	405	47	Chase	Jesse	3	1		1		2			1	1			9		
Somerset	405	48	Davis	James	3	3		1	1	2			1	1			12		
Somerset	405	49	Bourne	Stephen		1		1		1	3			1			7		
Somerset	405	50	Bourne	Sarah		1								3			4		
Somerset	405	51	Shaw	John		1		1		3			1	2			8		
Somerset	406	1	Bourne	Samuel			1			2			1				4		
Somerset	406	2	Bourne	Frances			1						1	1			3		
Somerset	406	3	Chase	Gideon 2d	1	1		1		3			1				7		
Somerset	406	4	Chase	Patience Wido	1	1	1				2	1					6		
Somerset	406	5	Chase	Silas		1	2		1	2	2			3			11		
Somerset	406	6	Chase	Paul		1		1		1	1	2		1			7		
Somerset	406	7	Chase	Abner			1			1	1						3		
Somerset	406	8	Chase	Moses		1		1		1	1	1	1	1			7		
Somerset	406	9	Chase	Ichobod	1			1						4			6		
Somerset	406	10	Chase	Antepas	1			1		3			1				6		
Somerset	406	11	Chase	Stephen 2d	1			1		1			1				4		
Somerset	406	12	Stead	Stephen				1		1				1			3		
Somerset	406	13	Eddy	John	1	1		1		1	2		1				7		
Somerset	406	14	Chase	Oliver	2	2		1					1	1			7		
Somerset	406	15	Read	Samuel	1	1			1	3	3	2	1	1			13		
Somerset	406	16	Chase	Francis	2	2		1		1			1				7		
Somerset	406	17	Edminster	James				1			1		1				3		
Somerset	406	18	Shove	Nathll		1		1		1							3		
Somerset	406	19	Chase	Matthew				1					1				2		
Somerset	406	20	Chase	Asa		3		1		1			1				6		
Somerset	406	21	Purrinton	Clark	2	1	2	1		1	2		1				10		
Somerset	406	22	Purrinton	Widow		1	1			1			1				4		
Somerset	406	23	Chase	Gideon		1		1					1				3		
Somerset	406	24	Butterworth	Wido			1			1			1				3		
Somerset	406	25	Butterworth	Caleb			1			1		1					3		
Somerset	406	26	Peirce	Jonathan Junr		1	1		1	2	2			1			8		
Somerset	406	27	Baker	Jonathan	2			1		1			1				5		
Somerset	406	28	Peirce	Wido Hannah						1		5		1			7		
Somerset	406	29	Peirce	James		1			1	5				1			8		
Somerset	406	30	Peirce	David					1	1	4			2			8		
Somerset	406	31	Peirce	Ebenezer	1			1		1			1				4		
Somerset	406	32	Peirce	Jonathan				1									1		
Somerset	406	33	Peirce	David Jun	3			1		2			1				7		
Somerset	406	34	Peirce	Jonathan 3d	3			1					1				5		
Somerset	406	35	Purrinton	Edward	2	1		1		1	1		1				7		
Somerset	406	36	Chase	Joseph		1		1		1	1		1				5		
Somerset	406	37	Gibbs	Robert				1					1				2		
Somerset	406	38	Gibbs	Samuel	3			1					1				5		
Somerset	406	39	Gibbs	Robert 2d		3		1		2			1				7		
Somerset	406	40	Peirce	Obadiah	2			1		3			1				7		
Somerset	406	41	Brayton	Daniel			1	1		1			2				5		
Somerset	406	42	Luther	William				1						1			2		
Somerset	406	43	Weaver	Nathll	2			1		1			1				5		
Somerset	406	44	Weaver	James	1		1			1		1					4		
Somerset	406	45	Augar	Joshua	1									2			3		
Somerset	406	46	Morrison	James			1			2			1				4		
Somerset	406	47	Brown	John		1	2		1			2		1			7		
Somerset	406	48	Brown	John Jur	1			1					1				3		
Somerset	406	49	Gibbs	Henry	4	1			1	1	1		1				9		
Somerset	407	1	Chase	Allen		1			1			2		1			5		
Somerset	407	2	Chase	Guillford			1			1			1				3		
Somerset	407	3	Chase	Allen Junr	2			1		2			1				6		
Somerset	407	4	Luther	Barton	1	2		1		2			1				7		
Somerset	407	5	Luther	Benja	2		1			2			1				7		
Somerset	407	6	Chase	Elizh Wido										2			2		
Somerset	407	7	Luther	David			2	1		1		1		1			6		
Somerset	407	8	Lawton	William		3		1				2		1			7		
Somerset	407	9	Earl	Benja		1		1	1	1			1				5		
Somerset	407	10	Read	Nathan		2			1	1			1				5		
Somerset	407	11	Read	John			2		1	1			1				5		
Somerset	407	12	Chase	Daniel	1	2			1	1		4		1			10		

63

TOWN	PG#	LN#	LAST NAME	FIRST NAME	FREE WHITE MALES					FREE WHITE FEMALES					TOTAL ALL OTHER	TOTAL SLAVES	TOTALS	DISTRICT/ TOWNSHIP	NOTES
					under 10	10 to 16	16 to 26	26 to 45	45 and over	under 10	10 to 16	16 to 26	26 to 45	45 and over					
Somerset	407	13	Wilbour	John		1		1					1				3		
Somerset	407	14	Marble	Benja		2			1		1		1				5		
Somerset	407	15	Marble	Elias	1		1					1					3		
Somerset	407	16	Buffinton	Joseph	1	2		1			2		1				7		
Somerset	407	17	Norton	Elijah	1				1				1				3		
Somerset	407	18	Buffinton	James		1		1			2		1				5		
Somerset	407	19	Manchester	Stephen	3			1	1	1	1		3				9		
Somerset	407	20	Slead	Eliz Wido	1	4	1				2		1				9		
Somerset	407	21	Slead	Edward	2			1		3			1				7		
Somerset	407	22	Luther	Amos	3			1		1	1		1				7		
Somerset	407	23	Slead	Jonathan		2			1	1	4		1				9		
Somerset	407	24	Brayton	John	2	2		1		2	2		1		1		11		
Somerset	407	25	Wilbour	Daniel		3			1	3			2				9		
Somerset	407	26	Wilbour	Elisha		1	1		1	3			1				7		
Somerset	407	27	Shearman	Gido		2		1					1				4		
Somerset	407	28	Sherman	Preserved	1	1		1		2			1				6		
Somerset	407	29	Slead	William	1		1		1	1	2		1				7		
Somerset	407	30	Wilbour	Daniel Jr	1		1					1					3		
Somerset	407	31	Shearman	Caleb		1		1				1	1				4		
Somerset	407	32	Chase	William	2			1		2	2		1				8		
Somerset	407	33	Trip	Mial	1			1		3			1				6		
Somerset	407	34	Slead	Charles		4			1	1			1				7		
Somerset	407	35	Slead	Charles Jr	1		1			3	1	1					7		
Somerset	407	36	Anthony	Gardner	2	2	1		1	3	3		1	1			14		
Somerset	407	37	Anthony	John		2			1	2			1				6		
Somerset	407	38	Anthony	Caleb	3	1			1	3			1				9		
Somerset	407	39	Anthony	Israel			1			1	1		1				4		
Somerset	407	40	Chase	Nathan	1			1		2	5		1				10		
Somerset	407	41	Anthony	William				1					1				2		
Somerset	407	42	Anthony	Saml	1		1			2			1				5		
Somerset	407	43	Anthony	Stephen	3			1		2	2		1				9		
Somerset	407	44	Anthony	Peleg			1			1		1					3		
Somerset	407	45	Lee	John	2			1		3	1		1				8		
Somerset	408	1	Vendiome	Wido								1	1				2		
Somerset	408	2	Luther	Bathsheba						3	2		1				6		
Somerset	408	3	Luther	Ellis	1		1						1				3		
Somerset	408	4	Wood	Otis	3	1			1	1		1					7		
Somerset	408	5	Chase	Philip		2		1		2			1				6		
Somerset	408	6	Shearman	Peleg		1	1		1	2			1				6		
Somerset	408	7	Sherman	Robert	2			1		1			1				5		
Somerset	408	8	Gray	Joseph	3	1			1	2	1		1				9		
Somerset	408	9	Sherman	Daniel	2			1		1			1				5		
Somerset	408	10	Morse	Joseph	3			1					1				5		
Somerset	408	11	Anthony	Hezekiah	2			1		1			1				5		
Somerset	408	12	Winslow	Ebenzr	2	2	2		1		2		1				10		
Somerset	408	13	Mason	Job	3	1			1	1	1		1				8		
Somerset	408	14	Bayley	Edward			1					1					2		
Somerset	408	15	Sisson	Gilbert		1			1				1				3		
Somerset	408	16	Slead	Capt											5		5		
Somerset	408	17	Anthony	David	1	2	3		1	3	2	2		1			15		
Somerset	408	18	Chase	Israel			1			1			1				3		
Somerset	408	19	Chase	Ruth									1				1		
Somerset	408	20	Bowen	Saml	2	1	1						1				5		
Somerset	408	21	Allen	James	2		1			1		1					5		
Somerset	408	22	Marble	Saml	1	2	1						1				5		

TOWN	PG#	LN#	LAST NAME	FIRST NAME	FREE WHITE MALES under 10	10 to 16	16 to 26	26 to 45	45 and over	FREE WHITE FEMALES under 10	10 to 16	16 to 26	26 to 45	45 and over	TOTAL ALL OTHER	TOTAL SLAVES	TOTALS	DISTRICT/ TOWNSHIP	NOTES
Swansea	396	1	Bosworth	Elisha				1						1			2		
Swansea	396	2	Buffinton	Daniel	1	2		1		2			1				7		
Swansea	396	3	Chase	William	1	2		1		2			1				7		
Swansea	396	4	Buffinton	Job	2			1		1			1				5		
Swansea	396	5	Gibbs	John				1		3			1				5		
Swansea	396	6	Butterworth	Benj	1		1					1					3		
Swansea	396	7	Buffinton	John	1	3		1		2	1		1				9		
Swansea	396	8	Chase	Benjamin		2	1	1			2		1				7		
Swansea	396	9	Baker	Samuel	1	1		1		1	2	1	1				8		
Swansea	396	10	Earl	Thomas				3					2				5		
Swansea	396	11	Baker	Daniel				1					1				2		
Swansea	396	12	Chase	John	2	2	3	1			2		1				11		
Swansea	396	13	Chase	James	1	4	1		1	3	2		1				13		
Swansea	396	14	Chase	Edward	1	5		1	1	1	1		1				11		
Swansea	396	15	Slead	Elisha	2			1		2			1				6		
Swansea	396	16	Slead	Howland	1			1		2			1				5		
Swansea	396	17	Martin	James	1	2		1		2	2	1	1				10		
Swansea	396	18	Brayton	Preserved		2		1		1	2	1					7		
Swansea	396	19	Chase	Philip	1		1				1	1					4		
Swansea	396	20	Slead	Benja	1	2			1	2	5		1				12		
Swansea	396	21	Chase	Jonathan	2	4			1	1	3		1	2			14		
Swansea	396	22	Slead	John	2		1					1	1				5		
Swansea	396	23	Earl	Caleb		1	2		1			1		2	1		8		
Swansea	396	24	Slead	Ezra	2			1		1	1	1	1				7		
Swansea	398	1	Luther	Philip	1			1		1			1				4		
Swansea	398	2	Chase	Samuel	1			1		2			1				5		
Swansea	398	3	Connell	Seabry	2	2		1		2			1				8		
Swansea	398	4	Pratt	John	4			1		1			3				9		
Swansea	398	5	Lewin	John				1					1				2		
Swansea	398	6	Lewin	Thomas	2			1		1	2		1				7		
Swansea	398	7	Lewin	Nathaniel				1		4	2		1				8		
Swansea	398	8	Hill	Titus											7				
Swansea	398	9	Slead	Philip	1		1	1	1	1		1		1			7		
Swansea	398	10	Washburn	Mettiah				1					2				3		
Swansea	398	11	Chase	Stephen		3		1		3			1				8		
Swansea	398	12	Chase	Richard		1		1		1	1		2				6		
Swansea	398	13	Mason	William		1		1		2	1		1				6		
Swansea	398	14	Bowers	Joseph				1					1				2		
Swansea	398	15	Whalon	Joseph	1			1					2				4		
Swansea	398	16	Luther	John	1			1		1			1				4		
Swansea	398	17	Luther	Simeon	1	1		1	1				1				5		
Swansea	398	18	Rounds	Philip	1		1			1		1					4		
Swansea	398	19	Chase	John 3d	2			1		2		1	1				7		
Swansea	398	20	Hix	Robert			1	2		1		1	1	2			8		
Swansea	398	21	Eddy	Reserved	1			1		2	2	1		1			8		
Swansea	398	22	Chase	Hezekiah	1	1	2	1		1	1	1		1			9		
Swansea	398	23	Obrian	John	1	1	3	1		1	1		1				9		
Swansea	398	24	Whalan	Clark			1						1				2		
Swansea	398	25	Wood	Nathaniel				1					1				2		
Swansea	398	26	Eddy	Job				1		1	2		3	1			8		
Swansea	398	27	Castle	Nicholas	3	1	2	1		1			1				9		
Swansea	398	28	Luther	Richard				1			1	1		2			5		
Swansea	398	29	Terry	James				1		2			1	1			5		
Swansea	398	30	Baker	Jere											2		2		
Swansea	398	31	Castle	Richd	2		1				1	1					5		
Swansea	398	32	Johnson	Jonathan	1	1	1	1	1		1	1		1			8		
Swansea	398	33	Pullen	John	3			1		2		1	1				8		
Swansea	398	34	Chase	Silvester	1			1		2	2		2				8		
Swansea	398	35	Pero	Tom and											6		6		
Swansea	398	36	Winslow	John	1	1	1	1		3		1	1				9		
Swansea	398	37	Gray	John		1		1		1	1		1				5		
Swansea	398	38	Trafton	Elias D	2			1		1	1		1				6		
Swansea	398	39	Wortham	Joseph	1			1		2			1				5		
Swansea	398	40	Buffinton	Samuel			2		1		2			1			6		
Swansea	398	41	Buffinton	Elisha	1			1		3			1				6		
Swansea	398	42	Gardner	Saml 2d	4			1		2	1		2				10		
Swansea	398	43	Mason	David		3	3		1	4			1	1			13		
Swansea	398	44	Potter	Simeon				1		1			1				3		
Swansea	398	45	Wilbour	Joshua		1	2		1	1			1				6		
Swansea	399	1	Gardner	Wido	1	1				1			1	1			5		
Swansea	399	2	Gardner	Saml	1	3	2	2	1	1	1		2	1			14		
Swansea	399	3	Gardner	Peleg	1		2			1	4			1			9		
Swansea	399	4	Thurston	Varnum	1			1					1				3		
Swansea	399	5	Gardner	Joseph		1		1					1	1			4		
Swansea	399	6	Gardner	John		1		1		1	2		1				6		
Swansea	399	7	Gardner	Peleg Junr	3			1		1			1				6		
Swansea	399	8	Anthony	Job	3			1				1	1				6		
Swansea	399	9	Eddy	William	1	1			1	1	5		1				10		
Swansea	399	10	Chase	Royal	1	1		1		1	1		1				6		

TOWN	PG#	LN#	LAST NAME	FIRST NAME	FREE WHITE MALES					FREE WHITE FEMALES					TOTAL ALL OTHER	TOTAL SLAVES	TOTALS	DISTRICT/ TOWNSHIP	NOTES
					under 10	10 to 16	16 to 26	26 to 45	45 and over	under 10	10 to 16	16 to 26	26 to 45	45 and over					
Swansea	399	11	Vose	John				1		1			1	1			4		
Swansea	399	12	Munro	Stephen 2d			1	1					1				3		
Swansea	399	13	Luther	Job	2	1		1		3	1	1					9		
Swansea	399	14	Kingsley	Thomas		1			1	1		1	1	1			6		
Swansea	399	15	Kingsley	Simeon	1			1		2			1				5		
Swansea	399	16	Kingsley	Jonathan			2	1		3			1				7		
Swansea	399	17	Luther	Silas		1		1				1	1	1			5		
Swansea	399	18	Luther	Joseph	2			1		2			1				6		
Swansea	399	19	Luther	Jane			1			4			1				6		
Swansea	399	20	Luther	Upham		3	1		1	3				1			9		
Swansea	399	21	Luther	Mary	2							1	1	1			5		
Swansea	399	22	Brown	Elisha	2	1	1	1	1	3	2		1				12		
Swansea	399	23	Sisson	Richard		1		2		1	1			1			6		
Swansea	399	24	Brown	William				1				1		1			3		
Swansea	399	25	Brown	William Jnr		1						1					2		
Swansea	399	26	Brown	Jarvis				1						1			2		
Swansea	399	27	Brown	Seth	1	1		1	1	2	1	1		1			9		
Swansea	399	28	Brown	John		2		1	1	3	3			1			11		
Swansea	399	29	Gardner	Alexander		3		1		1	1			1	1		8		
Swansea	399	30	Jones	Simeon	2	1		1		3			1				8		
Swansea	399	31	Luther	Giles				1					1	3			5		
Swansea	399	32	Baker	Joseph			1			3	1		1	1			7		
Swansea	399	33	Luther	Obadiah	1		1	1		1	1		1	1			7		
Swansea	399	34	Luther	Manson	2	1	1	1		1	1		1	1			9		
Swansea	399	35	Slead	William	1		1			1		1					4		
Swansea	399	36	Chase	Wido									1	1			2		
Swansea	399	37	Luther	Samuel	2	1		1					2				6		
Swansea	399	38	Luther	Harlow		1	1		1			1		2			6		
Swansea	399	39	Wood	Simeon	1	1		1		3	2	1	1				10		
Swansea	399	40	Buffinton	Benja	2		3	1				1	2	1			10		
Swansea	399	41	Buffinton	Gardner			1	1				1	1				4		
Swansea	399	42	Buffinton	John 2d	1			1		1			1				4		
Swansea	399	43	Buffinton	Benja Jr			1			1		1					3		
Swansea	399	44	Lewin	John 2d			3	1						1			5		
Swansea	399	45	Chase	Abner	1			1		2			1				5		
Swansea	399	46	Lewin	Hale	3	1		1		1	1		1				8		
Swansea	400	1	Short	John				1						2			3		
Swansea	400	2	Luther	David				1						1			2		
Swansea	400	3	Trott	Jona				1						1			2		
Swansea	400	4	Kingsley	Benja	1			1					1				3		
Swansea	400	5	Kingsley	Barton	1			1					1				3		
Swansea	400	6	Kingsley	James	2			1					1				4		
Swansea	400	7	Kingsley	Amos		1	2	1					1	1			6		
Swansea	400	8	Luther	Barnabas	1		2					2					5		
Swansea	400	9	Luther	Theophilus	1	2		1		1	2		1				8		
Swansea	400	10	Hales	Lurana		3						2		1			6		
Swansea	400	11	Hale	Levi	2			1		1		1	1				6		
Swansea	400	12	Chase	Jabez				1						1			2		
Swansea	400	13	Chase	Jabez Junr	1			1		4		1					7		
Swansea	400	14	Wood	Enos			1					1		1			3		
Swansea	400	15	Mason	Mary								1		1			2		
Swansea	400	16	Mason	Christopher		1		1				1		1			4		
Swansea	400	17	Mason	Eber	1		1			1		1					4		
Swansea	400	18	Hollis	Ruel	2			1		1			1				5		
Swansea	400	19	Wood	David	1			1				1		1			4		
Swansea	400	20	Mason	Barnabas		2		1		2	1		1				7		
Swansea	400	21	Wood	Aaron		3		1		3		1	1				9		
Swansea	400	22	Wood	Jonathan	1	1		1					2	1			6		
Swansea	400	23	Wood	Caleb		1		1		1	1			1			5		
Swansea	400	24	Wood	William	1			1		1		1	1				5		
Swansea	400	25	Wood	John	2			1		1		1	1				6		
Swansea	400	26	Gibbs	Wido	1					2				1			4		
Swansea	400	27	Luther	Barton	1			1	1		1		1	1			6		
Swansea	400	28	Handy	Thomas		1			1	3	2			1			8		
Swansea	400	29	Mason	Daniel	1			1		2	1	1					6		
Swansea	400	30	Hale	John				1					1	1			3		
Swansea	400	31	Hale	David	2	3		1		2	1		1				10		
Swansea	400	32	Martin	Job	3			1				1		1			6		
Swansea	400	33	Martin	John				1				1	1				3		
Swansea	400	34	Mason	Joshua		1			1			1		2			5		
Swansea	400	35	Mason	Benajah			1					1					2		
Swansea	400	36	Mason	Caleb Junr	4	2			1	1				1			9		
Swansea	400	37	Mason	Caleb		1		1		1				1			4		
Swansea	400	38	Marble	Wm	2			1		1			1				5		
Swansea	400	39	Martin	Benja		2	4	1			2			2			11		
Swansea	400	40	Marble	Benja	2	2		1	1	1		2		1			10		
Swansea	400	41	Mason	Jeremiah	2	1		1		3	3		1				11		
Swansea	400	42	Mason	Peleg					1					2			3		
Swansea	400	43	Cornell	Asa	3			1		1	2		1				8		

TOWN	PG#	LN#	LAST NAME	FIRST NAME	FREE WHITE MALES					FREE WHITE FEMALES					TOTAL ALL OTHER	TOTAL SLAVES	TOTALS	DISTRICT/ TOWNSHIP	NOTES
					under 10	10 to 16	16 to 26	26 to 45	45 and over	under 10	10 to 16	16 to 26	26 to 45	45 and over					
Swansea	400	44	Smith	Thomas	2	1		1		1			1				6		
Swansea	400	45	Pearce	Philip	1	1	1		1	2	3		1				10		
Swansea	400	46	Mason	Simeon				1						1			2		
Swansea	400	47	Mastin & Aldrich	Widos	2	1				2	1		1	2			9		
Swansea	401	1	Mason	Isaac				1					2				3		
Swansea	401	2	Mason	Ezra	4			1		2	2		2				11		
Swansea	401	3	Mason	Isaac Jur			1						1				2		
Swansea	401	4	Chaffey	Wido			0		0			1		2			3		
Swansea	401	5	Pearce	Job		1		1						1			3		
Swansea	401	6	Mason	Benja		1		1				1	1	1			5		
Swansea	401	7	Chase	Jerethmeel	2			1		3			1				7		
Swansea	401	8	Fitch	William			1					1		1			3		
Swansea	401	9	Castle	Allen	1			1				3	1				6		
Swansea	401	10	West	Ephraim			1					1	1				3		
Swansea	401	11	Cornell	Elisha				1					2	2			5		
Swansea	401	12	Phillips	Ruth									1	1			2		
Swansea	401	13	Earl	Weston	3			1						1			5		
Swansea	401	14	Chase	James 2d	1	2	1		1	2	3			1			11		
Swansea	401	15	Cornell	Stephen		1		1					2	2			6		
Swansea	401	16	Francis	Ruben		1	1	1			1			1			5		
Swansea	401	17	Briggs	Nathan				1		2	2		1				6		
Swansea	401	18	Chase	Enoch		1		1						1			3		
Swansea	401	19	Chase	Ruben	2			1					1				4		
Swansea	401	20	Wheaton	Jona				1						1			2		
Swansea	401	21	Wheaton	Mial	3	1		1		1			1				7		
Swansea	401	22	Chase	Uriah		1		1		1			1				4		
Swansea	401	23	Peirce	Martha									1				1		
Swansea	401	24	King	Job			1	1				1	1				4		
Swansea	401	25	Horton	Job			1	1		1			1				4		
Swansea	401	26	Lee	Stephen	1	1		1		2	2		1				8		
Swansea	401	27	Luther	Sarah		1						3	1				5		
Swansea	401	28	Luther	Childs		1				1	1						3		
Swansea	401	29	Peirce	Mial		3		1		3	2		1				10		
Swansea	401	30	Burns	D.				1					1	1			3		
Swansea	401	31	Ingalls	Elkanah	2			1		2	1		1				7		
Swansea	401	32	West	John	1	1		1		2	1		1	1			8		
Swansea	401	33	Lewis	Patience		1								1			2		
Swansea	401	34	Mason	John	1		1					1					3		
Swansea	401	35	Lewis	Thomas Jr	3	1	1				1		1				7		
Swansea	401	36	Lewis	Thomas		1		1						1			3		
Swansea	401	37	Simmons	Abigail	1					1			1				3		
Swansea	401	38	Lewis	Anna & Mercy										2			2		
Swansea	401	39	Bullock	Stephen			1							2			3		
Swansea	401	40	Hale	Wido						2			1				3		
Swansea	401	41	Chase	Hezekiah	1		1	1			1						4		
Swansea	401	42	Winslow	Humphrey	1			1		1			1				4		
Swansea	401	43	Luther	Calvin	1			1	1	1			1	1			6		
Swansea	401	44	Luther	Aaron	2			1		2		1	1				7		
Swansea	401	45	Portergen	Benanuel										2			2		
Swansea	401	46	Lawton	James		2	2		1	1	2			1			9		
Swansea	402	1	Lawton	James Jr			1			2	1						4		
Swansea	402	2	Luther	Eben	2			1		1			1				5		
Swansea	402	3	Luther	Moses				1						1			2		
Swansea	402	4	Weaver	Peter				1						1			2		
Swansea	402	5	Usher	Edward	2			1		3			1				7		
Swansea	402	6	Luther	Caleb Wido	3	3				2	2		1				11		
Swansea	402	7	Sisson	Isaac	1	1		1		2	2		1				8		
Swansea	402	8	Luther	Theophilus	3	1		1		1	1		1				8		
Swansea	402	9	Shearman	Wido	3					2	1		1				7		
Swansea	402	10	Luther	Wido									1	1			2		
Swansea	402	11	Luther	Samuel		1		1		3	2		1				8		
Swansea	402	12	Stead	Peleg		3		1		4			1				9		
Swansea	402	13	Chase	Ruben		1	1	1					1	1			5		
Swansea	402	14	Burk	Ruben			1					1					2		
Swansea	402	15	Wood	Seth	1	1		1		1			1				5		
Swansea	402	16	Luther	Stephen	1	1		1		2	2		1				8		
Swansea	402	17	Sisson	Gardner	1		1			2	1						5		
Swansea	402	18	Woodmancy	John				1						1			2		
Swansea	402	19	Luther	James				1						1			2		
Swansea	402	20	Luther	James Jr	2	1	2		1	3	2	1		1			13		
Swansea	402	21	Gardner	William	1	2	2		2	3	1			1			12		
Swansea	402	22	Brown	Dan											5		5		
Swansea	402	23	Mathewson	Hannah											7		7		
Swansea	402	24	Sisson	Eleck	3			1		1			1	1			7		
Swansea	402	25	Luther	Mercy	1					2			1				4		
Swansea	402	26	Mason	Mehitable									1	1			2		
Swansea	402	27	Luther	Betsy	2							1					3		
Swansea	402	28	Handy	Samuel	1			1		1		1					4		
Swansea	402	29	Sisson	John			1			2			1				4		

67

TOWN	PG#	LN#	LAST NAME	FIRST NAME	FREE WHITE MALES					FREE WHITE FEMALES					TOTAL ALL OTHER	TOTAL SLAVES	TOTALS	DISTRICT/ TOWNSHIP	NOTES
					under 10	10 to 16	16 to 26	26 to 45	45 and over	under 10	10 to 16	16 to 26	26 to 45	45 and over					
Swansea	402	30	Cole	Constant		1	1		1					1			4		
Swansea	402	31	Cole	Aaron			1						1				2		
Swansea	402	32	Munro	Stephen	1	2		1			1			1			6		
Swansea	402	33	Kingsley	Hezekiah		1		1						1			3		
Swansea	402	34	Kingsley	Hezekiah Jr	2	1		1		1	1		1				7		
Swansea	402	35	Butterworth	Benja	2	1		1	1	1			1				7		
Swansea	402	36	Sisson	Gideon				1				2	2	1			6		
Swansea	402	37	Salisbury	Daniel		1		1						1			3		
Swansea	402	38	Bushe	John			1							1			2		
Swansea	402	39	Mason	John Esqr		1		1		1			1	1			5		
Swansea	402	40	Peirce	Nathan		1	1							1			3		
Swansea	402	41	Chase	Job	2	1		1		2	1		1				8		
Swansea	402	42	Robinson	John	1	1		1		2	1		1				7		
Swansea	402	43	Kingsley	Rose											4		4		
Swansea	402	44	Mason	Joseph	1	1	1	1		1	2		1				8		
Swansea	402	45	Mason	Job		1	1	1			1		1				5		
Swansea	402	46	Mason	Charles				1					1	1			3		
Swansea	402	47	Mason	Joel Jr	1		1			1		1					4		
Swansea	402	48	Strange	John	1			1		2			1				5		
Swansea	402	49	Kingsley	Asa			2	2	1	3			2	3			13		
Swansea	402	50	Martin	Benja				1	1					2			4		
Swansea	403	1	Short	Simeon	1			1		3			1	1			7		
Swansea	403	2	Luther	Samuel	1			1		4			1				7		
Swansea	403	3	Bears	Wido						1			1				2		
Swansea	403	4	Dagget	Jethro	1	1		1		1	1	1					6		
Swansea	403	5	Peck	Ambrose		2	1		1	2	2	1		1			10		
Swansea	403	6	Thompson	Charles		1		1		1	1			1			5		
Swansea	403	7	Saunders	Jacob	1			1		2				2			6		
Swansea	403	8	Saunders	Daniel		1						1					2		
Swansea	403	9	Saunders	Benja	1		1	1		2	1		1				7		
Swansea	403	10	Barney	Ruben	1			1		2	1		1				6		
Swansea	403	11	Chase	Jacob		1	1	1		2	2		1				8		
Swansea	403	12	Barney	Daniel	1			1		1	1		1				5		
Swansea	403	13	Childs	James				1			1		1				3		
Swansea	403	14	Barney	Peleg	2			1		1	2		1				7		
Swansea	403	15	Barney	Jonathan	2		2	1		2	2		1				10		
Swansea	403	16	Mason	Alexander		1			1	1	1		1				5		
Swansea	403	17	Franklin	Lemuel	3	1	1		1	1	1			1			9		
Swansea	403	18	Smith	Constant	2	2			1		1		1				7		
Swansea	403	19	Barney	Josiah				1						1			2		
Swansea	403	20	Barney	Joseph	1			1		3	1		1				7		
Swansea	403	21	Peirce	Fanny						1	1		1				3		
Swansea	403	22	Franklin	Shubal				1						1			2		
Swansea	403	23	Bryant	Wido										2			2		
Swansea	403	24	Chase	Simeon	2	2		1		2	2			2			11		
Swansea	403	25	Luther	Peleg	1	1		1		2	1		1				7		
Swansea	403	26	Luther	Job	0	1		1					1				3		
Swansea	403	27	Luther	Mathew				1						1			2		
Swansea	403	28	Miller	Widow		1								1			2		
Swansea	403	29	Cole	Ebenizr		1			1		1	2		1			6		
Swansea	403	30	Peck	Thomas	3			1						1			5		
Swansea	403	31	Peck	Peleg Junr			1			1		1					3		
Swansea	403	32	Peck	Peleg		3			1		1	2		1			8		
Swansea	403	33	Garnet	James											5		5		
Swansea	403	34	Scot	Samuel				1				1	1				3		
Swansea	403	35	Handy	Russell	1	2		1		2	1		1				8		
Swansea	403	36	Pearce	David		1	1	1		2	1		1				7		
Swansea	403	37	Pearce	Martin				1		2			1				4		
Swansea	403	38	Holmes	Ebenezer				1					1	1			3		
Swansea	403	39	Pearce	David Junr			1	1		3		1					6		
Swansea	403	40	Martin	Noble	2			1		1				1			5		
Swansea	403	41	Martin	Anna Wido								1		1			2		
Swansea	403	42	Martin	Jonathan	1				1			1	1	1			5		
Swansea	403	43	Martin	Stephen				1		2				1			4		
Swansea	403	44	Wheeler	Daniel				1		1	1		1				4		
Swansea	403	45	Wardwell	Wido	1					1			1				3		
Swansea	403	46	Wood	Barney		1	1						1				3		
Swansea	403	47	Church	Peter blk											4		4		
Swansea	403	48	Bozworth	Joseph	1	2		1		1	1		1				7		
Swansea	403	49	Mason	Edward		3			1				1				5		
Swansea	403	50	Mason	Mary Jr Wido								1	1				2		
Swansea	403	51	Horton	Jabez			1			1		1					3		
Swansea	403	52	Mason	Noble	3	3			1	1		4		1			13		
Swansea	403	53	Chase	Caleb				1			1			2			4		
Swansea	404	1	Mason	James		1							1				2		
Swansea	404	2	Chase	Saml	1	4			1	1		2	1				10		
Swansea	404	3	Chase	Henry			1	1					1				3		

68

TOWN	PG#	LN#	LAST NAME	FIRST NAME	FREE WHITE MALES under 10	10 to 16	16 to 26	26 to 45	45 and over	FREE WHITE FEMALES under 10	10 to 16	16 to 26	26 to 45	45 and over	TOTAL ALL OTHER	TOTAL SLAVES	TOTALS	DISTRICT/ TOWNSHIP	NOTES
Taunton	356	1	Smith	Hannah Wido	*	*	*	*	*	*	*	*	*	*			*		
Taunton	356	2	Shelley	Samuel				1									1		
Taunton	356	3	Cornish	Alice Wido						1		1	1				3		
Taunton	356	4	Smith	Sarah Wido		1	2						1				4		
Taunton	356	5	Dunham	Joseph			1			1		1		2			5		
Taunton	356	6	Ingell	Jonathan		1		1				1		1			4		
Taunton	356	7	French	Jona			1	1		2	1			1			6		
Taunton	356	8	Phillips	Lucy Wido	1		1							1			3		
Taunton	356	9	Johnson	William		2		1				1					4		
Taunton	356	10	Godfrey	Theodorah										1			1		
Taunton	356	11	Caswell	Prince											2		2		
Taunton	356	12	Fisher	Thomas											7		7		
Taunton	356	13	Godfrey	Richard			1	1	1	1	1	1		1			7		
Taunton	356	14	Stoddard	Miles			1		1	1				1			4		
Taunton	356	15	Stoddard	Elijah	2			1				1	1				5		
Taunton	356	16	Carver	William			1					1	1				3		
Taunton	356	17	Wood	Benjamin				1						1			2		
Taunton	356	18	Macomber	Stephen			1		1	1	1			1			5		
Taunton	356	19	Crossman	Seth			1				1						2		
Taunton	356	20	Adams	Seth	1	1		1					1				4		
Taunton	356	21	Hay	George	2			1		2			1				6		
Taunton	357	1	Padelford	David	3			1		1			2				7		
Taunton	357	2	Hathaway	Charlotte	2					1			1				4		
Taunton	357	3	Sever	William		1	1			1		1					4		
Taunton	357	4	Caswell	Richard					1	2			1				4		
Taunton	357	5	Thrasher	John		1	1		1	1				1			5		
Taunton	357	6	Vickery	David	1	1			1	1		3	2		1		10		
Taunton	357	7	Cooper	Benjamin			1			1			1				3		
Taunton	357	8	Pratt	Dier	1	2	1		1	3	1	1	2	1			13		
Taunton	357	9	Stephens	Ebenezer				1									1		
Taunton	357	10	Hewett	Salmon			1			1		1					3		
Taunton	357	11	Dunham	Jacob	1		1			1		1					4		
Taunton	357	12	Thayer	Seth	1			1			2	1		1			6		
Taunton	357	13	Macomber	James			1		1			1		1			4		
Taunton	357	14	Angell	John				1			1	2	1				5		
Taunton	357	15	Sumner	Ebenezer	2	2		1				1	1	1	1		9		
Taunton	357	16	Shaw	John			1		1	1	2	1		2			8		
Taunton	357	17	Littlefield	John	1			1		1			1				4		
Taunton	357	18	Hart	John	2	1		1			1	1	1				7		
Taunton	357	19	Macomber	Nathan	1	1	1		1			2	1				7		
Taunton	357	20	Ranville	John Demi		2		1		1				1			5		
Taunton	357	21	Presbrey	William Junior				1		1			1				3		
Taunton	357	22	Stephens	Barzilla		1	1	1		1	1			1			6		
Taunton	357	23	Dean	Israel	1			1					2	2			6		
Taunton	357	24	Ingell	Abiacher	1		1	1					2		1		6		
Taunton	357	25	Caswell	Nathaniel	2	2			1	1	2			1			9		
Taunton	357	26	Danforth	Asa	3			1		2	1		1	1			9		
Taunton	357	27	Willis	Mehitable Wido			1							1			2		
Taunton	357	28	Cooper	William	1		1					1		1			4		
Taunton	357	29	Right	John			1			1		1					3		
Taunton	357	30	Hatch	Estus		1			1					1			3		
Taunton	357	31	Cooper	James			1	1				1		1			4		
Taunton	357	32	Godfrey	Abigail Wido	1	1							1				3		
Taunton	357	33	Haskins	Jacob	2	1		1	1	1		1		1			8		
Taunton	357	34	Wood	Ephraim	2	1			1			1	2				7		
Taunton	358	1	Cooper	Elizabeth Wido									1				1		
Taunton	358	2	Jewett	Abraha	1			1			1			1			4		
Taunton	358	3	Tisdale	Ephraim	1	1	1		1	1	1			2			8		
Taunton	358	4	Pitts	Rhoba Wido		2		1			1			1			5		
Taunton	358	5	Phillips	Jacob	1	2		1		1		2	1				8		
Taunton	358	6	Thrasher	Elkanah	3			1						1			5		
Taunton	358	7	Read	George 2d	1				1		1	1	1				5		
Taunton	358	8	Wiliams	Richard	3	2		1		1	1		1				9		
Taunton	358	9	Dean	Abner				1				1	1				3		
Taunton	358	10	Williams	Ebenezer	1	1	2		1	2	1	2		1			11		
Taunton	358	11	Presbrey	John		2		1		2		2	1				8		
Taunton	358	12	Hood	Benj Landon	3	1						2		1			8		
Taunton	358	13	Hodges	Abijah Junior	1		1	1		2	1	1	1				8		
Taunton	358	14	Godfrey	John	1	2	2		1	1			1				8		
Taunton	358	15	Adams	Abijah Junior				1		4			1				6		
Taunton	358	16	Ladelford	Samuel	1	1		1	1	1		1	1				7		
Taunton	358	17	Godfrey	Job	1			2	1			3		1			9		
Taunton	358	18	Dean	Philip	1			1		2	3		1	1			9		
Taunton	358	19	Pierce	Elisha		2			1	1	1	1		1			7		
Taunton	358	20	Williams	Nathaniel	3	2	1		2	1	2	1	1	1			14		
Taunton	358	21	Shores	John	1			1					1				3		
Taunton	358	22	Ingall	Jonathan Junr		3			1	2		4		1			11		
Taunton	358	23	Coggeshall	Sarah Wido		1	3			1		1	1				7		
Taunton	358	24	Wild	Samuel Junior	1			1	1	2	1		1	1			8		

TOWN	PG#	LN#	HEADS OF HOUSEHOLD LAST NAME	FIRST NAME	FREE WHITE MALES under 10	10 to 16	16 to 26	26 to 45	45 and over	FREE WHITE FEMALES under 10	10 to 16	16 to 26	26 to 45	45 and over	TOTAL ALL OTHER	TOTAL SLAVES	TOTALS	DISTRICT/ TOWNSHIP	NOTES
Taunton	358	25	Williams	Elijah					1	2		1					4		
Taunton	358	26	Hood	Joseph	2	1	1		1	1	1	2	1				10		
Taunton	358	27	Sever	William			2		1		1			1			5		
Taunton	358	28	Sever	John	2			1		1	1		1				6		
Taunton	358	29	Richmond	Jonathan	1	1			1	1	1	4	1				10		
Taunton	358	30	Cooper	Seth					1		1			1			3		
Taunton	358	31	Carver	David		2	3		1	1	1	2		1			11		
Taunton	358	32	Robinson	James				1		1			1				3		
Taunton	358	33	Lincoln	David					1			1		1			3		
Taunton	358	34	Carver	Nathan	1		3		1	2	1		1				9		
Taunton	358	35	Macomber	Jonathan	1		1		1	1	1		1				6		
Taunton	358	36	Hood	John	2			1		2			1				6		
Taunton	358	37	Cushman	Zebedee	1		1		1	3	2		1				9		
Taunton	358	38	Smith	John W.	1		1	1		1	2		1		1		8		
Taunton	358	39	Stall	William		1	1	1		3	1		1				8		
Taunton	358	40	Daggett	Simeon	2	4		2				2	1		1		12		
Taunton	358	41	Shaw	Isaac	2	1	1	2		4		1	1				12		
Taunton	358	42	Babbit	Ziba	1	2		1		2	1		1				8		
Taunton	359	1	Barney	Joseph			1	1			1		1		1		5		
Taunton	359	2	Tisdale	Joseph	1	2	1		1	2	2		1				10		
Taunton	359	3	Gulliver	Gershom	2	1	2	1			1		1				8		
Taunton	359	4	Harvey	Phebe Wido									1	1			2		
Taunton	359	5	Babbit	Ebenezer	1			1		1	1	1		1			6		
Taunton	359	6	Wilbore	Jedediah Junr	3			1			1						5		
Taunton	359	7	Field	Zebulon	3	3			1	3	1		1				12		
Taunton	359	8	Caswell	Ebenezer		1	1		1			2		2			7		
Taunton	359	9	Wilbore	Joshua	1				1				1				3		
Taunton	359	10	Luscombe	Richard		2			1		1	2		1			7		
Taunton	359	11	Williams	George			1	1	1		1		1				5		
Taunton	359	12	Tisdale	Deborah Wido	4	1	2			2	1		1				11		
Taunton	359	13	Crosman	Otis	1	3			1	1	1	1					8		
Taunton	359	14	Hodges	James	4		1	1		3	1		1	1			12		
Taunton	359	15	Truscott	Abigail Wido		1				2	1		1				5		
Taunton	359	16	Harris	Benjamin	1			1		2			1		1		6		
Taunton	359	17	Padilford	John	3		1	1			1		1				7		
Taunton	359	18	Washburn	Isaac	2	1	2		1	1	1	1	1				10		
Taunton	359	19	King	Job			3		1	2		2		1			9		
Taunton	359	20	Brewer	Daniel		1	1	1	1	1		2		1			8		
Taunton	359	21	Dean	Ebenezer Junior	2	1		2		1	1		1				8		
Taunton	359	22	Hicks	Gideon	1		1		1	1	1	1					6		
Taunton	359	23	Hilton	Amos	3	1			1	1	1	1	1				9		
Taunton	359	24	Burt	George		1		1		1	1			1			5		
Taunton	359	25	Belcher	Benjamin	2			1				1	1				5		
Taunton	359	26	Johnson	Seth				1		2	2	3					8		
Taunton	359	27	Blake	Edward	4	2			1	2	2		1				12		
Taunton	359	28	Read	Uriah	2			1		3	2	1	1				10		
Taunton	359	29	Lu	Amos	2			1		3	3	1	1				11		
Taunton	359	30	Hathaway	Stephen	1	1	2	1		2	1		1				10		
Taunton	359	31	Lincoln	Benjamin	1	1	1		1	2	1	2		1			10		
Taunton	359	32	Dean	Rufus	1	1	1	2			1	4					10		
Taunton	359	33	Leonard	Ichabod	1			2	1					1			5		
Taunton	359	34	Pratt	Samuel		2	1		1	1	1					2	8		
Taunton	359	35	Weatherby	Thomas	1	3	1	2				1	1				9		
Taunton	359	36	Cott	Jonathan			3		1	3	1		1		1		10		
Taunton	359	37	Hull	Isaac											6		6		
Taunton	359	38	Leonard	Rufus	1		2		1	2	2	1		1			10		
Taunton	359	39	Townshend	John	1	1		1	1			2		1			7		
Taunton	359	40	Leonard	Samuel	2	1	7		1	1	2	1	1		4		20		
Taunton	359	41	Crocker	Samuel				1		2		1			1		5		
Taunton	359	42	McChorter	John				1					1	1			3		
Taunton	360	1	Crocker	Josiah		2		1					1	1	1		6		
Taunton	360	2	Williams	Cyrus		1		1			1		1		2		6		
Taunton	360	3	Wilson	William			1			4			1				6		
Taunton	360	4	Boon	Susanna								1		1			2		
Taunton	360	5	Pedelford	Seth		1	1		1	1	2	3	1		1		11		
Taunton	360	6	Wilson	Robert	1				1				1				3		
Taunton	360	7	White	Saul	1	1	1		1	2		2	1				9		
Taunton	360	8	Dean	Joseph	2	1	3		1	3		1	2				13		
Taunton	360	9	Hart	James Junior	3			1					1				5		
Taunton	360	10	Bolkcom	David	2	2	1	1		1			1		2		10		
Taunton	360	11	Godfrey	Rufus	2			1		2	2		1				8		
Taunton	360	12	Phillips	Charles	1			1		4			1				7		
Taunton	360	13	Hodges	Samuel	3		1	1		1			1				7		
Taunton	360	14	Allen	Barney	2	1	2		1	1		1		1	1		10		
Taunton	360	15	Potter	Simeon				1									1		
Taunton	360	16	Pierce	Samuel		1							1				2		
Taunton	360	17	Sidens	Martin			1			4			1				6		
Taunton	360	18	Burt	Joseph	2			1					1	1			5		
Taunton	360	19	Porter	John	1	1	1	1		1		2	1	1			9		

TOWN	PG#	LN#	LAST NAME	FIRST NAME	FREE WHITE MALES					FREE WHITE FEMALES					TOTAL ALL OTHER	TOTAL SLAVES	TOTALS	DISTRICT/ TOWNSHIP	NOTES
					under 10	10 to 16	16 to 26	26 to 45	45 and over	under 10	10 to 16	16 to 26	26 to 45	45 and over					
Taunton	360	20	Harlow	Phebe Wido						2			2	1			5		
Taunton	360	21	Tillinghast	Nicholas	1			1		3	1		1	1	1		9		
Taunton	360	22	Dean	Abiezer	1	1	1	1		3	3		1				11		
Taunton	360	23	Leonard	Abiather	3			1		3			1				8		
Taunton	360	24	Seabury	John W.	1		1	1		3	1		1				8		
Taunton	360	25	Fales	Samuel	1	2	7	3	3	5	2	2	1	1	1		28		
Taunton	360	26	Sherburn	Hannah Wido									1	1			2		
Taunton	360	27	Fish	Hannah Wido							1	1	1				3		
Taunton	360	28	Spinney	Benjamin	1	1		1		2			1				6		
Taunton	360	29	Barstow	Wido				1						1			2		
Taunton	360	30	White	Elijah				1		3			1				5		
Taunton	360	31	Tisdale	Simeon		6	3		1		1	1		2			14		
Taunton	360	32	Tubbs	Isaac	1	2	1		1	1			1	1			8		
Taunton	360	33	Briggs	Dean	3			1		2			1				7		
Taunton	360	34	Witherell	David	2			1		2			1				6		
Taunton	360	35	Vickery	Content Wido						1			1	1			3		
Taunton	360	36	Briggs	John		2		1					1				4		
Taunton	360	37	Harvey	Ephraim	1			1			1		1				4		
Taunton	360	38	Howard	Joseph	1			1					1				3		
Taunton	360	39	Burt	Isaac Junior	2	1			1		1	2	1				8		
Taunton	360	40	Stacey	Amos	3			2		4			2				11		
Taunton	360	41	Crosman	Robert Junr	4	1		1		1	2		1				10		
Taunton	360	42	Smith	Allen				1		4			1	1			7		
Taunton	361	1	Shores	Jonathan	1			1		2			1				5		
Taunton	361	2	Crosman	Ebenezer			2		1				1	1			5		
Taunton	361	3	Luscombe	Robert		1	1		1			2		1			6		
Taunton	361	4	Harding	Prince											2		2		
Taunton	361	5	Crosman	Simeon 2d		1		1		3	2		1				8		
Taunton	361	6	Luscombe	Abijah Junior			1			3		1					5		
Taunton	361	7	Phillips	Eleazer	1			1		1			1				4		
Taunton	361	8	Seckett	James				1						1			2		
Taunton	361	9	Ball	Abijah Junior				1						1			2		
Taunton	361	10	Burt	Rachel											2		2		
Taunton	361	11	Burt	James	2	2	1		1	2	1		1				10		
Taunton	361	12	Lincoln	Elizabeth Wido	1		1	1				1	1				5		
Taunton	361	13	Wilson	Susannah Wido			1			1			1				3		
Taunton	361	14	Presbrey	Seth	2	2	1		1			1		1			8		
Taunton	361	15	Macomber	Seth				1		1	2			1			5		
Taunton	361	16	Presbrey	William		1	1		1			1		1			5		
Taunton	361	17	Heffords	Samuel	1			1				1					3		
Taunton	361	18	Burt	Edward	2			1		3			1				7		
Taunton	361	19	Soper	Oliver	1		1		1	1			1	1			6		
Taunton	361	20	Padilford	Peleg	1	1	2	2	1			1	1	1			10		
Taunton	361	21	Dean	Edward	1			1		2	2	1	1				10		
Taunton	361	22	Macomber	Joshua Wms	2	1		1		2		1	1				8		
Taunton	361	23	Gammands	William	1	1	1			1		1					5		
Taunton	361	24	Hart	James	1		3		2			1		1			8		
Taunton	361	25	Dean	Sarah Wido										1			1		
Taunton	361	26	Dean	Ebenezer			1	1	1			1	1	1	1		7		
Taunton	361	27	Dean	Caleb		1		1		4			2				8		
Taunton	361	28	Dean	Luther	4	2		1		1			2				10		
Taunton	361	29	Lincoln	Robert			1			2			1				4		
Taunton	361	30	Dean	Elizabeth Wido		1						2	1	1			5		
Taunton	361	31	Dean	Lemuel		1		1					1				3		
Taunton	361	32	Caswell	Joseph				1		2	2		1				6		
Taunton	361	33	Caswell	Ebenezer Junior	3			1		1			1	1			7		
Taunton	361	34	Padelford	Philip	1	1		1	1	2	1		1		3		11		
Taunton	361	35	Staples	Job		1		1		2			1				5		
Taunton	361	36	Padelford	Edward			2		1	1	1			2			7		
Taunton	361	37	King	Elijah	4	1		1		1			1				8		
Taunton	361	38	Padelford	Jonathan		1			1			3		1			6		
Taunton	361	39	Stephens	Asa	1			1		1			1				4		
Taunton	361	40	Padelford	James	3			1		1	2		1				8		
Taunton	361	41	Padelford	Joshua	1	1	1	1		1			1	1			7		
Taunton	362	1	Padelford	Zachariah				1					1				2		
Taunton	362	2	King	Turner				1		1			1				3		
Taunton	362	3	Thomas	Richard	1			1		2			1				5		
Taunton	362	4	Padelford	Joseph	2			1		2	3		1				9		
Taunton	362	5	Adams	Peter											5		5		
Taunton	362	6	Eliot	John	1		2		1		1		1	1			7		
Taunton	362	7	Eliot	George			1	1						1			3		
Taunton	362	8	Eliot	Joseph	1	2	2		1	4		1	1				12		
Taunton	362	9	Eliot	Benjamin				1				1		2			4		
Taunton	362	10	King	Josiah		1	1	1	1	1				1			6		
Taunton	362	11	Robinson	Ebenezer	1	1		2		3	1		1				9		
Taunton	362	12	Richmond	Abraham		1				1		1					3		
Taunton	362	13	Richmond	Asa		1		1				1		1			4		
Taunton	362	14	Richmond	Stephen				1					1				2		
Taunton	362	15	Richmond	Noah	1			1		1			1				4		

Town	PG#	LN#	Last Name	First Name	FWM under 10	FWM 10 to 16	FWM 16 to 26	FWM 26 to 45	FWM 45 and over	FWF under 10	FWF 10 to 16	FWF 16 to 26	FWF 26 to 45	FWF 45 and over	Total All Other	Total Slaves	Totals	District/Township	Notes
Taunton	362	16	Richmond	Abiel	1		3	1	1		2	1		1			10		
Taunton	362	17	Richmond	Edward	2	1		1		1			1				6		
Taunton	362	18	Richmond	Elijah	1	1		1	1			1		1			6		
Taunton	362	19	Richmond	Seth	1				1		1			1			4		
Taunton	362	20	Briggs	Timothy					1					1			2		
Taunton	362	21	Caswell	Barnabas	2			1		1	1		1				6		
Taunton	362	22	Fry	Benjamin	2			1		1		1					5		
Taunton	362	23	Cain	Thomas	3	1		1		3	1		1				10		
Taunton	362	24	Perkins	David Junior	1			1		2			1	1			6		
Taunton	362	25	Barrows	George	1			1		1			1				4		
Taunton	362	26	Cain	John	2	1		1			1		1	1			7		
Taunton	362	27	Dean	Rebecca	1						1	1		1			4		
Taunton	362	28	Curtis	Jonathan	1			1		1		1					4		
Taunton	362	29	Cain	Moses				1			2		2				5		
Taunton	362	30	Johnson	Nathaniel	2	1		1		1			1				6		
Taunton	362	31	Andrews	Nathaniel			1	1					1				3		
Taunton	362	32	Raymond	Benjamin	2			1		2			1				6		
Taunton	362	33	Cain	Samuel				1		2				1			4		
Taunton	362	34	Richmond	Joseph		1	1		1	2	1			1			7		
Taunton	362	35	Williams	Isaac				1						1			2		
Taunton	362	36	Staples	George Junior		1		1				1		1			4		
Taunton	362	37	Padelford	Solomon	3			1		2	1		1				8		
Taunton	362	38	Caswell	Moses				1		1	1						3		
Taunton	362	39	Williams	Ebenezer Junr	2			1				1					4		
Taunton	362	40	Codding	Elisha	3			1		2			1				7		
Taunton	362	41	Codding	Abiather	2			1					1				4		
Taunton	362	42	Caswell	Samuel	5			1		1			1				8		
Taunton	363	1	Caswell	John	2	1	1		1	2	1	1		1			10		
Taunton	363	2	Caswell	Job		1		1				1	1	1			5		
Taunton	363	3	Staples	Ebenezer	4	1		1		1			1				8		
Taunton	363	4	Staples	Noah				1						1			2		
Taunton	363	5	Staples	Joshua	3		1			1	1		1				8		
Taunton	363	6	Caswell	Abiel				1					1				2		
Taunton	363	7	Caswell	William	2			1			1		1				5		
Taunton	363	8	Caswell	Abigail Wido										1			1		
Taunton	363	9	Dean	Isaac		1	1	1						1			4		
Taunton	363	10	Barney	William	1		2		1	1			1				6		
Taunton	363	11	Williams	Lemuel			1	1				1		1			4		
Taunton	363	12	Williams	George 2d			1	1				1		1			4		
Taunton	363	13	Andrews	Henry	2			1		2	1	1					7		
Taunton	363	14	Harvey	Jonathan				1			2	1	1				5		
Taunton	363	15	Sickell	Silas Junior				1		4	1		1				7		
Taunton	363	16	Sickell	Silas				1			1		1				3		
Taunton	363	17	Staples	Samuel		2	2	1		1	1		1				8		
Taunton	363	18	Staples	George		1		1		1	1		1				5		
Taunton	363	19	Johnson	James	1			1		2			1				5		
Taunton	363	20	Richmond	Alexander			1	1					1	1			4		
Taunton	363	21	Elms	Abner	2	1		1		1			1				6		
Taunton	363	22	Dean	Solomon		1		1		2	1		1				6		
Taunton	363	23	Danforth	John			1	1				1		1			4		
Taunton	363	24	Dean	Abiel			1	1				1		1			4		
Taunton	363	25	Dean	David				1									1		
Taunton	363	26	Dean	Charles	1			1	1			1					4		
Taunton	363	27	Dean	Elkanah		1		1		2	2		1				7		
Taunton	363	28	Dean	Seth				1						1			2		
Taunton	363	29	Dean	Seth Junior	2	1		1		3			1				8		
Taunton	363	30	Hall	Joseph			1	1					1	1			4		
Taunton	363	31	Hall	Josias				1					1				2		
Taunton	363	32	Hall	Zilpha Wido		1					1	3		1			6		
Taunton	363	33	White	Jacob	1			1		2			1				5		
Taunton	363	34	Robinson	Increase	1		1		1	2	2	1		1			9		
Taunton	363	35	Dean	Obed	1	1		2				1		2			7		
Taunton	363	36	Dean	Abel				1					1				2		
Taunton	363	37	Dean	Ezra				1					1				2		
Taunton	363	38	Hall	Ebenezer	3			1		2	1	1	1				9		
Taunton	363	39	Dean	James	1	1		1		2	1	1	1				8		
Taunton	363	40	Dean	George Junior	2			1					1				4		
Taunton	363	41	Dean	George				1					1				2		
Taunton	363	42	Williams	Nathaniel	1	1	1		1	2	1	2	1	1			11		
Taunton	363	43	Gardner	Samuel	1			1			1	1	1				5		
Taunton	363	44	Linscombe	Francis	1			1						2			4		
Taunton	364	1	Bouton	Robert	1			1		2			1				5		
Taunton	364	2	Wilbore	Jedediah		1			1		2			1			5		
Taunton	364	3	Wilbore	John	1			1		3			1				6		
Taunton	364	4	Wilbore	Stephen	1		1	1				1	1	1			6		
Taunton	364	5	Leonard	Gilbert	2			1		2	1		1				7		
Taunton	364	6	Burbank	Abner	1			1		1		1					4		
Taunton	364	7	Leonard	Abiather		2			1			1		1			5		
Taunton	364	8	Dean	Walter				1		2		1					4		
Taunton	364	9	Leonard	Zadoc	2	1		1		3	1		1				9		

TOWN	PG#	LN#	LAST NAME	FIRST NAME	FREE WHITE MALES					FREE WHITE FEMALES					TOTAL ALL OTHER	TOTAL SLAVES	TOTALS	DISTRICT/ TOWNSHIP	NOTES
					under 10	10 to 16	16 to 26	26 to 45	45 and over	under 10	10 to 16	16 to 26	26 to 45	45 and over					
Taunton	364	10	Woodward	David				1			1			2			4		
Taunton	364	11	Seckett	Job	3	1		1	1		1		1	1			9		
Taunton	364	12	Harvey	James	2	1		1		2	2	1	1				10		
Taunton	364	13	Hunt	Job				1					1				2		
Taunton	364	14	Cannedy	Noble	2	1		1		2	1		2				9		
Taunton	364	15	Seckett	Moses Junior	1	2	1		1	2	2		1				10		
Taunton	364	16	Richmond	Reuben	2	1		1		1		1	1				7		
Taunton	364	17	Clarke	Ezra	1	1	1	1		1		1	1	1			8		
Taunton	364	18	Richmond	Sarah Wido										1			1		
Taunton	364	19	Hathaway	Job	3	2				2	2		1				11		
Taunton	364	20	Caswell	Joshua		2		1						1			4		
Taunton	364	21	Hoskins	Henry	2	2		1		1			1				7		
Taunton	364	22	Mirick	Obed	1			1		1		1					4		
Taunton	364	23	Thompson	Samuel				1				1					2		
Taunton	364	24	Hoskins	Ruth			1							1			2		
Taunton	364	25	Hathaway	Mary								1		1			2		
Taunton	364	26	Cole	Joseph	3			1		1			1				6		
Taunton	364	27	Williams	Gideon	3	1	1	1		1	1	2		1			11		
Taunton	364	28	Hoskins	John	2	1		1		1		2					7		
Taunton	364	29	Pierce	Lydia Wido		1								1			2		
Taunton	364	30	Pierce	Simeon				1				1					2		
Taunton	364	31	Hoskins	William		2	1		1	2				1			7		
Taunton	364	32	Eaton	John	2			1		1		1					5		
Taunton	364	33	Winslow	Job			2	1	2			1					6		
Taunton	364	34	Hoard	Prudence Wido								1	1				2		
Taunton	364	35	Anthony	Edmund	3	1	1	1		1	1	1	1				10		
Taunton	364	36	Clarke	Amos	2			1		2			1				6		
Taunton	364	37	Paul	Edward	2	1	3		1	2	1	2	1				13		
Taunton	364	38	Paul	Seth				1					1				2		
Taunton	364	39	Paul	Jeremiah	1	1	1	1		2			1	1			8		
Taunton	364	40	Staples	Nathaniel				1					1				2		
Taunton	364	41	Staples	Seth		1						1					2		
Taunton	364	42	Macomber	Abiel	1		1		2	2	1		1				8		
Taunton	364	43	Macomber	Ichabod	1			1			1	1					4		
Taunton	364	44	Macomber	Elijah		2			1				1				4		
Taunton	365	1	Andrews	Jedidiah	1			1		1			1				4		
Taunton	365	2	Macomber	Rufus	2			1	1	1			1				6		
Taunton	365	3	Dean	Job				1						1	1		3		
Taunton	365	4	Hack	Nathan		1		1						2			4		
Taunton	365	5	Hack	Nathan Junior	2			1		2			1				6		
Taunton	365	6	Lincoln	Waitstill								1		2			3		
Taunton	365	7	Blake	grinfill	2	1	2		1	2	2	1	1				12		
Taunton	365	8	Townshend	Job Junr	1	1	1			1			1				5		
Taunton	365	9	Jones	Sylvester	4	1		1			1		1				8		
Taunton	365	10	Jones	Benjamin Junior	1			1					1				3		
Taunton	365	11	Richmond	Walker		1	1		1	1	1	1					6		
Taunton	365	12	Richmond	Abner	2	1		1		1		1	1	1			8		
Taunton	365	13	Walker	James	5	1		1					1	1			9		
Taunton	365	14	Perry	Joseph	1			1		2			1				5		
Taunton	365	15	Read	Joseph				1					1	1			3		
Taunton	365	16	Chace	Paul		1		1						1			3		
Taunton	365	17	Hack	Tobey											2		2		
Taunton	365	18	White	Abijah Junior	2	2		1		3	1		1				10		
Taunton	365	19	Bayliss	Gustavus A.			1			2			1				4		
Taunton	365	20	Townshend	Job	1		1		1	1	1	1		1			7		
Taunton	365	21	Sayer	Thomas											5		5		
Taunton	365	22	Barney	Jonathan			2	1									3		
Taunton	365	23	Barney	Oliver	2		1						1	1			5		
Taunton	365	24	Danforth	Oliver		1		1				2	2	2			8		
Taunton	365	25	Lever	Ebenezer	1		1		1	1	2			1			7		
Taunton	365	26	Potter	Scipio											6		6		
Taunton	365	27	Thayer	Jonathan				1		1		1		1			4		
Taunton	365	28	Thayer	Jonathan Junr			1						1				2		
Taunton	365	29	Hodges	Henry			1	1			1	2		2			7		
Taunton	365	30	Lincoln	Nathaniel	1		1				1	1					4		
Taunton	365	31	Fish	Samuel		1				1				2			4		
Taunton	365	32	Dean	Leonard	2		1			1			1				5		
Taunton	365	33	Fisher	Moses		1		1						1			3		
Taunton	365	34	Haskins	Stephen				1						1			2		
Taunton	365	35	Wild	Samuel	1		1			2			2				6		
Taunton	365	36	Stacey	Lemuel	2		1			1			1				5		
Taunton	365	37	Wild	Rachel										1			1		
Taunton	365	38	Lincoln	Nidebiah	3			1		1	2		1				8		
Taunton	365	39	Dean	Enos	3				1	2	1		1				8		
Taunton	365	40	Lee	Abiather	1	2	1		1		1	2		1			9		
Taunton	365	41	Lincoln	Elisha			1	1			1		2	1			6		
Taunton	365	42	Lincoln	Gideon			1	1					2	1			5		
Taunton	365	43	Cobb	Nathan			2		1	1		1		1			6		
Taunton	365	44	Lincoln	Abner	2	1			1		1	2	1				8		
Taunton	365	45	Lincoln	Isaac				1		1				1			3		
Taunton	366	1	Lincoln	Caleb	2			1		4	1		2	2			12		
Taunton	366	2	Pain	David	2				1		1		1				5		
Taunton	366	3	Read	Joseph 2d		1	1			2		2		1			8		
Taunton	366	4	Lincoln	James			1						1				2		
Taunton	366	5	Briggs	Elisha				1		1			1				4		
Taunton	366	6	Lee	Thomas		2	2		1			2	1				9		
Taunton	366	7	White	Cornelius	2		2		1	3	1	1					10		
Taunton	366	8	Walker	Peter		2	2		1		1	1	1	2			10		
Taunton	366	9	Walker	Peter Junior	1	1	1					1					4		

73

TOWN	PG#	LN#	LAST NAME	FIRST NAME	\<10	10 to 16	16 to 26	26 to 45	45 and over	\<10	10 to 16	16 to 26	26 to 45	45 and over	TOTAL ALL OTHER	TOTAL SLAVES	TOTALS	DISTRICT/ TOWNSHIP	NOTES
Taunton	366	10	Vickery	Elijah	2	1		1		2			1				7		
Taunton	366	11	Howland	Cuff											8		8		
Taunton	366	12	Briggs	Ezra	3			1		1		2	1				8		
Taunton	366	13	Pratt	Rufus	2			1		1			1				5		
Taunton	366	14	Bolton	Seth				1		4	1		1				7		
Taunton	366	15	Lincoln	Benjamin 2d	1	1	1		1	2	2	2		1			11		
Taunton	366	16	Lee	George	1			1		3	1		1				7		
Taunton	366	17	Briggs	Daniel 3d	3	1		1				1					6		
Taunton	366	18	Sumner	Seth	1			1		2			1				5		
Taunton	366	19	Sumner	Jezaniah			2		2	1	2		1				8		
Taunton	366	20	Bullock	James	2			1		1			1				5		
Taunton	366	21	Hall	Elisha	1			1		1			1				4		
Taunton	366	22	Brown	George	2			1		1	1		2				7		
Taunton	366	23	Willard	Thankfull Wido								2		1			3		
Taunton	366	24	Hack	Peter		1		1		1	2		1				6		
Taunton	366	25	Baker	Simeon			2	1					1				4		
Taunton	366	26	French	Nathaniel	1			1			1	1	1				5		
Taunton	366	27	Jones	Benjamin				1					1				2		
Taunton	366	28	Washburn	Hutchins	3			1					1	1			6		
Taunton	366	29	Baker	Abijah	1			1		1		1					4		
Taunton	366	30	Baker	Walker	4			1		1			1				7		
Taunton	366	31	Pratt	Elizabeth Wido	1	1	2			2		1		1			8		
Taunton	366	32	Pratt	Nehemiah	1				1	1	1		1	1			6		
Taunton	366	33	Pratt	Enos	2			1		3			1				7		
Taunton	366	34	Harvey	Lydia Wido						1				2			3		
Taunton	366	35	Lincoln	Joshua	3			1		1			1				6		
Taunton	366	36	Brown	Calvin Fille	1			1		2	2		1				7		
Taunton	366	37	Crosman	Job	1			1		1			1				4		
Taunton	366	38	Lincoln	Josiah		1	3	1	1			1	2	1			10		
Taunton	366	39	French	Sarah Wido									1				1		
Taunton	366	40	Read	John		2	3		1	1	1		1				9		
Taunton	366	41	Green	David		1						1					2		
Taunton	366	42	Brown	Newport											4		4		
Taunton	366	43	Lincoln	Asa	1	1	1	1		3	2		1				10		
Taunton	366	44	Knap	Elijah		1	1	1					1				4		
Taunton	366	45	Shores	Benjamin		1	1	1				1		1	1		6		
Taunton	366	46	Pratt	Hannah Wido										2			2		
Taunton	367	1	Dean	Sylvester	2	1	1	1		1			1				7		
Taunton	367	2	Phillips	Edward	1	1		1		3			1				7		
Taunton	367	3	Davis	William			3	1		1	1	1					7		
Taunton	367	4	Sproal	James	2	1		2		3	1	2	1		1		13		
Taunton	367	5	Swift	Foster		2	1	1		1	2		1		1		9		
Taunton	367	6	Crosman	Leonard		1		1				1	1				4		
Taunton	367	7	Luscombe	Otis		1		1		2			1	1	1		7		
Taunton	367	8	Crosman	Robert		1			1	1			2				5		
Taunton	367	9	Richmond	Benjamin	1		1		1	1	1		1				6		
Taunton	367	10	Crosman	Mary Wido								1	1				2		
Taunton	367	11	Mason	Bethiah	2					1			1				4		
Taunton	367	12	Holmes	Gershom		1		1		1			1				4		
Taunton	367	13	Volleson	Leonard	2			1		1	1	1	1				7		
Taunton	367	14	Foster	Timothy			1	1			1	1	1	1			6		
Taunton	367	15	Porter	Leonard		1	1			1		1					4		
Taunton	367	16	Porter	Mary Wido		2			1	1	1		1				6		
Taunton	367	17	Foster	John	1	2		1		2			1				7		
Taunton	367	18	Shores	Abraham				1						1			2		
Taunton	367	19	Prentice	Joseph				1		3		1					5		
Taunton	367	20	Wilson	Robert Junr				1		1		1					3		
Taunton	367	21	Hodges	Abijah		1		1	1	1				2			6		
Taunton	367	22	Fisher	Moses Junr	1			1		1			1				4		
Taunton	367	23	Macomber	Abiather		1		1		3			1				6		
Taunton	367	24	Codding	James	1	1			1				1	1			5		
Taunton	367	25	Porter	Ester Wido									2	1			3		
Taunton	367	26	Lee	Benjamin	2			1		1			1				5		
Taunton	367	27	Porter	Lincoln				1		1							2		
Taunton	367	28	Hill	David											10		10		
Taunton	367	29	Burt	Zilpha Wido		2	2			1	1	1		1			8		
Taunton	367	30	Codding	James Junr	1	1		1		1	1	1	1				7		
Taunton	367	31	Codding	Samuel		1	2		1	1			1	1			8		
Taunton	367	32	Walker	Eliakim				1	1		1		1	1			5		
Taunton	367	33	Walker	James 2d				1					1				2		
Taunton	367	34	Tisdale	Tabatha Wido				1	1					1			3		
Taunton	367	35	Burt	Daniel				1	1			1	1	1			5		
Taunton	367	36	Knap	Edward	2			1		1			1				5		
Taunton	367	37	Knap	Ephraim	1				1	3	1		1				7		
Taunton	367	38	Tisdale	Hannah Wido						3	1	1		3			8		
Taunton	367	39	Tisdale	James	1	1	1		1	1	1	2	2	1			11		
Taunton	367	40	Burt	Henry					1			1	1	1			4		
Taunton	367	41	Burt	Abel	1	2			1	1				1			6		
Taunton	367	42	Lincoln	Elijah	1			1		2			1				5		
Taunton	367	43	Lincoln	John				1					1	1			3		
Taunton	367	44	Pratt	Aaron		1	3		1			1		1			7		
Taunton	367	45	Lincoln	James 2d	4			1					1				6		
Taunton	367	46	Crosman	Benjamin	3	1			1	2	1	1					9		
Taunton	367	47	Crosman	Simeon	1	1	1		1	1	2	2		1			10		
Taunton	368	1	Hoskins	Preserved	2			1		2	2		1	1			9		
Taunton	368	2	Gardner	Freeman	2			1		1			1				5		
Taunton	368	3	Andrews	Samuel	1			1				1					3		
Taunton	368	4	Andrews	Abigail Wido									1	1			2		
Taunton	368	5	Woodward	George	2	2			1					1			6		
Taunton	368	6	Hunt	Stephen	1	1		1					1				4		

TOWN	PG#	LN#	LAST NAME	FIRST NAME	FREE WHITE MALES under 10	10 to 16	16 to 26	26 to 45	45 and over	FREE WHITE FEMALES under 10	10 to 16	16 to 26	26 to 45	45 and over	TOTAL ALL OTHER	TOTAL SLAVES	TOTALS	DISTRICT/ TOWNSHIP	NOTES
Taunton	368	7	Hunt	Jail Widow								1	2	1			4		
Taunton	368	8	Dean	Nathaniel	2	2	2		1	2			1		1		11		
Taunton	368	9	Gary	Seth	2	2		1		3	1		1				10		
Taunton	368	10	Hodges	William	4		1			2	2		1				10		
Taunton	368	11	Hunt	Enoch	2	2		1		3	1	1					10		
Taunton	368	12	Cobb	Rufus			2	2					1	1			6		
Taunton	368	13	Mason	Philip	1			1		1	1	2		1			7		
Taunton	368	14	Stacey	Job Junior	4	1							1				6		
Taunton	368	15	Cobb	Sarah										1			1		
Taunton	368	16	Burt	David		1	2		1	1	1			1			7		
Taunton	368	17	Howard	Susanna Wido		1	1			1		1		1			5		
Taunton	368	18	Stacey	James		1				1		2	1	1			6		
Taunton	368	19	Hoskins	John		2		1		2		1	1				7		
Taunton	368	20	Read	George				1						1			2		
Taunton	368	21	Read	Oliver	3	1		1		1			1				7		
Taunton	368	22	Read	Isaiah					1	2	2	2	1				8		
Taunton	368	23	Dean	Ebenezer 3d	2		1	1		2			1				7		
Taunton	368	24	Godfrey	Isaac	2		1		1	1	2		1				8		
Taunton	368	25	Leonard	William		2	2		1		2		1	2			10		
Taunton	368	26	Williams	Richard 2d	1		1					1					3		
Taunton	368	27	Leonard	Joseph			1			2		1					4		
Taunton	368	28	Thayer	John Junior	3	1		1		2	1		1	1			10		
Taunton	368	29	Leonard	Benjamin Junr		2		1						1			4		
Taunton	368	30	Harvey	John	1	1		1		2	2		1	1			9		
Taunton	368	31	Thayer	John		2		1					1	1			5		
Taunton	368	32	Crane	George	2	1		1		2	1	1	1				9		
Taunton	368	33	Field	Nathaniel Junr	1	1		1				1					4		
Taunton	368	34	Sears	Sarah Wido	1					1		1					3		
Taunton	368	35	Leonard	Daniel	2			1		4		1					8		
Taunton	368	36	Thayer	Abiather	1	1		1		1		1					5		
Taunton	368	37	Harvey	David	1	2	2		1			1		1			8		
Taunton	368	38	Harvey	Henry	1	2			3			2		3			11		
Taunton	368	39	Harvey	Joel		2			1	4	1	2	1				11		
Taunton	368	40	Willis	Nehemiah	1	1			1	2	2	1	1				9		
Taunton	368	41	Woodward	Ambros	1	2	2		2	1				2			11		
Taunton	368	42	Harvey	Thomas			1			1		1	1				4		
Taunton	368	43	Short	Luther	1		1					1	1				4		
Taunton	368	44	Briggs	Daniel Junior				1					1	1			3		
Taunton	368	45	Briggs	Daniel				1					1	1			3		
Taunton	368	46	Torrey	Levi		1			1	2				1			5		
Taunton	368	47	Briggs	Job		1			1		1	3		1			7		
Taunton	369	1	Pratt	Seth	3			1	1	1	1		1				8		
Taunton	369	2	Hewett	Thomas		1	1		1	2		1	1				7		
Taunton	369	3	Allen	Lewis	2		1	1		1	1		1				7		
Taunton	369	4	Wheeler	Benjamin	1	2		1		2	2		1				9		
Taunton	369	5	Stacey	Job				1						1			2		
Taunton	369	6	Clerk	Sarah Wido			1			1		1		1			4		
Taunton	369	7	Hodges	Thomas		1		1		1		3		1			7		
Taunton	369	8	Willis	Sumner			1	1				1		3			6		
Taunton	369	9	Willis	John	1	1		1		2	1		2				8		
Taunton	369	10	Leonard	Elijah 3d	2		1					1					4		
Taunton	369	11	Williams	Guilford	1		1			3		1					6		
Taunton	369	12	Woodward	Caleb	1				1	1		2	1				6		
Taunton	369	13	Witherell	Allen	1		1			2		1					5		
Taunton	369	14	Smith	Isaac			1			2		1					4		
Taunton	369	15	White	Timothy	1		1	1		2		1					6		
Taunton	369	16	White	John Junior		2		1	1	2	1			1			8		
Taunton	369	17	White	Benjmain	1		1			1		1					4		
Taunton	369	18	White	John		1			1					1			3		
Taunton	369	19	Chamberlain	Samuel	1			1		1		1					4		
Taunton	369	20	Witherell	Solomon	1	1	1	1		1	1		1				7		
Taunton	369	21	Field	Abiezer	1	1	1	1			1		1				6		
Taunton	369	22	Lincoln	Ezekiel	1		1		1		1	1		1			6		
Taunton	369	23	Witherell	Thomas	1	2				2		1					6		
Taunton	369	24	Wilbore	Isaiah	1		1			1			1				4		
Taunton	369	25	Wilbore	Joseph				1						1			2		
Taunton	369	26	Wilbore	Abishai	2	1		1					1				5		
Taunton	369	27	Holmes	Thomas			1	1		3		1					6		
Taunton	369	28	Dean	David 2d	1			1		1			1				4		
Taunton	369	29	Pollard	John	1	2		1		2	1		1				8		
Taunton	369	30	Lincoln	Luther											6		6		
Taunton	369	31	Lincoln	Stephen	1		3		1	1	2	1		1			10		
Taunton	369	32	Leonard	Solomon	1	2		1		1	1	1	1				8		
Taunton	369	33	Field	James	1	1			1	1		1		1			6		
Taunton	369	34	Lincoln	Thomas	1	2		1		4	1	1	1				11		
Taunton	369	35	Field	Bethuel		1						1					2		
Taunton	369	36	Field	Nathaniel	1		1	1	2	1	1			1			8		
Taunton	369	37	Smith	James	1	1		3	1	4	1	1		1			13		
Taunton	369	38	Smith	George		1						1					2		
Taunton	369	39	Bassett	Daniel	1				1	1				1			4		
Taunton	369	40	Woodward	Paul					1				1	2			4		
Taunton	369	41	Lincoln	Mary Wido		1	1			1			1	1			5		
Taunton	369	42	Jones	Joanna Wido										2			2		
Taunton	369	43	Lincoln	Samuel		1	2		1			2		2			8		
Taunton	370	1	Smith	Abraham	1	1			1		1			1			5		
Taunton	370	2	White	Abraham	3		1		1	2			1				7		
Taunton	370	3	Bassett	Jeremiah	2	2	1		2	2	1		1	2			13		
Taunton	370	4	Smith	Noah				1				1							
Taunton	370	5	Skiff	Abraham	1		1						1				3		
Taunton	370	6	Willis	Noah			1	1			2						4		

TOWN	PG#	LN#	LAST NAME	FIRST NAME	FREE WHITE MALES under 10	10 to 16	16 to 26	26 to 45	45 and over	FREE WHITE FEMALES under 10	10 to 16	16 to 26	26 to 45	45 and over	TOTAL ALL OTHER	TOTAL SLAVES	TOTALS	DISTRICT/ TOWNSHIP	NOTES
Taunton	370	7	Eddy	Apollos		1			1	1	1			1			5		
Taunton	370	8	Eddy	Apollos Junior	1		2					1					4		
Taunton	370	9	Ball	Jacob				1	1					1			3		
Taunton	370	10	Eddy	Paul	1	1	1		1	1	2	2		1			10		
Taunton	370	11	Eddy	Asahel		1		1		2	1	1					6		
Taunton	370	12	Eddy	Mercy						1		1		1			3		
Taunton	370	13	Eddy	Abishai		2		1		3	1		1				8		
Taunton	370	14	Leonard	Job	2			1		4	2		1				10		
Taunton	370	15	Leonard	Benjamin		1	1	1						1			5		
Taunton	370	16	Dean	Oliver				1		1		1		1			4		
Taunton	370	17	Dean	Hannah Wido		1							1				2		
Taunton	370	18	Leonard	Nathaniel		1	2		1	3	2		1				10		
Taunton	370	19	Warner	Noah	1			1		2			1				5		
Taunton	370	20	Williams	Benjamin Junr	1	1	1		1			1		1			6		
Taunton	370	21	Barney	John	1			1		1	1	3		1			8		
Taunton	370	22	Barney	Adolphus	1		1					1					3		
Taunton	370	23	Dean	Elijah 2d	1		1				1	1	1				5		
Taunton	370	24	Dean	Cyrus	2		1					1					4		
Taunton	370	25	Austin	Abiather	1			1		1	1		1				5		
Taunton	370	26	Wilbore	Henry				1		5	2		1				9		
Taunton	370	27	Field	Zebulon Junr	2		1	1		2	2		1	1			10		
Taunton	370	28	Turner	Abner	1			1			1		1				4		
Taunton	370	29	Dean	Ruth Wido			2						1				3		
Taunton	370	30	Dean	David 3d			1			2							3		
Taunton	370	31	Lincoln	Hart	1		1	1		3			1	1			8		
Taunton	370	32	Lincoln	Abijah	1	1	2		1		1		1				7		
Taunton	370	33	Austin	Solomon	2		1	1		1			1	1			7		
Taunton	370	34	Dean	Reul	1			1					1				3		
Taunton	370	35	Willis	Elisha	2			1					1				4		
Taunton	370	36	Owen	Sarah									1	1			2		
Taunton	370	37	Lincoln	Elijah	3			1				1					5		
Taunton	370	38	Woodward	Peter			1	1					1				3		
Taunton	370	39	Tucker	Joseph 2d				1		3	1		1				6		
Taunton	370	40	Woodward	Abijah	2	1	1	1					1				6		
Taunton	370	41	Leonard	Silas	1		1	1		1			1				5		
Taunton	371	1	Tucker	Joseph					1			2		1			4		
Taunton	371	2	Gary	Zephaniah			1		1	1		1		1			5		
Taunton	371	3	Newton	Richard	1			1		2			1				5		
Taunton	371	4	Barney	Jacob	2	2	3	1	1		1		1	2			13		
Taunton	371	5	Danforth	William	1			1		2			1				5		
Taunton	371	6	Burbank	Joseph	2	1		1		2	1		1				8		
Taunton	371	7	Leonard	Charles	1		1						1		1		4		
Taunton	371	8	Dean	Abishai	2	2		1					1				6		
Taunton	371	9	Leonard	Willliams	1			1	1	2		1					6		
Taunton	371	10	Leonard	Molly Wido							1		1				2		
Taunton	371	11	Neal	George					1	1			1				3		
Taunton	371	12	Dearborn	Benjamin		1			1	1		1		1			5		
Taunton	371	13	Woodward	Daniel	2	1	1	1		1	1	1	1				9		
Taunton	371	14	Leonard	James Junior	1			1		4	1		1				8		
Taunton	371	15	Leonard	James		1			1	1	2			1			6		
Taunton	371	16	Leonard	Jemima Wido										3			3		
Taunton	371	17	Lincoln	Moses	1			1		1			1				4		
Taunton	371	18	Williams	Thomas			1		1				1				3		
Taunton	371	19	Harding	Chloe											1		1		
Taunton	371	20	Tiffany	Cyrus											4		4		

TOWN	PG#	LN#	LAST NAME	FIRST NAME	FREE WHITE MALES					FREE WHITE FEMALES					TOTAL ALL OTHER	TOTAL SLAVES	TOTALS	DISTRICT/ TOWNSHIP	NOTES
					under 10	10 to 16	16 to 26	26 to 45	45 and over	under 10	10 to 16	16 to 26	26 to 45	45 and over					
Westport	327	1	Almy	Job					1				1				2		
Westport	327	2	Almy	William	1	2	2	1		2	1	1	1				11		
Westport	327	3	Allen	Humphrey	2				1	3	3	1	1				11		
Westport	327	4	Allen	Daniel					1					1			2		
Westport	327	5	Almy	Mary					1				1	2			4		
Westport	327	6	Almy	Ebenezer			2		1		1	1		1			6		
Westport	327	7	Allen	Thomas	1		2	1	1	1	1	1		1			9		
Westport	327	8	Allen	William	1	1		1		1	2	1	1				8		
Westport	327	9	Allen	George		1	1		1	2		2		1			8		
Westport	327	10	Allen	Abraham	1	1	1		1		1			1			6		
Westport	327	11	Anthony	Sarah										1			1		
Westport	327	12	Allen	Adam	1			1		1	2	2	1				8		
Westport	327	13	Allen	Pardon	1			1		2			2				6		
Westport	327	14	Allen	John	1			1	1	1			1				5		
Westport	327	15	Allen	Wilson				1		3			1				5		
Westport	327	16	Allen	David		1				1		1					3		
Westport	327	17	Anthony	John		2		1					1				4		
Westport	328	1	Brightman	Thos		1	1	1				1	1				5		
Westport	328	2	Brownell	Sylvester	1	3	1	1		4		3	2	1			16		
Westport	328	3	Brownel	Nathaniel	4			1		1			1	1			8		
Westport	328	4	Brightman	John		1		2					1				4		
Westport	328	5	Brightman	Israel		1	2		1	1		1		1			7		
Westport	328	6	Brownell	Abner	3	1		1		1	1		1				8		
Westport	328	7	Brightman	Joseph				1			1		1				3		
Westport	328	8	Brownell	William				1					1				2		
Westport	328	9	Brownell	Peleg	1			1		2	1		1	1			7		
Westport	328	10	Brownell	Benjm Senr		1			1			1	1	1			5		
Westport	328	11	Brightman	Henry 2nd				1			1		1				3		
Westport	328	12	Brightman	William		2		1					1				4		
Westport	328	13	Brownell	Shadrach		1		1		2	1		1				6		
Westport	328	14	Browenll	Thomas		2		1		3	1	1					8		
Westport	328	15	Browenll	Jeremiah	3			1		1			1				6		
Westport	328	16	Baker	Job	1	1		1		2			1				6		
Westport	328	17	Brownel	George 2d				1		1	1			1			4		
Westport	328	18	Brownel	George		2		1			1	2		1			7		
Westport	328	19	Brightman	George	1		2		1		2	2					8		
Westport	328	20	Brownell	Mary									1				1		
Westport	328	21	Brownell	Josiah	3	1		1		1	1	1	1				9		
Westport	328	22	Borden	Edward		1	1		1				1		2		6		
Westport	328	23	Borden	Gidion	3	1		1		2			1				8		
Westport	328	24	Burden	Isaiah	2	3	1	1			1		1				9		
Westport	328	25	Boomer	Daniel	1	1		1		1		1	1				6		
Westport	328	26	Brownell	Ezekiel	2	1		1				2					6		
Westport	328	27	Brownell	Benjm		1		1			3		1				6		
Westport	328	28	Baker	James	1			1		2			1				5		
Westport	328	29	Baker	Charles		1				4		1	1				7		
Westport	328	30	Baker	Ebenezar	1	2	1	1		4			1				10		
Westport	328	31	Burden	Peter Black											5		5		
Westport	328	32	Brownell	Paul	1		1	1		1			1				5		
Westport	328	33	Briggs	Thomas	2		1	1		1				1			6		
Westport	328	34	Brownell	Luther	1			1				1					3		
Westport	328	35	Brownell	Ruth	1					3		1	2				7		
Westport	328	36	Brownell	Prince	1		1	1					1				4		
Westport	328	37	Brownell	Cornelius		1			1		1		1				4		
Westport	328	38	Brownell	Sarah									1	1			2		
Westport	328	39	Butts	Sarah						3			1				4		
Westport	328	40	Briggs	William		1		1		1		1		1			5		
Westport	328	41	Butts	Peleg			1			3		1					5		
Westport	329	1	Briggs	Gardner	1		1			2			1				5		
Westport	329	2	Briggs	Lovet	2		1		1	1		1		1			7		
Westport	329	3	Briggs	Ephraim	1	1			1	4	1			1			9		
Westport	329	4	Butts	Chase				1				1	1				3		
Westport	329	5	Bessee	Abijah	1	2		1				1	1				6		
Westport	329	6	Brownell	James		1		1				2	1				5		
Westport	329	7	Brownell	Elizabeth				1					2				3		
Westport	329	8	Brownell	Benjm Junr	1	2		1		3	1	1	1				10		
Westport	329	9	Brightman	Gardner	1			1			1		1				4		
Westport	329	10	Baker	Robert	1	2	2	1		3	1		1				11		
Westport	329	11	Brightman	Blis	1	1							1	1			4		
Westport	329	12	Cory	Isaac			1		1	1	1	2	2	1	1		10		
Westport	329	13	Cory	Joseph	3	1		1		1			1				7		
Westport	329	14	Cornell	Gidion			2	1					1				4		
Westport	329	15	Cuffe	Paul											11		11		
Westport	329	16	Case	Amy									1				1		
Westport	329	17	Case	Wanton	1	1	3		1	1				1			8		
Westport	329	18	Case	Moses	2	1		1		2	1		1				8		
Westport	329	19	Cory	Thomas			1	1		1	1	1	1				6		
Westport	329	20	Cory	Benjamin	2	3			1	3		2	1				12		
Westport	329	21	Cory	Jubiter											2		2		
Westport	329	22	Cory	Glasco											5		5		
Westport	329	23	Cornell	Stephen		1		1				1	1				4		
Westport	329	24	Cornell	Abraham				1					1				2		
Westport	329	25	Cornell	John	1			1	1	1			1	1			6		
Westport	329	26	Cornell	Thomas				1	1			1	1	1			5		
Westport	329	27	Cornell	Pardon	2			1		1			1				5		
Westport	329	28	Cornell	Peleg	2	2		1		2	1		1				9		
Westport	329	29	Cornell	Govet		1		1					1				3		
Westport	329	30	Cornell	Christopher		1		1		2	1	1		1			7		
Westport	329	31	Cornell	Daniel	1	1		1		1			1				5		
Westport	329	32	Cornell	Susannah								1	1				2		

TOWN	PG#	LN#	HEADS OF HOUSEHOLD		FREE WHITE MALES					FREE WHITE FEMALES					TOTAL ALL OTHER	TOTAL SLAVES	TOTALS	DISTRICT/ TOWNSHIP	NOTES
			LAST NAME	FIRST NAME	under 10	10 to 16	16 to 26	26 to 45	45 and over	under 10	10 to 16	16 to 26	26 to 45	45 and over					
Westport	329	33	Cuffe	John											5		5		
Westport	329	34	Cornell	Philip	2			1		1			1				5		
Westport	329	35	Cornell	John	2	2		1					1				6		
Westport	329	36	Church	Constant		1		1		1	1		1				5		
Westport	329	37	Croel	John	1	2		1		1		1	1				7		
Westport	329	38	Carr	Eseck	2		1			1			1	1			6		
Westport	329	39	Cadman	Hannah							1		1	1			3		
Westport	329	40	Castelo	Ramon		1		1		3	2		1				8		
Westport	329	41	Cornell	Rebeccah										2			2		
Westport	329	42	Capron	John				1			1		1				3		
Westport	329	43	Cornell	Charles				1					1	1			3		
Westport	329	44	Crocker	Robert	1		1	1		2	1		1	1			8		
Westport	330	1	Case	Esther	2	1				2			1				6		
Westport	330	2	Chushman	Ichabod	1			1					1				3		
Westport	330	3	Childs	Aaron											4		4		
Westport	330	4	Cottle	John											6		6		
Westport	330	5	Case	Adam	2	1		1		1	1	1					7		
Westport	330	6	Davis	Elijah	2			1					1				4		
Westport	330	7	Davis	Benjamin		1	1	1			1	1	1	1	1		7		
Westport	330	8	Davis	Gidion	1	1		1		3	3		1				10		
Westport	330	9	Davis	John	2	1	3		1	1		1		1			10		
Westport	330	10	Devol	Benjamin		1	1	1		1			1	1			6		
Westport	330	11	Dier	Zacheus	1	1	1		2				1				6		
Westport	330	12	Dier	John	1			1		1			1	1			5		
Westport	330	13	Dean	Micah			1	1					1				3		
Westport	330	14	Devol	Pardon				1		2		1	1				5		
Westport	330	15	Devol	John				1									1		
Westport	330	16	Devol	Samuel		2		1					1				4		
Westport	330	17	Davis	Stephen			1	1		1		1					4		
Westport	330	18	Davis	Philip Stephonson		1		1		1			1				4		
Westport	330	19	Davis	Philip	2			1				1					4		
Westport	330	20	Devol	David					1				1				2		
Westport	330	21	Devol	Daniel 2d					1	4			1				6		
Westport	330	22	Denis	Robert	2			1					1				4		
Westport	330	23	Denis	John	1		1						1				3		
Westport	330	24	Davis	Abner		1				1			1				3		
Westport	330	25	Devol	Benjamin 2nd		2		1		1				2			6		
Westport	330	26	Davis	Eben		2		1		2		1		1			7		
Westport	330	27	Devol	Daniel 1st				1						1			2		
Westport	330	28	Davis	Thomas	2			1		1			1				5		
Westport	330	29	Davis	Aaron	2			1		1			1				5		
Westport	330	30	Dier	Preserved	2			1		2			1				6		
Westport	330	31	Dier	Bershebe						1		1					2		
Westport	330	32	Dier	Head			1										1		
Westport	330	33	Dier	Joseph			1						1				2		
Westport	330	34	Davis	Nicholas	2			1		1			1				5		
Westport	330	35	Devol	Berjona				1					1	1			3		
Westport	330	36	Devol	Reuben	3		1						1				5		
Westport	330	37	Davis	Abial			1	1					1	1			4		
Westport	331	1	Davis	Abial Junr		1		1		1			1				4		
Westport	331	2	Devol	Abner	2	1		1		2	2		1				9		
Westport	331	3	Davis	John 1st				1			1	1		1			4		
Westport	331	4	Devol	Jeremiah				1					1				2		
Westport	331	5	Davis	Jonathan				1		1				1			3		
Westport	331	6	Devol	Barney		1	1		1	1		1	1		1		7		
Westport	331	7	Devol	Joshua	2	1	1						1				5		
Westport	331	8	Deck	Exter											4		4		
Westport	331	9	Earl	John		1	1		1	1	1			2			7		
Westport	331	10	Earl	Robert	2	1		1		2	2	2	1				11		
Westport	331	11	Earl	Benjamin			1			1			1				3		
Westport	331	12	Earl	Elizabeth								1	2				3		
Westport	331	13	Earl	Wanton			1				1		1				3		
Westport	331	14	Earl	George			1							1			2		
Westport	331	15	Fisher	John	1			1		3	2		1				8		
Westport	331	16	Fisher	Job			1	1					1	1			4		
Westport	331	17	Frelove	George		1							1				2		
Westport	331	18	Gifford	William Free Miller	1		1		1	2	2		1				8		
Westport	331	19	Gifford	Abraham	1		1						1				3		
Westport	331	20	Gifford	Abraham Blk Smith	1	2		1		1	1	1	1				8		
Westport	331	21	Gifford	John Constable	5	1		1		1		4	1				13		
Westport	331	22	Gifford	Christopher		1		1		1	1		1	1			6		
Westport	331	23	Gifford	William Wm. Son		1		1					1	1			4		
Westport	331	24	Gifford	Joseph		2	1	1		1	2	2		2			11		
Westport	331	25	Gifford	Richard	1			1		3			1				6		
Westport	331	26	Gifford	Russel	1			1		1		1					4		
Westport	331	27	Gifford	Warren	1	1							1				3		
Westport	331	28	Gifford	Elijah	1	1		1					1				4		
Westport	331	29	Gifford	Elijah Junr			1			2			1				4		
Westport	331	30	Gifford	Ephraim	1			1		1			1				4		
Westport	331	31	Gifford	Stephen	2			2					1				5		
Westport	331	32	Gifford	George Ch. Son	3	2		1		1		1		1			9		
Westport	331	33	Gifford	Perry	1	1	1						1				4		
Westport	332	1	Gifford	Jonathan	1	1		1		2	1	1	1				8		
Westport	332	2	Gifford	Benjamin					1	1				1			3		
Westport	332	3	Gifford	George	2			1		1		1					5		
Westport	332	4	Gifford	Warren Jn Son			1			1			1				3		
Westport	332	5	Gifford	Luthern Jn Son			1						1				2		
Westport	332	6	Gifford	John Blk. Smith	2	1	1		1	1			1	1			8		
Westport	332	7	Gifford	Jonathan Mor. Son	2			1		1			1				5		
Westport	332	8	Gifford	Warren Mor. Son	1	1		1		1			1				5		

TOWN	PG#	LN#	LAST NAME	FIRST NAME	FREE WHITE MALES					FREE WHITE FEMALES					TOTAL ALL OTHER	TOTAL SLAVES	TOTALS	DISTRICT/ TOWNSHIP	NOTES
					under 10	10 to 16	16 to 26	26 to 45	45 and over	under 10	10 to 16	16 to 26	26 to 45	45 and over					
Westport	332	9	Gifford	Meriam									5	1			6		
Westport	332	10	Gifford	James	2		1		1	4	1	1	1	1			12		
Westport	332	11	Gifford	Ichabod		1		1					1				3		
Westport	332	12	Gifford	Wilbour	2			1		1	1		1				6		
Westport	332	13	Howland	Beriah	2				1	1		1					5		
Westport	332	14	Handy	Ely	1		1	1		2			1				6		
Westport	332	15	Harrard	Abigail		2				1		3		1			7		
Westport	332	16	Hicks	Barney	1		1		1	1	1	1	1				7		
Westport	332	17	Hicks	Thomas	1	1		1		1			1	1			6		
Westport	332	18	Hicks	William		1		1			1			1			4		
Westport	332	19	Howland	Prince		2		1		1	2			1			7		
Westport	332	20	Howard	Daniel	2	1	1		1	3	2	2		1			13		
Westport	332	21	Howland	Philip	1				1					1			3		
Westport	332	22	Howland	John					1		2			1			4		
Westport	332	23	Howland	Henry				1	1					1			3		
Westport	332	24	Howland	Jethro		1	1						1				3		
Westport	332	25	Howland	Henry Junr		1		1					1				3		
Westport	332	26	Howland	Humphrey		1	1		1			1					4		
Westport	332	27	Hicks	Benjamin				1		1		1					3		
Westport	332	28	Hammond	Humphrey				1		2		1					4		
Westport	332	29	Howland	Nancy						1	1		1				3		
Westport	332	30	Howland	John Son	3	3		1		2			1				10		
Westport	332	31	Howland	Sibil								2		1			3		
Westport	332	32	Howland	Isaac	1	1	1	1					1				5		
Westport	332	33	Hart	Samuel	2				1	2			1				6		
Westport	333	1	Haly	Joseph			1						1				3		
Westport	333	2	Heart	Sandford				1		2	1		1				5		
Westport	333	3	Heart	Eben	3	2		1		3	1	1	1				12		
Westport	333	4	Hull	Susannah											4		4		
Westport	333	5	Hart	Cate											2		2		
Westport	333	6	Howland	Charles	2	1			1	1	2		1				8		
Westport	333	7	Irish	Joseph	1			1					1				3		
Westport	333	8	Jucket	Ebenezer	4			1		2		1					8		
Westport	333	9	Kerby	Nathaniel	1		3		1	1	2			1			9		
Westport	333	10	Kerby	Stephen		1			2	2	1			1			7		
Westport	333	11	Kerby	Justice					1			2		1			4		
Westport	333	12	Kerby	Wesson		1	1	1		1		2		1			7		
Westport	333	13	Kerby	Peace		1				2	1		1				5		
Westport	333	14	Kerby	David		1	1						1	1			4		
Westport	333	15	Kerby	Richard		1	1					2	3	1			8		
Westport	333	16	Kerby	Robert	1	1	2	1		1	1			1			8		
Westport	333	17	Kerby	Robert 2d				1			1	1					3		
Westport	333	18	Kerby	John			1	1		1			1				4		
Westport	333	19	Kerby	Nathaniel Blacksmith	1	1	2		2	2	1	3		1			13		
Westport	333	20	Kerby	Abner	1			1		1		1					4		
Westport	333	21	Kerby	Rachel										2			2		
Westport	333	22	Knight	John				1		1		2		1			5		
Westport	333	23	Kerby	Pardon		1				2			1				4		
Westport	333	24	Lawton	George		1	3	1					1	1			7		
Westport	333	25	Lamonyan	John	1	1		1	1	3	1		1	1			10		
Westport	333	26	Lincoln	Abraham		1	1	1					1				4		
Westport	333	27	Little	Charles		1				2		1					4		
Westport	333	28	Macomber	Nathaniel	3	1			1	1	2		1				9		
Westport	333	29	Macomber	William 2d			1	1	1			2	1	1			7		
Westport	333	30	Macomber	Charles	1			1		3			1				6		
Westport	333	31	Macomber	Wanton	1			1		3	1		1				7		
Westport	333	32	Macomber	Abiel 2d		1			1					1			3		
Westport	334	1	Macomber	Humphrey	2	1	1	1	1	1	1	1	1	1			11		
Westport	334	2	Macomber	William 1st					1				1	1			3		
Westport	334	3	Manchester	Gilbert	2	1		1		3			1				8		
Westport	334	4	Manchester	Thomas				1				1		2			4		
Westport	334	5	Macomber	Peter	1	1		1		1			1				5		
Westport	334	6	Mayhew	Hilliard	1			1		1		1	1				5		
Westport	334	7	Manchester	James Point		1	1	1		1			1	1			7		
Westport	334	8	Milk	Lemuel		1		1				1		1			4		
Westport	334	9	Mosher	John				1					1	1			3		
Westport	334	10	Milk	Job		2	1	1				1	1	1			8		
Westport	334	11	Macomber	Abiel Senr				1					2	1			4		
Westport	334	12	Macomber	Levy	2	1							1				4		
Westport	334	13	Macomber	Wesson	1		2		1	3	2	2	1				12		
Westport	334	14	Macomber	Abigail			2					1	1	1			5		
Westport	334	15	Maccowen	Daniel	3			1						1			5		
Westport	334	16	Mosher	Edmond		1	1		1	2				1			6		
Westport	334	17	Manchester	Edward	3			1		2			1				7		
Westport	334	18	Mosher	Joshua	1	1		1		3	1		1				8		
Westport	334	19	Mayhew	Jonathan		1						1					2		
Westport	334	20	Manchester	James L. Son	1	1	1		1	1			1	1			7		
Westport	334	21	Manchester	Joseph				1					1				2		
Westport	334	22	Manchester	Archibald				1			1			1			3		
Westport	334	23	Manchester	Philip	2	2	3		1		1		1				10		
Westport	334	24	Macomber	Bethiah									1	1			2		
Westport	334	25	Mosher	Brice	1		1			1			1				4		
Westport	334	26	Macomber	Mary										1			1		
Westport	334	27	Mosher	Abigail						1		1	1	1			4		
Westport	334	28	Macomber	Samuel	2	1	1		1	3	1			1			10		
Westport	334	29	Mosher	Wesson				1		3			1				5		
Westport	334	30	Macomber	Isaac		1							1	1			3		
Westport	334	31	Macomber	George		1	1	1					1				4		
Westport	334	32	Macomber	Noah	2	2			1				3	1			9		
Westport	334	33	Mosher	Ephraim	1		1					1		1			4		

TOWN	PG#	LN#	LAST NAME	FIRST NAME	FREE WHITE MALES					FREE WHITE FEMALES					TOTAL ALL OTHER	TOTAL SLAVES	TOTALS	DISTRICT/ TOWNSHIP	NOTES
					under 10	10 to 16	16 to 26	26 to 45	45 and over	under 10	10 to 16	16 to 26	26 to 45	45 and over					
Westport	334	34	Potter	Peleg				1						1			2		
Westport	334	35	Palmer	Mary										1			1		
Westport	334	36	Potter	Nathaniel		1		1	1				1	1			5		
Westport	335	1	Parker	J. Avery	1	1		1		3	1		1				8		
Westport	335	2	Petty	Isaac		2	2		1		1	1		1			8		
Westport	335	3	Potter	Abner		1	2		1	1				1			6		
Westport	335	4	Potter	Mohes					1					1			2		
Westport	335	5	Potter	Edward				1			1			1			3		
Westport	335	6	Potter	Stephen		1	1		1		1	2	1		1		8		
Westport	335	7	Peckham	Jonathan		1			1	2		2	1				7		
Westport	335	8	Potter	Barney					1	1			1	1			4		
Westport	335	9	Potter	Ichabod 2d	2			1		1				1			5		
Westport	335	10	Potter	Wesson	3	1		1		1				1			7		
Westport	335	11	Palmer	John			1	1	1			1	1				5		
Westport	335	12	Potter	Elias			1							1			2		
Westport	335	13	Potter	Elijah		1		1	1	1			1	1			5		
Westport	335	14	Palmer	Henry	2			1					1				4		
Westport	335	15	Potter	Rebeccah										2			2		
Westport	335	16	Potter	Ichabod Son	1			1				1		1			4		
Westport	335	17	Petty	James			1		1	2		2		1			7		
Westport	335	18	Peckham	Elizabeth		2								1			3		
Westport	335	19	Petty	John	3			1		1				1			6		
Westport	335	20	Petty	Sarah						2		1		1			4		
Westport	335	21	Petty	William				1		4	1	4		1			11		
Westport	335	22	James	Petty				1		2				1			4		Name probably reversed
Westport	335	23	Petty	Rebeccah		1				1		1	1	1			5		
Westport	335	24	Petty	Joshua	1	2		1	1	2	1	1		1			10		
Westport	335	25	Peck	James				1		2			1				4		
Westport	335	26	Potter	John	2			1		1			1				5		
Westport	335	27	Potter	Philip	1			1					1				3		
Westport	335	28	Philips	Edward		1				1	1						3		
Westport	335	29	Peron	William											5		5		
Westport	335	30	Richmond	Perez	1	1	2	1	1	1	2	2		1			12		
Westport	335	31	Records	William	1	3	3	1		2	2			1			13		
Westport	335	32	Russel	David		1			1				1	2			5		
Westport	335	33	Russel	Seviah				2	3			1		1			7		
Westport	335	34	Robertson	William		1						2		1			4		
Westport	335	35	Richmond	London											4		4		
Westport	335	36	Soule	Nathaniel	1	1	1		1	2		1		1			8		
Westport	335	37	Soule	Henry		1			1			1		1			4		
Westport	335	38	Soule	Lemuel	2	1			1	1	1		1				7		
Westport	335	39	Soule	David	3			1		3	1		1				9		
Westport	335	40	Soule	Jona			1	1					1	2			5		
Westport	335	41	Soule	Wesson					1					1			2		
Westport	336	1	Soule	Hiram	1			1					1				3		
Westport	336	2	Soule	Benjamin 2d	1			1		1				1			4		
Westport	336	3	Shearman	Gideon	1		1	1		1	3		1				8		
Westport	336	4	Soule	Benjamin Senr				1				1		1			3		
Westport	336	5	Shearman	Preserved		1		1	1	1	1	2		1			7		
Westport	336	6	Shearman	Alice								1		1			2		
Westport	336	7	Sisson	Jonathan			1	1					1	2			5		
Westport	336	8	Sisson	Wilson	1	1	1	1		3		1					8		
Westport	336	9	Sisson	William	1	2		1		2			1				7		
Westport	336	10	Soule	Joseph			1	1	1					1			4		
Westport	336	11	Sisson	Philip			1	1					2	1			5		
Westport	336	12	Snell	Peter				1				4		1			6		
Westport	336	13	Sisson	Richmond				1					1	1			3		
Westport	336	14	Sisson	Hannah	3					2			1	1			7		
Westport	336	15	Sandford	Philip	1	1	1		1			1	1	1			7		
Westport	336	16	Soule	Oliver	1			1	1	1	1			1			6		
Westport	336	17	Sandford	Rescom		1	1						1				3		
Westport	336	18	Snell	Benjamin	1	2			1	1	1						6		
Westport	336	19	Soule	Jacob	3			1						1			5		
Westport	336	20	Soule	Sarah								1		1			2		
Westport	336	21	Sisson	Peleg	3			1					1				5		
Westport	336	22	Sisson	Content		1							1	1			3		
Westport	336	23	Snell	James	1			1		1							3		
Westport	336	24	Shearman	Job	2			1		2	1	1	1				8		
Westport	336	25	Slaid	Samuel		1				1		1					3		
Westport	336	26	Sandford	Thomas			1			2		1					4		
Westport	336	27	Sandford	David	2		1			1		1					5		
Westport	336	28	Snell	Job	3	2	1	1	1	3	1		1				13		
Westport	336	29	Tripp	Daniel				1						1			2		
Westport	336	30	Tripp	Luthern			1			2		2					5		
Westport	336	31	Taber	Philip	1	1		1		1			1	1			6		
Westport	336	32	Tripp	David	2	1	1	1	1	1		2	1	1			11		
Westport	336	33	Tripp	John	2	1		1		2	2		1				9		
Westport	336	34	Tripp	Joshua	1			1		1			1				4		
Westport	336	35	Tripp	Preserved	2		2	1					1				6		
Westport	337	1	Tallman	Gideon		1	1		1	1	1		1	2			8		
Westport	337	2	Tallman	Jonathan				1		1		1		1			4		
Westport	337	3	Tibbets	John				1		1		1		1			4		
Westport	337	4	Tripp	Elizabeth										1			1		
Westport	337	5	Tripp	Isaac			1							1			2		
Westport	337	6	Tripp	James	2	1		1		2	1			1			8		
Westport	337	7	Tripp	Anthony				1					1	2			4		
Westport	337	8	Tripp	Philip	2	1	1					1					5		
Westport	337	9	Tripp	Patience	1	2				2	1	1					7		
Westport	337	10	Tripp	Lovel	1			1		1	1			1			5		
Westport	337	11	Tripp	Edmond	3	2			1	1		1	1	2			12		

80

TOWN	PG#	LN#	LAST NAME	FIRST NAME	FREE WHITE MALES under 10	10 to 16	16 to 26	26 to 45	45 and over	FREE WHITE FEMALES under 10	10 to 16	16 to 26	26 to 45	45 and over	TOTAL ALL OTHER	TOTAL SLAVES	TOTALS	DISTRICT/ TOWNSHIP	NOTES
Westport	337	12	Taber	Oseck		1	1	1		1	1	1	1	1			8		
Westport	337	13	Tripp	George	2	1				4	1		1				10		
Westport	337	14	Tripp	Perry				2	2								4		
Westport	337	15	Tripp	Daniel Mason	2	1			1				1	1			6		
Westport	337	16	Tibbets	Henry	2	1				2	1		1				8		
Westport	337	17	Tripp	Wilson			1		1		2		1	2			7		
Westport	337	18	Tripp	Ichabod Junr				1						2			3		
Westport	337	19	Tripp	Elihew	1			1		2		1					5		
Westport	337	20	Tripp	Jonathan	1			1	1	1			1	1			6		
Westport	337	21	Tripp	Thomas		1			1			1	1	2			6		
Westport	337	22	Taber	Mary Wd									1	1			2		
Westport	337	23	Tomkins	Gilbert	3	1		1		2			2				9		
Westport	337	24	Taber	Joseph	1		1			1		1					4		
Westport	337	25	Tripp	Tullinghast			1			1		1					3		
Westport	337	26	Tripp	Caleb	2	1		1		2	1		1				8		
Westport	337	27	Tripp	Nathaniel	1		1	1		2		1	1	1			8		
Westport	337	28	Tripp	Lot	3		1			1			1				6		
Westport	337	29	Tripp	Job	2		1			1	1		1				6		
Westport	337	30	Tilson	Jacob				1				1	1	1			4		
Westport	337	31	Tripp	Culbert		1		1		1		1					4		
Westport	337	32	Tripp	Ebenezer	1	1	1	1			1	2		2			9		
Westport	337	33	Tripp	Benjamin				1						1			2		
Westport	337	34	Tripp	Jacob				1		2	1		1				5		
Westport	337	35	Tripp	Charles	2		1			1	1		1				6		
Westport	337	36	Tripp	Ebenezer 2d	1	1	1			1			1				5		
Westport	337	37	Tallman	James				1						1			2		
Westport	337	38	Tripp	Ezekiel		1				1	1	1					4		
Westport	337	39	Tripp	Nathan	1	1		1		3	1	2	1				10		
Westport	337	40	Taber	Thomas	1			1		3	1		1	1			8		
Westport	337	41	Tripp	Constant				1						1			2		
Westport	337	42	Tallman	Ezekiel	1			1	1	3	2	1	1				10		
Westport	338	1	Underwood	Nicholas	3	3		1					3	1			11		
Westport	338	2	White	Jonathan Junr	1		1			1		1					4		
Westport	338	3	White	Jonathan				1						1			2		
Westport	338	4	Walkins	William			1	1		1		1					4		
Westport	338	5	Wood	Israel		1		1					1	1			4		
Westport	338	6	Whote	Holder	3			1		2	1		1				8		
Westport	338	7	White	Silvenus			2	1		1	1	1	1				7		
Westport	338	8	White	Obed	1			1		1	2		1				6		
Westport	338	9	White	Zerothmael	2		1						1		1		4		
Westport	338	10	White	Cornelius	1		1			1			1	1			5		
Westport	338	11	Wing	Prince	1	1		1		1		3	1				8		
Westport	338	12	Wing	David	1	1	1	1		2	2		1				9		
Westport	338	13	Wing	Edward	1		1	1		1			1				5		
Westport	338	14	Wing	Joseph		2		1					1				4		
Westport	338	15	Wilcox	Samuel			1	1					1				3		
Westport	338	16	Wilcox	Benjamin		2	2	1					1				6		
Westport	338	17	White	Peleg		1				1	1						3		
Westport	338	18	White	Roger		1	2	1		2	1	1					8		
Westport	338	19	White	George		2	1			2	1		2				8		
Westport	338	20	Wilcox	Abner		1		1		1		1					4		
Westport	338	21	Wood	Thomas				1			1						2		
Westport	338	22	White	William		1	2	1			1		1				6		
Westport	338	23	Wood	George		1	1	1		1	1		1				6		
Westport	338	24	Wood	Peleg	1	1							1				3		
Westport	338	25	Wait	John		1	1	1		1			1				5		
Westport	338	26	Woodle	Phinehas	2	1	1	1		2		1					8		
Westport	338	27	Wood	Robert				1					1				2		
Westport	338	28	Weaver	Joseph	2		1			2	1		1				7		
Westport	338	29	Wood	William	1		1	2					1	1			6		
Westport	338	30	Wood	Arnold	1		1						1				3		
Westport	338	31	Wood	John		1	1	1					1	1			5		
Westport	338	32	Wilcox	Daniel	1		1		1			1					4		
Westport	338	33	Wilcox	John			1	1				1	1				4		
Westport	339	1	Wilcox	William		1		1	1	1		1	1				6		
Westport	339	2	Wilcox	Silvenus				1					1				2		
Westport	339	3	Wilcox	Culbert		1		1				1	1				4		
Westport	339	4	Wait	Rebeccah									2				2		
Westport	339	5	White	William 2d		2	1			2		2					7		
Westport	339	6	Woodle	Thomas	3	1		1		2	1						8		
Westport	339	7	Wainer	Thomas											2		2		
Westport	339	8	Wainer	Michael											9		9		
Westport	339	9	Weedon	John		1		1		1			1				4		
Westport	339	10	Woodle	Gersham Junr	2		1			1	1		1				6		
Westport	339	11	Woodle	George	1		1			1	1	1					5		
Westport	339	12	Woodle	Richard	1		1			1		1					4		
Westport	339	13	Wood	Mary	1							1	1				3		
Westport	339	14	Windsor	Lydia									3				3		

TOWN	PG#	LN#	LAST NAME	FIRST NAME	FREE WHITE MALES					FREE WHITE FEMALES					TOTAL ALL OTHER	TOTAL SLAVES	TOTALS	DISTRICT/ TOWNSHIP	NOTES
					under 10	10 to 16	16 to 26	26 to 45	45 and over	under 10	10 to 16	16 to 26	26 to 45	45 and over					
Attleboro	322	36	*	*	1	1	1		1	1	1	1	1	2			10		
Attleboro	322	34	*	Ebenezer		1		1					1				3		
Attleboro	320	34	*	Ephraim	2			1				1		1			5		
Rehoboth	296	2	Abel	Caleb	1		1	1	3	1		1					9		
Rehoboth	308	28	Abel	Medbery		1		1	1	1		1					5		
Rehoboth	296	1	Abel	Robert			1										1		
Taunton	358	15	Adams	Abijah Junior				1	4	1			1				6		
New Bedford	418	8	Adams	Elizabeth		2	2			1			1				6		
Rehoboth	297	13	Adams	John Jun			3	1	1	3			1				10		
New Bedford	418	18	Adams	Knowles		1		1		1			1				4		
Taunton	362	5	Adams	Peter											5		5		
Taunton	356	20	Adams	Seth	1	1		1					1				4		
New Bedford	420	11	Adams	Wally		1		1				1		1			4		
New Bedford	418	12	Akin	Bartholomew	1	2			2	1	1	1					8		
New Bedford	418	13	Akin	Deborah		1				1			1				3		
Dartmouth	340	12	Akins	Jacob	1		2			1	1						5		
Dartmouth	340	11	Akins	James		1		2		1		2					6		
Dartmouth	340	3	Akins	John		1	1	1		1	1	1	1	2			9		
Dartmouth	340	8	Akins	Mary		1				1	1						3		
Dartmouth	340	10	Akins	Ruth	1					1		1					3		
Dartmouth	341	17	Akins	Thomas	1			1		1		1					4		
Dartmouth	340	9	Akins	Timothy	1	1	1		1		1						7		
Dartmouth	341	19	Akins	William	1			1	1		1						5		
New Bedford	418	9	Alden	John		1	2		1		2		2				8		
New Bedford	418	11	Alden	John Jun	2			1		1	1	1					6		
Raynham	372	18	Alden	Lois									1				1		
New Bedford	418	10	Alden	Otis	1			1				1					3		
Easton	388	3	Alger	Benjamin		1		1		1	1		1				4		
Attleboro	319	15	Alger	Isaac		1		1		1		1	2				6		
Easton	388	2	Alger	Isaac	1	2		1	2	2			1				7		
Rehoboth	297	8	Allen	Abner	1		2				1	1					5		
New Bedford	420	2	Allen	Abraham	2	1		1		1			1				6		
Westport	327	10	Allen	Abraham	1	1	1		1	1			1				6		
Westport	327	12	Allen	Adam	1			1		2	2	1					8		
Rehoboth	297	10	Allen	Amaziah	1		1			1		1					6		
New Bedford	418	5	Allen	Anthony		1											1		
Taunton	360	14	Allen	Barney	2	1	2		1	1		1		1	1		10		
Dartmouth	340	18	Allen	Benjamin			2						1				3		
Rehoboth	316	1	Allen	Benjamin			1				1	1					3		
Attleboro	320	51	Allen	Bicknall			1			1		1					3		
Rehoboth	302	10	Allen	Comfort	2					1							4		
Dartmouth	340	17	Allen	Daniel		1		1		1							3		
Westport	327	4	Allen	Daniel				1					1				2		
New Bedford	420	3	Allen	David	5			1	1			3	1				11		
Westport	327	16	Allen	David		1				1		1					3		
Rehoboth	297	15	Allen	Deborah															Enumeration left blank
Rehoboth	300	35	Allen	Deborah						1		2					3		
Dartmouth	341	18	Allen	Ebenezar		1				1		1					3		
Dartmouth	341	14	Allen	Ebenezar 2nd	1		1					1					4		
New Bedford	418	2	Allen	Ebenezer	2	3		1		1	1		1				9		
Rehoboth	297	6	Allen	Ebenezer			1			1			1				3		
New Bedford	420	7	Allen	Eleazer	1			1					1				3		
Mansfield	384	3	Allen	Elijah	2		1				1						4		
Rehoboth	297	14	Allen	Elisha			1					1					2		
New Bedford	418	15	Allen	Elizabeth	1					2	1	1	1				6		
Rehoboth	300	36	Allen	Elizabeth		1		1	1	1		1					5		
Rehoboth	316	2	Allen	Ephraim		2		1	1	2	1						9		
New Bedford	418	4	Allen	Eunice		1						2	1				4		
Easton	388	5	Allen	Experience															Enumeration left blank
New Bedford	420	5	Allen	Francis			1										1		
Rehoboth	297	11	Allen	George			1			2		1					5		
Westport	327	9	Allen	George		1	1		1	2		2	1				8		
New Bedford	418	26	Allen	Humphrey	1			1					1				3		
Westport	327	3	Allen	Humphrey	2			1		3	3	1	1				11		
Rehoboth	302	11	Allen	Isaiah	1			1	1	1			1				6		
New Bedford	418	24	Allen	James		1	2			2	1		1				8		
Rehoboth	297	5	Allen	James	1		1	1	1	1	2		1				8		
Somerset	408	21	Allen	James	2		1			1			1				5		
New Bedford	418	25	Allen	James 2nd	3	1	1	1		2	1	1	1				11		
Dartmouth	341	5	Allen	Jedediah	1	1				2		1					8		
New Bedford	418	1	Allen	Jethro	1		4		1	1	1	1	1				10		
Dartmouth	340	22	Allen	Jethrow			1					1					2		
New Bedford	418	19	Allen	Job		1						1					2		
Freetown	292	24	Allen	John		1				3		1			1		6		
Rehoboth	297	7	Allen	John		1		1		1		1					5		
Westport	327	14	Allen	John	1			1	1	1		1					5		
Rehoboth	305	16	Allen	Jonathan	2	2		1	1			1					10		
New Bedford	420	6	Allen	Jonathan				1									1		
New Bedford	420	1	Allen	Jonathan 2d	1	1				1		1					5		
Dartmouth	341	1	Allen	Joseph		1	1	4			1	1					11		
Mansfield	384	2	Allen	Joseph	1		1		1	2	1		1				7		
Rehoboth	316	3	Allen	Josiah	2	1	1						1				10		

82

TOWN	PG#	LN#	HEADS OF HOUSEHOLD		FREE WHITE MALES					FREE WHITE FEMALES					TOTAL ALL OTHER	TOTAL SLAVES	TOTALS	DISTRICT/ TOWNSHIP	NOTES
			LAST NAME	FIRST NAME	under 10	10 to 16	16 to 26	26 to 45	45 and over	under 10	10 to 16	16 to 26	26 to 45	45 and over					
Dartmouth	340	15	Allen	Judah		1		1		2			1				5		
Taunton	369	3	Allen	Lewis	2		1	1		1	1		1				7		
Dartmouth	341	12	Allen	Margaret	1					1	1		1				4		
Mansfield	384	1	Allen	Micah	1		1		1		1			4			8		
Dartmouth	340	1	Allen	Obediah	2	1		1					1				5		
Rehoboth	297	4	Allen	Oliver		1					1						3		
Westport	327	13	Allen	Pardon	1			1		2			2				6		
New Bedford	418	7	Allen	Paul	1	2		1		3	1		1				9		
New Bedford	420	4	Allen	Peleg	1	1		1		2			1				6		
Dartmouth	341	3	Allen	Philip			1		2			1					6		
New Bedford	420	9	Allen	Robert	2	2		1		2	1	1	1				10		
Dartmouth	341	11	Allen	Ruben	1		1		2			1					6		
New Bedford	418	6	Allen	Rufus		2	3		1				1				7		
Dartmouth	341	4	Allen	Russel	2	1		1	1	2	1		2				10		
Rehoboth	297	9	Allen	Samuel		1	1	1			1	1	1				6		
Rehoboth	297	3	Allen	Samuel 2d	1	1		1	1	1	1						6		
New Bedford	418	3	Allen	Silvanus		1			1		1		1				4		
Rehoboth	296	3	Allen	Stephen	1		1	1				1	1				5		
Dartmouth	341	2	Allen	Sylvanus		1		1			1		1				4		
Dartmouth	340	16	Allen	Thomas		2		1			1		1				5		
Dartmouth	341	6	Allen	Thomas			1			2		1					6		
Dartmouth	341	13	Allen	Thomas	1			2					1				4		
Westport	327	7	Allen	Thomas	1		2	1	1	1	1	1		1			9		
New Bedford	418	16	Allen	William		1		3				2					6		
Westport	327	8	Allen	William	1	1		1		1	2	1	1				8		
Westport	327	15	Allen	Wilson		1		3					1				5		
Dartmouth	341	8	Almy	Christopher		1							1				2		
Westport	327	6	Almy	Ebenezer			2		1		1	1		1			6		
Dartmouth	340	14	Almy	George		1		1		1			1				4		
Dartmouth	340	2	Almy	Jiles			1		1	2		1					8		
Westport	327	1	Almy	Job			1				1						2		
Dartmouth	341	23	Almy	Joseph									3				3		
Westport	327	5	Almy	Mary			1					1	2				4		
Dartmouth	340	4	Almy	Peleg	1		1			1		1					7		
Dartmouth	341	10	Almy	Richard		1					1						2		
Dartmouth	341	9	Almy	Thomas		1					1						3		
Westport	327	2	Almy	William	1	2	2	1		2	1	1	1				11		
Easton	388	6	Ames	Jotham		1		1		1			1				5		
Easton	388	1	Ames	Permenas		1		1		2			1				5		
Dartmouth	340	21	Andrew	John		1					1						4		
Dartmouth	340	20	Andrew	Mary		2		1					1				4		
Dartmouth	340	19	Andrew	Stephen			1			1			1				3		
New Bedford	420	10	Andrews	Abial	2			1					1				4		
Taunton	368	4	Andrews	Abigail Wido								1	1				2		
Dighton	413	26	Andrews	David	2			1		3		1	1	1			9		
Dighton	413	35	Andrews	Elkanah	3	2			1	1			1		1		9		
Raynham	373	10	Andrews	George			1		1	1	1	1	1				6		
Taunton	363	13	Andrews	Henry	2			1		2	1	1					7		
Taunton	365	1	Andrews	Jedidiah	1		1			1			1				4		
Dighton	414	13	Andrews	John	3	1		1					1	1			7		
Raynham	375	4	Andrews	John	2	3		1		2			1				9		
Dighton	413	30	Andrews	Joseph	2			1		1			1	1			6		
Raynham	378	1	Andrews	Joseph	2			1					1				4		
Raynham	374	24	Andrews	Nathan	2	1		1		1	1	2	1				9		
Taunton	362	31	Andrews	Nathaniel			1	1					1				3		
Raynham	374	12	Andrews	Nathaniel Junr	1			1		2			1	1			6		
Raynham	372	37	Andrews	Reuben	1			1	2	2	1		1				8		
Raynham	375	7	Andrews	Rufus	1			1		1	1	1	1				6		
Taunton	368	3	Andrews	Samuel	1		1						1				3		
Dighton	412	45	Andrews	Stephen	2	1	1	1		2			1				8		
Dighton	413	36	Andrews	Thomas		2		1		1	1						5		
Dighton	409	7	Andrews	William	1	1		1	1	1			1				5		
Raynham	373	7	Andrews	Zephaniah	4	2		1					1				8		
Berkley	275	2	Andros	Thomas	3	1		1		3	2	1					11		
Taunton	357	14	Angell	John				1		1		2	1				5		
New Bedford	418	14	Anible	Isaac			1										1		
Rehoboth	297	12	Anthony	Abner	1			1					1				3		
Dartmouth	340	5	Anthony	Abraham										5			5		
Dartmouth	341	16	Anthony	Caleb	1		1		2			1	1				10		
Somerset	404	45	Anthony	Caleb			1		2			1					4		
Somerset	407	38	Anthony	Caleb	3	1		1		3			1				9		
Dartmouth	341	21	Anthony	Daniel		1		1				1					4		
New Bedford	420	12	Anthony	Daniel	2	1		1		1	1						6		
Somerset	408	17	Anthony	David	1	2	3		1	3	2	2		1			15		
Taunton	364	35	Anthony	Edmund	3	1	1	1		1	1	1	1				10		
Somerset	407	36	Anthony	Gardner	2	2	1		1	3	3		1	1			14		
Dartmouth	341	22	Anthony	Gidion		1		1				1					6		
Somerset	408	11	Anthony	Hezekiah	2			1		1			1				5		
Somerset	407	39	Anthony	Israel		1				1	1		1				4		
Dartmouth	340	13	Anthony	Jacob			1	2					1				4		
Swansea	399	8	Anthony	Job	3							1					6		

TOWN	PG#	LN#	LAST NAME	FIRST NAME	FREE WHITE MALES					FREE WHITE FEMALES					TOTAL ALL OTHER	TOTAL SLAVES	TOTALS	DISTRICT/ TOWNSHIP	NOTES
					under 10	10 to 16	16 to 26	26 to 45	45 and over	under 10	10 to 16	16 to 26	26 to 45	45 and over					
New Bedford	420	13	Anthony	John											6		6		
Somerset	407	37	Anthony	John		2			1	2				1			6		
Westport	327	17	Anthony	John		2			1				1				4		
Dartmouth	340	7	Anthony	Joseph												4	4		
Somerset	407	44	Anthony	Peleg			1			1		1					3		
Dartmouth	340	6	Anthony	Quanh												5	5		
Rehoboth	314	41	Anthony	Reuben	1		1	2		1		1					8		
Somerset	407	42	Anthony	Saml	1			1		2			1				5		
Westport	327	11	Anthony	Sarah									1				1		
Dartmouth	341	15	Anthony	Simon									2			2	2		
Somerset	407	43	Anthony	Stephen	3			1		2	2		1				9		
Dartmouth	341	20	Anthony	William		1		1					1	1			4		
New Bedford	418	23	Anthony	William											4		4		
Somerset	407	41	Anthony	William				1					1				2		
Rehoboth	309	13	Antrum	Darius			1						1				2		
Rehoboth	297	1	Armington	Asa	1			1				1					6		
Rehoboth	309	11	Armington	Benjamin	1			1		1			1				4		
Rehoboth	296	4	Armington	John				1		1			1				3		
Rehoboth	309	12	Armington	Joseph	3	2	2	1	2	1	1	1	1	1			18		
Rehoboth	297	2	Armington	Walker		1							1				3		
New Bedford	420	8	Armstrong	Susanna	1								1				2		
Norton	379	3	Arnold	Asa	1			1		1			1				4		
Raynham	378	2	Arnold	David		1	1	1	1	1		1	1				7		
Raynham	378	3	Arnold	John	1			1	1	1			1				5		
Freetown	292	5	Ashley	Abraham	4	1	2	1		2	1	1					12		
Freetown	292	29	Ashley	Abraham Jr			1			4			1				6		
Freetown	293	6	Ashley	Barnabas		1		1		1			1				4		
Freetown	292	30	Ashley	Enoch	1			1				1					3		
Freetown	292	16	Ashley	Micah	1		1		1	3	3		1				10		
Freetown	292	28	Ashley	Percival		1		1						1	1		4		
Freetown	293	5	Ashley	Percival Junr	3			1		1			1				6		
Freetown	292	10	Ashley	Taber	2		1						1				4		
New Bedford	418	22	Ashley	William			1						1		1		3		
Attleboro	321	54	Atherton	Daniel			1			2			1				4		
Mansfield	384	4	Atherton	Phillip	1	2		1					1	1			6		
Attleboro	318	42	Atherton	Rufus	1			1					1	1			4		
Attleboro	318	37	Atwell	William L		1		1	1								3		
Dighton	410	23	Atwood	George	2			2		2			1				7		
Dighton	413	21	Atwood	James	2	1		1		1			1				6		
Dighton	410	24	Atwood	John		1	1					1					3		
Berkley	274	4	Atwood	Joseph			2	1				3	1	1			8		
Dighton	410	31	Atwood	Joseph		1		2		1			1	1			6		
Dighton	410	42	Atwood	Sylv Jr	2	1		1		2	1		1				8		
Dighton	410	41	Atwood	Sylvest				1					2	2			5		
Somerset	406	45	Augar	Joshua	1								2				3		
Dartmouth	341	7	Auker	Joseph									1						
Taunton	370	25	Austin	Abiather	1			1		1	1		1				5		
Dighton	414	34	Austin	Abijah			1			1			1				3		
Norton	379	1	Austin	David	1	1	1		1	1	3	1					9		
New Bedford	418	20	Austin	Joseph		1		1	1	1	1			1	1		8		
Dighton	410	32	Austin	Seth		3			1		1			1			6		
Taunton	370	33	Austin	Solomon	2		1	1		1			1	1			7		
Norton	379	2	Austin	Stephen				1					1				2		
Easton	388	4	Austin	William			1			2			1				4		
Dighton	414	33	Austin	Zachariah				1			1	3	1				6		
New Bedford	418	17	Ayers	Edward			1			1	2		1				5		
New Bedford	418	21	Ayers	Joseph	1	1		1		2	2	2	1	1			11		
Norton	379	23	B*n	Seth	4	2		1		2			1				10		
Norton	379	7	Babbet	Edward	2		1	1		2			2				8		
Berkley	276	10	Babbit	Abijah		1			1	1		1	1				5		
Norton	379	9	Babbit	Betty			2			1	1						4		
Berkley	280	8	Babbit	Dean	2			1		1			1				5		
Freetown	281	11	Babbit	Ebenezer	1			1		2			1				5		
Taunton	359	5	Babbit	Ebenezer	1				1	1		1	1	1			6		
Freetown	282	32	Babbit	Ebenezer 2d	2			1					2				6		
Berkley	275	4	Babbit	Elkanah		1	1		1					1			4		
Dighton	409	14	Babbit	Gideon		2	1		1					1			5		
Berkley	276	11	Babbit	Isaac	1			1		2			1				5		
Berkley	275	5	Babbit	Isaac 2nd	1		1	1		1		1					5		
Berkley	276	2	Babbit	John		1	2		1			1		1			6		
Berkley	275	6	Babbit	Warren			2			1		1					4		
Taunton	358	42	Babbit	Ziba	1	2		1		2	1		1				8		
Dartmouth	342	10	Babcock	Benjamin				1	2				1			5			
New Bedford	420	23	Babcock	Joseph				1		1	1	1					4		
Dartmouth	342	12	Babcock	Peleg	2		1	1					1			6			
New Bedford	420	22	Babcock	Phebe	1	1	2			2	1	1		1			9		
Attleboro	321	34	Backman	Howland	1	1	1	1		2	1	1					8		
Attleboro	321	57	Bacon	Ebenezer		1	2	1	1	2	3	3		1			14		
Mansfield	384	18	Bailey	Abner				2		1		3	1	1			8		
Mansfield	384	15	Bailey	Samuel				1	1			1	1				4		
Easton	388	7	Bailey	Seth	1		2		1	2			1				7		
Taunton	366	29	Baker	Abijah	1			1		1			1				4		

| TOWN | PG# | LN# | HEADS OF HOUSEHOLD | | FREE WHITE MALES | | | | | FREE WHITE FEMALES | | | | | TOTAL ALL OTHER | TOTAL SLAVES | TOTALS | DISTRICT/ TOWNSHIP | NOTES |
			LAST NAME	FIRST NAME	under 10	10 to 16	16 to 26	26 to 45	45 and over	under 10	10 to 16	16 to 26	26 to 45	45 and over					
Dartmouth	342	11	Baker	Benjamin	1		1	1				1	1				5		
Westport	328	29	Baker	Charles		1		1		4		1					7		
Swansea	396	11	Baker	Daniel					1				1				2		
Westport	328	30	Baker	Ebenezar	1	2	1	1		4		1					10		
Dartmouth	342	3	Baker	Jabez				1				1	1				3		
Rehoboth	298	31	Baker	James	1		1						2				6		
Rehoboth	303	19	Baker	James	1		1						1				5		
Westport	328	28	Baker	James	1			1		2			1				5		
Swansea	398	30	Baker	Jere											2		2		
Rehoboth	304	7	Baker	Jeremiah				1			1		1				3		
Westport	328	16	Baker	Job	1	1		1		2			1				6		
Dartmouth	342	1	Baker	John			1	1					1				6		
Somerset	406	27	Baker	Jonathan	2		1			1		1					5		
Rehoboth	303	18	Baker	Joseph	1			1		2	1	1	1				7		
Swansea	399	32	Baker	Joseph			1			3	1		1	1			7		
Rehoboth	303	37	Baker	Joseph Jr		1		2			1						4		
Dartmouth	342	4	Baker	Lemuel		1		1				1					4		
Rehoboth	304	8	Baker	Lewin		2	1				1						5		
Rehoboth	298	32	Baker	Nathaniel		1		1		1		1					4		
Rehoboth	303	20	Baker	Nathaniel		1		1		1		1	1				5		
Rehoboth	303	41	Baker	Phebe							1	1					5		
Westport	329	10	Baker	Robert	1	2	2	1		3	1		1				11		
Rehoboth	304	35	Baker	Samuel	1	2	1			1	1	1					7		
Swansea	396	9	Baker	Samuel	1	1			1	1	2	1		1			8		
Dighton	414	25	Baker	Seth	2	1				1		1	1				7		
Taunton	366	25	Baker	Simeon		2		1						1			4		
Dartmouth	342	5	Baker	Stephen	3	1	1	1			1	2	1				10		
Taunton	366	30	Baker	Walker	4		1			1			1				7		
Attleboro	319	67	Balcom	Benjamin	2		1				1	1					5		
Attleboro	320	29	Balcom	Daniel	2		1			1		1	1	1			7		
Attleboro	319	12	Balcom	Elijah	1	1		1				1	1	1			6		
Attleboro	319	52	Balcom	Jacob	1	1		1			2		1				6		
Attleboro	319	19	Balcom	Mary	2	1		1			2		1				7		
Attleboro	319	18	Balcom	Nathan		1		2	2	1	2	2	1				11		
Attleboro	320	24	Balcom	Saml	1			1		1	1	1		1			6		
Attleboro	319	35	Balcom	William				1		1		1					3		
Rehoboth	302	24	Baldwin	Nathan		1	1	1		1	1						6		
Dartmouth	342	9	Baley	Zuacke											3		3		
Norton	379	19	Balkcom	Alexander				1				1	1				3		
Norton	379	20	Balkcom	David		2		1		1	1	1					7		
Norton	379	22	Balkcom	Jacob			1			1		1					3		
Norton	379	21	Balkcom	James	3		1			1		1					6		
Norton	379	18	Balkcom	Samuel	1	1		2		1		1					6		
Attleboro	318	62	Balkom	Enoch		2	1					1	1				5		
Taunton	361	9	Ball	Abijah Junior				1					1				2		
Taunton	370	9	Ball	Jacob			1	1					1				3		
Dartmouth	342	6	Bard	Mary	3								1				4		
Dartmouth	341	36	Bard	Molly	2	1				1	1						5		
Somerset	405	34	Bardine	John				1					1				2		
New Bedford	421	5	Barker	Abraham		1											1		
New Bedford	421	17	Barker	Joshua	1		2					2					5		
New Bedford	421	6	Barker	Thomas											3		3		
Freetown	284	13	Barnaby	Ambrose		4	1	1			4	1					12		
Taunton	370	22	Barney	Adolphus	1		1					1					3		
Rehoboth	298	17	Barney	Benajer	1		1				1	1					4		
Rehoboth	304	15	Barney	Caleb		1		1		1							4		
Rehoboth	304	14	Barney	Christopher		1	1					1					3		
Rehoboth	298	18	Barney	Cyrenius		1		2		1							5		
Swansea	403	12	Barney	Daniel	1		1			1	1	1					5		
Taunton	371	4	Barney	Jacob	2	2	3	1	1		1	1	2				13		
Rehoboth	311	18	Barney	James		1		1			1						3		
Taunton	370	21	Barney	John	1			1		1	1	3	1				8		
Rehoboth	309	24	Barney	Jonathan	1	1	2	1				1					7		
Swansea	403	15	Barney	Jonathan	2		2	1		2	2	1					10		
Taunton	365	22	Barney	Jonathan		2											3		
Swansea	403	20	Barney	Joseph	1			1		3	1	1					7		
Taunton	359	1	Barney	Joseph			1	1				1		1	1		5		
Swansea	403	19	Barney	Josiah				1					1				2		
Rehoboth	309	21	Barney	Nathaniel		1	1					1					4		
Taunton	365	23	Barney	Oliver	2		1					1	1				5		
Rehoboth	315	8	Barney	Paul									4				4		
Swansea	403	14	Barney	Peleg	2		1			1	2	1					7		
Swansea	403	10	Barney	Ruben	1		1			2	1	1					6		
Rehoboth	304	16	Barney	William		1		1				1					3		
Taunton	363	10	Barney	William	1	2		1		1		1					6		
Rehoboth	304	9	Barns	John	2	1				1		1					8		
New Bedford	420	43	Barrow	Thomas	3		1			2	1	1					8		
Attleboro	322	8	Barrows	Aaron		1		1			1		1				4		
Attleboro	322	5	Barrows	Benjm	2	1		2			1	1	1				8		
Attleboro	320	20	Barrows	Elijah				1		3		1	1				7		
Attleboro	322	1	Barrows	Ezra		1	1	1		2		2					7		

TOWN	PG#	LN#	LAST NAME	FIRST NAME	FWM under 10	FWM 10 to 16	FWM 16 to 26	FWM 26 to 45	FWM 45 and over	FWF under 10	FWF 10 to 16	FWF 16 to 26	FWF 26 to 45	FWF 45 and over	TOTAL ALL OTHER	TOTAL SLAVES	TOTALS	DISTRICT/ TOWNSHIP	NOTES
Taunton	362	25	Barrows	George	1				1	1			1				4		
Freetown	290	30	Barrows	Isaac	4			1		1	1		1				8		
Dighton	409	3	Barrows	John			1		1				1	1			4		
Attleboro	320	19	Barrows	Joseph		2	1		1		1	2		2			9		
Attleboro	322	9	Barrows	Milton	1			1		2			1				5		
Attleboro	322	7	Barrows	Phillbrook	3	2			1	1	2	2	1				12		
Attleboro	322	10	Barrows	Priscilla									1	1			2		
Taunton	360	29	Barstow	Wido			1						1				2		
Easton	388	10	Bartlett	Isaac	3		2	1					1	1			8		
Easton	388	13	Bartlett	Peter	1		1						1	1			4		
New Bedford	420	29	Bartlett	Silvanus	1		1	1					1				4		
Easton	389	6	Bartlett	Susannah	2	1								1			4		
Rehoboth	303	26	Barton	Hail	2	1		1		1	3		1				9		
Norton	380	5	Basset	Daniel				1		2			2				5		
Norton	380	7	Basset	Isaac	1		3	1		2	1		1				9		
Taunton	369	39	Bassett	Daniel	1				1	1				1			4		
Taunton	370	3	Bassett	Jeremiah	2	2	1		2	2	1		1	2			13		
Attleboro	319	44	Bassett	Joshua	3			1		2			1				7		
Easton	388	11	Bates	Benjamin		1	1		1	1			1				5		
Mansfield	384	6	Bates	Benjamin	1		3		1	2	1		1				9		
Mansfield	384	11	Bates	John				1		2			1				4		
New Bedford	420	30	Bates	Joseph	3	1			1	2	1		1				9		
Mansfield	384	8	Bates	Leavit		1	1		1	1	2		1				7		
Norton	380	4	Bates	Leavit				1		1			1				3		
New Bedford	420	18	Bates	Nathan				1					1				2		
Attleboro	318	61	Bates	Saml		1	1	1		1		3		1			8		
Attleboro	319	57	Bates	Solomon	2	1		1	1			1		1			7		
Mansfield	384	9	Bates	Spencer	1		1						1				3		
New Bedford	420	41	Bates	Worth		1	2	1		2	1		1				8		
Dighton	409	6	Baylee	Hodijah		2	1		1	1	1		1	1			7		
Dighton	409	4	Baylee	Thomas		1	1	1		1			1				5		
Dighton	409	1	Baylee	William		2		1				2		1			6		
Somerset	408	14	Bayley	Edward		1							1				2		
Dighton	411	16	Baylies	Thomas S	2	2	2		2				1				9		
New Bedford	420	15	Baylis	Frederic	2			1		1			1				5		
Taunton	365	19	Bayliss	Gustavus A.				1		2			1				4		
Swansea	403	3	Bears	Wido						1			1				2		
Dartmouth	342	25	Bedon	Benjamin			1	1		2		1					6		
Dartmouth	341	30	Bedon	Henry		1				1		1					3		
Dartmouth	341	32	Bedon	Richard		1				1	1						6		
Dartmouth	342	26	Bedon	Richard			1			1			1				3		
Dartmouth	342	24	Bedon	Ruth				2					1				3		
Dartmouth	341	31	Bedon	Sampson		1				2	1						8		
Rehoboth	298	37	Beers	Mary									1				1		
New Bedford	421	1	Beetle	Henry	2	1		1		2	1	1		1			9		
Taunton	359	25	Belcher	Benjamin	2			1		1			1				5		
Freetown	288	30	Bennet	Benjamin Jr	1			1		1			1				4		
Freetown	288	29	Bennet	Isaac	1			1		1	1		1	1			6		
Dartmouth	342	23	Bennet	John				1					1				2		
Freetown	286	12	Bennet	Peter				1					1				2		
New Bedford	421	19	Bennett	Benjamin				1			1		1				3		
New Bedford	421	10	Bennett	Daniel				1		2	2		1				6		
New Bedford	420	37	Bennett	Edward			1	1	1		1	2	1		2		9		
New Bedford	420	27	Bennett	Elisha	2	1		1			1		1				6		
New Bedford	420	33	Bennett	Gilbert	1			1		1	1		1				5		
New Bedford	421	23	Bennett	Jeremiah			1	1					1				3		
New Bedford	420	28	Bennett	Joseph	3			1		2			1				7		
New Bedford	420	38	Bennett	Joseph 2d	3			1		2			1				7		
New Bedford	420	34	Bennett	Meribah									2	1			3		
New Bedford	420	26	Bennett	Robert	2	1	2		1	1			2	1			10		
New Bedford	421	18	Bennett	Thomas	1		1		1	1	2	1	1				8		
New Bedford	420	36	Bennett	William		1		1						1			3		
Norton	379	16	Benson	John	4			1		1	1		1				8		
Somerset	405	9	Benson	William	2			1		2	1		1				7		
Westport	329	5	Bessee	Abijah	1	2		1				1	1				6		
Rehoboth	310	6	Bicknal	Peter		2		1		2			1				6		
Attleboro	322	56	Bicknell	Thoms	1	2	1		1	1	1	1		1			9		
Mansfield	384	7	Billings	Benjamin		1	1						1	1			4		
Mansfield	384	14	Bird	Elijah	2	1		1		2	1		1	1			9		
Easton	389	3	Bisby	Sauel		1		1		2	1	1		1			7		
Freetown	291	10	Bisemore	John	2			1		1	1		1				6		
Rehoboth	309	30	Bishop	Comfort	2		1	2		2			1	1			9		
Rehoboth	309	31	Bishop	Ebenezer				1					2				3		
Rehoboth	309	27	Bishop	John		2	1	1					1				5		
Rehoboth	309	29	Bishop	Phanuel		1		1				1	1				4		
Attleboro	320	17	Bishop	Zephaniah	1	1	3	1		1		2		1			10		
Dartmouth	342	8	Biss	Arnold			1			4	2	1	1				10		
Rehoboth	306	14	Blacington	Samuel	1	1	2			1		1	1				7		
Rehoboth	307	18	Black	Eliphalet		1	1					1	1				5		
Attleboro	322	67	Blackington	David	2		1					1	1	2			7		
Attleboro	321	7	Blackington	Joel	1	1	1			2			1				6		
Attleboro	322	49	Blackington	Jona					1		1		1				3		

TOWN	PG#	LN#	LAST NAME	FIRST NAME	M <10	M 10-16	M 16-26	M 26-45	M 45+	F <10	F 10-16	F 16-26	F 26-45	F 45+	TOTAL ALL OTHER	TOTAL SLAVES	TOTALS	DISTRICT/TOWNSHIP	NOTES
Attleboro	321	8	Blackington	Mary								1		1			2		
Attleboro	321	10	Blackington	Oliver			1		1	1				1			4		
Attleboro	321	11	Blackington	Oliver Junr	1	1	1			4	2	1					10		
Attleboro	321	12	Blackington	Othnial		2		1		1			1				5		
Attleboro	321	18	Blackington	Otis	2		1	1		1			1				6		
Attleboro	321	17	Blackington	Peter				1						1			2		
Attleboro	321	19	Blackington	Peter Junr	2		1			1	1	1					6		
Attleboro	321	6	Blackington	Saml				1				1		1			3		
Attleboro	321	22	Blackington	Wm	2		1						1				4		
Dartmouth	342	16	Blackman	Ebenezer	1	1		1	1	2	1		1				10		
New Bedford	420	32	Blackmore	John	1			1		2			1	1			6		
Taunton	359	27	Blake	Edward	4	2			1	2	2		1				12		
Taunton	365	7	Blake	grinfill	2	1	2		1	2	2	1	1				12		
Mansfield	384	5	Blanchard	Judith	1			2					1	1			5		
Norton	380	6	Blandin	Benja	1	1	1		1	2	1			3			10		
Rehoboth	300	42	Blanding	Christopher	1	1		1	1	1	1		1				11		
Attleboro	320	9	Blanding	Daniel	1	1	2	1			1	1		1			9		
Attleboro	320	18	Blanding	Noah	1		1	1		1		1	1				7		
Rehoboth	299	31	Blanding	William	1	1	1	1	1	2	1		1				10		
Freetown	282	27	Bliffens	Anson	2		1				1		1				5		
Freetown	286	16	Bliffins	Vallintine	3		1			1	1		1				7		
Rehoboth	306	11	Bliss	Abedial	1		1		3	2		1					11		
Rehoboth	302	15	Bliss	Abel	1	1	1		3	1		1					9		
Rehoboth	308	33	Bliss	Abel	1		1		3	1	1						8		
Rehoboth	299	39	Bliss	Abel 2nd	1		1					1					3		
Rehoboth	302	13	Bliss	Abiah				1				1	1				3		
Rehoboth	302	14	Bliss	Abiah Junr	1	1	2		4	1		1					11		
Rehoboth	301	22	Bliss	Asa	1	1	1		3	2		1					11		
Rehoboth	299	9	Bliss	Asahel	1		1	1	1	1	1		1				7		
Rehoboth	299	12	Bliss	Charles			1		1	1		1					5		
Rehoboth	314	10	Bliss	Cromel 2nd		1				1							3		
Rehoboth	315	6	Bliss	Elizabeth								3					3		
Rehoboth	299	10	Bliss	Ephraim			1						1				2		
Rehoboth	302	18	Bliss	Jacob	2		1	1		2	1	3					10		
Rehoboth	307	30	Bliss	Jacob Jr															Enumeration left blank
Rehoboth	298	44	Bliss	James	1	1	1		2	2	1		1				11		
Rehoboth	299	8	Bliss	James 2nd	2		1		2	1		1					7		
Rehoboth	306	16	Bliss	John	1	2		1			1		1				10		
Rehoboth	305	43	Bliss	Joseph	1	1		1		1	2	1					7		
Rehoboth	299	7	Bliss	Lydia	1	2				2			1				7		
Rehoboth	299	38	Bliss	Nathan	1	1		1		1			1				5		
Rehoboth	299	4	Bliss	Nathaniel		1	2					1	1				5		
Attleboro	318	33	Bliss	Newman	2		1			1		1					5		
Rehoboth	302	16	Bliss	Noah	1	1		1			1		1				6		
Rehoboth	299	11	Bliss	Obediah			1		1				1				4		
Rehoboth	300	43	Bliss	Oliver		2		1		1	2	1					7		
Freetown	283	8	Bliss	Phebe										2			2		
Rehoboth	299	20	Bliss	Samuel		1	1			1	1						4		
Rehoboth	300	29	Bliss	Samuel			1	1				1					3		
New Bedford	420	40	Bliss	William	2	2				1	1		1				8		
Somerset	404	6	Blithens	Royal				1						1			2		
New Bedford	420	16	Blossom	Benjamin	1		2		1	4	1	1	1				11		
Freetown	289	26	Blossom	Charity								1	1				2		
Freetown	289	20	Blossom	Elijah	1		1			2	1		1				7		
New Bedford	420	21	Blossom	Joseph	3			1		3		1					8		
Freetown	289	29	Blossom	Rufus	1			1		1			1				4		
New Bedford	420	17	Blossom	Samuel		1	1			1		1					4		
Rehoboth	307	12	Bois	George			1						1				5		
Taunton	360	10	Bolkcom	David	2	2		1	1				1		2		10		
New Bedford	420	25	Bolles	Prudence		1						1					2		
Raynham	376	1	Bolton	Gamaliel		1						1					2		
Freetown	291	29	Bolton	John		3		1		4		1					9		
Freetown	292	2	Bolton	Jonathan		1			1					1			3		
Raynham	374	39	Bolton	Seth				1				1		1			3		
Taunton	366	14	Bolton	Seth			1			4	1	1					7		
Rehoboth	308	43	Bonna		1					1							2		First name left blank
New Bedford	421	8	Bonney	Samuel			2			1	1						4		
Easton	388	20	Bonney	William	2	1			1				1				5		
Raynham	373	24	Boodry	John	1			1		2			1				5		
Raynham	373	23	Boodry	Joseph		1			1	2				1			5		
Freetown	289	25	Boomer	Daniel		1	1		1	1		2		1			7		
Westport	328	25	Boomer	Daniel	1	1		1		1		1	1				6		
Freetown	289	10	Boomer	Ephraim	2			1		1	1		1				6		
Freetown	288	26	Boomer	James	3			2		1			1	2			9		
Freetown	288	25	Boomer	Martin	2	2	2		1	2			2	1			10		
Freetown	289	2	Boomer	Nathaniel	1	1		1		2			1				6		
Taunton	360	4	Boon	Susanna								1		1			2		
Dartmouth	342	20	Booth	Anthony			1						1				2		
New Bedford	421	22	Booth	Benjamin	1			1		3			1				6		
New Bedford	421	21	Booth	Isaiah				1				1		1			3		
Freetown	289	28	Booth	Jesse	2			1				1	1				5		

TOWN	PG#	LN#	LAST NAME	FIRST NAME	FWM under 10	FWM 10 to 16	FWM 16 to 26	FWM 26 to 45	FWM 45 and over	FWF under 10	FWF 10 to 16	FWF 16 to 26	FWF 26 to 45	FWF 45 and over	TOTAL ALL OTHER	TOTAL SLAVES	TOTALS	DISTRICT/ TOWNSHIP	NOTES
Dartmouth	342	17	Booth	Moten		1	1		3	1		1					9		
Berkley	276	15	Booth	Samuel			1			1			1				3		
Freetown	287	23	Borden	Aaron	1	1		1		1			1				5		
Freetown	287	29	Borden	Abel	2			1		2	1		1				7		
Freetown	288	14	Borden	Abner	3			1					1				5		
Dartmouth	342	21	Borden	Alexander		1			3	1							6		
Freetown	288	4	Borden	Arnold	2			1					1				4		
Freetown	288	6	Borden	Daniel					1	1	1		1				4		
Westport	328	22	Borden	Edward		1	1		1				1		2		6		
Freetown	290	1	Borden	George		1	1		1		1	2		1	1		8		
Freetown	288	7	Borden	George 2d	3		2	2	1		1	2		1			12		
Westport	328	23	Borden	Gidion	3	1			1	2			1				8		
Freetown	292	1	Borden	John		1			1				1				3		
Freetown	284	24	Borden	Joseph	1	1		1		2	1		1				7		
Freetown	287	20	Borden	Louisa Wid		1							1				2		
Freetown	285	4	Borden	Mary Wid.	1	1		1		1	1		1				6		
Freetown	285	6	Borden	Nathan	2	1	2	1		1	2		1				10		
Freetown	285	11	Borden	Perry		2		1			2		1		2		8		
Freetown	285	7	Borden	Richard	3	1		1		1			1				7		
Freetown	287	30	Borden	Seth	1			1		2			1				5		
Freetown	285	12	Borden	Simeon P	1	1	1	1		2	1		1				9		
Freetown	287	26	Borden	Stephen					1			1	2	1			5		
Freetown	293	30	Borden	Stephen					1				1				2		
Freetown	285	8	Borden	Thomas	3	2	2	1	1	3	1	1	1				15		
Freetown	288	9	Borden	Thomas 2d	1			1					1				3		
Freetown	287	31	Borden	William	2			1		1			1				5		
Somerset	404	43	Borland	Frances	2	3			1		2		1				9		
Rehoboth	300	10	Boroen	Nathan	2		1		3	1			1				12		
Rehoboth	308	37	Boston	Richard			1	3				1					5		
Rehoboth	304	36	Bosworth	Amos		3		1		1			1				6		
Swansea	396	1	Bosworth	Elisha				1					1				2		
Rehoboth	303	22	Bosworth	Ichabod	1			1	1				1				4		
Rehoboth	303	23	Bosworth	Ichabod Jr	1		1		1	1							4		
New Bedford	420	24	Bosworth	Joseph			1						1				2		
Rehoboth	298	27	Bosworth	Peleg	1	3		1		1			1				7		
Attleboro	318	52	Bourn	Andrew	1		3	2	1		1	3		1			12		
Attleboro	319	48	Bourn	Seth	2	1			1	1	1		1	1			8		
Rehoboth	307	29	Bourn	Stephen	1	2		1	3	2	1	1					11		
Somerset	406	2	Bourne	Frances			1					1	1				3		
Somerset	406	1	Bourne	Samuel			1			2			1				4		
Somerset	405	50	Bourne	Sarah		1								3			4		
Somerset	405	49	Bourne	Stephen		1			1	1	3		1				7		
Taunton	364	1	Bouton	Robert	1			1		2			1				5		
New Bedford	421	16	Bowdish	James			1				1		1				3		
Dartmouth	342	22	Bowdsh	William	1	1		2		1	1		1				7		
Freetown	285	10	Bowen	Abraham	2			1		2			1				6		
Rehoboth	305	2	Bowen	Amy										1			2		
Rehoboth	309	25	Bowen	Barzillia	1		1						1				3		
Dighton	413	31	Bowen	Benamiel	1			1		3	2		1				8		
Rehoboth	302	21	Bowen	Benjamin		1		2		1							3		
Rehoboth	311	32	Bowen	Benjamin		1				1		1					5		
Attleboro	320	62	Bowen	Betty										2			2		
New Bedford	421	13	Bowen	Charles											4		4		
Rehoboth	309	16	Bowen	Cyrrel			1	1									2		
Rehoboth	307	32	Bowen	Eleazer	3			1	2				1				7		
Rehoboth	310	13	Bowen	Eleazer															Enumeration left blank
Rehoboth	309	15	Bowen	Elizabeth									1				1		
Rehoboth	302	20	Bowen	Ephraim		1		1		1							4		
Rehoboth	303	6	Bowen	Ephraim	1		1		1	1	1						7		
Rehoboth	310	11	Bowen	Ichabod			1	1		1			1				5		
Dighton	414	39	Bowen	Jeremiah	1	1	1		1	3			1				8		
Rehoboth	304	3	Bowen	Jeremiah			1		1			1					3		
Rehoboth	310	5	Bowen	Joel	2		1		3	3		1					13		
Rehoboth	302	34	Bowen	John		1		1			1	1	1				5		
Somerset	405	19	Bowen	John	1		1	1	1	1	4		1				10		
Rehoboth	305	7	Bowen	Marten			1	2					1				6		
Rehoboth	309	23	Bowen	Mary		1						2	1				4		
Freetown	285	9	Bowen	Nathan	2		3		1	1	1	2	1				11		
Rehoboth	307	14	Bowen	Noah	1			1	1				1				8		
Rehoboth	307	33	Bowen	Numan		1		3					1				6		
Rehoboth	309	14	Bowen	Ruth						3			1				4		
Somerset	408	20	Bowen	Saml	2	1	1						1				5		
Rehoboth	310	12	Bowen	Samuel			1	1		1	1		1				5		
Rehoboth	309	32	Bowen	Simeon			1			1			1				3		
Rehoboth	310	7	Bowen	Simeon Jr	2		1		1	3			1				8		
Rehoboth	306	13	Bowen	Stephen			1		2			1	1				7		
Attleboro	318	39	Bowen	Uriah	1	1		1					1				4		
Rehoboth	302	19	Bowen	Uriah			1			2			1				4		
Rehoboth	308	24	Bowen	Uriah Jr		1							1				3		
Dighton	414	36	Bowen	Zenas	2		1						1				4		
Rehoboth	307	24	Bowers	Asa				1			1		1				5		
Somerset	405	6	Bowers	Cash V Flora											3		3		
Somerset	405	16	Bowers	David Widow of									1	1			2		

TOWN	PG#	LN#	LAST NAME	FIRST NAME	FREE WHITE MALES					FREE WHITE FEMALES					TOTAL ALL OTHER	TOTAL SLAVES	TOTALS	DISTRICT/ TOWNSHIP	NOTES
					under 10	10 to 16	16 to 26	26 to 45	45 and over	under 10	10 to 16	16 to 26	26 to 45	45 and over					
Rehoboth	307	23	Bowers	Edward	1		1	3		1		1					7		
Somerset	405	45	Bowers	Jonathan		2		1		4	1		1				9		
Swansea	398	14	Bowers	Joseph				1					1				2		
Somerset	405	8	Bowers	Mary Widow				1					2				3		
Somerset	405	46	Bowers	Philip	3	1		1		1	4	1					11		
Somerset	405	7	Bowers	Rose											1		1		
Rehoboth	312	40	Bowers	Sylvester			1				1						2		
Rehoboth	307	22	Bowers	Sylvester Jr			1						3				5		
Dartmouth	342	19	Bowles	Ezra		1		1		1							4		
Berkley	280	19	Boyce	John	1			1		1		1	1				5		
Freetown	281	4	Boyce	William	2			1		2	1	1					7		
Dighton	412	27	Bozworth	Isiah		1							1				2		
Swansea	403	48	Bozworth	Joseph	1	2		1		1	1	1					7		
Somerset	404	34	Bragg	Henry			1			1			2				4		
Dighton	413	38	Bragg	John		1	1	1				2	2				7		
Berkley	276	4	Bragg	Samuel	1		1			1	1						4		
Freetown	292	32	Braley	Amos	2		1			2		1					6		
Freetown	293	1	Braley	Asa	1		1			2		1					5		
Freetown	291	26	Braley	Benjamin	4		1			1		1					7		
Freetown	291	28	Braley	Ephraim	1	1		1		2	1		1				7		
Freetown	292	31	Braley	Ezekel	1	2		1			2		1				7		
Freetown	291	23	Braley	Nathaniel	1	1	2	1					1				6		
New Bedford	420	31	Braley	Seth	1		1					1					3		
Freetown	291	25	Braley	William			1			1		1					3		
Norton	379	13	Braman	Silvanus	2		1	1				1	1				6		
Norton	379	17	Braman	Thomas	1		1	1				1	1				5		
Rehoboth	311	22	Branch	Aholiab			1			2			1		4				
Freetown	288	11	Braton	Benjamin		1	1					1					4		
Freetown	288	15	Braton	Frances				1				1	1				3		
Rehoboth	314	45	Brayton	Alderman									1		1				
Somerset	406	41	Brayton	Daniel			1	1		1			2				5		
Rehoboth	305	17	Brayton	David	2		1	1		1	1	1					9		
Somerset	407	24	Brayton	John	2	2		1		2	2		1		1		11		
Dighton	413	17	Brayton	Ned											5		5		
Swansea	396	18	Brayton	Preserved		2		1		1	2		1				7		
Rehoboth	315	3	Brayton	Sip											8		8		
Easton	388	18	Brett	Calvin	2	1		1		2	1	1	1				10		
Taunton	359	20	Brewer	Daniel		1	1	1	1	1		2	1				8		
Raynham	374	37	Briant	David	1	1	1					1	1				6		
Berkley	280	23	Briant	Jonathan			1	1			1	1	1				5		
Berkley	279	26	Briggs	Abial		1	1	1			1	1	1				6		
Dighton	410	1	Briggs	Abiezer	3	1		1		1	3		1				10		
Dighton	409	38	Briggs	Abner	4	1		1		1	1	1					9		
Freetown	281	10	Briggs	Abner	2		1	1		1		1					6		
Berkley	278	29	Briggs	Abraham				1		2	2		1				6		
Berkley	279	18	Briggs	Amata Wid							1	1	1				3		
Berkley	279	15	Briggs	Amos 2d	1	1	1		2	3	1	1					10		
Berkley	281	13	Briggs	Amos 3d	1		1			1		1					4		
Dartmouth	342	2	Briggs	Caleb		1	1			1					3				
Dartmouth	341	33	Briggs	Daniel			1					1			2				
Norton	379	6	Briggs	Daniel	3		1			2		2					8		
Taunton	368	45	Briggs	Daniel				1				1	1				3		
Taunton	366	17	Briggs	Daniel 3d	3	1		1				1					6		
Taunton	368	44	Briggs	Daniel Junior				1				1	1				3		
Attleboro	319	29	Briggs	Davis	2	1		1		2							6		
Taunton	360	33	Briggs	Dean	3		1			2		1					7		
Dighton	409	22	Briggs	Ebz				1			4	1					6		
Dighton	411	26	Briggs	Edward		1				1	1						3		
Dighton	411	25	Briggs	Eliakim		1							1				2		
Dighton	409	41	Briggs	Eliakim 2d			1	1		4	1						8		
Freetown	282	31	Briggs	Elijah			1	1					1				3		
Taunton	366	5	Briggs	Elisha			1			1	1		1				4		
Freetown	282	30	Briggs	Ephraim	4		1			1		1	1				8		
Westport	329	3	Briggs	Ephraim	1	1		1		4	1						9		
Berkley	275	3	Briggs	Ezra			1	1					1				5		
Taunton	366	12	Briggs	Ezra	3		1	1			2	1					8		
Berkley	277	9	Briggs	Fobes	1		1			2		1					5		
Westport	329	1	Briggs	Gardner	1		1			2		1					5		
Berkley	279	22	Briggs	George	2	2	1					1					6		
Dighton	409	28	Briggs	George	1	1		1	1	2	2	2	1				11		
Freetown	294	26	Briggs	George		1	1			3		1					6		
Berkley	276	22	Briggs	Gershom	2			1		1		1					5		
Dartmouth	341	35	Briggs	Hannah								1	1		2				
Berkley	278	15	Briggs	Hathaway	1			1		3	1	1					7		
Norton	379	14	Briggs	Hezekiah	3	1	1					1					6		
Berkley	277	29	Briggs	Israel	2			1		1		1			1		6		
Mansfield	384	10	Briggs	Jacob		1		1				1	1	1			6		
Dighton	410	38	Briggs	James	1	4		1		1	1		3				11		
Dighton	413	41	Briggs	James 2d	1			1		1	1		1				5		
Berkley	276	21	Briggs	Jedidiah		2	2	1	1	2	1	3	1	1			14		
Berkley	279	17	Briggs	Job			1					1					2		
Taunton	368	47	Briggs	Job				1			1	3	1				7		

89

TOWN	PG#	LN#	LAST NAME	FIRST NAME	FREE WHITE MALES					FREE WHITE FEMALES					TOTAL ALL OTHER	TOTAL SLAVES	TOTALS	DISTRICT/ TOWNSHIP	NOTES
					under 10	10 to 16	16 to 26	26 to 45	45 and over	under 10	10 to 16	16 to 26	26 to 45	45 and over					
Berkley	278	14	Briggs	John		1	2		1	2	1	1	1	1			10		
Dartmouth	341	26	Briggs	John			1		4			1			7				
Freetown	282	12	Briggs	John			3	1	1	1		1		1			8		
Norton	379	15	Briggs	John		1	1		1			1		1			5		
Taunton	360	36	Briggs	John		2			1					1			4		
Freetown	283	25	Briggs	John 2d	1	1	1		1	2	2		1				9		
Norton	379	5	Briggs	Jonathan	3				2	1	3		1				10		
Dartmouth	342	13	Briggs	Joseph		3							1		4				
Freetown	283	15	Briggs	Joseph		1		1		4		1		1			8		
Berkley	276	27	Briggs	Keturah Wid															
Westport	329	2	Briggs	Lovet	2		1		1	1		1		1			7		
Attleboro	320	27	Briggs	Margaret	1	1					1	2	1	1			7		
Berkley	279	32	Briggs	Mary Wid					1			1	1				3		
Dighton	411	23	Briggs	Matthew	1	1	1		1		2	1		1			8		
Berkley	279	30	Briggs	Nathan		2		1		1		1		1			6		
Dighton	409	29	Briggs	Nathan			1	1						1			3		
Swansea	401	17	Briggs	Nathan				1		2	2		1				6		
Attleboro	320	63	Briggs	Nathl		1			1			2		1			5		
Norton	380	8	Briggs	Nehemiah	3			1		2			1				7		
Dighton	409	40	Briggs	Saml			1	1						1			3		
Dighton	410	2	Briggs	Saml 2d				1						1			2		
Dighton	409	23	Briggs	Saml 3d	1	3		1		4			1				10		
Berkley	279	9	Briggs	Sarah	1						1		1				3		
Berkley	276	23	Briggs	Seth		1		1						1			3		
Norton	380	9	Briggs	Simeon				1				1	2				4		
Mansfield	384	19	Briggs	Solomon				1	1		1		1				4		
Attleboro	320	35	Briggs	Stephen	1	2		1		2			1				7		
Berkley	276	26	Briggs	Thomas			1	1			1	1	1				5		
Westport	328	33	Briggs	Thomas	2		1	1		1				1			6		
Taunton	362	20	Briggs	Timothy				1						1			2		
Norton	379	4	Briggs	Timothy Jr	1		1		1	1				1			5		
Dartmouth	341	34	Briggs	Wesson		1	1	1		1		1			6				
Dartmouth	342	14	Briggs	William			1						1		2				
Westport	328	40	Briggs	William		1		1	1	1		1		1			5		
Dighton	410	3	Briggs	Zebedec	2			1		3			1	1			8		
Freetown	287	9	Brightman	Benjamin	2			1		1	1		1				6		
Westport	329	11	Brightman	Blis	1	1		1						1			4		
Westport	329	9	Brightman	Gardner	1			1			1		1				4		
Freetown	287	10	Brightman	George		1		1	2	2		2		1			9		
Freetown	289	21	Brightman	George	3	1		1		1	3		1	1			11		
Westport	328	19	Brightman	George	1		2		1		2	2					8		
Freetown	287	12	Brightman	Henry		1		1				1		1			4		
Westport	328	11	Brightman	Henry 2nd				1			1			1			3		
Westport	328	5	Brightman	Israel		1	2		1	1		1		1			7		
New Bedford	421	3	Brightman	John		1	1					1					3		
Westport	328	4	Brightman	John		1			2				1				4		
Freetown	287	13	Brightman	Jonathan	2			1		1			1				5		
Freetown	287	14	Brightman	Joseph				2				1		1			4		
Westport	328	7	Brightman	Joseph				1		1			1				3		
Freetown	284	27	Brightman	Joseph Jr	1	3	2		1				1				8		
Freetown	287	11	Brightman	Pardon			1			2		1					4		
Freetown	288	23	Brightman	Peleg	4			1			1		1				7		
Westport	328	1	Brightman	Thos		1	1	1				1	1				5		
Dartmouth	341	24	Brightman	Wanton	2		1		1		1	1			8				
Westport	328	12	Brightman	William		2		1					1				4		
Freetown	288	21	Brightman	Joseph 3d			1			2			1				4		
Mansfield	384	16	Brintnell	Ebenezer			1	1					1				3		
Mansfield	384	17	Brintnell	Ebenezer Jr	3		1			2			1				7		
Mansfield	384	13	Brintnell	Job		1		1		1	1	2		1			7		
Mansfield	384	12	Brintnell	Nathaniel	1			1				1		2			5		
Raynham	376	19	Britten	Henry	1		2	1		1	1	1					7		
Raynham	376	20	Britten	Nathaniel	2				1	1	2	1	1				8		
Raynham	376	18	Britten	Robert				1				1	1	2			5		
Easton	388	17	Britton	John	2	1	2		1	3			1				10		
Easton	389	1	Britton	Joshua	2		1			3			1				7		
Easton	389	2	Britton	Pendleton		1		1						1			3		
Easton	388	16	Britton	William	1	1	2		1		1	1		1			8		
Easton	388	19	Britton	Zachariah				1						1			2		
Freetown	289	9	Bron	Frances				1		1	1		2	1			6		
Freetown	291	13	Brosman	Olive	2						1		1	1			5		
Westport	328	15	Browenll	Jeremiah	3			1		1			1				6		
Westport	328	14	Browenll	Thomas		2			1	3	1	1					8		
Freetown	284	31	Browmall	Jonathan	3	2			1	1	1		1	3			12		
Rehoboth	310	10	Brown	Aaron			1		1			1	1				4		
Rehoboth	300	14	Brown	Abel		1	1		3			1	1				7		
Rehoboth	309	35	Brown	Anna		3						2		1			6		
Dartmouth	342	18	Brown	Benjamin	1	1		1	2	1		1	1				8		
Dartmouth	342	15	Brown	Benjamin Jr			1						1		4				
Freetown	283	26	Brown	Benjamin W.	1	1		1					1				4		
Taunton	366	36	Brown	Calvin Fille	1			1		2	2		1				7		
Swansea	402	22	Brown	Dan											5		5		
Attleboro	322	45	Brown	David	4	1			1		1						8		

TOWN	PG#	LN#	LAST NAME	FIRST NAME	FREE WHITE MALES under 10	10 to 16	16 to 26	26 to 45	45 and over	FREE WHITE FEMALES under 10	10 to 16	16 to 26	26 to 45	45 and over	TOTAL ALL OTHER	TOTAL SLAVES	TOTALS	DISTRICT/ TOWNSHIP	NOTES
Rehoboth	300	15	Brown	David			1	1					1	1			4		
Attleboro	322	53	Brown	David the 2nd	1			1				1					3		
New Bedford	420	35	Brown	Dedford											2		2		
Somerset	404	17	Brown	E. Wid		1						1	1	1			4		
Swansea	399	22	Brown	Elisha	2	1	1	1	1	3	2	1					12		
Attleboro	319	54	Brown	Ezera	1	1	2	1		2	1		1	1			10		
Taunton	366	22	Brown	George	2		1			1	1		2				7		
Rehoboth	309	36	Brown	Gideon 2d	1	2		1				1	1				6		
Freetown	287	24	Brown	Hannah Wid		1							1	1			3		
Rehoboth	300	16	Brown	James			1	1			1	1		1			5		
Swansea	399	26	Brown	Jarvis				1					1				2		
Rehoboth	297	18	Brown	John			1			1	1		1				5		
Somerset	404	18	Brown	John	1		1			2		1					5		
Somerset	406	47	Brown	John		1	2	1				2	1				7		
Swansea	399	28	Brown	John		2		1	1	3	3		1				11		
Rehoboth	307	28	Brown	John 2nd	1	2		1	1	1	3	1					11		
Rehoboth	299	17	Brown	John 3rd			1		2		1						4		
Somerset	406	48	Brown	John Jur	1		1					1					3		
Rehoboth	310	9	Brown	Jonathan			1	1			1						5		
Freetown	294	3	Brown	Josiah		1				3			1				5		
Rehoboth	310	8	Brown	Nathaniel		1					1	1					4		
Taunton	366	42	Brown	Newport											4		4		
Rehoboth	309	37	Brown	Oliver	1		1		1	1	2		1				8		
Rehoboth	307	27	Brown	Samuel		1		1					2				6		
Rehoboth	308	23	Brown	Samuel Jr		2	1				1						5		
Rehoboth	309	34	Brown	Sarah							1	1					2		
New Bedford	421	4	Brown	Scipio											6		6		
Swansea	399	27	Brown	Seth	1	1		1	1	2	1	1					9		
Dighton	412	21	Brown	William		1	1		1	1	1	1		1			7		
Swansea	399	24	Brown	William				1				1		1			3		
Swansea	399	25	Brown	William Jnr		1						1					2		
Rehoboth	314	37	Brown	Zebedee	2	1		2		1	1	1				10			
Westport	328	18	Brownel	George		2		1		1	2		1				7		
Westport	328	17	Brownel	George 2d				1		1	1		1				4		
Westport	328	3	Brownel	Nathaniel	4			1			1		1	1			8		
Westport	328	6	Brownell	Abner	3	1		1		1	1		1				8		
Westport	328	27	Brownell	Benjm		1		1			3		1				6		
Westport	329	8	Brownell	Benjm Junr	1	2		1		3	1	1	1				10		
Westport	328	10	Brownell	Benjm Senr		1						1	1	1			5		
Westport	328	37	Brownell	Cornelius		1		1				1		1			4		
Westport	329	7	Brownell	Elizabeth				1					2				3		
Westport	328	26	Brownell	Ezekiel	2	1							2				6		
Westport	329	6	Brownell	James			1	1				2	1				5		
New Bedford	420	19	Brownell	John	1			1					2				4		
Westport	328	21	Brownell	Josiah	3	1		1		1	1	1	1				9		
Westport	328	34	Brownell	Luther	1			1				1					3		
Westport	328	20	Brownell	Mary										1			1		
Westport	328	32	Brownell	Paul	1		1	1		1			1				5		
Westport	328	9	Brownell	Peleg	1		1	1		2	1		1	1			7		
Westport	328	36	Brownell	Prince	1		1	1						1			4		
New Bedford	420	20	Brownell	Robert			1					1					2		
Westport	328	35	Brownell	Ruth	1					3			1	2			7		
Westport	328	38	Brownell	Sarah									1	1			2		
Westport	328	13	Brownell	Shadrach		1		1		2	1		1				6		
Westport	328	2	Brownell	Sylvester	1	3	1	1		4		3	2	1			16		
New Bedford	421	2	Brownell	Uriah			1		1	2		1					5		
Westport	328	8	Brownell	William					1				1				2		
Norton	380	3	Bruton	William				1		3		1					5		
Easton	388	8	Bryant	Dependence F	1		1			1			1				4		
New Bedford	420	44	Bryant	Gamaliel				1		1			1				3		
New Bedford	420	45	Bryant	Gamaliel Jr				1		3		1			1		6		
Raynham	373	11	Bryant	Lemuel		1				1			1				3		
Swansea	403	23	Bryant	Wido									2				2		
Easton	388	14	Buck	Barnabas	1		1			1			1				4		
Easton	388	15	Buck	Benjamin	2		1			3			1				7		
Easton	389	5	Buck	Nathan	2		1					2					1		
Easton	389	4	Buck	Tertius			1			1			1				3		
Easton	388	12	Buck	Thomas				1					2	1			4		
Rehoboth	307	10	Bucklin	Barrak			1				1	1					4		
Rehoboth	309	18	Bucklin	David	1	1	1			1							6		
Rehoboth	309	19	Bucklin	Ebenezer	1			1	1				2				6		
Rehoboth	309	17	Bucklin	George	1		1	1					1				4		
Rehoboth	309	20	Bucklin	James	1	2		1		1	2		1				8		
Rehoboth	307	13	Bucklin	James 2nd			1						1				2		
Rehoboth	307	9	Bucklin	Joseph	1	1						2	1				6		
Rehoboth	307	11	Bucklin	Joseph 2nd			1			1	2	1					6		
Somerset	405	33	Buffington	Benka	1	2		1		5		1					10		
Dartmouth	342	7	Buffington	Stephen		1	1	1			1		1				5		
Somerset	404	46	Buffinton	Benja	4	1		1		2		1					9		
Swansea	399	40	Buffinton	Benja	2		3	1			1	2	1				10		
Swansea	399	43	Buffinton	Benja Jr			1			1			1				3		
Swansea	396	2	Buffinton	Daniel	1	2		1		2			1				7		
Swansea	398	41	Buffinton	Elisha	1			1		3			1				6		
Swansea	399	41	Buffinton	Gardner			1	1				1	1				4		
Somerset	407	18	Buffinton	James			1	1		2			1				5		

TOWN	PG#	LN#	LAST NAME	FIRST NAME	FREE WHITE MALES					FREE WHITE FEMALES					TOTAL ALL OTHER	TOTAL SLAVES	TOTALS	DISTRICT/ TOWNSHIP	NOTES
					under 10	10 to 16	16 to 26	26 to 45	45 and over	under 10	10 to 16	16 to 26	26 to 45	45 and over					
Swansea	396	4	Buffinton	Job	2			1		1			1				5		
Swansea	396	7	Buffinton	John	1	3			1	2	1		1				9		
Swansea	399	42	Buffinton	John 2d	1			1		1			1				4		
Somerset	405	36	Buffinton	Jona		1		1		4	1						7		
Somerset	407	16	Buffinton	Joseph	1	2		1			2			1			7		
Somerset	404	44	Buffinton	Moses		2			1		2			2			7		
Swansea	398	40	Buffinton	Samuel			2		1		2		1				6		
Easton	388	9	Buler	Atherton															Enumeration left blank
Rehoboth	299	1	Bullock	Aaron	2	1		1	1		1	1	1				8		
Rehoboth	304	39	Bullock	Abel		1		1				1	1				4		
Rehoboth	298	7	Bullock	Asa	1			1	3	1	1		1				9		
Rehoboth	298	2	Bullock	Barrak	1	1	1	1		4		2					10		
Rehoboth	302	8	Bullock	Benjamin	1			1	2	1		1		1			8		
Rehoboth	298	10	Bullock	Calvin	1	1		1		2	1		1				8		
Rehoboth	299	2	Bullock	Ebenezer		1		1		1	1	1					7		
Rehoboth	298	13	Bullock	Eleazer			1				1		1				3		
Rehoboth	305	6	Bullock	Jabez	3	1	1					1	1				7		
Rehoboth	309	33	Bullock	Jabez 2nd		1	1					1					4		
Rehoboth	306	12	Bullock	James		1	1	1				1	1				5		
Taunton	366	20	Bullock	James	2			1		1			1				5		
Freetown	282	28	Bullock	Jessee					1				1				2		
Rehoboth	298	12	Bullock	Kent	1			1	1	2	1	1					8		
Rehoboth	304	24	Bullock	Richard	1		1	1	1	1		1					7		
Attleboro	317	17	Bullock	Richd	1	1		1		1	1						5		
Rehoboth	298	11	Bullock	Samuel	2	1	1	1		2	1	1					9		
Rehoboth	298	3	Bullock	Stephen	1			1		2		1	1				6		
Swansea	401	39	Bullock	Stephen			1						2				3		
Rehoboth	298	4	Bullock	Stephen Jr			1			1			1				4		
Rehoboth	311	25	Bullock	Thomas	1			1		1		1					6		
Rehoboth	298	9	Bullock	William			1			1		1					3		
New Bedford	420	39	Bumpus	Silvester	1		2		1	1	2	1		1			9		
Dighton	414	28	Bun	Nathll	1	1		1		1	1	1					6		
New Bedford	421	7	Bunker	Sheubael		1		1		1	1	1					5		
Taunton	364	6	Burbank	Abner	1			1		1		1					4		
Freetown	282	5	Burbank	Isaac			1	1	1		1	2		1			7		
Freetown	282	6	Burbank	Isaac Jnr	1			1		1	1	1					5		
Taunton	371	6	Burbank	Joseph	2	1		1		2	1	1					8		
Westport	328	24	Burden	Isaiah	2	3	1	1			1		1				9		
Westport	328	31	Burden	Peter Black											5		5		
New Bedford	420	14	Burges	Isaiah	1	2		1		1			2				7		
Swansea	402	14	Burk	Ruben			1						1				2		
Somerset	405	30	Burke	Benjamin				1			1		1				3		
Swansea	401	30	Burns	D.					1			1	1				3		
Rehoboth	306	2	Burr	Cromwel		1	1	1		1							4		
Rehoboth	305	21	Burr	Elisha		1	1				1						3		
Freetown	293	29	Burr	Elizabeth Wid						2		1					3		
Rehoboth	306	1	Burr	Isaac	1	1	1		1	1		1					6		
Rehoboth	305	20	Burr	Nathaniel		1	1	1		1	2	1					8		
New Bedford	421	11	Burrill	Joshua	1	1		1		2	1	1					7		
Taunton	367	41	Burt	Abel	1	2		1		1		1					6		
Berkley	277	4	Burt	Abner		1	2	3	1			1	3	1			12		
Berkley	277	19	Burt	Abner Junr	1		1	1		2		1					6		
Dighton	413	18	Burt	Clothier			2	1					1				4		
Taunton	367	35	Burt	Daniel			1	1			1	1	1				5		
Norton	300	1	Burt	David	2	2	2	1		1							8		
Taunton	368	16	Burt	David		1	2		1	1	1		1				7		
Norton	380	2	Burt	David Jr	1			1		2		1					5		
Norton	379	8	Burt	Dinah		1						1	1				3		
Berkley	277	3	Burt	Edmond		1			1	1		1					4		
Taunton	361	18	Burt	Edward	2			1		3			1				7		
Taunton	359	24	Burt	George		1		1		1	1		1				5		
Taunton	367	40	Burt	Henry				1			1	1	1				4		
Taunton	360	39	Burt	Isaac Junior	2	1		1			1	2	1				8		
Taunton	361	11	Burt	James	2	2	1	1		2	1		1				10		
Berkley	278	3	Burt	John	1	1		1					1				4		
Berkley	278	2	Burt	Joseph				1					1				2		
Norton	379	10	Burt	Joseph				1		1		1	2				5		
Taunton	360	18	Burt	Joseph	2			1				1	1				5		
Norton	379	11	Burt	Joseph Jr	2			1		1		1	1				6		
Taunton	361	10	Burt	Rachel									2				2		
Rehoboth	306	15	Burt	Rufus	1		1			1		1					7		
Berkley	277	2	Burt	Simeon	1	2	3		1	1	1	2		1	1		13		
Berkley	277	1	Burt	Stephen	3		3		1	2	2	1	2				14		
Freetown	290	15	Burt	Thomas		1		1					1				3		
Norton	379	12	Burt	William	2	1	1		1	1	1	1	1	1			10		
Taunton	367	29	Burt	Zilpha Wido		2	2			1	1	1		1			8		
Swansea	402	38	Bushe	John			1						1				2		
Dighton	409	19	Butlar	Kate		1							1				2		
New Bedford	421	12	Butler	Benjamin		1		1				2		1			5		
New Bedford	421	14	Butler	Benjamin Jr			1			2	1		1				5		
New Bedford	421	20	Butler	Daniel			1			3		1	1				6		
New Bedford	421	15	Butler	Obadiah	2			1					1	1			5		

TOWN	PG#	LN#	LAST NAME	FIRST NAME	FREE WHITE MALES					FREE WHITE FEMALES					TOTAL ALL OTHER	TOTAL SLAVES	TOTALS	DISTRICT/ TOWNSHIP	NOTES
					under 10	10 to 16	16 to 26	26 to 45	45 and over	under 10	10 to 16	16 to 26	26 to 45	45 and over					
New Bedford	420	42	Butler	Peter	1			1		2		1	1	1			7		
New Bedford	421	9	Butterfield	Easther											1		1		
Swansea	396	6	Butterworth	Benj	1		1						1				3		
Swansea	402	35	Butterworth	Benja	2	1		1	1	1			1				7		
Somerset	406	25	Butterworth	Caleb		1				1			1				3		
Rehoboth	309	28	Butterworth	Oliver			1				2		1				4		
Somerset	406	24	Butterworth	Wido		1				1			1				3		
Dartmouth	341	25	Butts	Abraham	1			1		2	1						7		
Westport	329	4	Butts	Chase				1				1		1			3		
Freetown	289	3	Butts	David	1			1		3			1				6		
Freetown	287	3	Butts	Gideon			1	1				1		1			4		
Dartmouth	341	29	Butts	Peleg		1			2	1							4		
Westport	328	41	Butts	Peleg				1		3		1					5		
Westport	328	39	Butts	Sarah						3			1				4		
Dartmouth	341	27	Butts	Stephen	2			1	1	1			1				7		
Dartmouth	341	28	Butts	Stephen 2nd		1		1		1							3		
Raynham	372	5	Byram	William	1	2		1		2		2		1			9		
Westport	329	39	Cadman	Hannah								1	1	1			3		
Raynham	373	42	Cain	Benjamin	1			1		2	1	2	1				8		
Taunton	362	26	Cain	John	2	1		1		1		1		1			7		
Taunton	362	29	Cain	Moses					1			2		2			5		
Taunton	362	33	Cain	Samuel				1		2				1			4		
Taunton	362	23	Cain	Thomas	3	1		1		3	1		1				10		
New Bedford	422	28	Cairsley	Elijah	2		1						1				4		
New Bedford	422	27	Cairsley	Thomas	1			1		3			1				6		
Rehoboth	302	3	Cambel	Rode									1				1		
Raynham	372	19	Campbell	Joshua	1			1		2			1				5		
Raynham	372	6	Campbell	Oliver	1			1		4			1	1			8		
Rehoboth	304	25	Campbell	Sylvanus		1		1		1							5		
Somerset	404	14	Candage	John		1						1					2		
Taunton	364	14	Cannedy	Noble	2	1		1		2	1	2					9		
New Bedford	422	32	Cannon	John	2	2		1		2		2	1				10		
New Bedford	422	13	Cannon	Phillip	1	1	2	1		1			1				7		
Attleboro	318	58	Capron	Elijah		2	1	1				2		1			7		
Norton	380	24	Capron	Elisha	1			1		3			1				6		
Westport	329	42	Capron	John					1			1		1			3		
Attleboro	318	57	Capron	Otis		1		1		2		1		1			6		
Rehoboth	310	20	Carben	Robert	1		1						1				3		
New Bedford	422	26	Card	Jonathan	1		1	1					1				4		
Dighton	411	9	Carey	Daniel	2			1		2			1				6		
Dighton	411	10	Carey	Wido		1						3		1			5		
Attleboro	320	64	Carlile	Betty	1					1	1						3		
Rehoboth	310	16	Carpent	Ashel		2		1		3	3	1					10		
Rehoboth	299	28	Carpenter	Abel	1	1		1	1	1			1				7		
Rehoboth	312	44	Carpenter	Amos			1										1		
Rehoboth	299	33	Carpenter	Amy								1	1				2		
Rehoboth	309	26	Carpenter	Aseph		1		1	1	1		2					6		
Rehoboth	307	36	Carpenter	Benjamin	1	2		1		1			1				10		
Rehoboth	310	15	Carpenter	Benjamin		1		1				1					4		
Rehoboth	301	8	Carpenter	Caleb	1			1	2	1	1						7		
Rehoboth	308	22	Carpenter	Caleb		1	1	1		1		1		1			6		
Rehoboth	312	41	Carpenter	Caleb				1				1	3	1			7		
Rehoboth	307	34	Carpenter	Caleb 2nd		1	1	1		1		1		1			6		
Rehoboth	312	42	Carpenter	Caleb 2rd	2		1		3				1				7		
Rehoboth	299	32	Carpenter	Christopher		1	1			1		2					6		
Attleboro	319	60	Carpenter	Cyrel		1	1		1	1	1			1			6		
Attleboro	320	7	Carpenter	Daniel		1	1	2		1	1			1			7		
Rehoboth	310	14	Carpenter	Daniel	2	1		1	1	1		1					10		
Rehoboth	309	38	Carpenter	Daniel Jr		1		1		1							3		
Attleboro	320	4	Carpenter	Daniel Junr	2			2					1				5		
Rehoboth	299	44	Carpenter	Ebenezer		1						1					3		
Rehoboth	307	26	Carpenter	Elihu		1				1							3		
Rehoboth	307	35	Carpenter	Elihu	2			1		1	1	1					11		
Attleboro	318	20	Carpenter	Elisha		1	1	1				3		1			7		
Rehoboth	301	7	Carpenter	Elizabeth		1	1			2			1				5		
Rehoboth	307	15	Carpenter	Ezeikel															Crossed out
Attleboro	322	3	Carpenter	Ezekiel	1	1	2	1	1			1	1	1			9		
Rehoboth	299	30	Carpenter	James	1				4			1	1				8		
Attleboro	322	65	Carpenter	John		2	1					1					4		
Attleboro	323	10	Carpenter	John		1		1		2	2						6		
Rehoboth	306	20	Carpenter	John				1				1					2		
Rehoboth	310	17	Carpenter	Jonathan	1		1	1	1	1			1				6		
Attleboro	320	44	Carpenter	Josiah	1		1		1			2	1	1			7		
Rehoboth	307	37	Carpenter	Mary		3			2	2			1				8		
Attleboro	322	25	Carpenter	Nathan	2		1			1			1				5		
Attleboro	320	61	Carpenter	Noah								1	3				5		
Rehoboth	314	38	Carpenter	Noah		1						1					3		
Rehoboth	300	28	Carpenter	Obediah	2	1		1	3	1	1	1	1				13		
Rehoboth	313	1	Carpenter	Oliver		1	1						1				4		
Rehoboth	309	39	Carpenter	Otis		1							1				5		
Norton	380	20	Carpenter	Peter		1	1	1	1					1			5		
Rehoboth	298	34	Carpenter	Peter	1	1		1		1	1						5		
Rehoboth	300	46	Carpenter	Peter 2d	2	1			1	1							6		

93

TOWN	PG#	LN#	LAST NAME	FIRST NAME	FREE WHITE MALES					FREE WHITE FEMALES					TOTAL ALL OTHER	TOTAL SLAVES	TOTALS	DISTRICT/ TOWNSHIP	NOTES
					under 10	10 to 16	16 to 26	26 to 45	45 and over	under 10	10 to 16	16 to 26	26 to 45	45 and over					
Attleboro	318	7	Carpenter	Samuel		1	1	1		1		1		1			6		
Rehoboth	301	1	Carpenter	Samuel	1			1	1			1					5		
Rehoboth	299	23	Carpenter	Stephen	1	1		1	2	1		1					9		
Rehoboth	299	24	Carpenter	Thomas	1		1			1		1					6		
Rehoboth	299	43	Carpenter	Thomas			1	1					1				3		
Rehoboth	306	21	Carpenter	Thomas	1		1		2	1	2	1					9		
Rehoboth	300	45	Carpenter	Thomas 2d	1			1			2	1	1				6		
Rehoboth	306	22	Carpenter	Thoms 2nd															Crossed out
Freetown	283	11	Carpenter	William			1			1			1		1		4		
Norton	380	19	Carpenter	William	3		2		1	1	3	1	1				12		
Easton	389	11	Carr	Caleb	1			1		1			2	1			6		
Westport	329	38	Carr	Eseck	2			1		1			1	1			6		
New Bedford	422	14	Carriwill	Phillip											5		5		
Raynham	375	2	Carter	Stanley	4		1	1		2	1		1				10		
Dighton	414	1	Cartwright	Daniel		1	1		1		1		1				5		
Dighton	413	43	Cartwright	Daniel Jr	2	2		1	1	1			1				8		
Dighton	413	44	Cartwright	Jona	1							1					2		
Taunton	358	31	Carver	David		2	3		1	1	1	2		1			11		
Raynham	376	8	Carver	Jabez	1		1		1	2	1		1				7		
Raynham	372	26	Carver	John		1	1		1			1		1			5		
Taunton	358	34	Carver	Nathan	1		3		1	2	1		1				9		
Taunton	356	16	Carver	William				1			1	1					3		
Dighton	411	7	Carwell	Elijah		4	1		1			2		2			10		
Westport	330	5	Case	Adam	2	1		1		1	1	1					7		
Westport	329	16	Case	Amy									1				1		
Westport	330	1	Case	Esther	2	1				2			1				6		
Rehoboth	298	30	Case	Gardner		1	1		3	1		1			8				
New Bedford	422	25	Case	Job	1			1		3	1		1				7		
Dighton	414	24	Case	Jonathan J	3	1		1		1		1					7		
Rehoboth	303	31	Case	Joseph	2	1	1		4	2	1					11			
Westport	329	18	Case	Moses	2	1		1		2	1		1				8		
Dartmouth	342	31	Case	Rachel		1						1			2				
Westport	329	17	Case	Wanton	1	1	3		1				1				8		
Attleboro	323	1	Casse	Bowdoin	1		1	1			1	1	1				6		
Westport	329	40	Castelo	Ramon		1			1	3	2		1				8		
Swansea	401	9	Castle	Allen	1			1		3		1					6		
Swansea	398	27	Castle	Nicholas	3	1	2		1	1			1				9		
Swansea	398	31	Castle	Richd	2		1			1	1						5		
Taunton	363	6	Caswell	Abiel				1			1						2		
Taunton	363	8	Caswell	Abigail Wido									1				1		
Berkley	278	4	Caswell	Abner				1		1			1				3		
Berkley	278	7	Caswell	Abraham	2	1		1		2			1				7		
Taunton	362	21	Caswell	Barnabas	2			1		1	1		1				6		
Taunton	359	8	Caswell	Ebenezer		1	1		1			2		2			7		
Taunton	361	33	Caswell	Ebenezer Junior	3			1		1			1	1			7		
Berkley	278	6	Caswell	Ephraim	1		1	1					1	1			5		
Taunton	363	2	Caswell	Job			1		1			1	1	1			5		
Taunton	363	1	Caswell	John	2	1		1		2	1	1	1				10		
Taunton	361	32	Caswell	Joseph				1		2	2		1				6		
Taunton	364	20	Caswell	Joshua		2		1					1				4		
Taunton	362	38	Caswell	Moses				1		1		1					3		
Taunton	357	25	Caswell	Nathaniel	2	2		1		1	2		1				9		
Taunton	356	11	Caswell	Prince											?		2		
Taunton	357	4	Caswell	Richard				1		2			1				4		
Taunton	362	42	Caswell	Samuel	5			1		1			1				8		
Taunton	363	7	Caswell	William	2			1		1			1				5		
New Bedford	422	16	Cathaway	Lot											3		3		
Freetown	283	2	Chace	Augustine	1			1		4	1		1				8		
Freetown	284	7	Chace	Beloney	1		1	1		2	2		1				8		
Freetown	286	19	Chace	Benjamin	2			1					1				4		
New Bedford	422	42	Chace	Benjamin	1			1		2		2		1			7		
Freetown	294	18	Chace	Benjamin 2d			1	1					1				3		
Freetown	283	6	Chace	Darius	2	2	2		1	1	1			1			10		
Freetown	286	30	Chace	Dudlee	3			1				1	1				6		
Freetown	285	16	Chace	Ebenezer				1		2			1				4		
Freetown	293	20	Chace	Edward	2	1	1	1		1		1	1				8		
Berkley	278	24	Chace	Ezra	2		2	1		2	3	1	1	1			13		
Freetown	283	1	Chace	Gilbert	3		1	1		2		1	1				9		
Freetown	291	5	Chace	Greenfield	1			1		3	1	2		1			9		
Berkley	280	17	Chace	Hannah									1				1		
Freetown	294	1	Chace	Isaac	1					2			1				4		
New Bedford	422	47	Chace	Jared	2	1		1		1	2		1				8		
Freetown	282	26	Chace	Jessee			1						1				2		
Freetown	285	31	Chace	Job	2	1		1		1	2		1				8		
Attleboro	320	57	Chace	John	2	3	1	1		1	1		2				11		
New Bedford	422	18	Chace	Joseph		1	4			1		1					7		
New Bedford	422	44	Chace	Michael	2			1		1			1				5		
Freetown	294	19	Chace	Michal				1		1	2		1				5		
Freetown	283	9	Chace	Noah		2		1		3			1				7		
Freetown	291	8	Chace	Otis	2			1		2		1					6		
Taunton	365	16	Chace	Paul		1		1					1				3		

TOWN	PG#	LN#	LAST NAME	FIRST NAME	Free White Males under 10	10 to 16	16 to 26	26 to 45	45 and over	Free White Females under 10	10 to 16	16 to 26	26 to 45	45 and over	TOTAL ALL OTHER	TOTAL SLAVES	TOTALS	DISTRICT/ TOWNSHIP	NOTES
Freetown	294	17	Chace	Phillip				1		3	2		1				7		
Freetown	294	20	Chace	Seth			2		1					1			5		
Berkley	279	14	Chace	Simeon	1	1	2	1		3	1		1				10		
Freetown	294	16	Chace	Phebe Wid						1			2				3		
New Bedford	422	15	Chadwick	John	1			1					2				4		
Rehoboth	309	44	Chaffe	Bradock	1			1	2	1	1	1					8		
Rehoboth	310	26	Chaffe	Daniel			1	1					1				7		
Rehoboth	314	13	Chaffe	Ephraim		1	1		3				1				6		
Rehoboth	310	21	Chaffe	Jonathan	1	2		1	1			1	1				7		
Rehoboth	310	22	Chaffe	Jonathan		1	1		2			1					7		
Rehoboth	314	15	Chaffe	Jonathan															Enumeration left blank
Rehoboth	309	45	Chaffe	Joseph	1	1		1	2				1				8		
Rehoboth	310	25	Chaffe	Nathaniel		2		1		1		1	1				6		
Rehoboth	301	38	Chaffe	Samuel				1				1	2	1			6		
Rehoboth	312	46	Chaffe	Samuel				1		2	1		2				6		
Rehoboth	308	8	Chaffe	Shubel				1		1			1				3		
New Bedford	422	43	Chaffee	John	3	1		1	1			1		1			8		
Swansea	401	4	Chaffey	Wido		0		0			1		2				3		
Raynham	374	42	Chamberlain	James			1	3					1				5		
Taunton	369	19	Chamberlain	Samuel	1			1		1		1					4		
Dartmouth	343	7	Chandeler	Jeremiah	1		1			2		1		1			8		
Rehoboth	310	1	Chandler	Jacob		2		1	2	1	1	1					9		
New Bedford	422	37	Chandler	Joshua			1			2			1				4		
Freetown	288	12	Chandler	Walter	1			1		1		1	1				5		
Mansfield	385	15	Chapman	John	2			1		1		1					5		
Dighton	413	5	Chase	Aaron	2	1		1		2	2		1				9		
Dartmouth	342	37	Chase	Abner		2	2				1		1				6		
Somerset	406	7	Chase	Abner		1					1	1					3		
Swansea	399	45	Chase	Abner	1			1		2			1				5		
Dartmouth	343	19	Chase	Allen		1		1			1						4		
Somerset	407	1	Chase	Allen		1					2		1				5		
Somerset	407	3	Chase	Allen Junr	2		1			2			1				6		
Somerset	406	10	Chase	Antepas	1		1			3			1				6		
New Bedford	422	31	Chase	Ariel	1			1		1		1					4		
Somerset	406	20	Chase	Asa		3		1			1		1				6		
Dartmouth	343	2	Chase	Benjamin			1		1				1				3		
Swansea	396	8	Chase	Benjamin		2	1	1			2		1				7		
Swansea	403	53	Chase	Caleb				1			1		2				4		
Dighton	413	2	Chase	Caleb Jr	4			1		1	2		1				9		
Freetown	290	12	Chase	Chloe Wid	1					1			1				3		
Somerset	404	10	Chase	Collins			1			1		1					3		
Somerset	407	12	Chase	Daniel	1	2		1		1		4		1			10		
Dartmouth	343	6	Chase	David			1	2					1				4		
Dartmouth	343	21	Chase	David			1				1		1				3		
Dartmouth	343	25	Chase	Ebenezer	1			1		1	1		1				5		
Swansea	396	14	Chase	Edward	1	5		1	1	1	1		1				11		
Somerset	407	6	Chase	Elizh Wido									2				2		
Swansea	401	18	Chase	Enoch		1		1					1				3		
Dartmouth	343	31	Chase	Ezekiel	1			1		2	2		1				9		
Somerset	405	1	Chase	Ezra				1			1		1				3		
Somerset	405	2	Chase	Ezra Jun	1		1				1						3		
Somerset	406	16	Chase	Francis	2	2		1		1			1				7		
Somerset	406	23	Chase	Gideon		1		1					1				3		
Somerset	406	3	Chase	Gideon 2d	1	1		1		3			1				7		
Somerset	407	2	Chase	Guillford				1			1		1				3		
Swansea	404	3	Chase	Henry			1	1					1				3		
Swansea	398	22	Chase	Hezekiah	1	1	2		1	1	1	1		1			9		
Swansea	401	41	Chase	Hezekiah	1		1	1					1				4		
Somerset	406	9	Chase	Ichobod	1			1						4			6		
Somerset	405	18	Chase	Isaac				1		2	1		1				5		
Somerset	408	18	Chase	Israel				1		1			1				3		
Swansea	400	12	Chase	Jabez				1						1			2		
Swansea	400	13	Chase	Jabez Junr	1			1			4		1				7		
Swansea	403	11	Chase	Jacob		1	1	1		2	2		1				8		
Somerset	404	3	Chase	James	2	1			1	1	3		1				9		
Swansea	396	13	Chase	James	1	4	1		1	3	2		1				13		
Swansea	401	14	Chase	James 2d	1	2	1		1	2	3		1				11		
Somerset	404	38	Chase	James 3d	4	1		1			1	1					8		
Dartmouth	343	20	Chase	Jeremiah		1					1	1					4		
Swansea	401	7	Chase	Jerethmeel	2			1		3		1					7		
Somerset	405	47	Chase	Jesse	3	1		1		2			1	1			9		
Swansea	402	41	Chase	Job	2	1		1		2	1		1				8		
Dartmouth	343	1	Chase	John		1		1					2				4		
Dartmouth	343	22	Chase	John		1					1						3		
Swansea	396	12	Chase	John	2	2	3		1	2			1				11		
Swansea	398	19	Chase	John 3d	2			1		2		1	1				7		
Swansea	396	21	Chase	Jonathan	2	4		1		1	3		1	2			14		
Somerset	406	36	Chase	Joseph		1		1		1	1		1				5		
Somerset	406	19	Chase	Matthew				1						1			2		
Somerset	406	8	Chase	Moses		1			1	1	1	1	1	1			7		
Somerset	407	40	Chase	Nathan	1			1		2	5		1				10		

TOWN	PG#	LN#	LAST NAME	FIRST NAME	M<10	M10-16	M16-26	M26-45	M45+	F<10	F10-16	F16-26	F26-45	F45+	TOTAL ALL OTHER	TOTAL SLAVES	TOTALS	DISTRICT/TOWNSHIP	NOTES
Dartmouth	342	38	Chase	Nathaniel	1	1		1			2		1			6			
Somerset	406	14	Chase	Oliver	2	2		1					1	1			7		
Somerset	406	4	Chase	Patience Wido	1	1	1				2		1				6		
Somerset	406	6	Chase	Paul		1		1		1	1	2		1			7		
Somerset	408	5	Chase	Philip		2		1			2		1				6		
Swansea	396	19	Chase	Philip	1		1				1	1					4		
Dartmouth	343	23	Chase	Preserved		1			1		1					3			
Swansea	398	12	Chase	Richard		1		1		1	1	2					6		
Swansea	399	10	Chase	Royal	1	1		1		1	1		1				6		
Swansea	401	19	Chase	Ruben	2			1					1				4		
Swansea	402	13	Chase	Ruben		1		1	1				1	1			5		
Somerset	408	19	Chase	Ruth									1				1		
Swansea	404	2	Chase	Saml	1	4		1	1		2		1				10		
Swansea	398	2	Chase	Samuel	1			1		2		1					5		
Somerset	404	28	Chase	Shadrach				1		2			1				4		
Somerset	406	5	Chase	Silas		1	2	1		2	2		3				11		
Swansea	398	34	Chase	Silvester	1			1		2	2		2				8		
Swansea	403	24	Chase	Simeon	2	2		1		2	2		2				11		
Dartmouth	343	18	Chase	Simeon	1			1		1		1			5				
Dartmouth	343	17	Chase	Simeon Junr		1					1				4				
Somerset	405	15	Chase	Stephen	2	1		1			1	1					6		
Swansea	398	11	Chase	Stephen		3			1	3			1				8		
Somerset	406	11	Chase	Stephen 2d	1			1		1			1				4		
Swansea	401	22	Chase	Uriah		1		1		1			1				4		
Swansea	399	36	Chase	Wido									1	1			2		
Somerset	407	32	Chase	William	2			1		2	2		1				8		
Swansea	396	3	Chase	William	1	2		1		2			1				7		
Attleboro	321	28	Cheever	Daniel	1		1			2			2				6		
Attleboro	321	9	Cheever	George		1	1					1					3		
Westport	330	3	Childs	Aaron											4		4		
Swansea	403	13	Childs	James			1			1		1					3		
Easton	389	7	Chipman	Jacob	1			1		2			1				5		
New Bedford	421	28	Church	Benjamin		1	1			1	1		1				5		
New Bedford	421	29	Church	Benjamin Jr		1				1	1	1					4		
Freetown	287	25	Church	Betsey Wid	3	3	1			2		3		1			13		
New Bedford	421	30	Church	Charles	1	2		1		2		2	2				10		
New Bedford	422	12	Church	Charles 2d	1	1	1	1				1					5		
Westport	329	36	Church	Constant		1		1		1	1		1				5		
New Bedford	422	11	Church	Elizabeth		1					1		1				3		
Dighton	410	40	Church	Frances	2			1					1				4		
Dighton	410	22	Church	Gamaliel	1		1	1		1		2	1	1			8		
New Bedford	421	35	Church	Gamaliel	2		1			1		1					5		
New Bedford	422	10	Church	Gilbert		1						1					2		
Freetown	287	27	Church	Joseph	1		1		1	1	2	2		1			9		
New Bedford	421	36	Church	Joseph	2	1	1		1	1	1	1	1				9		
Swansea	403	47	Church	Peter blk											4		4		
New Bedford	422	8	Church	Stephen	1		1			1			1				4		
New Bedford	422	7	Churchill	David		1			1	1			1				4		
New Bedford	422	6	Churchill	Jedidah									1				1		
New Bedford	422	36	Churchill	Thomas	1			1		1		2					5		
Westport	330	2	Chushman	Ichabod	1			1					1				3		
Attleboro	320	54	Clafflin	Calvin			1			1		1					3		
Attleboro	320	3	Clafflin	Charles			1			1		1	1	1			5		
Attleboro	318	27	Clafflin	Comfort			1			1			1		1		4		
Attleboro	320	56	Clafflin	Daniel	1			1		1	1	1					5		
Norton	380	23	Clafflin	Nathaniel		2		1		1	1		1				6		
Attleboro	318	28	Clafflin	Nehemiah		1		1		3			1				6		
Attleboro	318	67	Clafflin	Noah		3	2					2					7		
Attleboro	318	25	Clafflin	Phineas	1	1	1	1				2	1	1			8		
Attleboro	318	23	Clafflin	Phineas Junr	1		1					1					3		
Attleboro	318	26	Clafflin	Rufus		1				2		1					4		
New Bedford	422	9	Claghorn	George	1	2		1		2	1	3		1			11		
Norton	380	14	Clap	David	1	1	1		2	1	2		2				10		
Mansfield	385	1	Clap	Elkanah		1		1	1	2	1		1	1			8		
Freetown	285	19	Clark	Asa	2	2		1	1				1				7		
Norton	380	25	Clark	Asa	1			1		2			1				5		
New Bedford	421	24	Clark	David		2	1	1				1		1			6		
Somerset	404	35	Clark	Henry	2		1			1	1	1					6		
New Bedford	421	31	Clark	John		2							2				4		
Norton	380	21	Clark	Pitt	1			1		1			1	1			5		
Freetown	283	5	Clark	Richard	3	1		1		1		1					7		
Freetown	291	9	Clark	Seth	1		1					1					3		
Freetown	286	3	Clark	Theophelus				1					1				2		
Freetown	286	4	Clark	Theophelus Jr	1		2	1		3	1		1				9		
Norton	380	22	Clark	William		1		1		2			1				5		
Taunton	364	36	Clarke	Amos	2			1		2		1					6		
Taunton	364	17	Clarke	Ezra	1	1	1	1		1	1	1	1				8		
New Bedford	421	40	Clasby	Lot	1		1	1		1			1				5		
Berkley	278	30	Clemmons	Lydia									1				1		
Taunton	369	6	Clerk	Sarah Wido			1			1		1		1			4		

TOWN	PG#	LN#	LAST NAME	FIRST NAME	FREE WHITE MALES					FREE WHITE FEMALES					TOTAL ALL OTHER	TOTAL SLAVES	TOTALS	DISTRICT/ TOWNSHIP	NOTES
					under 10	10 to 16	16 to 26	26 to 45	45 and over	under 10	10 to 16	16 to 26	26 to 45	45 and over					
Freetown	284	12	Cleveland	Ambros	1	2		1		7	1	1	1				14		
Freetown	286	29	Cleveland	Benjamin			1	1				2		1			5		
Freetown	286	31	Cleveland	David	1	1		1			1	1	1				6		
Freetown	287	5	Cleveland	Elphas	2			1		2			1				6		
Freetown	288	31	Cleveland	Jonathan	1		1	1	1	2		1	1				8		
Dighton	410	33	Clouston	Hannah		1							1	2			4		
Mansfield	385	3	Cobb	Benjamin				1					1				2		
Mansfield	385	5	Cobb	Benjamin Junr	3	1	1			1		1		1			8		
Mansfield	385	9	Cobb	Daniel			1					1	1				3		
Mansfield	385	4	Cobb	David	2			1					1				4		
Norton	380	16	Cobb	Elisha	1	1	1	1		4	2	1	1				12		
Mansfield	385	6	Cobb	John	1	1		1		1			1				5		
Mansfield	385	13	Cobb	Jonathan	2			1		2			1				6		
Norton	380	11	Cobb	Lyman	1			1		3			1	1			7		
Mansfield	385	7	Cobb	mason	3	2			1				1				7		
Taunton	365	43	Cobb	Nathan			2		1	1		1		1			6		
Norton	380	12	Cobb	Pliny	1		1			1		1					4		
Taunton	368	12	Cobb	Rufus			2		2			1		1			6		
Mansfield	385	8	Cobb	Salmon	2			1		2	2		1				8		
Taunton	368	15	Cobb	Sarah									1				1		
Norton	380	10	Cobb	Silas			2	2	2	2	1	1	1		1		12		
Norton	380	15	Cobb	William				1				1	1				3		
Taunton	362	41	Codding	Abiather	2			1					1				4		
Taunton	362	40	Codding	Elisha	3			1		2			1				7		
Taunton	367	24	Codding	James	1	1		1				1	1				5		
Taunton	367	30	Codding	James Junr	1	1		1			1	1	1				7		
Mansfield	385	14	Codding	Samuel	4	1	1	1			2		1	1			11		
Taunton	367	31	Codding	Samuel		1	2		1	1	1		1	1			8		
Dighton	414	29	Codding	William		1		1				1		1			4		
New Bedford	422	23	Coggenhall	John Jr	1		4				1	1					7		
New Bedford	422	35	Coggeshall	Gideon	1		1	1		4	2		1				10		
New Bedford	422	34	Coggeshall	John		2	1	2				1	1		1		8		
Taunton	358	23	Coggeshall	Sarah Wido	1	3				1		1	1				7		
Berkley	277	10	Colby	Jeremiah			1					1					2		
Rehoboth	306	18	Cole	Aaron	1	2		1	1	1	1						12		
Swansea	402	31	Cole	Aaron		1						1					2		
Rehoboth	309	43	Cole	Allen		2				1		1					5		
Rehoboth	306	19	Cole	Amos			1						1				2		
Rehoboth	303	44	Cole	Constant	2	1		1		1	2		1				9		
Swansea	402	30	Cole	Constant		1	1	1					1				4		
Rehoboth	310	28	Cole	David		1		1				1					3		
Swansea	403	29	Cole	Ebenizr		1		1		1	2		1				6		
Rehoboth	309	40	Cole	Joseph	1	1		1	1	1			1				6		
Taunton	364	26	Cole	Joseph	3			1		1			1				6		
Raynham	374	17	Cole	Joseph Junr		1											1		
Rehoboth	298	26	Cole	Nehemiah	1	1		1	1	1			1				6		
Rehoboth	302	36	Cole	Otis		1		2				1					5		
Attleboro	320	65	Cole	Richard				1		2	2	2	1				8		
Rehoboth	302	29	Cole	Simeon	1	1		2	2	1	1	1	1				11		
Rehoboth	306	17	Cole	Simeon															Enumeration left blank
Attleboro	321	45	Cole	Timothy	2				1	2	1		1				7		
Rehoboth	309	41	Cole	William	1			1	3	1	1		1				9		
New Bedford	422	40	Cole	Archipus		1	1			3			1				6		
New Bedford	422	30	Coleman	Benjamin			1						1				2		
Dartmouth	343	9	Collins	Benjamin		2		1		1							6		
Raynham	374	31	Collins	Pomp											5		5		
Dartmouth	343	10	Collins	Richard				1					1				2		
Dartmouth	343	24	Collins	Richard		1				1		1	1				6		
Dartmouth	343	4	Collins	William		1	1					1					3		
Freetown	290	2	Combs	Elnathan	1			1		1			1				4		
Attleboro	319	58	Comings	David	2			2					3	1			8		
Rehoboth	306	23	Conant	Timothy		2		1		2	1	1					9		
New Bedford	422	20	Congdon	Caleb	2			1		3		1	1				8		
New Bedford	422	33	Congdon	John		1		1		1		1	1		1		6		
New Bedford	422	21	Congdon	Joseph				1					1				2		
Freetown	291	6	Conley	John	1			1		1			1				5		
Swansea	398	3	Connell	Seabry	2	2		1		2			1				8		
Dartmouth	343	28	Cook	Audra		1	1			2			1				5		
Dartmouth	343	29	Cook	Benjamin										6			6		
Freetown	288	16	Cook	Elihu	2		1	1		1			1				6		
Freetown	285	5	Cook	John	2			1					1				4		
New Bedford	422	1	Cook	Pardon		1			1	2	1	1	1				7		
New Bedford	422	2	Cook	Paul				1					1				2		
New Bedford	421	41	Cook	Robert			1			1		1					3		
New Bedford	422	45	Coombs	Ithamar	3			1					1				5		
Rehoboth	309	42	Coomer	John				1					1				2		
Taunton	357	7	Cooper	Benjamin				1		1			1				3		
Rehoboth	307	40	Cooper	David	1	1	1		1	3	1	1	1				13		
Taunton	358	1	Cooper	Elizabeth Wido									1				1		
Taunton	357	31	Cooper	James		2		1					1				4		
Rehoboth	310	27	Cooper	Nathaniel		2		1	1	1	2		1				8		

TOWN	PG#	LN#	LAST NAME	FIRST NAME	FREE WHITE MALES					FREE WHITE FEMALES					TOTAL ALL OTHER	TOTAL SLAVES	TOTALS	DISTRICT/ TOWNSHIP	NOTES
					under 10	10 to 16	16 to 26	26 to 45	45 and over	under 10	10 to 16	16 to 26	26 to 45	45 and over					
Attleboro	319	59	Cooper	Noah		2	1	1	1			2	1	1			9		
Taunton	358	30	Cooper	Seth				1			1			1			3		
Taunton	357	28	Cooper	William	1		1						1	1			4		
Mansfield	385	16	Copeland	Amasa	1		1						1				3		
Norton	380	17	Copeland	Asa		3	1		1	3	1			1			10		
Easton	389	8	Copeland	Elijah		1			1	1	2			1			6		
Easton	389	9	Copeland	Elijah Jr	2			1			1		1				5		
New Bedford	421	33	Copeland	Elisha		1		1		2	2		1				7		
Easton	389	10	Copeland	Josiah	2	2		1		1			1	1			8		
Mansfield	385	2	Copeland	Moses		1	1	1		1	2			1			7		
Norton	380	18	Copeland	Samuel	1	2			1	1			1	1			7		
Mansfield	385	10	Copeland	William	1	1	1		1	2	1	1		1			9		
New Bedford	422	39	Cornal	Levi				1		2			1				4		
Westport	329	24	Cornell	Abraham				1					1				2		
Dartmouth	343	14	Cornell	Amos		1	1						2		5				
Swansea	400	43	Cornell	Asa	3			1		1	2		1				8		
Westport	329	43	Cornell	Charles				1				1	1				3		
Westport	329	30	Cornell	Christopher		1		1		2	1	1		1			7		
Westport	329	31	Cornell	Daniel	1	1				1			1				5		
Swansea	401	11	Cornell	Elisha				1					2	2			5		
Dartmouth	342	27	Cornell	Eunice	1					1			1		3				
Dartmouth	342	28	Cornell	Gidion		1	1	1	2		1		1		7				
Westport	329	14	Cornell	Gidion			2	1					1				4		
Westport	329	29	Cornell	Govet		1		1					1				3		
Dartmouth	343	33	Cornell	Isaac				1			1	1			3				
Dartmouth	343	15	Cornell	John	1		1		2		1				8				
Westport	329	25	Cornell	John	1			1	1	1			1	1			6		
Westport	329	35	Cornell	John	2	2		1					1				6		
Westport	329	27	Cornell	Pardon	2			1		1			1				5		
Westport	329	28	Cornell	Peleg	2	2		1		2	1		1				9		
Westport	329	34	Cornell	Philip	2			1		1			1				5		
Westport	329	41	Cornell	Rebeccah										2			2		
Dartmouth	343	32	Cornell	Richard		1							1		3				
Dartmouth	342	30	Cornell	Sarah					3		1	1			6				
Dartmouth	342	32	Cornell	Stephen		1		1					1		3				
Swansea	401	15	Cornell	Stephen		1			1				2	2			6		
Westport	329	23	Cornell	Stephen			1		1			1		1			4		
Dighton	410	9	Cornell	Stephen Jr	1			1		1			1				4		
Westport	329	32	Cornell	Susannah									1	1			2		
Westport	329	26	Cornell	Thomas			1	1		1	1	1					5		
Dartmouth	342	29	Cornell	Timothy			1						2		3				
Dartmouth	343	16	Cornell	William		1		1		1					4				
Taunton	356	3	Cornish	Alice Wido						1			1	1			3		
New Bedford	421	27	Cornish	Hananiah				1						2			3		
New Bedford	421	34	Cornish	Patience								2	2	1			5		
Westport	329	20	Cory	Benjamin	2	3			1	3			2	1			12		
Westport	329	22	Cory	Glasco											5		5		
Westport	329	12	Cory	Isaac			1		1	1	1	2	2	1	1		10		
Westport	329	13	Cory	Joseph	3	1		1		1			1				7		
Westport	329	21	Cory	Jubiter											2		2		
Westport	329	19	Cory	Thomas		1		1	1		1		1	1			6		
Dartmouth	342	35	Cory	William		2	1		3				1		9				
Taunton	359	36	Cott	Jonathan			3		1		3	1		1	1		10		
Westport	330	4	Cottle	John											6		6		
Freetown	292	8	Cottle	Samuel	1				1		1		1				4		
Freetown	292	7	Cottle	Thomas		1	1		1		1	2		1			7		
Freetown	289	14	Cotton	Thomas	4			1			1		1				7		
Berkley	281	11	Cotton	William		1		1					1				3		
New Bedford	422	22	Coval	William	4	1	2		1	1	1		1				11		
New Bedford	422	46	Cowen	Luella		1				1	1	1					4		
Dartmouth	343	30	Cowing	Ebenezer		2		1		1			1		5				
Dartmouth	343	12	Cowing	Joshua	1		1		2	1			1		9				
Dartmouth	343	13	Cowing	Mary			1					1	1		3				
Dartmouth	343	11	Cowing	Zebah		1	1			1			1		4				
Dighton	412	26	Crandle	John			1				1	1	1				4		
New Bedford	421	26	Crandon	Consider			1						1				2		
New Bedford	421	32	Crandon	John			1										1		
New Bedford	421	39	Crandon	Joseph	1		1			1			1				4		
New Bedford	422	5	Crandon	Phillip	2			1					1				4		
New Bedford	421	25	Crandon	Thomas				1									1		
Berkley	276	18	Crane	Abel			1		1		1		1				4		
Berkley	276	17	Crane	Abiather	1			1	1	3			1				7		
Berkley	276	20	Crane	Anna Wd		2						1	1				4		
Berkley	276	16	Crane	Benjamin	1				1	2	2		1				7		
Berkley	280	13	Crane	Benjamin 2d	1				1				1				3		
Berkley	275	9	Crane	Bernice			1		1			1		1			4		
New Bedford	422	41	Crane	Cesar											2		2		
Berkley	279	25	Crane	Ebenezer		1			1		2			2			6		
Berkley	280	5	Crane	Elisha			2		1				3	1			7		
Taunton	368	32	Crane	George	2	1		1		2		1	1	1			9		
Berkley	279	29	Crane	Henry	1		1						1				3		
Raynham	375	15	Crane	Henry			1		1					1			3		
Berkley	276	19	Crane	Luther	4		1	1		2	2		1				11		

TOWN	PG#	LN#	LAST NAME	FIRST NAME	FWM under 10	FWM 10–16	FWM 16–26	FWM 26–45	FWM 45+	FWF under 10	FWF 10–16	FWF 16–26	FWF 26–45	FWF 45+	TOTAL ALL OTHER	TOTAL SLAVES	TOTALS	DISTRICT/ TOWNSHIP	NOTES
Berkley	280	15	Crane	Nathaniel				1		2			1				4		
Norton	380	13	Crane	Terry	2		1	1			1		1				6		
Dartmouth	343	8	Crank	George												6	6		
Berkley	277	22	Cranson	Bathsheba								1		1	1		3		
Attleboro	321	56	Cranston	Jason			1	1		1			1				4		
Freetown	291	31	Crapo	Benjamin	1		1						1				3		
Freetown	292	3	Crapo	Joshua				1				2	2	1			6		
Freetown	292	6	Crapo	Peter	1	1	2	1		3			1				9		
Dartmouth	343	26	Crapo	Peter Junr			1	1					2				5		
Dartmouth	343	27	Crapo	Richard			1	2					1				4		
Dartmouth	342	33	Crapo	Ruben		1						1					3		
Dartmouth	342	36	Craw	David			1	1					1				5		
Dartmouth	343	34	Craw	Nathan			1	3					1				7		
Mansfield	385	12	Crawley	Abraham	1	2		1		2		1	1	1			9		
New Bedford	422	24	Crocker	Joshua			1	1		4	1	3	1				11		
Taunton	360	1	Crocker	Josiah			2	1					1	1	1		6		
Westport	329	44	Crocker	Robert	1		1	1		2	1		1	1			8		
New Bedford	422	29	Crocker	Rowland	2	1		1				1	1				6		
Taunton	359	41	Crocker	Samuel				1		2			1		1		5		
Westport	329	37	Croel	John	1	2		1		1			1	1			7		
Taunton	367	46	Crosman	Benjamin	3	1		1		2	1	1					9		
Taunton	361	2	Crosman	Ebenezer		2		1					1	1			5		
Raynham	373	6	Crosman	Elhanan	1		1					1					3		
Norton	380	26	Crosman	Elisha	1		1			2			1				5		
Raynham	373	3	Crosman	Gabriel	1	2		1					1				5		
Taunton	366	37	Crosman	Job	1		1			1			1				4		
Taunton	367	6	Crosman	Leonard		1	1					1	1				4		
Taunton	367	10	Crosman	Mary Wido							1		1				2		
Taunton	359	13	Crosman	Otis	1	3		1				1	1	1			8		
Taunton	367	8	Crosman	Robert		1		1		1				2			5		
Taunton	360	41	Crosman	Robert Junr	4	1		1		1	2		1				10		
Taunton	367	47	Crosman	Simeon	1	1	1	1		1	2	2	1				10		
Taunton	361	5	Crosman	Simeon 2d		1				3	2		1				8		
Mansfield	385	11	Crosman	Thephilus		3		1					1				5		
New Bedford	422	19	Cross	Latham				1					1				2		
Taunton	356	19	Crossman	Seth			1						1				2		
Dartmouth	342	34	Crossman	Zelotes			1						1				2		
New Bedford	421	38	Crowel	John			1			1			1				3		
Rehoboth	305	40	Crowell	James	1		1			1	2		1				6		
Berkley	279	12	Cudworth	David	1	1	2	1					1				6		
Freetown	281	7	Cudworth	David	1		1						1				3		
Freetown	294	22	Cudworth	David 2d	1		1			1			1				4		
Freetown	283	12	Cudworth	Dolly Wid.		1						2	1				4		
Freetown	283	13	Cudworth	Drinkwater		1						1					2		
Freetown	281	6	Cudworth	Jessee				1			1	1		1			4		
Freetown	294	27	Cudworth	Jessee	2		1			1		1					5		
Freetown	281	2	Cudworth	Phebe Wid								2	1				3		
Freetown	281	3	Cudworth	William	2		1			2			1				6		
Westport	329	33	Cuffe	John											5		5		
Westport	329	15	Cuffe	Paul											11		11		
Dartmouth	343	5	Cummings	Benjamin	1			1	2	3	1	1					11		
Dighton	409	33	Cummings	David			1					1					2		
Dighton	413	8	Cummings	John		2		1		1	2		1				7		
Dighton	413	10	Cummings	Jona	1	1	1						1				4		
Somerset	405	12	Cummings	Noble	1	2	1			2	2	1					9		
Dighton	414	12	Cummings	William	1	1	1	1					1				5		
Freetown	285	17	Cummons	Alanson	2			1						1			4		
Freetown	291	15	Cummons	Jail			1			3		1					5		
Freetown	285	18	Cummons	Phillip	2	1		1		3			1				8		
New Bedford	421	37	Cunningham	Stephen		2	2	1				1	1				7		
Dighton	411	42	Curtin	Jonathan			1	1					1				3		
Dighton	411	43	Curtin	Jonathan Jr	1		1						1				3		
Taunton	362	28	Curtis	Jonathan	1			1			1		1				4		
Rehoboth	310	19	Cushin	Charles			1		1			1	1				8		
Rehoboth	307	39	Cushin	Jacob	2	1				1	2		1				9		
Rehoboth	307	38	Cushin	Josiah	2			1		1	1		1				6		
Rehoboth	310	18	Cushing	Level			1						1				3		
New Bedford	422	3	Cushman	Elisha				1									1		
New Bedford	422	17	Cushman	Ezra	2	1	3	2				1	1	1	1		12		
Attleboro	317	4	Cushman	Joseph	2	1		1		2			1	1			8		
New Bedford	422	4	Cushman	Mary	1	1						1	1				4		
New Bedford	422	38	Cushman	Mial	1	1		1					1				4		
Dartmouth	343	3	Cushman	Obed	1			1	1	2	1	1					9		
Taunton	358	37	Cushman	Zebedee	1		1			3	2		1				9		
Rehoboth	300	23	Cushon	David		1	1					1	1				4		
Attleboro	319	21	Cutting	Aaron	1	2							1				4		
Attleboro	321	30	Cutting	David	2		1			1			1				5		
Attleboro	319	22	Cutting	James		2	1	1		2		1					8		
Attleboro	319	23	Cutting	Oliver				1		1	2		1	1			6		
Freetown	286	9	Dagget	Benjamin				1		2	1		1				5		
Rehoboth	307	42	Dagget	Jacob	1		2		2			1	1				10		
Rehoboth	302	7	Dagget	James			1						1				6		

TOWN	PG#	LN#	LAST NAME	FIRST NAME	FREE WHITE MALES					FREE WHITE FEMALES					TOTAL ALL OTHER	TOTAL SLAVES	TOTALS	DISTRICT/ TOWNSHIP	NOTES
					under 10	10 to 16	16 to 26	26 to 45	45 and over	under 10	10 to 16	16 to 26	26 to 45	45 and over					
Rehoboth	313	4	Dagget	James		2	1	1			1		1			6			
Swansea	403	4	Dagget	Jethro	1	1		1		1	1	1					6		
Rehoboth	310	4	Dagget	Levi			1	3		2		1				9			
Rehoboth	310	3	Dagget	Robert		1	1		1	2		1				10			
Rehoboth	302	6	Dagget	Timothy		1		1					1			3			
Rehoboth	313	2	Dagget	William 2nd			1					1				6			
Rehoboth	310	2	Dagget	Willm			3	1				2	1			7			
Attleboro	321	33	Daggett	*			1			2		1					4		
Attleboro	321	32	Daggett	E*	2	1	1			1	1						6		
Attleboro	321	35	Daggett	Elihu		1	1		1	1	2	1					7		
Attleboro	321	31	Daggett	Elijah	1	2	1	1		3	1	1					10		
Attleboro	322	35	Daggett	Isaac		1	2		1	1	1	2	1				9		
Attleboro	318	68	Daggett	Jesse				1		1		1					3		
Attleboro	319	8	Daggett	Joab	4	3		1		2		2		2			14		
Attleboro	319	9	Daggett	John			2	1	1	1		1		1			8		
Attleboro	318	31	Daggett	Joseph					1	2		1					4		
Norton	380	37	Daggett	Josiah	1			1		1			1				4		
Attleboro	320	22	Daggett	Reuben	2			1	1		1			1			6		
Taunton	358	40	Daggett	Simeon	2	4		2				2	1		1		12		
Taunton	357	26	Danforth	Asa	3			1		2	1		1	1			9		
Norton	380	34	Danforth	Elijah			3	1	1	1	1						8		
Taunton	363	23	Danforth	John		1		1				1		1			4		
Taunton	365	24	Danforth	Oliver		1			1	2	2		2				8		
Norton	380	35	Danforth	Thomas	2	1		1		3	1	1		1			10		
Taunton	371	5	Danforth	William	1			1		2		1					5		
Rehoboth	306	24	Darby	Abner			1		3			1				6			
Rehoboth	311	35	Darby	Abner		1		1	2	1		1				8			
Rehoboth	306	25	Darby	John				1								1			
New Bedford	423	17	Darnon	Joseph	1			1		1	1		1		1		6		
New Bedford	423	18	Darnon	Joseph Jun			1				2						3		
Freetown	289	18	Davis	Aaron	1	1		1	1	2			2	1			9		
New Bedford	423	30	Davis	Aaron	1		1		1	3	1	1	1				9		
Westport	330	29	Davis	Aaron	2			1		1			1				5		
Westport	330	37	Davis	Abial			1	1					1	1			4		
Westport	331	1	Davis	Abial Junr			1		1	1		1					4		
Westport	330	24	Davis	Abner			1				1		1				3		
New Bedford	423	32	Davis	Abraham	1	1		1		1	1		1				6		
Somerset	404	33	Davis	Arthur	2	2		1		1			1				7		
Rehoboth	301	18	Davis	Barney			1			1			1			3			
Somerset	404	11	Davis	Benj			2		1				1	2			6		
Somerset	405	14	Davis	Benja Jun		1		1		4	2	1	1				10		
Freetown	289	13	Davis	Benjamin			1			1		1					3		
Westport	330	7	Davis	Benjamin		1	1	1		1	1		1		1		7		
Freetown	290	11	Davis	Cornelius		2	1		1			1		1			6		
Freetown	287	2	Davis	Cornelius Jr	1			1		1		1					4		
Rehoboth	298	5	Davis	Daniel		1	1	1		1	1		1			6			
Rehoboth	298	6	Davis	Daniel Jr			1		1	1						5			
New Bedford	424	3	Davis	David	1	1		1		5	1		1				10		
Westport	330	26	Davis	Eben		2			1	2	1		1				7		
Freetown	289	4	Davis	Edmond	1		1			2		1					5		
Freetown	290	18	Davis	Eleazer	1			1	1	1			1	1			6		
Westport	330	6	Davis	Elijah	2			1					1				4		
Westport	330	8	Davis	Gidion	1	1		1		3	3		1				10		
New Bedford	423	24	Davis	Humphrey	1			1		1			1				4		
Dartmouth	343	41	Davis	James				1					1			2			
Freetown	290	17	Davis	James	1		1					1		1			4		
New Bedford	423	46	Davis	James		2	1		1			3		1			8		
Somerset	405	48	Davis	James	3	3		1	1	2			1	1			12		
New Bedford	423	29	Davis	James 2nd	4			1					1				6		
New Bedford	424	1	Davis	James 2nd	1	1	1		1	4	1	2	1	1			13		
New Bedford	423	25	Davis	Jethro	2			1				1		1			5		
Dighton	411	24	Davis	John	2	3			1	2	1	1		1			11		
Westport	330	9	Davis	John	2	1	3		1	1		1		1			10		
Westport	331	3	Davis	John 1st				1			1	1		1			4		
Freetown	291	16	Davis	Jonathan	1			1						1			3		
Westport	331	5	Davis	Jonathan				1	1					1			3		
Freetown	286	11	Davis	Jonathan Jr	1			1		2			1				5		
Freetown	289	19	Davis	Joseph		1	3	1	1	3			1	1			11		
Rehoboth	306	26	Davis	Joseph	1	2		1			1		1			7			
Freetown	290	14	Davis	Kiah	2	1			1	1		1		1			7		
New Bedford	423	27	Davis	Nathan	1	1		1		1		2		1			8		
Freetown	290	21	Davis	Nichademos				2			1	1	2				6		
New Bedford	423	23	Davis	Nicholas			2	1		2			1				6		
Westport	330	34	Davis	Nicholas	2			1		1			1				5		
New Bedford	423	26	Davis	Nicholas 2nd			1	1		1			1				4		
Freetown	282	19	Davis	Paul	1			1		1			1				5		
Westport	330	19	Davis	Philip	2			1					1				4		
Westport	330	18	Davis	Philip Stephonson		1		1		1			1				4		
Dartmouth	343	37	Davis	Richard			1				1	1	1			5			
New Bedford	423	38	Davis	Russell		1	1					1					3		
New Bedford	423	28	Davis	Ruth								1					1		
Somerset	404	31	Davis	Silas		1		1					1				3		
Westport	330	17	Davis	Stephen		1			1	1			1				4		

100

TOWN	PG#	LN#	HEADS OF HOUSEHOLD		FREE WHITE MALES					FREE WHITE FEMALES					TOTAL ALL OTHER	TOTAL SLAVES	TOTALS	DISTRICT/ TOWNSHIP	NOTES
			LAST NAME	FIRST NAME	under 10	10 to 16	16 to 26	26 to 45	45 and over	under 10	10 to 16	16 to 26	26 to 45	45 and over					
Freetown	284	20	Davis	Thomas			1	1					1				3		
Westport	330	28	Davis	Thomas	2			1			1		1				5		
Freetown	286	14	Davis	Wd Dinah			1						1				2		
Dartmouth	343	40	Davis	William			1			1		1			6				
Rehoboth	305	14	Davis	William	2		1	4		1		1			10				
Taunton	367	3	Davis	William			3	1		1	1	1					7		
Attleboro	321	60	Davis	Aaron			1		1			1		1			4		
Attleboro	320	53	Davison	Andrew			1			2			1				4		
Rehoboth	305	13	Davison	William			1						1		3				
Freetown	288	2	Davol	Abner				1					1				2		
Freetown	287	19	Davol	Pardon		1	2		1	1		1		2			8		
Attleboro	322	14	Day	Charles			1			2		1	1				5		
Attleboro	322	13	Day	Eliphaz		1	1		1			1		1			5		
Attleboro	317	24	Day	Jeremiah		3			1			1	1	1			7		
Attleboro	321	46	Day	Loammi	1	2	1		1			1		1			7		
Berkley	281	1	Dean	Aaron	2			1		3			1				7		
Taunton	363	36	Dean	Abel				1					1				2		
Taunton	363	24	Dean	Abiel		1		1			1		1				4		
Taunton	360	22	Dean	Abiezer	1	1	1	1		3	3		1				11		
Taunton	371	8	Dean	Abishai	2	2		1					1				6		
Taunton	358	9	Dean	Abner				1					1	1			3		
Raynham	372	23	Dean	Benaiah	1	2	2	1		2	1		1				10		
Freetown	294	25	Dean	Benjamin	3	1		1		1			1				7		
Taunton	361	27	Dean	Caleb		1		1		4			2				8		
Taunton	363	26	Dean	Charles	1		1	1				1					4		
Taunton	370	24	Dean	Cyrus	2		1						1				4		
Berkley	280	27	Dean	David		1			1	1		1	1	1			6		
Taunton	363	25	Dean	David				1									1		
Taunton	369	28	Dean	David 2d	1			1		1			1				4		
Taunton	370	30	Dean	David 3d				1		2							3		
Berkley	280	28	Dean	David Jur	1			1		1			1				4		
Taunton	361	26	Dean	Ebenezer		1	1	1				1	1	1	1		7		
Taunton	368	23	Dean	Ebenezer 3d	2	1	1			2			1				7		
Taunton	359	21	Dean	Ebenezer Junior	2	1		2		1	1		1				8		
Taunton	361	21	Dean	Edward	1			1		2	2	2	1	1			10		
Taunton	370	23	Dean	Elijah 2d	1			1				1	1	1			5		
Taunton	361	30	Dean	Elizabeth Wido		1						2	1	1			5		
Taunton	363	27	Dean	Elkanah			1		1	2	2		1				7		
Taunton	365	39	Dean	Enos	3				1	2	1		1				8		
Attleboro	318	4	Dean	Ephraim & Asa	4	2		2		4		2	1	4			19		
Taunton	363	37	Dean	Ezra				1					1				2		
Taunton	363	41	Dean	George				1					1				2		
Taunton	363	40	Dean	George Junior	2		1					1					4		
Taunton	370	17	Dean	Hannah Wido		1						1					2		
Raynham	376	3	Dean	Hoitstill Wid										1			1		
Taunton	363	9	Dean	Isaac		1	1	1									4		
Taunton	357	23	Dean	Israel	1			1					2	2			6		
Berkley	280	31	Dean	James			2	1				2			1		6		
Taunton	363	39	Dean	James	1	1		1		2	1	1	1				8		
Berkley	280	32	Dean	James Junr			1			1	1		1				4		
Taunton	365	3	Dean	Job				1					1		1		3		
Raynham	373	19	Dean	Job 2d	1		1	2			1	2	1				8		
Raynham	376	11	Dean	Job 2d	3	3		1		1		3	1				12		
Raynham	375	42	Dean	Johith		1		1		4		1					7		
Raynham	373	17	Dean	Jonathan				1					1				2		
Raynham	374	16	Dean	Jonathan 3d	3			1		1	1		1				7		
Raynham	373	18	Dean	Jonathan Junr	2	1		1					1				5		
Berkley	280	29	Dean	Joseph		1		1					1				3		
Raynham	375	40	Dean	Joseph				1					1				2		
Taunton	360	8	Dean	Joseph	2	1	3	1		3		1	2				13		
Raynham	375	41	Dean	Joseph Junr	1	1		1		1			1				5		
Raynham	372	14	Dean	Josiah		2	4	1		1		2		1			11		
Raynham	376	7	Dean	Lazell	2			1		2	1		1				7		
Taunton	361	31	Dean	Lemuel		1		1						1			3		
Taunton	365	32	Dean	Leonard	2			1		1			1				5		
Freetown	281	1	Dean	Levi	1	1	1	2		1			2				8		
Raynham	376	30	Dean	Linus	3			1		1			1				6		
Taunton	361	28	Dean	Luther	4	2		1		1			2				10		
Berkley	281	2	Dean	Mary Wid		2	1					1		1			5		
Westport	330	13	Dean	Micah			1	1					1				3		
Raynham	375	34	Dean	Nathaniel	2	2	1	1					2	1			10		
Taunton	368	8	Dean	Nathaniel	2	2	2		1	2			1	1	1		11		
Taunton	363	35	Dean	Obed	1	1			2			1		2			7		
Taunton	370	16	Dean	Oliver				1		1	1		1				4		
Taunton	358	18	Dean	Philip	1			1		2	3		1	1			9		
Taunton	362	27	Dean	Rebecca	1					1		1		1			4		
Taunton	370	34	Dean	Reul	1			1					1				3		
Taunton	370	29	Dean	Ruth Wido		2								1			3		
Dighton	409	9	Dean	Saml	3			1			1	1	1				7		
Taunton	361	25	Dean	Sarah Wido									1				1		
Raynham	374	7	Dean	Seth			2	1		4	2	1	1				11		
Taunton	363	28	Dean	Seth				1					1				2		

TOWN	PG#	LN#	HEADS OF HOUSEHOLD LAST NAME	FIRST NAME	FREE WHITE MALES under 10	10 to 16	16 to 26	26 to 45	45 and over	FREE WHITE FEMALES under 10	10 to 16	16 to 26	26 to 45	45 and over	TOTAL ALL OTHER	TOTAL SLAVES	TOTALS	DISTRICT/ TOWNSHIP	NOTES
Taunton	363	29	Dean	Seth Junior	2	1		1		3			1				8		
Taunton	363	22	Dean	Solomon		1		1		2	1		1				6		
Raynham	375	22	Dean	Stephen			1		1		1	2		1			6		
Raynham	375	20	Dean	Stephen Junr	1		1			1		1		1			5		
Taunton	367	1	Dean	Sylvester	2	1	1	1		1			1				7		
Raynham	374	15	Dean	Thomas		1		1			1	1	1				5		
Berkley	280	30	Dean	Walter	1			1					2	1			5		
Taunton	364	8	Dean	Walter			1			2		1					4		
Berkley	275	10	Dean	Weltha Wid	2	2							2	1			7		
Taunton	359	32	Dean	Rufus	1	1	1	2		1	4						10		
Norton	380	28	Deane	Asahel	2		1		1	1	1	1	1				8		
Norton	380	36	Deane	Asahel Jun	1		1	1		1	1	1	1				7		
Norton	380	27	Deane	Daniel		1		1					1				3		
Easton	389	31	Deane	Edward	1				1				1				3		
Easton	389	20	Deane	Elisha				1				1	1				3		
Easton	389	21	Deane	Elisha Junr	2			1		1	1		1				6		
Easton	389	19	Deane	James		1	1	1					1	1	1		5		
Easton	389	32	Deane	James 2d			1			3		1					5		
Norton	380	31	Deane	Nathan				1			1	1					3		
Norton	380	32	Deane	Nathan Jr	3	2		2		1		2	1				11		
Norton	380	29	Deane	Noah	1	1		1		1	1		1				6		
Norton	380	30	Deane	Pliny	2		1	1		1		1	1				7		
Norton	380	33	Deane	Richard	2	1	3		1	1	2		1				11		
New Bedford	423	40	Deane	William			1					1					2		
Taunton	371	12	Dearborn	Benjamin		1		1		1		1	1				5		
Rehoboth	313	3	Debens	Charles			1									1			
Westport	331	8	Deck	Exter											4		4		
New Bedford	423	41	Delano	Abisha	1			1		1		1			3		7		
New Bedford	423	43	Delano	Allerton	1			1		1			1				4		
New Bedford	423	15	Delano	Amaziah	1			1					1				3		
New Bedford	423	11	Delano	Calvin		1		1			2		1				5		
New Bedford	422	49	Delano	Dinah		1							1				2		
New Bedford	423	7	Delano	Ephraim		1	1	1			4		1				8		
New Bedford	423	39	Delano	Gideon				1									1		
New Bedford	423	35	Delano	Hannah	2								1				3		
New Bedford	423	1	Delano	Jabez	2			1					1		1		5		
New Bedford	423	5	Delano	John	2	1	1	1			1	1	1				8		
New Bedford	423	13	Delano	John	2	2		1		2	1		1				9		
New Bedford	423	20	Delano	Joseph		1	2		1	1	1	1	1				8		
New Bedford	422	48	Delano	Joshua	1	4	3		1	2		2		1			14		
New Bedford	423	16	Delano	Marcy	1								1				2		
New Bedford	423	12	Delano	Nathan	1			1		4	1		1				8		
New Bedford	423	6	Delano	Paul	1	1	1						1				4		
New Bedford	423	8	Delano	Reuben		1		1			2	1	1				6		
New Bedford	423	3	Delano	Richard	2			1		2			1		1		7		
New Bedford	423	14	Delano	Seth	1			1					1				3		
New Bedford	423	2	Delano	Thomas		2	1		1	1	1		1				7		
New Bedford	423	44	Delano	Thomas 2nd	1			1		2	1		1				6		
Freetown	294	4	Demoranoil	Josiah	1			1		1			1				4		
Dartmouth	344	1	Demoranvel	Nehemiah		1		1		1					4				
Dartmouth	343	42	Demoranvel	Shoman		1		4			1				6				
Westport	330	23	Denis	John	1		1					1					3		
Westport	330	22	Denis	Robert	2		1					1					4		
Somerset	405	31	Dennis	Arther	2	2			1	2	4		1				12		
Somerset	405	32	Dennis	John				1									1		
Freetown	287	17	Dennison	James		1		1		1	1		1	1			6		
Freetown	293	8	Denno	Nathaniel		2	1	1		3	1	1	1				10		
Attleboro	320	8	Derry	John	1		2	1		1	2		1				8		
Dartmouth	343	38	Derry	Lucina											7		7		
Norton	380	38	Derry	Wilks			1			1		1					3		
Attleboro	317	30	Devens	John	3		1					2					6		
Dartmouth	343	39	Devil	Job	2		1						1		5				
Westport	331	2	Devol	Abner	2	1		1		2	2	1					9		
Westport	331	6	Devol	Barney		1	1		1	1	1	1		1			7		
Westport	330	10	Devol	Benjamin		1	1	1		1		1	1				6		
Westport	330	25	Devol	Benjamin 2nd		2		1			1		2				6		
Westport	330	35	Devol	Berjona				1				1	1				3		
Westport	330	27	Devol	Daniel 1st				1					1				2		
Westport	330	21	Devol	Daniel 2d				1		4			1				6		
Dartmouth	343	35	Devol	David	2	2	1		1		2	1				11			
Westport	330	20	Devol	David				1				1					2		
Westport	331	4	Devol	Jeremiah				1				1					2		
Westport	330	15	Devol	John				1									1		
Westport	331	7	Devol	Joshua	2	1		1					1				5		
Westport	330	14	Devol	Pardon			1			2	1	1					5		
Westport	330	36	Devol	Reuben	3		1					1					5		
Westport	330	16	Devol	Samuel		2		1					1				4		
New Bedford	423	9	Dexter	William				1									1		
Dartmouth	343	36	Dick	Silas											10		10		
Easton	389	28	Dickerman	Ebenezer		1		1					1				3		
Easton	389	29	Dickerman	James	2			1		2			1				6		
Easton	389	37	Dickerman	Nehemiah		1							1				2		
Westport	330	31	Dier	Bershebe						1		1					2		

TOWN	PG#	LN#	LAST NAME	FIRST NAME	FREE WHITE MALES under 10	10 to 16	16 to 26	26 to 45	45 and over	FREE WHITE FEMALES under 10	10 to 16	16 to 26	26 to 45	45 and over	TOTAL ALL OTHER	TOTAL SLAVES	TOTALS	DISTRICT/ TOWNSHIP	NOTES
Westport	330	32	Dier	Head			1										1		
Westport	330	12	Dier	John	1			1		1			1	1			5		
Westport	330	33	Dier	Joseph				1					1				2		
Westport	330	30	Dier	Preserved	2				1	2			1				6		
Westport	330	11	Dier	Zacheus	1	1	1		2				1				6		
New Bedford	424	2	Dillingham	Bejamin Jr			2	1		2		1					6		
New Bedford	423	22	Dillingham	Benjamin		1	3	1	1			2		1			9		
New Bedford	423	21	Dillingham	Cornelius				1				1					2		
Berkley	280	7	Dillingham	John	2			2		2		1					7		
Mansfield	385	21	Doane	Dwight	3			2		1	1	1					8		
Mansfield	385	20	Doane	Elijah			1		1	1			1				4		
New Bedford	423	19	Doane	Elizabeth								2					2		
Mansfield	385	17	Doane	Isaac			1		1			1	1	1			5		
Mansfield	385	19	Doane	John			3		1			2	1	1			8		
Mansfield	385	18	Doane	William			1	1		1			1				4		
Mansfield	385	24	Doane	William 2d	2			1		2			1				6		
Freetown	294	2	Dodson	Jonathan				1									1		
Freetown	287	8	Dodson	Jonathan 2d	1	1			1	1				2			6		
New Bedford	423	36	Doty	Elihu			1					1	1				3		
Dartmouth	344	2	Doty	John			1	1	1	1		1			9				
New Bedford	423	37	Doty	Theodore			1										1		
Easton	389	35	Downing	Moses		1		1		2	1		1				6		
Easton	389	23	Drake	Adam		2		1		1	1		1				6		
Mansfield	385	26	Drake	Benjamin	1			1				1					3		
Easton	389	16	Drake	Bethuel		2		1		1	1		1	1			7		
Easton	389	17	Drake	Bethuel Jr			1			2			1				4		
Easton	389	36	Drake	Cyrus			1					1					2		
Easton	389	40	Drake	Edward	2	1		1		2			1				7		
Easton	389	14	Drake	Elijah	2			1		1			1				5		
Easton	389	15	Drake	Elijah Jr			1			1			1				3		
Easton	389	26	Drake	Elizabeth	3		1			1	1	1	1				8		
Easton	389	39	Drake	Isaac			1				1		1				3		
Easton	389	12	Drake	Jonah				1					1				2		
Easton	389	27	Drake	Joseph				1					2				3		
Easton	389	22	Drake	Lot	3	2		1				1	1				8		
Mansfield	385	25	Drake	Oliver	2	3		1		2			1				9		
Norton	380	39	Drake	Otis	3			1		1			2				7		
Easton	389	38	Drake	Patty	2								1				4		
Easton	389	25	Drake	Robert	1		1		1	1	2		1				7		
Easton	389	30	Drake	Thomas	1	3	2		1	3			1				11		
Easton	389	13	Drake	Timothy	2			1		2			1				6		
Easton	389	24	Drake	Titus	4			1					1				6		
Easton	389	33	Drake	Zachariah	2			1			1	3		1			8		
Attleboro	317	23	Draper	Ebenezer				1			1	1		1			4		
Attleboro	322	28	Draper	Ebenezer the 2nd	1			1		1			1				4		
Attleboro	322	59	Draper	James		1	1			2	1	1		1			7		
Attleboro	321	43	Draper	John	2	1	1	1			2	1	1				9		
Attleboro	322	60	Draper	Lewis	2			1			1	1					5		
Attleboro	317	25	Draper	Stephen		2	1	1		1		1		1			7		
New Bedford	423	34	Drew	Benjamin	1			1		2			1				5		
New Bedford	423	10	Drew	Isaac			1		1			1		1			4		
Easton	389	34	Drew	John	2	1		2		1	1		1	2			10		
New Bedford	423	4	Drew	Joshua		3	1	1		4		1	2				12		
New Bedford	423	48	Drew	Josiah	1		1		1		1		2				6		
Easton	389	18	Drew	Nicholas	1			1		2			1				5		
New Bedford	423	31	Drew	Sarah									1				1		
Rehoboth	311	26	Drier	William			1					2			3				
Berkley	280	24	Drinkwater	Desire									2				2		
Rehoboth	305	38	Drown	Frederic	1		1	1				2	1		7				
Rehoboth	300	19	Drown	Jesse		1						1			3				
Rehoboth	305	39	Drown	Jonathan		1						1	1		3				
Rehoboth	300	18	Drown	Nathaniel		1		1		1		1	1		6				
Rehoboth	300	17	Drown	Roial		1				1		1			6				
New Bedford	423	33	Dudley	George	2			1		1			1				5		
Freetown	282	20	Duglap	Daniel	1	2		2		1		1	1				8		
New Bedford	423	42	Dunbar	Fanny	2	2				2	1		1				8		
Attleboro	319	61	Dunham	Abial	1	1			1	1	1	2		2			9		
Mansfield	385	23	Dunham	Elizabeth									1	2			3		
New Bedford	423	45	Dunham	George L.			1			1			1				3		
Taunton	357	11	Dunham	Jacob	1			1		1			1				4		
Attleboro	319	40	Dunham	John		1	1			2	1		1				6		
Taunton	356	5	Dunham	Joseph			1			1			1	2			5		
Attleboro	320	31	Dunham	Sarah								1		1			2		
Mansfield	385	22	Dunham	William	4	3			1	2			1				11		
New Bedford	423	47	Durfee	James	2		1	1		4			1				9		
Freetown	285	1	Durffee	Benjamin	2	1		1	1		1	2	1				9		
Freetown	285	3	Durffee	Charles	1			1	1	3	2		3	1			12		
Freetown	293	11	Durffee	David		1			1				1				3		
Freetown	288	17	Durffee	Ruth Wid						1			1				2		
Freetown	289	12	Durffee	Thomas			1			1			1				3		
Somerset	407	9	Earl	Benja		1		1	1		1			1			5		
Westport	331	11	Earl	Benjamin			1			1			1				3		
Swansea	396	23	Earl	Caleb		1	2		1				1	2	1		8		

103

TOWN	PG#	LN#	HEADS OF HOUSEHOLD LAST NAME	FIRST NAME	FREE WHITE MALES under 10	10 to 16	16 to 26	26 to 45	45 and over	FREE WHITE FEMALES under 10	10 to 16	16 to 26	26 to 45	45 and over	TOTAL ALL OTHER	TOTAL SLAVES	TOTALS	DISTRICT/ TOWNSHIP	NOTES
Westport	331	12	Earl	Elizabeth							1		2				3		
Westport	331	14	Earl	George				1					1				2		
New Bedford	424	18	Earl	Job	1	1		1				2	1				6		
Westport	331	9	Earl	John		1	1	1		1	1		2				7		
Somerset	404	19	Earl	Oliver	1			1		1			1				4		
Westport	331	10	Earl	Robert	2			1		2	2	2	1				11		
Swansea	396	10	Earl	Thomas				3					2				5		
Westport	331	13	Earl	Wanton			1			1			1				3		
Swansea	401	13	Earl	Weston	3			1					1				5		
New Bedford	424	15	East	George				1					1				2		
Dartmouth	344	4	Easton	Walter	1	1	1	1		1	1	1			7				
Dartmouth	344	3	Eastons	Joseph	1	1	1	2		1		1			7				
Taunton	364	32	Eaton	John	2			1		1		1					5		
Norton	380	41	Eddy	Abiel				1					1				2		
Taunton	370	13	Eddy	Abishai		2		1		3	1	1					8		
Taunton	370	7	Eddy	Apollos		1		1		1	1		1				5		
Taunton	370	8	Eddy	Apollos Junior	1		2					1					4		
Taunton	370	11	Eddy	Asahel		1		1		2		1					6		
Norton	380	43	Eddy	Elijah	1	1	1	1			1	1		1			7		
Norton	380	42	Eddy	Ezra			1	1					1				3		
New Bedford	424	16	Eddy	Job		1											1		
Swansea	398	26	Eddy	Job				1		1	2		3	1			8		
New Bedford	424	17	Eddy	John	1			1		1			1				4		
Norton	380	44	Eddy	John	1			1					1				3		
Somerset	406	13	Eddy	John	1	1		1		1	2		1				7		
Dighton	413	4	Eddy	Joshua	3		1			1		1					6		
Somerset	405	42	Eddy	Lydia Wido		1							1				2		
Taunton	370	12	Eddy	Mercy						1		1		1			3		
Taunton	370	10	Eddy	Paul	1	1	1	1		1	2	2		1			10		
Norton	380	40	Eddy	Rachel			1				1			1			3		
Swansea	398	21	Eddy	Reserved	1			1		2	2	1		1			8		
Norton	380	45	Eddy	Samuel		1		1		1	1		1	1			7		
Swansea	399	9	Eddy	William	1	1		1		1	5		1				10		
Dartmouth	344	5	Eddy	Zephaniah			1			1			1		3				
Somerset	406	17	Edminster	James			1			1		1					3		
Freetown	286	5	Edmister	Noah			1	1			1		1				4		
Rehoboth	311	33	Edson	Ebenezer	1	2		1	1	1			1		8				
Rehoboth	304	4	Edson	Nathan			1	1		2		1			6				
New Bedford	424	10	Eldredge	Amos	1	1		1		1	1		1				6		
New Bedford	424	7	Eldredge	Elnathan	2		2		1			1		1			7		
New Bedford	424	6	Eldredge	Isaiah				1					1				2		
New Bedford	424	4	Eldredge	John				1					1				2		
New Bedford	424	5	Eldredge	Killey			1			3	1		1				6		
New Bedford	424	8	Eldredge	Rebecca	1							1					2		
New Bedford	424	9	Eldredge	Salathiel	1			1					1	1			4		
Freetown	287	16	Eldridge	Gideon	1			1					1	1	2		6		
Taunton	362	9	Eliot	Benjamin				1				1	2				4		
Taunton	362	7	Eliot	George			1	1					1				3		
Taunton	362	6	Eliot	John	1		2	1		1			1	1			7		
Taunton	362	8	Eliot	Joseph	1	2	2		1	4	1		1				12		
Mansfield	385	27	Eliot	Nehemiah									1				1		
Rehoboth	313	6	Ellis	Ashur			1			1		1			5				
New Bedford	424	13	Ellis	Elijah				1		1			1				3		
Attleboro	322	61	Ellis	Jabez	1	1	1	1						1			5		
Rehoboth	313	5	Ellis	James			1			1		1			5				
Attleboro	322	71	Ellis	Joel	1		1				1	1					4		
New Bedford	424	12	Ellis	John				1									1		
New Bedford	424	14	Ellis	Luke		1	1			4	2	1	1				10		
Attleboro	322	62	Ellis	Richd	1	1	2		1				1	1			7		
Raynham	372	31	Ellis	Sarah Wid							1		1	2			4		
New Bedford	424	11	Ellis	Seth				1					1	1			3		
Dighton	411	11	Elmes	Elkanah				1						1			2		
Taunton	363	21	Elms	Abner	2	1		1		1			1				6		
Freetown	288	20	Elsbree	Boomer	3	1	3		1		1			1			10		
Freetown	289	11	Elsbree	Ephraim			1			1	1	1					4		
Rehoboth	306	5	Engals	Edmun		3		1		1		1			6				
Freetown	282	25	Ennis	William			1				1	1	1				4		
Somerset	404	29	Evans	Caleb	4			1					1				6		
Somerset	404	27	Evans	Jacob	4	1		1		1	1			2			10		
Freetown	291	4	Evens	Gilford	1	1		1		1	1						5		
Freetown	283	27	Evens	John	3		1		1	1	2	1		1			10		
Freetown	294	5	Evens	Mary Wid							1			1			2		
Berkley	279	20	Evens	William	2	1		1		2	1	1	1				10		
Attleboro	319	65	Everet	Abijah		2	1	1		1			2	1			8		
Attleboro	321	25	Everet	Saml	1		1	1		2	2	2					9		
Rehoboth	300	44	Fairbrother	William	1	2		1	2	1			1		8				
Attleboro	321	50	Fales	Peter	1	3			1					1			6		
Taunton	360	25	Fales	Samuel	1	2	7	3	3	5	2	2	1	1	1		28		
Attleboro	322	46	Farebrother	Thoms		1	1			1	3	2		1			9		
Berkley	279	6	Farrington	Abial		1	1			1			1				4		
Dartmouth	344	13	Faunce	Thomas	1	1	1	1		1	3		2		10				
Easton	390	3	Ferguson	George			2		1		1						5		

TOWN	PG#	LN#	LAST NAME	FIRST NAME	FWM under 10	FWM 10-16	FWM 16-26	FWM 26-45	FWM 45+	FWF under 10	FWF 10-16	FWF 16-26	FWF 26-45	FWF 45+	TOTAL ALL OTHER	TOTAL SLAVES	TOTALS	DISTRICT/TOWNSHIP	NOTES
Taunton	369	21	Field	Abiezer	1	1	1	1			1		1				6		
Taunton	369	35	Field	Bethuel		1						1					2		
Norton	381	11	Field	Darius	1		1			1		1					4		
Norton	381	12	Field	David			1					1					2		
Attleboro	321	61	Field	Ebenezer	1		2		1	2	1	1					8		
Taunton	369	33	Field	James	1	1			1	1		1	1				6		
Rehoboth	299	37	Field	John			1		1			1				4			
Attleboro	318	47	Field	Jos	1	1		1					1	2			6		
Mansfield	385	33	Field	Joseph	2			1		1	2		1				7		
Taunton	369	36	Field	Nathaniel	1		1	1	2	1	1		1				8		
Taunton	368	33	Field	Nathaniel Junr	1	1		1				1					4		
Mansfield	385	35	Field	Richard				1					1				2		
Norton	381	7	Field	Solomon	2			1		3		2					8		
Mansfield	385	36	Field	William	1			1		2		1					5		
Taunton	359	7	Field	Zebulon	3	3			1	3	1		1				12		
Taunton	370	27	Field	Zebulon Junr	2		1	1		2	2		1	1			10		
Easton	390	6	Fillebrown	Bethuel	3			1		3			1				8		
Mansfield	385	34	Fillebrown	Catharine	1			1		1			2	1			6		
Dighton	409	34	Fish	Daniel	2	1			1	1	3	1		1			10		
Dighton	413	3	Fish	Robert		1			1				1	1			4		
Somerset	404	36	Fish	Widow	1					1			1				3		
Taunton	360	27	Fish	Hannah Wido						1	1	1					3		
Taunton	365	31	Fish	Samuel		1				1			2				4		
Rehoboth	301	19	Fisher	Ana	1								1			2			
Rehoboth	310	29	Fisher	Daniel	1			1		1	1	1				5			
Rehoboth	310	30	Fisher	Daniel Jr			1	1			1					4			
Attleboro	319	16	Fisher	David		1	1	1		1			1				5		
Attleboro	319	31	Fisher	David		1		1				1					3		
Mansfield	385	39	Fisher	Jacob	1	1						1					3		
Westport	331	16	Fisher	Job			1	1					1	1			4		
Attleboro	319	30	Fisher	Joel	2	1			2	4	3	2		2			16		
Westport	331	15	Fisher	John	1			1		3	2		1				8		
Rehoboth	313	7	Fisher	Joshua	1	1		1	1	1		2	1			9			
Mansfield	385	31	Fisher	Lemuel			1		1			2		2			6		
Taunton	365	33	Fisher	Moses			1		1					1			3		
Taunton	367	22	Fisher	Moses Junr	1			1		1			1				4		
Dartmouth	344	10	Fisher	Nathan															Enumeration left blank
Mansfield	385	32	Fisher	Nathan	1	2		1		3	2		1				10		
Attleboro	319	33	Fisher	Peter		2			1	1	2		1	1			8		
Attleboro	323	2	Fisher	Samuel	2		1			1		1					5		
Mansfield	385	29	Fisher	Samuel		2			1			1	1				5		
Mansfield	385	30	Fisher	Samuel Jr	1		1					1					3		
Dartmouth	344	7	Fisher	Seth	1	1				1		1	1			5			
Taunton	356	12	Fisher	Thomas											7		7		
Dartmouth	344	11	Fisher	William	1		1	1				1	1			5			
New Bedford	424	22	Fisk	Brownell	1			1		3			1				6		
New Bedford	424	23	Fisk	David	1			1		1	1		1				5		
New Bedford	424	28	Fisk	Preserved			1			1			1				3		
New Bedford	424	24	Fisk	Turner		1		1		1		1	1				5		
Swansea	401	8	Fitch	William								1		1			3		
Attleboro	322	27	Fitton	John		1		1			1		2				5		
Rehoboth	313	8	Fitts	David	1		1	1			1					5			
Easton	390	1	Fobes	Libeus				1			1		2				4		
Raynham	373	9	Fobes	Perez				1					1				2		
New Bedford	424	25	Folger	Obed	1	1		1		2			1				6		
Attleboro	320	16	Follet	Jona		1	2	1	1	1	1		1				8		
Rehoboth	305	9	Follet	Robert		1		1				1				5			
Rehoboth	306	7	Forbs	Daniel	1			1		2		1				6			
Easton	390	4	Ford	Joseph	1			1		1			1				4		
Somerset	405	17	Forrester	Wido	1					1		1					3		
Attleboro	319	27	Foster	Elexander		1		1			1		1				4		
Attleboro	319	28	Foster	Elexander Junr	3	1	3			1	1	2					11		
Freetown	293	12	Foster	Gload		1		1			1						3		
Attleboro	321	51	Foster	John	2		1			1	1	1					6		
Freetown	292	23	Foster	John	1	1	1		1	1	1	2	1		1		10		
Taunton	367	17	Foster	John	1	2		1		2			1				7		
Attleboro	319	53	Foster	Joseph		1	1	1		2			1				6		
Norton	381	8	Foster	Joseph	1			1		1				1			4		
Norton	381	10	Foster	Josiah	1		1					1					3		
New Bedford	424	29	Foster	Peter		2				2			1				5		
Taunton	367	14	Foster	Timothy		1		1		1	1	1	1				6		
Rehoboth	306	3	Fowler	Isaac		1	1		1	1	1					8			
Dartmouth	344	8	Fowler	Thomas										2		2			
Mansfield	385	28	Francis	Apollos	2		1	1		1		1	1				7		
Rehoboth	300	26	Francis	John		1						1				4			
Norton	381	1	Francis	Levi		1			1	1			1				4		
Mansfield	385	38	Francis	Levi Jur	1			1		2			1				5		
Dartmouth	344	9	Francis	Nathan	1			1		2	3	1				9			
Dighton	414	40	Francis	Peleg		2		1				1		1			5		
Dighton	415	1	Francis	Peleg Jr		1				2		1					4		
Swansea	401	16	Francis	Ruben			1		1			1		1			5		
Norton	381	4	Francis	Tisdale	1			1		2			1	1			6		
Rehoboth	305	19	Franklin	Daniel		1		1			1					6			

TOWN	PG#	LN#	LAST NAME	FIRST NAME	FREE WHITE MALES under 10	10 to 16	16 to 26	26 to 45	45 and over	FREE WHITE FEMALES under 10	10 to 16	16 to 26	26 to 45	45 and over	TOTAL ALL OTHER	TOTAL SLAVES	TOTALS	DISTRICT/ TOWNSHIP	NOTES
Swansea	403	17	Franklin	Lemuel	3	1	1		1	1	1			1			9		
Norton	381	5	Franklin	Record				1					1	1			3		
Swansea	403	22	Franklin	Shubal				1						1			2		
Rehoboth	298	19	Frankton	Elisha			1	2		1							6		
Raynham	373	21	Frazier	Charles	4	1		1			1		1				8		
Norton	381	9	Frazier	Hugh		1		1					1				3		
Dartmouth	344	6	Freborn	Cuffe											6		6		
Freetown	288	22	Freelove	Thomas		2	1	1		3			1				8		
Norton	381	2	Freeman	Bethiah			2			2	1	1	1				7		
New Bedford	424	21	Freeman	Charles B.		1	1			1		1					4		
Attleboro	317	13	Freeman	Daniel	2			1		1			1				5		
Attleboro	320	40	Freeman	Ezra				1		3			1	1			6		
Norton	381	3	Freeman	John	2			2		3			1				8		
Rehoboth	315	7	Freeman	Joseph											5		5		
New Bedford	424	19	Freeman	Obed		2		1				4	1				8		
Attleboro	318	3	Freeman	Thoms				1					1	1			3		
Attleboro	317	16	Freeman	William	2			1		2			1				6		
Westport	331	17	Frelove	George			1					1					2		
Dartmouth	344	12	Frelove	John			1					1					2		
Rehoboth	307	43	French	Abel	1		1		3	1	1	1					10		
Berkley	277	12	French	Content Wid									1				1		
Berkley	277	20	French	Ebenezer				1				1					2		
Berkley	277	15	French	Elijah				1				1					2		
Rehoboth	310	31	French	Elkana Jr	1	2	1		4		2	1					13		
Rehoboth	298	45	French	Elkanah	1	2	1		4		2	1					13		
Rehoboth	307	41	French	Elkanah	1			1		1			1				4		
Berkley	275	8	French	Ephraim	2		1			1		1					5		
Attleboro	320	45	French	Ezra	2	1		1		2	1	1	2				10		
Berkley	277	14	French	Israel	1			1					1				3		
Berkley	277	18	French	Israel Junr		1	1	1		1	1	1		1			7		
Berkley	276	25	French	James	1		1	1		1	2	2		1			9		
Norton	381	6	French	James	2			1		1			1	1			6		
Rehoboth	307	44	French	James	1	1		1		1	1	1	1				7		
Rehoboth	313	9	French	James Jr	1		1		3	1		1					7		
Rehoboth	307	45	French	John	2		1	1		1		1					8		
Taunton	356	7	French	Jona			1		1	2	1		1				6		
Berkley	277	21	French	Keziah									1				1		
Berkley	277	11	French	Levi		1		1		1	2	2	1				8		
Berkley	277	6	French	Nathan	1			1	2	1	1	2	2				10		
Taunton	366	26	French	Nathaniel	1			1		1	1		1				5		
Berkley	277	16	French	Phillip	1		1	1		3			1				7		
Berkley	277	13	French	Samuel	1	1	1	1				1	2				7		
Rehoboth	313	10	French	Samuel				1				1	2				4		
Rehoboth	313	11	French	Samuel Jr	1		1			1		1					7		
Taunton	366	39	French	Sarah Wido									1				1		
Attleboro	320	14	French	Thoms	1		3	1		2	2		1				10		
Raynham	373	16	French	William				1					1				2		
Taunton	362	22	Fry	Benjamin	2			1		1			1				5		
Attleboro	318	34	Fuller	Abial	1	1	1		1		1	1	1	1			8		
Rehoboth	310	32	Fuller	Asa			1			2		1					6		
Easton	390	5	Fuller	Barzillia	2			1		2			1				6		
Rehoboth	310	24	Fuller	Benjamin	1	3		1	1	1		1	1				9		
Rehoboth	308	35	Fuller	Benjamin 2nd		2		1	1	1			1				8		
Attleboro	318	5	Fuller	Caleb		1	2	2				1	3	1			10		
Attleboro	318	14	Fuller	Darius	3			1		1	1		1				7		
Attleboro	318	36	Fuller	Ebenezer	4	2	2					2		1			11		
New Bedford	424	26	Fuller	Francis	2			1		1	2	1	1				8		
Attleboro	318	16	Fuller	Frederick	2		1	1		1	1	1					7		
Rehoboth	298	36	Fuller	Giberd		1	1					1					4		
Easton	390	2	Fuller	Isaac		2		1		1		1	1				6		
Mansfield	385	37	Fuller	Isaac	1		1			1		1					4		
Attleboro	320	25	Fuller	Jedithan	1							1	1				3		
Rehoboth	302	38	Fuller	Jesse			1	2	2			1					7		
Rehoboth	308	29	Fuller	Jesse			1	2	2			1					7		
New Bedford	424	27	Fuller	John			1		1			1					3		
Attleboro	318	9	Fuller	Jos		1		1		2		1	2				7		
New Bedford	424	30	Fuller	Mary			1			1	1	1	1				5		
Rehoboth	302	39	Fuller	Nathaniel	1			1		1	1	2	2				8		
Rehoboth	310	33	Fuller	Noah		1		1		1	1	1					6		
New Bedford	424	20	Fuller	Peter		1	1		1	2	1		1				8		
Attleboro	318	15	Fuller	Stephen		1		1		1			1				4		
Attleboro	321	21	Fuller	Stephen the 2nd		2		1		2		1					6		
Rehoboth	302	9	Fuller	Timothy	1			1	3		1	2					9		
Rehoboth	308	31	Fuller	Timothy	1			1	3		1	2					9		
Attleboro	320	46	Fuller	Zelotes			1	1	1			1					4		
Attleboro	320	38	Fullers	Daniel	2		1			1							4		
Rehoboth	313	13	Gage	Benjamin	1	1	1		1	1	1						8		
Taunton	361	23	Gammands	William	1	1	1			1							5		
Swansea	399	29	Gardner	Alexander		3		1	1	1			1	1	1		8		
New Bedford	425	8	Gardner	Andrew	4	1		1		1			1				8		
Rehoboth	314	43	Gardner	Edward		1		1					1				3		
Taunton	368	2	Gardner	Freeman	2			1		1							5		

TOWN	PG#	LN#	LAST NAME	FIRST NAME	FREE WHITE MALES					FREE WHITE FEMALES					TOTAL ALL OTHER	TOTAL SLAVES	TOTALS	DISTRICT/ TOWNSHIP	NOTES
					under 10	10 to 16	16 to 26	26 to 45	45 and over	under 10	10 to 16	16 to 26	26 to 45	45 and over					
Rehoboth	303	43	Gardner	James	1	1		1	1	1	2		1				9		
Swansea	399	6	Gardner	John		1		1		1	2		1				6		
Swansea	399	5	Gardner	Joseph		1		1					1	1			4		
Swansea	399	3	Gardner	Peleg	1		2		1		4			1			9		
Swansea	399	7	Gardner	Peleg Junr	3			1		1			1				6		
Attleboro	321	13	Gardner	Saml	1			1				1					3		
Swansea	399	2	Gardner	Saml	1	3	2	2	1	1	1		2	1			14		
Swansea	398	42	Gardner	Saml 2d	4			1		2	1		2				10		
Taunton	363	43	Gardner	Samuel	1			1				1	1	1			5		
Dighton	412	11	Gardner	Stephen	2			1	1	3	1		1				9		
Swansea	399	1	Gardner	Wido	1	1						1	1	1			5		
Swansea	402	21	Gardner	William	1	2	2		2	3	1		1				12		
Attleboro	318	21	Garfield	Jonathan		1		1		1		2		1			6		
Swansea	403	33	Garnet	James											5		5		
Taunton	368	9	Gary	Seth	2	2		1		3	1		1				10		
Taunton	371	2	Gary	Zephaniah		1		1	1	1		1		1			5		
Berkley	277	28	Gavin	Paul	2			1		1			1	1			6		
Easton	390	13	Gay	Solomon		1		1		4			1				7		
New Bedford	425	4	Gelat	David			1										1		
New Bedford	424	31	Gelat	John	3			1	1	2	1		1				9		
Attleboro	317	10	George	William			1	1		3	1		1				7		
New Bedford	424	42	Gerish	John	1			1				1					3		
New Bedford	425	7	Gerish	John		1			1			2		1			5		
New Bedford	424	33	Gibbs	Alfred		1				1		1					3		
New Bedford	424	34	Gibbs	Ancel		1	1										2		
Somerset	406	49	Gibbs	Henry	4	1			1	1	1		1				9		
Swansea	396	5	Gibbs	John				1			3			1			5		
Somerset	406	37	Gibbs	Robert				1						1			2		
Somerset	406	39	Gibbs	Robert 2d		3		1			2		1				7		
New Bedford	424	35	Gibbs	Rowland			1										1		
Somerset	406	38	Gibbs	Samuel	3			1					1				5		
Swansea	400	26	Gibbs	Wido	1					2			1				4		
Attleboro	321	41	Gibson	Lamont			1			1			1				3		
Dartmouth	344	16	Gidley	Henry		2				1	3	2					8		
Dartmouth	344	15	Gidley	Samuel	2		1			2		1					9		
Dartmouth	344	14	Gidley	Thomas		1			2				1				5		
Dartmouth	345	4	Gidly	Benjamin		2						2					6		
New Bedford	424	37	Gifford	Abner			1										1		
Dartmouth	344	23	Gifford	Abraham	1		1		2	1	1	1					8		
Westport	331	19	Gifford	Abraham	1			1					1				3		
Westport	331	20	Gifford	Abraham Blk Smith	1		2		1		1	1	1	1			8		
Dartmouth	344	35	Gifford	Anne	2	1							1				4		
Westport	332	2	Gifford	Benjamin				1	1					1			3		
Westport	331	22	Gifford	Christopher		1			1	1	1		1	1			6		
Dartmouth	344	26	Gifford	David	1	2		1	1		1		2				8		
Dartmouth	344	34	Gifford	David 2d	1			2	1			1					6		
Dartmouth	344	27	Gifford	Elihew		3		1		1	1		1				8		
Westport	331	28	Gifford	Elijah	1		1		1				1				4		
Westport	331	29	Gifford	Elijah Junr			1			2			1				4		
Westport	331	30	Gifford	Ephraim	1			1		1			1				4		
Westport	332	3	Gifford	George	2			1		1			1				5		
Westport	331	32	Gifford	George Ch. Son	3	2			1	1		1					9		
Dartmouth	344	33	Gifford	Gidion			1	1		2	1						5		
Westport	332	11	Gifford	Ichabod		1			1				1				3		
Dartmouth	344	28	Gifford	Isaac			1		2				1				5		
Dartmouth	344	31	Gifford	James			1		1				1				4		
New Bedford	424	39	Gifford	James	2	1	3		1	3	1	1		1			13		
Westport	332	10	Gifford	James	2			1		4	1	1	1	1			12		
Dartmouth	345	3	Gifford	Jeremiah	1	2		2		1	1						9		
Westport	332	6	Gifford	John Blk. Smith	2	1	1		1	1			1				8		
Westport	331	21	Gifford	John Constable	5			1		1			4	1			13		
Dartmouth	345	1	Gifford	Jonathan		2		1	1		2		1				7		
Westport	332	1	Gifford	Jonathan	1	1			1	2	1	1	1				8		
Westport	332	7	Gifford	Jonathan Mor. Son	2			1		1			1				5		
Dartmouth	344	19	Gifford	Joseph		1			1		1						4		
Dartmouth	344	32	Gifford	Joseph	1			2				1	1				5		
Westport	331	24	Gifford	Joseph		2	1		1	1	2	2		2			11		
Dartmouth	344	25	Gifford	Josiah		1						1	1				4		
Dartmouth	344	36	Gifford	Luis	1			1	2	1			1				8		
Westport	332	5	Gifford	Luthern Jn Son			1						1				2		
Westport	332	9	Gifford	Meriam								5	1				6		
Dartmouth	344	18	Gifford	Nathaniel			1	2		1							6		
New Bedford	425	12	Gifford	Noah	2			1		1			1				5		
Westport	331	33	Gifford	Perry	1	1		1					1				4		
Westport	331	25	Gifford	Richard	1			1		3			1				6		
New Bedford	425	13	Gifford	Ruamy	1		2			1		2	1				7		
Westport	331	26	Gifford	Russel	1			1		1			1				4		
Dartmouth	344	20	Gifford	Samuel		2	1			1		1	1				7		
Dartmouth	344	30	Gifford	Silas		1		1		1							4		
Dartmouth	345	2	Gifford	Silus Wdo									4				4		
Dartmouth	344	24	Gifford	Stephen	1	2				2		1					8		
New Bedford	425	9	Gifford	Stephen			1				1		2				4		

TOWN	PG#	LN#	HEADS OF HOUSEHOLD		FREE WHITE MALES					FREE WHITE FEMALES					TOTAL ALL OTHER	TOTAL SLAVES	TOTALS	DISTRICT/ TOWNSHIP	NOTES
			LAST NAME	FIRST NAME	under 10	10 to 16	16 to 26	26 to 45	45 and over	under 10	10 to 16	16 to 26	26 to 45	45 and over					
Westport	331	31	Gifford	Stephen	2			2					1				5		
Dartmouth	344	22	Gifford	Thomas		1				1			1				3		
New Bedford	424	41	Gifford	Thomas	2		1		1	2	1		1	1			9		
New Bedford	425	11	Gifford	Thomas				1					1				2		
Dartmouth	344	17	Gifford	Timothy		1	1	1		1	1	3	2				10		
Westport	331	27	Gifford	Warren	1		1						1				3		
Westport	332	4	Gifford	Warren Jn Son			1			1		1					3		
Westport	332	8	Gifford	Warren Mor. Son	1	1		1		1		1					5		
Westport	332	12	Gifford	Wilbour	2		1			1	1	1					6		
Dartmouth	344	29	Gifford	William	1	1			1			1					6		
New Bedford	424	40	Gifford	William	1			1		2		1					5		
Westport	331	18	Gifford	William Free Miller	1		1		1	2	2	1					8		
Westport	331	23	Gifford	William Wm. Son		1			1			1	1				4		
Dartmouth	345	5	Giford	Benjamin		1		2			1						6		
Easton	390	17	Gilbert	Apollos		1					1						2		
Mansfield	385	42	Gilbert	Daniel		4	2						1		1		8		
Mansfield	385	40	Gilbert	David	1			1				2					4		
Norton	381	15	Gilbert	George		1	2	1		1		1	1				7		
Mansfield	385	41	Gilbert	James			1					1	1				3		
New Bedford	425	3	Gilbert	John		1		2		1		1					5		
Norton	381	14	Gilbert	John	1	1		1			2		1				6		
Easton	390	18	Gilbert	Nathaniel		1		1		2		1					5		
Somerset	404	16	Gillet	Peter	1	1		1		2		1					6		
Dartmouth	344	21	Gillis	John		1						1					6		
Raynham	372	10	Gilmore	Elisha	3	1		1		1	1	2	1				10		
Raynham	376	10	Gilmore	John	1		2	1	1		2		1				8		
Raynham	375	38	Gilmore	John Junior		1	1	1		2		1	2				8		
Easton	390	12	Gilmore	Joshua	3	1	2	1			1		1				9		
Raynham	374	32	Gilmore	Toby											9		9		
Attleboro	318	56	Gilmore	William	1		1				1						3		
Rehoboth	306	27	Glading	James		1			1		1	1				8			
Rehoboth	306	28	Gladinig	William		1		2			1					5			
Dighton	412	24	Godbey	Seth			2					2					4		
Easton	390	7	Godfrey	Abigail								1	1				2		
Taunton	357	32	Godfrey	Abigail Wido	1	1						1					3		
Norton	381	16	Godfrey	Gersham	1			1		1		1					4		
Taunton	368	24	Godfrey	Isaac	2		1		1	1	2		1				8		
Norton	381	17	Godfrey	James	1	3		1		1		1	1				8		
Taunton	358	17	Godfrey	Job	1		2	1	1		3		1				9		
Taunton	358	14	Godfrey	John	1	2	2		1	1		1					8		
Easton	390	8	Godfrey	Joseph		1		1				1					3		
Easton	390	9	Godfrey	Joseph Jr	1	2	1	1		1		1					7		
Norton	381	19	Godfrey	Mary							1	1					2		
Taunton	356	13	Godfrey	Richard		1	1	1		1	1	1	1				7		
Taunton	360	11	Godfrey	Rufus	2		1		2	2	1						8		
Norton	381	18	Godfrey	Samuel			2				2		1	1			6		
Taunton	356	10	Godfrey	Theodorah							1						1		
Rehoboth	301	14	Goff	Aaron	2		1	1			1					5			
Rehoboth	300	3	Goff	Amos	1	1		1		1	1	1				6			
Rehoboth	303	25	Goff	Amos	1		1			2	1	1				5			
Rehoboth	301	44	Goff	Asa	2	1		1			1		1			7			
Rehoboth	307	21	Goff	Caleb		1		2	1	1		1				6			
Rehoboth	300	4	Goff	Charles		1		2		1						4			
Rehoboth	301	40	Goff	Constant	1		1	1			1					5			
Dighton	412	9	Goff	Enoch		1		1			1						3		
Dighton	412	10	Goff	Enoch Junr			1				1						2		
Rehoboth	302	2	Goff	Israle		1		2	1	1						7			
Berkley	279	21	Goff	John	2	2	2	1	1	1		1	1				11		
Rehoboth	306	29	Goff	Levi															Enumeration left blank
Rehoboth	300	9	Goff	Levi Junior		1		2			1					4			
Rehoboth	300	1	Goff	Lovel		1		1	1	1		1				5			
Rehoboth	299	13	Goff	Nathan	1		1		1	1		1				5			
Rehoboth	304	1	Goff	Nathaniel	1		1					1				4			
Freetown	293	25	Goff	Paul		1					1	1				3			
Rehoboth	300	7	Goff	Samuel	1		1	2	1		1	1				11			
Dighton	414	35	Goff	Shubal	1	1		1		5	1	1					10		
Rehoboth	306	30	Goff	Squier Jr															Enumeration left blank
Rehoboth	300	5	Goff	Squire			1				1					2			
Rehoboth	301	10	Goff	Squire		1		3	2		1					8			
Rehoboth	305	24	Goff	Sylvester		1		3			1					7			
Freetown	282	24	Goff	Thomas	2	1		1		1		1				6			
Dighton	412	13	Gooding	Ephraim	4	1		1		1	1		1	1			10		
Dighton	410	26	Gooding	George			1	1				1					3		
Dighton	410	27	Gooding	Joseph		2		1		1		1					5		
Dighton	410	28	Gooding	Joseph Jr		2	1	1		1		1					6		
Dighton	410	25	Gooding	Matthew	2			1		1	1	1	1				7		
Rehoboth	313	15	Gooduff	Isaac		1		2			1					5			
Easton	390	15	Goodwin	Daniel	1		1		1		2	1					6		
Rehoboth	301	15	Gooff	Abel	2		1		1		1	1				7			
Rehoboth	313	14	Gooff	Ezra		1					1	2				8			
Rehoboth	300	2	Gooff	James	1		1	1			1	1				8			
Rehoboth	301	3	Gooff	Joseph			1		1		1	1				4			

TOWN	PG#	LN#	LAST NAME	FIRST NAME	FREE WHITE MALES					FREE WHITE FEMALES					TOTAL ALL OTHER	TOTAL SLAVES	TOTALS	DISTRICT/ TOWNSHIP	NOTES
					under 10	10 to 16	16 to 26	26 to 45	45 and over	under 10	10 to 16	16 to 26	26 to 45	45 and over					
Rehoboth	301	4	Gooff	Joseph Jr			1				1						2		
Rehoboth	301	11	Gooff	Levi Junior		1	1	1	1	2	1	1					9		
Rehoboth	301	2	Gooff	Richard	1			1		1		1					7		
New Bedford	424	36	Gordon	William	2	1	1		1	2		2	1	1			11		
Easton	390	16	Goward	Francis	1		1	1				1					4		
Easton	390	19	Goward	Mary			1					1		1			3		
New Bedford	425	2	Graham	Michael				1									1		
Rehoboth	308	42	Graham	Rebeckah							1	1	2				4		
Rehoboth	313	12	Grand	Benjamin	2			1		1							4		
Attleboro	321	23	Grant	Elias			1	1				1					3		
Rehoboth	304	12	Grant	Thomas	1	1		1				2	1				6		
Raynham	372	8	Graves	Samuel	2			1					1				4		
Swansea	398	37	Gray	John		1		1		1	1		1				5		
Somerset	408	8	Gray	Joseph	3	1		1		2	1		1				9		
New Bedford	424	38	Green	Christopher	1		1						1	1			4		
Taunton	366	41	Green	David		1							1				2		
Mansfield	386	1	Green	Roland		1		1		1	1		1		1		6		
Mansfield	386	2	Green	Roland Jur			1						1				2		
New Bedford	425	10	Green	Thomas			1			1			1				3		
New Bedford	425	5	Green	Caleb		2		1		2			1				6		
Berkley	280	10	Gregory	Elisha	1	1	1	1					1	1			6		
New Bedford	425	14	Greive	David	1			1		3	1	1	1				8		
Norton	381	13	Grey	John		1	1	1					2				5		
New Bedford	424	32	Grinnel	Benjamin	3	1	1	1		2			1				9		
New Bedford	425	1	Grinnel	Cornelius	2	2		1		1			1				7		
Freetown	282	8	Grinnel	Oliver	1			1		1			1				4		
New Bedford	425	6	Grinnel	Susanna	1		1			1	4		2	1			10		
Mansfield	385	52	Grover	Abiel		1		1		2			1				5		
Mansfield	386	4	Grover	Benjamin		1		1		1	3		1				7		
Mansfield	385	43	Grover	David			2		1				1				4		
Mansfield	385	44	Grover	David Jur	1			1		2	2		1				7		
Mansfield	385	45	Grover	Jesse			1						1				2		
Mansfield	385	47	Grover	Joseph			1						1				2		
Mansfield	385	49	Grover	Levi		1		1				2	1				5		
Mansfield	385	46	Grover	Samuel	2			1					1				4		
Mansfield	385	51	Grover	Samuel			1			1			1				3		
Mansfield	385	50	Grover	Seth		2		1		2			1				6		
Mansfield	386	3	Grover	Simeon			1			1	1	1					4		
Mansfield	385	48	Grover	Thomas				1					1				2		
Mansfield	386	5	Grover	William	1	1	1	1				1	1	1			7		
Attleboro	322	30	Guild	Ebenz	1		2			1	1						5		
Attleboro	321	27	Guild	Jos	1	2			1	1	1						6		
Easton	390	10	Guild	Samuel	1	1	1		1	2	1		1				8		
Easton	390	11	Guild	Samuel Jur			1						1				2		
Norton	381	20	Guillo	Francis	1	2		1		2			1				7		
Taunton	359	3	Gulliver	Gershom	2	1	2	1				1		1			8		
Freetown	293	19	Gurney	Silas		1		1		1	2		1				6		
Raynham	372	34	Gushee	Elijah	1		2		1	1	1		1				7		
Raynham	372	33	Gushee	Samuel		1		1		1		1	1				5		
Raynham	372	36	Gushee	Seth			1					2					3		
Easton	390	14	Gwinell	Hannah	1					3			1				5		
Taunton	365	4	Hack	Nathan		1		1					2				4		
Taunton	365	5	Hack	Nathan Junior	2		1		2		1						6		
Taunton	366	24	Hack	Peter		1		1		1	2	1					6		
Taunton	365	17	Hack	Tobey											2		2		
Raynham	373	14	Hacket	Asahel	3			1		1			1	2			9		
Swansea	400	31	Hale	David	2	3		1		2	1		1				10		
Dighton	414	37	Hale	Job		1				1		1					3		
Rehoboth	298	22	Hale	Job	1	1		1	2				1		7				
Swansea	400	30	Hale	John				1				1	1				3		
Swansea	401	40	Hale	Wido						2			1				3		
Swansea	400	11	Hale	Levi	2			1		1		1	1				6		
Swansea	400	10	Hales	Lurana		3				2			1				6		
Raynham	374	5	Hall	Abigail Wid			1	1					1				3		
Raynham	372	15	Hall	Amos				1					2				3		
Raynham	373	38	Hall	Asa	1			1		2			1				5		
Norton	381	37	Hall	Brian	2	1		1		2	1		2				9		
Raynham	372	20	Hall	Caleb	1			1					1				3		
Taunton	363	38	Hall	Ebenezer	3			1		2	1	1	1				9		
Raynham	373	41	Hall	Edmund			3	1					1	1			6		
Taunton	366	21	Hall	Elisha	1			1		1			1				4		
Mansfield	386	6	Hall	Elkanah	2		1	1		2			1				7		
Attleboro	319	24	Hall	Ephraim	2			1		1	2		1	1			8		
Raynham	372	13	Hall	Hannah Wid	1							1		2			4		
Raynham	375	24	Hall	Hannah Wid	1					2	2		1				6		
Raynham	373	1	Hall	Job	1	1				1		3	1				8		
Attleboro	319	10	Hall	John			1			1							3		
Norton	381	39	Hall	John	1			1	1					1			4		
Norton	381	40	Hall	John 3d	1			1		2	1		1				6		
Raynham	374	25	Hall	Joseph			1	1			2		1				5		
Taunton	363	30	Hall	Joseph				1				1	1				4		

109

TOWN	PG#	LN#	LAST NAME	FIRST NAME	FREE WHITE MALES					FREE WHITE FEMALES					TOTAL ALL OTHER	TOTAL SLAVES	TOTALS	DISTRICT/ TOWNSHIP	NOTES
					under 10	10 to 16	16 to 26	26 to 45	45 and over	under 10	10 to 16	16 to 26	26 to 45	45 and over					
Raynham	373	37	Hall	Joseph 2d			1	1									2		
Attleboro	318	13	Hall	Josiah		1	1	1				1	1				5		
Taunton	363	31	Hall	Josias				1					1				2		
Raynham	372	16	Hall	Lewis			2	1	1				1				5		
Raynham	373	2	Hall	Luther				1					1				2		
Raynham	372	32	Hall	Mason	1			1		2			1				5		
Raynham	372	43	Hall	Nathan					1					2			3		
Raynham	372	44	Hall	Nathan Junior					1			1	1				3		
Raynham	375	35	Hall	Nathaniel	1		1	1	1				1				5		
Raynham	372	12	Hall	Reuben		1	2		1	1	2	2		1			10		
Raynham	375	18	Hall	Samuel		1		1					1				3		
Raynham	375	25	Hall	Seth	4			1		1			1				7		
Norton	381	38	Hall	Silas	2			1		1			1				5		
Raynham	373	43	Hall	Silas		1		1		1	1		1				5		
Raynham	375	33	Hall	Stephen		1		1		1			1	1			5		
Raynham	373	35	Hall	William				1									1		
Taunton	363	32	Hall	Zilpha Wido		1						1	3	1			6		
Westport	333	1	Haly	Joseph			1		1				1				3		
New Bedford	425	32	Hamblin	Wealthy	1					1			1				3		
New Bedford	426	9	Hammond	Alden	1			1						1			3		
New Bedford	425	27	Hammond	Barnabas	4	1	1	1		1	1	2	1				12		
New Bedford	426	18	Hammond	Barzilla	1	1	1	1					1				5		
New Bedford	426	21	Hammond	Heart	1					1			1				3		
Westport	332	28	Hammond	Humphrey			1			2		1					4		
New Bedford	426	19	Hammond	Jabez	1			1						1			3		
New Bedford	426	24	Hammond	Jabez Jr	1			1		2			1				5		
New Bedford	427	11	Hammond	Mary		1								3			4		
New Bedford	425	31	Hammond	Prince			1			3		1					5		
New Bedford	425	20	Hammond	Richard	1	1		1		2	1		1				7		
New Bedford	425	30	Hammond	Sarah	1					2	1		1				5		
New Bedford	425	26	Hammond	Seth	2		1		1	1		1	1				7		
New Bedford	427	4	Hammond	Thomas	1			1		1		2	1		1		7		
Westport	332	14	Handy	Ely	1		1	1		2			1				6		
New Bedford	425	37	Handy	Gamaliel		1		1					1				3		
Dartmouth	345	33	Handy	George		1		1				1				3			
New Bedford	425	33	Handy	Isaac	3			1					1				5		
Dartmouth	345	9	Handy	John	3	1		1	2				1	1		9			
New Bedford	425	29	Handy	Rose		1							1				2		
Swansea	403	35	Handy	Russell	1	2		1		2	1		1				8		
Swansea	402	28	Handy	Samuel	1			1		1		1					4		
New Bedford	425	28	Handy	Thomas					1				1				2		
Swansea	400	28	Handy	Thomas		1		1		3	2		1				8		
Rehoboth	313	27	Handy	William		1				1		1				4			
Easton	390	25	Haney	Elisha		1		1	1				1	1			5		
Rehoboth	313	24	Hannon	John		1	2				1		2			6			
Norton	381	46	Haradon	Isaac	1			1		3			1				6		
Mansfield	386	7	Harden	John	2		1		1	1		2	1	1			9		
Taunton	371	19	Harding	Chloe											1		1		
Attleboro	322	26	Harding	Jona	2		1			1		1					5		
Taunton	361	4	Harding	Prince											2		2		
Mansfield	386	14	Hardon	David		3	2		1	1	1		1	1			10		
Mansfield	386	13	Hardon	Isaac		1				4			1	1			7		
Mansfield	386	15	Hardon	Jacob	1	1		1		2		2	1				8		
Mansfield	386	12	Hardon	Susannah									1	1			2		
Rehoboth	313	22	Hare	Jonathan	1	1		1		1	1		1			9			
Taunton	360	20	Harlow	Phebe Wido						2		2	1				5		
Easton	390	22	Harlow	Ruben	2	1		1		1			1				6		
Westport	332	15	Harrard	Abigail		2				1		3	1				7		
Rehoboth	313	23	Harris	Benjamin		1		1	2	1		1				7			
Taunton	359	16	Harris	Benjamin	1			1		2		1			1		6		
Somerset	405	24	Harris	John			1			2		1					4		
Mansfield	386	20	Harris	Thomas		1	2	1		1			1				6		
Freetown	287	18	Harrison	John		1		1		2	1		2				7		
Westport	333	5	Hart	Cate											2		2		
Dartmouth	345	45	Hart	Hannah								3				3			
Taunton	361	24	Hart	James	1		3	2					1	1			8		
Taunton	360	9	Hart	James Junior	3		1						1				5		
Taunton	357	18	Hart	John	2	1		1			1	1	1				7		
Dartmouth	345	44	Hart	Joseph		1		1		2	1		1			7			
New Bedford	426	36	Hart	Lemison	1			1		2	1		1				6		
Westport	332	33	Hart	Samuel	2			1		2			1				6		
Dartmouth	345	47	Hart	William	1	1		1		3			1	1		8			
Taunton	368	37	Harvey	David	1	2	2		1				1	1			8		
Taunton	360	37	Harvey	Ephraim	1		1			1		1					4		
Taunton	368	38	Harvey	Henry	1	2			3			2		3			11		
Taunton	364	12	Harvey	James	2	1		1		2	2	1	1				10		
Taunton	368	39	Harvey	Joel		2			1	4	1	2	1				11		
Taunton	368	30	Harvey	John	1	1		1		2	2		1	1			9		
Taunton	363	14	Harvey	Jonathan					1			2	1	1			5		
Taunton	366	34	Harvey	Lydia Wido						1				2			3		
Taunton	359	4	Harvey	Phebe Wido								1	1				2		
Taunton	368	42	Harvey	Thomas		1		1		1			1				4		

110

TOWN	PG#	LN#	LAST NAME	FIRST NAME	FREE WHITE MALES					FREE WHITE FEMALES					TOTAL ALL OTHER	TOTAL SLAVES	TOTALS	DISTRICT/ TOWNSHIP	NOTES
					under 10	10 to 16	16 to 26	26 to 45	45 and over	under 10	10 to 16	16 to 26	26 to 45	45 and over					
Mansfield	386	18	Haskel	zuriel					1					1			2		
Freetown	291	17	Haskell	Benjamin	3	1		1		1	1		1				8		
Freetown	291	22	Haskell	Isaac	1	1		1		2			1				6		
Freetown	291	21	Haskell	John	1	1	1						1	1			5		
Freetown	291	19	Haskell	Josiah	1	1		1		3			1	1			8		
Freetown	291	24	Haskell	Josiah 2d	2			1		1			1				5		
New Bedford	426	33	Haskell	Roger	1		1	1				1			1		6		
Freetown	289	27	Haskell	William	1	1						1					3		
Freetown	293	9	Haskens	Abner	1	1		1		1	1	1					6		
Freetown	292	18	Haskens	Anthony	1	1						1					3		
Freetown	286	2	Haskens	Elijah	1					2			1				5		
Freetown	294	8	Haskens	Nathaniel		1		1		2	1		1				6		
Berkley	278	25	Haskens	Phillip	1		2		1		2	3		1			10		
Berkley	279	16	Haskens	Ruth Wid	3		2					3		1			9		
Taunton	357	33	Haskins	Jacob	2	1		1	1	1			1	1			8		
Rehoboth	306	31	Haskins	John	2	3		1				1	1			9			
New Bedford	426	45	Haskins	Jonathan				1		1			1				3		
Taunton	365	34	Haskins	Stephen				1					1				2		
New Bedford	426	17	Haskins	William	2		2	1		1	1		1				8		
Taunton	357	30	Hatch	Estus		1		1					1				3		
New Bedford	426	16	Hatch	James		1	1	1		1	1		1				6		
New Bedford	427	1	Hatch	Seth			1			1			1				3		
Freetown	284	6	Hathaway	Abial			1			1			1				3		
Berkley	276	5	Hathaway	Abijah				1						3			4		
Berkley	276	6	Hathaway	Abijah Jnr	2	2	1			1		1	1				9		
Raynham	372	9	Hathaway	Abraham	1	1	1		1	1	1	1		1			8		
Berkley	276	8	Hathaway	Alice Wid								3		1			4		
New Bedford	425	40	Hathaway	Arthur	2	2		1		2	1		1				9		
Berkley	276	9	Hathaway	Barzilla	2	1				1			1	1			6		
Berkley	276	7	Hathaway	Benanuel			1			1			1				3		
Berkley	279	27	Hathaway	Benjamin			1	1	1			1		1			5		
Berkley	280	16	Hathaway	Benjamin Jr			1			2			1				4		
New Bedford	425	22	Hathaway	Bridget									2				2		
Freetown	282	15	Hathaway	Calven				1					2				3		
Taunton	357	2	Hathaway	Charlotte	2					1			1				4		
New Bedford	425	23	Hathaway	Clark	1			1	1	1			1				5		
Freetown	283	31	Hathaway	Cloather	2			1		1			1				5		
New Bedford	427	23	Hathaway	Deborah	1								1				2		
Freetown	283	22	Hathaway	Deborough Wid.									1				1		
Freetown	283	32	Hathaway	Dorcas Wid.										3			3		
Freetown	285	15	Hathaway	Dudlee		2	3	1	1	1		2	1				11		
New Bedford	425	35	Hathaway	Eleazer	1	1			1	2		1	1				7		
New Bedford	427	14	Hathaway	Elihu				2		1			1	1			5		
Freetown	289	16	Hathaway	Elisha	1				1			2	2	1			7		
Dartmouth	345	26	Hathaway	Elizabeth			1					1	2		4				
New Bedford	425	17	Hathaway	Elizabeth	1	2						3					6		
Berkley	275	14	Hathaway	Elkanah			1						1				2		
New Bedford	426	8	Hathaway	Elnathan				1					1				2		
Berkley	279	28	Hathaway	Enoch	1			1		1	1	1					5		
Dighton	414	19	Hathaway	Ephraim				1				1	2				4		
Freetown	294	23	Hathaway	Ephraim				1				1	1				3		
Dighton	414	11	Hathaway	Ephraim Jr	1	2		1	1	1	2		1				9		
Berkley	276	1	Hathaway	Ezra		1				1	1	1	1	1			7		
New Bedford	425	34	Hathaway	George	1			1					1				3		
Freetown	283	19	Hathaway	Gilbert	2	2	1		1	1	1	1		2			11		
Freetown	294	11	Hathaway	Gilford	1			1		1			1				4		
Freetown	294	14	Hathaway	Gilford 2d	1	1		1		1			1				5		
New Bedford	427	3	Hathaway	Hannah			1						1	1			3		
New Bedford	427	19	Hathaway	Hannah			1							1			2		
Berkley	279	23	Hathaway	Henry	2	2	2	1		1			1				9		
Dartmouth	345	43	Hathaway	Henry	1		1	1		1		1			5				
New Bedford	427	6	Hathaway	Humphrey	3	1	1					1	1				7		
Dighton	409	15	Hathaway	Isaac			1		1	4	2		1				9		
New Bedford	427	22	Hathaway	Isaac			1	1				1					3		
Freetown	290	28	Hathaway	Israel	1	1	1			1			1				6		
New Bedford	426	12	Hathaway	Jabez			1					1	1				3		
Freetown	284	19	Hathaway	Jail	1	1		1	1	1	1		2				8		
Freetown	289	31	Hathaway	Jail	1			1		1			1				4		
Freetown	294	7	Hathaway	James			1					1	1				3		
New Bedford	427	20	Hathaway	James			1						1				2		
Dighton	411	27	Hathaway	Job											4		4		
Taunton	364	19	Hathaway	Job	3	2		1		2	2		1				11		
Dighton	414	2	Hathaway	John	4	1			1	1	1	3		3			14		
Freetown	283	29	Hathaway	John	1			1		1		1			1		5		
Freetown	293	26	Hathaway	John	4	1		1		1			1	1	1		10		
New Bedford	426	14	Hathaway	John				1			1	1		1			4		
Freetown	283	17	Hathaway	Joseph	4		1		1	2	1		1				10		
Freetown	283	28	Hathaway	Joseph	1			1		1			1	1	3		8		
Dighton	414	18	Hathaway	Joshua			1	1						3			5		
Dighton	414	17	Hathaway	Joshua Jr	1			1			1		1				4		
Dighton	410	34	Hathaway	Leonard	2		1			1	1		1				6		
New Bedford	426	1	Hathaway	Lois									1				1		

TOWN	PG#	LN#	LAST NAME	FIRST NAME	FREE WHITE MALES					FREE WHITE FEMALES					TOTAL ALL OTHER	TOTAL SLAVES	TOTALS	DISTRICT/ TOWNSHIP	NOTES
					under 10	10 to 16	16 to 26	26 to 45	45 and over	under 10	10 to 16	16 to 26	26 to 45	45 and over					
Freetown	294	6	Hathaway	Malbone	3			1		1			1				6		
Dartmouth	345	42	Hathaway	Maltiah		1							1			2			
Taunton	364	25	Hathaway	Mary								1		1			2		
Freetown	289	30	Hathaway	Mary Wid	1							1	1	1			4		
Freetown	290	24	Hathaway	Micah			1			2		1					4		
New Bedford	425	45	Hathaway	Micah		1	2		1	1	3	3					11		
Berkley	275	7	Hathaway	Nathaniel	2			1		4			1				8		
Freetown	283	20	Hathaway	Nathaniel	1			1		3	1		1	1			8		
New Bedford	427	5	Hathaway	Nathaniel			1			2			1				4		
Freetown	283	3	Hathaway	Nicholas	1			1		1			1				4		
New Bedford	427	15	Hathaway	Noah	2			1		1			1				5		
New Bedford	426	6	Hathaway	Obed		1		1					1	1			4		
Dartmouth	345	41	Hathaway	Paul	2			1	2	3	1					11			
Berkley	276	3	Hathaway	Peter	1			1		1		1					4		
Berkley	279	11	Hathaway	Phillip				1		1		1					3		
Freetown	283	30	Hathaway	Phillip	1			1		1		1			1		5		
Freetown	283	7	Hathaway	Phillip 2d	2		1	1			1	1		1			7		
New Bedford	427	21	Hathaway	Prince	1			1					1				3		
New Bedford	425	24	Hathaway	Reuben			1					3	1				5		
New Bedford	427	7	Hathaway	Richard		1	4		1	2	1	1		1	1		12		
Freetown	287	1	Hathaway	Robert	1	2		1		2	1		1				8		
New Bedford	425	19	Hathaway	Robert			2		1			3		1			7		
Freetown	294	12	Hathaway	Sally Wid		1				1			1				3		
Freetown	284	3	Hathaway	Samuel	2	1	2	1		2	2		1				11		
New Bedford	425	42	Hathaway	Samuel			1		1		3		1				8		
New Bedford	426	7	Hathaway	Samuel			1		1	1	1			1			5		
New Bedford	427	16	Hathaway	Seth			1		1					1			3		
Freetown	284	10	Hathaway	Silas	3	2	1		1	2	1	1	1				12		
New Bedford	427	18	Hathaway	Silvanus	1			1					1				3		
Berkley	275	15	Hathaway	Stephen					1								1		
Dighton	412	25	Hathaway	Stephen	1			1	1	2		1					6		
New Bedford	425	44	Hathaway	Stephen		1	2		1	1	1	3		1			10		
Taunton	359	30	Hathaway	Stephen	1	1	2	1	1	2		1		1			10		
Freetown	284	2	Hathaway	Thomas	1			1				1	1				4		
New Bedford	426	3	Hathaway	Thomas			1			2		1					4		
Freetown	283	18	Hathaway	Weltha Wid.	1							1		2			4		
Dighton	414	23	Hathaway	William	1	1	3		1	3	1		1				11		
Freetown	290	26	Hathaway	William				1					1				2		
New Bedford	427	9	Hathaway	William	1			1		1			1				4		
New Bedford	427	25	Hathaway	William Jr		1					1						2		
Freetown	290	25	Hathaway	Zepheniah		1		1					1	1			4		
Freetown	290	23	Hathaway	Zepheniah Jr	2			1		2			1				6		
Attleboro	322	41	Hatting	George	2		1						1				4		
Attleboro	319	20	Hawes	Eli	1			1		1	1		1				5		
Taunton	356	21	Hay	George	2			1		2			1				6		
Easton	390	33	Hayden	Charles		1	1				1		1				4		
Easton	390	31	Hayward	Abner				1				2		1			4		
Easton	390	32	Hayward	Ebinezer	1		1		1	1	1			1			6		
Easton	390	21	Hayward	Edward	4	1			1	1	1	1					9		
Easton	390	23	Hayward	Jonathan	1		1			1			1				4		
Easton	390	20	Hayward	Joshua	1			1		5	2		1				10		
Easton	390	24	Hayward	Oliver	1	3	2	1		3		1	1				12		
New Bedford	426	25	Hazard	Thomas	2	1	1	1		1	1	2	1		2		12		
Somerset	405	43	Head	Caleb		2				1	1		1				6		
Dartmouth	345	7	Head	Henry		1	1			2	2		1			8			
Somerset	405	37	Head	Job		1		1		4			1				7		
Somerset	405	38	Head	Job Junr		1				1		1					3		
Dartmouth	345	20	Head	John	1	1	1	1	2	2			1			11			
Somerset	405	20	Head	Baker	3	2		1		2	1		1				10		
Norton	382	1	Heard	Enos			1			1		1					3		
Westport	333	3	Heart	Eben	3	2		1		3	1	1	1				12		
Westport	333	2	Heart	Sandford				1		2	1		1				5		
New Bedford	426	35	Heffords	Jonathan	3	1		1		1	1		1				8		
Taunton	361	17	Heffords	Samuel	1			1					1				3		
Somerset	405	10	Hellon	John	2			1		1	2		1				7		
New Bedford	426	37	Helm	John	2			1		1			1				5		
Dighton	412	43	Henry	Alexnader	1		1			1		1		1			5		
New Bedford	426	22	Henshaw	William	2	1	3	1			1		1				9		
Berkley	278	22	Hervery	James	2			1				1	1				5		
Berkley	277	24	Hervery	William			1						1				2		
Norton	381	41	Hervey	Josiah				1					1	1			3		
Raynham	375	13	Hewett	Rufus	1		1			1			1				4		
Taunton	357	10	Hewett	Salmon		1							1				3		
Taunton	369	2	Hewett	Thomas		1	1	1		2			1	1			7		
Raynham	375	36	Hewitt	Richard	1		1			1			1				4		
New Bedford	426	13	Hicks	Abraham	3	1				2			1				8		
Westport	332	16	Hicks	Barney	1		1			1	1	1	1				7		
Westport	332	27	Hicks	Benjamin		1				1		1					3		
Dartmouth	345	21	Hicks	Daniel		1	1		1			1				5			
Dartmouth	345	12	Hicks	Deborah									2			2			
New Bedford	425	15	Hicks	Galen			1					1	1				3		
Taunton	359	22	Hicks	Gideon	1		1		1	1	1	1					6		

TOWN	PG#	LN#	HEADS OF HOUSEHOLD		FREE WHITE MALES					FREE WHITE FEMALES					TOTAL ALL OTHER	TOTAL SLAVES	TOTALS	DISTRICT/ TOWNSHIP	NOTES
			LAST NAME	FIRST NAME	under 10	10 to 16	16 to 26	26 to 45	45 and over	under 10	10 to 16	16 to 26	26 to 45	45 and over					
Dartmouth	345	8	Hicks	Thomas			1						2				3		
Westport	332	17	Hicks	Thomas	1	1	1			1			1	1			6		
Westport	332	18	Hicks	William		1		1			1			1			4		
Dighton	412	33	Hide	James											8		8		
Rehoboth	315	5	Hill	Barbary										4			4		
New Bedford	426	40	Hill	Benjamin	2		1		1	4	2		1				11		
Rehoboth	313	25	Hill	Benjamin		1		1	1	1		1					6		
Rehoboth	313	30	Hill	David		1		1		1	1	1	1				6		
Taunton	367	28	Hill	David											10		10		
Rehoboth	313	31	Hill	David Jr		1		1				1					4		
Rehoboth	313	20	Hill	James			1			1		2					4		
Norton	381	45	Hill	Joseph				1				1					2		
Attleboro	318	41	Hill	Leonard	1		1	1		2	1		1	1			8		
Somerset	405	5	Hill	Ruth							1		1				2		
Swansea	398	8	Hill	Titus											7				
New Bedford	426	15	Hillman	Zachariah	1	2		1		2	1		1				8		
New Bedford	425	18	Hills	Jabez	1		1			1			1				4		
Taunton	359	23	Hilton	Amos	3	1		1		1	1	1	1				9		
Rehoboth	300	12	Hilton	Edward	1		1			1		1					5		
Rehoboth	304	44	Hilton	John			1				1		1				4		
Freetown	282	10	Hinds	Ebenezer	1	2			1	1	2	2		1			10		
Freetown	285	30	Hinds	Ebenezer Junr	1		1					1					3		
New Bedford	426	2	Hitch	Elget		1		1						1			3		
New Bedford	425	39	Hitch	George				1			1	2		1			5		
New Bedford	426	20	Hitch	George Jr			1			1			1				3		
New Bedford	425	25	Hitch	Hardy	1		1						2				4		
New Bedford	425	43	Hitch	Samuel		3					1	1		1			7		
Mansfield	386	22	Hitchcock	Thomas			1			2			2				5		
Rehoboth	299	16	Hix	Azariah		1	1					1	2				5		
Rehoboth	299	3	Hix	Hezekiah		1	1	1	1		1		1				7		
Rehoboth	304	38	Hix	Jacob			1				1		1				4		
Rehoboth	299	18	Hix	Jotham	1	1				1			1				5		
Rehoboth	306	35	Hix	Jotham 2nd			1			1							2		
Rehoboth	304	34	Hix	Nathan	2			1	2	2			1				8		
Rehoboth	302	25	Hix	Nathan 2	2	1	1		1	1		1					11		
Rehoboth	306	32	Hix	Nathan 2nd	2	1	1	1		1							11		
Swansea	398	20	Hix	Robert			1	2		1		1	1	2			8		
Rehoboth	303	12	Hix	Stephen	1			1	1	1	2	1					10		
Somerset	405	25	Hoar	Gideon	1	5	1		1	2	1			1			12		
Berkley	276	24	Hoard	David			1						1	1			3		
Raynham	373	8	Hoard	David	1	1			1	2			1				6		
Taunton	364	34	Hoard	Prudence Wido									1	1			2		
Taunton	367	21	Hodges	Abijah		1		1	1		1			2			6		
Taunton	358	13	Hodges	Abijah Junior	1		1	1		2	1	1	1				8		
Norton	381	36	Hodges	David		2				2		1	1				7		
Mansfield	386	19	Hodges	Elijah				1					1				2		
Norton	381	25	Hodges	Elijah	1			1				2	1				5		
Mansfield	386	9	Hodges	Elisha	2		1			2	1		1				7		
Norton	381	24	Hodges	George		1		1					1				3		
Taunton	365	29	Hodges	Henry			1	1			1	2		2			7		
Norton	381	30	Hodges	Isaac		1			1	1			1				4		
Norton	381	34	Hodges	Isaac Junr	2	2	1	1		2		1	1				10		
Norton	381	23	Hodges	James	1		4	1		1	2	1	1				12		
Taunton	359	14	Hodges	James	4		1	1		3	1		1	1			12		
Mansfield	386	11	Hodges	Jesse		1		1		1	1		1				5		
Mansfield	386	8	Hodges	Job				1					1	1			3		
Mansfield	386	10	Hodges	John	3	1		1		1			1				7		
Norton	381	27	Hodges	John				1		2	2	1	1				7		
Norton	381	28	Hodges	Jonathan	1	1	1	1		2			1				7		
Norton	381	29	Hodges	Joseph		1	1		1	1	1		1				7		
Norton	381	35	Hodges	Joseph 2d	1			1		3			1				6		
Norton	381	33	Hodges	Josiah		1	1	1						1			4		
Norton	381	21	Hodges	Leonard	1			1				1	1				4		
Mansfield	386	16	Hodges	Nathaniel		2	2			2			1	1			9		
Norton	381	32	Hodges	Rufus		1		1									2		
Taunton	360	13	Hodges	Samuel	3		1	1		1			1				7		
Norton	381	31	Hodges	Seth	1		1	1		2	1		1				7		
Taunton	369	7	Hodges	Thomas		1			1	1		3		1			7		
Norton	381	26	Hodges	Tisdale	1	1	3		1			2		1			9		
Taunton	368	10	Hodges	William	4			1		2	2		1				10		
Swansea	400	18	Hollis	Ruel	2			1		1			1				5		
Swansea	403	38	Holmes	Ebenezer				1					1	1			3		
Attleboro	321	53	Holmes	Elizabeth	2	2	1		1	2	1	1		1			11		
Taunton	367	12	Holmes	Gershom		1			1	1		1	1				4		
New Bedford	427	12	Holmes	James				1					1	1			3		
New Bedford	425	36	Holmes	John	2		1	1		2			1				7		
Norton	382	2	Holmes	John		1		1		1			1				4		
Raynham	374	40	Holmes	John			1			1			1				3		
Attleboro	321	24	Holmes	Joseph	1	1		1		2	1	1		1			8		
New Bedford	426	5	Holmes	Joseph	2			1		3			1				7		
Raynham	374	33	Holmes	Otis	2			1					1				4		
Attleboro	318	46	Holmes	Samuel			2		1	1		1		1			6		

113

TOWN	PG#	LN#	LAST NAME	FIRST NAME	FREE WHITE MALES under 10	10 to 16	16 to 26	26 to 45	45 and over	FREE WHITE FEMALES under 10	10 to 16	16 to 26	26 to 45	45 and over	TOTAL ALL OTHER	TOTAL SLAVES	TOTALS	DISTRICT/ TOWNSHIP	NOTES
Attleboro	322	39	Holmes	Samuel		1		1		1			1				5		
Taunton	369	27	Holmes	Thomas			1	1		3			1				6		
New Bedford	427	8	Holmes	William	1	1		1		3			1				7		
Taunton	358	12	Hood	Benj Landon	3	1			1				2	1			8		
Somerset	404	7	Hood	John	3	2		1					1				7		
Taunton	358	36	Hood	John	2			1		2			1				6		
Taunton	358	26	Hood	Joseph	2	1	1		1	1	1	2	1				10		
Somerset	404	8	Hood	William		1				1		1					3		
New Bedford	427	13	Hopkins	John	2			1		2			1				6		
Rehoboth	311	28	Hor	Jacob		1		1				2	1				7		
Rehoboth	311	29	Hor	Jacob Jr			1						1				3		
Rehoboth	306	33	Horten	Barnard		1		1		1	2		1				6		
Rehoboth	304	37	Horten	Volentine				1					1				3		
Rehoboth	301	43	Horton	Aaron			1					1					3		
Rehoboth	299	25	Horton	Abial	1	1		1	1	1			1				6		
Norton	381	22	Horton	Benjamin		1				3		1		1			6		
Rehoboth	304	42	Horton	Comfort		2		1	1	2	1		1				9		
Rehoboth	301	42	Horton	Constant				1			1		1				3		
Rehoboth	305	28	Horton	Conten	1	1				1	1		1				5		
Rehoboth	301	41	Horton	Daniel	1	1		1	2	1	1						8		
Rehoboth	303	11	Horton	Eliphlet		1		2				1					6		
Swansea	403	51	Horton	Jabez		1				1		1					3		
Rehoboth	302	42	Horton	James		2		1		1	1	1					7		
Rehoboth	304	43	Horton	Job	1	1		1				1					4		
Swansea	401	25	Horton	Job		1		1		1				1			4		
Freetown	290	19	Horton	Jonathan				1		1			1	1			4		
Rehoboth	302	46	Horton	Joseph		3	1	1	2	1	1	2					11		
Rehoboth	300	6	Horton	Nathan		1		1			1		1				5		
Rehoboth	302	41	Horton	Nathan	1	1		1		1			1	1			9		
Dighton	410	4	Horton	Seth	1			1		1			1				4		
Rehoboth	300	8	Horton	Shubel		1				1			1				5		
Dighton	415	2	Horton	Solomon	1	2	3	1	1		1	1	1				11		
Rehoboth	303	36	Horton	Thomas		1	1	1		1			1				6		
Rehoboth	314	42	Horton	Wheeler		1		1		1							5		
Rehoboth	303	42	Horton	William	1			1	1	1		2					7		
Rehoboth	303	40	Horton	William 3rd		1				1							2		
Rehoboth	298	29	Horton	Willm		1	1					1					4		
Dartmouth	345	40	Hoskins	George	2	1		1			2		1				8		
Taunton	364	21	Hoskins	Henry	2	2		1		1			1				7		
Taunton	364	28	Hoskins	John	2	1		1		1		2					7		
Taunton	368	19	Hoskins	John		2			1			2	1	1			7		
Taunton	368	1	Hoskins	Preserved	2			1		2	2	1	1				9		
Taunton	364	24	Hoskins	Ruth		1							1				2		
Taunton	364	31	Hoskins	William		2	1		1	2				1			7		
New Bedford	426	11	House	Benjamin				1									1		
New Bedford	426	10	House	John	1	2		1		1			1	1			7		
New Bedford	427	24	House	Sheubal		1				1		1					3		
Attleboro	320	41	How	William		1				1	2						4		
New Bedford	425	38	Howard	Abner			2		1	6	1		1				11		
Easton	390	34	Howard	Barnabas	3	1		1			1		1				7		
Easton	390	28	Howard	Calvin	1			1		4			1				7		
Westport	332	20	Howard	Daniel	2	1	1		1	3	2	2		1			13		
Easton	390	29	Howard	Elijah	1	2			1		2		1				7		
Easton	390	30	Howard	Joseph	2	2	1		1	2		1	1	1			11		
Taunton	360	38	Howard	Joseph	1			1					1				3		
Raynham	376	14	Howard	Molly Wid	1								1				2		
Easton	390	26	Howard	Nehemiah		1			1				1	1			4		
Easton	390	27	Howard	Roland	3			1		1	1	2		1			9		
Raynham	376	22	Howard	Rufus		1							1				2		
New Bedford	427	10	Howard	Solomon		1	1		1		1	2					6		
Taunton	368	17	Howard	Susanna Wido		1	1			1		1		1			5		
Raynham	376	31	Howard	William	3	2	2	1		2	1	1	1				13		
Dartmouth	345	27	Howland	Asa		1						2	2				5		
Dartmouth	345	14	Howland	Benjamin				1					1				2		
New Bedford	426	41	Howland	Benjamin	2			1				1	1				5		
Westport	332	13	Howland	Beriah	2			1		1		1					5		
Dartmouth	345	30	Howland	Cady								2					2		
Dartmouth	345	32	Howland	Caleb	1	1		1	1	2	1	1					8		
Westport	333	6	Howland	Charles	2	1			1	2	1		1				8		
New Bedford	426	27	Howland	Cornelius			1	1		3	1		1				7		
Taunton	366	11	Howland	Cuff											8		8		
Dartmouth	345	29	Howland	Daniel	1			1	2	1			1				9		
Dartmouth	345	37	Howland	David		1		4			1						6		
Freetown	283	23	Howland	George		1			1	3	1	1	1				8		
Dartmouth	345	16	Howland	Gideon	1		1	1				2	2				7		
New Bedford	426	28	Howland	Gideon		1		1				2					4		
Dartmouth	345	39	Howland	Gideon 2d		3		1	1	1	1	1					8		
New Bedford	426	34	Howland	Gilbert	3		1	1		1	1	1					8		
Dartmouth	345	10	Howland	Henry	1		1		2			1	1				8		
Westport	332	23	Howland	Henry				1	1					1			3		
Westport	332	25	Howland	Henry Junr		1							1				3		
New Bedford	426	32	Howland	Humphrey	1	3	1	1		1			1	1			9		
Westport	332	26	Howland	Humphrey		1	1		1				1				4		
Dartmouth	345	13	Howland	Isaac	1	1		1	1	1	1	1	1				11		

114

| | | | HEADS OF HOUSEHOLD | | FREE WHITE MALES | | | | | FREE WHITE FEMALES | | | | | | | | | |
TOWN	PG#	LN#	LAST NAME	FIRST NAME	under 10	10 to 16	16 to 26	26 to 45	45 and over	under 10	10 to 16	16 to 26	26 to 45	45 and over	TOTAL ALL OTHER	TOTAL SLAVES	TOTALS	DISTRICT/TOWNSHIP	NOTES
New Bedford	426	31	Howland	Isaac					1			2		1	1		5		
Westport	332	32	Howland	Isaac	1	1	1	1					1				5		
New Bedford	426	29	Howland	Isaac Jun				1				1	1				3		
New Bedford	426	30	Howland	James		1	1	1	1		1		1				6		
Westport	332	24	Howland	Jethro			1	1					1				3		
Freetown	292	27	Howland	Job Jr	1		1	1		1			1				5		
Dartmouth	345	18	Howland	John	1		1		1	1		1	1				9		
Dartmouth	345	46	Howland	John	1	2		1	1	2		1					12		
New Bedford	426	42	Howland	John	1	1	3		1	2	1	1	2		1		13		
Westport	332	22	Howland	John					1		2		1				4		
Westport	332	30	Howland	John Son	3	3		1		2			1				10		
Dartmouth	345	24	Howland	Jonathan		1		1	1	1	1	1					7		
New Bedford	427	2	Howland	Jonathan	2	1				1	1		1				7		
Dartmouth	345	19	Howland	Joseph			1				1		1				4		
Dartmouth	345	34	Howland	Joseph			2		3				1				6		
New Bedford	426	43	Howland	Joseph		1		2				1	1		1		6		
Dartmouth	345	31	Howland	Joshua			1			2			1				5		
Freetown	283	24	Howland	Joshua		1		1				2		1			5		
Dartmouth	345	25	Howland	Lucy		1	1			1	2		2				7		
Dartmouth	345	28	Howland	Luthern		1		1					2				4		
New Bedford	426	23	Howland	Mathew	2	1	3		1	1	1		1				10		
Westport	332	29	Howland	Nancy							1	1	1				3		
Dartmouth	345	11	Howland	Nathaniel	1	1	1		4	1	1	1	1				12		
New Bedford	426	39	Howland	Peleg	3		1	1			1	1	1				8		
Dartmouth	345	38	Howland	Pero										4	4		4		
Westport	332	21	Howland	Philip	1			1					1				3		
Westport	332	19	Howland	Prince		2		1		1	2		1				7		
Dartmouth	345	36	Howland	Reserved	1		1				1	1					6		
New Bedford	427	17	Howland	Reuben	1		1	1		1		1	1				6		
Westport	332	31	Howland	Sibil								2	1				3		
Dartmouth	345	15	Howland	Stephen		1		2			1						6		
Dartmouth	345	6	Howland	Thomas	1		1	1			1		1				6		
Dartmouth	345	17	Howland	Thomas		1		1			1						4		
New Bedford	426	44	Howland	Timothy	1	2	1						1				6		
Dartmouth	345	35	Howland	Warren		1		1	4	1		1					8		
New Bedford	426	26	Howland	Weston	2		1	1		1			1		1		7		
Dartmouth	345	23	Howland	William	1		1		2	1		1					6		
New Bedford	425	41	Howland	Wing		2	2		1	3	1	2	1				12		
Easton	390	35	Howward	Deane		1		1				1					3		
Rehoboth	313	29	Hudson	Reuben		1		1			1	1	1				5		
Taunton	359	37	Hull	Isaac											6		6		
Dartmouth	345	22	Hull	John	2			1	1			2					8		
Westport	333	4	Hull	Susannah											4		4		
Rehoboth	313	28	Humphrey	David		1		1	2	1	1						6		
Rehoboth	311	17	Humphrey	Jonathan	2	3		1	3	1			1				11		
Rehoboth	314	23	Hunt	Chris															Enumeration left blank
Taunton	368	11	Hunt	Enoch	2	2		1			3	1	1				10		
Rehoboth	312	45	Hunt	Hezekiah		2		2		1	1		2				8		
Taunton	368	7	Hunt	Jail Widow							1		2	1			4		
Mansfield	386	17	Hunt	James				1							3		4		
Taunton	364	13	Hunt	Job				1					1				2		
Rehoboth	313	16	Hunt	John		1		1			1						3		
Rehoboth	313	21	Hunt	John 2nd	1		1		1		1						5		
Attleboro	320	60	Hunt	Joseph	2	1	2		1		2		1				9		
Norton	381	42	Hunt	Joseph		1	2		1		1	1		1			7		
Norton	381	44	Hunt	Josiah		1	1				1	2	2				7		
Rehoboth	313	19	Hunt	Josiah			1		1		1	1					5		
Rehoboth	313	18	Hunt	Nathaniel	3		1		1		1	1					9		
Rehoboth	313	17	Hunt	Peter	1		1		1	2		1					8		
Mansfield	386	21	Hunt	Quincy	1			2		1			1	1			6		
Norton	381	43	Hunt	Samuel	5	1		1		1		1	1				10		
Rehoboth	300	21	Hunt	Simeon			2	1		1	1	1	1				7		
Taunton	368	6	Hunt	Stephen	1	1		1					1				4		
Rehoboth	313	26	Hunt	William		2	1		1	1			1				6		
Freetown	290	16	Hunter	Elexander	1	1			1	2			1				6		
Raynham	374	41	Huron	Benjamin		1						1					2		
New Bedford	426	38	Hussey	Isaiah			1		2	1			1				5		
New Bedford	425	21	Huttleston	Henry	1	1		1		1			1				5		
New Bedford	425	16	Huttleston	Peleg			1	1		1		2					5		
New Bedford	426	4	Huttleston	Thomas	1		1						1				3		
Rehoboth	313	32	Ide	Abel	1		1		1				1				5		
Attleboro	318	17	Ide	Amos		1		1	1	2		2		1			8		
Rehoboth	313	33	Ide	Ezra			1		2				1				6		
Attleboro	317	12	Ide	Ichabod	1		1	1		3		1		2			9		
Attleboro	317	14	Ide	Jacob	1	1	1		1	3	1		1				9		
Rehoboth	313	34	Ide	John	2		1					1					8		
Rehoboth	307	46	Ide	Mary						2		1					4		
Dighton	412	16	Ide	Nathan		1		1		1	1		1	1			6		
Attleboro	317	15	Ide	Nathaniel	1			1		2		2	1				7		
Rehoboth	313	36	Ide	Nathaniel	1	2	2	1		2		1					8		
Rehoboth	313	35	Ide	Willm	1		1		1			1					5		
Rehoboth	311	21	Iney	Benjamin			1						1				2		
Taunton	358	22	Ingall	Jonathan Junr		3			1	2		4	1				11		
Swansea	401	31	Ingalls	Elkanah	2		1			2		1					7		

TOWN	PG#	LN#	LAST NAME	FIRST NAME	FWM <10	FWM 10-16	FWM 16-26	FWM 26-45	FWM 45+	FWF <10	FWF 10-16	FWF 16-26	FWF 26-45	FWF 45+	TOTAL ALL OTHER	TOTAL SLAVES	TOTALS	DISTRICT/ TOWNSHIP	NOTES
Rehoboth	304	32	Ingals	Elkanah	1	1		1		1		1	1				6		
Rehoboth	298	33	Ingals	Hezekiah	1	1		1			5		1				9		
Taunton	357	24	Ingell	Abiacher	1		1	1					2		1		6		
Taunton	356	6	Ingell	Jonathan		1			1			1	1				4		
Attleboro	319	7	Ingraham	Comfort			2	1	2			1	1	1			8		
Attleboro	318	60	Ingraham	Elijah	1		2	1		2			1				7		
Attleboro	322	24	Ingraham	Jeremiah	1	1	1		1	1	1	2	1				9		
New Bedford	428	14	Ingraham	Paul				1			1	1					3		
New Bedford	428	13	Ingraham	Thomas		1	2		1	1	2	1		1			9		
New Bedford	428	9	Ingraham	Timothy		1	2	1	1	1		1		1			8		
Westport	333	7	Irish	Joseph	1			1					1				3		
Freetown	292	15	Jabez	George		2	1		2	1	1	2	1				10		
Norton	382	4	Jackson	Hezekiah		1		1		1			1				4		
Attleboro	322	68	Jackson	James	1	1		1		2	2		1				8		
Norton	382	3	Jackson	Nathaniel			1		1			1		1			4		
Attleboro	322	42	Jackson	Samuel	2	1	2		1	1	2		1				10		
Rehoboth	313	38	Jacobs	Allen		1		1					2				4		
Rehoboth	308	1	Jacobs	Calvin	1		1	1		1			2				6		
New Bedford	427	32	Jacobs	David			1			1			1				3		
Rehoboth	313	37	Jacobs	John	2			1					2	1			8		
Westport	335	22	James	Petty				1			2			1			4		Name probably reversed
New Bedford	428	15	James	William		2						2					4		
Rehoboth	314	39	Jenings	Nathan		1	1			1		1					4		
Rehoboth	314	40	Jenings	Squier Jr		1		1				1					7		
Rehoboth	307	25	Jenks	Levi		1		3				1					9		
New Bedford	427	31	Jenne	Abner	1	1		1		1	1		1	1			7		
New Bedford	427	36	Jenne	Caleb		1	1	1		3			1				7		
New Bedford	428	11	Jenne	Caleb Jr	2		2	1				2					7		
New Bedford	427	30	Jenne	David	1			1		2			1				5		
New Bedford	427	42	Jenne	Elizabeth			2							1			3		
New Bedford	427	27	Jenne	Israel	2	1		1		2	1	1		1			9		
New Bedford	427	29	Jenne	Jabez	1			1					1	1			4		
New Bedford	428	10	Jenne	Jahariel		1		1		2		1	1				6		
New Bedford	427	43	Jenne	Jeptha	1			1		1			1				4		
New Bedford	427	37	Jenne	Jethro					1			1		1			3		
New Bedford	428	3	Jenne	Job		1	1	2	1		1	2		1			9		
New Bedford	428	6	Jenne	John	2			1		2			1		1		7		
New Bedford	427	38	Jenne	Jonathan	1	1	1	1					1				5		
New Bedford	427	45	Jenne	Josiah			1										1		
New Bedford	427	33	Jenne	Levi	3	1	2		1	2	1		2				12		
New Bedford	427	40	Jenne	Marcy						1		1					2		
New Bedford	427	28	Jenne	Nathaniel			1							2			3		
New Bedford	427	39	Jenne	Patience									1	2			3		
New Bedford	428	16	Jenne	Patience										1			1		
New Bedford	428	8	Jenne	Peleg	2		3						1				6		
New Bedford	427	44	Jenne	Reuben	2		1	1		1			1				6		
New Bedford	427	41	Jenne	Sarah										1			1		
New Bedford	428	1	Jenne	Sarah			1			1	1	1		1			5		
New Bedford	428	4	Jenne	Seth			1						1	1			3		
New Bedford	427	35	Jenne	Weston	2			1					1				4		
New Bedford	428	7	Jenne	Weston2nd		1							1				2		
New Bedford	428	5	Jenne	William			1			1							2		
Taunton	358	2	Jewett	Abraha	1			1		1			1				4		
Norton	382	5	Jewitt	Jedediah	1			1		1			1				4		
Attleboro	322	15	Jillson	Daniel	2	1		1		1	1	1					7		
Attleboro	317	11	Jillson	Levi		1		1		1	2		2				7		
Attleboro	317	7	Jillson	William		1					1						?		
Easton	390	37	Johnson	David	2			1		2			1				6		
New Bedford	427	34	Johnson	Ebenezer		1											1		
Easton	390	38	Johnson	Edward											4		4		
Freetown	292	26	Johnson	Ichabod				1	3				2	1			7		
Taunton	363	19	Johnson	James	1			1		2			1				5		
Swansea	398	32	Johnson	Jonathan	1	1	1	1	1		1	1		1			8		
Taunton	362	30	Johnson	Nathaniel	2	1			1	1			1				6		
New Bedford	428	12	Johnson	Samuel											7		7		
Taunton	359	26	Johnson	Seth				1		2	2	3					8		
Taunton	356	9	Johnson	William		2			1				1				4		
Dartmouth	346	4	Jones	Abial		1		1			1						5		
Easton	390	36	Jones	Abigail									3	1			4		
Dighton	413	11	Jones	Asa	1	1		1		3	1		1				8		
Taunton	366	27	Jones	Benjamin				1					1				2		
Taunton	365	10	Jones	Benjamin Junior	1			1					1				3		
Rehoboth	313	40	Jones	Ebenezer	1		1		3	3	1						9		
Dighton	410	18	Jones	Henry					1		2		1				4		
Dighton	413	14	Jones	Isaac	2			1			1	2	2				8		
New Bedford	427	26	Jones	Isaiah	1	1	2	1					1				6		
Rehoboth	308	39	Jones	Jenken		1		2	1			1					7		
Dighton	413	34	Jones	Jeremiah			1			1		1					3		
Taunton	369	42	Jones	Joanna Wido										2			2		
Dighton	411	14	Jones	John	1			1		1			1				4		
Rehoboth	299	34	Jones	John			1			1		1					3		
Dighton	414	26	Jones	Jonathan		2		1		1	2		1				7		
Rehoboth	308	40	Jones	Josiah		1	1	1		1		1					6		
Raynham	372	17	Jones	Nehemiah	1			1		2			1				5		
Dighton	413	9	Jones	Salathiel	3	1		1	1	1		1	1				9		
Raynham	372	24	Jones	Samuel			1	1		2			1				5		

| | | | HEADS OF HOUSEHOLD | | FREE WHITE MALES | | | | | FREE WHITE FEMALES | | | | | | | | | |
TOWN	PG#	LN#	LAST NAME	FIRST NAME	under 10	10 to 16	16 to 26	26 to 45	45 and over	under 10	10 to 16	16 to 26	26 to 45	45 and over	TOTAL ALL OTHER	TOTAL SLAVES	TOTALS	DISTRICT/TOWNSHIP	NOTES
Berkley	280	4	Jones	Sargent	2		1						1				4		
Raynham	372	3	Jones	Seth		1			1				1	1			4		
Swansea	399	30	Jones	Simeon	2	1		1		3		1					8		
Taunton	365	9	Jones	Sylvester	4	1		1			1	1					8		
Dighton	413	12	Jones	Wido											2		2		
Rehoboth	313	39	Jones	William	1			1	2	1	2	1					8		
Attleboro	319	56	Jones	Wm					1						2		3		
Dartmouth	346	2	Jones	Zebedee		1		3					1				5		
Dartmouth	346	3	Jones	Zepheniah		1		2					1				4		
Berkley	277	23	Jones	Zephiniah		1			1			2		2			6		
Dartmouth	346	5	Jonson	Laurance											4		4		
New Bedford	428	2	Joseph	Christopher	2	1		1				1	1	1			7		
Dartmouth	346	1	Joy	Samuel		1		1				1	1				4		
Westport	333	8	Jucket	Ebenezer	4			1		2		1					8		
Freetown	292	4	Jucket	Micah	3	1			1		1	1					7		
Freetown	293	21	Jucket	Stephen	1		1					1	1				4		
Freetown	285	28	Jucket	Thankfull			1				1	1		1			4		
Somerset	405	22	Kain	Robert				1					1				2		
Somerset	405	29	Kain	Robert Jr		2		1		2	1		1				7		
New Bedford	428	28	Keen	Ebenezer		1		1				1	1				4		
New Bedford	428	29	Keen	Ebenezer Jr			1			1			1		1		4		
New Bedford	428	27	Keen	Jesse	2	1		1			1	1	1				7		
Easton	391	9	Keith	Alexander			1			2	1	1					5		
Raynham	375	26	Keith	Asa	2	1	2	1				1	1				8		
Easton	390	41	Keith	Benjamin			1	1					1				3		
Easton	391	11	Keith	Bethiah			1						1	3			5		
Easton	391	5	Keith	David		1	2		1		1	2		1			8		
Easton	391	12	Keith	David				1		1		1		1			4		
Easton	390	39	Keith	Josiah	2	1		1			2		1				7		
Easton	390	40	Keith	Lemuel		1	2		1	1	1		1				7		
Easton	391	4	Keith	Mary		1							1				2		
Easton	391	10	Keith	Nehemiah		1				1			1		1		4		
Easton	391	3	Keith	Scot	2	1	1		1	1	1	1		1			9		
Norton	382	8	Keith	Seth	1	1	1		1		1	2		1			8		
Somerset	405	3	Kellog	Joseph			1			2	1		1				5		
New Bedford	428	21	Kempton	Asa	1			1		3			1				6		
New Bedford	428	39	Kempton	David	2			1		3	2		1				9		
New Bedford	428	32	Kempton	Elijah	2			1		2	3		1				9		
New Bedford	428	37	Kempton	Ephraim				1		1		1	2	1	1		7		
New Bedford	428	38	Kempton	Ephraim Jr		1	2	1		1		1		1	1		8		
New Bedford	428	23	Kempton	James	2	3		1		1		2	1	1			11		
New Bedford	428	24	Kempton	Jonathan	1	1		1		4	1		1				9		
New Bedford	428	40	Kempton	Joseph				1					2				3		
New Bedford	428	34	Kempton	Manasseh			2	2	1				1	1	1		8		
New Bedford	428	35	Kempton	Manasseh Jr	2	1	5	1		2		1	1				13		
New Bedford	428	33	Kempton	Obed	1	1		1			2		1				6		
New Bedford	428	18	Kempton	Paul		1							1				2		
New Bedford	428	30	Kempton	Sarah										1			1		
New Bedford	428	22	Kempton	Stephen		1		1		1		1	1				5		
New Bedford	428	36	Kempton	Thomas		2			1	1				2			6		
New Bedford	428	20	Kempton	William		2			1	2	1	1	1				8		
New Bedford	428	26	Kempton	William Jr	1		1						1				3		
Rehoboth	307	20	Kenedy	David	1			1	1				1				4		
Rehoboth	313	41	Kent	Elijah & Son	2			2		1	1	1	2				14		
Rehoboth	313	45	Kent	Elizabeth									1				1		
Rehoboth	302	12	Kent	Ezekel		1	1	1		1	2		1				7		
Rehoboth	306	36	Kent	Ezkiel			1			1			1				3		
Rehoboth	313	44	Kent	Ezra			1		1	1		1					6		
Rehoboth	313	43	Kent	Jabez EB		1				1	1						3		
Rehoboth	314	1	Kent	James		1		1		1			1				4		
Rehoboth	314	2	Kent	John		1		2					1				4		
Rehoboth	306	34	Kent	Joseph	2			1				1	1				5		
Rehoboth	313	42	Kent	Josiah	1	2			1	1	1						7		
Rehoboth	313	46	Kent	Noah			1	1					1				3		
Westport	333	20	Kerby	Abner	1		1			1		1					4		
Dartmouth	346	8	Kerby	Benjamin		1		1		1			1				6		
Westport	333	14	Kerby	David		1		1					1	1			4		
Westport	333	18	Kerby	John			1	1		1			1				4		
Westport	333	11	Kerby	Justice				1				2	1				4		
Dartmouth	346	10	Kerby	Luthern		1		1				1					4		
Westport	333	9	Kerby	Nathaniel	1	3		1		1	2		1				9		
Westport	333	19	Kerby	Nathaniel Blacksmith	1	1	2		2	2	1	3	1				13		
Westport	333	23	Kerby	Pardon		1						2	1				4		
Westport	333	13	Kerby	Peace		1						2	1	1			5		
Westport	333	21	Kerby	Rachel										2			2		
Dartmouth	346	7	Kerby	Rescom			1					1					6		
Westport	333	15	Kerby	Richard		1		1				2	3	1			8		
Westport	333	16	Kerby	Robert	1	1	2		1			1	1	1			8		
Westport	333	17	Kerby	Robert 2d			1					1					3		
Dartmouth	346	6	Kerby	Silas			1						2				6		
Westport	333	10	Kerby	Stephen		1				2		1	1				7		
Dartmouth	346	9	Kerby	Wesson		1						1					2		
Westport	333	12	Kerby	Wesson		1		1	1	1		2	1				7		
New Bedford	428	25	Killey	amos	2	1		1				2					7		
Rehoboth	303	33	Kilton	John 2nd	1		1		1	2		1	1				8		
Rehoboth	303	32	Kilton	Nathaniel		1							1				2		
Easton	391	2	Kimball	Isaac			1			1		1					3		

TOWN	PG#	LN#	LAST NAME	FIRST NAME	FREE WHITE MALES under 10	10 to 16	16 to 26	26 to 45	45 and over	FREE WHITE FEMALES under 10	10 to 16	16 to 26	26 to 45	45 and over	TOTAL ALL OTHER	TOTAL SLAVES	TOTALS	DISTRICT/ TOWNSHIP	NOTES
Easton	391	1	Kimball	Samuel	2			1	1	3			1	1			9		
Dighton	409	8	Kimble	Asa	1		1			1	1	1					5		
Raynham	374	27	King	Barzilla			1			1		1					3		
Raynham	374	28	King	Benjamin	1		1		2			1		1			6		
Norton	382	10	King	Calvin	1	1		1		1			1				5		
Taunton	361	37	King	Elijah	4	1		1		1			1				8		
Raynham	373	20	King	George	1				1				1				3		
Raynham	374	13	King	Isaac	2	1		1		1			1				6		
Swansea	401	24	King	Job		1		1				1	1				4		
Taunton	359	19	King	Job		3		1		2		2		1			9		
Norton	382	7	King	John	1		1		1			1	1	2			7		
Raynham	374	20	King	John					2			2		1			5		
Raynham	373	4	King	John Junior	1			1		1	3	3		1			10		
Norton	382	11	King	Josiah	1				1	1			1	1	1		5		
Taunton	362	10	King	Josiah		1	1	1	1	1				1			6		
Raynham	374	22	King	Nathan	2	1	2	1		2	1	1	1	1			12		
Raynham	372	11	King	Philip		1	2		1	1	1		1				7		
Rehoboth	299	40	King	Robert	1	1		1			2		1				8		
Raynham	374	14	King	Silas	2	1		1		1			1				6		
Raynham	374	18	King	Stephen	4			1		1		1	1				8		
Taunton	362	2	King	Turner				1		1			1				3		
Swansea	400	7	Kingsley	Amos		1	2		1				1	1			6		
Swansea	402	49	Kingsley	Asa		2	2	1		3			2	3			13		
Swansea	400	5	Kingsley	Barton	1		1						1				3		
Swansea	400	4	Kingsley	Benja	1		1						1				3		
Rehoboth	303	1	Kingsley	David		2		1		1	2	1					7		
Swansea	402	33	Kingsley	Hezekiah		1			1				1				3		
Swansea	402	34	Kingsley	Hezekiah Jr	2	1		1		1	1		1				7		
Swansea	400	6	Kingsley	James	2			1					1				4		
Swansea	399	16	Kingsley	Jonathan		2		1		3		1					7		
Swansea	402	43	Kingsley	Rose											4		4		
Swansea	399	15	Kingsley	Simeon	1			1		2			1				5		
Swansea	399	14	Kingsley	Thomas		1			1	1	1	1	1				6		
Easton	391	8	Kingsman	Edward	2	1		1		2			1				7		
New Bedford	428	19	Kinney	Jacob	1	1	2	1					1				6		
New Bedford	428	17	Kinney	Samuel		1		1				1					3		
Easton	391	7	Kinsley	Benjamin			1		1	1	1		1				5		
Easton	391	6	Kinsley	Zebudiah	1	1		1		1		4	1				9		
Raynham	372	30	Knap	Atherton		1	2	1		1		1	1				7		
Taunton	367	36	Knap	Edward	2			1		1			1				5		
Raynham	372	42	Knap	Eliab	2	1			2	1	1	1	1				9		
Taunton	366	44	Knap	Elijah		1	1	1					1				4		
Taunton	367	37	Knap	Ephraim	1			1		3	1		1				7		
Raynham	372	27	Knap	Philip		1	1	1					1				4		
Raynham	372	29	Knap	Sarah Wid									1				1		
Rehoboth	305	8	Knap	Seth	1		1	1	1	1		1					6		
Dartmouth	346	12	Knap	Eben			1					1					2		
Dartmouth	346	11	Knapp	Asael		1		1		2		1					7		
Norton	382	9	Knapp	Daniel		1	1		1		1	1	1				6		
Mansfield	386	23	Knapp	John		1		2					1	1	1		5		
Mansfield	386	24	Knapp	John Jur			1				1						2		
Dighton	410	45	Kneeder	Thomas		1		1					1				3		
Westport	333	22	Knight	John				1	1	1		2	1				5		
Norton	382	6	Knowles	Asa	1		1			1			1				4		
Dighton	411	1	Knowles	Jonathan	2			1		1			1				5		
Taunton	358	16	Ladelford	Samuel	1	1		1	1	1		1	1				7		
Rehoboth	301	35	Lake	Eletheam	1			1		1		1					6		
Rehoboth	298	40	Lake	Laben	1	2		1		1	1	1					9		
Westport	333	25	Lamonyan	John	1	1		1	1	3	1		1	1			10		
New Bedford	428	41	Landers	Jane	2					1			1				4		
Mansfield	386	29	Lane	Abiel		1		1		1			1				4		
Rehoboth	300	41	Lane	Amos		2		1		1	1	1					6		
Norton	382	22	Lane	Daniel	3			1		1		1					6		
Mansfield	386	26	Lane	Ebenezer		1		1		1			1				4		
Norton	382	18	Lane	Ephraim		1	3		1	1	1		1				8		
Norton	382	21	Lane	Isaac		1		1		1		1					4		
Attleboro	322	70	Lane	Jona			1		1	2			1				5		
Mansfield	386	25	Lane	Joseph	1	1		1		1	1		1				6		
Attleboro	322	69	Lane	Levi	1		1						1				3		
Mansfield	386	27	Lane	Seth				1				1					2		
Mansfield	386	28	Lane	Seth Junr	1		1	1		1	1		1				6		
Norton	382	17	Lane	William	2			1		3		2					8		
New Bedford	428	44	Langworthy	John	1		2						1		1		6		
Dartmouth	346	15	Lapham	Humphrey	2		1		2	1		1					8		
Dartmouth	346	17	Lapham	Mary		1							1				2		
Dartmouth	346	16	Lapham	Nicholas		1		1		1							3		
Freetown	292	9	Laramee	Benjamin Jun	2	2		1		1	1		1				8		
Freetown	293	4	Laramee	John		1		1	1	3			2	1			9		
Easton	391	17	Lathrop	Ambrose															Enumeration left blank
Easton	391	15	Lathrop	Edmund		1	1						1				3		
Easton	391	21	Lathrop	Isaac	1	1	2		1	2	2	1		1			11		
Easton	391	30	Lathrop	Isaac 2d			1						1				2		

TOWN	PG#	LN#	HEADS OF HOUSEHOLD		FREE WHITE MALES					FREE WHITE FEMALES					TOTAL ALL OTHER	TOTAL SLAVES	TOTALS	DISTRICT/ TOWNSHIP	NOTES
			LAST NAME	FIRST NAME	under 10	10 to 16	16 to 26	26 to 45	45 and over	under 10	10 to 16	16 to 26	26 to 45	45 and over					
Easton	391	22	Lathrop	John			2	1		1	2		1				7		
Easton	391	23	Lathrop	John 2d	1		1			1		1					4		
Easton	391	33	Lathrop	Joseph		1		1		2	1		1				6		
Easton	391	34	Lathrop	Joseph 2d				1						2			3		
Easton	391	28	Lathrop	Solomon	2	1		1		2		1	1				8		
Freetown	289	1	Law	James			1			2			1				4		
Dartmouth	346	13	Lawton	Abraham											4		4		
Rehoboth	314	3	Lawton	Caleb	1		1	1				1			4				
Freetown	287	15	Lawton	Daniel	4	2			1	4	1		1				13		
Freetown	288	32	Lawton	George	3	1					1		2	1			8		
Westport	333	24	Lawton	George			1	3	1				1	1			7		
Freetown	288	24	Lawton	Hannah Wid		1							2	1			4		
Swansea	401	46	Lawton	James		2	2	1		1	2		1				9		
Swansea	402	1	Lawton	James Jr			1			2		1					4		
Freetown	291	2	Lawton	Job	2		1						1				4		
Dartmouth	346	18	Lawton	Jonathan			1	1		1		1			5				
Rehoboth	299	29	Lawton	Sebray			1		1			1	1	1	8				
Rehoboth	299	35	Lawton	Thomas			1	2					1		5				
Somerset	407	8	Lawton	William		3			1			2		1			7		
Norton	382	31	Lazell	Ebenezer	1			1					1				3		
Easton	391	16	Leach	Abisha	2	1	3	1	1		1		1				10		
Raynham	375	21	Leach	Asa	1	1		1		3			1				7		
Raynham	375	27	Leach	Eliphalet			1			1		1					3		
Easton	391	32	Leach	Rufus			2						1				3		
Dighton	415	12	Lee	Abiather	1		1					1					3		
Taunton	365	40	Lee	Abiather	1	2	1		1		1	2	1				9		
Taunton	367	26	Lee	Benjamin	2			1		1			1				5		
Taunton	366	16	Lee	George	1			1		3	1		1				7		
Rehoboth	303	39	Lee	Israel			1					1			4				
Somerset	407	45	Lee	John	2			1		3	1		1				8		
Swansea	401	26	Lee	Stephen	1	1			1	2	2		1				8		
Taunton	366	6	Lee	Thomas		2	2		1	2	1		1				9		
Taunton	360	23	Leonard	Abiather	3			1		3			1				8		
Taunton	364	7	Leonard	Abiather		2			1		1		1				5		
Mansfield	386	30	Leonard	Abiel					1					1			2		
Mansfield	386	31	Leonard	Abijah	1		2			1	1	1	1				8		
Taunton	370	15	Leonard	Benjamin		1	1	1	1				1				5		
Taunton	368	29	Leonard	Benjamin Junr			2	1					1				4		
Taunton	371	7	Leonard	Charles	1		1						1		1		4		
Raynham	373	15	Leonard	Cuff											10		10		
Taunton	368	35	Leonard	Daniel	2			1		4			1				8		
Easton	391	31	Leonard	David	1		1					1					3		
Raynham	374	1	Leonard	Eliakim	2			1		1			1				5		
Raynham	372	7	Leonard	Elijah				2	1				1	1			5		
Taunton	369	10	Leonard	Elijah 3d	2		1					1					4		
Easton	391	18	Leonard	Eliphalet			1	1			1			2			5		
Easton	391	19	Leonard	Eliphalet Jr	1		1	1		3		1	1				8		
Raynham	373	40	Leonard	Gamaliel					1				1				2		
Norton	382	16	Leonard	George		1		1	2	1	1	1	2				9		
Taunton	364	5	Leonard	Gilbert	2			1		2	1		1				7		
Taunton	359	33	Leonard	Ichabod	1			2	1				1				5		
Easton	391	25	Leonard	Isaac	1	1		1		1			1				5		
Easton	391	20	Leonard	Jacob	2			1		1			1				5		
Taunton	371	15	Leonard	James		1			1	1	2		1				6		
Taunton	371	14	Leonard	James Junior	1			1		4	1		1				8		
Taunton	371	16	Leonard	Jemima Wido										3			3		
Taunton	370	14	Leonard	Job	2			1		4	2		1				10		
Norton	382	19	Leonard	Jonathan		1	1		1	1		2	1				7		
Taunton	368	27	Leonard	Joseph			1			2		1					4		
Raynham	372	4	Leonard	Joshua	1			1	1	1			1				5		
Raynham	374	3	Leonard	Mary Wid		3							1				4		
Taunton	371	10	Leonard	Molly Wido								1	1				2		
Taunton	370	18	Leonard	Nathaniel		1	2		1	3	2		1				10		
Mansfield	386	32	Leonard	Nehemiah	2	2			2	1	1	1		2			11		
Taunton	359	38	Leonard	Rufus	1		2	1		2	2	1	1				10		
Easton	391	29	Leonard	Samuel		1			1	4	2	1	1				10		
Raynham	376	34	Leonard	Samuel	1	1		1					1				4		
Taunton	359	40	Leonard	Samuel	2	1	7		1		1	2	1	1	4		20		
Raynham	373	30	Leonard	Samuel 3d	1	1		1		3			1				7		
Raynham	376	21	Leonard	Samuel Junr	1	1		1		2	1		1				7		
Raynham	375	1	Leonard	Seth				2					2				4		
Taunton	370	41	Leonard	Silas	1		1	1		1			1				5		
Raynham	375	3	Leonard	Simeon	3	2			1	1			1				8		
Raynham	373	39	Leonard	Simeon 2d				1		1			1				3		
Taunton	369	32	Leonard	Solomon	1	2		1		1	1	1	1				8		
Norton	382	23	Leonard	Thomas	1		1	1		1		1					5		
Raynham	374	2	Leonard	Thomas	2			1					1				8		
Taunton	368	25	Leonard	William		2	2		1	2		1		2			10		
Taunton	371	9	Leonard	Willliams	1			1	1	2		1					6		
Taunton	364	9	Leonard	Zadoc	2	1		1		3	1		1				9		
Raynham	372	2	Leonard	Zephanah			1		1			1		1			4		
Taunton	365	25	Lever	Ebenezer	1		1		1	1	2			1			7		
New Bedford	428	42	Levett	Joseph			1			1			1				3		
Swansea	399	46	Lewin	Hale	3	1	1			1	1	1					8		

TOWN	PG#	LN#	LAST NAME	FIRST NAME	FREE WHITE MALES under 10	10 to 16	16 to 26	26 to 45	45 and over	FREE WHITE FEMALES under 10	10 to 16	16 to 26	26 to 45	45 and over	TOTAL ALL OTHER	TOTAL SLAVES	TOTALS	DISTRICT/ TOWNSHIP	NOTES
Swansea	398	5	Lewin	John					1					1			2		
Swansea	399	44	Lewin	John 2d			3	1						1			5		
Swansea	398	7	Lewin	Nathaniel				1		4	2	1					8		
Swansea	398	6	Lewin	Thomas	2			1		1	2	1					7		
Dighton	415	8	Lewis	Aaron	1	1	1	1		1	1			1			7		
New Bedford	429	4	Lewis	Abner				1						1			2		
Swansea	401	38	Lewis	Anna & Mercy										2			2		
Dighton	410	10	Lewis	Benja	2	2		1			2		1				8		
Rehoboth	300	25	Lewis	Daniel			1					1	1		4				
Dartmouth	346	14	Lewis	John										4	4				
Swansea	401	33	Lewis	Patience		1								1			2		
New Bedford	428	43	Lewis	Robinson	1			1				1					3		
Swansea	401	36	Lewis	Thomas			1		1					1			3		
Swansea	401	35	Lewis	Thomas Jr	3	1		1			1		1				7		
Dighton	415	7	Lewis	Timothy	1			1		3	1		1				7		
Norton	382	25	Lincoln	Abiel				1						4			5		
Norton	382	26	Lincoln	Abiel Jr	2	1	2		1	2		2	1				11		
Taunton	370	32	Lincoln	Abijah	1	1	2		1		1		1				7		
Norton	382	30	Lincoln	Abner			1			1			1				3		
Taunton	365	44	Lincoln	Abner	2	1			1		1	2	1				8		
Westport	333	26	Lincoln	Abraham		1	1		1				1				4		
Raynham	376	2	Lincoln	Ambros	2	2		1		1	1		1				8		
Norton	382	27	Lincoln	Asa	2	1			1	1		1		1			7		
Taunton	366	43	Lincoln	Asa	1	1	1	1		3	2		1				10		
New Bedford	429	1	Lincoln	Benjam	1	1	2	1				2					7		
Taunton	359	31	Lincoln	Benjamin	1	1	1		1	2	1	2		1			10		
Taunton	366	15	Lincoln	Benjamin 2d	1	1	1		1	2	2	2		1			11		
Taunton	366	1	Lincoln	Caleb	2			1		4	1		2	2			12		
Norton	382	12	Lincoln	David				1						2			3		
Taunton	358	33	Lincoln	David				1				1		1			3		
Norton	382	13	Lincoln	David Jun		3	1		1					1			6		
Taunton	367	42	Lincoln	Elijah	1			1		2			1				5		
Taunton	370	37	Lincoln	Elijah	3			1				1					5		
Taunton	365	41	Lincoln	Elisha			1	2		1			2				6		
Taunton	361	12	Lincoln	Elizabeth Wido	1		1	1				1	1				5		
Taunton	369	22	Lincoln	Ezekiel	1		1			1	1			1			6		
Taunton	365	42	Lincoln	Gideon			1	1					2	1			5		
Norton	382	28	Lincoln	Hannah										2			2		
Taunton	370	31	Lincoln	Hart	1		1	1		3			1	1			8		
Dartmouth	346	19	Lincoln	Isaac				1					1	2	5				
Taunton	365	45	Lincoln	Isaac			1	1		1			1				3		
Taunton	366	4	Lincoln	James				1					1				2		
Taunton	367	45	Lincoln	James 2d	4			1					1				6		
Taunton	367	43	Lincoln	John				1					1	1			3		
Taunton	366	35	Lincoln	Joshua	3			1	1				1				6		
Taunton	366	38	Lincoln	Josiah		1	3	1	1		1	2		1			10		
Norton	382	14	Lincoln	Levi		1		1		3	1	1					7		
Dighton	411	17	Lincoln	Lott	4	2		1		2							9		
Norton	382	15	Lincoln	Luther	2		2	1		3			1	1			10		
Taunton	369	30	Lincoln	Luther											6		6		
Norton	382	29	Lincoln	Marcy			1	1						2			4		
Taunton	369	41	Lincoln	Mary Wido		1	1			1			1	1			5		
Taunton	371	17	Lincoln	Moses	1			1		1			1				4		
Taunton	365	30	Lincoln	Nathaniel	1			1				1	1				4		
Taunton	365	38	Lincoln	Nidebiah	3			1		1	2		1				8		
Easton	391	24	Lincoln	Paul		1	2		1		2			1			7		
Taunton	361	29	Lincoln	Robert				1		2			1				4		
Norton	382	24	Lincoln	Rufus				1		1	2		1				5		
Taunton	369	43	Lincoln	Samuel		1	2		1			2		2			8		
Rehoboth	311	34	Lincoln	Sandford			1		2	1		1			6				
Norton	382	20	Lincoln	Simeon	3			1		1	1		1				7		
Taunton	369	31	Lincoln	Stephen	1		3		1	1	2	1		1			10		
Taunton	369	34	Lincoln	Thomas	1	2		1		4	1	1		1			11		
Taunton	365	6	Lincoln	Waitstill								1		2			3		
Rehoboth	298	41	Lindsey	Benjamin	1			1	1	2		1			8				
Rehoboth	300	27	Lindsey	John	2	1		1		1	1		1		9				
Taunton	363	44	Linscombe	Francis	1			1						2					
Dartmouth	346	21	Liscom	Richard			1	2				1			6				
Attleboro	318	38	Liscomb	Samuel		2	1		1	2			2				8		
Dartmouth	346	22	Little	Barker	3			1		3		1			8				
Westport	333	27	Little	Charles			1			2		1					4		
Dartmouth	346	23	Little	Nathaniel			1					1			3				
Easton	391	13	Littlefield	Abiah															Enumeration left blank
Easton	391	14	Littlefield	Daniel															Enumeration left blank
Easton	391	27	Littlefield	Ebenezer	2			1		1				1			5		
Taunton	357	17	Littlefield	John	1			1		1				1			4		
New Bedford	429	3	Littlefield	Sarah											7		7		
Easton	391	26	Littlefield	Seth	1		1		1	1	2		1				7		
Dighton	412	22	Lockwood	James	1	1			1	1			1				5		
Attleboro	321	59	Lombard	James			1			1			1				3		
Mansfield	386	34	Lovel	David		2			1				1	3			7		
Mansfield	386	33	Lovel	Isaac		2			1				1	2			6		
New Bedford	429	2	Lowden	John			1			1			1				3		
Taunton	359	29	Lu	Amos	2					3	3	1	1				11		

TOWN	PG#	LN#	LAST NAME	FIRST NAME	FREE WHITE MALES					FREE WHITE FEMALES					TOTAL ALL OTHER	TOTAL SLAVES	TOTALS	DISTRICT/ TOWNSHIP	NOTES
					under 10	10 to 16	16 to 26	26 to 45	45 and over	under 10	10 to 16	16 to 26	26 to 45	45 and over					
Freetown	292	12	Lucus	Elijah		2	2	1		3		1	1				10		
Attleboro	320	58	Lune	Daniel		1		1					1				3		
Taunton	361	6	Luscombe	Abijah Junior			1			3		1					5		
Taunton	367	7	Luscombe	Otis		1		1		2			1	1	1		7		
Taunton	359	10	Luscombe	Richard		2			1		1	2		1			7		
Taunton	361	3	Luscombe	Robert		1	1		1			2		1			6		
Swansea	401	44	Luther	Aaron	2			1		2		1	1				7		
Somerset	407	22	Luther	Amos	3			1		1	1		1				7		
Swansea	400	8	Luther	Barnabas	1		2						2				5		
Somerset	407	4	Luther	Barton	1	2		1		2			1				7		
Swansea	400	27	Luther	Barton	1			1	1	1	1			1			6		
Somerset	408	2	Luther	Bathsheba							3	2		1			6		
Dighton	413	32	Luther	Benja	2	2	1		1	1	1		1	1			10		
Somerset	407	5	Luther	Benja	2		1			2			1				7		
Freetown	288	1	Luther	Benjamin		1	1		1	1			1				5		
Swansea	402	27	Luther	Betsy	2							1					3		
Swansea	402	6	Luther	Caleb Wido	3	3				2	2	1					11		
Swansea	401	43	Luther	Calvin	1			1	1	1		1		1			6		
Swansea	401	28	Luther	Childs		1				1		1					3		
Somerset	407	7	Luther	David			2	1		1		1		1			6		
Swansea	400	2	Luther	David				1						1			2		
Somerset	404	41	Luther	David Junr		1					1	1					3		
Somerset	404	22	Luther	Dyer		1						1					2		
Swansea	402	2	Luther	Eben	2		1			1		1					5		
Somerset	408	3	Luther	Ellis	1		1					1					3		
Swansea	399	31	Luther	Giles				1				1	3				5		
Swansea	399	38	Luther	Harlow		1	1	1				1	2				6		
Swansea	402	19	Luther	James				1					1				2		
Swansea	402	20	Luther	James Jr	2	1	2	1		3	2	1		1			13		
Swansea	399	19	Luther	Jane		1					4	1					6		
Swansea	399	13	Luther	Job	2	1		1		3	1	1					9		
Swansea	403	26	Luther	Job	0	1		1					1				3		
Swansea	398	16	Luther	John	1			1		1			1				4		
Dartmouth	346	20	Luther	Jonathan			1						1		3				
Swansea	399	18	Luther	Joseph	2		1			2			1				6		
Swansea	399	34	Luther	Manson	2	1	1		1	1	1		1	1			9		
Swansea	399	21	Luther	Mary	2							1	1	1			5		
Swansea	403	27	Luther	Mathew				1						1			2		
Swansea	402	25	Luther	Mercy	1					2			1				4		
Swansea	402	3	Luther	Moses				1						1			2		
Swansea	399	33	Luther	Obadiah	1			1	1	1	1		1	1			7		
Swansea	403	25	Luther	Peleg	1	1		1		2	1		1				7		
Swansea	398	1	Luther	Philip	1			1		1			1				4		
Swansea	398	28	Luther	Richard				1			1	1		2			5		
Swansea	399	37	Luther	Samuel	2	1		1					2				6		
Swansea	402	11	Luther	Samuel		1		1		3	2		1				8		
Swansea	403	2	Luther	Samuel	1			1		4			1				7		
Swansea	401	27	Luther	Sarah			1						3	1			5		
Swansea	399	17	Luther	Silas		1		1			1		1	1			5		
Swansea	398	17	Luther	Simeon	1	1		1	1				1				5		
Swansea	402	16	Luther	Stephen	1	1			1		2	2		1			8		
Somerset	405	39	Luther	Theophelus	1			1		3			1				6		
Swansea	400	9	Luther	Theophilus	1	2		1		1	2		1				8		
Swansea	402	8	Luther	Theophilus	3	1		1		1	1		1				8		
Swansea	399	20	Luther	Upham		3	1	1		3			1				9		
Swansea	402	10	Luther	Wido									1	1			2		
Somerset	406	42	Luther	William				1						1			2		
Rehoboth	300	31	Lyon	Aaron			2			1		1					4		
Rehoboth	308	27	Lyon	Aaron		1	1			1	1	1					5		
Attleboro	320	67	Lyon	John		1			1	1			1				4		
Rehoboth	310	34	Lyon	Obediah	1		1						1				5		
Rehoboth	300	37	Lyon	Samuel		1		1		1	1	1					6		
Rehoboth	308	26	Lyon	Samuel Jr	3	1						1					5		
Rehoboth	300	32	Lyon	William		1							1				2		
Westport	334	15	Maccowen	Daniel	3			1						1			5		
Freetown	284	8	Mackson	Jonathan	2	1		1		2			1	1			8		
Rehoboth	311	23	Macliss	Thomas			1						1				2		
Taunton	367	23	Macomber	Abiather		1	1			3		1					6		
Taunton	364	42	Macomber	Abiel	1		1		2			2	1	1			8		
Westport	333	32	Macomber	Abiel 2d		1			1					1			3		
Westport	334	11	Macomber	Abiel Senr					1				2	1			4		
Westport	334	14	Macomber	Abigail			2					1	1	1			5		
Dartmouth	346	27	Macomber	Anson	3	1	1		2	1	1				12				
Westport	334	24	Macomber	Bethiah									1	1			2		
Westport	333	30	Macomber	Charles	1		1			3			1				6		
Dartmouth	347	17	Macomber	Constant	1			1					1		7				
Easton	391	44	Macomber	Daniel		1			1			1	1				4		
Rehoboth	311	31	Macomber	Elemuel		1	1				2						4		
Berkley	277	27	Macomber	Elijah	2		1		1	1		2	1				8		
Dartmouth	346	24	Macomber	Elijah	1			1	2			1	1		8				
Taunton	364	44	Macomber	Elijah		2			1					1			4		

TOWN	PG#	LN#	LAST NAME	FIRST NAME	FREE WHITE MALES under 10	10 to 16	16 to 26	26 to 45	45 and over	FREE WHITE FEMALES under 10	10 to 16	16 to 26	26 to 45	45 and over	TOTAL ALL OTHER	TOTAL SLAVES	TOTALS	DISTRICT/ TOWNSHIP	NOTES
Norton	382	41	Macomber	Ezra	1			1		3			1				6		
Westport	334	31	Macomber	George		1	1						1				4		
Westport	334	1	Macomber	Humphrey	2	1	1	1	1	1	1	1	1	1			11		
Taunton	364	43	Macomber	Ichabod	1				1			1	1				4		
Westport	334	30	Macomber	Isaac			1					1		1			3		
Berkley	277	30	Macomber	James					1				1				2		
Taunton	357	13	Macomber	James			1		1			1		1			4		
Berkley	280	3	Macomber	Joel	2			1		1		1					5		
Rehoboth	311	36	Macomber	John	2			1			2		1			6			
Taunton	358	35	Macomber	Jonathan	1		1		1	1	1		1				6		
Taunton	361	22	Macomber	Joshua Wms	2	1		1				2	1				8		
Westport	334	12	Macomber	Levy	2		1						1				4		
Westport	334	26	Macomber	Mary									1				1		
Taunton	357	19	Macomber	Nathan	1	1	1		1			2	1				7		
Westport	333	28	Macomber	Nathaniel	3	1			1	1	2		1				9		
Westport	334	32	Macomber	Noah	2	2			1			3	1				9		
Dartmouth	346	25	Macomber	Perry	1		1		2	2	1					9			
Westport	334	5	Macomber	Peter	1	1		1		1			1				5		
Taunton	365	2	Macomber	Rufus	2			1	1	1			1				6		
Freetown	293	13	Macomber	Samuel	1			1		1		1					4		
Westport	334	28	Macomber	Samuel	2	1	1		1	3	1		1				10		
Taunton	361	15	Macomber	Seth				1	1	1	2		1				5		
Taunton	356	18	Macomber	Stephen			1		1	1	1		1				5		
Berkley	278	1	Macomber	Venns	1		1			1							3		
Westport	333	31	Macomber	Wanton	1			1		3	1		1				7		
Berkley	278	23	Macomber	Wd Susan	1												2		
Westport	334	13	Macomber	Wesson	1		2		1	3	2	2	1				12		
Westport	334	2	Macomber	William 1st				1					1	1			3		
Westport	333	29	Macomber	William 2d			1	1	1			2	1	1			7		
Norton	382	38	Makepeace	David	1			1		1		1					4		
Mansfield	386	35	Makepeace	Isaac		2		1		5		1					9		
Norton	382	36	Makepeace	Lysander				1		3		1		1			6		
Norton	382	35	Makepeace	Masa		1					1	1		1			4		
Raynham	374	38	Makepeace	Seth	1	1		1		2			1				6		
Norton	382	37	Makepeace	William					1			3		1			5		
Raynham	376	35	Makepeace	William		1			1	1	1		1				5		
Raynham	376	36	Makepeace	William Junr	2			1					1				4		
Westport	334	22	Manchester	Archibald				1		1			1				3		
Westport	334	17	Manchester	Edward	3			1			2		1				7		
Westport	334	3	Manchester	Gilbert	2	1		1		3			1				8		
Westport	334	20	Manchester	James L. Son	1	1	1		1	1			1	1			7		
Westport	334	7	Manchester	James Point		1	1	1	1	1			1	1			7		
New Bedford	429	27	Manchester	Job				1				1		1			3		
Westport	334	21	Manchester	Joseph				1					1				2		
Westport	334	23	Manchester	Philip	2	2	3		1		1		1				10		
Somerset	407	19	Manchester	Stephen	3			1		1	1			3			9		
Westport	334	4	Manchester	Thomas				1				1	2				4		
Easton	391	41	Manley	Abiah			1					1					2		
Easton	391	42	Manley	Daniel	1			1		1		2					5		
Easton	391	35	Manley	David		1	1		1		1			1			5		
Easton	391	36	Manley	David Jr	1			1		1			1				4		
Easton	391	39	Manley	Seth					1			1		1			3		
Easton	391	40	Manley	Seth Jr	4			1		1			1				7		
Easton	391	37	Manley	William			2							1			3		
Attleboro	317	29	Mann	Newton	1	1		2		1	1		1				7		
Rehoboth	303	30	Marbel	Stephen				1		2	1	2				6			
Somerset	407	14	Marble	Benja		2			1			1		1			5		
Swansea	400	40	Marble	Benja	2	2		1	1	1		2		1			10		
Somerset	407	15	Marble	Elias	1		1					1					3		
Somerset	405	4	Marble	George	3	1	1	1			1		1				8		
Dighton	411	2	Marble	James				1				1					2		
Somerset	404	9	Marble	Joseph	3	1		1				1	1				7		
Somerset	404	30	Marble	Lloyd	1		1			1		1					3		
Somerset	408	22	Marble	Saml	1	2	1					1					5		
Somerset	404	25	Marble	Thomas	1			1			1		1				4		
Somerset	405	23	Marble	Thomas 2d	1	1		1		1	2		1				7		
Swansea	400	38	Marble	Wm	2			1		1			1				5		
Easton	392	3	March	Anthony											4		4		
Rehoboth	301	16	Marker	Burden			1	1		1	1	1				7			
Rehoboth	301	20	Marker	John				1			2		1			4			
Rehoboth	301	21	Marker	John Jun			1		2			1				6			
Rehoboth	305	30	Marten	Hail			1		2			1				7			
Rehoboth	303	4	Marten	Hezekiah	2	2		1		1	2	1	1			11			
Norton	382	39	Martin	Amos		2	2		1			2		1			8		
Swansea	403	41	Martin	Anna Wido							1		1				2		
Rehoboth	311	20	Martin	Asa	1		1		3	1		1				9			
Swansea	400	39	Martin	Benja		2	4			1		2		2			11		
Swansea	402	50	Martin	Benja				1	1					2			4		
Rehoboth	301	30	Martin	Calvin		1	1		3				1			7			
Rehoboth	306	38	Martin	Daniel		1		1					1			4			
Rehoboth	305	29	Martin	Edward	1			1					2			4			
Rehoboth	303	3	Martin	Ephraim	2	1	1		2	1			2			11			
Rehoboth	301	27	Martin	George W.		1			1	1			1			6			
New Bedford	429	10	Martin	Hannah											3		3		

TOWN	PG#	LN#	LAST NAME	FIRST NAME	M under 10	M 10 to 16	M 16 to 26	M 26 to 45	M 45 and over	F under 10	F 10 to 16	F 16 to 26	F 26 to 45	F 45 and over	TOTAL ALL OTHER	TOTAL SLAVES	TOTALS	DISTRICT/TOWNSHIP	NOTES
Rehoboth	298	15	Martin	James	1		1				1		1	1		5			
Swansea	396	17	Martin	James	1	2		1		2	2		1	1			10		
Attleboro	320	47	Martin	Job				1				2		1			4		
Swansea	400	32	Martin	Job	3			1			1		1				6		
Attleboro	318	64	Martin	John			2		1			1		1			5		
Rehoboth	308	34	Martin	John	1		1		3	1		1				9			
Swansea	400	33	Martin	John			1				1	1					3		
Swansea	403	42	Martin	Jonathan	1			1		1	1		1				5		
Rehoboth	302	5	Martin	Marther									1			1			
Swansea	403	40	Martin	Noble	2			1		1			1				5		
Swansea	403	43	Martin	Stephen				1		2			1				4		
Rehoboth	301	33	Martin	Sylvenus		1						1				2			
Rehoboth	301	31	Martin	Valentine		1		1	2			1				5			
Rehoboth	301	32	Martin	Valentine Jr		1					1	1				4			
Norton	382	40	Martin	William	2			1		2	2		1				8		
Freetown	281	12	Marvill	Charles	1		1	1		2			1				6		
Dighton	412	42	Masden	Hannah	1								1				2		
Swansea	403	16	Mason	Alexander		1			1	1	1		1				5		
Dighton	409	32	Mason	Amos	1	1	1		1	1	2			1			8		
Rehoboth	303	38	Mason	Avis		2							1			3			
Swansea	400	20	Mason	Barnabas		2			1	2	1		1				7		
New Bedford	429	25	Mason	Benajah				1			1		1				3		
Swansea	400	35	Mason	Benajah		1						1					2		
Swansea	401	6	Mason	Benja		1			1			1	1	1			5		
Taunton	367	11	Mason	Bethiah	2						1		1				4		
Rehoboth	314	6	Mason	Caleb				1				1	2			4			
Swansea	400	37	Mason	Caleb		1		1		1				1			4		
Swansea	400	36	Mason	Caleb Junr	4	2		1		1				1			9		
Swansea	402	46	Mason	Charles			1					1	1				3		
Swansea	400	16	Mason	Christopher		1			1		1		1				4		
Swansea	400	29	Mason	Daniel	1					2		1	1				6		
Rehoboth	314	5	Mason	David			1		2			1				5			
Swansea	398	43	Mason	David		3	3		1	4			1	1			13		
Swansea	400	17	Mason	Eber	1		1			1		1					4		
Swansea	403	49	Mason	Edward		3			1				1				5		
Rehoboth	304	26	Mason	Elisha	2	1	1	1	3	1		1	1			14			
Swansea	401	2	Mason	Ezra	4			1		2	2		2				11		
Freetown	292	19	Mason	Hezekiah	1		1	1						1			4		
Attleboro	320	37	Mason	Isaac	1		1	1		1		1		1			6		
Swansea	401	1	Mason	Isaac				1				2					3		
Swansea	401	3	Mason	Isaac Jur		1						1					2		
Rehoboth	314	4	Mason	James		1		1			1		2			5			
Swansea	404	1	Mason	James		1						1					2		
Swansea	400	41	Mason	Jeremiah	2	1		1		3	3		1				11		
Somerset	408	13	Mason	Job	3	1				1	1	1					8		
Swansea	402	45	Mason	Job		1	1	1			1	1					5		
Swansea	402	47	Mason	Joel Jr	1		1			1		1					4		
Attleboro	319	32	Mason	John	1			2		2	2		1				8		
Dighton	412	12	Mason	John	2			1		1		1					5		
Rehoboth	306	9	Mason	John	1			1	2	2	1					7			
Rehoboth	311	42	Mason	John	1			1	2	2	1					7			
Swansea	401	34	Mason	John	1		1					1					3		
Swansea	402	39	Mason	John Esqr		1		1		1			1	1			5		
Rehoboth	314	8	Mason	Jonathan	2		1		2			1				8			
Rehoboth	303	28	Mason	Joseph	1			1	1	2		1		1		10			
Swansea	402	44	Mason	Joseph	1	1	1	1		1	2		1				8		
Swansea	400	34	Mason	Joshua		1			1		1			2			5		
Swansea	400	15	Mason	Mary								1	1				2		
Swansea	403	50	Mason	Mary Jr Wido							1		1				2		
Swansea	402	26	Mason	Mehitable									1	1			2		
Rehoboth	314	7	Mason	Nathan			1	3		1		1	2			9			
Swansea	403	52	Mason	Noble	3	3		1		1	4		1				13		
Swansea	400	42	Mason	Peleg				1					2				3		
Taunton	368	13	Mason	Philip	1			1		1	1	2	1				7		
New Bedford	429	30	Mason	Reuben	1	1	1	1		1	2	1	1				9		
Swansea	400	46	Mason	Simeon				1						1			2		
Swansea	398	13	Mason	William		1		1		2	1		1				6		
Swansea	400	47	Mastin & Aldridge	Widos	2	1				2	1		1	2			9		
Swansea	402	23	Mathewson	Hannah											7		7		
Attleboro	321	38	Maxcy	Benja	3			1					1				5		
New Bedford	429	16	Maxfeld	Isaac		1				1			1				3		
New Bedford	429	17	Maxfeld	Joseph	3		1			1			1				6		
New Bedford	429	28	Maxfeld	Warren	1			1				1					3		
New Bedford	429	15	Maxfeld	Zadock		1	1		1		1	3		1			8		
Dartmouth	347	4	Maxfield	Abraham		1	1		1		1	1					7		
Dartmouth	347	2	Maxfield	David		1	1		4			1					7		
Dartmouth	346	33	Maxfield	Edmond		1	1	2			1		1				6		
Dartmouth	347	3	Maxfield	John			1					1					2		
Dartmouth	347	1	Maxfield	Timothy			1	1		1	3	1					8		
Dartmouth	346	34	Maxfield	Zadock		1		3		1		1	1				7		
Attleboro	322	55	May	Elisha		2	2	1				2		1			8		
Westport	334	6	Mayhew	Hilliard	1			1		1		1	1				5		

TOWN	PG#	LN#	LAST NAME	FIRST NAME	FWM under 10	FWM 10 to 16	FWM 16 to 26	FWM 26 to 45	FWM 45 and over	FWF under 10	FWF 10 to 16	FWF 16 to 26	FWF 26 to 45	FWF 45 and over	TOTAL ALL OTHER	TOTAL SLAVES	TOTALS	DISTRICT/ TOWNSHIP	NOTES
New Bedford	429	23	Mayhew	Jeremiah		1	1		1		1			1	1		6		
Westport	334	19	Mayhew	Jonathan		1							1				2		
Taunton	359	42	McChorter	John				1						1	1		3		
New Bedford	428	31	McKenzie	Martin	2			1					1				4		
New Bedford	431	1	McPherson	John		1	1	1		1		1					5		
New Bedford	429	26	Medar	William	1			1		2	1		1				6		
Rehoboth	300	30	Medbury	Abel		1		1		1		1					5		
Rehoboth	300	33	Medbury	Ebenezer	2		1	1	2			1					8		
Rehoboth	308	2	Medbury	Ebenezer			1										2		
Rehoboth	308	3	Medbury	Ebenezer 2nd	3		1		2			1					7		
Rehoboth	310	37	Medbury	John	3	1		1				1					9		
Rehoboth	311	43	Medbury	Nathan		1		3	1		2	2					10		
Rehoboth	311	45	Medbury	Nathaniel	1			1			1	1					4		
Rehoboth	311	44	Medbury	Siah	1		1		2	1	1						8		
Rehoboth	312	2	Medbury	Thomas	1	1	1					1					4		
New Bedford	429	12	Mendal	Ellis	2		1	1	2	1		1	1	1			10		
New Bedford	429	14	Mendal	Lemuel				1			1	1					3		
New Bedford	429	7	Mendal	Thomas	1	1	1	1			1		1				6		
New Bedford	429	31	Meranville	Simeon	2			1	4	2		1					10		
Freetown	284	1	Merrick	Isaac		1	2	1		2			1				7		
New Bedford	429	29	Merrihew	Peter	2			1	3			1	1				8		
Dartmouth	346	35	Michal	Elkanah			1		1			1					3		
Dartmouth	346	36	Michel	Nathan		1					1						3		
Freetown	286	17	Miles	Abigail Wid						2		1		1			4		
Westport	334	10	Milk	Job	2	1	1			1	1	1	1				8		
Westport	334	8	Milk	Lemuel		1		1			1		1				4		
Rehoboth	302	32	Millard	Aaron		1	1			1		1					7		
Rehoboth	302	44	Millard	Hezekiah		1	1					1					3		
Rehoboth	305	27	Millard	Jacob		1	1	1		1							4		
Rehoboth	302	4	Millard	Josiah		1					1						2		
Rehoboth	302	31	Millard	Spice		1	1	1	1	1	1	1					7		
Rehoboth	314	16	Miller	Clark		1					1						2		
Freetown	290	5	Miller	David		1	2		1	1	1	1					8		
Attleboro	318	55	Miller	Elkenah	1			1			1						3		
Rehoboth	310	36	Miller	Ellis	2		1		3		1						8		
Dighton	415	6	Miller	Henry		1					1						2		
Rehoboth	311	40	Miller	James				1		1	1	1					4		
Rehoboth	314	44	Miller	James 2nd		1		1		1		1					5		
Freetown	290	9	Miller	Jeb	2			1		2		1					6		
Dartmouth	347	10	Miller	John		1		2			1	1					7		
Rehoboth	305	32	Miller	John		1		1		2		1					5		
Rehoboth	311	39	Miller	John 2nd			1				1						2		
Rehoboth	314	17	Miller	Joseph		1		2		1							4		
Rehoboth	310	35	Miller	Mary	1		1	1	1		1	2					8		
Rehoboth	302	45	Miller	Nathaniel	2	1	1			1							7		
Rehoboth	298	14	Miller	Philop	2	1		1		2		1					8		
Freetown	286	32	Miller	Robert	1	1	1	1		1	1		1				7		
New Bedford	429	13	Miller	Robert		1		1				1					3		
Rehoboth	304	28	Miller	Samuel			1	2	1		1						8		
Rehoboth	304	29	Miller	Samuel 2nd		1		1		1		1					4		
Swansea	403	28	Miller	Widow		1						1					2		
Rehoboth	304	2	Miller	William			1		1		1						3		
Berkley	278	28	Mirich	Ebenezer	1			1		2	1	1	1				7		
Berkley	278	8	Mirich	Nathan				1					1				2		
Berkley	278	5	Mirich	Simeon	2			1		2		1					6		
Taunton	364	22	Mirick	Obed	1			1		1		1					4		
Easton	391	46	Mitchel	Abiel			1			1	3		1				6		
New Bedford	429	9	Mitchel	David				1			1		1				3		
Easton	392	2	Mitchel	Eliphalet	1			1				1					3		
New Bedford	429	8	Mitchel	Seth	1		1	1		1		1					5		
Easton	391	38	Mitchel	Thomas		3	1	1		4	1		1				11		
Easton	392	1	Mitchel	Timothy	1			1		1		1					4		
Easton	391	43	Monk	George	1		1		1				2				5		
Attleboro	318	30	Moore	Alice									2				2		
Attleboro	318	29	Moore	Joanna			1					2	1				4		
Rehoboth	315	4	Moore	Robert									3		3				
Norton	382	42	Morey	Cesar											8		8		
Norton	382	32	Morey	Ruhanah			1					2	1	1			5		
Norton	382	33	Morey	Samuel	1		1	1		1	1		2	1			8		
Somerset	406	46	Morrison	James				1		2		1					4		
Attleboro	322	18	Morse	Charles	1			1		1	1	1					5		
Attleboro	319	34	Morse	Elijah	1		2	1		1			1				6		
Easton	391	45	Morse	Ephraim	1		1			3		1					6		
Somerset	408	10	Morse	Joseph	3			1				1					5		
Attleboro	322	19	Morse	Stephen P	2		1					1					4		
Attleboro	322	16	Morse	William				1			1	1	1				4		
Attleboro	322	17	Morse	Wm Junr	1		1		1			1					4		
Freetown	293	15	Morse	Abraham	1		1	1		2			1				6		
New Bedford	429	6	Morton	Jethro	1	1		1		3	1		1				8		
Freetown	285	26	Morton	Job				1					1				2		
Freetown	285	25	Morton	Nathaniel		2		2		1			2				7		
Freetown	285	24	Morton	Nathaniel Jr		1		1		2	1						5		
New Bedford	429	5	Morton	Seth									3				4		
Westport	334	27	Mosher	Abigail						1		1	1	1			4		
New Bedford	429	11	Mosher	Abner	2		1				1						4		

TOWN	PG#	LN#	LAST NAME	FIRST NAME	FREE WHITE MALES					FREE WHITE FEMALES					TOTAL ALL OTHER	TOTAL SLAVES	TOTALS	DISTRICT/ TOWNSHIP	NOTES
					under 10	10 to 16	16 to 26	26 to 45	45 and over	under 10	10 to 16	16 to 26	26 to 45	45 and over					
Dartmouth	347	5	Mosher	Barney				1					1				2		
Dartmouth	347	6	Mosher	Barney Junr	4	1	1		1			1					9		
New Bedford	429	21	Mosher	Benjamin					1		1		1				3		
Westport	334	25	Mosher	Brice	1		1			1		1					4		
Dartmouth	346	28	Mosher	Ebenezer		1		1		1		1					5		
Westport	334	16	Mosher	Edmond		1	1		1	2			1				6		
New Bedford	429	18	Mosher	Elihu			2		1	1		1	1				6		
Dartmouth	347	15	Mosher	Elijah		1						1					4		
Dartmouth	346	32	Mosher	Elizabeth								1	2				4		
Westport	334	33	Mosher	Ephraim	1		1					1		1			4		
Dartmouth	347	12	Mosher	George	1			1			1		1				4		
Dartmouth	347	7	Mosher	Hannah								1	1				2		
Dartmouth	347	16	Mosher	Isaac		1		1		1							4		
Dartmouth	347	11	Mosher	Jesse	1			1		1		1					4		
Dartmouth	346	30	Mosher	Jethrow		1					1						3		
Dartmouth	347	13	Mosher	John	2	1		1	1	2		1					10		
Westport	334	9	Mosher	John				1				1	1				3		
Dartmouth	347	14	Mosher	John Junr		1			1			1					4		
Westport	334	18	Mosher	Joshua	1	1		1		3		1					8		
Dartmouth	347	8	Mosher	Lemuel		2		1		1		1					5		
Dartmouth	346	29	Mosher	Maxon	1	1		1		1	1		1				7		
New Bedford	429	19	Mosher	Phillip	2			1		1			1		1		6		
Dartmouth	346	26	Mosher	Ruben		1				1							2		
New Bedford	429	24	Mosher	Ruth									1				1		
New Bedford	429	20	Mosher	Samuel	1			1		3		1	1				7		
Dartmouth	346	31	Mosher	Stephen			1			2		1					4		
Westport	334	29	Mosher	Wesson				1		3		1					5		
Rehoboth	314	46	Moss	Pero											5		5		
Dartmouth	347	9	Mott	Thomas			1	1	1		1	1	1				6		
Rehoboth	305	41	Moulton	Chase		1	1		2	1	1						8		
Rehoboth	306	6	Moulton	Stephen	2	2	1			1		1					8		
Rehoboth	304	41	Moulton	William	1		1		2	1		1					7		
Attleboro	321	52	Mowey	James	1		1			1							3		
Rehoboth	312	1	Munro	Allen	1		1		1	1		1					6		
Rehoboth	306	37	Munro	Benjamin		2	1	1				1					6		
Norton	382	34	Munro	Nathaniel	2			1		2				1			6		
Swansea	402	32	Munro	Stephen	1	2			1	1				1			6		
Swansea	399	12	Munro	Stephen 2d		1	1					1					3		
Rehoboth	311	46	Mur	Nathan		1	1	1					1				4		
New Bedford	429	22	Myrick	Mathew	1			1				1					3		
Rehoboth	300	13	Nash	Jonathan		1		1			1						4		
New Bedford	429	42	Nash	Simeon	1	2			1		2		1				7		
Taunton	371	11	Neal	George				1		1			1				3		
Somerset	404	32	Neel	James	1	2		1		1		1					6		
Norton	382	48	Newcomb	Asa	1		1	1		1			1				5		
Norton	382	49	Newcomb	John	2	1	1		2	2	1	2	1	1			13		
Mansfield	386	37	Newcomb	Jonathan			3		2	1		1		3			10		
Norton	382	45	Newcomb	Joseph		2			1			1	1				5		
Norton	382	46	Newcomb	Josiah	1	1		1				1	1				5		
Norton	382	47	Newcomb	Richard	1	1		1		2		1	3	1			10		
Norton	382	44	Newcomb	Samuel				1					1				2		
Norton	382	43	Newcomb	Silvester	1			1		2			2				6		
Attleboro	322	38	Newel	Samuel		3	1	2		1		1	2	1			11		
Attleboro	322	37	Newel	Samuel Junr	2		1				1	1					5		
Berkley	276	13	Newhall	Darius	1	1	1		1	2	2		1				9		
Berkley	276	12	Newhall	Nehemiah		1		1				1	1				4		
Berkley	276	14	Newhall	Nehemiah Jr	3		1	1				1					6		
Norton	383	5	Newland	David	1			1		3		1					6		
Norton	383	3	Newland	Enos	1			1		2		1					5		
Mansfield	386	36	Newland	Jacob		2		2		1	1		1	1			8		
Norton	383	1	Newland	Jeremiah	1		1	1				2	1				6		
Norton	383	2	Newland	Jonathan				1				1	1				3		
New Bedford	429	44	Newport	Prince									1		1		2		
Taunton	371	3	Newton	Richard	1			1		2			1				5		
Berkley	280	22	Nicholas	Aaron				1		2	1	2	1				7		
Berkley	280	9	Nicholas	Edward				1					1				2		
Freetown	282	13	Nicholas	Eleazer	1	2		2		2			3				10		
Berkley	280	21	Nicholas	Hannah Wid									1	1			2		
Berkley	280	6	Nicholas	James		1	2	1				2		1			7		
Berkley	279	24	Nicholas	Joseph	1			1		1		1					4		
Rehoboth	304	30	Nichols	Israel		1		1			1						4		
Rehoboth	304	31	Nichols	Israel Jun		1	1				1						6		
Rehoboth	304	33	Nichols	Joseph	1		1				1						3		
Easton	392	4	Niles	Elijah	2			1		1	1		2				7		
Dighton	412	28	Norton	Benja		1				1		1					3		
New Bedford	429	37	Norton	Constant		1		1		2			1				5		
Somerset	407	17	Norton	Elijah	1			1					1				3		
New Bedford	429	32	Norton	Hannah		1					1	1	1				4		
Rehoboth	308	41	Norton	John	1		1		2				1				6		
Attleboro	319	26	Norton	Thoms	2	2	2		1			1		1			9		
Norton	383	4	Norton	William				1				1	1				3		
Raynham	373	12	Noyes	Samuel	3	1		1		1		1	1				7		
Rehoboth	305	12	Numan	Daniel			1		2								5		

125

TOWN	PG#	LN#	LAST NAME	FIRST NAME	FREE WHITE MALES					FREE WHITE FEMALES					TOTAL ALL OTHER	TOTAL SLAVES	TOTALS	DISTRICT/ TOWNSHIP	NOTES
					under 10	10 to 16	16 to 26	26 to 45	45 and over	under 10	10 to 16	16 to 26	26 to 45	45 and over					
Rehoboth	305	11	Numan	David			1		2			1					4		
Rehoboth	308	4	Numan	David 2nd		2	1					1					6		
Rehoboth	314	11	Numan	Jesse		1	1	1	1	1	1	1					7		
Rehoboth	310	23	Numan	Nathan			1		1			1					5		
Rehoboth	305	10	Numan	Samuel		1		1			1	1					4		
New Bedford	429	41	Nye	Barnabas		1		1				3		1			6		
New Bedford	429	34	Nye	Daniel		1		1				1					3		
New Bedford	429	39	Nye	Jonathan	1	1		1		4	2	1					10		
New Bedford	429	33	Nye	Mary						1	1	1					3		
New Bedford	429	43	Nye	Nathan	1		1		1			1		1			5		
New Bedford	429	40	Nye	Obed		1		1				2		1	1		6		
New Bedford	429	36	Nye	Stephen	1			1		1		1					4		
New Bedford	429	35	Nye	Thomas	2			1				2	1				6		
New Bedford	429	38	Nye	Thomas Junr	2	1		1		3	1	1					9		
Swansea	398	23	Obrian	John	1	1	3		1	1	1		1				9		
New Bedford	429	45	Onan	John			2		1	1		1					5		
New Bedford	430	2	Onan	Joshua			1					1					2		
New Bedford	430	1	Onan	Simeon		1		1			1		2				5		
Rehoboth	308	5	Ormsbee	Abraham Jr		1	1		2	2		1					9		
Rehoboth	305	22	Ormsbee	Daniel		1		1		2	1	1					7		
Rehoboth	306	10	Ormsbee	Luis	2		1			1		1					8		
Attleboro	321	37	Orne	James Junr			1			2			1				4		
Rehoboth	301	39	Ornsbee	Abraham		1		1			1		1				4		
Rehoboth	301	37	Ornsbee	Benjamin			1		1			1					3		
New Bedford	430	3	Ornsby	Brownell	2			1	1			1					5		
Mansfield	386	38	Osgood	John				1					1				2		
Taunton	370	36	Owen	Sarah								1	1				2		
New Bedford	430	47	Packard	Abijah		1	1			1		1					4		
Easton	392	9	Packard	Barnabas	2	2		1		3		1					9		
Easton	392	11	Packard	Calvin	1	1		1		1	1	1					6		
Easton	392	25	Packard	James	2			1	1			1	2				7		
Easton	392	20	Packard	Jedidiah	1	1		1		3		1					7		
Easton	392	21	Packard	Jedidiah 2d		1											1		
Dartmouth	347	22	Packard	Joel	1		1			1		1					4		
Easton	392	5	Packard	Joseph				1					1				2		
Freetown	282	3	Paddock	Josiah			2		1			1					4		
Taunton	357	1	Padelford	David	3			1		1			2				7		
Taunton	361	36	Padelford	Edward		2		1		1	1		2				7		
Taunton	361	40	Padelford	James	3			1		1	2	1					8		
Taunton	361	38	Padelford	Jonathan		1			1			3	1				6		
Taunton	362	4	Padelford	Joseph	2			1		2	3	1					9		
Taunton	361	41	Padelford	Joshua	1	1	1	1		1			1	1			7		
Taunton	361	34	Padelford	Philip	1	1		1	1	2	1		1		3		11		
Taunton	362	37	Padelford	Solomon	3			1		2	1		1				8		
Taunton	362	1	Padelford	Zachariah				1					1				2		
Taunton	359	17	Padilford	John	3		1	1				1	1				7		
Taunton	361	20	Padilford	Peleg	1	1	2	2	1			1	1	1			10		
Dartmouth	347	27	Page	Ebenezar									1		1		2		
Taunton	366	2	Pain	David	2			1			1		1				5		
Freetown	293	24	Pain	Ebenezer 2d	1			1		1			1				4		
Freetown	291	12	Pain	Gilford				1		1			1				3		
Freetown	291	14	Pain	Ichabod	1			1				1					3		
Freetown	294	10	Pain	Job			2	1			1	1	1				6		
Mansfield	387	6	Pain	Joel	2	1				1	2		1				8		
Freetown	290	20	Pain	John				1			1		1	1			4		
Mansfield	386	39	Pain	John		1		1	1	2		1		1			7		
Freetown	290	27	Pain	John 2d			1	1				1		1			4		
Rehoboth	312	3	Pain	Jonathan	1			1		1	2		1				7		
Freetown	291	11	Pain	Joseph	1	1			1	2			1	1			7		
Freetown	291	3	Pain	Mary Wid	1	1	1					1		1			5		
Rehoboth	312	6	Pain	Nathaniel			1						1	1			3		
Rehoboth	312	8	Pain	Nathaniel Jr	1			1		2	2		1				9		
Rehoboth	312	7	Pain	Pelig	1		1	2		2	1		1				8		
Freetown	294	13	Pain	Warden	1	1			1	2		2		2			9		
Freetown	282	11	Paine	Ebenezer	1	2	1		1	1	1	2		1			10		
Dartmouth	347	31	Palmer	Abigail							2		1				4		
Westport	335	14	Palmer	Henry	2			1				1					4		
Rehoboth	301	6	Palmer	John			1		1			1					4		
Westport	335	11	Palmer	John			1	1	1			1	1				5		
Norton	383	16	Palmer	Joseph		1		1		3			1				6		
Dighton	412	41	Palmer	Mary		1						1					2		
Westport	334	35	Palmer	Mary									1				1		
Somerset	404	39	Palmer	Wido		1				1	2		1				5		
Dartmouth	347	37	Parce	Clothier		1		1					1		3				
Norton	383	6	Parker	Daniel		1	1		1		1	1	2	1			8		
Freetown	293	10	Parker	Elijah	2	2	2	1		2	1		1		1		12		
New Bedford	430	29	Parker	Elventon				1									1		
Westport	335	1	Parker	J. Avery	1	1				3	1		1				8		
New Bedford	430	39	Parker	Jonathan	3			1		1			1				6		
New Bedford	431	14	Parker	Nathan		1				1		1					3		
New Bedford	431	9	Parker	William	2	1	2		1	2			1				9		
New Bedford	430	12	Parker	Zalmena			1										1		
Attleboro	319	51	Parmenter	Caleb	1	1	2			1			1				6		
Freetown	285	29	Parris	Desire		1	1					1		1			4		
Berkley	278	27	Parris	Olive	1							1					2		

126

TOWN	PG#	LN#	LAST NAME	FIRST NAME	M under 10	M 10 to 16	M 16 to 26	M 26 to 45	M 45 and over	F under 10	F 10 to 16	F 16 to 26	F 26 to 45	F 45 and over	TOTAL ALL OTHER	TOTAL SLAVES	TOTALS	DISTRICT/TOWNSHIP	NOTES
Norton	383	7	Pattin	John				2	1				2				5		
Taunton	364	37	Paul	Edward	2	1	3		1	2	1	2	1				13		
Taunton	364	39	Paul	Jeremiah	1	1	1	1		2		1	1				8		
Dighton	410	21	Paul	Lemuel	1	2		1		3	1		1				9		
Dighton	415	10	Paul	Peter	3	2		1		1	1		1				9		
Dighton	410	17	Paul	Richard	2	1		1					1				5		
Taunton	364	38	Paul	Seth				1						1			2		
Dighton	410	6	Paul	William	3	1			1	3	1	3		1			13		
Dighton	410	19	Paul	Zebedee			1						1	1			3		
Berkley	279	4	Paull	Benjamin	3	1			1		1	1	1				8		
Berkley	278	17	Paull	Ebenezer	1			1	1			4	1	1			9		
Berkley	278	11	Paull	Ebenezer 2d			2		1		2	2		1			8		
Berkley	279	8	Paull	Isaac	2			1		3	2		1	1			10		
Berkley	279	10	Paull	Israel		1	1	1		3	1	1	1				9		
Berkley	277	8	Paull	Jacob	1			1		1		1					4		
Berkley	279	7	Paull	James	2		1	1		2	3	1	1				11		
Berkley	277	25	Paull	John 1st					1	1				1			3		
Berkley	277	17	Paull	John 2d					1	2	1			2			6		
Berkley	278	9	Paull	Joseph		1		1				2	1				5		
Berkley	277	26	Paull	Roger	1			1		4			1				7		
Berkley	279	5	Paull	Samuel	2		1	1		2	2		2				10		
Dartmouth	347	26	Peabody	Daniel	1		1				1	1	1				5		
Dartmouth	347	25	Peabody	Peleg	1							1					2		
New Bedford	430	42	Pearce	Cesar											6		6		
Swansea	403	36	Pearce	David		1	1	1		2	1		1				7		
Swansea	403	39	Pearce	David Junr		1	1	1		3		1					6		
Attleboro	318	50	Pearce	Ezekiel		1		1			2		1				5		
Attleboro	322	29	Pearce	Jeremiah			1		1			1					3		
Swansea	401	5	Pearce	Job	1			1					1				3		
New Bedford	431	11	Pearce	Joseph		1	2	1		3	1	1	1				10		
Swansea	403	37	Pearce	Martin			1			2			1				4		
Swansea	400	45	Pearce	Philip	1	1	1		1	2	3		1				10		
Rehoboth	305	3	Pears	Comfort		1				1		1					6		
Rehoboth	302	23	Pears	Ebenezer		2		3		2		1					9		
Rehoboth	303	29	Pears	Henery	1		1	1		1	2		1				8		
Rehoboth	298	28	Pears	Isaac	1		1	3		1	1	1	1				12		
Rehoboth	303	2	Pears	Israel	2		1		1		2	1					8		
Rehoboth	301	24	Pears	James			1				1						6		
Rehoboth	305	1	Pears	John		1	2			1	1	1					7		
Rehoboth	303	24	Pears	Joseph	1	1		1	1	2	2	1					11		
Rehoboth	304	45	Pears	Joseph 2d	1		1		1			1	1				7		
Rehoboth	301	46	Pears	Nathan		1					1						3		
Rehoboth	301	45	Pears	Nathaniel	1			1	1								3		
Rehoboth	303	27	Pears	Nathaniel 2nd	1		1		1	1		1					7		
Rehoboth	298	25	Pears	Peleg	2	1	1		1	1	1		1				10		
Rehoboth	303	21	Pears	Preserved	1		1		2	3		1					10		
Rehoboth	305	33	Pears	Richard			1			1	1	1	1				5		
Rehoboth	305	34	Pears	Robert		1		1		1							3		
Rehoboth	302	35	Pears	Samuel	2		1	1				1					8		
Rehoboth	299	19	Pears	Stephen		1		1		1		1					4		
Rehoboth	303	15	Pearse	Barnard	2		1		1			1					6		
Rehoboth	303	13	Pearse	Joshua		1		2	1	2	2		3				12		
Rehoboth	303	14	Pearse	Leonard		1		1				1					4		
Rehoboth	305	4	Pearse	Noah			1	1		1		1					5		
Rehoboth	305	5	Pearse	Squeir	1		1		3		2	1					9		
New Bedford	430	11	Pease	Abner			1				1	1					3		
Rehoboth	314	14	Peck	Abiah			1						1				3		
Rehoboth	301	34	Peck	Allen		2	1	1			2		1				9		
Rehoboth	299	27	Peck	Ambrose			1			1		1					3		
Swansea	403	5	Peck	Ambrose		2	1		1	2	2	1		1			10		
Rehoboth	310	40	Peck	Charles	1			1		1		1					5		
Rehoboth	312	9	Peck	Comfort		1		1			1	1					5		
Rehoboth	312	11	Peck	Comfort Jr	2		1		3			1					8		
Rehoboth	312	4	Peck	Cyrrel	3		1		2		1	1					10		
Rehoboth	312	13	Peck	Darius		1		1			1						3		
Rehoboth	310	39	Peck	Ebenezer	1			1		1			1				4		
Rehoboth	314	9	Peck	Ebenezer 2nd						1							1		
Rehoboth	302	30	Peck	Ebenzer 2nd			1	1	2	1							6		
Rehoboth	311	4	Peck	Edmond		1						1					5		
Rehoboth	299	15	Peck	Elemuel		1						1					2		
Attleboro	319	63	Peck	Elizabeth									3				3		
Rehoboth	301	29	Peck	George		1	1		3			1					6		
Rehoboth	298	8	Peck	Gideon 2d	1			1	3	1		1					9		
Rehoboth	299	26	Peck	Gideon 2d			1	1				1					4		
Rehoboth	307	31	Peck	Henery		2	1	1		2	1		1				8		
Rehoboth	306	42	Peck	James	1			1	1	1		1					7		
Rehoboth	312	10	Peck	James			1		2			1					6		
Attleboro	322	47	Peck	Jeremiah	3	3	1			1	2	1	1				12		
Rehoboth	306	44	Peck	Jethnial		1	1	1				1	1				5		
Rehoboth	310	41	Peck	John	1	2											4		
Attleboro	319	64	Peck	Jonathan	1			1	1			1		1			5		
Rehoboth	298	23	Peck	Jonathan		2		1					1				4		
Rehoboth	298	24	Peck	Jonathan Jr	1	1	1		3	1		1					9		

TOWN	PG#	LN#	HEADS OF HOUSEHOLD LAST NAME	FIRST NAME	FREE WHITE MALES under 10	10 to 16	16 to 26	26 to 45	45 and over	FREE WHITE FEMALES under 10	10 to 16	16 to 26	26 to 45	45 and over	TOTAL ALL OTHER	TOTAL SLAVES	TOTALS	DISTRICT/ TOWNSHIP	NOTES
Rehoboth	301	36	Peck	Joseph		1							1				5		
Rehoboth	304	5	Peck	Josiah				1		1	1	1					4		
Rehoboth	304	6	Peck	Josiah Jr			1		1			1					4		
Rehoboth	308	9	Peck	Marry									1				1		
Rehoboth	299	14	Peck	Mary				1					1				2		
Rehoboth	304	13	Peck	Nicholas		3		1					1				5		
Rehoboth	306	41	Peck	Oliver	2	1		1	1			1	1				9		
Rehoboth	309	8	Peck	Otis	1	1		1		2	3		1				9		
Swansea	403	32	Peck	Peleg		3			1	1	2		1				8		
Swansea	403	31	Peck	Peleg Junr			1			1		1					3		
Rehoboth	298	42	Peck	Phillip	1	1	1	1		1	3		1				9		
Rehoboth	301	28	Peck	Samuel	1		1	1			1		1				5		
Rehoboth	312	12	Peck	Solmomon	1		1		2			1					6		
Rehoboth	311	5	Peck	Stephen			1			1			1				3		
Rehoboth	310	42	Peck	Thomas			1		3				1				8		
Swansea	403	30	Peck	Thomas	3			1						1			5		
Westport	335	25	Peck	James			1			2		1					4		
Rehoboth	302	33	Peckam	Aaron	2			1	1	1	2	1	1				14		
Dartmouth	347	38	Peckham	Bristol										3			3		
Dartmouth	347	28	Peckham	Caleb				1		2	3	1	1				11		
Westport	335	18	Peckham	Elizabeth		2							1				3		
Dartmouth	347	29	Peckham	Isaiah			1					1					2		
New Bedford	430	18	Peckham	Isaiah	2			1		3			1				7		
Dartmouth	347	30	Peckham	James		1		3				1					6		
New Bedford	431	3	Peckham	John			1				1		1	1	1		5		
New Bedford	430	35	Peckham	John Jur	1		2			1		1					5		
Westport	335	7	Peckham	Jonathan		1		1		2		2	2	1			7		
New Bedford	430	19	Peckham	Lucy										2			2		
New Bedford	431	4	Peckham	Mary										1			1		
New Bedford	430	20	Peckham	Peleg			1	1						1			3		
New Bedford	431	5	Peckham	William	1		1			2			1	1			6		
Freetown	288	5	Peckum	Barbor	1			1		2	2		1				7		
Taunton	360	5	Pedelford	Seth		1	1		1	1	2	3	1		1		11		
Rehoboth	312	14	Peeks	Thomas		1					1						3		
Somerset	404	1	Peirce	Asa	3	1		1		1	1	1	1				9		
Freetown	283	14	Peirce	Bethnel	3	2	1	1		1			1				9		
Dighton	409	10	Peirce	Caleb	1	2	1	1			1	1					7		
Somerset	406	30	Peirce	David				1		1	4			2			8		
Somerset	406	33	Peirce	David Jun	3			1		2			1				7		
Berkley	280	25	Peirce	Ebenezer				1					1				2		
Freetown	283	4	Peirce	Ebenezer		1		1					1				3		
Somerset	406	31	Peirce	Ebenezer	1			1		1			1				4		
Berkley	280	26	Peirce	Ebenezer Junr	2	1		1		2			1				7		
Berkley	281	10	Peirce	Elisha			1	1						1			3		
Swansea	403	21	Peirce	Fanny						1	1		1				3		
Dighton	412	18	Peirce	Holmes		1	1			1		1					4		
Dighton	412	14	Peirce	Jabez		1		1						1			3		
Somerset	406	29	Peirce	James		1		1		5			1				8		
Dighton	414	6	Peirce	John	2	1		1		2	2		1	1			10		
Somerset	406	32	Peirce	Jonathan				1									1		
Somerset	406	34	Peirce	Jonathan 3d	3			1					1				5		
Somerset	406	26	Peirce	Jonathan Junr		1	1		1	2	2			1			8		
Freetown	286	21	Peirce	Lydia Wid						1			1				2		
Swansea	401	23	Peirce	Martha										1			1		
Somerset	404	2	Peirce	Mial				1						1			2		
Swansea	401	29	Peirce	Mial		3		1		3	2		1				10		
Swansea	402	40	Peirce	Nathan		1		1					1				3		
Dighton	414	38	Peirce	Nathll	3	1		1		2			1				8		
Somerset	406	40	Peirce	Obadiah	2			1		3			1				7		
Dighton	412	15	Peirce	Thomas	1			1		1		1					4		
Somerset	406	28	Peirce	Wido Hannah						1	5		1				7		
Dighton	413	19	Pells	George	1	1	2		1	1	2		1				9		
Dighton	415	15	Pendleton	Gidion	1	1	1		1	2			1				7		
Norton	383	11	Penno	Peter	2		3			2	1	1		1			11		
Mansfield	387	3	Penny	John				1						1			2		
Freetown	294	15	Perkens	David	1			1		4			1				7		
Dartmouth	347	23	Perkins	Benjamin		1		5				1					7		
Taunton	362	24	Perkins	David Junior	1			1		2			1	1			6		
New Bedford	431	12	Perkins	Henry	2			1		3	2	4		1			13		
Swansea	398	35	Pero	Tom and											6		6		
Westport	335	29	Peron	William											5		5		
Rehoboth	308	6	Perren	Daniel			1		1			1					4		
Rehoboth	308	7	Perren	Zepheriah Sen			1	1	3			1	1				7		
Rehoboth	312	43	Perrin	Thomas			1		1			1					7		
Rehoboth	312	5	Perry	Constant	1		1	1		1	1						6		
Rehoboth	311	24	Perry	David Jr	1	2		2		1	1		2				9		
New Bedford	430	44	Perry	Ebenezer	1			1	1		1		1				5		
Dighton	413	28	Perry	Edward				1					1	1			3		
Attleboro	320	33	Perry	Ephraim	1		*	*		*	*	1					2		
Rehoboth	306	45	Perry	Ezra		2		1	1	2	2		1				9		
Rehoboth	311	30	Perry	Ezra		1		1			1		1				5		
Rehoboth	306	46	Perry	Ezra Jr	1		1		1	1		1					8		
New Bedford	430	4	Perry	Freeman	2			1		1		1	1				6		

128

TOWN	PG#	LN#	LAST NAME	FIRST NAME	FREE WHITE MALES					FREE WHITE FEMALES					TOTAL ALL OTHER	TOTAL SLAVES	TOTALS	DISTRICT/ TOWNSHIP	NOTES
					under 10	10 to 16	16 to 26	26 to 45	45 and over	under 10	10 to 16	16 to 26	26 to 45	45 and over					
Norton	383	10	Perry	Ichabod		1	1		1	2		1		1			7		
Attleboro	320	32	Perry	Isaac		1		1				1		2			5		
Attleboro	323	8	Perry	Jacob	1		1	1		1	1			2			7		
Easton	392	12	Perry	James			2	1			1			1			5		
Easton	392	13	Perry	James Jur				1		2		1	2	1			7		
Rehoboth	302	37	Perry	Jesse		3	1	1		2		1	1				9		
Rehoboth	310	38	Perry	John	1		1			1	2		1				6		
Attleboro	323	13	Perry	Joseph	1		1			1	1	1					5		
Dighton	415	17	Perry	Joseph	1		1	1		1		3		1			8		
Rehoboth	301	5	Perry	Joseph		1	1			1			1				5		
Taunton	365	14	Perry	Joseph	1		1			2		1					5		
Rehoboth	306	40	Perry	Josial		2	1	1		2	1		1				8		
New Bedford	430	28	Perry	Lemuel		1		1				3	2				7		
Dighton	410	30	Perry	Luther		1						1					2		
Norton	383	9	Perry	Nathan		2	2	1		1	2	2		1			11		
Rehoboth	300	34	Perry	Noah	1	3	1				1	2					8		
Dighton	412	23	Perry	Saml Junr	2		1	1		2		1					7		
Easton	392	10	Perry	Samuel	2			1			1			1			5		
New Bedford	431	6	Perry	Samuel				1					1	1	1		4		
New Bedford	431	7	Perry	Samuel Jun	2		1	1		1	1	1					7		
Dighton	414	27	Perry	Simeon		2		1		1	2			1			7		
Dighton	413	29	Perry	Sylvester	2	1		1		2	1	1					8		
Rehoboth	306	39	Perry	Timothy		1		1		1	1	1					5		
Rehoboth	303	16	Perry	William			1			1		2		1			5		
Rehoboth	301	12	Pettis	Ezekiel		1	1	1					1				5		
Rehoboth	306	43	Pettis	Ezekiel		1	1	1					1				5		
Somerset	405	11	Pettis	Henry	1		1			1	2	1					7		
Dartmouth	347	18	Petty	David			1	1		1		1					7		
Westport	335	2	Petty	Isaac		2	2		1	1	1			1			8		
Westport	335	17	Petty	James		1		1		2	2			1			7		
Westport	335	19	Petty	John	3		1			1			1				6		
Westport	335	24	Petty	Joshua	1	2	1	1		2	1	1	1				10		
Westport	335	23	Petty	Rebeccah		1				1		1	1	1			5		
Westport	335	20	Petty	Sarah						2		1		1			4		
Dartmouth	347	42	Petty	Simpson	1		1			1	1	1					5		
Westport	335	21	Petty	William			1	4		1		4		1			11		
Westport	335	28	Philips	Edward		1				1	1						3		
Dartmouth	347	39	Philips	Ira	2		1	2		1		1					9		
Dighton	410	15	Phillips	Abiezer		2	1			1	2		1				7		
Dighton	413	13	Phillips	Abiezer Jr	2		1			3	3	1					10		
Berkley	281	9	Phillips	Abigal Wid		1							1				2		
Easton	392	23	Phillips	Asa		1	1	1		1		1		2			7		
Dighton	410	12	Phillips	Baylies		1						1					2		
Taunton	360	12	Phillips	Charles	1		1			4			1				7		
Norton	383	15	Phillips	Daniel		2		1				1		1			5		
Berkley	281	7	Phillips	Ebenezer	1			1									2		
Freetown	294	9	Phillips	Ebenezer Junr			2			1				1			4		
Taunton	367	2	Phillips	Edward	1	1	1			3			1				7		
Taunton	361	7	Phillips	Eleazer	1		1			1			1				4		
Dighton	409	27	Phillips	Elizt Wido	2	1	1			1	2	1		1			9		
Dighton	410	16	Phillips	Ephraim	2	1	1			1		1		1			7		
Easton	392	24	Phillips	Jacob				1				2	2	1			6		
Taunton	358	5	Phillips	Jacob	1	2	1			1		2	1				8		
Berkley	281	8	Phillips	John	1		1						2				4		
Mansfield	387	4	Phillips	John		2		1		1				1			5		
Taunton	356	8	Phillips	Lucy Wido	1	1								1			3		
Berkley	276	30	Phillips	Mary Wid									1				1		
Berkley	277	7	Phillips	Nathaniel		1		1				1					3		
Freetown	284	29	Phillips	Peirce	2	2	1			2		1	1				9		
New Bedford	430	27	Phillips	Peter				1					1				2		
Berkley	275	11	Phillips	Phebe									1				1		
Berkley	276	28	Phillips	Ralph	1			1		1	1		1				5		
Berkley	279	31	Phillips	Ralph Jun	2	1						1					4		
Swansea	401	12	Phillips	Ruth									1	1			2		
Dighton	410	11	Phillips	Saml	1		2	1		1			1				7		
Berkley	276	29	Phillips	Samuel		2	1			2	2		1				8		
Easton	392	22	Phillips	Silas		2	1			1	1	1					6		
Freetown	282	14	Pickens	Samuel	2	1	1			2	1	1	1				9		
New Bedford	430	23	Pickhens	John									1				1		
New Bedford	430	24	Pickhens	Thaddeus	1		1						1				3		
Rehoboth	300	20	Pidge	Benjamin	2	3	1	1		1	1	1	2				12		
Attleboro	318	48	Pidge	David	1	1	1		1	2	3			1			10		
Taunton	358	19	Pierce	Elisha		2		1		1	1	1		1			7		
Taunton	364	29	Pierce	Lydia Wido			1							1			2		
Taunton	360	16	Pierce	Samuel			1						1				2		
Taunton	364	30	Pierce	Simeon			1						1				2		
Freetown	292	21	Pigesley	Joseph	2	3		1		2	2	1	1				12		
Freetown	291	27	Pigesley	Robert	2		1			1	2	1					7		
Attleboro	319	55	Pike	Moses			1	1		2		1		1			6		
New Bedford	430	17	Pinkham	Andrew	1		1						1				3		
Attleboro	322	23	Pitcher	Keziah									2				2		
Dighton	410	13	Pitts	Philip	1		1			2			1				5		
Taunton	358	4	Pitts	Rhoba Wido		2	1					1		1			5		

TOWN	PG#	LN#	LAST NAME	FIRST NAME	FREE WHITE MALES					FREE WHITE FEMALES					TOTAL ALL OTHER	TOTAL SLAVES	TOTALS	DISTRICT/ TOWNSHIP	NOTES
					under 10	10 to 16	16 to 26	26 to 45	45 and over	under 10	10 to 16	16 to 26	26 to 45	45 and over					
Somerset	404	21	Place	James	1			1		1	1		1				5		
New Bedford	430	46	Plumb	Joshua	1			1		1			2				5		
Taunton	369	29	Pollard	John	1	2			1	2	1		1				8		
Raynham	376	9	Pollard	John Junior	1		1						1				3		
Dighton	410	43	Pool	Isaac	4		2		1	2	2	3		2			16		
Easton	392	19	Pool	John	2			1		1		2					6		
Dighton	410	44	Pool	Jonah				1		2			1	1			5		
Dartmouth	347	40	Pool	Safinas	2		1			2		1			9				
Easton	392	6	Pool	Samuel	1	1	1		1				1	1			6		
New Bedford	430	31	Pope	Ebenezer				1					1				2		
New Bedford	430	8	Pope	Edmund			1		1	1	2		1				6		
New Bedford	431	2	Pope	Edward		2	1		2		3		2	2			12		
New Bedford	430	16	Pope	Ephraim				1				1					2		
New Bedford	430	7	Pope	Freeman	2		1					2	1				6		
New Bedford	430	26	Pope	Jonathan	1		1	1		2		1					6		
New Bedford	430	32	Pope	Lemuel			1										1		
New Bedford	430	30	Pope	Marcy								1					1		
New Bedford	430	9	Pope	Nathaniel	4				1			2					7		
New Bedford	430	15	Pope	Samuel		1	1		1	1	1	1	1				7		
New Bedford	430	21	Pope	Seth				1					1				2		
New Bedford	430	6	Pope	Thomas	1			1		2			1				5		
New Bedford	430	10	Pope	William	1		1					1	1				4		
New Bedford	431	8	Pope	Worth	1		2	1		2		1	1				8		
New Bedford	430	25	Pope	Yet Seth	1				1	3	1		1				7		
Freetown	282	22	Porter	Benjamin	1	1	2		2			2	2				10		
Freetown	282	16	Porter	Benjamin 2d	1			1				1					3		
Taunton	367	25	Porter	Ester Wido								2	1				3		
Taunton	360	19	Porter	John	1	1	1	1	1		2	1	1				9		
Taunton	367	15	Porter	Leonard			1	1		1	1						4		
Taunton	367	27	Porter	Lincoln				1		1							2		
Taunton	367	16	Porter	Mary Wido		2			1	1	1		1				6		
Freetown	282	23	Porter	Robert	1	1	1	1		1			1				6		
Berkley	275	1	Porter	Tisdale				1		1		1					3		
Swansea	401	45	Portergen	Benanuel									2				2		
Dartmouth	347	33	Potter	Abner	1	1			1	1			1		5				
Westport	335	3	Potter	Abner		1	2		1	1			1				6		
Westport	335	8	Potter	Barney					1	1		1	1				4		
Westport	335	5	Potter	Edward				1		1		1					3		
Westport	335	12	Potter	Elias				1					1				2		
Westport	335	13	Potter	Elijah		1		1	1	1		1					5		
Dartmouth	347	19	Potter	Gardner			1			1	1				6				
Attleboro	320	59	Potter	Holliman	3	1	1	1		1		1					8		
Dartmouth	347	36	Potter	Humphrey	2	2		1				1			7				
Westport	335	9	Potter	Ichabod 2d	2			1		1		1					5		
Westport	335	16	Potter	Ichabod Son	1			1			1		1				4		
Westport	335	26	Potter	John	2			1			1		1				5		
New Bedford	431	13	Potter	Jonathan	3			1		2	2		1				9		
Dartmouth	347	34	Potter	Joshua	1			1		2		1	1		6				
Westport	335	4	Potter	Mohes					1				1				2		
Westport	334	36	Potter	Nathaniel		1		1	1			1	1				5		
New Bedford	430	34	Potter	Pardon			2	1		2		2					7		
Westport	334	34	Potter	Peleg					1				1				2		
Westport	335	27	Potter	Philip	1			1			1						3		
Dartmouth	347	35	Potter	Prince		2		1		3	1	1			8				
Westport	335	15	Potter	Rebeccah									2				2		
Taunton	365	26	Potter	Scipio											6		6		
Swansea	398	44	Potter	Simeon				1	1			1					3		
Taunton	360	15	Potter	Simeon				1									1		
New Bedford	430	36	Potter	Southworth	1		1					1					3		
New Bedford	430	40	Potter	Stephen	1			1		1		1					4		
Westport	335	6	Potter	Stephen		1	1		1	1	2	1		1			8		
New Bedford	430	38	Potter	Thurston		1		1				1	1				4		
Dartmouth	347	41	Potter	Weaver			1					1			3				
Westport	335	10	Potter	Wesson	3	1		1		1		1					7		
Dartmouth	347	32	Potter	Wm Holiday	2		1		2	2		1			8				
Somerset	405	27	Potts	Widow			1			2			1				4		
Norton	383	14	Powers	Edward					1		1	1	1				4		
Taunton	367	44	Pratt	Aaron		1	3	1			1		1				7		
Mansfield	386	43	Pratt	Amasa			1				1						2		
New Bedford	431	10	Pratt	Amos	1	1		1		1			1	1			6		
Easton	392	8	Pratt	Caleb	3			1					1				5		
Freetown	292	25	Pratt	David		1		1			1	1					4		
Mansfield	386	42	Pratt	David			1		1	1	2		1				6		
Taunton	357	8	Pratt	Dier	1	2	1		1	3	1	1	2	1			13		
Taunton	366	31	Pratt	Elizabeth Wido	1	1	2			2		1	1				8		
Taunton	366	33	Pratt	Enos	2			1		3			1				7		
Taunton	366	46	Pratt	Hannah Wido									2				2		
Dighton	414	16	Pratt	Jabez		2			1	5			1				9		
Mansfield	386	40	Pratt	John	1		2		1		1		1				6		
Swansea	398	4	Pratt	John	4			1		1			3				9		
Mansfield	386	41	Pratt	John Jur	3	2		1		2		1	2				11		
Dighton	414	15	Pratt	Jona			1		1					3			5		
Easton	392	18	Pratt	Jonathan			1	1	1		1			1			5		
Norton	383	17	Pratt	Joseph				1						1			2		
Easton	392	7	Pratt	Josiah			1			1		1					3		
Mansfield	387	2	Pratt	Josiah	2			1		1			1				5		

130

			HEADS OF HOUSEHOLD		FREE WHITE MALES					FREE WHITE FEMALES									
TOWN	PG#	LN#	LAST NAME	FIRST NAME	under 10	10 to 16	16 to 26	26 to 45	45 and over	under 10	10 to 16	16 to 26	26 to 45	45 and over	TOTAL ALL OTHER	TOTAL SLAVES	TOTALS	DISTRICT/TOWNSHIP	NOTES
Mansfield	387	1	Pratt	Josiah Jr			1	1		2		2					6		
New Bedford	430	41	Pratt	Lewis	1			1					1				3		
Mansfield	387	7	Pratt	Lucy						1		1		1			3		
Taunton	366	32	Pratt	Nehemiah	1				1	1	1		1	1			6		
Taunton	366	13	Pratt	Rufus	2			1		1			1				5		
Taunton	359	34	Pratt	Samuel		2	1		1	1	1		2				8		
Easton	392	14	Pratt	Seth			2	1					1				4		
Taunton	369	1	Pratt	Seth	3		1	1		1	1		1				8		
Mansfield	387	5	Pratt	Spencer		2			1		1		1				5		
Dartmouth	347	21	Pratt	Thomas			1		2	1	1	1			8				
Easton	392	15	Pratt	William		1		1	1			1	1				5		
Freetown	282	2	Pratt	William	4	2		1			1		1				9		
Easton	392	16	Pratt	William 2d		1			1				2	1			5		
Easton	392	17	Pratt	William 3d	1	1		1					1				4		
Taunton	367	19	Prentice	Joseph				1		3		1					5		
Taunton	358	11	Presbrey	John		2		1		2		2	1				8		
Taunton	361	14	Presbrey	Seth	2	2	1		1			1		1			8		
Norton	383	8	Presbrey	Simeon	2	2	2	1		3			1	1			12		
Taunton	361	16	Presbrey	William		1	1		1			1		1			5		
Taunton	357	21	Presbrey	William Junior			1			1			1				3		
Raynham	374	35	Presho	James				1					1				2		
Raynham	376	32	Presho	Joseph	2			1		2	1		1				7		
Raynham	375	17	Presho	Sampson	2	2		1		2	1		1				9		
Raynham	374	36	Presho	Zadoc	5			1		1			2				9		
Attleboro	319	5	Price	Edward		1	1	1		1		2					6		
New Bedford	430	14	Price	John	1			1		2		2	1				7		
New Bedford	430	37	Price	Oliver	3	1			1	3			1				9		
New Bedford	430	33	Price	Simeon		1		1		1			1	1			5		
Dartmouth	347	20	Prince	Elizabeth										4	4				
Dartmouth	347	24	Prince	Job										3	3				
Norton	383	13	Prior	Hepzebah										1			1		
New Bedford	430	43	Prior	Susanna										1			1		
New Bedford	430	22	Procter	Josiah				1					1	1			3		
New Bedford	430	5	Procter	Samuel		1	2		1				1	1	2		8		
New Bedford	430	13	Procter	Susanna	1	1	1			1		2	1				7		
New Bedford	430	45	Proud	John	1	1			1	1	2	3		1			10		
Norton	383	12	Puffin	Benjamin		1		1					1	1			4		
Swansea	398	33	Pullen	John	3			1		2		1		1			8		
Somerset	406	21	Purrinton	Clark	2	1	2	1		1	2		1				10		
Somerset	406	35	Purrinton	Edward	2	1		1		1	1		1				7		
Somerset	406	22	Purrinton	Widow		1	1				1		1				4		
Dartmouth	348	2	Quan	Deborah										3	3				
Dartmouth	348	1	Quan	James										6	6				
Dartmouth	348	3	Quan	Joseph										10	10				
Dartmouth	348	4	Quan	Martha										3	3				
Easton	392	26	Quinley	James			1			1			1				3		
New Bedford	431	17	Randall	Putnam	1		1			1		1					4		
Easton	392	31	Randell	Abiah				1				2		1			4		
Easton	392	41	Randell	Abner		2		1				2		1			6		
Easton	392	28	Randell	Absolon				1					1				2		
Easton	393	3	Randell	Apollos	1			1		2			1				5		
Easton	392	43	Randell	Barnabas				1									1		
Easton	392	40	Randell	Caleb	1		1	1		1		1					5		
Easton	392	34	Randell	Daniel	2			1		2			1				6		
Easton	393	12	Randell	Daniel	2			1		2	1		1				7		
Easton	393	9	Randell	Ebinezer			1	1		1			1				4		
Easton	392	44	Randell	Ephraim	1	3		1			2			1			8		
Easton	393	4	Randell	Hopestill	1	1	1		1	1		1	1	1			8		
Easton	392	39	Randell	Job	3	2		1		2	1	1	1				12		
Easton	392	32	Randell	John		2	2	1					2				7		
Easton	393	8	Randell	John 2d	4			1		2			1				9		
Easton	392	33	Randell	Jonathan	1		1			4			1				8		
Easton	393	7	Randell	Luther	2			1		1	1		1				6		
Easton	393	2	Randell	Nehemiah	1			1				1	1	1			5		
Easton	393	5	Randell	Phinehas	4								1				6		
Easton	392	38	Randell	Robert					1				1				2		
Easton	392	42	Randell	Solomon			1	1				2		1			5		
Easton	393	6	Randell	Thomas	2	4		1					1	1			9		
Easton	393	11	Randell	Thomas	4	2		1					1	1			9		
Easton	392	35	Randell	Timothy	1	1		1		3	1		1				8		
Easton	393	10	Randell	Timothy	1	1		1		3	1		1				8		
Easton	393	1	Randell	Ziba		2		1		1		1					6		
Taunton	357	20	Ranville	John Demi		2		1		1				1			5		
Taunton	362	32	Raymond	Benjamin	2			1		2			1				6		
Norton	383	18	Raymond	Ephraim	1		2	1		3	1	1	1				10		
Dighton	413	27	Raymond	Saria						1	1		1				3		
New Bedford	431	47	Raynolds	Michael	1			1					1				3		
New Bedford	432	1	Raynolds	William	3	1		1		2	1		1	1			9		
Attleboro	319	49	Read	Abel		1		1		4			1	1			8		
Rehoboth	312	16	Read	Abel				1					1			2			
Easton	392	30	Read	Abijah			2		1		1	1		1			6		
Rehoboth	311	2	Read	Amos			1	1					1			3			
Attleboro	317	22	Read	Arnon	1		1						1				3		
Attleboro	317	19	Read	Azael		1	1							3			5		
Berkley	278	26	Read	Barney	1		1			1			1				4		

TOWN	PG#	LN#	LAST NAME	FIRST NAME	FWM under 10	FWM 10 to 16	FWM 16 to 26	FWM 26 to 45	FWM 45 and over	FWF under 10	FWF 10 to 16	FWF 16 to 26	FWF 26 to 45	FWF 45 and over	TOTAL ALL OTHER	TOTAL SLAVES	TOTALS	DISTRICT/ TOWNSHIP	NOTES
Rehoboth	312	20	Read	Bashabee										2			2		
Freetown	282	21	Read	Benjamin	3	1	1		1	1	2		1				10		
Freetown	293	28	Read	Benjamin Jun				1				1					2		
Freetown	289	15	Read	Braton			1			2		1	1				5		
Attleboro	318	18	Read	Daniel			1			1				2			4		
Freetown	284	25	Read	Daniel	4			2	1				2	1			10		
Somerset	405	44	Read	David	2		1			1	3		1	1			9		
Freetown	284	30	Read	Dolly		1							3	3			7		
Attleboro	322	20	Read	Ebenezer	1			1		2		1					5		
Dighton	415	11	Read	Ebenezer		3		1		2	1	1	1				9		
Freetown	287	7	Read	Elizabeth Wid										1			1		
Attleboro	318	43	Read	Ephraim		1	1	1	1	1		1		1			7		
Freetown	284	4	Read	George	2	1		1					1				5		
Taunton	368	20	Read	George				1					1				2		
Freetown	289	6	Read	George 2d	3			2					1	1			7		
Taunton	358	7	Read	George 2d	1			1			1	1		1			5		
Freetown	289	8	Read	Gideon	1			1		3			1	1			7		
Taunton	368	22	Read	Isaiah				1		2	2	2	1				8		
Freetown	293	22	Read	James	1			1					1		1		4		
Attleboro	318	45	Read	Joel	2	2		1		2	1	3	1	1			14		
Somerset	407	11	Read	John			2	1		1			1				5		
Taunton	366	40	Read	John		2	3	1		1	1		1				9		
Attleboro	323	7	Read	Jona	1		1	1				1					4		
Freetown	284	23	Read	Jonathan	2		3	1		1		1	2	1			11		
Freetown	287	6	Read	Jonathan Jr	2			1		2			1				6		
Freetown	289	7	Read	Joseph	1	1	1		1		1	3		2			10		
Taunton	365	15	Read	Joseph				1					1	1			3		
Taunton	366	3	Read	Joseph 2d		1	1	1		2		2		1			8		
Attleboro	317	18	Read	Levi			1					1					2		
Freetown	287	28	Read	Mary Wid		1		1					2	1			5		
Attleboro	318	44	Read	Moses	1			1					1	2			5		
Freetown	289	5	Read	Nathan	2			1		2			1		4		10		
Somerset	407	10	Read	Nathan		2		1			1		1				5		
Attleboro	318	19	Read	Nathan	1			1		1			1				4		
Freetown	289	17	Read	Oliver	2			1		1	2		1				7		
Rehoboth	310	45	Read	Oliver			1			2							3		
Taunton	368	21	Read	Oliver	3	1		1		1			1				7		
Rehoboth	310	46	Read	Oliver Jr			1					1					4		
Rehoboth	312	15	Read	Perres		1		1			1	1					5		
Rehoboth	314	36	Read	Peter			1						1				2		
Attleboro	317	21	Read	Saml				1				1					2		
Somerset	406	15	Read	Samuel	1	1		1		3	3	2	1	1			13		
Rehoboth	311	1	Read	Simeon	1	1		1	1	1			1				6		
Attleboro	317	20	Read	Thoma		1		1		1			1				4		
Taunton	359	28	Read	Uriah	2			1		3	2	1	1				10		
Somerset	405	13	Read	Wid						1		1	1				3		
Attleboro	317	3	Read	William	1			1		1	1		1				5		
Easton	392	29	Read	William	3	2		1			1		1				8		
Freetown	281	13	Read	William			3		1			3	1				8		
Easton	392	36	Record	Amasa			1		1	1			1		1		5		
Westport	335	31	Records	William	1	3	3	1		2	2		1				13		
Dartmouth	348	28	Reed	Benjamin	2	2	1		2	2			1	1			11		
Rehoboth	298	1	Reed	Elijah A.		1	1						1				4		
Dartmouth	348	31	Reed	Elijah Warren		1		3					1				6		
Dighton	409	20	Reed	Jemima									2	1			3		
Dartmouth	348	29	Reed	John	1		1			2			1				8		
Dighton	413	7	Reed	Joshua	2		1						1				4		
Dartmouth	348	33	Reed	Lemuel	1			1	2	1			1				8		
Dighton	413	6	Reed	Loved		2		1		1	1		1				6		
Rehoboth	308	11	Reed	Nathan			1			1	3		1				6		
Rehoboth	308	12	Reed	Nathaniel	2		1		3	1	1	1					9		
Rehoboth	308	36	Reed	Rachel		1				1	1		1				5		
Dighton	409	21	Reed	Samuel	4	1			1	1			1				8		
Rehoboth	307	8	Reed	Sarrah & Huldah									2				2		
Dighton	409	17	Reed	Seth	1			1		1	1		1				5		
Dighton	412	5	Reed	Simeon				4	1				1				6		
Dighton	412	6	Reed	Simeon Junr		1		1		1	1		1				5		
Dartmouth	348	32	Reed	Thomas			1						1				2		
Rehoboth	310	44	Reed	Thomas	2			1		1		1	1				9		
Dartmouth	348	30	Reed	Thomas Junr		2	1		1	3	1		1				12		
Dartmouth	348	26	Reed	William	1	1			3			1					8		
Dighton	413	1	Reed	William	3	1		1		1	1		1				8		
Rehoboth	312	19	Reed	Renuff Philip			1	1				1					3		
Dartmouth	349	13	Reynolds	Benjamin	2			1					1				4		
Attleboro	321	26	Richard	John	2		2	1				1	1	1			8		
Berkley	278	18	Richard	Verdy									1				1		
Attleboro	321	5	Richards	Avery	1			1		3	1		1				7		
Attleboro	321	3	Richards	David		1	1					2					5		
Attleboro	321	40	Richards	Edwd Junr	4			1		1			1				7		
Attleboro	321	39	Richards	Jesse	2	1	1	1					1				6		
Attleboro	322	31	Richards	Joseph A				1		1							2		
Attleboro	321	1	Richards	Luther	2	1		1		2			1				8		
Attleboro	322	66	Richards	Lydia	3	1							2				6		

TOWN	PG#	LN#	LAST NAME	FIRST NAME	FREE WHITE MALES under 10	10 to 16	16 to 26	26 to 45	45 and over	FREE WHITE FEMALES under 10	10 to 16	16 to 26	26 to 45	45 and over	TOTAL ALL OTHER	TOTAL SLAVES	TOTALS	DISTRICT/ TOWNSHIP	NOTES
Attleboro	321	4	Richards	Nathan	1			1		1			1				4		
Attleboro	321	2	Richards	Edwd	1				1				2				4		
Attleboro	318	63	Richardson	Abiathar		1	1		2	1		2		1			8		
Attleboro	318	59	Richardson	Abiathar Junr			3	1				1	1				6		
Attleboro	319	37	Richardson	Benja	1		1			1		2		1			6		
Attleboro	319	45	Richardson	Caleb	2	1		1	1			1	1				7		
Attleboro	319	1	Richardson	Daniel				1		2			1				4		
Attleboro	319	2	Richardson	Daniel Jr	3	1		1		1							6		
Mansfield	387	10	Richardson	Ebenezer				1		2		1					4		
Attleboro	319	14	Richardson	Francis	1		1			1		1					4		
Norton	383	19	Richardson	George	1		1					1					3		
Attleboro	319	38	Richardson	Seth	2		2	1		2	3	1	1	1			13		
Mansfield	387	9	Richardson	Stephen				1					1				2		
Mansfield	387	11	Richardson	Thomas			1			1		1					3		
Attleboro	319	4	Richardson	Vinton			1		1	1			1				4		
Attleboro	318	51	Richardson	Wm	1		1	1		1		2					6		
Norton	383	20	Richmand	George	1			1	3	1	2		1				9		
Taunton	362	16	Richmond	Abiel	1		3	1	1		2	1		1			10		
Dighton	412	44	Richmond	Abigail			2			1		4		1			8		
Taunton	365	12	Richmond	Abner	2	1		1		1		1	1	1			8		
Taunton	362	12	Richmond	Abraham		1				1		1					3		
Taunton	363	20	Richmond	Alexander			1	1				1	1				4		
Taunton	362	13	Richmond	Asa		1			1			1		1			4		
Taunton	367	9	Richmond	Benjamin	1		1		1	1	1			1			6		
Taunton	362	17	Richmond	Edward	2	1		1		1			1				6		
Taunton	362	18	Richmond	Elijah	1	1		1	1			1		1			6		
Dighton	409	2	Richmond	Ezra				1					2				3		
Raynham	374	23	Richmond	Ezra	1					1	1	1	1				6		
Dighton	413	39	Richmond	Gamiel		1			1	3	1		1				7		
Dighton	412	47	Richmond	Jim											6		6		
Dighton	413	24	Richmond	John	1			1		2	1	1		1			7		
Rehoboth	312	21	Richmond	John R	1	2	1	1			2		1	1			9		
Dighton	409	13	Richmond	Jonah	3	3	3		1		2			1			13		
Freetown	294	21	Richmond	Jonathan	1			1		2	1		1				6		
Taunton	358	29	Richmond	Jonathan	1	1			1	1	1	4	1				10		
Taunton	362	34	Richmond	Joseph		1	1		1	2	1			1			7		
Westport	335	35	Richmond	London											4		4		
Taunton	362	15	Richmond	Noah	1			1		1		1					4		
Freetown	282	4	Richmond	Paddoch			1						1				2		
Westport	335	30	Richmond	Perez	1	1	2	1	1	1	2	2		1			12		
Taunton	364	16	Richmond	Reuben	2	1		1		1		1	1				7		
Freetown	285	32	Richmond	Samuel	2	1		1	1	2		1		1			9		
Taunton	364	18	Richmond	Sarah Wido									1				1		
Raynham	373	13	Richmond	Seth	1	1	1	1	1	1			1				7		
Taunton	362	19	Richmond	Seth	1			1			1			1			4		
Taunton	362	14	Richmond	Stephen				1						1			2		
Dighton	413	22	Richmond	Thomas B.	3		2		1		2	1		1			10		
Taunton	365	11	Richmond	Walker		1	1		1	1	1	1					6		
Dighton	412	38	Richmond	William	1		2	1	1	2			1	1			9		
Freetown	286	1	Richord	Isaac		1		1			1						3		
Dartmouth	348	7	Rickdson	Sarah		2				3		1					6		
New Bedford	431	45	Rickelson	Abraham	2			1		2			1		1		7		
New Bedford	431	36	Rickelson	Charles			1										1		
New Bedford	431	31	Rickelson	Daniel		1	1		1			1	1		1		6		
New Bedford	431	32	Rickelson	Joseph		1	1					1					3		
Dartmouth	348	15	Ricketson	Clark	1		1		1			1					4		
Dartmouth	349	1	Ricketson	Cook			1				1		1				6		
Dartmouth	348	13	Ricketson	Henry	1		1	2				1					6		
Dartmouth	348	14	Ricketson	John			1					2	2				6		
Dartmouth	349	8	Ricketson	Peleg		1						1	1				3		
Dartmouth	348	23	Rider	Abigale									2				2		
Dartmouth	348	19	Rider	Benjamin		1		1			1	1					4		
Freetown	290	4	Rider	Benjamin	1		1			1		1					4		
Dartmouth	348	25	Rider	Henry		1				1	1						4		
Dartmouth	348	22	Rider	John		1				1		1					4		
Dartmouth	348	20	Rider	Rowland		1						1					3		
Dartmouth	348	24	Rider	Samuel	1			1		1		1					5		
Dartmouth	348	21	Rider	William	2			1		1	1		1				6		
Taunton	357	29	Right	John			1			1		1					3		
Rehoboth	306	4	Right	Joseph			1			2	1	1					6		
New Bedford	431	37	Right	Thomas			1						2				3		
Easton	392	37	Ripley	Samu		2		1				1	1				5		
Easton	392	27	Riply	Abiel	1			1		3		1					6		
Attleboro	317	2	Robbins	Ezekiel				1					1				2		
Westport	335	34	Robertson	William		1						2	1				4		
Raynham	375	30	Robinson	Abishai			1			1		1					3		
Attleboro	319	3	Robinson	Ebenezer	1		1					2	1				5		
Taunton	362	11	Robinson	Ebenezer	1	1		1		3	1		1				9		
Raynham	375	37	Robinson	Eliab			1	1				1	1				4		
Attleboro	322	4	Robinson	Ezekiel		1	1	2	1			1		1			7		
Attleboro	317	6	Robinson	George	2		2	1		2			1				8		
Attleboro	321	36	Robinson	George W	1	1		1	1	2		1					7		

TOWN	PG#	LN#	LAST NAME	FIRST NAME	FREE WHITE MALES under 10	10 to 16	16 to 26	26 to 45	45 and over	FREE WHITE FEMALES under 10	10 to 16	16 to 26	26 to 45	45 and over	TOTAL ALL OTHER	TOTAL SLAVES	TOTALS	DISTRICT/ TOWNSHIP	NOTES
Somerset	404	12	Robinson	Gideon			1					1					2		
Raynham	374	9	Robinson	Godfrey	3		1	1		1			1				7		
Raynham	374	8	Robinson	Hendrick	1	2		1		1	1		1				7		
Taunton	363	34	Robinson	Increase	1		1		1	2	2	1	1				9		
Taunton	358	32	Robinson	James			1			1			1				3		
Attleboro	318	11	Robinson	Joel			1	1		1			1				4		
Raynham	375	32	Robinson	John	1		1		1	1	1			1			6		
Swansea	402	42	Robinson	John	1	1		1		2	1		1				7		
Somerset	404	40	Robinson	Joseph	2	1			1	2	2				1		9		
Raynham	374	11	Robinson	Josiah	1				1	1	1	2	1				7		
Attleboro	318	35	Robinson	Josie	1		1			2		2					6		
Raynham	374	10	Robinson	Nathan	3	2		1		1	1		1				9		
Attleboro	318	54	Robinson	Nathaniel		1	5		1	1		2	1				11		
Rehoboth	300	38	Robinson	Noah															Enumeration left blank
Rehoboth	310	43	Robinson	Noah	1		1		3			1	1		8				
Attleboro	323	15	Robinson	Obed	5		3	2		3	1	1	1				16		
Rehoboth	308	10	Robinson	Rachel						1		1			2				
Attleboro	318	12	Robinson	Saml	2		1		1			1		2			7		
Raynham	375	23	Robinson	Seth	1	2			1	2	1	1	1	2			11		
New Bedford	431	21	Robinson	William			1				1			1			3		
Attleboro	323	3	Robinson	Zephariah	1			1		1	1			2			6		
Rehoboth	312	17	Rodliaf	Frederic	2	1		1	1				1		10				
New Bedford	431	46	Rodman	Samuel	2		1		1	1	2	3	1		1		12		
Mansfield	387	8	Rogers	Benjamin					1			1	1				3		
Mansfield	387	12	Rogers	Daniel			1					1					2		
Dartmouth	348	27	Rogers	Gidion	1			1	3	2	1	1					9		
Freetown	288	8	Rogers	Jeremiah	2			1		1	2		1				7		
Dartmouth	349	14	Rogers	John			1			1		1					3		
Rehoboth	301	23	Rogerson	John	1		1					1					5		
Attleboro	323	14	Roginson	Robert	2	1	2	1		3		1					10		
Freetown	292	11	Ronnalds	Micah			1			1		1		1			4		
Dighton	415	16	Rose	Nath	1			1					1				4		
Dighton	415	14	Rose	Thomas			2		1			2	2	1			8		
Dighton	410	35	Rose	Thomas Jr	3			1		2			1	1			8		
New Bedford	431	33	Ross	William	1			1		2	1		1				6		
New Bedford	431	35	Rotch	Joseph					1			1	1	1			4		
New Bedford	431	26	Rotch	Thomas			1	1				1	1	1			5		
New Bedford	431	25	Rotch	William		1			1	2	2	1	2		1		10		
New Bedford	431	27	Rotch	William Jun	2	1	3	2		1	2		3		2		16		
Rehoboth	307	6	Round	Abner			1		1	1							4		
Rehoboth	303	10	Round	Amos			1					1					3		
Rehoboth	308	38	Round	Amos 2		1		1		1							3		
Rehoboth	303	8	Round	Chase	1		1			3	2		1				9		
Rehoboth	309	9	Round	Enos	1		1						1				3		
Rehoboth	303	17	Round	Georg	2		1	2				1					6		
Attleboro	319	39	Round	Hezekiah	2	1			1	1	2	3	1				11		
Rehoboth	307	2	Round	Jabez		3		1		1	1	1					7		
Rehoboth	303	9	Round	John			2		1		1	1					8		
Rehoboth	307	5	Round	Lane		1			1	2		1					5		
Rehoboth	303	7	Round	Marten	1			1		2		1					5		
Rehoboth	305	15	Round	Nathaniel	1			1		1		1					4		
Rehoboth	307	4	Round	Simeon	1	2		1		1	1	1					9		
Rehoboth	307	3	Round	Sylvester	1	1	1		3	2	1	1					11		
Rehoboth	303	5	Round	Nathaniel			1		2	2	1	1					8		
Somerset	404	20	Rounds	Chase			1			1		1					3		
Rehoboth	299	22	Rounds	Esther		1				1	1	1					4		
Rehoboth	302	40	Rounds	James			1		3			1					5		
Swansea	398	18	Rounds	Philip	1		1			1		1					4		
Freetown	285	20	Rounsevill	Levi		2		1			2			1			6		
Freetown	285	22	Rounsevill	Phillip	3	1	2		1	1	1	1	1				11		
Freetown	285	21	Rounsevill	Thomas	1	3	1		1			4	1				11		
Freetown	285	23	Rounsevill	William	1			1		2		1					5		
Freetown	292	17	Rounswill	Abner	1			1		2		1					5		
Freetown	293	16	Rounswill	Gabriel Wid	1	2	1			3		1					8		
New Bedford	431	18	Rouse	John			1			2		1					4		
Rehoboth	312	18	Rude	William			1	1		1		1					4		
Freetown	286	22	Runnolds	John	2			1				1	1				5		
Dartmouth	349	6	Russel	Barney		1	1					1					3		
Dartmouth	349	9	Russel	Clark	1		1	1		1		1					5		
Dartmouth	349	5	Russel	David			1					1					2		
Westport	335	32	Russel	David		1			1			1	2				5		
Dartmouth	348	5	Russel	Elihu			1	1		1							4		
Dartmouth	348	11	Russel	Elijah			1	1		3		1					6		
Dartmouth	348	17	Russel	Elizabeth								2	1				3		
Dartmouth	348	9	Russel	Humphrey	1		1			2	1	1	1				7		
Dartmouth	349	2	Russel	Isaac				1					1				2		
Dartmouth	348	12	Russel	Jonathan			2	2		1		1					8		
Dartmouth	348	6	Russel	Joseph	1		1		3	1		1					9		
Dartmouth	349	4	Russel	Joseph			1	2		1		1					6		
Dartmouth	349	3	Russel	Luthern		2	1					1	1				5		
Dartmouth	348	18	Russel	Michael			1			1			4	2			8		
Dartmouth	348	8	Russel	Otes			1		2			1	1				6		
Dartmouth	349	12	Russel	Paul		1			1	1	2						6		
Dartmouth	348	16	Russel	Perry		2	1				1						4		

TOWN	PG#	LN#	LAST NAME	FIRST NAME	FREE WHITE MALES under 10	10 to 16	16 to 26	26 to 45	45 and over	FREE WHITE FEMALES under 10	10 to 16	16 to 26	26 to 45	45 and over	TOTAL ALL OTHER	TOTAL SLAVES	TOTALS	DISTRICT/ TOWNSHIP	NOTES
Dartmouth	348	10	Russel	Philip			1			2	1						6		
Westport	335	33	Russel	Seviah			2	3			1		1				7		
Dartmouth	349	7	Russel	Stephen	1		1						1				5		
Dartmouth	349	10	Russel	Stephen			1		1				1				5		
Dartmouth	349	11	Russel	William	1	1	1		3	1							7		
New Bedford	431	42	Russell	Abraham	4			4			3		1		7		19		
New Bedford	431	29	Russell	Barnabas	1	1	1		1	5	2	2	1	1	1		16		
New Bedford	431	38	Russell	Caleb				1		1			1				3		
New Bedford	431	39	Russell	Caleb Jur			2	1		2			1				7		
New Bedford	431	28	Russell	Charles	1	1		1		1	1	1	1				7		
New Bedford	431	24	Russell	Gilbert		1		1		4	2	1	1		1		11		
New Bedford	431	19	Russell	John		1	1	1						1			4		
New Bedford	431	43	Russell	John J	1		1			1			1				4		
New Bedford	431	22	Russell	Jonathan	2			1			1	1	1				6		
New Bedford	431	41	Russell	Joseph				1				1	1				3		
New Bedford	431	40	Russell	Pero											3		3		
New Bedford	431	15	Russell	Phillip	3		1			2		1					7		
New Bedford	431	44	Russell	Seth	1			1				1	1				4		
New Bedford	431	23	Russell	Seth Jun		1		1		1	1	1			2		7		
New Bedford	431	34	Russell	William	1	1	1		1	1	1		1				7		
New Bedford	431	20	Russell	William 2nd	1		1		1	1	3	1		1			9		
New Bedford	431	30	Russell	William Jr	2	1	3	1		1		1		1			10		
New Bedford	431	16	Russell	Wing	1		1			1			1				4		
Freetown	281	15	S*intine	Thomas	1		1			1		1	1				5		
Freetown	287	32	Saben	Samuel	3			1		1			1				6		
Rehoboth	307	19	Sabin	Dolly			1	1		1	1	3					7		
Attleboro	318	40	Sabin	Vessel	1			1					1				3		
Rehoboth	308	13	Sabin	William		1		1		1		1					4		
Attleboro	320	52	Saddler	John	2		1	1		3		1	1				9		
Swansea	402	37	Salisbury	Daniel		1		1					1				3		
Freetown	292	13	Saller	Silas	1	1		1				1		1			5		
Freetown	284	16	Sallintine	David	1	1		1	1			2		1	1		9		
Freetown	284	14	Sallintine	Wid. Mary			2			1	1	1	1				6		
Freetown	284	15	Sallintine	William	1		1	2	2	1		4	1	2	1		15		
Attleboro	322	43	Sally	Nelly		1				1		1					3		
Rehoboth	299	46	Salsburg	William		1		2				1					5		
Rehoboth	311	41	Salsbury	Hezekiah	1		1			1		1					4		
Rehoboth	312	38	Salsbury	Samuel		1		3			1						5		
New Bedford	432	15	Sampson	Isacher	5		1	1		1		1					9		
Freetown	290	6	Samson	Ebenezer	2			1		1			1	1			6		
Freetown	290	10	Samson	John	1	2		1		2			1				7		
Dartmouth	350	29	Sandford	David	1		1	1			1						6		
Westport	336	27	Sandford	David	2			1		1		1					5		
Dartmouth	350	20	Sandford	Elisha		1	1				1	1					4		
Dartmouth	350	17	Sandford	George		1					1						2		
Dartmouth	350	19	Sandford	Isaac	1					1		1					5		
Dartmouth	350	21	Sandford	John		1		3			1						6		
Dartmouth	350	23	Sandford	Paul		1					1						2		
Dartmouth	350	18	Sandford	Peleg		1		2		1	1						6		
Westport	336	15	Sandford	Philip	1	1	1	1		1	1		1				7		
Westport	336	17	Sandford	Rescom		1	1				1						3		
Dartmouth	351	12	Sandford	Richard	1		1		1		1						6		
Westport	336	26	Sandford	Thomas			1		2		1						4		
Dartmouth	350	24	Sandford	William	1		1	2			1						5		
Berkley	278	19	Sanford	George				1				2					3		
Berkley	278	21	Sanford	George Junr	4		1		2		1	1					9		
Berkley	278	20	Sanford	Joseph	3	2	1		1			1					8		
Attleboro	320	30	Sanford	Paul	1	1	3	1		3			1				10		
Berkley	275	12	Sanford	Robert		1				2	1	1					5		
Attleboro	320	26	Sanford	Saml	2		1				1		1				5		
Freetown	288	19	Sanford	Stephen	1		1			1	1						4		
Swansea	403	9	Saunders	Benja	1		1	1		2	1		1				7		
Swansea	403	8	Saunders	Daniel		1					1						2		
Swansea	403	7	Saunders	Jacob	1		1			2			2				6		
Taunton	365	21	Sayer	Thomas											5		5		
Swansea	403	34	Scot	Samuel		1					1	1					3		
Taunton	360	24	Seabury	John W.	1		1	1		3	1		1				8		
Taunton	368	34	Sears	Sarah Wido	1					1		1					3		
Taunton	361	8	Seckett	James				1					1				2		
Taunton	364	11	Seckett	Job	3	1		1	1	1			1	1			9		
Taunton	364	15	Seckett	Moses Junior	1	2	1		1	2	2		1				10		
Berkley	278	13	Seekels	John		1					1						2		
Dartmouth	350	45	Sekel	Caleb		1		2			1						4		
Easton	393	13	Selee	Nathan	2			1	1	3	1		1				9		
Rehoboth	299	36	Servis	Reuben		1						1					3		
Taunton	358	28	Sever	John	2			1		1		1	1				6		
Taunton	357	3	Sever	William		1	1			1		1					4		
Taunton	358	27	Sever	William			2		1	1			1				5		
New Bedford	432	23	Sharpes	Hezekiah											2		2		
Dighton	410	14	Shaw	Abraham	1			1		2			1				5		
Norton	383	39	Shaw	Benjamin		1		1		1			1				4		
Easton	393	20	Shaw	Eliphalet	3		1						1				5		
Somerset	404	26	Shaw	Eliphalet	1		1			4	1		1				8		
Taunton	358	41	Shaw	Isaac	2	1	1	2		4		1	1				12		
Dighton	413	20	Shaw	Jabez	1			2					1				4		

135

TOWN	PG#	LN#	LAST NAME	FIRST NAME	FREE WHITE MALES					FREE WHITE FEMALES					TOTAL ALL OTHER	TOTAL SLAVES	TOTALS	DISTRICT/ TOWNSHIP	NOTES
					under 10	10 to 16	16 to 26	26 to 45	45 and over	under 10	10 to 16	16 to 26	26 to 45	45 and over					
Dighton	413	42	Shaw	Jahaziah				1		3	2	1					7		
Somerset	405	51	Shaw	John		1		1		3		1	2				8		
Taunton	357	16	Shaw	John			1	1		1	2	1	2				8		
Raynham	375	39	Shaw	Jonathan	1	1		1		2		1					6		
Raynham	373	32	Shaw	Joseph				1					1				2		
Raynham	373	31	Shaw	Joseph Junior			1	1		1		1					4		
Easton	393	14	Shaw	Joshua	1			1					1				3		
Dighton	410	8	Shaw	Lavina							1		3				4		
Raynham	372	1	Shaw	Mason		1	1	1					1				4		
Raynham	374	4	Shaw	Nathaniel		1		1			1	1	1				5		
Rehoboth	309	3	Shaw	Nathaniel & Son			1	1	2			1	1				9		
Easton	393	19	Shaw	Nicholas			1		1			1					3		
Somerset	405	35	Shaw	Oliver		1		1		2		1					5		
Raynham	373	28	Shaw	Samuel	2			1		2		1					6		
Norton	383	38	Shaw	Sarah	2							1	2				5		
Raynham	373	33	Shaw	Silas		1	1	1		1	1		1				6		
New Bedford	432	10	Shaw	William	4		1	1		2	1		1	1			11		
Somerset	404	15	Shea	John			1			1		1	1				4		
Dartmouth	349	28	Shearman	Abraham			1	2		1		1					6		
Westport	336	6	Shearman	Alice							1		1				2		
Dartmouth	349	29	Shearman	Barney	1	1		1			1		2				7		
Dartmouth	349	27	Shearman	Benjm			1				1	1					3		
Dartmouth	349	26	Shearman	Benjm Junr	1		1	2		1		1					8		
Dartmouth	350	34	Shearman	Butler			1	1	1				1				4		
Dartmouth	351	5	Shearman	Butler 2nd			1	1				1					5		
Dartmouth	350	31	Shearman	Caleb		1	1			2	1	1					8		
Somerset	407	31	Shearman	Caleb		1		1				1	1				4		
Dartmouth	351	6	Shearman	Charles			1	2		2		1					8		
Dartmouth	350	36	Shearman	Daniel			1						2				4		
Dartmouth	350	26	Shearman	David	1	1	1	1			1		1				5		
Dartmouth	351	2	Shearman	Deavenport			1	3		1							7		
Dartmouth	350	4	Shearman	Elihu			1	1		1							3		
Dartmouth	350	9	Shearman	George		2		1		2	1		1				7		
Westport	336	3	Shearman	Gideon	1		1	1		1	3	1					8		
Somerset	407	27	Shearman	Gido		2		1					1				4		
Dartmouth	350	35	Shearman	Ira			1	3	1		1						6		
New Bedford	432	13	Shearman	Isaac	1		1	1		2	3	1					9		
New Bedford	432	2	Shearman	Jabez			1			2		1					4		
Dartmouth	350	38	Shearman	James			1	2		1		1		3			11		
Dartmouth	350	33	Shearman	Jerih	1	1		1		1							5		
Westport	336	24	Shearman	Job	2		1			2	1	1	1				8		
New Bedford	432	9	Shearman	John 2nd			1	1		1		1					4		
Dartmouth	350	39	Shearman	Jonathan	1			1		1	1	1					5		
Dartmouth	350	14	Shearman	Josiah		1					2	2					5		
Dartmouth	351	8	Shearman	Josiah		1					1						2		
Dartmouth	350	30	Shearman	Mary		1		1		1	1						4		
Norton	383	32	Shearman	Mary	1		1	1					4				7		
Dartmouth	350	28	Shearman	Paul		1				2	1	1					6		
Dartmouth	350	3	Shearman	Peleg		2	2	1				1					6		
Somerset	408	6	Shearman	Peleg		1	1		1		2		1				6		
Dartmouth	350	6	Shearman	Peleg 2d		1					1						3		
Dartmouth	350	27	Shearman	Philip			1	1	1			1	2				6		
Westport	336	5	Shearman	Preserved		1			1	1	1	2		1			7		
Dartmouth	350	32	Shearman	Prince			1				1		1				3		
Dartmouth	350	8	Shearman	Ruben		1	1	2				1	1				8		
Dartmouth	350	11	Shearman	Russel		2	1	1				1					7		
Dartmouth	350	10	Shearman	Shadrach	1		1	1	4	2		2	3				16		
Dartmouth	351	1	Shearman	Timothy			1			1	1	1					4		
Swansea	402	9	Shearman	Wido	3					2	1	1					7		
Dartmouth	350	2	Shearman	William			1	1					2				4		
Dartmouth	351	3	Shearman	Zoath	2		1	3				1					8		
Dartmouth	351	4	Sheldon	John	1			1	3	2		1					10		
Norton	383	41	Shelley	Joseph		1			1	1			1	2			6		
Taunton	356	2	Shelley	Samuel				1									1		
Raynham	376	6	Shelly	Eliab		1	1		1		2		1	1			7		
Norton	383	22	Shepard	Jacob	1	1	1	1	1		1	1		1			8		
Easton	393	16	Shepard	Samuel	1			1		2			1				5		
Mansfield	387	22	Shepard	Seth	1		1		1	1			2				6		
Rehoboth	312	22	Shependson	Zebadiah			1					2					3		
Rehoboth	312	27	Sheperson	Benager			1			2		1					4		
Dartmouth	350	43	Shepherd	Abner	1							1					6		
Dartmouth	351	10	Shepherd	Barney		1	1	2				1					6		
Dartmouth	351	9	Shepherd	John			1				1	1					3		
Taunton	360	26	Sherburn	Hannah Wido							1	1					2		
Somerset	404	42	Sherdon	John			1	1	1								3		
Somerset	404	37	Sherdon	William	3			1			2		2				8		
Somerset	408	9	Sherman	Daniel	2			1		1		1					5		
Somerset	407	28	Sherman	Preserved	1	1		1		2			1				6		
Somerset	408	7	Sherman	Robert	2			1		1			1				5		
Freetown	288	10	Sherman	Silas	2			1				1							
Freetown	282	1	Shore	Joseph		1		1					1				3		
Freetown	293	27	Shore	Mary Wid	1		1			2		1	1				6		
Taunton	367	18	Shores	Abraham				1					1				2		
Taunton	366	45	Shores	Benjamin			1	1	1		1		1	1	1		6		
Taunton	358	21	Shores	John	1			1				1					3		

TOWN	PG#	LN#	LAST NAME	FIRST NAME	FREE WHITE MALES under 10	10 to 16	16 to 26	26 to 45	45 and over	FREE WHITE FEMALES under 10	10 to 16	16 to 26	26 to 45	45 and over	TOTAL ALL OTHER	TOTAL SLAVES	TOTALS	DISTRICT/ TOWNSHIP	NOTES
Taunton	361	1	Shores	Jonathan	1			1		2			1				5		
Rehoboth	312	28	Shores	Zephaniah		2		1		1	1		1				6		
Rehoboth	309	5	Short	Daniel		1		1	1	1			1				5		
Rehoboth	311	9	Short	Ebenezer		1		1		1	1						5		
Rehoboth	305	31	Short	Ebenzer			1		1	1		1					5		
Swansea	400	1	Short	John				1					2				3		
Taunton	368	43	Short	Luther	1			1			1		1				4		
Rehoboth	309	4	Short	Philip		1		2	1	1		1					9		
Swansea	403	1	Short	Simeon	1			1		3		1	1				7		
Rehoboth	311	6	Shory	Abel		2	1		5			1					10		
Rehoboth	308	14	Shory	Abel 2nd			1		1	2		1					7		
Rehoboth	311	8	Shory	Jacob			1					1					2		
Rehoboth	311	3	Shory	John				1				1	1				3		
Rehoboth	311	7	Shory	Zepheniah						1	1	1					3		
Berkley	280	11	Shove	Asa		1	1		1	1		2		1			7		
Freetown	281	5	Shove	Azrah	1	1	1		1	3			1				8		
Berkley	280	1	Shove	Edward		1	2		1		1		2	1			8		
Berkley	280	14	Shove	George		1	2		1	1		3		1			9		
Berkley	280	20	Shove	Hannah Wid						1	1	1					3		
Somerset	406	18	Shove	Nathll		1			1		1						3		
Berkley	280	12	Shove	Samuel		1		1		3		1					6		
Berkley	280	2	Shove	Theophelus			1					1					2		
Somerset	404	4	Shove	Theophelus		3			1	2	1		1				8		
Berkley	280	18	Shove	William			1	1			1	2	1				6		
Rehoboth	312	26	Showry	Sarah									2				2		
Taunton	363	16	Sickell	Silas				1			1		1				3		
Taunton	363	15	Sickell	Silas Junior				1		1	4	1		1			7		
Taunton	360	17	Sidens	Martin			1			4			1				6		
Swansea	401	37	Simmons	Abigail	1					1		1					3		
Freetown	284	18	Simmons	Abraham	1		1	1				1	1				5		
Freetown	286	20	Simmons	Abraham Jun	1		1		1	1							4		
Somerset	404	5	Simmons	Brown	1	1		1		1	2	4		1			11		
Rehoboth	303	35	Simmons	Comfort	1	1	1		3	2	1	1					11		
Dighton	410	5	Simmons	Constant		1	1	1	1			3		1			8		
Dighton	409	26	Simmons	Constant 2d	1		1					1					3		
Dighton	414	7	Simmons	Edward	2	1			1	3		1					8		
Rehoboth	304	27	Simmons	Edward		1	1	1		2		1					8		
Dighton	414	5	Simmons	Eliphalet	2			1		1	1	1					6		
Freetown	284	22	Simmons	Harvey	2			2		2			1		1		8		
Dighton	409	31	Simmons	Jereh				1					1				2		
Freetown	286	28	Simmons	Job			1			1		1					3		
Freetown	291	18	Simmons	John				1					1				2		
Dighton	409	30	Simmons	Joshua		1		1		4	2		1				9		
Dighton	414	22	Simmons	Mercy		1	1			2	2	1					7		
Dighton	412	37	Simmons	Seth	1	1	1		1	1	1	1					7		
Freetown	286	23	Simmons	Silvester	1	1				2			1				6		
Raynham	376	25	Simmons	Thomas	2			1		1			1				5		
Rehoboth	303	34	Simmons	Thomas			1			1		1			3				
Somerset	405	28	Simmons	Zephaniah	2	2	1	1	1	1	1	1					10		
Dighton	409	25	Simons	Hannah Wido		1				1	1		1				4		
Rehoboth	315	2	Sips	Stephen											4		4		
New Bedford	432	17	Sisson	Benjamin	2	2		1		2	2		1				10		
Westport	336	22	Sisson	Content		1						1		1			3		
Swansea	402	24	Sisson	Eleck	3			1		1		1	1				7		
Swansea	402	17	Sisson	Gardner	1		1			2		1					5		
Swansea	402	36	Sisson	Gideon				1			2	2	1				6		
Somerset	408	15	Sisson	Gilbert		1		1					1				3		
Westport	336	14	Sisson	Hannah	3						2	1	1				7		
Swansea	402	7	Sisson	Isaac	1	1		1		2	2	1					8		
Swansea	402	29	Sisson	John				1		1			1				4		
New Bedford	432	6	Sisson	Jonathan		1	1			1			1				4		
Westport	336	7	Sisson	Jonathan		1		1					1	2			5		
New Bedford	432	16	Sisson	Mary									1				1		
Westport	336	21	Sisson	Peleg	3			1					1				5		
Westport	336	11	Sisson	Philip			1	1				2	1				5		
Swansea	399	23	Sisson	Richard		1				2	1	1		1			6		
Westport	336	13	Sisson	Richmond				1				1	1				3		
Dartmouth	350	15	Sisson	Stephen			1	2			1	1				7			
Westport	336	9	Sisson	William	1	2		1		2		1					7		
Westport	336	8	Sisson	Wilson	1	1	1	1		3		1					8		
Taunton	370	5	Skiff	Abraham	1		1					1					3		
Berkley	278	16	Skiff	Isaac		1					1						2		
Mansfield	387	14	Skinner	David		1		1			2		1				5		
Mansfield	387	26	Skinner	David Jr				1		2	1	1					5		
Mansfield	387	32	Skinner	Ezra	1	2		1		3	1		1				9		
Mansfield	387	29	Skinner	Hewit	1		1			3		1		1			7		
Mansfield	387	18	Skinner	Isaac	1			1				1					3		
Mansfield	387	16	Skinner	Jacob	1	1	2		1	1			1				7		
Mansfield	387	15	Skinner	James	1			1		4	1	1	1				9		
Mansfield	387	33	Skinner	Otis			1			1		1					3		
Mansfield	387	17	Skinner	Robert	1	1		1		2		1					6		
Mansfield	387	24	Skinner	Rufus		1					1		1				3		

TOWN	PG#	LN#	LAST NAME	FIRST NAME	FWM <10	FWM 10-16	FWM 16-26	FWM 26-45	FWM 45+	FWF <10	FWF 10-16	FWF 16-26	FWF 26-45	FWF 45+	TOTAL ALL OTHER	TOTAL SLAVES	TOTALS	DISTRICT/TOWNSHIP	NOTES
Mansfield	387	19	Skinner	Thomas				1						1			2		
Mansfield	387	20	Skinner	Thomas Jur	1		1		1	2	2	1		1			9		
Mansfield	387	28	Skinner	William				1		3			1				5		
Norton	383	40	Skinner	Zophir	1			1				1					3		
Mansfield	387	31	Slack	Lewis	3			1	1				1				6		
Attleboro	322	2	Slack	Samuel		1		1	1	1		3	1				8		
Dartmouth	350	42	Slaid	Edward	1	1		1	1	1	1		1			8			
Westport	336	25	Slaid	Samuel			1			1		1	1				3		
Swansea	396	20	Slead	Benja	1	2			1	2	5			1			12		
Somerset	408	16	Slead	Capt											5		5		
Somerset	407	34	Slead	Charles		4			1		1	1	1				7		
Somerset	407	35	Slead	Charles Jr	1		1			3	1	1					7		
Somerset	407	21	Slead	Edward	2			1		3			1				7		
Swansea	396	15	Slead	Elisha	2			1		2			1				6		
Somerset	407	20	Slead	Eliz Wido	1	4	1				2		1				9		
Swansea	396	24	Slead	Ezra	2			1		1	1	1		1			7		
Swansea	396	16	Slead	Howland	1			1		2			1				5		
Swansea	396	22	Slead	John	2		1					1	1				5		
Somerset	407	23	Slead	Jonathan		2			1	1	4			1			9		
Swansea	398	9	Slead	Philip	1		1	1	1	1	1			1			7		
Somerset	407	29	Slead	William	1		1		1	1	2		1				7		
Swansea	399	35	Slead	William	1		1			1		1					4		
Dartmouth	349	20	Slocum	Caleb		1		1		1							3		
Dartmouth	349	25	Slocum	Ceasar									3				3		
Dartmouth	351	11	Slocum	Christopher		1		1				1					3		
Dartmouth	349	18	Slocum	Elihu	2	1		1	1	1		1					11		
Dartmouth	350	37	Slocum	Elihu 2nd		1					1	1					5		
Dartmouth	349	22	Slocum	Giles		1		1			1	1					6		
Dartmouth	350	25	Slocum	Holder		1		1					1	2			5		
Dartmouth	349	17	Slocum	Jonas	1	1		1	3	2		1					10		
Dartmouth	349	16	Slocum	Jonathan			1			1	1	1					4		
Dartmouth	349	15	Slocum	Jonathan Junr		1						1					5		
Dartmouth	349	21	Slocum	Peleg 1st	1		1	1				3	1				7		
Dartmouth	351	7	Slocum	Peleg 2nd		1		1					1				3		
Rehoboth	315	1	Slocum	Prime										8			8		
Dartmouth	350	7	Slocum	Santo									3				3		
Rehoboth	312	25	Smith	Abial		1		1					1	1			4		
Norton	383	34	Smith	Abisha	1			1		3	2	1					8		
Freetown	285	14	Smith	Abner	1		1	1	1		1	1	1	1			8		
Taunton	370	1	Smith	Abraham	1	1		1		1			1				5		
Taunton	360	42	Smith	Allen			1			4			1	1			7		
Norton	383	25	Smith	Anna	1		2			1			1				5		
Rehoboth	309	1	Smith	Aron		1		2				1	1			6			
Norton	383	28	Smith	Arunah	3			1		2		1	1				8		
Dighton	409	36	Smith	Asa	2		1			1		1					5		
Dartmouth	349	31	Smith	Benjamin	1		1		2	1		1				7			
Dartmouth	349	37	Smith	Benjamin			1						1			2			
Dartmouth	350	40	Smith	Benjamin Jr			1			1		1				4			
Dartmouth	350	41	Smith	Benjamin Junr		1					1					5			
Dartmouth	349	39	Smith	Collins	1		1		3			1				8			
Swansea	403	18	Smith	Constant	2	2			1		1		1				7		
Attleboro	319	41	Smith	Cyrel		1	1					1		1			4		
Dighton	409	37	Smith	Daniel		1				1		1					3		
Attleboro	321	44	Smith	David		1			2		1	3		2			9		
Norton	383	23	Smith	David				1						1			2		
Dartmouth	349	19	Smith	Deliverance		1			2	1						5			
Raynham	376	23	Smith	Ebenezer			1						1				2		
Freetown	293	23	Smith	Edward			1			2		1	1				5		
Dartmouth	350	1	Smith	Elihu			1		2				1			5			
Rehoboth	308	46	Smith	Ezekiel		1		1				1	1			5			
Dartmouth	349	32	Smith	George	1	1	1	1					1	1		6			
Taunton	369	38	Smith	George			1						1			2			
Dartmouth	349	23	Smith	George 2nd	1	1	1		2	1			1	1		10			
Freetown	293	17	Smith	Gilbert	2			1		1			1				5		
Dartmouth	349	24	Smith	H. Benjamin		1	1			1						6			
Taunton	356	1	Smith	Hannah Wido	*	*	*	*	*	*	*	*	*	*			*		
Dartmouth	350	12	Smith	Henry	1	1		1				1	1			5			
Rehoboth	311	37	Smith	Huldah							1	1	1				3		
Dartmouth	349	34	Smith	Increas			1						1			2			
Raynham	376	26	Smith	Isaac				1						1			2		
Taunton	369	14	Smith	Isaac				1		2			1				4		
Norton	383	37	Smith	Jacob		1	1		1		1	1	1				6		
Dighton	413	40	Smith	James	1	2			1	1	1	4		1			11		
Taunton	369	37	Smith	James	1	1	3		1	4	1	1		1			13		
Dartmouth	349	38	Smith	Jiles	1		1		3	1						7			
Dartmouth	350	46	Smith	John	1			1		1		1	1			5			
Dighton	409	5	Smith	John	3	2	2		1	1		1	2	1			13		
Rehoboth	299	21	Smith	John		1		1		1			1				4		
Rehoboth	307	7	Smith	John		2	1		1	1		1	1				8		
Rehoboth	308	44	Smith	John 2nd		1		1			1		1	1			5		
Taunton	358	38	Smith	John W.	1		1	1		1	2		1		1		8		
Norton	383	29	Smith	Jonathan		1		1		3			1				6		
Rehoboth	305	42	Smith	Joseph			1	1					1				4		
Rehoboth	297	16	Smith	Joshua				1	1		1		1				5		

TOWN	PG#	LN#	LAST NAME	FIRST NAME	FREE WHITE MALES					FREE WHITE FEMALES					TOTAL ALL OTHER	TOTAL SLAVES	TOTALS	DISTRICT/ TOWNSHIP	NOTES
					under 10	10 to 16	16 to 26	26 to 45	45 and over	under 10	10 to 16	16 to 26	26 to 45	45 and over					
Rehoboth	314	12	Smith	Joshua Jr				1	2				1				7		
Dartmouth	350	44	Smith	Lowrey			1		1	1							5		
Dartmouth	349	33	Smith	Mary	1	1						1	1	1			5		
Dartmouth	349	30	Smith	Meribah									2				2		
Rehoboth	309	2	Smith	Narthaniel	2			1	1	1	2		1				10		
Mansfield	387	21	Smith	Nicholas					1					2			3		
Taunton	370	4	Smith	Noah				1		1			1				3		
Rehoboth	308	45	Smith	Oliver	2		1		2	1	1						9		
Dartmouth	349	40	Smith	Peleg		1	1				1		1				5		
Dartmouth	349	35	Smith	Perry			1		1				1				6		
Dartmouth	350	5	Smith	Ruben				1	2	1			1				7		
Dighton	409	24	Smith	Saml	1	2		1	1	2	3			1			11		
Dartmouth	349	36	Smith	Samuel		1		1			1						4		
Rehoboth	297	17	Smith	Samuel	1		1			1		1	1				5		
Taunton	356	4	Smith	Sarah Wido		1	2						1				4		
Norton	383	24	Smith	Seth		1		1						1			3		
Mansfield	387	30	Smith	Spencer	1		1			2			1				5		
Dighton	409	35	Smith	Stephen	1			1						1			3		
Mansfield	387	25	Smith	Stephen	2	1		1		1	2			1			8		
Dighton	410	20	Smith	Stephen Jr	1		1			4	1		1				8		
Swansea	400	44	Smith	Thomas	2	1		1		1			1				6		
Norton	383	21	Smith	Timothy			1	1	1	1		2		1			7		
Dighton	412	46	Smith	William					1					1			2		
Raynham	376	28	Smith	William	1	1			1	1		1		1			6		
Raynham	376	24	Smith	William Junior	1		1			2		1					5		
Freetown	289	23	Snell	Amos					1					1	3		5		
Freetown	289	24	Snell	Amos Jr	2			1		2			1		4		10		
Dighton	414	9	Snell	Anthony			1						1				2		
Westport	336	18	Snell	Benjamin	1	2		1		1	1						6		
Freetown	289	22	Snell	George	2		1			2	2		1		2		10		
Westport	336	23	Snell	James	1								1				3		
Westport	336	28	Snell	Job	3	2	1	1		3	1		1				13		
Dighton	414	14	Snell	John		1		1					1	1			4		
Attleboro	320	6	Snell	Lorana						1			1				2		
Westport	336	12	Snell	Peter					1				4	1			6		
Easton	393	17	Snow	Calvin	2	1		1		4	1		1				10		
Raynham	375	29	Snow	Ebenezer					1					1			2		
Raynham	375	28	Snow	Ebenezer Junior	2	1		1		1	1		1				7		
Mansfield	387	13	Snow	Reuben		1	1	1	1				1	1			6		
Raynham	372	22	Snow	Solomon	1	1			1			1		1			5		
Easton	393	22	Snow	William	3			1		1			1	1			7		
Taunton	361	19	Soper	Oliver	1		1	1		1			1	1			6		
Westport	336	2	Soule	Benjamin 2d	1		1			1		1					4		
Westport	336	4	Soule	Benjamin Senr				1				1		1			3		
Westport	335	39	Soule	David	3		1			3		1					9		
Westport	335	37	Soule	Henry		1		1					1	1			4		
Westport	336	1	Soule	Hiram	1		1						1				3		
Westport	336	19	Soule	Jacob	3			1						1			5		
Westport	335	40	Soule	Jona			1	1					1	2			5		
Westport	336	10	Soule	Joseph			1	1						1			4		
Westport	335	38	Soule	Lemuel	2	1		1		1	1		1				7		
Westport	335	36	Soule	Nathaniel	1	1	1	1		2		1		1			8		
Westport	336	16	Soule	Oliver	1		1	1		1	1						6		
Westport	336	20	Soule	Sarah									1	1			2		
Westport	335	41	Soule	Wesson				1						1			2		
Freetown	284	5	Southwick	Joshua			1						1				2		
Dartmouth	350	22	Sowle	William	1		1	1				1			4				
Taunton	360	28	Spinney	Benjamin	1	1				2			1				6		
New Bedford	432	3	Spooner	Benjamin			1	1		1	1	1		1			6		
New Bedford	432	24	Spooner	Elnathan		2		1	1	1			2	1			8		
Dighton	414	3	Spooner	James	1		1	1					1				4		
New Bedford	432	22	Spooner	John	1			1		3			1				6		
Attleboro	321	29	Sprague	John		1	1	1		2		2		1			8		
Rehoboth	299	5	Sprague	Samuel		1	1	1		1	2		3				9		
Taunton	367	4	Sproal	James	2	1		2		3	1	2		1	1		13		
Taunton	360	40	Stacey	Amos	3			2		4			2				11		
Taunton	368	18	Stacey	James		1		1				1	2	1			6		
Taunton	369	5	Stacey	Job				1						1			2		
Taunton	368	14	Stacey	Job Junior	4	1							1				6		
Taunton	365	36	Stacey	Lemuel	2					1		1	1				5		
Dartmouth	350	13	Stafford	Lilly		1		2				1	1	1	7				
Taunton	358	39	Stall	William		1	1	1		3	1		1				8		
Dighton	410	29	Standish	David			1			3	1	1	1				7		
Attleboro	323	9	Stanley	Amos			1		1				1	1			4		
Norton	383	36	Stanley	Benjamin			1		1	1		1	2	1			7		
Attleboro	321	58	Stanley	Catherine	2	1				1	2		1				7		
Attleboro	323	12	Stanley	George	1	1	1			1	1	1					6		
Attleboro	323	4	Stanley	Jesse	1	1		1	1	1		3	2	1			12		
Attleboro	323	6	Stanley	Jona	1	2	1		1	2		1	1	1			10		
Attleboro	323	5	Stanley	Stephen	1	1		1		2			1				6		
Attleboro	322	40	Stanley	Wm	1		2	2					2	1			8		
Taunton	363	3	Staples	Ebenezer	4	1				1			1				8		
Taunton	363	18	Staples	George		1			1		1	1		1			5		
Taunton	362	36	Staples	George Junior		1			1				1	1			4		
Taunton	361	35	Staples	Job		1		1		2			1				5		

TOWN	PG#	LN#	LAST NAME	FIRST NAME	FREE WHITE MALES under 10	10 to 16	16 to 26	26 to 45	45 and over	FREE WHITE FEMALES under 10	10 to 16	16 to 26	26 to 45	45 and over	TOTAL ALL OTHER	TOTAL SLAVES	TOTALS	DISTRICT/ TOWNSHIP	NOTES
Berkley	278	10	Staples	Joseph		1		1			1		1				4		
Taunton	363	5	Staples	Joshua	3		1	1		1	1	1					8		
Taunton	364	40	Staples	Nathaniel				1					1				2		
Taunton	363	4	Staples	Noah				1					1				2		
Taunton	363	17	Staples	Samuel		2	2	1		1	1		1				8		
Taunton	364	41	Staples	Seth			1					1					2		
Attleboro	319	17	Starkey	Amos	1	1		1		1		1					6		
Attleboro	318	32	Starkey	Sarah							1		1				2		
Attleboro	319	25	Starkey	Sibil	2		1					1	2	1			7		
Attleboro	319	11	Starkey	Thoms	1			1					1	1			4		
Attleboro	319	62	Starkey	Thoms Junr	3	1	1			2		1					8		
Rehoboth	307	16	Starkweather	Ephraim			1					1			2				
Rehoboth	307	17	Starkweather	Oliver	1		1			1		1			6				
Swansea	402	12	Stead	Peleg		3		1		4			1				9		
Somerset	406	12	Stead	Stephen				1		1			1				3		
Mansfield	387	27	Stearns	Isaac	1	1		1		2			1				6		
Easton	393	24	Stearns	Simeon				1			1	1					3		
Dighton	411	8	Stephen	Saml		2		1		1	3		1				8		
Taunton	361	39	Stephens	Asa	1		1			1		1					4		
Taunton	357	22	Stephens	Barzilla		1	1	1		1	1		1				6		
Dighton	411	5	Stephens	Benja				1				2	1				4		
Dighton	415	13	Stephens	Benja Jr			1			1		1					3		
Taunton	357	9	Stephens	Ebenezer				1									1		
Dighton	411	6	Stephens	John		3		1				1	1				6		
Rehoboth	312	23	Stephens	Samuel		1	1	2		2	1	1			9				
Dighton	409	11	Stetson	Ebenz			1	1		2	2		1				7		
New Bedford	432	4	Stetson	Joseph			1				1		1				3		
New Bedford	432	12	Stetson	Nathaniel	1	3	1	1		1		1	1				9		
New Bedford	432	14	Stetson	William			1			1		1					3		
New Bedford	432	18	Stevens	Eunice		2						1		1			4		
New Bedford	432	21	Stevens	Job	1		1			1		1					4		
New Bedford	432	5	Stevens	Seth	1		1	1		4	1	1	1				10		
New Bedford	432	20	Stevens	William			1						1				2		
Taunton	356	15	Stoddard	Elijah	2		1					1	1				5		
Taunton	356	14	Stoddard	Miles		1	1			1			1				4		
New Bedford	432	7	Stoddard	Nichols	2		1			1		1	1				6		
New Bedford	432	8	Stoddard	Noah	1	1	1	1		1	1		1				7		
New Bedford	432	19	Stoddard	Samuel		1	1						1				3		
Easton	393	23	Stokes	Ira	1		1			2			1				5		
Easton	393	15	Stone	Ephraim	2		1						1				4		
Norton	383	26	Stone	Nathaniel	3	1	1		1	4	2	2	1				15		
Easton	393	21	Stone	Solomon	2		1			3	1	1					8		
Norton	383	35	Storey	Elijah	2	2	1			2	1		1				9		
Easton	393	18	Storey	Thomas		2	1	1		1			1				6		
Norton	383	30	Storey	Thomas			1	1				2		2			6		
Norton	383	27	Storey	William	1		1	1		2			1				6		
Freetown	281	8	Strange	Charles	2	1	1	1		3	2	1	1	1			13		
Freetown	281	9	Strange	John	1	2		1			1	2					8		
Swansea	402	48	Strange	John	1			1		2			1				5		
Berkley	279	19	Strange	Joseph			1						1				2		
Freetown	285	13	Strange	Lot			1		1	1	2	2		1			8		
Freetown	291	7	Strange	William	2			1		1			1				5		
Attleboro	323	16	Stratton	Lemuel	1			1		1	1	2	1				7		
Dartmouth	350	16	Stratton	Udel			2				1				3				
Taunton	357	15	Sumner	Ebenezer	2	2	1				1	1	1		1		9		
Taunton	366	19	Sumner	Jezaniah			2		2	1	2		1				8		
Taunton	366	18	Sumner	Seth	1		1			2			1				5		
Attleboro	322	58	Swan	Dutey	1		1					1					3		
Attleboro	322	57	Swan	Robert	1	1		1				1					4		
Somerset	404	23	Swasey	Jerathmeel	1	3		1		1	2		1				9		
Somerset	405	21	Swasey	Joseph	2		1			3	2		1				9		
Somerset	404	24	Swasey	Polly Wido		1					1		1				3		
Mansfield	387	23	Sweet	Benjamin		1	2	1					1	1			6		
Attleboro	320	5	Sweet	Gideon	2	2	1	1	1	1	1	3	1	1			14		
Attleboro	320	2	Sweet	Gideon Junr		1				1	1						3		
Attleboro	318	53	Sweet	Henry	2			1	1	1	2	2	1	1			11		
Norton	383	33	Sweet	John	1		1			1	1		1				5		
Attleboro	319	42	Sweet	Michael	1		1		1			1	1	1			6		
Norton	383	31	Sweet	Michael	2	2	1			3		1	1				10		
Attleboro	319	66	Sweet	Nathaniel				1						2			3		
Attleboro	320	15	Sweet	Thoms	1	1		1	1	2	1						8		
Attleboro	318	6	Sweet	Zebadiah		1	2	1					1				5		
Attleboro	322	6	Sweeting	John				2						2			4		
Attleboro	321	49	Swetland	Clark		2		1		3	1	1					8		
Attleboro	322	50	Swetland	George			1			1		1	1				4		
Attleboro	322	51	Swetland	John				1		1		1	1				4		
Attleboro	322	52	Swetland	Oliver	1	1	1			2	1	1					7		
Attleboro	321	47	Swetland	William			2	1			2	2		1			8		
Attleboro	321	48	Swetland	William the 2nd	1	1		1			2	2	1				8		
Attleboro	321	42	Swettland	Bowen	5		2	1		5			1				14		
New Bedford	432	11	Swift	Asa	2			1					1	1			5		
Taunton	367	5	Swift	Foster		2	1	1		1	2		1		1		9		
Dartmouth	351	24	Taber	Amos	1			1							6				

TOWN	PG#	LN#	HEADS OF HOUSEHOLD		FREE WHITE MALES					FREE WHITE FEMALES					TOTAL ALL OTHER	TOTAL SLAVES	TOTALS	DISTRICT/ TOWNSHIP	NOTES
			LAST NAME	FIRST NAME	under 10	10 to 16	16 to 26	26 to 45	45 and over	under 10	10 to 16	16 to 26	26 to 45	45 and over					
Dartmouth	351	31	Taber	Benjamin	1	1	1			1		1			8				
Westport	337	24	Taber	Joseph	1		1			1		1					4		
Westport	337	22	Taber	Mary Wd								1	1				2		
Westport	337	12	Taber	Oseck		1	1	1		1	1	1	1	1			8		
Westport	336	31	Taber	Philip	1	1			1	1			1	1			6		
Westport	337	40	Taber	Thomas	1			1		3	1		1	1			8		
Dighton	414	8	Talbot	Elka		2	1			1		1					5		
Dighton	413	33	Talbot	Hannah		1	2						1				4		
Dighton	412	32	Talbot	Jedediah		1		1					1				3		
Dighton	414	10	Talbot	Joseph	1	3		1	1		1	3		1			11		
Dighton	413	37	Talbot	Joseph 2d	1			1		1			1				4		
Dighton	411	35	Talbot	Josiah	2	1	2		1	2	1	1		2			12		
Dighton	413	15	Talbot	Saml	2	1	1		1			2		1	1		9		
Dighton	413	16	Talbot	Silas	1			1		3	1						6		
Dighton	412	34	Talbot	Zepha	3				1	1	1			1			7		
Westport	337	42	Tallman	Ezekiel	1			1	1	3	2	1	1				10		
Westport	337	1	Tallman	Gideon		1	1		1	1	1		1	2			8		
Westport	337	37	Tallman	James				1					1				2		
Westport	337	2	Tallman	Jonathan				1		1	1			1			4		
Attleboro	317	5	Tate	Sally		1	1							1			3		
Easton	393	35	Taylor	David	3			1		2	1		1				8		
Dighton	409	39	Teaston	Seth			2		2				4	1			9		
Freetown	290	8	Terry	Ebenezer	2	2	1					1	1	1			9		
Swansea	398	29	Terry	James					1	2			1	1			5		
Freetown	284	9	Terry	Job		2			1	1		1	1				6		
Freetown	288	27	Terry	Robert	3			2		1			1	2			9		
Freetown	288	28	Terry	Robert Jr		1		1		1	1		1				5		
Freetown	291	1	Terry	Zepheniah			2	1	1	1	2		1				8		
Berkley	281	4	Tew	Abigal Wid	1	1				1	2		1				6		
Berkley	281	3	Tew	Dan		1	2	1		1		2	2	1			10		
Berkley	281	5	Tew	Henry				1				2		2			5		
Berkley	281	6	Tew	Henry Junr	2	1	2		1	2	1		1				10		
Berkley	281	12	Tew	Margaret Wid								2		1			3		
Attleboro	320	48	Thatcher	Peter	1		1	1	1	1	3			2			10		
Taunton	368	36	Thayer	Abiather	1	1		1		1			1				5		
Mansfield	387	37	Thayer	Christopher				1					1				2		
Easton	393	32	Thayer	Jacob		2	1		1	2	1		1				8		
Taunton	368	31	Thayer	John			2	1					1	1			5		
Taunton	368	28	Thayer	John Junior	3	1		1		2	1		1	1			10		
Taunton	365	27	Thayer	Jonathan				1	1			1		1			4		
Taunton	365	28	Thayer	Jonathan Junr			1						1				2		
Easton	393	26	Thayer	Nathaniel	2	1	1	1	1	2	1	1	1				11		
Mansfield	387	38	Thayer	Remember	1								1	1			3		
Easton	393	34	Thayer	Samuel	2	1		1		2	1		1				8		
Taunton	357	12	Thayer	Seth	1			1				2	1	1			6		
Easton	393	31	Thayer	Stephen	3	1		1		1	1		1	1			9		
Freetown	288	3	Thomas	Elihu	2		1			1			1				5		
Freetown	293	14	Thomas	Jedidiah	1		1						1				3		
Taunton	362	3	Thomas	Richard	1			1		2			1				5		
Swansea	403	6	Thompson	Charles		1		1		1	1		1				5		
Easton	393	28	Thompson	David		1		1					1				3		
Easton	393	29	Thompson	David Jr	1			1		4			1				7		
Taunton	364	23	Thompson	Samuel				1				1					2		
Taunton	358	6	Thrasher	Elkanah	3			1					1				5		
Taunton	357	5	Thrasher	John		1	1		1	1			1				5		
Rehoboth	304	22	Threeshear	Aaron	1	1	1			1			1		8				
Rehoboth	311	38	Threeshear	Asa		1							2		3				
Rehoboth	304	23	Threeshear	Barnabas				1		1	1		1		4				
Attleboro	317	27	Throop	Amos		1		2				1		2			6		
Rehoboth	304	18	Thurber	Benjamin		1		1		1	1				6				
Rehoboth	298	21	Thurber	Daniel		1		1		1	2	1			6				
Rehoboth	304	19	Thurber	David		1		3			1				6				
Rehoboth	304	21	Thurber	James 2nd		1						1			2				
Rehoboth	304	17	Thurber	Leonard			1			1			1		3				
Rehoboth	305	18	Thurber	Nathaniel		1		2		2			1	1	8				
Rehoboth	304	20	Thurber	Reuben		1							1		4				
Freetown	290	13	Thurston	Edward			2	1		2		2	2	1			10		
Freetown	286	25	Thurston	Peleg	1		2	1					1				5		
Freetown	286	27	Thurston	Samuel				1				2			1		4		
Freetown	286	24	Thurston	Thomas			2	1					1	1			5		
Swansea	399	4	Thurston	Varnum	1		1						1				3		
Westport	337	16	Tibbets	Henry	2	1		1		2	1		1				8		
Westport	337	3	Tibbets	John				1		1		1		1			4		
Attleboro	318	22	Tiffany	Betsey	1							1	1				3		
Taunton	371	20	Tiffany	Cyrus											4		4		
Attleboro	319	36	Tiffany	Daniel		1		1		1		1	1				5		
Attleboro	318	24	Tiffany	Ebenezer	2	1		1	1	1	1		1	1			9		
Attleboro	319	47	Tiffany	Noah	3	2		1		2	1	2	1				12		
Mansfield	387	36	Tiffany	William				1					1				2		
Easton	393	33	Tilden	David		1		1		2			1				5		
Taunton	360	21	Tillinghast	Nicholas	1			1		3	1		1	1	1		9		
Westport	337	30	Tilson	Jacob				1				1	1	1			4		
Raynham	375	14	Timberlake	James	1		1						1				3		

TOWN	PG#	LN#	LAST NAME	FIRST NAME	FREE WHITE MALES					FREE WHITE FEMALES					TOTAL ALL OTHER	TOTAL SLAVES	TOTALS	DISTRICT/ TOWNSHIP	NOTES
					under 10	10 to 16	16 to 26	26 to 45	45 and over	under 10	10 to 16	16 to 26	26 to 45	45 and over					
Attleboro	322	21	Tingley	Lucy	1	1						1		1			4		
Attleboro	322	33	Tingley	Thomas Junr			1			1		1					3		
Attleboro	322	32	Tingley	Thoms				1			1	1	1				4		
Attleboro	322	22	Tingley	Timothy	3			1			1		1				6		
Freetown	285	27	Tinkam	Arther	2		1			1		1					5		
Freetown	282	9	Tisdale	Abigail Wid.						1			1				2		
Taunton	359	12	Tisdale	Deborah Wido	4	1	2			2	1	1					11		
Taunton	358	3	Tisdale	Ephraim	1	1	1		1	1	1		2				8		
Taunton	367	38	Tisdale	Hannah Wido						3	1	1	3				8		
Taunton	367	39	Tisdale	James	1	1	1		1	1	1	2	2	1			11		
Easton	393	27	Tisdale	John	2	1	1	1		2	1	1					9		
Taunton	359	2	Tisdale	Joseph	1	2	1		1	2	2	1					10		
Norton	383	42	Tisdale	Polly						1	1						2		
Taunton	360	31	Tisdale	Simeon		6	3		1	1	1		2				14		
Taunton	367	34	Tisdale	Tabatha Wido			1	1					1				3		
Berkley	277	5	Tisdale	Thomas		1	2						1				4		
Rehoboth	312	24	Titas	Comfort		1				1						3			
Rehoboth	308	15	Tittas	Comfort	1		1			1		1				4			
Norton	383	43	Titus	Ebenezer		1	1		1		2	3		2			10		
Attleboro	317	9	Titus	John	1		1					1					3		
Mansfield	387	35	Titus	Joseph	1			1		1		1	1				5		
Attleboro	317	26	Titus	Peter	2		1	1				1					5		
Attleboro	318	10	Titus	Rbecca									2				2		
Attleboro	317	1	Titus	Samuel	1	1		1	1	2	1						8		
Norton	383	47	Titus	Silvester	1		1			1		1					4		
Attleboro	317	8	Titus	Simeon		1	1		1			1	1				5		
Attleboro	320	28	Titus	Timothy	3		1			1	1	1	1				8		
Berkley	274	3	Tobey	Appolos	2		1				1	1					5		
Berkley	274	2	Tobey	Nathaniel	1	1	1		1		2		1				7		
Berkley	274	1	Tobey	Samuel		1	3	1	1	1	2	1	1				12		
Dartmouth	351	13	Toby	Cornelius		1		1			1		1			6			
Mansfield	387	34	Todd	Archibald	1	1		1		1	1		1				6		
Westport	337	23	Tomkins	Gilbert	3	1		1		2			2				9		
Freetown	284	28	Tompkins	Benjamin			1			5		1					7		
Taunton	368	46	Torrey	Levi		1			1	2			1				5		
Freetown	286	6	Torry	Benjamin		1		1		1		1					4		
Freetown	286	7	Torry	Susannah Wd								1	1				2		
Dighton	415	9	Tosolong	Leander											3		3		
Attleboro	323	11	Town	Gideon	3		1		1	1		3					9		
Berkley	278	12	Townsand	Gilbert	2	1		1					1	1			6		
Taunton	365	20	Townshend	Job	1			1		1	1		1				7		
Taunton	365	8	Townshend	Job Junr	1	1	1			1		1					5		
Taunton	359	39	Townshend	John	1	1		1	1			2	1				7		
Dartmouth	351	30	Trafford	Joseph	1			1	1	2	1					7			
Dighton	409	18	Trafton	Benja		1	1		1		1		1				5		
Swansea	398	38	Trafton	Elias D	2		1			1	1	1					6		
Dighton	409	16	Trafton	Snow			1			3		1					5		
Somerset	407	33	Trip	Mial	1		1			3		1					6		
Dartmouth	351	15	Tripp	Abner		1	2			1						5			
Westport	337	7	Tripp	Anthony			1				1	2					4		
Westport	337	33	Tripp	Benjamin			1					1					2		
Westport	337	26	Tripp	Caleb	2	1		1		2	1	1					8		
Westport	337	35	Tripp	Charles	2		1			1	1	1					6		
Westport	337	41	Tripp	Constant			1					1					2		
Westport	337	31	Tripp	Culbert		1	1			1		1					4		
Westport	336	29	Tripp	Daniel			1					1					2		
Westport	337	15	Tripp	Daniel Mason	2	1						1	1				6		
Westport	336	32	Tripp	David	2	1	1	1	1	1	2		1	1			11		
Westport	337	32	Tripp	Ebenezer	1	1	1				1	2		2			9		
Westport	337	36	Tripp	Ebenezer 2d	1	1	1				1		1				5		
Westport	337	11	Tripp	Edmond	3	2		1		1	1	1	1	2			12		
Westport	337	19	Tripp	Elihew	1		1			2	1						5		
Westport	337	4	Tripp	Elizabeth									1				1		
Dartmouth	351	16	Tripp	Ephraim			1			1		1				4			
Mansfield	387	39	Tripp	Ephraim	1	2	1		2	1		1		2			10		
Westport	337	38	Tripp	Ezekiel			1			1	1	1					4		
Westport	337	13	Tripp	George	2	1		1		4	1	1					10		
Westport	337	18	Tripp	Ichabod Junr				1					2				3		
Westport	337	5	Tripp	Isaac		1	1										2		
Westport	337	34	Tripp	Jacob			1			2	1	1					5		
Westport	337	6	Tripp	James	2	1				1	2	1					8		
Westport	337	29	Tripp	Job	2		1			1	1	1					6		
Dartmouth	351	23	Tripp	John		1		1			1		1			5			
Westport	336	33	Tripp	John	2	1		1		2	2	1					9		
Westport	337	20	Tripp	Jonathan	1		1	1		1			1	1			6		
Westport	336	34	Tripp	Joshua	1			1		1			1				4		
Westport	337	28	Tripp	Lot	3		1			1		1					6		
Westport	337	10	Tripp	Lovel	1			1			1	1		1			5		
Westport	336	30	Tripp	Luthern			1			2		2					5		
Westport	337	39	Tripp	Nathan	1	1	1			3	1	2	1				10		
Westport	337	27	Tripp	Nathaniel	1		1	1		2		1	1	1			8		
Dartmouth	351	28	Tripp	Othnial		1						2	1			4			
Westport	337	9	Tripp	Patience	1	2				2	1		1				7		
Westport	337	14	Tripp	Perry				2	2								4		
Westport	337	8	Tripp	Philip	2	1	1					1					5		

142

TOWN	PG#	LN#	HEADS OF HOUSEHOLD		FREE WHITE MALES					FREE WHITE FEMALES					TOTAL ALL OTHER	TOTAL SLAVES	TOTALS	DISTRICT/ TOWNSHIP	NOTES
			LAST NAME	FIRST NAME	under 10	10 to 16	16 to 26	26 to 45	45 and over	under 10	10 to 16	16 to 26	26 to 45	45 and over					
Westport	336	35	Tripp	Preserved	2		2	1					1				6		
Westport	337	21	Tripp	Thomas		1			1			1	1	2			6		
Westport	337	25	Tripp	Tullinghast			1			1		1					3		
Dartmouth	351	27	Tripp	William			1				1		1			3			
Westport	337	17	Tripp	Wilson			1		1		2		1	2			7		
Swansea	400	3	Trott	Jona				1						1			2		
Taunton	359	15	Truscott	Abigail Wido		1					2	1		1			5		
Somerset	405	26	Tubb	Samuel		2	2		1		2		1				8		
Taunton	360	32	Tubbs	Isaac	1	2	1		1	1		1		1			8		
Berkley	279	13	Tubbs	Samuel	3	2		1		3			1				10		
Dartmouth	351	19	Tucker	Abraham		1	1						1			3			
Norton	383	44	Tucker	Asahel	3			1		1		1	1				7		
Dartmouth	351	22	Tucker	Benjamin	1	1		1	1		1		1				7		
Dartmouth	351	21	Tucker	Berzilla			1	1					1			3			
Dartmouth	351	18	Tucker	Edward		1		3				1					5		
Dartmouth	351	32	Tucker	Henry	2	1	1		1			1		1			8		
Norton	383	46	Tucker	Hezekiah	2		1	1		1	2	1	1	1			10		
Dartmouth	351	29	Tucker	Holder			1			1	2					5			
Norton	383	45	Tucker	Jedediah				1		1			2	1			5		
Norton	383	48	Tucker	Jereth		1						1					2		
Dartmouth	351	20	Tucker	John		2		1		2	2					9			
Mansfield	387	40	Tucker	John											4		4		
Dartmouth	351	26	Tucker	Jonathan	1		1	1		1		1		1		7			
Dartmouth	351	17	Tucker	Joseph		1		1			1		1			4			
Taunton	371	1	Tucker	Joseph				1			2		1				4		
Taunton	370	39	Tucker	Joseph 2d			1			3	1		1				6		
Rehoboth	298	35	Tucker	Joshua			1		4			1					6		
Dartmouth	351	25	Tucker	Rebeccah								2				2			
Dartmouth	351	14	Tucker	Sambo										5		5			
Taunton	370	28	Turner	Abner	1			1				1		1			4		
Rehoboth	300	24	Turner	Amos		1		1		1			1				4		
Easton	393	25	Turner	Bethael	1	2		1		3	1		1				9		
Easton	393	30	Turner	Elijah	2			1		2	2	1	1				9		
Rehoboth	302	17	Turner	Ephraim	2			1		1	1	1					6		
Rehoboth	308	30	Turner	Ephram	1	1		1		1	1	1					6		
Freetown	285	2	Turner	John	2			1				1	1				5		
Rehoboth	307	1	Turner	Judah							1		1				2		
Rehoboth	300	22	Turner	Nathan		1						2					3		
Rehoboth	302	22	Turner	William		1		2				1					5		
Attleboro	318	1	Tyler	Ebenezer	1	1	2		1	2	1		1				9		
Attleboro	320	50	Tyler	Ebenezer the 2nd	1	2	2			1	2	3					11		
Attleboro	318	8	Tyler	Walter		1		1			1	1					4		
Attleboro	318	2	Tyler	Zelotes	1		1		1	4		1	1	1			10		
Attleboro	321	55	Tyron	Wm	1		1		1	1	1	1					6		
Westport	338	1	Underwood	Nicholas	3	3		1				3	1				11		
Dighton	414	21	Upham	Abijah	1		1			1	1	1					5		
Dighton	414	20	Upham	Barnet				1					1				2		
Dartmouth	351	34	Upham	James		1						1				3			
Berkley	275	13	Upton	Adonijah		1		1									2		
Swansea	402	5	Usher	Edward	2			1		3			1				7		
Dartmouth	351	33	Valentine	Lydia											4		4		
Somerset	408	1	Vendiome	Wido								1	1				2		
Norton	384	1	Verry	William	1		1	1		2	2		2	1			10		
Rehoboth	312	31	Vial	Allen			1	1				1	1				4		
Rehoboth	312	30	Vial	Benjamin			1			1			1				3		
Rehoboth	312	34	Vial	Constant		1		1		1		1					4		
Rehoboth	314	18	Vial	Hezekiah	1		1		1			1					5		
Rehoboth	312	33	Vial	John		2	1			2		1					6		
Rehoboth	312	29	Vial	Nathaniel	1		1	3				1					7		
Rehoboth	312	32	Vial	Rachel								2	2				4		
Attleboro	320	23	Viccory	Ruth		1	1						1				3		
Taunton	360	35	Vickery	Content Wido								1	1	1			3		
Taunton	357	6	Vickery	David	1	1			1	1		3	2		1		10		
Taunton	366	10	Vickery	Elijah	2	1		1		2			1				7		
Rehoboth	301	17	Vicory	Robert	2		1		2	1		1					8		
Taunton	367	13	Volleson	Leonard	2			1		1	1	1	1				7		
Swansea	399	11	Vose	John			1		1			1	1				4		
Easton	393	36	Vose	Reuben	1		1			3	1	1					7		
Easton	394	12	Wade	David	5		2	1		1	2	1	1	1			14		
Rehoboth	314	20	Wade	Ichabod	1			1		1		1					4		
Dartmouth	352	17	Wade	John	1			1			1	1	2			7			
Rehoboth	309	10	Wade	Luis	5			1		1	2		1				10		
Easton	394	39	Wade	Thomas	2	1		1		3			1				8		
Dartmouth	352	19	Wady	Humphrey		1	1						1			3			
Westport	339	8	Wainer	Michael											9		9		
Westport	339	7	Wainer	Thomas											2		2		
Dartmouth	352	20	Wait	Henry	2			1		2		1				6			
Westport	338	25	Wait	John		1	1	1		1			1				5		
Westport	339	4	Wait	Rebeccah									2				2		
Attleboro	320	66	Walcott	Benjm	3	1	1		1		1	2	1				10		
Attleboro	321	14	Walcott	Moses				1			1			1			3		
Attleboro	321	15	Walcott	Moses Junr		1		1		2	1		1				6		
Attleboro	321	16	Walcott	Pentecost		1	1		1	1	1		1				6		
Dighton	411	39	Waldren	Elijah					3					2			5		
Dighton	412	1	Waldron	Abraham				5	1				2	1			9		

TOWN	PG#	LN#	HEADS OF HOUSEHOLD LAST NAME	FIRST NAME	FREE WHITE MALES under 10	10 to 16	16 to 26	26 to 45	45 and over	FREE WHITE FEMALES under 10	10 to 16	16 to 26	26 to 45	45 and over	TOTAL ALL OTHER	TOTAL SLAVES	TOTALS	DISTRICT/ TOWNSHIP	NOTES
Dighton	412	2	Waldron	Abraham Jr	1			1				1					3		
Dighton	412	3	Waldron	Benja			1					1					2		
Dighton	411	13	Waldron	Benja 2d	2		1			1			1				5		
Dighton	411	15	Waldron	George	1		4		1			2	1				9		
Dighton	411	12	Waldron	George Jr	1			1		2			1				5		
Dighton	414	32	Waldron	Joseph		1	1	1	1	1	1	1		1			8		
Dighton	412	4	Waldron	Robert			1					1					2		
Dighton	412	7	Walker	Ebenezer				1			1	2	1				5		
Mansfield	388	20	Walker	Eleazer		1		1	1	2	1	1	1				8		
Dighton	411	41	Walker	Eliakim		1						1					2		
Taunton	367	32	Walker	Eliakim			1	1			1	1	1				5		
Rehoboth	308	17	Walker	Ephraim	1	1		1		1	1	1	1		8				
Rehoboth	308	25	Walker	Ephraim 2nd	1	3		1	1	1		1	1		10				
Dighton	414	31	Walker	George	1			1		2			1				5		
Rehoboth	314	25	Walker	George H			1			1		1		2	7				
Somerset	404	13	Walker	Gilbert			1		1	3		1	1				7		
Taunton	365	13	Walker	James	5	1		1				1	1				9		
Taunton	367	33	Walker	James 2d			1					1					2		
Dighton	411	3	Walker	John	2			1		2			1				6		
Rehoboth	314	24	Walker	John			1					1			2				
Dighton	411	19	Walker	Jonathan		2		1					1	2			6		
Dighton	411	20	Walker	Jonathan Jr	1			1		2			1				5		
Rehoboth	314	26	Walker	Joseph		1		2				2		1	6				
Rehoboth	308	16	Walker	Luis	2		1	2		1	1				8				
Rehoboth	308	18	Walker	Moses	1		1	2			1	1			6				
Rehoboth	308	19	Walker	Moses 2nd		1	1	3		1	1				10				
Dighton	411	18	Walker	Nathll	2	3		1	1	1		3		1			12		
Dighton	411	38	Walker	Nehemiah	2		1	1				1		1			6		
Dighton	411	40	Walker	Perez		1		1						1			3		
Dighton	414	30	Walker	Perez Junr	1			1		2			1				5		
Taunton	366	8	Walker	Peter		2	2	1		1	1	1	2				10		
Taunton	366	9	Walker	Peter Junior	1	1	1					1					4		
Rehoboth	300	11	Walker	Phillip	1	1		1		1	1		2		8				
Rehoboth	312	35	Walker	Richard	1			1	1	1		1	1	1	7				
Rehoboth	308	20	Walker	Richard 2nd															Enumeration left blank
Dighton	410	39	Walker	Sylvester	1			1		2			1				5		
Rehoboth	312	36	Walker	Timothy	1	3		1	3	1	1				10				
Dighton	410	36	Walker	William	1	3	2		1	1	1		1				10		
Dighton	410	37	Walker	William Jr			1			2			1				4		
Westport	338	4	Walkins	William		1		1		1		1					4		
Easton	394	29	Ward	Joseph		2	1		1	3		1	1				9		
Dighton	414	4	Wardwell	Josiah	2	1		1		2	1		1				8		
Swansea	403	45	Wardwell	Wido	1							1	1				3		
Dighton	412	35	Ware	George	1	1		1		2	2	1	1	2			11		
Taunton	370	19	Warner	Noah	1			1		2			1				5		
Raynham	373	36	Warren	Thomas		1		1						1			3		
Dartmouth	352	34	Washborn	Bazaleal	2			1	2	1	1	1			10				
Dartmouth	352	31	Washborn	Ira	1		1	1		1	1				7				
Dartmouth	352	8	Washborn	Peter	1			1		2					4				
Easton	394	38	Washburn	Hugh				1		1	1		1				4		
Taunton	366	28	Washburn	Hutchins	3			1					1	1			6		
Taunton	359	18	Washburn	Isaac	2	1	2		1	1		1	1	1			10		
Raynham	372	40	Washburn	Israel	4	2			1		1		1				9		
Norton	384	26	Washburn	Malatiah				1						1			2		
Swansea	398	10	Washburn	Mettiah				1						2			3		
Raynham	372	39	Washburn	Nehemiah	5		1	1		1	3		1				12		
Raynham	372	41	Washburn	Oliver	1			1		4	1		1				8		
Raynham	374	34	Washburn	Seth	1		2	1		4	1	1					11		
Dartmouth	352	7	Waste	Nathan		1	1			1	1				4				
Mansfield	387	44	Waterman	Mary								1	1				2		
Freetown	284	26	Watson	Elkanah	1	1		1		1		1					6		
Rehoboth	298	16	Watson	John	2	2		1			2		2		9				
Mansfield	388	13	Weatherby	Ebenezer			1			2		1					4		
Easton	394	34	Weatherby	Nathaniel	2		1	1		1	1	1	1				8		
Taunton	359	35	Weatherby	Thomas	1	3	1	2				1	1				9		
Rehoboth	314	35	Weaton	Peter	1		2						1		4				
Freetown	282	17	Weaver	Benjamin		2	1		1	1	1		1		1		8		
Somerset	406	44	Weaver	James	1		1			1		1					4		
Westport	338	28	Weaver	Joseph	2			1		2	1		1				7		
Somerset	406	43	Weaver	Nathll	2			1		1			1				5		
Swansea	402	4	Weaver	Peter					1					1			2		
Freetown	284	21	Weaver	Sheffield		1		1		3	1	1	1	1			9		
Rehoboth	301	26	Webber	James		1					1				4				
Rehoboth	301	25	Webber	John			1			2		1			6				
Rehoboth	305	36	Weber	Nathaniel	1		1				1		1		7				
Rehoboth	305	45	Weber	Richard	1	1		1	1	1	1		1		7				
Freetown	283	16	Webester	Simeon P	1			1		2			1	1			6		
Dartmouth	352	26	Webster	Abigail					1			1	1				3		
Westport	339	9	Weedon	John		1			1			1		1			4		
Dartmouth	352	5	Weeks	Joshua	1		1		2			1			7				
Raynham	372	28	Welbore	Meshach	2			1		2		1	1				7		
Mansfield	387	43	Wellman	Ebenezer	1		1			2			1				5		
Mansfield	388	7	Wellman	Isaac			1		1			1		2			5		

TOWN	PG#	LN#	LAST NAME	FIRST NAME	FREE WHITE MALES under 10	10 to 16	16 to 26	26 to 45	45 and over	FREE WHITE FEMALES under 10	10 to 16	16 to 26	26 to 45	45 and over	TOTAL ALL OTHER	TOTAL SLAVES	TOTALS	DISTRICT/ TOWNSHIP	NOTES
Mansfield	388	14	Wellman	John	1				1				2				4		
Attleboro	322	11	Wellman	Lot	1			1		1			1				4		
Attleboro	322	12	Wellman	Rhoda			1						2	1			4		
Dighton	415	3	Wescoat	Cornelius				1					1				2		
Dighton	415	5	Wescoat	John	2	1		1		1	1		2				8		
Dighton	415	4	Wescoat	Richard			1			1		1					3		
Rehoboth	305	23	West	Amost	1	2		1		1		2	1				8		
Rehoboth	305	26	West	Benjamin			1		2	1		1					6		
Swansea	401	10	West	Ephraim			1				1	1					3		
Rehoboth	305	25	West	Henery	1			1					1				3		
Swansea	401	32	West	John	1	1			1	2	1		1	1			8		
Rehoboth	311	12	West	Joseph	1		1		1	1		1					7		
Dighton	410	7	West	Nathan			1			2		1					4		
Rehoboth	311	13	West	Oliver	1		1	1		1			1				6		
Easton	394	32	West	Peleg	1		1			1			1				4		
Norton	384	29	West	Robert			1					1					2		
Freetown	292	14	Westcoat	Benjamin				1				1					2		
Freetown	292	22	Westcoat	Thomas	2	2				3			1				9		
Freetown	291	20	Westcoat	William			1			2		2	1				6		
Easton	394	7	Wetherell	Abijah		2		1						1			4		
Easton	394	8	Wetherell	Abijah Jr	2			1		4	1		1				9		
Mansfield	388	12	Wetherell	Benjamin		1		1			1			1			4		
Dighton	411	21	Wetherell	Daniel	1		3		1		2	2					9		
Easton	394	22	Wetherell	Darius	2			1		1			1				5		
Mansfield	388	1	Wetherell	Solomon	1	2	1	1	1	1			2				9		
Attleboro	319	46	Wetherell	Tisdale	1		1					1		1			4		
Swansea	398	24	Whalan	Clark			1					1					2		
Easton	394	13	Whalock	Lymon		2		1		1	1		1	2			8		
Dartmouth	352	24	Whalon	Daniel		1		1		2	2						7		
Dartmouth	352	35	Whalon	Joseph			1		2			2					6		
Swansea	398	15	Whalon	Joseph	1			1					2				4		
Mansfield	387	49	Wheaton	Calvin	2			2		1			2				7		
Easton	394	11	Wheaton	Daniel	2			1		1			1				5		
Norton	384	4	Wheaton	George		2		1				1		1			5		
Swansea	401	20	Wheaton	Jona				1						1			2		
Rehoboth	298	43	Wheaton	Jonathan	1		1			2		1					8		
Rehoboth	300	40	Wheaton	Joseph	1	1		1		1		1					7		
Rehoboth	302	1	Wheaton	Joseph	1			1	2	2	2	1	1				11		
Norton	384	5	Wheaton	Laban	1	1		1	1	1		1	1				7		
Rehoboth	299	6	Wheaton	Lewis	1	1	1		5		1	1					11		
Rehoboth	311	19	Wheaton	Lucas	1			1		1		1	2				10		
Swansea	401	21	Wheaton	Mial	3	1		1		1			1				7		
Rehoboth	298	20	Wheeler	Aaron	2	1		1		1		2	1				10		
Rehoboth	309	6	Wheeler	Barnard		1	1		1	2		1					8		
Dighton	412	8	Wheeler	Benjamin	4	3	1	1		2	2			1			15		
Taunton	369	4	Wheeler	Benjamin	1	2		1		2	2		1				9		
Dartmouth	352	9	Wheeler	Calven		1					1		1				4		
Rehoboth	302	26	Wheeler	Comfort	3		1					1					6		
Rehoboth	304	11	Wheeler	Cyrel			1		3			1					7		
Swansea	403	44	Wheeler	Daniel			1			1	1		1				4		
Rehoboth	301	9	Wheeler	Huldah	1				1				1				5		
Rehoboth	305	37	Wheeler	Jarvis			1		3		1						5		
Rehoboth	305	35	Wheeler	Jeremiah		2		1			1		1				5		
Rehoboth	299	45	Wheeler	Jeremiah Jr	1	1		1			2		1				7		
Rehoboth	309	7	Wheeler	Job			1		2		1						5		
Rehoboth	309	22	Wheeler	Job			1		2		1						5		
Dighton	411	22	Wheeler	John		2			1	2				1			6		
Rehoboth	302	28	Wheeler	Mason			1			1	1		1				4		
Rehoboth	302	27	Wheeler	Nathan			1	2				1					5		
Rehoboth	308	32	Wheeler	Philip	1		1	2		1		1					8		
Rehoboth	304	40	Wheeler	Rusel	1		1	1		1							4		
Rehoboth	301	13	Wheeler	Samuel			1	1				1					4		
Rehoboth	305	46	Wheeler	William			1	1				1					6		
Dighton	412	48	Wheelor	Phebe											5		5		
Rehoboth	298	39	Whiaker	Margret									3		3		3		
Mansfield	388	16	Whilbore	Benjamin			1			2			1				4		
Attleboro	322	63	Whipple	Ephraim			1			1			1				3		
Attleboro	322	64	Whipple	Jenkes	2		1			2		1					6		
Rehoboth	298	38	Whitaker	Daniel			1					2					3		
Rehoboth	305	44	Whitaker	Noah	1	3		1			2		1				8		
Rehoboth	308	21	Whitaker	Peter	2			1	1	1			1				8		
Rehoboth	312	39	Whitaker	Richard		1		1	1			1	1				5		
Attleboro	320	49	Whitaker	Richd	3	2	1			2		1	1				11		
Taunton	365	18	White	Abijah Junior	2	2		1		3	1		1				10		
Norton	384	23	White	Abraham			1	1						1			3		
Taunton	370	2	White	Abraham	3		1			2			1				7		
Easton	394	25	White	Adonijah	3			1		1			1				6		
Mansfield	387	48	White	Amos	1			1		1		1	1				5		
Raynham	372	35	White	Apollos	1			1		1			1				4		
Raynham	375	19	White	Asa	1		2	1		3	1		1				9		
Taunton	369	17	White	Benjmain	1		1			1		1					4		
Taunton	366	7	White	Cornelius	2		2		1		3	1	1				10		
Westport	338	10	White	Cornelius	1			1		1			1	1			5		
Mansfield	388	18	White	Daniel		1			1			1		1			4		

TOWN	PG#	LN#	LAST NAME	FIRST NAME	FREE WHITE MALES					FREE WHITE FEMALES					TOTAL ALL OTHER	TOTAL SLAVES	TOTALS	DISTRICT/ TOWNSHIP	NOTES
					under 10	10 to 16	16 to 26	26 to 45	45 and over	under 10	10 to 16	16 to 26	26 to 45	45 and over					
Raynham	375	8	White	Daniel			1	1		1		1					4		
Easton	394	19	White	David	2			1		3			1				7		
Mansfield	388	10	White	David			1	1					1				3		
Freetown	293	7	White	Ebenezer			1			1			1				3		
Mansfield	388	23	White	Ebenezer	1		1	1	1	1		1		1			7		
Attleboro	322	44	White	Edward	1		1			2		1					5		
Easton	394	36	White	Edward			2		1	1	1		1				6		
Mansfield	388	9	White	Eliab			1		1				1	1			4		
Raynham	376	27	White	Elijah				1		1	1		1				4		
Taunton	360	30	White	Elijah			1			3			1				5		
Westport	338	19	White	George		2	1			2	1			2			8		
Raynham	375	9	White	Hannah Wid							1			2			3		
Easton	394	37	White	Howard			1						1				2		
Raynham	374	30	White	Isaac	2			1		2		1	2				8		
Raynham	375	10	White	Israel	3	1	1	1		2	1		1				10		
Taunton	363	33	White	Jacob	1			1		2			1				5		
Easton	394	20	White	John	2			1		1			1				5		
Mansfield	387	47	White	John		3		1					1				5		
Norton	384	19	White	John	1	2	1		1	1	1			1			8		
Taunton	369	18	White	John		1		1					1				3		
Taunton	369	16	White	John Junior		2	1		1	2	1			1			8		
Mansfield	388	15	White	Jonathan				1					1				2		
Westport	338	3	White	Jonathan				1					1				2		
Mansfield	388	21	White	Jonathan Jr			1		1	2	1	1		1			7		
Westport	338	2	White	Jonathan Junr	1		1			1			1				4		
Easton	394	26	White	Josiah			1	1					1				3		
Mansfield	387	46	White	Lemuel	1		1		1	1			1	1			6		
Mansfield	388	25	White	Leonard	1			1				1					3		
Mansfield	388	2	White	Matthew	1			1					1				3		
Mansfield	387	45	White	Mehetable	1	1				2				1			5		
Freetown	292	20	White	Merchant	2								1	1			5		
Mansfield	388	24	White	Nathan	2			1		2			1				6		
Westport	338	8	White	Obed	1				1		1	2	1				6		
Mansfield	388	26	White	Oliver			1						1				2		
Westport	338	17	White	Peleg		1				1	1						3		
Raynham	372	38	White	Perez	2			1		1			1				5		
Freetown	291	30	White	Perregrin		1	1	1	1			1		1			6		
Westport	338	18	White	Roger		1	2	1		2	1	1					8		
Easton	394	28	White	Royal					1	1	1		1				4		
Raynham	372	21	White	Rufus	3		1						1				5		
Freetown	293	2	White	Samuel	1	2		1		4			1				9		
Mansfield	388	19	White	Samuel				1		2			1				4		
Raynham	374	29	White	Samuel				1						1			2		
Mansfield	388	11	White	Sarah		1				1	1	1					4		
Taunton	360	7	White	Saul	1	1	1		1	2		2	1				9		
Westport	338	7	White	Silvenus		2		1		1	1	1					7		
Mansfield	388	8	White	Simeon	3		1		2	2	1		1	1			11		
Freetown	293	3	White	Thomas		1		1		2			2	1			6		
Taunton	369	15	White	Timothy	1		1	1		2			1				6		
Westport	338	22	White	William		1	2	1				1		1			6		
Westport	339	5	White	William 2d			2	1		2		2					7		
Norton	384	25	White	Zebulon	1	3			1	2		3		1			11		
Westport	338	9	White	Zerothmael	2			1					1		1		4		
Attleboro	321	20	Whiting	John	3		1			2			1				7		
Rehoboth	302	43	Whiting	William	1		1		2	1		1				7			
Rehoboth	314	28	Whitman	Frederic			1			1			1			3			
Rehoboth	314	30	Whitman	Israel		1		3		1		1				7			
Rehoboth	314	27	Whitman	Samuel	1		1			1		1				4			
Rehoboth	314	29	Whitman	Samuel Jr			1					1				2			
Dighton	412	30	Whitmarsh	Abial		1		1					1				3		
Freetown	293	18	Whitmarsh	Asa	2			1					1				4		
Dighton	412	39	Whitmarsh	Holmes Wido of	1	1				1			1				4		
Dighton	412	20	Whitmarsh	John	1	2	1		1	1	1		1				9		
Dighton	412	29	Whitmarsh	Jonathan	1	2			1	2			1				7		
Dighton	413	23	Whitmarsh	Matthew	1	1			1	1	1		1				7		
Dighton	412	31	Whitmarsh	Robert	2			1		2	1		1				7		
Dighton	412	17	Whitmarsh	Rufus			1		1			3		1			6		
Dighton	412	40	Whitmarsh	Sarah		1	1							1			3		
Dighton	412	19	Whitmarsh	Walter			1						1				2		
Westport	338	6	Whote	Holder	3			1		2	1		1				8		
Rehoboth	314	31	Wiett	Lemuel	1			1					2			4			
Taunton	369	26	Wilbore	Abishai	2	1		1					1				5		
Raynham	375	12	Wilbore	Adam			1						1				2		
Raynham	376	17	Wilbore	Apollos	1			1		1		1					4		
Raynham	376	29	Wilbore	Ebenezer	1	2		1		2	1		1				8		
Easton	394	14	Wilbore	Ebinezer	2	2		1		3	1			1			10		
Raynham	376	15	Wilbore	Elkanah			1	1					1	1			4		
Raynham	376	16	Wilbore	Elkanah Junr				1		1			1				3		
Norton	384	13	Wilbore	Ephraim	2	1	1		1	1	1			2			9		
Easton	394	15	Wilbore	George	3	2	1	1		2			1				10		
Taunton	370	26	Wilbore	Henry				1			5	2					9		
Raynham	372	25	Wilbore	Isaiah			1	1	1			1	1	1			6		
Taunton	369	24	Wilbore	Isaiah	1			1		1			1				4		
Raynham	375	11	Wilbore	Jacob	2				1		1	1		1			6		

Census table (page 147). FWM = Free White Males, FWF = Free White Females.

TOWN	PG#	LN#	LAST NAME	FIRST NAME	FWM under 10	FWM 10–16	FWM 16–26	FWM 26–45	FWM 45 & over	FWF under 10	FWF 10–16	FWF 16–26	FWF 26–45	FWF 45 & over	TOTAL ALL OTHER	TOTAL SLAVES	TOTALS	DISTRICT/ TOWNSHIP	NOTES
Taunton	364	2	Wilbore	Jedediah		1			1	2			1				5		
Taunton	359	6	Wilbore	Jedediah Junr	3			1				1					5		
Norton	384	28	Wilbore	Joel	1			1					1				3		
Taunton	364	3	Wilbore	John	1			1		3			1				6		
Taunton	369	25	Wilbore	Joseph				1					1				2		
Raynham	376	4	Wilbore	Joseph Junior	1	1		1		2			1				6		
Taunton	359	9	Wilbore	Joshua	1			1						1			3		
Raynham	375	6	Wilbore	Josiah		1	2	1					2	1			7		
Raynham	375	5	Wilbore	Libus		1	2						1				4		
Raynham	375	31	Wilbore	Samuel	4	1			1	1	1	2	1				11		
Raynham	376	13	Wilbore	Simeon			3		1	1		2		1			8		
Raynham	375	16	Wilbore	Simeon Junr	3			1		1		1					6		
Taunton	364	4	Wilbore	Stephen	1		1		1			1	1	1			6		
Raynham	376	12	Wilbore	Zephaniah	1		1	1		1		2					6		
Raynham	376	33	Wilbore	Zibean			1			1		1		1			4		
Somerset	407	25	Wilbour	Daniel		3		1		3				2			9		
Somerset	407	30	Wilbour	Daniel Jr	1		1					1					3		
Somerset	407	26	Wilbour	Elisha		1	1	1		3			1				7		
Freetown	290	7	Wilbour	Elizabeth Wid		1	1					1		1			4		
Freetown	287	21	Wilbour	Isaac	2	1		1		2	2	1					9		
Somerset	405	40	Wilbour	James	2	1		1		2			1				7		
Somerset	407	13	Wilbour	John		1	1					1					3		
Swansea	398	45	Wilbour	Joshua		1	2	1		1			1				6		
Dighton	411	4	Wilbour	Josiah	1		1					1					3		
Somerset	405	41	Wilbour	Mary Wido	1	2	1			2	1		1				8		
Dartmouth	352	2	Wilbur	David				1		2			1				4		
Dartmouth	352	32	Wilbur	Henry			1	1				1					4		
Dartmouth	352	33	Wilbur	Isaac			1	1		1	1						7		
Dartmouth	352	4	Wilbur	Jonathan		2		1		1	2	1	1				8		
Dartmouth	352	3	Wilbur	Stephen				1		1		1					5		
Westport	338	20	Wilcox	Abner		1		1		1			1				4		
Dartmouth	352	11	Wilcox	Benjamin	1			3		1							5		
Westport	338	16	Wilcox	Benjamin	2		2	1					1				6		
Westport	339	3	Wilcox	Culbert		1		1					1	1			4		
Westport	338	32	Wilcox	Daniel	1			1		1			1				4		
Dartmouth	352	18	Wilcox	Henry	1	1							1				3		
Westport	338	33	Wilcox	John			1	1					1	1			4		
Westport	338	15	Wilcox	Samuel		1		1						1			3		
Westport	339	2	Wilcox	Silvenus				1						1			2		
Dartmouth	352	15	Wilcox	Thomas	1	1	1	1		1		2	1				8		
Dartmouth	351	37	Wilcox	William	1	1		1		2			1				6		
Westport	339	1	Wilcox	William		1	1	1		1			1	1			6		
Norton	384	14	Wild	Benjamin	2	1		1		2	1		1				8		
Easton	394	31	Wild	John	2			1			1		1				5		
Taunton	365	37	Wild	Rachel										1			1		
Taunton	365	35	Wild	Samuel	1			1		2			2				6		
Taunton	358	24	Wild	Samuel Junior	1			1	1	2	1		1	1			8		
Attleboro	317	28	Wilder	John	3		1	1		3	1		1				11		
Taunton	358	8	Wiliams	Richard	3	2		1		1	1		1				9		
Freetown	281	14	Wilkenson	John	3			1		1	3		1				9		
Dartmouth	351	36	Wilkey	George		1		1		1							3		
Dartmouth	351	35	Wilkey	Peter				1		1	1		1				5		
Attleboro	319	13	Wilkinson	John			1	1				1		1			4		
Taunton	366	23	Willard	Thankfull Wido								2		1			3		
Raynham	373	26	Williams	Abiel	1		1		1			1	1	1			6		
Mansfield	388	22	Williams	Amasa	3			1		1			1				6		
Easton	394	6	Williams	Anna		1				1				1			3		
Mansfield	387	42	Williams	Bates		1				1		1					3		
Dartmouth	353	3	Williams	Benjamin	1	1		1				1		1			7		
Easton	394	21	Williams	Benjamin		1				3			1				5		
Mansfield	388	4	Williams	Benjamin		1		1					2	1			5		
Mansfield	388	17	Williams	Benjamin Jr		1				1			1				3		
Taunton	370	20	Williams	Benjamin Junr	1	1	1	1					1	1			6		
Taunton	360	2	Williams	Cyrus		1	1					1		1	2		6		
Mansfield	388	5	Williams	Daniel	2			1		2			1				6		
Dighton	411	36	Williams	David			2	1		1		3					7		
Mansfield	387	41	Williams	Ebenezer		1				1		1					3		
Taunton	358	10	Williams	Ebenezer	1	1	2		1	2	1	2		1			11		
Taunton	362	39	Williams	Ebenezer Junr	2			1					1				4		
Easton	394	3	Williams	Edward		1	3		1	3	1			1			10		
Mansfield	388	6	Williams	Elijah				1						1			2		
Taunton	358	25	Williams	Elijah				1		2		1					4		
Easton	394	18	Williams	Ezra	2			1		2	1	1					7		
Dighton	411	37	Williams	George		2	1	1		2			2	1			9		
Raynham	374	26	Williams	George		1	3	1	1	1			2	1			10		
Taunton	359	11	Williams	George			1	1	1				1	1			5		
Taunton	363	12	Williams	George 2d			1	1					1	1			4		
Dighton	411	33	Williams	George Jr	1		1	1		1			1				5		
Raynham	374	21	Williams	George Junr	2	1				1			1				5		
Taunton	364	27	Williams	Gideon	3	1	1		1	1	1	2		1			11		
Taunton	369	11	Williams	Guilford	1			1		3			1				6		
Taunton	362	35	Williams	Isaac				1						1			2		
Mansfield	388	3	Williams	Jacob	2			1		1	1	1					7		

147

Town	PG#	LN#	Last Name	First Name	Free White Males under 10	10 to 16	16 to 26	26 to 45	45 and over	Free White Females under 10	10 to 16	16 to 26	26 to 45	45 and over	Total All Other	Total Slaves	Totals	District/Township	Notes
Dartmouth	353	1	Williams	James	1	3		1			1		1				7		
Dighton	411	32	Williams	Jared	1			1				1	2				5		
Easton	394	10	Williams	John	1		3		1	3	1	3	1				13		
Mansfield	387	50	Williams	John	1	1	2		1	1		1	1				8		
Raynham	373	5	Williams	John			1		1	1		1		1			5		
Dighton	411	30	Williams	Jonathan	1				1	2	3		1				8		
Raynham	373	22	Williams	Jonathan	1	1		1		2	1		1				7		
Dartmouth	353	2	Williams	Joshua		1	1		2		1	1					9		
Dighton	411	31	Williams	Joshua				1		2			1				4		
Easton	394	23	Williams	Joshua	2			1				1	1				6		
Easton	394	5	Williams	Josiah			1		1		1	2					5		
Raynham	373	27	Williams	Lemuel		2		1			1						4		
Taunton	363	11	Williams	Lemuel			1		1			1		1			4		
Raynham	373	25	Williams	Macey	1			1		2			1				5		
Easton	394	4	Williams	Marlboro	1	2		1		1	2		1				8		
Dartmouth	353	4	Williams	Mary Wid	1		1		1		1	1					6		
Raynham	373	29	Williams	Nathan	1	1			1	2	1	1		1			8		
Taunton	358	20	Williams	Nathaniel	3	2	1		2	1		2	1	1			14		
Taunton	363	42	Williams	Nathaniel	1	1		1		2	1	2	1	1			11		
Raynham	374	19	Williams	Noah				1		1				2			4		
Easton	394	35	Williams	Oliver	2			1		1			1				5		
Taunton	368	26	Williams	Richard 2d	1		1					1					3		
Easton	394	16	Williams	Sarah		1	1	1		2	1		1	2			9		
Raynham	374	6	Williams	Silas	2			1		3			1				7		
Dighton	411	29	Williams	Simeon	1			1		1				2			5		
Raynham	373	34	Williams	Stephen		2		1				1		1			5		
Easton	394	27	Williams	Thomas	3	1		1		2	1	1	1				10		
Taunton	371	18	Williams	Thomas			1	1					1				3		
Dighton	411	34	Williams	William			1			1			1				3		
Norton	384	10	Willis	Beriah	3	1		1		1	1		1				8		
Taunton	370	35	Willis	Elisha	2			1					1				4		
Taunton	369	9	Willis	John	1	1		1		2	1		2				8		
Easton	394	17	Willis	Lemuel			1		1		1	2		1			6		
Taunton	357	27	Willis	Mehitable Wido			1							1			2		
Taunton	368	40	Willis	Nehemiah	1	1			1	2	2	1	1				9		
Taunton	370	6	Willis	Noah			1		1			2					4		
Easton	394	9	Willis	Phillip	1			1		4			1				7		
Taunton	369	8	Willis	Sumner			1	1				1		3			6		
Easton	394	1	Willis	Thomas		3			1	1	1	1					8		
Easton	394	2	Willis	Thomas Jr	2	2		1		4	1		1				11		
Rehoboth	300	39	Willmarth	Daniel	1	1		1	1	4		1					12		
Attleboro	320	42	Willmarth	Jona	3			1			1		2				7		
Rehoboth	311	27	Willmarth	Joseph		2		1	1	1			1				6		
Rehoboth	314	21	Willmarth	Mary							2		1				3		
Rehoboth	314	22	Willmarth	Thomas			1						1				2		
Attleboro	320	1	Wilmarth	Amos	1			1					1				3		
Attleboro	320	10	Wilmarth	Dan	1	1		1		2	1						6		
Attleboro	318	65	Wilmarth	Eliphalet					1			1	1				3		
Attleboro	318	66	Wilmarth	Eliphalet Junr		1	1		1	1	2		1				7		
Attleboro	320	36	Wilmarth	Elkanah					1				1				2		
Attleboro	320	55	Wilmarth	John	2			1		1	1		1				6		
Attleboro	320	13	Wilmarth	Larned	1	1	2			2	2			1			9		
Attleboro	319	43	Wilmarth	Martha	1		2			2	1		1				7		
Attleboro	320	12	Wilmarth	Nathan				1		1		1		1			4		
Attleboro	320	11	Wilmarth	Nathan Junr		1				1		1					3		
Attleboro	320	39	Wilmarth	Preston		1		1		2							4		
Attleboro	319	50	Wilmarth	Stephen	2			1		2			1	2			8		
Attleboro	320	43	Wilmarth	Stephen 2d	2			1		1			1				5		
Freetown	290	3	Wilson	David		3		1				1		1			6		
Taunton	360	6	Wilson	Robert	1			1					1				3		
Taunton	367	20	Wilson	Robert Junr			1			1		1					3		
Taunton	361	13	Wilson	Susannah Wido			1			1			1				3		
Taunton	360	3	Wilson	William			1			4			1				6		
Rehoboth	312	37	Windsor	Ira	1		1		1	1		1					6		
Westport	339	14	Windsor	Lydia										3			3		
Rehoboth	314	19	Windsor	Mary				1		1		1		1			6		
Westport	338	12	Wing	David	1	1	1		1	2	2	1					9		
Westport	338	13	Wing	Edward	1		1		1	1			1				5		
Dartmouth	352	1	Wing	John	1	1	1		2	2		1					9		
Westport	338	14	Wing	Joseph		2		1					1				4		
Dartmouth	352	23	Wing	Primus										3	3		3		
Westport	338	11	Wing	Prince	1	1		1				1	3				8		
Dartmouth	352	29	Winslow	Abigale								1	1				2		
Berkley	279	1	Winslow	Avery		2	1					1		1			5		
Berkley	279	2	Winslow	Avery Jun			1			1	1						3		
Dartmouth	352	25	Winslow	Benjam Junr			1		1	1			1				4		
Dartmouth	352	27	Winslow	Benjamin	1	1		1	1	1	2		1				8		
Freetown	283	21	Winslow	Benjamin	2			1	1	2			1	1			8		
Freetown	286	8	Winslow	David		1			1	2			1				5		
Berkley	279	3	Winslow	Ebenezer	1		1			1		1		1			5		
Somerset	408	12	Winslow	Ebenzr	2	2	2		1		2		1				10		
Freetown	282	18	Winslow	Ephraim	1	1		1	1	1	2	1	1	1			10		
Freetown	288	13	Winslow	Ezra	1			1					1	1			4		
Freetown	286	15	Winslow	George			1							1			2		

TOWN	PG#	LN#	LAST NAME	FIRST NAME	FREE WHITE MALES					FREE WHITE FEMALES					TOTAL ALL OTHER	TOTAL SLAVES	TOTALS	DISTRICT/ TOWNSHIP	NOTES
					under 10	10 to 16	16 to 26	26 to 45	45 and over	under 10	10 to 16	16 to 26	26 to 45	45 and over					
Freetown	290	22	Winslow	George 2d			1	1		1	1		1				5		
Swansea	401	42	Winslow	Humphrey	1			1		1		1					4		
Freetown	287	4	Winslow	Isaac	1			1		2	3	1					8		
Freetown	283	10	Winslow	James		1	3		1	1				2			8		
Freetown	290	29	Winslow	James 2d	1			1		2	1		1				6		
Dighton	411	28	Winslow	Job	1		1	1		2	1		1				7		
Taunton	364	33	Winslow	Job			2	1	2			1					6		
Dartmouth	352	28	Winslow	John			1	2		1		1			5				
Freetown	286	18	Winslow	John	3	2		1		2	1		1				10		
Swansea	398	36	Winslow	John	1	1	1	1		3		1	1				9		
Freetown	294	24	Winslow	John 2d				1				1					2		
Freetown	282	29	Winslow	Joseph	2	1		1		1	2	1	1				9		
Freetown	284	17	Winslow	Luther	2	1	3		1	1	1		1				10		
Freetown	286	26	Winslow	Luther Jr	2			1		2			1				6		
Freetown	286	13	Winslow	Nathan	1		2	1					2	1			7		
Dartmouth	352	22	Winslow	Nelson			1			1		1			5				
Freetown	282	7	Winslow	Oliver			3			2			1	1			7		
Dartmouth	352	21	Winslow	Richard			1						1		4				
Dartmouth	352	30	Winslow	Thomas			1		1	1					3				
Freetown	286	10	Winslow	William	3		2		1			1		1			8		
Freetown	284	11	Winslow	Abner		1	2	1		1	1	1		1			8		
Norton	384	7	Wiswall	Amasa	1		1	1		2	1		1	1			8		
Norton	384	6	Wiswall	Elijah	2		1	1		1			1	1			7		
Norton	384	12	Wiswall	Noah			2		1	1	1			1			6		
Rehoboth	314	47	Witeman	Richard										2	2				
Norton	384	15	Witherell	Abijah		1		1				1		1			4		
Taunton	369	13	Witherell	Allen	1		1			2		1					5		
Taunton	360	34	Witherell	David	2		1			2			1				6		
Norton	384	22	Witherell	Elisha			1					1					2		
Norton	384	27	Witherell	George	1		1						2				4		
Norton	384	16	Witherell	James	2	2						1		1			6		
Norton	384	20	Witherell	John		2		1				1		1			5		
Norton	384	21	Witherell	Samuel	1		1						1				3		
Taunton	369	20	Witherell	Solomon	1	1	1	1	1	1			1				7		
Raynham	376	5	Witherell	Solomon Junr			1			1		1					3		
Taunton	369	23	Witherell	Thomas	1		2			2		1					6		
Norton	384	8	Witherell	William			2	1				2	2				7		
Norton	384	9	Witherell	William Jun	2		1			1			1				5		
Attleboro	318	49	Withington	Thomas			1	1		2		1					5		
Freetown	288	18	Wodwell	Pardon		1				2		1					4		
Swansea	400	21	Wood	Aaron		3		1		3		1	1				9		
Westport	338	30	Wood	Arnold	1			1					1				3		
Swansea	403	46	Wood	Barney		1		1					1				3		
Taunton	356	17	Wood	Benjamin				1					1				2		
Swansea	400	23	Wood	Caleb		1		1		1	1		1				5		
Rehoboth	314	34	Wood	David	1		1			2		1			5				
Swansea	400	19	Wood	David	1			1				1		1			4		
Swansea	400	14	Wood	Enos			1					1		1			3		
Taunton	357	34	Wood	Ephraim	2	1		1				1	2				7		
Westport	338	23	Wood	George		1	1	1		1	1		1				6		
Westport	338	5	Wood	Israel		1							1	1			4		
Dartmouth	352	16	Wood	John	1	2		1	2	1	1	1			10				
Rehoboth	314	33	Wood	John			1	2		2		1			8				
Swansea	400	25	Wood	John	2			1		1		1	1				6		
Westport	338	31	Wood	John		1	1	1				1	1				5		
Dartmouth	352	14	Wood	Jonathan		1						1			3				
Rehoboth	311	14	Wood	Jonathan	1	2		1	1	2	1	1	1		10				
Swansea	400	22	Wood	Jonathan	1	1		1					2	1			6		
Rehoboth	311	16	Wood	Jonathan Jr		1						1			3				
Dartmouth	352	13	Wood	Josiah			1					1	1		3				
Rehoboth	314	32	Wood	Luis		1	1						1		3				
Dartmouth	352	12	Wood	Luthern		1	1						2		4				
Attleboro	322	54	Wood	Mary									2	1			3		
Westport	339	13	Wood	Mary	1								1	1			3		
Swansea	398	25	Wood	Nathaniel				1					1				2		
Rehoboth	311	15	Wood	Oliver		1						1			6				
Somerset	408	4	Wood	Otis	3	1		1		1		1					7		
Westport	338	24	Wood	Peleg	1		1					1					3		
Westport	338	27	Wood	Robert				1						1			2		
Swansea	402	15	Wood	Seth	1	1		1		1		1					5		
Swansea	399	39	Wood	Simeon	1	1		1		3	2	1	1				10		
Westport	338	21	Wood	Thomas				1				1					2		
Swansea	400	24	Wood	William	1			1		1		1	1				5		
Westport	338	29	Wood	William	1		1	2				1		1			6		
Dartmouth	352	10	Wood	Marlborough			1		1			1	1		7				
Rehoboth	304	10	Wood	John 2nd			1				1		1		4				
Attleboro	320	21	Woodcock	James				1					1	1			3		
Attleboro	319	6	Woodcock	Jonathan				1		1		1	1	1			6		
Easton	394	33	Woodcock	Martha	1								1	1			3		
Easton	394	24	Woode	Mary							1			1			2		
Easton	394	30	Woode	Mary						2	1			1			4		
Westport	339	11	Woodle	George	1			1		1	1	1					5		
Westport	339	10	Woodle	Gersham Junr	2		1			1	1		1				6		
Westport	338	26	Woodle	Phinehas	2	1	1		1	2		1					8		

TOWN	PG#	LN#	LAST NAME	FIRST NAME	M under 10	M 10 to 16	M 16 to 26	M 26 to 45	M 45 and over	F under 10	F 10 to 16	F 16 to 26	F 26 to 45	F 45 and over	TOTAL ALL OTHER	TOTAL SLAVES	TOTALS	DISTRICT/ TOWNSHIP	NOTES
Westport	339	12	Woodle	Richard	1			1		1		1					4		
Westport	339	6	Woodle	Thomas	3	1			1	2		1					8		
Dartmouth	352	6	Woodmancy	Gideon	2		1		1			1				6			
Swansea	402	18	Woodmancy	John					1				1				2		
Rehoboth	299	42	Woodmansie	Eleazer			1		2			1				8			
Rehoboth	299	41	Woodmansie	Squire				1	1				1			3			
Taunton	370	40	Woodward	Abijah	2	1	1	1					1				6		
Taunton	368	41	Woodward	Ambros	1	2	2		2	1		1		2			11		
Norton	384	11	Woodward	Anna										2			2		
Taunton	369	12	Woodward	Caleb	1				1	1		2	1				6		
Taunton	371	13	Woodward	Daniel	2	1	1	1		1	1	1	1				9		
Taunton	364	10	Woodward	David					1			1		2			4		
Norton	384	18	Woodward	Elkanah	1			1				1					3		
Norton	384	3	Woodward	Elkanah Jr	1		1					1					3		
Taunton	368	5	Woodward	George	2	2			1					1			6		
Norton	384	2	Woodward	Hannah					1		1	2		1			5		
Norton	384	24	Woodward	Isaac	2				1	3	1	2		1			10		
Rehoboth	311	11	Woodward	John		1		1		1		1				5			
Norton	384	17	Woodward	Josiah		1	3	2	1	1	1	1		3			13		
Norton	384	30	Woodward	Levi	2			1		1		1					5		
Taunton	369	40	Woodward	Paul					1	1				2			4		
Taunton	370	38	Woodward	Peter		1			1					1			3		
Rehoboth	311	10	Woodward	Samuel				1		3		3				7			
Rehoboth	306	8	Woodward	Samuel Jr		1		1					1			3			
Swansea	398	39	Wortham	Joseph	1			1		2			1				5		
Dighton	409	12	Wright	Benja	1	2	1		1	1	1		1				8		
Dighton	413	25	Wright	Joshua		1		1				1					3		
Dighton	412	36	Wright	Wido		1	1	1				3	1	1			8		
Freetown	287	22	Wrightington	James		1				3		1					5		
Attleboro	322	48	Young	Mary		1		1						1			3		

NOTES